A Critical Handbook of Children's Literature

Rebecca J. Lukens
Professor Emerita, Miami University

Jacquelin J. Smith
University of Northern Iowa

Cynthia Miller Coffel
Independent Writer

PEARSON

Boston • Columbus • Indianapolis • New York • San Francisco • Upper Saddle River
Amsterdam • Cape Town • Dubai • London • Madrid • Milan • Munich • Paris • Montreal • Toronto
City • São Paulo • Sydney • Hong Kong • Seoul • Singapore • Taipei • Tokyo

For those who love and respect children's literature

Vice President, Editor-in-Chief: Aurora Martínez Ramos
Editor: Erin Grelak
Associate Sponsoring Editor: Barbara Strickland
Editorial Assistant: Michelle Hochberg
Executive Marketing Manager: Krista Clark
Production Editor: Annette Joseph
Editorial Production Service: Electronic Publishing Services Inc.
Manufacturing Buyer: Megan Cochran
Electronic Composition: TexTech Inc./Jouve
Cover Designer: Linda Knowles

Credits and acknowledgments borrowed from other sources and reproduced, with permission, in this textbook appear on pages 359–360.

Many of the designations by manufacturers and sellers to distinguish their products are claimed as trademarks. Where those designations appear in this book, and the publisher was aware of a trademark claim, the designations have been printed in initial caps or all caps.

Library of Congress Cataloging-in-Publication Data

Lukens, Rebecca J.
  A critical handbook of children's literature / Rebecca J. Lukens, Jacquelin J. Smith, Cynthia Miller Coffel.—9th ed.
      p.   cm.
  Includes bibliographical references and index.
  ISBN-13: 978-0-13-705638-5
  ISBN-10: 0-13-705638-9
  1. Children's literature—History and criticism.   2. Children—Books and reading.   I. Smith, Jacquelin J.   II. Miller Coffel, Cynthia.   III. Title.
  PN1009.A1L84 2012
  809'.89282—dc23

                                                                                    2011034407

10 9 8 7 6 5 4 3 2 1

ISBN-13: 978-0-13-705638-5
ISBN-10: 0-13-705638-9

ABOUT THE AUTHORS

Rebecca Lukens graduated with honors from Concordia College in Minnesota, earned an M.A. from Syracuse University, and next worked on the editorial staff of a children's encyclopedia in New York. After a year on the faculty of St. Olaf College followed by her marriage, she taught at New York State College, Albany, and later at Ohio University, Chillicothe. After publication of a few children's stories, Miami University Department of English hired Lukens to teach children's literature—not "kiddy lit"—as well as technical and expository writing.

The first edition of *A Critical Handbook of Children's Literature* was published by Scott Foresman in 1976, and *A Critical Handbook of Literature for Young Adults* by HarperCollins in 1994. Lukens also co-edited a literature anthology, *Woman: An Affirmation*, published by D. C. Heath in 1979. Her latest publication, *It's Been Great*, is a memoir dedicated "to my children and theirs."

Lukens's retirement teaching has been with Miami University's Institute for Learning in Retirement; her favorite class she called "Laughter for Health and Sanity."

Jacquelin Smith is a career educator whose classroom and special education teaching experiences span grades two through eight. Children's literature has been a central focus throughout her teaching career, from its natural place with literacy learning to its content area connections. She has shared many cross-curricular teaching and learning strategies for literacy (IRA), science (NSTA), social studies (NCSS), and math (NCTM) using children's books at professional conferences and in publications with the National Council of Teachers of Mathematics; her work was featured in their journal, *Teaching Children Mathematics*, and she assisted with the book *The Wonderful World of Mathematics*. A lifelong learner, she earned her M.S. and special area certifications from the University of Northern Iowa where she has been an instructor of children's literature for more than ten years. She has an "ABD" Ph.D. from the University of Iowa where she focused her studies on critically examining children's literature.

Cynthia Miller Coffel is the author of *Thinking Themselves Free: Research on the Literacy of Teen Mothers*. She has taught literacy at the preschool, junior high, high school, and college levels, and currently works as a curriculum writer. Her research on children's and young adult literature has appeared in journals such as *The ALAN Review, Reader*, and *QSE*. Her work won the Jeffrey E. Smith award for nonfiction from *The Missouri Review* in 2007, and her literary essays have twice been listed among the notable essays of the year in The Best American Essays series. Her B.A. and M.S. are from Indiana University; her Ph.D. in literacy education is from the University of Iowa.

◉ CONTENTS

CHAPTER 7: SETTING   166

CHAPTER 8: POINT OF VIEW   190

CHAPTER 9: STYLE AND TONE   210

Each of the previous editions of *A Critical Handbook of Children's Literature* has addressed elements of change; change is present again in this edition of the handbook, perhaps more so, not only because two new authors (Jacquelin Smith and Cynthia Miller Coffel) are providing revisions to this edition, but more importantly because children's literature itself is continually changing in form and content. In the past decade there have been changes in the culture of the United States, in the culture of publishing, and in the culture of childhood. Eliza Dresang refers to these changes as *radical change,* and she attributes the fundamental changes taking place in literature for young readers to the "connectivity, interactivity, and access in the digital world."[1] Sylvia Pantaleo[2] considers radical change characteristics in literature as a historical phenomenon very much like those associated with postmodernism. Instances of the ways these kinds of changes affect children's literature will be reflected in the chapters you read in the ninth edition.

As we worked on this ninth edition, we made thoughtful decisions about the nature and number of changes to address. Changes in children's literature are complex in a field thick with multiple stakeholders and diverse audiences. The varied insights we considered reflect the vitality and robust nature of children's literature, and each choice necessitated a thoughtful process that honored both constancy and difference. The result is a handbook that remains rooted in its past while representing current trends in children's literature and providing a structure that encourages vigorous growth for the future.

The following sections reflect the emphasis of the ninth edition of *A Critical Handbook of Children's Literature,* beginning with a discussion of the elements that serve to maintain the heart and soul of the handbook.

The Importance of Books

The value of reading books has always permeated discussions of literature in general, and of current interest to lovers of children's books is whether there is even a future for books as we know them. Most readers will agree that books remain important, as do we, though style and form will most certainly continue to change. The addition of electronic devices such as the Kindle, the Nook, and the iPad has enlivened the discussion, but we agree with Eliza Dresang's stance that electronic formats can successfully coexist with and enhance material books as we know them.[3] Fortunately, the role of these handheld readers seems to be one of *encouraging* reading, providing yet another avenue to access the nearly 30,000 books published for juveniles each year between 2002 and 2009.[4] The number of books published and their availability are hopeful signs when we consider the current emphasis in education on prepackaged curricula, standardized tests for measuring reading achievement, and decreased focus on independent reading at home and school.

As with previous editions, we will not venture into specific issues of pedagogy, but we agree with Nancie Atwell's research-based observation that "book reading, which profits a reader, an author, and a democratic society, is also the single activity that consistently relates to proficiency in reading, according to the National Assessment of Educational Progress."[5] We advocate for the importance of the book for literacy learning and learning in a global society, which implies a strong recommendation for quality literature in the hands and minds of children and young adults. Margaret Meek said it best in her classic *How Texts Teach What Readers Learn*: "We learned to read completely and sensitively, because we gave ourselves . . . 'private lessons,' by becoming involved in what we read." Like Meek, we advocate for the inclusion of sharing and interaction with other people as a vital aspect of the process of learning how a book works and how the story goes.[6]

Literary Understanding

Just *how* books work remains a central focus of this edition of *A Critical Handbook of Children's Literature*. The importance of literary understanding and some facility with literary criticism permeates the field of children's literature. Literary critics within the field of children's literature frequently examine children's books in view of the ever-shifting perspectives of sociology, psychology, history, and culture. Texts are also seen as cultural artifacts to be viewed from particular literary stances ranging from "new criticism" to "reader response" to "cultural criticism" or through a Marxist or feminist lens.[7] In the absence of a unified system of literary criticism, we have included aspects of several theories concerning contemporary children's books. Central to our work is a belief that the essence of *literature* lies with the text (verbal and visual), its inherent structures, and the intertextuality that pervades the study of literature. The familiar format and genre structures popular to classifying children's literature and to helping younger readers appreciate the books they read have been updated;[8] each chapter dedicated to a particular literary element, format, or genre has been revised as well. But the importance of the reader, who provides information that informs *how* an author or illustrator achieves success with a particular genre of book or literary element, remains central to our work. The reader response criticism of Louise Rosenblatt will guide our approach to looking closely at children's books.

Louise Rosenblatt provided us with a strong reminder that the text is considered to be an important part of the balance between the reader, the text, and the context. Though the focus of this edition remains on the particular books we analyze, our approach is again not that of the New Critics, who view the text and its author as the primary source of meaning. We value the importance of the reader and the cultural context in the reading transaction to support the content within each chapter. We agree with Rosenblatt that powerful responses to literature, those that expand a reader's understanding, depend on careful selection and critical analysis. That is, the active reader is responsible for part of a literary response, but the literary work directs a portion as well.

Rosenblatt's reader response theory holds that valid literary criticism must come from the *reader as a reader*. Valid criticism must be about "the web of feelings, sensations, images, ideas, that [the reviewer or critic as reader] weaves between himself and the text." This does not mean that Rosenblatt completely rejected "objective" literary criticism. For Rosenblatt the text is important, too, as "the external pole in the process."[9] But objective literary criticism (i.e., criticism focused *only* on this external pole of the text)—no matter how insightful—cuts readers off "from their own aesthetic roots" with the ironic result of driving readers from the subject of the criticism: the text.[10]

Practitioner Donalyn Miller's outstanding practice of honoring the personal and aesthetic views of sixth-grade students in order to effectively mentor their progress with literary understanding is a wonderful example of Rosenblatt's ideas. Miller's young readers know the importance of not only articulating their personal responses, but also of returning to the literature to justify and clarify their impressions of a literature selection.[11] Louise Rosenblatt in *Literature as Exploration* also argues that it is important for the teacher to avoid imposing any "preconceived notions about the proper way to react to any work."[12] This places an important responsibility on the teacher, who must not only allow for personal interpretations of a children's book but also be aware of the literary qualities worthy of examination—a process that requires any reader to return to the book, to look again at what is there in light of personal connections or questions in need of clarification.

Margaret Mackey[13] describes the importance of returning to the book when she shares the limitations of a single reading for both students *and teachers* as they tackle the composite nature of quality literature and layered responses. Mackey's study related to findings from readers of adolescent literature, but we believe the same recommendation holds true for all readers, including the readers of this handbook. Consider Emily Gravett's *The Rabbit Problem;* readers encountering this picturebook will delight in the multiplying rabbits and the format resembling a hanging wall calendar that captures the year in which the story is set. Each month the expanding rabbit family and their habitat are revealed through interactive elements; readers will stop to open letters, fliers, and personal correspondence as they view one year in the life of a rabbit. An initial read would be partial and inadequate; a second reading would reveal elements of fantasy or perhaps how each of Gravett's techniques assists with the suspension of disbelief. Later still, a reader with interest in mathematics may recognize the Fibonacci number sequence revealed by the final pop-up pages. Each reading allows for a different level of interpretation by an increasingly informed reader.

The act of reading a book once or twice in and of itself does not assure the kind of response Rosenblatt and Mackey describe. For that reason we have increased the emphasis on literary response through mediated experiences that guide literature interpretation in a separate chapter that serves as a capstone to this edition. Reading aloud can be an interactive and responsive event, as can opportunities to respond in meaningful discussions that can take many forms. The connections between writing and appreciating how literature works are also important. By emphasizing and clarifying the ways reading aloud and encouraging spoken and written response to books lead to deepened literary understanding, teachers receive knowledge of practical value.

Understanding Books in the Company of Other Books

Books can be understood and analyzed individually, but they may best be understood in the company of other books. Examining a book in relation to other books provides a certain repetition that confirms and reaffirms a reader's understanding not just of the book, but how it "works." This concept is not new to literature; authors and illustrators are continually reading, writing, and creating in a world of literature the formats, genres, and literary techniques that have come before. It is an idea not found in previous editions of this handbook but one that will be a critical element in the ninth edition. We first introduce the concept of intertextuality here and provide further discussion in the next section, "To the Reader."

Intertextuality

All children's books are a plurality of other texts, containing subtle, but often purposeful, traces of other stories in both illustration and words. A book may initially be critiqued for the qualities it possesses, but the process of examining its literary content inevitably leads to other connections within and between other texts. Books depend upon, interact with, and generate other texts as writers and artists read, learn, and borrow from the writers and artists they admire. For example, in her science fiction novel, *When You Reach Me,* Rebecca Stead relies on the concept of the tesseract from Madeleine L'Engle's *A Wrinkle in Time.* In a different approach, Anthony Browne parodies paintings by great artists in his picturebook, *Willy's Pictures.* Characters from classic stories intermingle as J. Patrick Lewis weaves a story of the quest for imagination in *The Last Resort.* Roberto Innocenti's illustrations reveal more than half of this story's secrets. *The Last Resort* depends on a reader having a broad background in classic literature, but J. Patrick Lewis assists readers by providing informative back matter. The concept of intertextuality is not new to literature for adults, and because it is increasingly evident in books for children and young adults, we are incorporating ideas about intertextuality into our revisions of the handbook.

Stories lean on other stories, and texts are always understood in a relationship with other texts. We believe that books should not be considered in isolation. In this edition of *A Critical Handbook of Children's Literature* we rely on the theory of intertextuality and the belief that "intertextuality refers to all kinds of links between two or more texts."[14] This does not mean that a focus on the text ignores what the reader contributes "because a reader brings to a text all of the other texts she has read, as well as her own cultural context. An 'allusion only makes sense if the reader is familiar with the hypotext (the text alluded to).'"[15] The Ahlbergs' humor in their classic interactive picturebook, *The Jolly Postman or Other People's Letters,* relies on knowledge of European folktales in both the illustration and the texts.

Authors, like the Ahlbergs, borrow from other stories purposely, but children's books "are inherently intertextual, constituted by elements of other texts."[16] The intertextual links that exist between conventions such as genre or style[17] can be revealed by examining literature—a process that provides a keen understanding of literature and how it encourages reading, writing, and literacy.[18]

We will apply the concept of intertextuality as we recommend books related through genre, literary elements, topics, or concepts. A variety of textsets will present multiple books in relational ways that support readers' search for quality books. Lawrence Sipe[19] called the relationship between illustrations and words in picturebooks "synergy"; the larger understanding that comes from examining clusters of books can be called a kind of synergy as well. Just as David Lewis[20] represented the relationship between words and pictures by coining the term *picturebook* from the traditional *picture book,* we will refer to *text set* as a *textset* to reflect the synergy created by the interaction between multiple books whose similarities and differences can create something *more* in the mind of an involved reader.

Our textsets frequently represent the way books change and then inspire new growth—books that are original, yet clearly have roots in previously existing stories. Bill Thomson's *Chalk* reminds us of the classic *Harold and the Purple Crayon,* but the surreal illustrations combine fantasy with a feeling of reality that leaves readers with a very different set of possibilities. The beautifully illustrated winner of the 2011 Caldecott Medal, *A Sick Day for Amos McGee* by Philip Christian and Erin Stead, is reminiscent of the comforting *Goodnight Moon* by Margaret Wise Brown and Clement Hurd. The red balloon that accompanies the zoo animals' visit is symbolic of the many children's stories in which a sense of adventure is attached to a balloon, as with the *You Can't Take a Balloon into . . .* series by Jacqueline Preiss Weitzman and Robin Preiss Glasser. At the end of this preface, as in each chapter of this handbook, we provide a small textset offering examples of intertextuality in books for children.

We find promise in the metaphor of the rhizome: a plant whose root systems rely on interconnections, replication with variation, and multiple pathways for new growth. Eliza Dresang confirmed the power of this metaphor from plant biology in the preface of her classic *Radical Change: Books for Youth in a Digital Age,*[21] where she makes this very apt comparison to describe the networks of interrelationships in the digital world. Adapting this rhizome metaphor has current utility and will inform the structure and content within each chapter. Though not explicitly referenced, it will be represented in the ways we present examples of literature in related clusters. It will be especially evident when our selections include classics alongside currently established titles as well as those newly published, revealing how books lean on those that have come before. The metaphor also provides a structure for the variety of textsets in each chapter, whose styles reinforce the ways children's literature has radically changed in form, style, and the subjects it includes. Literature grows and changes in ways that are predictable, yet the novelty of new genre blends constantly surprises and pleases readers. Appreciating and fully understanding the many changes in children's literature requires a stance of active inquiry; readers of this handbook will benefit from the same approach as they realize the additions to the ninth edition.

What Is New to the Ninth Edition

Based on research in the field of children's literature, contributions of outside reviewers, and our own close examination of the eighth edition of *A Critical Handbook of Children's Literature,* the ninth edition reflects significant changes. Outlining what is new here, the preface introduces the significance of each point, and each will be realized throughout the chapters of this book.

- Extensive **Recommended Books** and other booklists, with new and current titles, are included in this edition. They are organized not only according to literary categories for children's literature, but also by topics and concepts of interest to contemporary readers.

- As mentioned, the literature we share will frequently be organized as **Textsets,** augmenting the updated lists of recommended titles for children and young adults. These additional sets of titles range from classics to currently popular to brand-new books and are designed not only to model what a textset can be, but also to introduce additional titles the reader may want to research.

- To invite inquiry and an appreciation for the ways books are interrelated, **Inquiry Points** are placed intermittently throughout each chapter to invite readers to engage with a concept, to inquire further about a new idea, or to research suggested titles.

- Following this preface a new introduction, **To the Reader,** will more efficiently organize many of the points from the previous "To the Teacher" and "To the Student." Both the preface and this unified introduction are addressed to you, "the reader," who may be a practicing or pre-service teacher, a librarian, a parent, or a course instructor; it is for any student of children's literature, though each person's background and approaches to the use of the book will certainly vary.

- Children's books are cultural artifacts. As such they reflect cultural changes. **Chapter 2, Issues and Fundamental Changes in Children's Literature,** reveals extensive revisions. Although it pulls threads from chapters in the previous edition, it is dedicated to some of the important changes currently affecting children's literature. In Chapter 2 we briefly share research on the effects of the digital age on children's books, ways children interact with wordless picturebooks, the growing interest in graphic and verse novels, and the impact of blended genres and postmodernism on children's picturebooks.

- **Chapter 3, Picturebooks,** focuses on the picturebook format, in which significant attention is given to illustration, including the artistic styles, media, and design features of contemporary picturebooks. Just as important is the attention the reader must give to the relationship between the illustrations and the verbal text, an emphasis in Chapter 3. The literature titles selected for this chapter and those recommended in the textset are almost completely revised. Readers of this handbook will find additional picturebook examples integrated into every chapter.

- **Chapter 9, Style and Tone,** is designed to show how these two elements share many qualities and how each can influence the other. Style, which largely consists of syntactical choices, influences tone. Combining these two shorter chapters from the previous edition allows readers to better understand this relationship and see how these two elements of a text influence each other.

- Interaction with literature through reading aloud, encouraging discussion, and independent reading have been added as important topics to **Chapter 14, A Lifetime of Reading,** to emphasize that neither reader nor context can be ignored when considering the selection and analysis of a children's book.

MyEducationKit™

Prepare with the Power of Classroom Practice. MyEducationKit's easy-to-assign homework and activities will engage your students and ensure that they come to class more prepared. It saves you the class time that would otherwise be spent reviewing the basics and lets you devote that time to higher-level learning experiences. Informed by evidence-based practice, MyEducationKit connects your course content to real classrooms with interactive exercises and activities that enhance students' learning and give them a deeper understanding of teaching.

- Prepare your students to analyze, reflect, and respond to **real classroom situations** with assignments that provide video, case studies, and authentic student and teacher artifacts.

- Search through more than **22,000 exemplary titles of children's and young adult literature** on Pearson's Children's and Young Adult Literature Database.

- Reflect on the craftsmanship behind quality children's and young adult literature using the **podcasts and conversations** with many of today's top writers and illustrators.

- Use the **lesson planning software** to develop high-quality lesson plans. The software also makes it easy to integrate your state's content standards into all of your lesson plans.

- Prepare your students to pass their teacher licensure exams by familiarizing them with **teacher certification test** requirements. This module includes descriptions of what is covered on each exam and opportunities to answer sample test questions.

SUMMARY

Children's literature remains familiar, yet the field includes continuous examples of change and originality. We strive to present you, the reader, with examples of books to encourage thoughtful examination of literature that inspires, enriches, and informs readers in the ways literature works. This preface outlines ways this edition adheres to previous editions of *A Critical Handbook of Children's Literature* and also presents elements of change readers will explore within the chapters of the ninth edition. The introductory chapter that follows contains some purposeful repetition of concepts and ideas from this preface. In addition, "To the Reader" will launch our pattern of updated literature for children and young adults, inquiry points that invite readers to interact with concepts, and textsets that model the many ways literature can be combined.

The useful organizing structure in the chapters of this handbook assists transactional reading and encourages informed multiple readings. When using this handbook, we strongly recommend reading or rereading some of the suggested books prior to or during each chapter, most notably E. B. White's *Charlotte's Web*. Readers will also find Patricia and Fredrick McKissack's nonfiction narrative, *Christmas in the*

TEXTSET

Intertextual References in Children's Picturebooks

Ahlberg, Allen. *Previously.* Bruce Ingman, Illus. Candlewick, 2007.
Favorite story characters are linked through their actions prior to the stories we know and love, such as what Jack and Jill were doing prior to their fateful walk up the hill.

Ahlberg, Janet, and Allen Ahlberg. *The Jolly Postman.* LB Kids, 2001.
Readers delight in overt references to folktales in the illustrations and interactive pieces in this classic book.

Almond, David. *Skellig.* Hodder, 1998. Delacorte, 1999.
Allusions to Blake's poetry.

Browne, Anthony. *Into the Forest.* Candlewick, 2004.

Browne, Anthony. *Me and You.* Farrar, Straus & Giroux, 2010.
Readers discover the story of Goldilocks and how she happened upon the home of the Three Bears in this dual-perspective version of the popular tale.

Browne, Anthony. *The Tunnel.* Knopf, 1990.
Two stories in which children experience strange events depending on allusions to popular folktale motifs.

Browne, Anthony. *Willy's Pictures.* Candlewick, 1999.

Browne, Anthony. *Willy the Dreamer.* Candlewick, 2002.
Browne alludes to famous paintings through parody as well and includes an appendix to build art appreciation.

Creech, Sharon. *Hate That Cat.* HarperCollins, 2008.

Creech, Sharon. *Love That Dog.* Perfection, 2003.

When a young boy learns to understand and appreciate various forms of poetry, readers understand the concept of intertextuality and how it is a natural part of literary learning.

Crummel, Susan Stevens. *The Little Red Pen.* Janet Stevens, Illus. Harcourt, 2011.
Poor Little Red Pen needs the help of the other school supplies to get her papers corrected— will they help?

L'Engle, Madeleine. *A Wrinkle in Time.* Farrar, Straus & Giroux, 1962.

Stead, Rebecca. *When You Reach Me.* Wendy Lamb, 2009.
Stead won the 2010 Newbery Medal for this book, which relies on the time travel and "tessering" first introduced by Madeleine L'Engle in her series starting with the 1962 classic *A Wrinkle in Time.*

Lewis, J. Patrick. *The Last Resort.* Roberto Innocenti, Illus. Creative Publications, 2002.
Allusions to classic literature makes this a great picturebook addition for young adults!

Miranda, Anne. *To Market, to Market.* Janet Stevens, Illus. Harcourt Brace, 1997.
Imagine the literal interpretation of the well-known nursery rhyme, "To Market, to Market"!

Seibold, J. Otto. *Re-Nurseried!! And Re-Rhymed!! Children's Classics.* Chronicle, 2010.
Appreciation of these hip and humorous fractured rhymes, such as 'Rain, Rain, don't go away,' depend on readers' familiarity with the original versions.

Shulevitz, Uri. *Snow.* Scholastic, 1998.
Award-winning picturebook artist Uri Shulevitz subtly integrates popular Mother Goose characters in this child's-wonder-in-the-snow story.

Wheeler, Lisa. *Spinster Goose: Twisted Rhymes for Naughty Children.* **Sophie Blackall, Illus. Atheneum, 2011.**	**Wiesner, David.** *The Three Pigs.* **Clarion, 2001.**
Spinster Goose is the stern headmaster at a reform school for totally unruly children; the lessons are told in sinister verse with contrasting illustrations by Sophie Blackall.	You will never read *The Three Pigs* in the same way once you experience this version that is thoroughly impacted by the postmodern. Wiesner alludes to his other originally fantastic picturebooks in the illustrations.

Big House, Christmas in the Quarters, very valuable. A contemporary picturebook such as David Macaulay's *Black and White* or David Wiesner's *The Three Pigs* will also foster appreciation for changes evident in contemporary picturebooks. Encouraging students to sample books across a variety of genres and formats before, during, and after reading certain chapters will also provide students with a complete sense of the field.

Acknowledgments

We are grateful to the many teachers, pre-service teachers, and librarians we consider our companions in the study of children's literature—those insightful readers we know through our teaching and learning experiences, professional networks, and scholarly reading. You'll see cited throughout this book the names of many scholars, critics, writers, and illustrators who continually enriched our thinking, challenging us to not only read some of the most wonderful children's books being published each year, but also to examine them critically. We are grateful as well to the professors in the University of Iowa's Language, Literacy, and Culture Division—in particular Dr. Cynthia Lewis—who opened the door for us to look at and think about texts, contexts, and children and young adult readers in new ways.

For reviews and suggestions, we thank the following: Debbie East, Indiana University; Jacqueline N. Glasgow, Ohio University; Bette P. Goldstone, Arcadia University; Tracey L. Kristo, Anoka-Ramsey Community College; and Stephanie R. White, Cameron University.

We are grateful, too, to the many colleagues who have used earlier editions of *A Critical Handbook of Children's Literature.*

NOTES

1. Eliza Dresang, *Radical Change: Books for Youth in a Digital Age* (New York: H. W. Wilson Company, 1999), p. 14.
2. Sylvia Pantaleo, "Readers and Writers as Intertexts: Exploring the Intertextualities in Student Writing," *Australian Journal of Language and Literacy,* 29(2), 2006, pp. 163–181.
3. We will frequently refer to Eliza Dresang's *Radical Change,* which has turned out to be quite prophetic in its discussion of the effects of digital media on children's books. Dresang advocates for a dual existence of the digital format and the handheld book—even before the advent of the Kindle, the Nook, the iPad, and various handheld reading devices.

4. According to Bowker's 2011 industry statistics for new book titles and editions from 2002 to 2009, publishing dipped slightly but rebounded at the end of this decade. Access this information at www.bowker.com/index.php/home.

5. Nancie Atwell, "The Case for Literature," *Education Week*, 29(21), Fall 2010, p. 32. Nancie Atwell is responding to the call for literacy experts to join in on a discussion about the inclusion of literature in the national standards established by the National Council of Teachers of English. Atwell teaches with literature at the Center for Teaching and Learning, in Edgecomb, Maine. She is highly respected for her books, *The Reading Zone* and *In the Middle*.

6. Margaret Meek, *How Texts Teach What Readers Learn* (Stroud, UK: The Thimble Press, 1988). Available from www.thimblepress.co.uk. Margaret Meek provides a wealth of private lessons for those interested in literature and literacy in the forty-eight pages of this very readable classic.

7. The importance of literary learning is discussed effectively in Glenna Sloan, *The Child as Literary Critic*: *Developing Literacy Through Literature, K–8* (New York: Teachers College Press, 2003). Sloan considers Northrup Frye's umbrella theory encompassing enough to fit the many theoretical stances applied to the study of children's literature and discusses its merit in "Northrop Frye in the Elementary Classroom," *Children's Literature in Education*, 40, June 2009, pp. 120–135.

8. Donalyn Miller, *The Book Whisperer* (San Francisco, CA: Jossey-Bass, 2009). This book masterfully guides sixth-grade students to go beyond their initial response in talking about books to consider the genre characteristics they find in their reading. It focuses on authors and genres, but does not introduce how "whispering" can go further with literary elements.

9. Louise Rosenblatt, *Literature as Exploration*, 5th ed. (New York: Modern Language Association of America, 1995), p. 139. *Literature as Exploration* is Louise Rosenblatt's groundbreaking work that outlines her response theory. The book was published during a time when readers and their personal, political, social, and cultural backgrounds were not emphasized in the process of literary criticism.

10. Louise Rosenblatt, *The Reader the Text, the Poem: The Transactional Theory of the Literary Work* (Carbondale, IL: Board of Trustees, Southern Illinois University. 1978), p. 140. This is Louise Rosenblatt's second book outlining her transactional theory of reading and her views on reader response.

11. *The Book Whisperer* details the respect teacher researcher Donalyn Miller has for children's ability to not only appreciate quality literature, but also to talk about it as budding literary critics.

12. Louise Rosenblatt, *Literature as Exploration*, 5th ed. (New York: Modern Language Association of America, 1995).

13. Margaret Mackey, "Many Spaces: Some Limitations of Single Readings," *Children's Literature in Education*, 24(3), 1993, pp. 147–163. Mackey convincingly shares her personal and professional experiences with building a relationship between readers and texts through multiple readings.

14. Maria Nikolajeva and Carole Scott, *How Picture Books Work* (New York: Garland Publishing, 2001), p. 227.

15. Maria Nikolajeva and Carole Scott, *How Picture Books Work* (New York: Garland Publishing, 2001), p. 228. Cited in Sylvia Pantaleo, "Readers and Writers as Intertexts." Sylvia Pantaleo also refers to their belief that "intertextuality may be culturally dependent."

16. Norman Fairclough, "Intertextuality in Critical Discourse," *Linguistics and Education*, 4, 1992, p. 270. Cited in Sylvia Pantaleo, "Readers and Writers as Intertexts."

17. Norman Fairclough, "Intertextuality in Critical Discourse," p. 271. Cited in Sylvia Pantaleo, "Readers and Writers as Intertexts."

18. Don Latham, "Empowering Adolescent Readers: Intertextuality in Three Novels by David Almond," *Children's Literature in Education*, 39, 2008, pp. 213–226. Don Latham describes how David Almond employs various types of intertextuality in three novels. Latham provides various interpretations of the term "intertextuality" and shares ways adolescent readers examined sets of texts related to Almond's work. The process empowered the young readers' meaning making.

19. Lawrence Sipe, "How Picturebooks Work: A Semiotically Framed Theory of Text–Picture Relationships," *Children's Literature in Education*, 29(2), 1998, pp. 97–108. Lawrence Sipe has elaborated on the synergy of picturebook interactions and other concepts related to picturebooks in *Storytime* (New York: Teacher's College Press, 2008).

20. David Lewis, *Reading Contemporary Picturebooks: Picturing Text* (London: Routledge-Falmer, 2001). Though the "picture book" was thoroughly explored by Perry Nodelman in *Words about Pictures: The Narrative Art of Children's Picture Books* (Athens, GA: University of Georgia Press, 1988). David Lewis was one of the first to really

delve into the changes occurring in contemporary picturebooks.

21. Eliza Dresang, *Radical Change: Books for Youth in a Digital Age* (New York: H. W. Wilson Company, 1999), pp. xv–xx, 3–16. The preface to this book, which uses this analogy to describe how books change and renew, has recently been published in a digital journal, *Contemporary Issues in Technology and Teacher Education,* 8(3), pp. 277–293.

RECOMMENDED BOOKS

AHLBERG, JANET, AND ALLEN AHLBERG. *The Jolly Postman.* LB Kids, 2001.

BAKER, JEANNIE. *Mirror.* Candlewick, 2010.

BROWN, MARGARET WISE. *Goodnight Moon.* Illustrated by Clement Hurd. HarperCollins, 1947.

BROWNE, ANTHONY. *Willy's Pictures.* Candlewick, 1999.

GRAVETT, EMILY. *The Rabbit Problem.* Simon & Schuster, 2010.

JOHNSON, CROCKETT. *Harold and the Purple Crayon.* HarperCollins, 1998.

L'ENGLE, MADELEINE. *A Wrinkle in Time.* Farrar, Straus & Giroux, 1962.

LEWIS, J. PATRICK. *The Last Resort.* Illustrated by Roberto Innocenti. Creative Publications, 2002.

MACAULAY, DAVID. *Black and White.* Houghton Mifflin, 1990.

MCKISSACK, PATRICIA, AND FREDRICK MCKISSACK. *Christmas in the Big House, Christmas in the Quarters.* Illustrated by John Thompson. Scholastic, 1994.

STEAD, PHILIP CHRISTIAN. *A Sick Day for Amos McGee.* Illustrated by Erin Stead. Roaring Book Press, 2010.

STEAD, REBECCA. *When You Reach Me.* Wendy Lamb, 2009.

THOMSON, BILL. *Chalk.* Marshall Cavendish, 2010.

WEITZMAN, JACQUELINE PREISS. *You Can't Take a Balloon into the Metropolitan Museum.* Illustrated by Robin Preiss Glasser. Penguin Putnam, 1998.

WHITE, E. B. *Charlotte's Web.* Harper, 1952.

WIESNER, DAVID. *The Three Pigs.* Clarion, 2001.

The Three Pigs

David Wiesner

David Wiesner incorporates intertextual connections when he alludes to his other picturebooks in the storyboards the pigs are examining.

TO THE READER

A Critical Handbook of Children's Literature is directed toward a college classroom audience of mature students who expect to work with children and books—whether as parents, librarians, or teachers. This handbook does not stand alone as a classroom text. As with any handbook, it is designed to guide and accompany meaningful inquiry into children's literature. Reading many children's books along with a variety of stories, poems, biographies, and informational books for children will enable any student of children's literature to become well acquainted with the wonderful children's and young adult books currently available. Thoughtfully applying critical criteria to this literature assists students with both responding to and evaluating it. In this ninth edition, the handbook expresses the same conviction as past editions have—that literature for children can be judged by standards similar to those used to judge writing for adults. Children, like adults, read to vicariously explore the world, escape the confining present, discover themselves, or become someone else. In addition, children join adults in their quest for knowledge and their desire for shared literary experiences mediated by a variety of quality books. Because adults—in the roles of teachers, librarians, or parents—help children choose books, we hope to put into your hands the best literature for these purposes.

The Purpose of *A Critical Handbook of Children's Literature*

Becoming an effective literacy teacher, librarian, or thoughtful consumer of children's books involves immersion in the literature written for children and young adults. This special kind of reading reminds us of children's natures and concerns, helping us see how we might guide children toward pleasurable literary experiences, enabling their journey of lifelong reading. The discovery of books that model important qualities of the various formats and genres of children's books and assist in developing critical reading of quality literature is an overarching goal of the revision of this handbook. We invite you to consider the major premises of this edition.

Carefully Examining Quality Literature

A Critical Handbook of Children's Literature remains committed to the idea expressed by the children's poet Walter de la Mare: "Nothing but the best in anything is good enough for the young." Within that guideline, we believe that learning to make critical judgments about what constitutes "the best" or what is "good enough" is vital for a balanced approach to literacy learning for all. How do we learn to analyze literature for children and make critical judgments?

Though the techniques for analysis are ordinary in themselves, an increased awareness of them provides valuable understanding. Throughout the book, the criteria by which one can first identify and then critically analyze quality fiction will be explained. Issues of character, plot, theme, setting, point of view, style, and tone will also be described and exemplified. In addition criteria for judging picturebooks, poetry, biography, and nonfiction informational books will be suggested. Learning to recognize such literary elements as character, plot, and theme helps readers understand the effects a writer achieves and appreciate the reasons for his or her choices. If we skip the evaluative process and avoid applying criteria for excellence, we remove from you—students who are studying children's literature—a valuable opportunity to think. It would be similar to turning children loose in the library or bookstore to learn very little beyond "what's out there."

It is this return to the literature that creates the need for you—current and future librarians, parents, and teachers—to learn to evaluate books for children. Reading for personal and critical response is not simply "picking the work apart." Rather than destroying the work and the reader's pleasure, the process of thinking in critical ways about what is read can provide opportunities for reading the word and the world differently. A response heard from concert pianist Eleanore Vail, in a lecture about music appreciation, seems to apply here: "You and I both love music, but I truly believe that what I know about it vastly increases my appreciation of it." This handbook helps you to examine literature and, in the process, increase your appreciation. It will also help you transfer that appreciation from the college classroom to children, especially when the books you read are of the best quality.

Louise Rosenblatt insisted that the best literature should be the substance of reading. How *do* we choose the best from the thousands of children's books published each year, as well as from the thousands that remain in print year after year?

Current Literature

Lively analysis and response to literature depend on quality books that resonate with contemporary readers. As has been the recent practice for this handbook, we have again updated the lists of recommended children's books for each chapter in our ninth edition, selecting titles that will elicit a layered literary response beyond a reader's initial, personal response. We have done more than simply provide lists of books with newer copyright dates: We have added new formats and blended genres. The picturebook format mirrors this reality, and we include titles with sophisticated illustration, designs, and topics. We have also given more emphasis to historical fiction in this edition. Topics for children's books are expanding, bringing new emphases and opening the door for inquiry not only into the world of the future, but also into an understanding of what has come before. Contemporary selections encourage thought about the global nature of our world, and books can provide thoughtful vicarious experiences for children.

Consider *Mirror*, the recently published and uniquely designed picturebook by Jeannie Baker. Readers of any age will be invited to consider the shared humanity that lies beneath presentations of cultural difference. In this fresh approach to the increasingly popular format of wordless picturebooks, *Mirror* invites exploration into diverse cultures while realizing the commonalities of global human experience, as well as showing the new interactive possibilities that exist for the handheld book. Two interrelated stories mirror one another, both in the physical turning of the pages with side-by-side books and with the daily activity of a family in Australia and another in Morocco. An overview discussion of *multicultural literature* is included in Chapter 2 of this edition, and the importance of this literature for our children who will be global citizens permeated our search for the books we include. This emphasis is reflected in our approach of infusing multicultural books throughout, rather than confining them to a separate chapter. Quality multicultural literature spans all genres and requires thoughtful analysis of its literary elements in much the same way other books do.

Selecting quality books is much more likely when the children's literature community of readers and reviewers is included. We are passionate consumers of children's books and seek the perceptions and expertise of colleagues and respected mentors through journals, conferences, and electronic discussion boards. We drew on several quality professional resources in our search for a variety of great children's books: the Children's Book Council, the American Library Association, the Rutgers Child Lit Listserv, the Bank Street Center for Children's Literature, the National Council of Teachers of English, and Oyate, to name but a few. Children's book awards, some of which are listed in Appendix A of this handbook, are also a fertile source of possibilities for books that can serve as mentor texts.

Lists are valuable, and they assist in the process of creating a landscape of books that inspire action and develop strong conceptual frameworks for learning about literature and life. In this edition of the handbook, we will strive to not only share quality books, but also to present many of these books in relationship to themes and literary elements. The resulting networks will create depth and perspective as they encourage individual choices and multiple opportunities to interact with a literary technique, format, or element. The increased access to interconnected books can demonstrate how literature for children has evolved in response to cultural change and that there is no single "best book." Rather, there are many possible "best books."

The handbook analyzes many of the children's books we considered to be positive examples of the literary elements, formats, and genres that comprise the field of children's literature—noteworthy titles from classics to favorites to those newly published. With this kind of expertise and our own experiences with literature, we have discovered many thought-provoking, important, and motivating titles for children and young adults. We invite you to select from this wide array and discover the ways carefully reviewing and evaluating children's literature sharpens critical skills as it familiarizes you with a wide range of titles.

Reading the Classics of Children's Literature

The concept of "the classic" is an important idea that we would be remiss to ignore. Mark Twain wrote that classics are books nobody wants to read but everybody wants to have read. This is not true for most of the classics of children's literature; readability is a prime reason these books have both been loved by children and admired by adults. Though there is some argument about how exactly to define a classic for children, we consider classics to be books that have worn well, with a strong impact on writers and readers, attracting admirers from one generation to the next. Classics can span all genres, from historical fiction to contemporary realism to fantasy and science fiction. Their impact extends to other writers and artists of children's literature, influencing the direction of children's book publishing in important ways.

Literature written for children has a relatively brief history, and books that have interested two or maybe even three generations are eligible to be called classics; they can be said to connect past and present and hold possibilities for the future.

For instance, the well-known science fiction novel *A Wrinkle in Time* by Madeleine L'Engle can be considered a classic. Unique in its 1962 debut, this 1963 Newbery Medal winner introduced concepts that are central to appreciating *When You Reach Me*, a 2010 Newbery Medal recipient. The story's premise of multiple dimensions and travel through time and space will likely intrigue readers for years to come.

Classic books have a strong impact on generations of writers and readers. For example, the importance of immigration to the history of United States is reflected in Eleanor Estes's *The Hundred Dresses* and Joseph Krumgold's *Onion John*. Both are classic stories of Eastern European immigrants from the 1950s with parallels to current discussions about immigration, which in turn may inform those sure to arise in the future. We can see their themes being revisited in currently popular historical fiction such as *Esperanza Rising* by Pam Muñoz Ryan or the picturebook memoirs, *La Mariposa* by Francisco Jimenez and Pat Mora's *Tomás and the Library Lady*. Shaun Tan's acclaimed graphic narrative, *The Arrival*, may become a classic in the future.

The elements keeping classics in continuous circulation probably include the significance of theme, the credibility of character, the continuing reality of the conflict, and the engaging quality of style. Even as the diversified family farm becomes extinct and cultural expectations for girls change, E. B. White's finest novel, *Charlotte's Web*, will continue to be loved. White's thorough portrayal of character, his choice of life-and-death conflict, his affectionately humorous tone, and his presentation of universal themes about friendship, satisfaction, and death are elements associated with classics rather than works whose popularity fades.

Another notable feature of classics in today's world is the likelihood that they will be *viewed* and experienced visually as well as read in their familiar bound paper formats. The 2006 movie version of *Charlotte's Web* assures additional circulation and the possibility of renewed readership of the book for generations to come. The qualities of *Alice's Adventures in Wonderland* as children's literature have also inspired its recent film version. *Alice* remains an incomparable work of nonsense; readers have never outgrown Carroll's wit, and his playful inventiveness remains unsurpassed. Similarly, Chris Van Allsburg's *The Polar Express*, Kay Thompson's *Eloise Takes a Bawth*, and Maurice Sendak's *Where the Wild Things Are* all contain themes of childhood that have allowed them to gain status as classics and as film. The appeal of classic stories can remain for a surprisingly long time, and classic stories from one generation are frequently appropriated by newer formats and styles that entice children in different ways. But their move from one art form to another and from book to film involves significant changes essential not only to the new art form, but also to make them appeal to today's children whose lives and expectations are so different from those of past generations.

In our view, a book that is a **classic** is one that influences other writers, illustrators, and readers who study and learn from classics and adapt them in important and timely ways. A classic inspires new growth, and it should be read in relationship with other books and in accordance with the times in which it was written and for its intended audience. The classics inspire stories and responses, connections and inquiry into numerous content areas—they mentor readers not only in their literacy with books but also with other kinds of texts such as film, drama, and artistic expression. Just as important, classic texts, indeed much of quality children's literature, because of the artistry of its language or the intelligence of its visuals, encourages reading aloud, literary and critical discussion, and writing.

Texts That Mentor

As in previous editions of *A Critical Handbook of Children's Literature* we will include a discussion of numerous books cited for their importance and contribution to different literary genres, formats, or elements, as well as for the joy they have brought to our personal literacy histories. We will frequently refer to books, established and new, whose quality is such that they stand the test of time, as **mentor** texts, realizing there is an expanding notion of which books across format and genre may be considered "the best," if the numerous awards for children's books are any indication. For this reason, some mentor texts, including picturebooks that have particular interest and versatility, will be shared across chapters, as with *Charlotte's Web* in previous editions. For example, we discuss David Macaulay's classic picturebook, *Black and White*, with its experiments in multiple plotlines and a resolution open to reader interpretation. Shortly thereafter, we discuss *The View from Saturday*, a contemporary children's novel told from the multiple perspectives of a diverse group of sixth-graders. Both were unique works that influenced other authors and illustrators to push at the boundaries of what a children's book could be. They are examples of mentor texts that rarely stand alone for very long.

Few children's books are fully realized in isolation. Books affect other books, explicitly or subtly, in much the same way various writers influence other writers. Each of the mentor books could be enjoyed on its own, but would be better appreciated in the company of other books that share literary aspects or important topics readers want to explore. This clustering of related books creates the possibility for an important book to remain in the hands of children a bit longer; newer books shared in the company of an established work of literature are enriched. Pairing an older but award-winning story of migrant workers, *Roosevelt Grady*, written in the early 1960s, with more recent stories of migrant workers, like Julia Alvarez's recent award-winning novel of migrant workers in Vermont, *Return to Sender,* or the unique migrant perspective in Maxine Trottier's *Migrant,* has an important effect. Having children *also* read Francisco Jimenez's immigration story, *The Circuit,* or the compelling story, *Dark Water* by Laura McNeal, along with a nonfiction presentation of stories about migrant workers, like Kathleen Krull's award-winning biography of Cesar Chavez, *Harvesting Hope,* further empowers readers with different ways of looking at a topic like immigration; they discover that there are often more than two sides to a story. Great books can serve as mentor texts that inspire readers, writers, and lovers of children's books to find related books on the shelves of their libraries and bookstores.

Texts in Combination

Our emphasis on literature (the classics, currently popular, and brand new) returns us to the idea of intertextuality introduced in the preface. Any book exists in a relationship with other books through its genre, format, literary elements, or author and illustrator techniques. That is, books are positioned not along a continuum, but in an intertextual landscape that allows them to be analyzed individually and collectively according to particular features. Books relate to multiple texts both present and past in numerous ways; "intertextuality" can refer to features like the illustration or design elements in the picturebook format. A reader intrigued by Joyce Sidman's 2011 Newbery Honor book, *Dark Emperor and Other Poems of the Night,* might search for other picturebooks that blend poetry with nonfiction, such as Tracie Vaughn Zimmer's *Cousins of Clouds: Elephant Poems.* Another reader of Sidman's fine book might connect with the message conveyed in the endpapers whose opening lavender conveys the evening; the orange of sunrise signals the night giving way to day at book's end. An exploration of books with significance in the endpapers, such as those of Roni Schotter and Giselle Potter's *The Boy Who Loved Words,* might follow. A single book encourages multiple connections; readers branch out to other books in accordance with their individual interests and the characteristics of the books they encounter.

This handbook's intertextual emphasis also relates to current practices that integrate children's literature into virtually all areas of the curriculum. It is valuable to help students see that literary connections occur within and between children's books, but it is also important that readers appreciate opportunities to connect literature with topics from healthy living, science, social studies, mathematics, music, or art. For example, the work of animal activist and conservationist, Dr. Jane Goodall, is accessible to younger readers in two biographies: *Me . . . Jane* by Patrick McDonnell and *The Watcher: Jane Goodall's Life with the Chimps* by Jeanette Winter. Children can compare the styles of writing or illustration in these two books, and explore their impact on the story a reader constructs about an important humanitarian. Or, young sports enthusiasts may marvel at Bill Thomson's realistic art that looks as though a camera is angling in for the varied perspectives of boys and girls actively involved in their favorite competitive sport in a trio of Carol Nevius picturebooks: *Karate Hour, Baseball Hour,* and *Soccer Hour.* Readers can apply what they learn from children's books to the world at large, to solving problems or exploring social issues.

Our selection of various texts recognizes the power of individual books but respects their connection with other quality children's books, through both subtle allusion and explicit references. The basic concept of "intertextuality" will be applied throughout this handbook. We envision a landscape of children's literature, growing in multiple directions, sprouting new genres, styles, formats, themes, and plot structures as readers and writers transact with and respond to multiple texts. Each chapter will include many children's books situated within **textsets**—clusters of related books. The following three textsets related to the classic *Eloise* picturebook series are each based on a different style or focal point to demonstrate a few of the many possibilities for this feature.

Kay Thompson and Hilary Knight's classic *Eloise* series enjoyed widespread popularity in the late 1950s and 1960s and also in the late 1990s when various episodes were reissued. Adults who remembered the books from childhood were eager to revisit them with grandchildren. When a new Eloise story by Kay Thompson was discovered, it was illustrated and published posthumously by Hilary Knight in 2002, forty years after the first *Eloise* book was a hit. *Eloise Takes a Bawth* immediately climbed to number one on the *New York Times* best-seller list.

One of the first books to feature an active young girl as a main character, the original Eloise was much loved by many girls and their parents. However, this pampered star of the book series may not be representative of current attitudes of girls. We see ways readers might update this character in the following textsets, which are a sample of the varied styles of textsets we will incorporate into the handbook. Some textsets are annotated, some are centered around a point of inquiry, and some are unannotated lists of books related to a particular concept.

An Annotated Textset: Extending a Classic

This annotated textset for *Eloise Takes a Bawth* shows the types of comments that may be provided for books within textset lists.

TEXTSET

Countering Ideology in *Eloise Takes a Bawth*

Eloise Takes a Bawth was published in 2002, but it reflects the same attitudes about gender and class as the original series did in the 1950s and 1960s. The fun look back at a classic character seems slightly out of place in today's world. Much of the story is revealed through the depictions of Eloise's pampered existence at the Plaza Hotel in New York. Though she has freedom from her absent parents (and a self-absorbed nanny who looks the other way), her movement is confined to "home." She can "do" only in her imagination, shown by Hilary Knight's pen-and-ink drawings. This textset's companion books provide additional possibilities for Eloise, showing empowered young girls in action around the world.

Adler, David A. *America's Champion Swimmer: Gertrude Ederle.* Terry Widener, Illus. Perfection Learning, 2005.

Each part of a picturebook has the potential to tell some of the story. The back flap of the new Eloise book jacket shares an endorsement from bathing beauty and film star, Esther Williams. Esther reveals a kinship she has with Eloise: "We don't swim fast, we swim pretty!" This parodic endorsement reveals that Eloise might benefit from finding out about another swimmer who *didn't* swim pretty—she swam *fast*—becoming the first woman to swim the English Channel (and faster than the men of the time). Gertrude Ederle's story is effectively told by David Adler.

Brown, Don. *Uncommon Traveler: Mary Kingsley in Africa.* Sandpiper, 2000.

Eloise is confined to the Plaza Hotel, with piles of toys. As she searches for things to do, it never occurs to her to find inspiration and stimulate her imagination by reading a book. Like Eloise, Mary also had intermittent visits from her father, and was confined—but in a Victorian manse. However, rather than find nothing but mischief, Mary is resourceful and independent, reading from her father's library. Finally free, she travels to Africa, experiencing wonderful adventures. Unlike Hilary Knight's illustrations, which carry the Eloise story, Don Brown's are less important than the biography he narrates.

Corey, Shana. *You Forgot Your Skirt, Amelia Bloomer.* Chesley McLaren, Illus. Scholastic, 2000.

Eloise loves fashion! Here is the story of another fashionable young woman, who designed appropriate clothes for women to play outside. Unlike Eloise, she also fought for women's suffrage.

Crew, Gary. *Bright Star.* Anne Spudvilas, Illus. Kane/Miller Book, 1997.

Wouldn't Eloise wonder about the restrictions on girls in the mid-1800s and what it took to realize the dream of becoming an astronomer? Gary Crew's nice fictional story is based on the true story of a girl from history. Anne Spudvilas's illustrations provide additional information about this time period.

Hazen, Barbara Shook. *Katie's Wish.* Emily Arnold McCully, Illus. Dial, 2002.

Eloise accomplishes goals only in her imagination. As with most of the young girl protagonists McCully illustrates, Katie overcomes adversity, the loss of her mother and the absence of her father. Unlike Eloise who was surrounded with abundance, Katie must survive the mid-1800s Irish potato famine. Katie finally realizes that it was not her childish actions that caused the famine, unlike

(continued)

Eloise, who sees little connection between her actions and the disaster at the Plaza Hotel.

Hopkinson, Deborah. *Maria's Comet*. Deborah Lanino, Illus. Aladdin, 2003.

This is a story of the childhood of the first professor of astronomy at Vassar. Eloise would benefit from meeting this young girl who also came from a little privilege, but took advantage of it in a positive way—to stretch herself and accomplish a goal.

McBrier, Page. *Beatrice's Goat*. Lori Lohstoeter, Illus. Atheneum, 2001.

Eloise has no concerns about money or responsibility in her world of privilege. The pricey damage done to the Plaza Hotel will simply be charged to her father. We don't know, but it's likely that Eloise has private schooling. Beatrice, on the other hand, is a young girl without many advantages who craves the opportunity to attend school. Receiving a goat (through Heifer International), she earns enough money to go to school.

McClintock, Barbara. *Dahlia*. Farrar, Straus & Giroux, 2002.

Eloise is missing strong female models and her energy and action are often unsupported; her identity is not examined. In this story about the nineteenth century, Charlotte is allowed to play outside with Bruno, her teddy bear, and the neighborhood boys. She struggles with what to do with the gift of a frilly doll, but receives support from her aunt as she learns to incorporate gender expectations into her lifestyle.

McCully, Emily Arnold. *The Pirate Queen*. Putnam, 1998.

Eloise envisions herself as a pirate during her bathtub escapades. She'd be surprised to know the story of an actual pirate in McCully's swashbuckling tale of Grania O'Malley, Ireland's famed lady pirate. She might also enjoy pairing this with Jane Yolen's *The Ballad of the Pirate Queens* (Harcourt, 1995).

A Listing Textset

This listing textset on children's play demonstrates the basic listing of books within a textset when provided without comments or inquiry text.

TEXTSET

Children's Constructive, Imaginative Play Alone and Together

Action is an important part of the plot of the Eloise series. But, in *Eloise Takes a Bawth* Eloise played by *herself*; her adventures are *only* in her imagination. She played actively in the bathtub, but the results were anything but constructive. We recommend adding these fictional stories that feature children playing alone and together creatively, constructively, and with imagination—or books that invite a reader to interact playfully and imaginatively. Boys are allowed!

Playing Together

Frazee, Marla. *A Couple of Boys Have the Best Weekend Ever*. Harcourt, 2008.

Gravett, Emily. *Monkey and Me*. Simon and Schuster, 2007.

Grey, Mini. *Traction Man is Here!* Alfred A. Knopf, 2005.

Lehman, Barbara. *Rainstorm.* Houghton Mifflin, 2007.

Lehman, Barbara. *The Red Book.* Houghton Mifflin, 2004.

Lehman, Barbara. *The Secret Box.* Houghton Mifflin, 2011.

Meade, Holly. *Inside! Inside! Inside!* Marshall Cavendish Children's Books, 2005.

Morrison, Toni. *The Big Box.* Giselle Potter, Illus. Jump at the Sun, 1999.

O'Connor, George. *KAPOW!* Simon and Schuster, 2004.

Zolotow, Charlotte. *William's Doll.* William Pène du Bois, Illus. HarperCollins, 1972.

Time Alone

Child, Lauren. *I Absolutely Must Do Coloring Now or Painting or Drawing.* Grosset & Dunlap, 2006.

Tullet, Hervé. *The Book with a Hole.* Tate Publishing, 2011.

Tullet, Hervé. *The Coloring Book.* Tate Publishing, 2009.

Tullet, Hervé. *Press Here.* Chronicle, 2011.

An Inquiry Textset

This inquiry textset for *Eloise Takes a Bawth* demonstrates the possibilities for delving deeper into the interconnectedness of books and the opportunities they provide to understand additional perspectives.

TEXTSET

What Might Eloise See Outside of the Plaza in New York City?

Setting is an important element in *Eloise Takes a Bawth*. If Eloise left the Plaza Hotel, she might have found other things to do—or other activities for her imaginary fun right there in New York City. Let's explore! What other stories across genres are available for young readers interested in New York City?

Collier, Bryan. *Uptown.* Henry Holt and Co., 2004.

Curtiss, A. B. *The Little Chapel That Stood.* Oldcastle Publishing, 2003.

Gerstein, Mordecai. *The Man Who Walked Between the Towers.* Square Fish, 2007.

Harwayne, Shelley. *Messages to Ground Zero: Children Respond to September 11, 2001.* Turtleback, 2001.

Hopkinson, Deborah. *Sky Boys: How They Built the Empire State Building.* James E. Ransome, Illus. Schwartz & Wade, 2006.

Melmed, Laura Krauss. *New York! New York! The Big Apple from A to Z.* Frané Lessac, Illus. HarperCollins, 2005.

Mullin, Michael. *Larry Gets Lost in New York City.* Sasquatch Books, 2010.

Platt, Richard. *Through Time: New York City.* Kingfisher, 2010.

Puck. *Wow! New York: Imagine a City Built with a Paper Clip.* Rey David Rojas, Illus. Duo Press, 2010.

Rappaport, Doreen. *Lady Liberty: A Biography.* Matt Tavares, Illus. Candlewick, 2008.

Rubbino, Salvatore. *A Walk in New York.* Candlewick, 2009.

Sasek, Miroslav. *This Is New York!* Universe, 2003.

Schulman, Janet. *Pale Male: Citizen Hawk of New York City.* Meilo So, Illus. Knopf, 2008.

Weitzman, Jacqueline Preiss. *You Can't Take a Balloon into the Metropolitan Museum.* Robin Glasser, Illus. Dial, 1998.

Interacting with This Edition

Teachers, parents, and librarians, through their interactions with children and books, are the mediators whose careful actions encourage readers. This is so whether the interactions with literature occur in a large- or small-group instructional setting, a one-on-one consultation, or an intensive tutoring context—a similar transaction takes place.

The process of reading, responding, and analyzing books for their literary qualities in the company of more experienced readers relies on a respect for questioning and for seeking understanding. A handbook is not an exhaustive description of any single topic; it introduces topics important, in our case, to making sense with children's literature. Examples to illustrate each topic are provided, but a spirit of inquiry will assist the reading process. To that end, we will periodically insert **Inquiry Points** that engage you, the reader, with the content of this handbook. These opportunities to clarify and extend the ideas we share will be useful for you not only during the reading of an individual chapter, but afterward as well. Designed for your learning, the inquiry points can be adapted for students of children's literature in other settings. The following inquiry point invites you to consider yourself as a reader who returns to the book to see more closely what is there and then views those insights in relation to other books.

The concept of "home" is common to children's stories, both literally and figuratively. Characters across genres are always leaving home, only to return again. Children of all ages engage with family, friends, or pets in settings that are both familiar and new. Think about the concept of the physical "house" in children's books. Virginia Lee Burton's *The Little House* has been enjoyed, with themes that have endured, since 1942. Its nostalgic look at urban sprawl has been reclaimed in Jeannie Baker's *Home*, published in 2004. A pairing of the books reveals the way technology has changed what can be presented visually in a picturebook. Pair *The Little House* again with the warm scratchboard illustrations in *The House in the Night*. The gold-enhanced black and white illustrations are more

INQUIRY POINT

Can you find other books that relate to the concept of "house" or "home"? Arrange the books so that the classics and most recently published books form a timeline from first to most recently published titles. How do the books build the concept of "house" or "home"? Look for patterns of similarity and difference in the books.

Baker, Jeannie. *Home.* Greenwillow, 2004.

Baker, Jeannie. *Mirror.* Candlewick, 2010.

Baker, Jeannie. *Window.* Walker, 2002.

Burton, Virginia Lee. *The Little House.* Houghton Mifflin, 1942.

Lewis, J. Patrick. *The House.* Creative Editions, 2009.

Swanson, Susan Marie. *The House in the Night.* Houghton Mifflin, 2008. ◉

akin to children's books from previous decades, and they give this 2008 Caldecott book a feeling of nostalgia and, perhaps, stability. In a third pairing, more sophisticated readers will be amazed at Roberto Innocenti's realistic paintings of a house's transformation over time in *The House*, while finding interest in the more global reach from its European setting. Jeannie Baker's aforementioned *Mirror* provides the reader with the sense that homes differ, yet are alike across cultures. These five related books can provide a glimpse of how children's books continually grow, change, and lean on each other.

Interacting with these books, or preparing a set of children's books that relate in a significant way, prepares you to begin thinking of the ways books work in combination. Throughout this handbook you will discover a number of textsets and inquiry points, from the very specific to those more general in nature. We invite readers to use these in ways that matter.

Active Reading

Periodically providing options for you, our readers, to stop and interact with the content of each chapter is an important feature of this handbook. We like the notion of experienced readers encouraging children's active and thoughtful reading by employing an attitude of inquiry toward their own reading. The inquiry points invite a transaction with important concepts for critically analyzing children's literature across genre and format. They encourage extensions such that any reader of the book will benefit from this process of learning about literature while learning *through* literature.

We will conclude our brief introduction with a reminder about Louise Rosenblatt's passion for an active stance during the act of reading for meaning. We also recognize the importance of Wolfgang Iser's concept of the implied reader, an idea that helps us see how writers of children's literature need to imagine the children they think will be reading their work. This theory suggests that readers need to be thoughtful, initially responding to the text personally, but then more closely examining the literature to interpret it. Finally, it is important to consider context; readers respond to literature in a multitude of ways based on the transaction between their own backgrounds and the possibilities discovered in the book. This triad—the book, the child, and the context—a solid study of selected literature, tempered by considerations of both the child and the cultural context—more fully realizes literature's mentoring potential and its impact on literacy learning.

A reference to Rosenblatt's reader response theory is relevant here for a number of reasons. Louise Rosenblatt describes reading as a transaction, or exchange between the reader and the book. The aesthetic—thinking, feeling, and experiencing—of reading literature must be recognized and can best be described as the experiences of pleasure *and* understanding. Rosenblatt describes another reading experience, what she calls "efferent" reading, referring to the acquisition of information through reading. A reader engaged with a passage for this purpose could take time to explore it further before moving ahead, analyzing, critiquing, and questioning. Reading takes readers where they are with what they have experienced, recognizing that different readers have different transactions. For example, many students who read *Charlotte's Web* by E. B. White react pleasurably to the understanding gained about emotions, thoughts, and behavior. Other students might limit an interpretation of this story to elucidation of what a general farm is like, even noting the science lesson on how the different parts of a spider's jointed leg enable it to spin a web. In Rosenblatt's terms, the group stresses the private aesthetic experience of understanding while certain students focus on the public element, the efferent or informative experience.

As you prepare to take advantage of what this handbook has to offer you as a future teacher, parent, or librarian, take a moment to examine the mentor text that has been a part of *A Critical Handbook of Children's Literature* from its beginnings. As with previous editions we make frequent references to the classic *Charlotte's Web;* reading this book prior to engaging with the first chapters will be an advantage to you as a reader. Processing your initial responses prior to any response to the book's literary merit will assist you as you consider the possibilities for this classic with today's child. We may feel amused and touched when we read *Charlotte's Web,* but how do we discuss it, decide its literary worth, or determine its value as a mentor text once the initial personal response has been considered? It is more effective to discuss criteria if each reader, each student of children's literature who reads this handbook, has *Charlotte's Web* in common.

INQUIRY POINT

Look at the cover of *Charlotte's Web.* What do you remember about this well-known book? If you have never read it, what do you *think* you know about this book? Make a three-column chart to jot down your impressions of your reading of this classic *before, during, and after.*

What was the effect of this book on you as a reader? Reread the book. This time, think about its genre or format and any literary qualities you have noticed. Were there things you wondered about—avenues of inquiry you would like to pur-

sue that you find interesting or important? Does the author or illustrator have additional work? Make a concept map or web of these points. Try to find at least two children's books that would connect with each question or topic you included. Reflect on what you discovered in your process and the decisions you made. Share your ideas with a colleague.

Consider your impressions as you work with this ninth edition! ◉

What I remember or *think* I know: In general, I remember	What I found during the reading:	This book has merit or problems within the following elements:
Characters:	Characters:	Characters:
Plot:	Plot:	Plot:
Setting:	Setting:	Setting:
Theme:	Theme:	Theme:
Style & Tone:	Style & Tone:	Style & Tone:
Point of View:	Point of View:	Point of View:
	In general, I noticed:	Your impressions of the qualities of this book:

SUMMARY

The study of critical theories as they apply to literature for both adults and children belongs in a college classroom, to be sure. But that emphasis is frequently for an audience different from students who plan to work effectively with children in a single-classroom experience of children's literature, who may need more practical ideas. As readers and writers, we are indebted to reader response theories, particularly those associated with Louise Rosenblatt. This approach is relevant during times when professionally sanctioned literacy standards promote the inclusion of children's literature as well as an appreciation and understanding of both the way it is organized and the literary elements of each genre. The current emphasis on books and their inherent qualities is important, and we believe that what and how children read matters.

Applying critical standards to children's literature suggests, even affirms, that children's literature is similar to adult literature and that children benefit from good literature. If literature of poor or mediocre quality is all children know, they may be persuaded that reading literature lacks importance for thinking about and understanding the world. This handbook takes the view that, with some small differences, literature for children should be judged by the same standards as literature for adults. Children are more apt to become lifetime readers when their earliest exposure is to literature of high quality and they are encouraged in their efforts to articulate the sense they make of it. Reader response theory provides both an important and relevant critical method, for it encourages a continual branching of new interpretations and responses. We encourage this approach with our readers, as they explore books and their attributes.

RECOMMENDED BOOKS

ALVAREZ, JULIA. *Return to Sender*. Knopf, 2009.

BAKER, JEANNIE. *Mirror*. Candlewick, 2010.

CARROLL, LEWIS. *Alice's Adventures in Wonderland*. Collector's Library, 2009.

ESTES, ELEANOR. *The Hundred Dresses*. Harcourt, 1944.

JIMENEZ, FRANCISCO. *The Circuit*. Houghton Mifflin, 1999.

JIMENEZ, FRANCISCO. *La Mariposa*. Houghton Mifflin, 1998.

KONIGSBURG, E. L. *The View from Saturday*. Atheneum, 1996.

KRULL, KATHLEEN. *Harvesting Hope: The Story of Cesar Chavez*. Illustrated by Yuyi Morales. Harcourt, 2003.

KRUMGOLD, JOSEPH. *Onion John*. Crowell, 1959.

L'ENGLE, MADELEINE. *A Wrinkle in Time*. Farrar, Straus & Giroux, 1962.

LEWIS, J. PATRICK. *The House*. Creative Editions, 2009.

MACAULAY, DAVID. *Black and White*. Houghton Mifflin, 1990.

MCDONNELL, PATRICK. *Me . . . Jane*. Little, Brown, 2011.

MCNEAL, LAURA. *Dark Water*. Knopf, 2010.

MORA, PAT. *Tomás and the Library Lady*. Illustrated by Raul Colón. Knopf, 1997.

NEVIUS, CAROL. *Baseball Hour*. Illustrated by Bill Thomson. Marshall Cavendish, 2008.

NEVIUS, CAROL. *Karate Hour*. Illustrated by Bill Thomson. Marshall Cavendish, 2004.

NEVIUS, CAROL. *Soccer Hour*. Illustrated by Bill Thomson. Marshall Cavendish, 2011.

RYAN, PAM MUÑOZ. *Esperanza Rising*. Scholastic, 2000.

SCHOTTER, RONI. *The Boy Who Loved Words*. Illustrated by Giselle Potter. Schwartz & Wade, 2006.

SENDAK, MAURICE. *Where the Wild Things Are*. HarperCollins, 1988.

SHOTWELL, LOUISA ROSSITER. *Roosevelt Grady*. Illustrated by Peter Burchard. World Publishing, 1963.

SIDMAN, JOYCE. *Dark Emperor and Other Poems of the Night*. Illustrated by Rick Allen. Houghton Mifflin, 2010.

STEAD, REBECCA. *When You Reach Me*. Wendy Lamb, 2009.

TAN, SHAUN. *The Arrival*. Arthur Levine, 2007.

THOMPSON, KAY, AND MART CROWLEY. *Eloise Takes a Bawth*. Illustrated by Hilary Knight. Simon & Schuster, 2002.

TROTTIER, MAXINE. *Migrant*. Illustrated by Isabelle Arsenault. Groundwood, 2011.

VAN ALLSBURG, CHRIS. *The Polar Express*. Houghton Mifflin, 1985.

WHITE, E. B. *Charlotte's Web*. Harper & Row, 1952.

WINTER, JEANETTE. *The Watcher: Jane Goodall's Life with the Chimps*. Schwartz & Wade, 2011.

Charlotte's Web

E. B. White / Illustrated by Garth Williams

Classic books motivate and influence other stories for many years. *Charlotte's Web* continues to inspire us.

CHAPTER ONE

Literature: What Is It?

The Value of Literature

"Literature," as the term is used here, does not include just any printed matter. Literature for children shares the qualities of literature in general; it's a matter of degree.

Readers may click through Guysread.com on the Internet, pick up *Time Magazine* in the supermarket, or look at the photographs in *National Geographic* at the doctor's office. Each of these provides information and vicarious experience, but they are not literature. Literature *may* give us information and vicarious experience, but it also offers much more. What sets a chapter of *Charlotte's Web* apart from a *Small Farm Today* article about animal life on a New England farm? What sets a page in *Christmas in the Big House, Christmas in the Quarters* apart from a list of dates about life on a Tidewater plantation just before the beginning of the Civil War? Many things, and they are at the heart of a definition of literature. Literature is traditionally described as the body of writing that exists because of its inherent imaginative and artistic qualities. The fine line drawn between literature (which is, in Louise Rosenblatt's terms, writing that we *live through* as we read it) and writing that is primarily scientific, intellectual, or philosophical (which we read in an *efferent* or information-receiving way) often wavers; we read these different kinds of texts for different purposes, expecting to come away with different kinds of knowledge.

Why do adults pick up and read a novel or a collection of poetry? Why do you? What is it that readers look for from literature that they don't find in the many factual accounts they read in newspapers? First, from literature of any kind, we seek *pleasure*—not to find a lesson in ecology, not to be taught about the natural habitat of the Louisiana brown pelican or about the perils of global warming. We choose literature that promises entertainment and, sometimes, escape. If other discoveries come to us, too, we are pleased and doubly rewarded.

However, our first motive for reading a novel, leafing through the pages of a picturebook, or chanting a poem is personal pleasure. We may lay the book aside with mixed feelings, but if there is no enjoyment, we reject it completely or leave it unfinished. For adults who have had a variety of experiences, who have known success and failure, who have had to face their own shaky ethical standards, the nature of pleasure in literature may be different from that for children.

We read for pleasure.

Because we are all different, the pleasures we seek as well as those we encounter may be very personal and, for that matter, may vary on different days or occasions. But what is required of us as critical readers is that we examine the pleasure a work of literature aspires to give. As critical readers we don't just stop with our personal pleasure: "I like it, and that's so personal that it cannot be debated." We go on, instead, to find in the work the sources of that personal enjoyment. Dennis Sumara suggests that reading and interpreting literature brings us the pleasure of transforming "imaginative occasions into productive insights."[1] These "surprising and purposeful insights" we find in reading literature may lie in a painful recognition of ourselves, a satisfying verification of our humanness, or in variations of the great questions of the philosopher Immanuel Kant: What must I know? What should I be? What can I hope? But some kind of pleasure is essential, whether the reader is eight or eighty-five years old.

Literature provides a second reward: *understanding*. This understanding comes from the exploration of the human condition and the revelation of human nature. It is not explicitly the function of literature, either for children or for adults, to try to reform humans, or to set up guidelines for behavior; however, it is the province of literature to observe and to comment, to open individuals and their society for our observation and understanding. Information alone may or may not contribute to understanding. We can know a person's height, weight, hair color, ethnic background, and occupation—this is information. But having information—overwhelming us and abundantly available now with the click of a mouse—does not necessarily create the conditions for deep insight. Until we are aware of temperament, anxieties, joys, and ambitions, we do not *know* that person.

Information is *part* of the story, and when we see it, we expect it to be relevant. The following passage from *Roll of Thunder, Hear My Cry* by Mildred Taylor, for example, contains both summarized and detailed information. Here it is Christmas morning:

> In addition to the books there was a sockful of once-a-year store-bought licorice, oranges, and bananas for each of us and from Uncle Hammer a dress and a sweater for me, and a sweater and a pair of pants each for Christopher John and Little Man. But nothing compared to the books. Little Man, who treasured clothes above all else, carefully laid his new pants and sweaters aside and dashed for a clean sheet of brown paper to make a cover for his book, and throughout the day as he lay upon the deerskin rug looking at the bright, shining pictures of faraway places, turning each page as if it were gold, he would suddenly squint down at his hands, glance at the page he had just turned, then dash into the kitchen to wash again—just to make sure.

The effect of the paragraph is not merely to tell about the Christmas presents, but also to reveal something about the characters and their lives. Here is a family devoted to reading, to education, to learning about the world beyond. Books are precious, so precious that they must be protected, and only clean hands may touch them. The home is furnished simply with a deerskin rug that must have been carefully skinned and cured for use. There may be a hunter in the family. This family values appearance and takes good care of their clothing, not taking it for granted; clothes are important as special Christmas gifts, as are fresh fruit and licorice. In order to be part of literature, information in a text must be carefully crafted and provided for important reasons.

This is not to say that all literature is necessarily fictional. There are texts—like our nonfiction **mentor text**, Coretta Scott King award winner *Christmas in the Big House, Christmas in the Quarters,* by Patricia and Fredrick McKissack—that primarily provide us with information, with facts that are true about history, science, mathematics, music, or art, but in which the writers have shaped and deepened the information to provide us with new insights into the world and ourselves. In the case of the McKissacks' book, for example, we see how within one household two different groups of people—the plantation owners and the plantation slaves—get ready for the Christmas of 1859 and what they think about as they prepare. The contrast between the thoughts and experiences of the whites and the blacks, along with the extensive notes the McKissacks present about that day in history, provide us with the deep insight we expect from literature. Literature can take many forms—memoir, information texts about science and new discoveries, histories of past events, even texts presented in both graphics and words. What makes a work literature is its ability to give significance to an experience described in terms of human lives—significance that helps us, whatever our age, to understand a little more about ourselves and others. In the most general terms, then, fictional or nonfictional literature is reading that, by means of imaginative and artistic qualities, provides pleasure and understanding.

Returning to the comparison of the *Small Farms Today* article and *Charlotte's Web,* we can feel fairly certain that although we may enjoy the process, we read the *Small Farms Today* article primarily for information, and we can also be reasonably sure that we read *Charlotte's Web* primarily for pleasure.

Literature has other more specific appeals for us as readers. Literature *shows human motives* for what they are, inviting the reader to identify with or react to a character. We may see into the mind of the character—or into the subconscious that even the character does not know. Through the writer's careful choice of details we come to see clearly the motivation for action. If in these chosen details we see some similarity to our own lives, we identify with the character, feeling that we understand the motives and can justify the deeds. Or seeing the error in judgment that the character fails to see, we understand. Seeing motives we disapprove of, we distrust, or seeing a reflection of our own mistakes, we forgive.

One goal of the writer is to make sense out of life.

Our fictional mentor text, E. B. White's *Charlotte's Web,* serves as a critical example here. It shows the complexity and growth of one character, Wilbur the pig, who at one moment cries out in panic, "I don't want to die! Save me, somebody! Save me!" However, months later his motive for action is selfless concern:

> "Templeton, I will make you a solemn promise. Get Charlotte's egg sac for me, and from now on I will let you eat first, when Lurvy slops me. I will let you have your choice of everything in the trough and I won't touch a thing until you're through."

The motives of Charlotte the spider, however, are born of pure sympathy and a desire to help Wilbur in his suffering. She says briskly that Wilbur will not die, and she weaves words into her web until late at night. A less-than-powerful child reader may identify with Wilbur, the powerless pig, but the adult who reads the book to the child may identify more readily with the selfless Charlotte. In order to call a book a piece of literature, it must have this ability to resonate for a reader at many different stages of life. Though *Charlotte's Web* is an older piece of literature, having been published in 1952, and though some aspects of the text show the limited perspective of its male, white, time-bound author (family farms are much less in evidence now; a young Fern of today might be more feisty, a state fair less safe and inviting), the book's expression of the importance of friendship, the inevitability of death, and its depiction of a life (Charlotte's) well lived, still provides lasting insights into the human experience. *Charlotte's Web* can be considered literature because it provides new insights into the human experience for a reader, at any age, no matter how many times it is read. *Charlotte's Web* can even be considered great literature, because it continues to attract readers well after the people for whom it was written are gone.

Literature offers many kinds of understanding.

Literature also *provides form for experience.* Aside from birth and death, real life has no beginnings or endings but is instead a series of stories without order, each story merging with other stories. Literature, however, makes order of randomness by organizing events and consequences, cause and effect, beginning and ending. When we look back on our lives, we notice the high spots: "the first time we met" or even "the day we sold the SUV." With the perspective given by distance in time, what once seemed trivial now seems important. When we look back, we may be unaware of sequence, because chronology is merely the random succession of life's disordered events. Literature, however, by placing the relevant episodes—"and the next time we met"—into coherent sequence, gives order and form to experience.

Fiction makes order from disparate events.

In *Charlotte's Web* White selects events that, among other things, demonstrate the purpose in Charlotte's life. When she says, "By helping you, perhaps I was trying to lift up my life a trifle," we see more clearly the pattern of Charlotte's behavior. Although she accepts the inevitability of death, she does not accept the prospect of passive waiting. Charlotte chooses instead to fill her days with order and purpose. As White directs our thoughts and alters our feelings in a chosen course, he gives form to the experience of the ongoing cycle of life.

Literature also may *reveal life's fragmentation.* Not a day goes by without our being pulled in one direction after another by the demands of friendship—"Please help." Of obligation—"I promised I would." Of pressure—"It's due tomorrow." And of money—"I wish I could afford it." Life is fragmented, and our daily experience proves it. However, literature, while it may remind us of our own and society's fragmentation, does not leave us there. It sorts the world into disparate segments we can identify and examine; friendship, greed, family, sacrifice, childhood, love, advice, old age, treasures, snobbery, and compassion are set before us for close observation. We will see in future pages how, in this increasingly fragmented and busy age, writers are expressing that fragmentation in new ways.

Literature helps us to identify and examine fragments of experience.

Although literature may be saying or revealing that life is fragmented, it simultaneously *helps us focus on essentials.* In *Christmas in the Big House, Christmas in the Quarters*, the McKissacks have ordered the chaotic experiences of the months and weeks before Christmas Day on the Virginia plantation so as to permit the reader to experience a part of life with different intensity but with new understanding. The McKissacks chose to write about a Christmas on the eve of the secession of the South, just after John Brown's raid on Harper's Ferry, in order to focus the reader's attention on the different perceptions of landowners and slaves at this time. The McKissacks

Literature helps us to see essentials—the meaning and unity of life.

seem to have wanted readers to be aware of the fact that while the white plantation owners celebrate Christmas, the slaves are quietly talking about freedom. In the process of giving order to life, the McKissacks sorted out what they considered the essential details from the nonessential. Undistracted by irrelevant experiences or minor anxieties, readers focus on what the McKissacks want them to see: that which they consider the essentials of action, people, events, and tensions. Because literature ignores the irrelevant and focuses on the essentials, significance becomes clear. As we read, our detachment helps us to see events and their possible influences. Challenged, we make choices, feel the excitement of suspense, and glow with the pride of accomplishment. Literature *says* that life is fragmented. What it *does* is something else: Literature provides a sense of life's unity and meaning.

Literature can *explore and suggest attitudes toward the institutions of society.* A group of people organized for specific purposes may become accepted as an institution, something bigger than separate individuals. This group's judgments can create a form of institutional control that establishes rules about behaviors we might like to determine for ourselves. The institutions of society—like government, family, church, and school, as well as forces that shape our jobs—urge and coerce us into conforming to standards. Literature clarifies our reactions to institutions by showing appropriate circumstances for submitting to or struggling against them.

Literature helps us explore attitudes toward the institutions of society.

In the institution called farming, for example, it is unprofitable to keep a runt pig, because fattening him will not pay a good return on the dollar. In *Charlotte's Web,* Wilbur's existence is in conflict with this institutional truth, and we see what a life-and-death struggle does to an immature innocent. We may not literally identify with Wilbur, but his struggle for life nonetheless has similarities to our own. Wilbur soon discovers who his friends are, how resourceful they can be, how hard they will work for another's safety, and even, in Templeton's case, what a person's price may be. Through Wilbur's struggle with the profit imperative in farming we discover in a small way the impersonal nature of society. In other stories we may discover that racism is institutionalized, or that although we individually hate war, it is sometimes ordered by institutions larger than ourselves. The variety of such conflicts seems infinite. *Christmas in the Big House, Christmas in the Quarters,* for example, challenges the historical institution of slavery. Readers will find many other children's books that similarly make us think and consider actions we might pursue when a problem needs to be solved in society.

Not only do institutions affect our lives, but nature does, too, and as with institutions, literature often *reveals nature as a force* with profound influence. Our natural environment constantly reminds us of its effects on our lives, whether with windstorms, as described in the classic, *The Storm Book* by Charlotte Zolotow, or the more imaginative *Hurricane* by David Wiesner, or with extreme cold and lack of sun and food, as described in nonfiction survival stories like Jacqueline Briggs Martin's *The Lamp, the Ice, and the Boat Called Fish.* Literature, by presenting humans involved in conflict with such weather, makes us see the power of nature on human life.

The natural world may influence us in varied ways.

Nature sometimes demands that humans exert all their powers against it. The now classic *Stone Fox* by John Reynolds Gardiner rivets readers to their seats as they cheer for Willy and his dog Spotlight to win an Iditarod race to save his grandfather's land. Now at its thirtieth anniversary, this book perfectly demonstrates that, although struggling cannot conquer nature, humans may struggle heroically and yet not be conquered. In such a conflict, the reader can applaud the human will.

Literature lets us see
into other lives.

Literature *provides vicarious experiences.* It is impossible for us to live any life but our own, in any time but our own life span, or in any other place but the present. Yet literature makes it possible for us to experience different times, places, and lives. Reading *Christmas in the Big House, Christmas in the Quarters* allows us to experience the Christmastime of a child living in slave quarters on a Virginia plantation, a child for whom winter is "shoe-wearing time," for whom school is a secret, forbidden "pit school" out in the woods, and for whom Christmastime means more, not less, work. We see how that child's parents react to the news of John Brown's raid on Harper's Ferry and also to the escape of a friend, and we feel a bit of what that child must have felt. Literature can provide us with windows through which we see the lives of people different from ourselves, people who live in different countries, speak different languages, value life in different ways than we do. Reading literature by and about people from places and times different from those we live in helps us ask new questions about our own place and time. Our comprehension becomes wider and deeper when our lives become textured with this new, vicarious experience. The possibilities for us to participate in lives other than our own become infinite, as numerous as the books on the library shelves.

The vicarious experience of literature entices and leads us into *meeting an artist-creator* whose medium, words or brush strokes, we know; whose subject, human nature, we live with; whose vision, life's meaning, we hope to understand. We are the student-novice before the artist. In the hands of a gifted writer or painter, we turn from being passive followers into passionate advocates calling new followers. The writer's skill with words, like the artist's ability with shape, color, and line, gives us a pleasure we want to share—and an understanding we have an urge to spread.

Literature for Children and Young Adults

As children's literature critic Peter Hunt writes,

> The children's book can be defined in terms of the implied reader. It will be clear, from a careful reading, who a book is designed for: whether the book is on the side of the child totally, whether it is for the developing child, or whether it is aiming somewhere over the child's head. [2]

Literature for
children can be
defined in terms of
the implied reader.

Another way of putting this is to say that children's literature is different from literature written for adults because of its audience. Children's literature can have all the complexity, resonance, insight, wit, and artistry we find in literature for adults; however, it has a double nature, different from the literature intended to be read only by adults.

Part of the "doubleness" of children's literature is its *dual* audience. Children's literature is written for two audiences: the adult who often buys and approves of the literature and the child who reads it. Children's literature is double also because, differently from adult literature, children's literature is not written by the kind of person who reads it. Children's literature is written by adults for children as adults imagine children to be. Children's literature, then, if it is written for its readers' pleasure, is also written for the pleasure of children as that pleasure is imagined by adult writers.

Like adults, children seek pleasure from a story, but the sources of their pleasure may be somewhat different. Because their experiences are more limited, children may not understand the same complexity in ideas as adults. To deal with this more limited understanding, the expression of ideas in children's books will perhaps be simpler than they are in many books for adults. Stories for children are often more directly told than are stories for adults, with fewer digressions and more obvious relationships between characters and actions, or between characters themselves—though, as we shall see in subsequent chapters, story lines in children's literature are becoming increasingly sophisticated. Though the best children's literature is not overtly didactic, with a moral at the end telling children how to behave, the persuasive intent of a story written for a child is often more explicit, easier to tease out, than is the intent of a story written for an adult. Because children are both more and less literal than adults, they may accept the fantastic more readily than many adults. Children are frequently more open to experimenting with a greater variety of literary forms than many adults will accept—from poetry to folktales, from adventure to fantasy.

When we speak of literature we most often think of the words on the page and the worlds those words create, but when we speak of children's literature we must include the picturebook format as well, with its ever-growing selection of art. Children's literature *provides visual worlds to enter into.* Texture, color, shape, and line, along with shading, contrast, perspective, and balance—these are some of the elements that accomplished children's artists of our time work and play with as they create wonderful new and familiar worlds for us in photographs or watercolors, pen or ink, acrylic or gouache, collage or cartoon. *Charlotte's Web* is a beautiful story, and the drawings of the great Garth Williams enhance the way we understand Wilbur. Once having read the book it becomes difficult to imagine Wilbur in any way other than as Williams has presented him. Who, having leafed through the book, can imagine a plantation Christmas without thinking of John Thompson's warm colors in *Christmas in the Big House, Christmas in the Quarters?* Who can read or hear the story of *The Three Pigs* by David Wiesner without imagining the puzzled and chagrined wolf as the story goes out of control? The great artists of children's literature bring pictures to the words we read, but also, as we will argue in this handbook, bring to the field of children's literature a great deal more.

Literature for children can provide visual worlds to enter into.

As we said earlier, children's literature is always written for children as adult writers imagine them; as society changes, some of the ways adults imagine children and childhood change. We believe that children are imagined somewhat differently now by the adult writers of children's literature than they were in previous decades. Influenced by the arguments of Eliza Dresang, Peter Hunt, Perry Nodelman, and Maria Nikolajeva, we believe that children's literature is still recognizable as a distinct and important body of literature, separate from literature for adults. Unlike literature written for adults, literature written especially for children grapples with questions of innocence at the same time as it seeks to provide knowledge.[3] Yet children's literature is becoming more like literature for adults as society changes. We will go into more detail about these changes in the next chapter.

We want briefly here, before we end this chapter, to clarify some of the differences between children's and young adult literature. There are two different kinds of literature that have been labeled "young adult." One kind of literature—*To Kill a Mockingbird, Lord of the Flies, Catcher in the Rye,* and *A Separate Peace,* for example— was originally written by adults for adults, but because an adolescent was a main character, or because the book captured something true about adolescence, has been incorporated into high school curricula, and taken on as a part of adolescent literature. Most books labeled "young adult literature" have been written expressly with adolescent readers in mind. Most young adult literature is therefore problematic in the same way that children's literature is: It is written by adults for teenagers, as those adult writers imagine teenagers to be.

In "The Harry Potter Novels as a Test Case for Adolescent Literature," Roberta Seelinger Trites provides a helpful explanation of the difference between children's and young adult literature. She writes that *Harry Potter and the Sorcerer's Stone,* the first book of the series, can be considered a children's book, because, as is essential in a children's book, it "portrays parents' love as omnipotent, and it provides a reassuring message about death."[4] The rest of the Harry Potter series, Trites writes, can be considered adolescent literature, because in these books Harry, Hermione, and Ron increasingly explore their sexuality, experience deaths that are frightening, and struggle against powerful institutions that structure their lives. The line between children's and young adult literature is thin and wavering, and there are other explanations for the differences between the two types, but we think this explanation is a provocative and helpful one. In this handbook we will describe both children's and young adult books that we consider to be literature.

Literature for children is somewhat different from literature for young adults.

New Books
Depend on Old Books

We want to reinforce a message from the introductory chapter: We will continuously focus on children's and young adult books that are considered **classics** now as well as books that we believe are classics in the making. We plan to group classic books of both kinds—books that have worn well, attracting readers from one generation to the next, as well as books that have broken new ground, influencing other writers and artists of children's literature—in textsets of related children's books. Textsets, as Lawrence Sipe tells us, contribute to literary competence because "the more stories we know, the greater number of critical tools we bring to bear on any particular story."[5]

Any writer is being influenced by, communicating with, and answering to particular writers who came before her.

We believe that in writing a book any writer is being influenced by, communicating with, and answering to particular writers who came before her. Rebecca Stead's *When You Reach Me* in some ways updates ideas that Madeline L'Engle played with throughout *A Wrinkle in Time.* In *House of Dolls,* a story in four chapters beautifully illustrated by Barbara McClintock, Francesca Lia Block pays homage to Rumer Godden's 1948 classic, *The Doll's House,* which Block's main character Madison Blackberry reads with her mother at the end of the story. We can be fairly certain that Mildred Taylor had read *To Kill a Mockingbird* many times when she wrote *Roll of Thunder, Hear My Cry*. Readers of old and new classics develop a "textual intelligence" [6] that helps them become more literate human beings and better readers and writers. The more quality children's literature readers know and understand, the greater the chance that brave new stories will be created in times to come.

INQUIRY POINT

Writers use others' texts as springboards for their own in many ways. This could be considered a kind of intertextuality, but it is not overt. The writer does not necessarily clearly quote or make reference to another writer who has influenced his work. One writer's novel about the life of a small pig inspires a younger writer to tell a similar story. A reader can only infer this relationship. Similarly, sometimes an adult story of a certain type—the slave narrative, for example—inspires a children's writer to try his hand at writing his own version of the same kind of story for younger readers, as Gary Paulson did in his faux slave narrative *Nightjohn*. Sometimes one writer will have learned aspects of his craft from studying another writer; one can surmise Jarret J. Krosoczka learned some of what he expresses in his wonderful graphic novel *Lunch Lady and the Cyborg Substitute* by reading Dav Pilkey's *Captain Underpants* series. ◉

SUMMARY

Literature at its best gives both pleasure and understanding. It explores what it is like to be a complicated human being living in a complicated world. If these phrases seem too abstract for children's and young adult literature, we can rephrase them in young people's terms:

… and back to pleasure and understanding.

What are people like?

Why are they like that?

What do they need?

What makes them do what they do?

Glimpses of answers to these questions are made visible in poetry or fiction by the elements of plot, character, point of view, setting, tone, and style of an imaginative work; they are brought to our awareness through perspective, color, shape, tone, or design of an artistic work. Nonfiction brings us into other worlds as well, providing us with images of real life and real ideas—mathematics, science, history. All of these kinds of well-crafted writing together constitute literature. Words are merely words, pictures merely pictures, but literature for any age is words and pictures chosen with skill and artistry to give readers delight and to help them understand themselves, others, and the world.

INQUIRY POINT

Writers of children's literature borrow from the adult literature written by others or that they themselves have written. Or, to be more exact, they can think through a problem in one genre and then in another, in their adult writing as well as in their children's writing. As you read E. B. White's *Charlotte's Web*, it can be informative to read White's nonfiction essay, "Death of a Pig," as well. How do you think one text influenced the other? ◉

TEXTSET

Pairing Up with Charlotte's Web

The textset for this chapter will invite you to examine issues and themes from the classic *Charlotte's Web*. Here we examine aspects of *Charlotte's Web* and pair them with some children's stories that might update, extend, clarify, or contrast with the original text. The different stories might also encourage new questions about *Charlotte's Web*.

The Book

White, E. B. *Some Pig!* HarperCollins, 2006.

The picturebook *Some Pig!* introduces readers to Wilbur using E. B. White's masterful text from the classic *Charlotte's Web*. The text is combined with artist Maggie Kneen's illustrations. This charming picturebook edition may introduce children to Fern and Wilbur, but does it satisfy the way *Charlotte's Web* can? Explore other picturebooks made up of excerpts from the original novel, such as *Wilbur's Adventure* from HarperCollins (2007).

The Author

White, E. B. *The Annotated Charlotte's Web.* Garth Williams, Illus. HarperCollins, 2006.

An exciting exploration of one of the best-loved classics of all times. *The Annotated Charlotte's Web* includes information from E. B. White's original drafts, cross-references, letters, criticism, and literary–cultural commentary. This illustrated book of annotations and notes provides many insights into the making of *Charlotte's Web*. A must for YA readers who might want to revisit *Charlotte's Web* and find out about the thoughts of its author.

The Setting

Fair

Part of *Charlotte's Web* takes place at a fair. Which of these fair books seem to be the closest to the descriptions of E. B. White?

Alter, Judy. *Meet Me at the Fair: County, State, and World's Fairs & Expositions.* Franklin Watts, 1997.

This nonfiction book with photographic art is filled with information about the history of America's fairs.

Frasier, Debra. *A Fabulous Fair Alphabet.* Beach Lane Books, 2010.

The Minnesota State Fair, a favorite site of the author/illustrator, is presented in scrapbook form.

Lewin, Ted. *Fair!* Lothrop, Lee & Shepard Books, 1997.

Lewin's trademark paintings bring to life the sights, sounds, and smells of a county fair, including animal, craft, and food judging, as well as the set up of a typical fair.

Farm

Bial, Raymond. *Portrait of a Farm Family.* Houghton Mifflin, 1995.

This classic of nonfiction is a photo essay story of a fourth-generation farm family and traces the daily routine from dawn to dusk, chores and all. Do you recognize any characters—Fern or Avery—in the children portrayed here?

Provenson, Alice, and Martin Provenson. *A Year at Maple Hill Farm.* Aladdin, 2001.

This book is a description of life on an old-fashioned farm like the one where Wilbur lives.

The book shows the farm through the seasons and celebrates changes in the lives of all the humans and animals living there.

Provenson, Alice, and Martin Provenson. *Our Animal Friends at Maple Hill Farm.* Aladdin, 1984.

This *New York Times* Outstanding Book of the Year choice creates a nostalgic view of the animals we imagine to be on the family farm, similar to *Charlotte's Web.*

 ## The Characters

Fern

Wolfman, Judy. *Life on a Pig Farm.* Learner Publishing Group, 2001.

The author describes the experiences of a young girl as she raises pigs as part of a 4-H project.

Wilbur

Jones, Carol. *Sausage: From Farm to You Series.* Chelsea House, 2003.

This book tells how fresh, cooked, and dried sausages are made in both small butcher shops and large meatpacking plants. The history of sausage is shared as well.

Masson, Jeffrey Moussaieff. *The Pig Who Sang to the Moon: The Emotional World of Farm Animals.* Ballantine, 2004.

A different view of the animals in *Charlotte's Web* and the lives they lead on modern large-scale farms for adolescent readers. There is nothing to say that middle-level and YA readers will not benefit from rereading a childhood classic and pairing it with a best-selling book that presents another perspective.

Rath, Sara. *Complete Pig.* Voyeur, 2004.

This nonfiction book contains all kinds of interesting and amusing facts, phrases, stories, folklore, and history about pigs, using photographs throughout. This book emphasizes our human relationship with pigs without delving deeply into modern large-scale swine production or animal welfare and environmental issues.

Charlotte

Bishop, Nic. *Spiders.* Scholastic, 2007.

This Sibert Award and Orbis Pictus Honor book for 2008 features beautiful photography and astonishing facts, showing spiders for the successful predators they are.

Templeton

Wersba, Barbara. *Walter: The Story of a Rat.* Donna Diamond, Illus. Front Street, 2005.

An unlikely friendship develops between Walter, literate rat, and Amanda Pomeroy, elderly writer of children's books. Filled with allusions to classic adult literature and beautifully illustrated, it is told from a rat's perspective, one who is resentful about the lack of rats as characters.

 ## The Plot

Montgomery, Sy. *The Good Good Pig: The Extraordinary Life of Christopher Hogwood.* Ballantine, 2007.

This true story takes place in the author's New England backyard. When she adopts a sickly runt from a litter of pigs, naming him Christopher Hogwood after the symphony conductor, raising him for slaughter isn't an option: Montgomery's a vegetarian and her husband is Jewish. This is a memoir and a great read-aloud to partner with *Charlotte's Web*, possibly in comparing the traits of Wilbur and Christopher.

Rush, Ken. *What about Emma?* Orchard, 1996.

In this tale, a dairy farm family comes on hard times and has to sell off their herd. Sue, the young protagonist that narrates the story, convinces her father to keep her favorite cow, Emma, who is ready to calve.

NOTES

1. Dennis J. Sumara, *Why Reading Literature in School Still Matters: Imagination, Interpretation, Insight* (Mahwah, NJ: Lawrence Erlbaum Associates, 2002), pp. 5, 9.
2. Peter Hunt, *Criticism, Theory, & Children's Literature* (Cambridge, MA: Basil Blackwell, 1991), p. 64.
3. Perry Nodelman, *The Hidden Adult: Defining Children's Literature* (Baltimore: Johns Hopkins Press, 2008), pp. 59–68.
4. Roberta Seelinger Trites, "The Harry Potter Novels as a Test Case for Adolescent Literature," *Style*, 35(3), 2001, pp. 472–485. The quotation is from page 472.
5. Lawrence R. Sipe, *Storytime: Young Children's Literary Understanding in the Classroom* (New York: Teachers College Press, 2008), p. 147.
6. Jim Burke, *The English Teachers Companion* (New York: Heinemann, 2007). On page 6, Burke defines *textual intelligence* by explaining that the word *text* originally meant "to weave," and that studies of the construction of texts "form the heart of textual intelligence."

RECOMMENDED BOOKS

BLOCK, FRANCESCA LIA. *House of Dolls*. HarperCollins, 2010.

GARDINER, JOHN REYNOLDS. *Stone Fox*. HarperCollins, 1992.

GODDEN, RUMER. *The Doll's House*. Viking Press, 1948.

KROSOCZKA, JARRET J. *Lunch Lady and the Cyborg Substitute*. Knopf, 2009.

LEE, HARPER. *To Kill a Mockingbird*. Harper, 1963.

L'ENGLE, MADELINE. *A Wrinkle in Time*. Laurel Leaf, 1976.

MARTIN, JACQUELINE BRIGGS. *The Lamp, the Ice, and the Boat Called Fish*. Sandpiper, 2005.

MCKISSACK, PATRICIA, AND FREDRICK L. MCKISSACK. *Christmas in the Big House, Christmas in the Quarters*. Scholastic, 1994.

PAULSON, GARY. *Nightjohn*. Laurel Leaf, 1995.

PILKEY, DAV. *The Adventures of Captain Underpants*. Blue Sky Press, 2005.

ROWLING, J. K. *Harry Potter and the Sorceror's Stone*. Scholastic, 2008.

STEAD, REBECCA. *When You Reach Me*. Wendy Lamb Books, 2009.

TAYLOR, MILDRED. *Roll of Thunder, Hear My Cry*. Dial, 1976.

WHITE, E. B. *Charlotte's Web*. Harper, 1952.

WIESNER, DAVID. *Hurricane*. Clarion, 1990.

WIESNER, DAVID. *The Three Pigs*. Clarion, 2001.

ZOLOTOW, CHARLOTTE. *The Storm Book*. HarperCollins, 1989.

MyEducationKit™

Go to the topics "Evaluating Children's Literature" and "Adolescent Literature" on the MyEducationKit for this text, where you can:

- Search the Children's Literature Database, housing more than 22,000 titles searchable in every genre by authors or illustrators, by awards won, by year published, and by topic and description.
- Explore genre-related Assignments and Activities, assignable exercises showing concepts in action through database use, video, cases, and student and teacher artifacts.
- Listen to podcasts and read interviews from some of the brightest and most enduring stars of children's literature in the Conversations.
- Discover web links that will lead you to sites representing the authors you learn about in these pages, classrooms with powerful children's literature connections, and literature awards.

Where is the heaven of lost stories?

The Dreamer

Pam Muñoz Ryan / Illustrated by Peter Sís

The issue of selection can involve censorship; readers may choose to not select a book that is in new or unfamiliar format.

CHAPTER TWO

Issues and Fundamental Change in Children's Literature

 ## Issues in Children's Literature Today

What are the main issues being discussed in the field of children's literature today?

What are some of the ways that children's literature has changed in the past two decades?

All children live in a world that is constantly changing, and these changes often enter their world through media that surrounds us. This exposure has changed the experience of childhood. Though childhood may never have been the time of innocence, safety, happiness, and simplicity that adults like to imagine it once was, we agree with David Elkind, psychologist, professor, and author of *The Hurried Child*, that because of the Internet, television, cell phones, and other digital devices, children today experience time, space, social relationships—even reality itself—differently from the ways earlier generations did. As Elkind states, "In many ways . . . digital children have a far different sense of reality than previous generations. This digital reality is extraordinarily rich and complex. Yet children are still children in many respects."[1]

Writers of children's literature are addressing a different, more visual, savvier audience of children than they were twenty, ten, even five years ago, in part because of a society in which media such as television and computers are more visible and available. Children today are apt to watch the television shows their parents watch, to wear clothes similar to those their parents wear, and, perhaps, to worry about some of the same societal issues their parents worry about.

Some believe that children today experience time, space, social relationships—even reality itself—differently from the ways earlier generations did.

15

One way to help children make sense of the complicated world in which we live is to share stories with them. They only hear certain kinds of stories on television, in the movies, or online. We believe that it's important to provide children with a greater variety of stories through books. Hearing, telling, and writing stories have always been ways that people make sense of their worlds. Though we expect and hope that children will continue to read the old beloved classics—*Charlotte's Web, The Hundred Dresses,* or *Make Way for Ducklings*—we also believe that many of the stories children read and hear today should be new—should be different from the old stories—in order to reflect, and to help children make sense of, this changed world.

But just as ideas about what childhood is really like have been slow to change, ideas about what makes a quality children's book have been slow to change. Such ideas have rarely kept pace with the changes in the literature available for children to read.

In this chapter we discuss both ideas about children's books and some of the new forms that children's books are taking. We also examine three issues currently associated with children's books, affecting the selection of quality children's writing. We first look at the growing use of series books in children's reading. Second, we discuss the need for an increase in children's books that address a more culturally diverse population. Finally, we address the increase in adult topics being addressed in children's books. We discuss current challenges to these adult topics in a section on censorship as well.

After addressing these issues and the ideas that surround them, we discuss more fundamental changes that we see taking place in the quality children's books that are being published today. Influenced by Eliza Dresang, we relate those fundamental changes to a more digitalized culture and to a changing culture of childhood. We discuss books that address risky topics, books that blend genres in a variety of ways, and new forms that have become increasingly popular, such as the graphic novel and the wordless picturebook. Finally, we look at the ways in which postmodern theory has influenced the presentation of stories in picturebooks.

First, we discuss series books and some of the ideas that surround them.

Series Books

Many stories are published as parts of a series, some of them with one uniting literary element such as genre, author, or character. Children seeking short contemporary action stories about sports may read Matt Christopher stories—one about baseball, another about soccer. Children seeking historical fantasy may read Mary Pope Osborne's series *The Magic Tree House*—one story about life in Victorian England, another about life during the Great Depression in the United States. When they read series books, children are typically involved with a particular character, though with mystery, historical fiction or biography, or nonfiction information books, the interest might also be with a time period, event, or topic. Fantasy and science fiction are popular genres for series, and many series books are written in the contemporary realism genre as well.

Author Gary D. Schmidt[2] mentions several different kinds of series books that children may enjoy. One series type in particular, whose characters remain constant throughout, as in the *Nancy Drew* series or the *Boxcar Children* series, has drawn the most criticism. The *Babysitters Club* series and the *Diary of a Wimpy Kid* series are frequently criticized for the very qualities that make this type of fiction so appealing: Easy to read and understand, these books move quickly with little description and much dialogue and come to satisfying conclusions. Often called formulaic novels, these books can reassure young readers whose reading fluency often increases over the series and who finally decide they have had enough and go on to other stories. However, the consistency and predictability may delay a reader's experiences with fresh characters and challenging plots. On the other hand, they do have positive aspects. Perhaps their greatest contribution to literature for children is the way they offer opportunity to share books while helping young readers discover pleasure in reading. Peer pressure—the fact that everybody else is reading books in a certain series—can certainly work to encourage more children to read. Lemony Snicket's parodic stories featuring Klaus and Violet in *A Series of Unfortunate Events* provide a twist to this type of series with a bit of dark humor that holds some allure for today's readers.

Another type of series, exemplified by J. R. R. Tolkien and J. K. Rowling, documents character growth, according to Schmidt, with plots that are separated though similar in thematic point. Such series are best enjoyed in sequence, and the series is sophisticated enough that younger readers can enjoy a volume more than once before moving on to the next book. This series offers space for the reader to grow right along with characters like Harry Potter, providing an antidote to static characters. The third type of series book Schmidt describes features a strong central character, like Beverly Cleary's Ramona, Lois Lowry's Anastasia, or Kay Thompson's Eloise. Character focus means that the order of the novels in the series is unimportant, even though our hero or heroine changes slightly throughout the series.

Some series books focus on a strong central character.

The fourth type of series identified by Schmidt is defined by subject and constitutes primarily biography and informational books. This is an increasingly valuable format. Nonfiction information book series, such as the *New True* books, typically feature many topics young readers want to investigate through an expository text structure. In addition, there are nonfiction series like the natural history books of Jean Craighead George (i.e., *One Day in the Desert* or *One Day in the Tropical Rainforest*) that feature well-researched topics but use a narrative structure.

There are more series books today than ever before, and there are better books in those series. Often in the past there were only series books of the formulaic type available, which critics denigrated for their lack of depth, but currently many challenging, varied, and imaginative books in all genres are being published in series. We believe that series books should be used with the same care as all children's literature and selected according to criteria appropriate to the book's genre, its reader, and the purpose it will serve. Each book in a biography series, for example, should be well researched, balanced, and accurately reflect the life of the person in light of the times in which they lived.

Thinking "Multiculturally"

What does it mean to think "multiculturally"? What does it mean to be "white"? According to the 2008 census projections, most citizens of the United States are "white." This largest "racial" or "ethnic" group in the United States is made up of a culturally diverse set of Caucasians—not only European people whose ancestors came from Germany, Austria, Italy, Poland, Russia, Greece, Ireland, and many other countries, but white people whose ancestors are from Latin American countries as well, people of white Hispanic ancestry. Though the United States is still over 75 percent "white," as a country we are now, and have been for some time, in the midst of a great societal change. Demographers predict that in forty years white people of non-Hispanic origin—whatever their cultural backgrounds—will be less than 50 percent of the population. Almost all other population categories (i.e., Asian, Black, American Indian/Alaskan Indian, Native Hawaiian/Pacific Islander) are projected to increase. This means that our ethnic and cultural makeup will continue to change. The literature we offer our children should reflect the population who will be reading it. However, although all children benefit from seeing themselves and others in children's books, these complexities of racial, ethnic, and cultural affinity continue to be a small slice of the children's books published.

It is still true that most of the faces in picturebooks—and most other kinds of children's books—are white.

Children's books feature more characters from varied countries and cultures than they did in 1965, when Nancy Larrick famously wrote about the "All-White World of Children's Books,"[3] but still, as Susan Lempke[4] wrote in *Horn Book Magazine* in 1999, most of the faces in the picturebooks are white. Statistics kept by the Cooperative Children's Book Center (CCBC) show that for 2007, of approximately 5,000 children's books published, only about 4 percent were authored by people of color, and slightly more than 6 percent were about people of color.[5]

The book selection process becomes even more important when we realize that it is still true that most of the people in the teaching profession are white middle-class women who are quite likely to be Christian, married, heterosexual, and middle-aged. Because so many teachers share these traits, it's important for all teachers—for the readers of this handbook—to learn as much as they can about the lives and beliefs of the children they teach. For example, because so many of the faces in the children's books are white, it's important for pre-service teachers to learn as much as they can about books that describe children from racial and ethnic groups other than their own. Reading *The Watsons Go to Birmingham, 1963* may both help an African American child feel confirmed and encourage him to learn something of the history of the civil rights movement. Reading *Sky Sisters* might help an Ojibwe girl feel closer to her own sister and learn a bit about the history of her people. When children read about people living in other parts of the world—as when a seven-year-old white boy reads about Lebanese Sami living in war-torn Beirut in *Sami and the Time of Troubles,* or when a black teen in Cedar Rapids reads about how Indian American Sameera navigates the political scene in Mitali Perkins's *First Daughter: Extreme American Makeover,* or when a Mexican American girl in San Francisco reads *Jalapeño Bagels,* and learns that other children

---

INQUIRY POINT

The illustrations in a picturebook provide additional layers for developing cultural understanding. Lynne Reiser discovered the complexities of illustration when she collaborated with six Costa Rican artists to create what she intended to be a picturebook parallel for her *Cherry Pies and Lullabies.* Read *Cherry Pies and Lullabies* and note the patterns in the book. Notice Reiser's illustrations. Read *Tortillas and Lullabies.* Look for the corresponding elements between the two books. What are the similarities and differences you see?

Now, access Lynne Reiser's article "Going from But to And,"[6] which tells the story of how *Tortillas and Lullabies* was created and what Lynne Reiser learned from the experience. Look through the books again. Note additional details. What surprised you? What caused you to reconsider your own thinking about selection of multicultural picturebooks?

have one white and one Hispanic parent—their worlds are widened, and their imaginations, perhaps, made more empathetic, more comfortable with difference.[7]

In the idea of "multiculturalism"—a problematic term in itself—we include people who are not considered mainstream based on categories other than the racial or ethnic. We encourage teachers to include in their classroom libraries books about children and adults who are different from the white middle-class mainstream regardless of religion, race, ability, gender, age, sexual orientation, socioeconomic status, body image, language, political beliefs, or ethnicity. To this end we advocate for the selection and inclusion of a wide array of children's books that represent lifestyle and cultural beliefs of as many children as possible.[8]

Fortunately, there is increasing acceptance of books that portray racial and ethnic diversity. Still, different people have different opinions. Readers' political and religious beliefs and their thoughts about the appropriateness, in children's books, of frank discussions of the body, socioeconomic class, and failures of United States policy often cause controversy. It is in part because of these controversies that many of these issues continue to be underrepresented in children's books.

The Issue of Censorship and Selection

Teachers must be sensitive to community concerns as well as to students' cognitive and social maturity, their needs and fears. There have been cases in which teachers pushed texts onto children who were too young to understand the concepts they contained. Community mores and parents' fears about children's knowledge or lack of it should certainly be respected. Still, when worried parents approach school administrators, teachers, or librarians about "inappropriate" books, teachers must know how to address such challenges. Some of these challenges develop into calls for censorship, often with books that have potential for mediating the cultural issues they effectively portray.

A highly convincing argument against censorship is expressed in the American Library Association's (ALA) document, "The Freedom to Read."[9] As the ALA notes, creative thought is unfamiliar and different, and until an idea is clarified and tested, it may be difficult to accept. We "need to know not only what we believe but why we believe it."[10] A totalitarian system, unlike democracy, silences those whose ideas challenge the controlling authorities. In a democratic society, new ideas must be proposed, clarified, tested, and, sometimes, modified. But first those new ideas must be heard.

In a democratic society, new ideas must be proposed, clarified, and tested.

Every book published is not worthy of endorsement, but considering that new ideas enlarge us, help our minds grow, and increase our understanding of possibilities, it is important to continually offer children new quality books. Censorship is restrictive; a group of individuals decides what may not be read, what should be excluded. Censorship is then in some sense anti-democratic. The democratic society we live in allows us to make our own decisions about how we live.

Censorship may appear to be an effective strategy for groups wanting to remove a particular book from library shelves, but history shows that "banning" a book in a culture where information freely circulates tends to increase interest and discussion. Sales of that censored book then soar. This allows the book to achieve a status it might not have earned on literary merit alone. In a similar vein, the day-to-day selection or refusal to select particular books may have, in reality, the effect of true censorship. Adults who choose books for children or supervise children as they find their own books need to keep in mind the goal of cultural sensitivity as well as the goal of intellectual freedom.

Inevitably children meet the diversity of our society when they leave home. They are best prepared for that diversity if they have been allowed by parents and teachers to think for themselves, if they have heard the ideas of others and been allowed to talk freely and courteously about those ideas, and if they have learned to evaluate them. As the ALA says in their "The Freedom to Read" document, "the answer to a 'bad' book is a good one, the answer to a 'bad' idea is a good one."

The ALA publication "Intellectual Freedom Brochure"[11] also lists several suggestions for combating censorship, paraphrased as follows:

- Make intellectual freedom part of the library mission.
- Educate people about the importance of intellectual freedom.
- Become advocates for freedom to think independently.
- Respond to requests for support when controversy arises.
- Be aware of relevant legislation or court cases.
- Support organizations that believe in this freedom.
- Start a local group that publicizes the right to read.
- Report attempted censorship incidents to the ALA.

Supporting Selection

In addition to the tips ALA provides, the National Council of Teachers of English (NCTE) runs an "Anti-Censorship Center," which contains helpful information about the issue of censorship, the teacher's responsibilities, and the organization's stance. Included on the NCTE website[12] are suggestions for how to talk to a parent who is making a complaint, as well as a document called "Citizens' Request for Reconsideration of a Work," which is a form that a parent can complete and turn in to the principal, teacher, or school board. One of the purposes of the form is to encourage emotional parents to look into their complaints about a book and gain perspective about the book and choices they have for their children. At the same time, teachers and the community can examine just how much they know about the book in question and remind everyone involved in the selection process of the book's merits.

text continues on page 23

Controversial Books for Children and Young Adults

The American Library Association keeps lists of the most frequently banned children's and young adult books for each year. This textset, which has been organized to show the wide variety of reasons children's books have been challenged over the years, lists only a very few of the many books that are banned or contested each year. This list is based, in part, on the American Library Association's most frequently challenged or banned lists, which can be found at www.ALA.org.

The ALA and the National Council of Teachers of English both provide excellent resources to assist with books and topics that have come under fire. However, many of the difficulties adults encounter when selecting a children's book happen because of personal and cultural reasons they may not anticipate. The bottom line is to know your books, the children, the context, and the way the book will be shared with a child.

 Controversial Picturebooks

Harris, Robie. *It's Perfectly Normal: Changing Bodies, Growing Up, Sex, and Sexual Health.* **Candlewick Productions. 1996.**

On the top of the American Library Association's ten most challenged books for 2005, this information picturebook has been denounced for depicting homosexuality, nudity, and birth control use, as well as for promoting sex education. The straightforward pictures in the book were found particularly objectionable.

Herrera, Carolina. *Nappy Hair.* **Joseph Cepeda, Illus. Alfred A. Knopf, 1998.**

This cheerfully illustrated picturebook uses the African American call-and-response tradition to humorously praise the curly hair of its protagonist, Brenda. The book was the center of a controversy

when a white teacher read the book to a group of African American children. Parents were upset, in part, by the pictures in the book, and in part because they did not think the teacher should have been talking about their children's hair. The issue of a European American teacher reading aloud in an African American dialect was also raised. The African American writer of the book defended the white teacher's choice. Pairing this story with *I Love My Hair* by Nikki Grimes, illustrated by E. B.Lewis or Belle Hooks's *Happy to Be Nappy*, illustrated by Chris Raschke, helps to place this story in a better context.

Richardson, Justin, and Peter Parnell. *And Tango Makes Three.* **Simon & Schuster Books for Young Readers, 2005.**

According to the American Library Association, this picturebook was the most challenged book of 2006, 2007, and 2008, as well as the most banned book of 2009. It is a simply illustrated true tale of two male chinstrap penguins, Silo and Roy, who live in New York's Central Park Zoo. The two penguins showed affection for each other and, when given an orphaned egg, took turns sitting on it. They then raised the baby penguin, Tango. The book has received numerous awards, including the ASPCA Henry Bergh children's book award but has also been attacked because it depicts homosexuality as it occurs in nature. The ALA reports that it has been banned or challenged because it is considered "anti-ethnic, anti-family," and concerns "homosexuality, religious viewpoint." In October of 2008 it was the center of an ACLU freedom of speech case, charged with promoting same-sex partnering and pairing.

Sendak, Maurice. *In the Night Kitchen.* **HarperCollins, 1970.**

According to the American Library Association, this picturebook was one of the top twenty-five most challenged books of the past two decades.

(continued)

A Caldecott Honor winner, it is the wittily illustrated story of Mickey's travels through a surreal baker's kitchen, where he helps an Oliver Hardy look-alike bake a cake. The book has been controversial primarily because it shows Mickey fully naked. In some libraries, patrons have defaced books to provide Mickey with pants. Others dislike the book because they see other images—like a milk bottle—as problematically sexual. Still others see allusions to the extermination of Jewish prisoners during the Holocaust and the Oliver Hardy look-alike as Hitler.

Steig, William. *Sylvester and the Magic Pebble.* **Simon & Schuster's Children's Publishing, 1970.**

In the 1970s, police associations complained about this book, and it was challenged in eleven states because of the satirical depiction of policemen as pigs. The book is the story of a donkey, Sylvester, who collects pebbles and one day comes across a pebble that magically grants him wishes. The book won the Caldecott Medal in 1970.

Zolotow, Charlotte. *William's Doll.* **William Pene Du Bois, Illus. HarperCollins, 1972.**

This classic children's book depicts a young boy whose preference is to play with a doll. "William wanted a doll. He wanted to hug it and cradle it in his arms." Rather than discourage his choice, his grandmother supports it. Readers at the time of publication objected, and even now object, to this gender-role reversal, preferring that the main character make the decision to play with boy toys.

Controversial Books for Older Children

Cormier, Robert. *The Chocolate War.* **Random House Children's Books, 1974.**

Ever since this book was published in 1974, it has made the most-challenged books lists. According to the ALA, it was fourth on the list of the one hundred most challenged books of this past decade.[13]

Considered one of the greatest young adult novels of all time, the book has received objections due to sexual situations, violence, and the depiction of secret societies and anarchic students.

Naylor, Phyllis Reynolds. *Alice* **series. Simon & Schuster, 1985, 1993, 1995, 1996, 2000, 2002, 2003, 2005, 2006.**

This series of approximately twenty books was second on the ALA's list of the one hundred most challenged books of the decade, right after the *Harry Potter* series. The series follows Alice from third grade through her senior year of high school; it has been banned or disputed for language and sexual situations.

Pullman, Phillip. *His Dark Materials* **series. Knopf Books for Young Readers, 1996, 2001, 2007.**

According to the American Library Association,[14] this fantasy series—*The Golden Compass, The Subtle Knife, and The Amber Spyglass*—was the second most challenged of 2008. It is eighth on their list of top one hundred banned or challenged books of the decade. The series was disputed because of anti-Christian themes.

Rowling, J. K. *Harry Potter* **series. Scholastic, 2000, 2001, 2002, 2004, 2006, 2008, 2009.**

These books topped the American Library Association's lists in 1999, 2000, and 2001. They were at the top of the one hundred most banned or challenged books of the decade. The books were considered anti-family as well as promoting witchcraft and an interest in the occult.

Schwartz, Alvin. *Scary Stories to Tell in the Dark.* **HarperCollins, 1984, 1986, 1991.**

The three books in this series topped the American Library Association's one hundred most challenged books of the decade. Objections included being "too scary," too violent, and for being "unsuited to age group."

The central concern, as always, is the selection of quality books that provide valuable literary models for students. Sensitive and well-informed selection that meets the needs of today's children and their cultural assets is of great importance.

Fundamental Changes

Earlier in this chapter we described the changes that are occurring in the experience of childhood, and how we believe writers of children's books are responding to those changes. In this section of the chapter we briefly discuss, first, Eliza Dresang's concept of "radical change" and how her theory relates to new trends in children's literature. Then we go into more depth about each of the changes she describes. We provide numerous examples of books that exemplify each of these changes in children's literature.

Radical Change

In her book *Radical Change: Books for Youth in a Digital Age* librarian Eliza T. Dresang describes ways children's books have changed. She attributes much of this change to the "digital age"—that is, *this* age, when children are surrounded by technology that provides many choices and means of interaction. Dresang's theory suggests that children born after 1977 require new, interactive, sophisticated kinds of books that mimic some of the qualities of the digital world that has always surrounded them. The interconnected, electronic "global village" is their reality, and many writers and artists working to create literature for children, Dresang suggests, recognize these dynamics and create literature that reflects these changes in society. [15]

Dresang notes three concepts she finds expressed throughout newer books that respond to our digital age. First, she says, these books provide children with increased connectivity as, for example, in the ways they provide connections to outside resources, linking readers to an expanded community in the ways that hypertext links on the computer do. Second, Dresang notes the increased interactivity created by these books, as, for example, in the ways they provide readers with more choices, with less direct and linear plots, with a more variable, nonsequential order to make sense of. Increasingly complex visual texts are encouraging a different kind of interaction. Finally, Dresang says these books, like television, bring the world into the sheltered home, providing children with increased access to subjects and styles of language that have never been addressed or used in children's books before.

Dresang marks 1991, when David Macaulay's Caldecott Medal–winning picturebook *Black and White* was published, as the time she first noticed these changes in children's books. *Black and White* is an example of a book with the increased interactivity Dresang describes, a never-before-seen form and format. *Black and White* tells not one simple plot with a beginning, middle, and end, but at least four stories that all occur on each page at the same time. In the same way that a reader reads **hypertext** on a computer, the reader of this book is required to choose which story to read first, and then, in order to truly understand the book, to try to reconstruct what happens while making connections among all four stories, all panels, at once. Most readers will need to complete this book multiple times in order to find a

Some believe that children born after 1977 require new, interactive, sophisticated kinds of books that mimic the digital world that has always surrounded them.

satisfying resolution within it. Providing readers with such choice and complexity in the picturebook format was new in 1991, but has become more prevalent, even expected, since that time.

Three Types of Changes

Dresang makes clear that the concepts she calls connectivity, interactivity, and access run through different genres of children's literature in many entangled ways. She identifies three types of change she sees in children's literature, each related to these ideas.

She describes changing perspectives. This includes books in which each chapter is told in a different character's voice or from a different point of view (providing increased interactivity), novels told in voices that have been unheard in the past (providing increased access), or in which young narrators tell their own stories directly, not speaking as one of the voices created by the omniscient, adult narrator, but in her own words (providing increased connectivity).

Dresang lists examples of changing boundaries: books using subjects, settings, and communities previously forbidden or unusual in children's literature; genre boundaries that are blurring; and endings that are messy, unresolved, or unhappy (providing increased access).

Finally, she describes changing forms and formats. This includes new uses of graphics—words typeset large or small or in colors or wobbly on the page to express emotion; art that works to expand, complement, comment on, limit, or completely contradict the words on the page; and plots and organizational strategies that are not linear or sequential (providing increased interactivity).

Being able to delineate these different kinds of changes from each other is not as important as being aware that they exist in children's literature today and may require child readers to use interpretive skills that children in the past have not had to use.

In the next portions of this chapter we will provide more detail about these and other recent changes found in children's literature.

> Since 1991, children's books have changed.

INQUIRY POINT

Dresang and others suggest that all three of the changes listed above can be found in Peter Sis's picturebook biography of Galileo, *Starry Messenger*. After finishing this section of the handbook, read *Starry Messenger*. Be on the lookout for examples of Dresang's categories. Write examples from the book under the three different categories. After attempting this once, read the book again. What else do you see?[16]

 Changing Perspectives

In her 1998 article "Exit Children's Literature," Maria Nikolajeva[17] suggests that some writers are making children's literature that seems less and less distinct from literature written for adults. Plots in children's literature, she says, are no longer as simple as they used to be, with clear beginning, middle, and end; some stories no longer have one set, permanent, setting; characters no longer have clear roles, and the story does not end with an "unambivalent message or moral."[18] Nikolajeva writes that much of children's literature has moved away from "what has been called the master plot of children's literature: home to departure to adventure to homecoming."[19] Plots in literature for children are more and more "polyphonic, [and] multi-voiced." The entire plot of a novel may take up just one slice of the main character's day, or two different stories may be going on at once, or many settings may be traversed in the course of the story.

More sophisticated plots are part of the increased connectivity, interactivity, and access Dresang notes, because in their sophistication they allow more access to adult ways of thinking, more interactivity between reader and text, and, in some cases, more connection with different kinds of characters.[20] This more sophisticated kind of plot can be seen, for example, in Sue Townsend's *The Secret Diary of Adrian Mole, Aged 13¾,* organized not with a distinct storyline, but as a fictitious diary that the reader is allowed to peek into. The poetic novel *Heaven,* by Angela Johnson, contains a sophisticated plot as well, in that there is no omniscient adult narrator guiding the reader to a particular conclusion and introducing all of the characters. Twelve-year-old Marley tells the story herself, in the first person; we see everything through her eyes, not through the eyes of an adult narrator. The only character the reader does not see through Marley's eyes is her Uncle Jack, whose letters to Marley provide a direct introduction. The acclaimed young adult novel *The Curious Incident of the Dog in the Nighttime* (the first book to be simultaneously released to the adult and YA market) is told from the point of view of Christopher Boone, a fifteen-year-old autistic savant, a mathematical genius who only eats red food; as he solves the mystery of his dog's murder, the reader must determine which of what he sees is real and which is colored by his peculiar way of understanding the world. Our nonfiction mentor text, *Christmas in the Big House, Christmas in the Quarters,* can be seen as an example of this more sophisticated plot because it contains no focal characters with whom the child reader is expected to identify; it also presents the reader with two very different points of view toward the events in history being described.

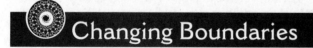

Changing Boundaries

Risky Topics

The boundaries of the children's book are changing in that more writers are addressing topics that Eliza Dresang has called "risky," subjects formerly considered off-limits for children, and even for young adults. Whether people consider these topics risky because they relate to the areas of culture we discussed at the outset of this chapter or to the assumptions we hold about young readers, they are of concern when adults decide to deselect books for children.

In her 1998 article "Outrageous Viewpoints: Teachers' Criteria for Rejecting Works of Children's Literature," Julie Wollman-Bonilla[21] describes her research into elementary pre-service teachers' reluctance to select children's books they thought might do any of the following:

1. Frighten or corrupt the children by introducing them to topics they shouldn't know about
2. Confuse children by representing values that are not accepted in the homes of mainstream America
3. Cause distress for children by identifying racism or sexism as social problems

Though many of the pre-service teachers believed in the importance of presenting multicultural works to students, when it came down to choosing books they would actually use in their classrooms, they wanted books that would unsettle no one. Many people, like the teachers Wollman-Bonilla describes, think that school studies should not admit the outside world; others believe that schools should encourage study and thought about the very troubles we see in the newspapers every day. Educators from first-grade teachers to college professors disagree about how much of the real world should enter their classrooms.

We want to introduce you to some thoughtfully written children's books of high quality that address some of the risky topics Dresang describes and Wollman-Bonilla's teachers fear. Our space is limited, so we only present three. The books are controversial because of social topics rather than personal topics, such as the mental health of a mother or the autism of a brother, though there are many books that address these more personal risky topics as well. Just because a book presents a more difficult topic doesn't mean it is a book worth reading. Many controversial children's books are overly simple; others are poorly written or designed. We encourage you to be aware of your own prejudices and fears as you begin to select books for children and to be conscientious and aware of the needs and concerns of your school and the community of which you are a part.

From Slave Ship to Freedom Road, written by Julius Lester and illustrated by Rod Brown, is an information picturebook that exemplifies many of the recent changes in children's literature. First, it is a picturebook about slavery, a topic that many adults might feel is inappropriate for children. Second, it is a picturebook intended for an audience of older children, not the traditional audience for the format. Third, the tone of both Lester's thought-provoking words and Brown's startling, raw paintings is more direct about the horrors of slavery than adults might expect from a children's picturebook. Fourth, this powerful book uses a multivoiced narrative style: The straightforward history of the African American journey from slave ship to plantation life to freedom is told both by a single narrator, who seems to be Lester himself, and, in italicized type, by individuals who experienced the history—the slave auctioneer, the plantation owner, and the slaves themselves. Finally, the book is different from the traditional children's picturebook in that Lester works to involve the reader directly, by asking questions of his child audience. He provides "imagination exercises" written "For White People" and others "For African Americans," suggesting, perhaps for the first time in children's literature, that white children and black children might read a text, especially one about slavery, in very different ways.

The Librarian of Basra: A True Story from Iraq, written and illustrated by Jeannette Winter, is a very different book that is somewhat controversial. This biography tells a story—reported in the *New York Times*—of Alia Muhammad Baker, a librarian in Iraq, to whom books were more valuable "than mountains of gold." It describes how Baker and her friends moved 30,000 books from the library and stored them in people's homes, so that they were not destroyed when a bomb hit the library building. The book, painted in a bright, folk-art style, is very gentle about the horrors of war. Though the role of the United States in the bombing is never mentioned, some children will know that the hands that hold the guns in some pictures are the hands of American soldiers. Stories of war are frequently considered risky for children, but this is especially so when the conflict is one that is ongoing and very present to the families of many younger readers. Endnotes provide more detail about the true incidents this book describes.

Educators from first-grade teachers to college professors disagree about how much of the real world should enter their classrooms.

Visiting Day by Jacqueline Woodson, illustrated by James Ransome, depicts the excitement of a young girl as she looks forward to seeing her father on visiting day in prison. We see the girl's grandmother fixing her hair and making sandwiches, as the girl imagines her father's preparations. Only on visiting day does her grandmother make fried chicken at 6:00 in the morning; only on visiting day does she get to tell her father everything that has happened during the month. Ransome paints the father as a warm, handsome man in khakis; we see his calendar marked off in anticipation of his daughter's visit as well. Children whose parents are incarcerated rarely have a chance to see this experience in a book just for them, and this absence reinforces the conflicting emotions they must feel. Though this book relates to a serious topic, the tone of this book is one of reassurance for the child. In an endnote, both artist and writer movingly discuss their experiences visiting family members who were in jail.

> ### INQUIRY POINT
>
> How might you introduce some of these and other controversial books with children? At what age do you think these different books should be introduced? How will you frame your introduction of the story? What kinds of comments do you feel unprepared for? Try to imagine how you would address those comments. You may find further titles for this in the textset at the end of this chapter. ⬤

Genre Blending

Along with changing boundaries by discussing topics usually reserved for adult audiences, contemporary writers and illustrators of children's books change boundaries in other ways as well. Maria Nikolajeva describes what she calls "genre eclecticism," which she considers the most prominent aspect of contemporary writing for children. The phrase "genre eclecticism" suggests that writers pick and choose from many genres to create blended works. Thus, the usual boundaries between genres are changing: between a book of fiction and a nonfiction book of history, between a book of poetry and one of information, or between a book of suspense and one of true science. In the next paragraphs we provide examples of some well-written and interestingly designed children's books whose boundaries are changing in this way.

The highly acclaimed visual text, *The Invention of Hugo Cabret* by Brian Selznick, is a novel in which different genres are blended. The book is about a young boy who lives secretly in a Paris train station and keeps time by winding the many clocks in the station every day. The book is also the true story of Georges Melies, a filmmaker in Paris from the early years of movie making as well as a magician and, in his last years, a toy seller in the Paris train station. The book combines charcoal drawings—reminiscent of black-and-white movie stills—that move the action of the plot along—close-ups of the boy's heel when he's running from the stationmaster, a train that gets larger and larger, closer and closer, with each flip of the page—and words that provide the details of the story. Blended genres combine a realistic mystery story and invented characters with the true history of early filmmaking into an incredible experience. This text "leans"[22] heavily upon other texts as well, including between its covers references to Charlie Chaplin as well as an iconic photograph of the early movie actor Buster Keaton hanging from a clock tower, in addition to photographs from Melies's own films. Considered by some a graphic novel, this book combines a satisfying and intricate story with an innovative format.

The Invention of Hugo Cabret and *The Dreamer* are examples of books in which genres blend.

The Dreamer by Pam Muñoz Ryan and Peter Sis is another book in which genres could be considered blended. In the book's Author Note, Ryan herself calls it a "book of fiction based on the events of Pablo Neruda's childhood." Though it is primarily a realistic tale, providing readers with one small slice of the Chilean poet's early years, it has elements of magical realism—a genre of writing associated with South American writers and also with the postmodern—as when, on the second page of the book, the numbers the young Neruda is looking at hold hands and fly around the room. The book has delightful graphic elements as well—small decorations by the master artist Peter Sis, which anticipate the events of each chapter, occasional pages with sounds written in large type, or wobbly words floating across the page. In an additional blend of genres, throughout the book Ryan has placed poetic questions that, she tells us in the back of the book, were inspired by Neruda's *Book of Questions*. Providing readers with some of Neruda's poetry in a sort of appendix at the back, this example of blended artistry would be a perfect introduction to the lives of artists or to poetry in general.

American Born Chinese by Gene Luen Yang received the Michael L. Printz Award and is a wonderful graphic blend that intertwines three different plotlines. Each of the stories could stand alone, but readers who recognize the ways the characters interrelate will construct a more satisfying resolution for The Monkey King, Jin Wang, and Danny; each learns to be comfortable in their own skin. This modern fable plays with Chinese cultural icons and stereotypes of "fresh-off-the boat" Chinese immigrants, as well as the angst felt by immigrants striving to blend their old culture with the new in the United States. The cartoon art is consistent within all three of the story segments, visually cueing the reader that this can be one story, and the plight of each character is similar in a blend of contemporary realism, folklore, and fantasy. This is a fresh approach to immigration and assimilation for young adult readers.

Changing Formats

When we speak of *format* we refer to the physical makeup of a printed or electronic work—its page size, typeface, binding, pictorial elements, cover, or margins.

Changing perspectives and boundaries are just two of the recent changes in children's books. In this section of this chapter, we describe three new formats that have developed in recent years: the verse novel, the graphic novel, and the wordless picturebook. When we speak of **format** we refer to the physical makeup of a printed or electronic work—its page size, typeface, binding, pictorial elements, cover, or margins.

Verse Novels

In the 2005 article "The Verse-Novel: A New Genre," Joy Alexander describes the **verse novel** as a form that "has only become prominent within the last ten years" (p. 269). Like the graphic novel and the wordless picturebook, the verse novel can be considered a new format in children's literature. Researchers argue about whether the verse novel can be considered a new genre, a blended genre, poetry, a different kind of realistic fiction, or just a new kind of format. Despite these arguments about categories, most of those who care about children's literature would agree that writing a story in blank verse form—in short sentences, as in a poem, with words that may contain sharp and vibrant visual imagery but do not rhyme—as compared to writing the same story in what Alexander calls "plain prose" is new. [23]

Just as Dresang sees many of the changes in children's books occurring in response to the digital revolution, Alexander links the evolution of the verse novel to the digital revolution as well. Some have suggested that along with the technological changes our society has recently seen, a new focus on orality has come about—that is, a focus on the word as it is spoken, rather than the word as written. Text messages, for example, while not exactly like what you might say to your neighbor, are not at all like a completely written-out text. Similarly, texting and message writing on social networking sites are more like the spoken than the written word. Some researchers, like Alexander, suggest that this movement toward orality is one of the reasons for the rise of the verse novel—reading them is more like listening to someone talk to you than reading a prose novel is.

Alexander suggests that the verse novel is most often used as the voice of a teenage character. Verse novels are often written in the first person, like a dramatic monologue. This format allows the writer to make it seem as if the narrator is speaking from the heart, directly to the reader; as Alexander puts it, the character "is 'telling it like it is,' with immediacy and reality" (p. 261).

Though verse novels originally were about contemporary children expressing contemporary problems, recently there has been what Myra Zarnowski[24] calls a "small but significant subgroup" dealing with historical issues. She lists the positive qualities of these historical fiction verse novels: historical accuracy, multiple perspectives on past events, vivid and sensory language, and details that provide empathy for people who lived in past times. Though many writers have been creating historical verse novels, Karen Hesse and Jen Bryant are two prominent ones.

Jen Bryant's debut novel, *The Trial,* blends elements readers enjoy from contemporary fiction with historical realism into a verse novel format. When Katie Leigh, the seventh-grade narrator of this novel, substitutes for her journalist uncle during the famous Lindbergh Baby Trial, she learns about her country and grows up a little. The trial of the man accused of kidnapping the aviation hero Charles Lindbergh's baby boy was called "the trial of the century," and it affects Katie in ways that she could not have imagined. The poems in *The Trial* create a context in which this media event occurred, providing readers glimpses of the economic realities of the time, the new influence of mass media, the nation's concerns about war, and the need to escape from everyday existence during the Great Depression. The arrangement of each

Some children's literature experts link the evolution of the verse novel to the digital revolution.

INQUIRY POINT

Select verse novels such as *Locomotion* by Jacqueline Woodson, *All the Broken Pieces* by Ann E. Burg, *Out of the Dust* by Karen Hesse, or *T4* by Ann Clare LeZotte. Look at the words on the pages. What difference does the increased white space make in your feelings about the book?

In some verse novels, each page or short section has a different title. How does this change your approach to each page or section?

Why do you think some writers do *not* use titles for each page?

Next, look at a page from Sonya Sones's verse novel, *One of Those Hideous Books Where the Mother Dies.* The page titled "Airplane Lunch" is written as a poem: "They/call/this/*chicken*?" How might you read this sentence differently if it were written in a more traditional way?

poem and the surrounding white space relieve the emotions readers are apt to feel as they read this powerful story.

Another unusual historical novel, by Margarita Engle (2009 Newbery Honor winner for *The Surrender Tree: Poems of Cuba's Struggle for Freedom*) is *Tropical Secrets: Holocaust Refugees in Cuba*. Historical fiction told in blank verse, it is the story of 13-year-old Daniel, who has escaped from Germany after the night of terror called Kristallnacht, in 1939. In blank verse he tells of his arrival, alone, in Havana. Soon Paloma, a wealthy 13-year-old Cuban girl, begins to tell about the arrival of the refugees from her point of view, as she gets to know Daniel and other Jewish refugees, and struggles with moral decisions she must make. We hear changing perspectives in these different voices, speaking directly in turn, and notice changing boundaries in the blend of historical fiction and verse. This beautifully written book—Paloma, sleeping in the dovecote says "I sleep surrounded by wings"—by an award-winning writer is also suspenseful, and will provide children with a glimpse of other children who took action in small but heroic ways in a difficult time.

Graphic Novels

Graphic novels are everywhere these days, including the elementary school classroom—with Jennifer Holm's delightful *Babymouse* series, Jeff Smith's award-winning saga about *Bone*, Dav Pilkey's *Captain Underpants* series with its Flip-O-Rama, and the practically wordless *Owly* series by Andy Runton—to name only a few of the most visible texts. Why have graphic novels become so popular recently? In *Understanding Comics*, a comic book about the history, theory, and making of comic books (also known as graphic novels), Scott McCloud,[25] one of the form's acknowledged masters, analyzes the graphic novel format both to give it the dignity he believes it deserves and to explain its power. He defines graphic novels, or comics, as "sequential visual art," which, he says, ask the reader to become more involved than purely word-based texts do; they are more "interactive," as Eliza Dresang might say.

McCloud argues that comic artists' use of "icons"—that is, abstractions—cartoony, simple pictures, not realistic drawings, and not words—use human beings' natural self-centeredness to make the texts seem to "glow with the life we lend them" (pp. 40–41). He says that cartoony images force readers to see the world within, whereas more realistic drawings help us see an outer world. McCloud states that one of the appeals of these novels is that "ours is an increasingly symbol-oriented culture" (p. 58) in which we need to learn to "read" signs and symbols every day in our lives; the increase in symbols has given artists of the graphic novel an ever-expanding iconography to work (and play) with. McCloud describes how readers' natural human desire for visual closure, that is, our tendency to imagine a whole when we see only its parts (assuming a whole person from a photo of feet), causes us to fill in partial pictures with our own imagined completion. We use that desire for closure, McCloud states, especially when reading from one panel of comic art to the next, one frame of action to the following. In between each panel or frame is the comic's **gutter**, or empty space. Between two panels in a graphic novel or comic anything can happen—any amount of time can go by, any amount of movement can occur—and the reader has to imagine what has happened between the panels, thus investing and involving herself fully in the world of the book.

In graphic works, McCloud explains, the artist shapes the panels themselves to his purposes. The different shapes and sizes affect the readers' experience. A longer panel can make readers think that a long period of time has occurred without the time frame being mentioned; when the artwork **bleeds** out to the edges of the panel, without the frame of a border, the panel may also suggest a timeless quality. Expressing time in graphic art is complicated, McCloud tells us, and expressing space and movement is complex as well. McCloud shows how graphic artists use line to express movement, and how the techniques of the graphic artist may be more akin to a filmmaker's than a writer's. McCloud convinces us that the graphic artist decides how he wants the reader to feel, where he wants the reader's eye to focus, and which aspect of the story he wants the reader to focus on.

Although once considered lesser than reading material with fewer pictures and more words, graphic novels have recently come into their own. The "low" art of graphic novels (if indeed we can consider it "low") has been combined with the "high" art of Shakespeare. Graphic novels exploit the full power of traditional narrative writing and art; graphic artists choose panel size, narration frames, forms of drawing, color, perspective, as well as particular words in order to ensure that the reader sees exactly what they want the reader to see. It may be that children who are having difficulty reading words are more sophisticated readers of visual images than children who read words well; it is certainly true that in our increasingly visual world, books will become increasingly visual too.

Graphic novels exploit the full power of traditional narrative writing and art.

The type of graphic novel called **manga** originated in Japan, where manga has a long history. The most recent style of manga is believed to have been introduced shortly after World War II, with its design perhaps influenced by the occupation of Japan by the United States. Very popular in Japan, manga are typically drawn in black and white, and the great Japanese artists of manga use techniques more related to the cinema than to the comic strip. In *Understanding Comics*, Scott McCloud suggests that the artists of Japanese manga have influenced comic book artists throughout the world. Currently, manga are so popular in the United States that some middle schools have manga clubs. Two manga that are particularly recommended by middle school students are *Fullmetal Alchemist* by Hiromu Arawawa and *One Piece* by Eichero Oda. One publisher uses the popularity of the manga to educate children in what are called Edu-manga. In Edu-manga, the popular character Astro-boy leads readers into new worlds.

Graphic novels—and other books increasingly using many kinds of art—come in many styles and in all genres. *The Librarian of Basra,* referred to earlier, for example, first appeared in graphic novel format by Mark Alan Stamaty. This story of Iraqi librarian Alia Muhammed Baker uses grey and beige panels to realistically depict Baker's brave actions, and the all-caps captions add to the intensity of this story. It provides much more visual information than a traditional picturebook would, allowing readers of all ages the opportunity to consider the destruction of war and the war in Iraq in particular. An endnote describes the invasion of Iraq reached Basra on April 6, 2003, but makes no mention of U.S. involvement in words or illustration.

To Dance: A Ballerina's Graphic Novel, written and drawn by Siena and Mark Siegel, is a different kind of graphic novel, a lovely memoir, painted in muted purples, pinks, blues, and grays. It tells the story of how a young Puerto Rican girl (Siena) became a ballerina with the American Ballet Theatre in New York. Readers learn how Siena grew in her art as well as about important moments in dance history—Mikhail Baryshnikov's defection from Russia, Gelsey Kirkland's performance of *Giselle*, and the death of the great choreographer George Ballanchine. Wordless paintings of dancers after Ballanchine's death are particularly moving.

Shaun Tan's award-winning tale of immigration and the experience of being a stranger in a strange land, *The Arrival*, is an example of another kind of graphic novel. Wordless, drawn in pale sienna and black and white, the paintings have the look of old-world photographs. In this novel, the main character experiences a new country of strange buildings, foreign languages, odd customs; we live through his difficult experiences with him as we look from frame to frame.

Finally, *Rapunzel's Revenge* by Shannon and Dean Hale is unlike any of the three previously described graphic novels. Created in the more traditional comic-book style, it offers a wild and witty updating of the fairy tale. In this version Rapunzel uses her long braids not just to climb down from the tower where she has been placed by her stepmother, but also to lasso, whip, and tie up the many bad guys she meets along her heroic journey to take the country back from the evil witch. Each of these graphic novels is completely different from the other, each is a sound example of the format, and each would be appropriate for elementary school students to read.

Wordless Picturebooks

Wordless picturebooks show us how the importance of the visual in today's culture has affected children's literature. In these picturebooks, illustrations carry the full responsibility for meaning. Through the focus and unity created by the pictures, through various artistic styles and media and the narrative style in which the pictures are presented, this special picturebook type presents the thread of story. Unlike wordless object, number, and concept books, wordless picturebooks tell a complete story visually. The increasing recognition being given this type of

Wordless picturebooks are increasingly winning awards.

picturebook is shown by the 2010 Caldecott Medal awarded to Jerry Pinkney for his beautiful wordless version of the Aesop Fable *The Lion and the Mouse*. Pinkney has been producing stunning watercolor picturebook illustrations for many years, but the top honor eluded him until his art connected with a unique design, in which a folklore type defined by its explicitly stated moral was successfully realized through illustration alone.

Wordless picturebooks provide complexity and detail, as well as continuity and consistency. For example, look at the many qualities in David Wiesner's *Flotsam*. The intricacy of the pictures offers enduring, if somewhat surreal pleasure. Complex double-page spreads are filled with the detail in a child's magical discovery of a vintage camera washed onto the seashore. The shore, village photo shop, and underwater camera shots reveal sea life in uncharacteristic actions and fantastic settings. Hours of looking could occupy a child taking in each of the creatures, their varied actions, and the use of **mise-en-abyme**—a visual or verbal text "embedded within another text as its miniature replica."[26] Readers will be surprised when the simple story of a visit to the beach gains intrigue by a visual journey as an imaginary camera pans out to show an increasingly distant perspective of the previous owner of the camera through time and space. Watercolor, surreal art, borders, endpapers, and the embossed casing combine, resulting in a totally successful wordless book.

Another intriguing wordless book using *mise-en-abyme* is Istvan Banyai's *Zoom*, which reverses the device of accumulation—rather than showing less and less of the image, more is shown as the focus decreases. Beginning with a close-up of a rooster's comb, the camera zoom works in reverse, taking the reader back and back as the pictures include more and more information. Children watch the rooster through the window; then one sees the whole house, which becomes part of a toy town, and next a child building the town, to a picture on the cover of a toy catalog held by a boy, and then to the boy sleeping by a pool, and so on until the pilot of a plane looks down at the town, then the country, and finally flies off into the atmosphere. The world revolves in space and becomes finally a speck in the universe. Each provocative picture shows proportion and position in space. *Re-Zoom* is Banyai's successful sequel.[27]

As in all books of a given category, variety in subject matter as well as in quality is infinite. A wordless picturebook that plays on our cultural fascination with dinosaurs, evolution, and time travel, *Time Flies,* is built around a natural history museum setting. A bird flies into the museum, in and out among the skeletal reconstructions of dinosaurs. Readers enjoy a surprise as the bird flies on, in and out of jaws and rib cages, as the setting transforms into prehistoric time and space. When the bird makes its way out through the Tyrannosaurus's tail, the setting transforms once more into a natural history museum. Oil paintings (all double-page spreads) use warm, burnished browns and reds for the museum, but cooler and more varied shades for the outdoor light of the prehistoric scenes. Unusual perspectives such as the bird juxtaposed with the dinosaur provide the contrast with strength and fragility. Rohmann's choice of representational art give a sense of reality to a story that is pure imagination, but older readers might enjoy thinking about theories connecting birds with dinosaurs. All ages can enjoy the metaphor in Eric Rohmann's title.

A book with a far more serious and complex storyline, Jeannie Baker's *Window;* illustrated in two- and three-dimensional collage, offers increasingly intricate pictures that are both curious and familiar. A mother and infant son gaze out their window and view a wooded lot in the country. As the child grows, the view changes: first a single house in the distance, then a small town, and finally a city appear. When the child is a grown man, that same window reveals too-close houses, billboards, traffic, litter, and stores; he loads a van with his possessions and moves away to a country lot, where he finds a country house and plans to raise his family in an environment like that of his own childhood. As he stands in the window with his own infant, he sees the city in the distance, and the river before him—but beyond is a sign advertising lots for sale. The cycle will repeat itself. The natural materials for the collage illustrations appropriately remind the reader of environmental conservation. The story makes a point about the changing countryside through urbanization as well as the inevitability of such change. The story's tone is regret, and the theme hints at the sad truth of the loss of country and a simple bucolic life.

Baker's sequel to *Window* is *Home,* in which Baker reverses the sequence of environmental damage. Set some years later, a child born into the clogged urban setting seen from her window witnesses the gradual process of reclamation. Together the citizens clean and clear up the neighborhood so that by the end of the wordless picturebook the collage art again reveals new trees and a blue river in the distance.

Wordless picturebooks are not entirely new; however, recently published selections reflect changes in style, tone, and design, just as all of children's literature does. Their nature has become increasingly sophisticated as in, for example, Bill Thomson's imaginative and surreal *Chalk.* This inventive wordless book for young children shows the highly unusual results of imagination on a rainy day. The sun comes out and the fun begins; readers see butterflies emerge from the sidewalk and other chalk drawings begin to move. Thomson's paintings seem to come alive!

The origin of these books is increasingly international; it is exciting to see them available to children in the United States. *Mirror* by Suzy Lee delights younger readers, but they may feel unsettled by its atypically sober ending. Korean born, Lee currently works in Singapore. Her earlier wordless book, *Shadow* features a similar young girl as the protagonist. Both books effectively use the books' gutter to create the story's climax, and both add a splash of color to the black and white drawings when emotion is critical to the story. In both stories, the protagonist is active, exploring her impact on the world around her: How does a shadow work? What is that image in the mirror?

The wordless style created by Switzerland's Peter Heuer adds a new character at the end of each story in his series. *Lola,* the first member of the set is now *Lola & Fred & Tom.* Heuer's motivation for the wordless books springs from the need to avoid the language barriers of Switzerland's four national languages. Katja Kamm is an award-winning German author/illustrator whose *Invisible* finds elements from each two-page spread disappearing into the colorful background as new elements appear. This wordless picturebook's style creates a game for young and old readers.

German Jorg Muller explores changes in his nation's countryside with seven trifold spreads. *The Changing Countryside* is a disheartening one, but children of all ages will recognize the message of preserving the landscape as they empathize with the story's hero—a Victorian Manse that finally succumbs to the wrecking ball. The trifolds arrive in a portfolio format, creating interesting possibilities for changing the order of events in this wordless book.

French artist Anne Villeneuve employs the wordless picturebook format to show the action-packed adventure of Turpin the taxi driver, who is trying to return a red scarf left in his cab. *The Red Scarf* plays with a familiar circus theme that depicts the frenetic adventure by including several small scenes on one page. The technique provides the reader with a feel for the hectic efforts of this well-meaning cabbie.

Wordless picturebooks frequently provide multiple story possibilities; they are "writerly" texts that involve the reader in the construction of the stories within. The power of the author is subverted in favor of the reader/writer as well as the illustrator. The notion of readers in control of the meaning of a book that is open to interpretation is associated with **postmodernism**, a movement that has impacted literature for some time. However, postmodern effects in children's books is a more recent phenomenon.

In wordless picturebooks, the power of the author is subverted in favor of the reader/ writer as well as the illustrator.

Postmodernism and Children's Books in Brief

We have shown you in this chapter some of the many ways that children's literature has changed over the past two decades, and we have shared one of the conceptual and theoretical frameworks researchers rely on when they consider contemporary children's literature: Eliza Dresang's radical change theory. Others frame these fundamental changes taking place in contemporary literature for children and young adults differently, associating them with the "broader historical, social, and cultural movement referred to as postmodernism."[28] The concept of postmodernism has been broadly used to describe changes, tendencies, and developments in philosophy, literature, art, and architecture during the last half of the twentieth century, and its effects have been felt in the field of literature for some time.

However, as the following quote[29] makes clear, "Postmodernism and its meaning is a contested terrain. One feature likely to be undisputed though is its rejection of unity, homogeneity, totality, and closure. . . . The postmodern perspective is a questioning one. It does provide an alternative discourse, a different way of thinking, that can be appropriated for a critical examination of texts." Our emphasis on inquiry and returning to any text for closer examination makes it natural for us to include the postmodern perspective in the discussion of important changes to children's books. As Coles and Hall state, "Postmodern texts have, as a significant feature, a breaking down of barriers."[30] At first glance their statement sounds as if these changes are straightforward in nature and limited to a single feature. But the possibilities are many, for any literary element of a children's book could provide a barrier to change.

We offer two examples of lines that have been crossed with the reminder that, for this handbook, we will limit our examples to literature for children and young adults. First, though most book reading for children assumes a left-to-right, top-to-bottom progression, the 1968 picturebook *Rosie's Walk* by Pat Hutchins veers from this traditional linear plot progression. Rosie the hen's trek across the pages is fraught with distraction, as the reader watches a trickster fox's repeated attempts to capture Rosie, yet she seems oblivious to the danger. Each humorous mishap gives readers a chance to interject their thoughts, allowing the "reading path to veer from the linear."[31] Reading a children's story in a traditional "new criticism" way—that is, doing a close reading of the work itself, with the belief that the answer to readers' questions is in the work only—results in an agreed-on, single best meaning, but contemporary texts may have words and images that reject a single interpretation and provide the possibility of multiple meanings. We have already alluded to the groundbreaking *Black and White* by David Macaulay,[32] in which readers' forward progress is split four

Black and White by
David Macaulay,
in which readers'
forward progress is
split four ways, was
a groundbreaking
picturebook.

ways (and more) as they make meanings from the story combinations available to them. When directionality veers significantly from the traditional left to right and top to bottom, readers need to find a way to frame recursive elements. A wordless example of this more postmodern style of writing can be found in *The Yellow Balloon* by Charlotte Dematons, in which readers must follow the elaborate "path" of a rogue balloon, placing the historical beside the fantastic, the familiar with the remote. When reading these books readers view and review multidimensionally, creating their own stories.

Besides altering normal progression, modern literature also often presents "truthful" representations of reality as comic scenes of mere entertainment. Postmodern literature replaces seriousness with parody and irony. But in the process of being playful, postmodern texts create a space for questioning the very "truths" they mock. For example, J. Patrick Lewis breaks a barrier by creating a children's book related to death that nevertheless includes visual and verbal puns. The dark humor of *Once upon a Tomb: Gravely Humorous Verses* parodies the epitaph at the same time as it presents the reader with ironic ways characters might die. An example: for the underwear salesman, "Our grief/Was brief."

Sophistication for Children

Adults are frequently skeptical about children's capacity to understand books with postmodern traits. In particular, they don't believe children will enjoy the nonlinear, multilayered, open-ended books that mimic the characteristics of the digital media. Others disagree, such as Jill McClay,[33] who echoes Dresang and McClelland: "Children encounter the postmodern at every turn in their fictional worlds. While many adults see the postmodern as a departure from or a comment on 'tradition' in literature, it *is* the tradition that children meet on television and in movies." And it *is* the new tradition of the Internet, hypertext software, even smart phone technologies. But as McClay found in her research into children's reactions to Macaulay's boundary-breaking *Black and White,* children's sense of what counts as a story or a book is still forming. Children were open to the possibilities *Black and White* presented, and each adjusted their approach to the book and made sense of the stories in their own ways.[34] Adults (teachers, parents, and librarians), on the other hand, tended to interpret the book with strategies they used successfully when reading traditional storybooks; they were less resourceful in dealing with the recursive and digressive pathways of postmodern picturebooks and the illustrations necessary to build their own interpretations. Adults' assumptions about books affected their comfort with selection of complex texts like *Black and White.*[35]

Adults tended to
interpret postmodern
picturebooks in less
resourceful and
successful ways than
children did.

As Margaret Meek[36] noted in her seminal work *How Texts Teach What Readers Learn*, adults tend to use one kind of reading for all. She noted that as we become more experienced readers, we can become less skilled. Children who have been immersed in a digital world are not only more comfortable with texts that show postmodern tendencies, but they may also find these books more appealing than other, more traditional books. It has also been suggested that the formats presented in more postmodern books might hold great appeal for contemporary children; the books might provide a jumping-off point for mediating how texts work, a new site for playing with the possibilities books still offer readers in our digital age.

One of the most valuable traits of postmodern picturebooks is their self-referential nature—that is, how they reveal their natures as books. Readers can learn about the way the digital world works from postmodern picturebooks; their parodic and intertextual nature call attention to their own construction; their secrets are revealed. **Metafiction**, which is part of the postmodern trend in picturebooks, is fiction that deals with the conventions of the writing of fiction. In these books storylines take a visible turn to other stories; characters reveal themselves as such; illustrators insert themselves into the story, showing their importance; readers are beckoned into the book and consulted throughout the reading process.[37]

We see these self-referential qualities as quite important because of their disruption of the lived-through experience traditionally associated with fiction; instead of offering the reader a secondary world, postmodern picturebooks offer a metafictive stance that draws attention to the text *as a text*. David Wiesner's very postmodern picturebook version of *The Three Pigs* is a good illustration not only of metafictive devices but also of postmodern attributes that can be found in children's and young adult books.[38]

The Three Pigs, which is famous for being a postmodern picturebook, continually refers to itself. It begins like the original story, but deconstruction starts right away. First, the reader notices one of the pigs in a corner of the page, saying that the wolf blew him "right out of the story!" Next, the same pig, who is outside of the frame of the picture, invites another pig to join him: "Come on—it's safe out here." On later pages, we see the pigs crawling out from what are clearly the pages of the book, and even making those pages into a paper airplane. By taking the characters right out of the story. Wiesner reminds the reader that this *is* a story, constructed (or built, or written) by a person.

The Three Pigs exemplifies postmodernism in at least six other ways. Each is listed below, with an example from Wiesner's book.

- *Multiplicity in pathways through the story and meanings.* This version of *The Three Pigs* does not go simply from beginning to middle and end, but digresses, interrupts itself, and includes other stories alongside or inside the main plot. The *nonlinear plot* in Wiesner's construction begins with the traditional plot, but breaks it up as the pigs choose to leave the story and as they enter into and out of other storyboards (notice how the illustrations show them browsing for another story with other characters). The story doesn't even end, and we don't know if the pigs live happily ever after, as they are in the process of constructing a new story at the end of the book.

- *Intertextuality with other kinds of texts.* Despite using the framework of the old story, *The Three Little Pigs,* Wiesner also makes references to other folkloric favorites, *The Loathesome Dragon* and *The Dish and the Spoon*. Wiesner lets children know that the pigs are not confined to their folklore world—they are now in a fantasy world and can interact with these stories as well. Children familiar with Wiesner's work will recognize allusions to *The Loathesome Dragon, Tuesday,* and *Free Fall.*

- *Subversion of literary traditions.* A tone of parody, irony, or subversion can be seen in *The Three Pigs*—the pigs are craftier, trickier, and less afraid of the wolf than they are in the original story (maybe they've heard Disney's song, *Who's Afraid of the Big Bad Wolf?*). The story subverts the power of the author when one of the pigs looks out from the page and acknowledges his readers, letting them know that they have power to co-create the story with the pigs. The author's traditional importance is also subverted by the many allusions to the illustrator's work, just as the story is subverted from the traditional, less by the words than the illustrations. The original tale's family characteristics are also subverted by the depiction of the pigs as brothers but of different breeds, with no mother to be the source of their resistance.

- *Blurring of distinctions. The Three Pigs* mixes high and low culture, subverts author and reader, and blends distinctions among traditional literary genres. Wiesner allows the pigs to take over the story, along with the reader. In fact they *rewrite* the story, blurring the distinction between the writer of the book and the book's characters themselves. In overturning the deference to text over illustration, just as traditional lore is subverted by modern fantasy, the reader realizes this story could not happen as it does without primary attention to the illustration.

- *Playfulness.* Readers are invited to treat the text as a semiotic playground all throughout this book. Children recognize the spirit of fun that permeates the pigs' adventures (once they embrace the freedom they've been given to co-author the story). The Wolf remains in the traditional story and never really "gets it," but who knows what story he might choose if he were to join in the fun.

As elsewhere in this handbook, we advocate for children *and* adults to read the story and then *reread* it to see what is there, making sense of it as literature. Books with postmodern attributes demand more than one reading, making this new subgenre[39] a perfect place for readers of all ages to think about close reading. We think it is important to remember that though these books have been classified as "postmodern," they are not really postmodern so much as they are affected *by* postmodernism in varying degrees. Lawrence Sipe[40] recommends placing the books along a continuum that recognizes this variance as well as the fact that a "postmodern picturebook" can be so for very different reasons. Some books have a small degree of influence, such as some of the fairy tale parodies. Others like *Black and White* and Wiesner's *The Three Pigs* have been infused with these qualities (and we recommend reading them both).

As with any category of children's literature—or maybe even *more* than any category—these books will continue to push boundaries and look for barriers to transgress or to illuminate. Kathleen O'Neil[41] delineates an important possibility for postmodern picturebooks: their power for promoting social justice responses. O'Neil selects postmodern children's books to illustrate the way they can still assist children in thinking about issues of morality. She says these books can impart social values despite the absence of overt moralizing and didacticism in this subgenre. Postmodern picturebooks can be a vehicle that encourages children to take a closer look at current issues in our world by stimulating readers to question and rethink the societal norms our postmodern culture prescribes. Other children's books can do this, but O'Neil advocates for postmodern books because of their purposeful subversion of traditions: "In keeping with the traditional purpose of children's books, postmodern picturebooks offer multiple opportunities for awakening children to cultural issues as well as providing models for responding to uncertainty and diversity."

"In short, a postmodern picturebook is one in which a traditional tale or plot is disrupted to present an alternative point of view or outcome, often in a way that questions the validity of conventional mores and leaves much of the meaning up to the reader. As a result, a thoughtful reading is necessary."[42] Linda De Haan's *King and King* parodies the fairy tale genre, disrupting the boy-meets-girl formula; a pastiche of illustrative styles keep the reader's eyes moving about the page, and there are intertextual references to European history. But O'Neil sees barrier breaking beyond a delightfully ironical twist to an old story, in the notion of marriage equity and an opportunity to imagine possibilities beyond the limits of traditional social expectations. Anthony Browne's excellent *Voices in the Park* is filled with allusions to popular Western culture, and the linear story path is disrupted as the story of a visit to the park is told from the perspective of each story character. Color and font provide visual cues to whose perspective is being shared. The barrier of social class as a topic for a children's book is crossed; its impact on the two families and the possible responses to the issues are left to the readers, who may find some of the accounts of the visit to the park disagreeable. The surreal artistic style adds to the effects and promotes additional critical analysis about what our world can or should be today and in the future.

Michele Anstey[43] brings us full circle with the reminder that postmodern picturebooks hold a special spot in children's literature, not only for their role in literacy, but also for their function in improving understanding of the political, social, cultural, and economic world, as well as for their connection to the digital world Eliza Dresang's theory of radical change includes. Anstey reminds us of our theme in this chapter: "Change is the overarching characteristic of the early 21st century and will continue to be so."

Postmodernism continues to influence children's literature. Adults preparing to select books for and with children will increasingly feel at ease with these creative members of the children's literature family, for they can be found in every genre. Spending a lot of time classifying runs counter to a postmodern spirit, but loose categories can help us see special features and consider their impact for readers.

SUMMARY

American society has changed in radical ways over recent decades. The pervasiveness of media, the instant access and connectivity provided by the Internet, and new technological avenues for communication have modified the ways we experience time and space, even the ways we experience reality itself. These technological changes have also altered the nature of childhood. Such changes have caused children's writers and artists to create new kinds of literature and art to address their savvier, more demanding audience of child readers. Issues that have long been sources of contention continue—the question over whether series books are worthy of children's time, the need for literature addressing our children's increasing social diversity, and the difficulties caused by risky topics in some books for parents and teachers—all are

text continues on page 41

TEXTSET

Postmodern Picturebooks

Metafictional/Self-Referential

Gerstein, Mordecai. *A Book*. Roaring Book Press, 2009.

Kanninen, Barbara. *A Story with Pictures*. Lynne Rowe Reed, Illus. Holiday House, 2007.

Smith, Lane. *It's A Book*. Roaring Book Press, 2010.

Stevens, Susan. *The Little Red Pen*. Janet Stevens, Illus. Harcourt, 2011.

Van Allsburg, Chris. *Bad Day at Riverbend*. Houghton Mifflin, 1995.

Whatley, Bruce. *Wait, No Paint!* Perfection, 2005.

Wiesner, David, *Art & Max*. Clarion, 2010.

Parody/Play/Ironic

Browne, Anthony. *Willy the Dreamer*. Candlewick, 1998.

Guarnaccia, Steven. *The Three Little Pigs: An Architectural Tale*. Abrams, 2010.

Portis, Antoinette. *This Is Not a Box*. HarperCollins, 2006.

Spiegelman, Art. *Open Me . . . I'm a Dog!* HarperCollins, 1997.

Novel Use of Literature or Genre Elements

Kitamura, Satoshi. *When Sheep Cannot Sleep*. Perfection, 1988.

Lester, Mike. *A Is for Salad*. Grosset & Dunlap, 2000.

Singer, Marilyn. *Mirror, Mirror: A Book of Reversible Verse*. Josee Massee, Illus. Dutton, 2010.

Nonlinearity

Kitamura, Satoshi. *Lily's Walk*. Dutton, 1987.

Lehman, Barbara. *Museum Trip*. Houghton Mifflin, 2006.

Stein, David Ezra. *Interrupting Chicken.* Candlewick, 2010.

Vere, Ed. *The Getaway*. Margaret McElderry, 2007.

Unusual Uses of Narrator Voice

Browne, Anthony. *Me and You*. Farrar, Straus and Giroux, 2010.

Browne, Anthony. *Voices in the Park*. DK Children, 1998.

Burningham, John. *Would You Rather . . .* HarperCollins, 1978.

Wiesner, David. *Flotsam*. Clarion, 2006.

Wiesner, David. *Sector 7*. Clarion, 1999.

Pastiche of Writing and Illustrative Styles

Gravett, Emily. *Little Mouse's Big Book of Fears*. Simon & Schuster, 2008.

Gravett, Emily. *Meerkat Mail*. Simon & Schuster, 2007.

Reibstein, Mark. *Wabi Sabi*. Ed Young, Illus. Little Brown, 2008.

Original Design

Bataille, Marion. *ABC3D*. Roaring Book, 2008.

Cottin, Menena. *The Black Book of Colors.* Rosana Faria, Illus.; Elisa Amado, Trans. Groundwood, 2008.

Gravett, Emily. *The Rabbit Problem.* Simon & Schuster, 2010.

Gravett, Emily. *Spells.* Simon & Schuster, 2009.

Muller, Jorg. *The Changing Countryside.* Heryin Books, 2006.

Spiegelman, Art. *Open Me . . . I'm a Dog!* HarperCollins, 1997.

Van Allsburg, Chris. *The Mysteries of Harris Burdick: Portfolio Edition.* Houghton Mifflin, 1996.

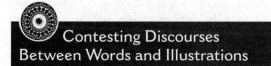
Contesting Discourses Between Words and Illustrations

Browne, Anthony. *Gorilla.* Knopf, 1991.

Burningham, John. *Come Away from the Water, Shirley.* Red Fox, 1992.

Burningham, John. *Time to Get Out of the Bath, Shirley.* Red Fox, 1987.

Intertextuality

Ahlberg, Allen. *The Jolly Postman.* Janet Ahlberg, Illus. LB Kids, 2001.

Browne, Anthony. *Into the Forest.* Walker, 2005.

Browne, Anthony. *Willy's Pictures.* Candlewick, 2000.

Browne, Anthony. *Willy the Dreamer.* Candlewick, 2002.

Lewis, J. Patrick. *The Last Resort.* Robert Innocenti, Illus. Creative Editions, 2002.

still sources of concern. These issues still require our thought and consideration. For example, in this chapter's textset describing some of the challenges and battles over children's books that have recently occurred, we suggest possible steps for teachers when books they want to use are challenged.

Writers and illustrators of children's texts have responded to our changing society in a variety of ways. We have outlined many such responses in this chapter. For example, children's books have become more like adult books, with more sophisticated plots, less clearly defined resolutions, and less reliable or more direct narrators. Children's books are also more apt to discuss risky topics than previously; one reason, we think, is that as children see more of the world through television, they need books that help them make sense of what they see. Finally, children's books are more apt to blur genres and content material now than they were in the past. A book can be about science, history, mathematics, animal life, and biography at once while also describing an imaginary world ruled by agreed-upon facts.

Along with changes in the boundaries of content and genre have come new formats. Specifically, in this chapter, we discussed the verse novel, listing some of the best historical fiction in verse as well. We also described the importance of graphic texts, describing some of the contributions this new format has made to children's literature. Other writers have attributed these new formats to the ways in which advanced technology has made our society both more oral and more visual.

Finally, we discussed the picturebook, a format that has been around for a long time, but which has also been changing in response to our changed culture. Wordless picturebooks and postmodern picturebooks can be seen as responses to our more visual, more fragmented culture in which, perhaps, there is no one simple truth to be presented to children, but a plethora of truths, voices, and perspectives. In the next chapter we continue our discussion of picturebooks, noting how these texts, the exciting new ones and the reassuring conventional ones, bring joy, curiosity, and pleasure to children while helping them think deeply about their world.

NOTES

1. David Elkind, "Technology's Impact on Child Growth and Development," *CIO* [online], September 22, 2003, pp. 1–3.

2. Gary D. Schmidt, "'So Here, My Dears, Is a New Oz Story': The Deep Structure of a Series," *Children's Literature Association Quarterly*, 14, Winter 1989, pp. 163–165.

3. Larrick's classic article was published in a book of the same name: *The All White World of Children's Books & African American Children's Literature*, edited by Osay-imwense Osa (Africa: World Press, 1995).

4. Susan Lempke stated in *Horn Book Magazine* that picturebooks do not reflect the diversity in our country. Of 216 picturebooks analyzed, 116 featured only all white characters. Only 7 of the 216 books featured African American characters. The article "The Faces in Picture Books" was reissued in the 2010 *Horn Book Magazine*, which may indicate that children's books continue to lag behind in their representation of ethnicity. Lempke's article has been reprinted and can be viewed in full online at www.hbook.com/whatsnew/default.asp.

5. The Cooperative Children's Book Center at the University of Wisconsin–Madison, School of Education, has kept records of the children's books by and about people of color since 1994, available at www.education.wisc.edu/ccbc/books/pcstats.htm. The categories for their research include African American, Asian, Hispanic, and Native American children's books.

6. Lynne Reiser. "Going from But to And: Challenges in Creating a Pair of Picture Books from Different Cultures," *The Horn Book*, 1998, pp. 578–586. (Accessible as a free pdf file on Google.com)

7. If you want to learn more about how to discuss race in your classroom, we suggest you read either *Talking Race in the Classroom* by Jane Bolgatz or *White Teacher* by Vivian Gussin Paley. Bolgatz's book is geared more toward high school teachers, but contains helpful suggestions about how to conduct difficult conversations. Paley's book is a classic, describing her own growth as a kindergarten teacher in a city classroom.

8. The eight categories of culture that structure the work of Elizabeth Knowles and Martha Smith, *Understanding Diversity Through Novels and Picturebooks* (New York: Libraries Unlimited, 2007) originated with the National Association of Independent Schools. These became so prevalent that the group has dropped the term "The Big 8" to emphasize other attributes that have equal (even greater) importance.

9. American Library Association, "The Freedom to Read," available at http://www.ala.org/ala/aboutala/offices/oif/statementspols/ftrstatement/freedomreadstatement.cfm. Other documents and helpful links related to censorship and the ALA-sponsored Banned Books Week can be found at: www.ala.org.

10. The Cooperative Children's Book Center, available at www.education.wisc.edu/ccbc/books/pcstats.htm.

11. American Library Association, "Intellectual Freedom," 2011, available at http://www.ala.org/template.cfm?section=basics&template=/contentmanagement/contentdisplay.cfm&contentid=24695.

12. The National Council of Teachers of English (NCTE) has helpful proactive tips for parents and educators related to selecting books and how to manage situations when a book has been challenged.

13. American Library Association, "OIF Lists 100 Most Challenged Books of the Decade," 2000, available at http://www.ala.org/ala/alonline/currentnews/newsarchive/2000/june2000/oiflists100most.cfm.

14. American Library Association, "Top Ten Most Frequently Challenged Books of 2008," 2011, available at http://www.ala.org/ala/issuesadvocacy/banned/frequentlychallenged/21stcenturychallenged/2008/index.cfm.

15. Eliza Dresang, *Radical Change: Books for Youth in a Digital Age* (New York: H. W. Wilson, 1999), p. 6.

16. Kathleen Horning, Merri V. Lingren, Hollis Rudiger, and Megan Schliesman, "Review of Starry Messenger by Peter Sis," *CCBC Choices*, 1996, p. 37.

17. Maria Nikolajeva, "Exit Children's Literature?" *The Lion and the Unicorn*, 22(2), 1998, pp. 221–236.

18. Vivi Edstrom, *Barnboken form. En studie I konsten att beratta*, 3rd ed. (Stockholm: Raben & Sjogren, 1994), pp. 19–57; Perry Nodelman, *The Pleasures of Children's Literature*, 2nd ed. (New York: Longman, 1992), pp. 154–164. Cited in Nikolajeva, "Exit Children's Literature?" p. 225.

19. Maria Nikolajeva, "Exit Children's Literature?" *The Lion and the Unicorn,* 22(2), 1998, p. 225.

20. Eliza Dresang, *Radical Change: Books for Youth in a Digital Age* (New York: H. W. Wilson, 1999).

21. Much of this section is adapted from Julie Wollman-Bonilla, "Outrageous Viewpoints: Teachers' Criteria for Rejecting Works of Children's Literature," *Language Arts,* 75(4), 1998, pp. 287–295.

22. Jane Yolen wrote the phrase "stories lean on other stories" in *Touch Magic: Fantasy, Fairy and Folklore in the Literature of Children* (New York: Philomel, 1981), p. 15.

23. Joy Alexander, "The Verse-Novel: A New Genre," *Children's Literature in Education,* 36(3), Spring 2005, pp. 269–283.

24. Myra Zarnowski, "Historical Novels in Verse: A Fusion Genre," *Journal of Children's Literature,* 36(1), Spring 2010.

25. Much of this section on graphic novels is paraphrased from Scott McCloud's seminal work, *Understanding Comics: The Invisible Art* (New York: Harper Perennial, 1993).

26. Maria Nikolajeva and Carole Scott, *How Picturebooks Work* (New York: Garland, 2001), p. 226.

27. See a good discussion of children's responses to wordless picturebooks using *mise en abyme* in Sylvia Pantaleo, "How Could That Be? Reading Banyai's *Zoom* and *Re-Zoom,*" *Language Arts,* 84(3), January 2007.

28. Sylvia Pantaleo and Lawrence Sipe comment on the various interpretations of the postmodern as it has affected children's literature in the introduction to *Postmodern Picturebooks: Play, Parody, and Self-Referentiality* (New York: Routledge, 2008).

29. Martin Coles and Christine Hall, "Breaking the Line: New Literacies, Postmodernism, and the Teaching of Printed Texts," *Reading Literacy and Language,* November 2001, p. 114. This classic article is often cited by current researchers applying the postmodern theory to contemporary children's books (e.g., Sylvia Pantaleo, Lawrence Sipe, and Maria Nikolajeva). Their discussion of changes is very readable and thorough.

30. Coles and Hall, "Breaking the Line," p. 112.

31. We are not convinced that *Rosie's Walk* is truly linear as claimed by Coles and Hall in "Breaking the Line." The book's copyright year was 1968, when breaking the "rules" for children's books was just beginning.

32. Jill McClay researched student interactions with this book and was one of the first to do so for a professional journal of children's literature following Dresang and McClelland's "Black and White: A Journey," *The Horn Book Magazine,* November–December 1995, pp. 704–710. Jill McClay, "Wait a Second . . . : Negotiating Complex Narratives in *Black and White,*" *Children's Literature in Education,* 31(2), 2000, pp. 91–106.

33. Eliza T. Dresang and Kate McClelland, "Black and White: A Journey," *The Horn Book Magazine,* November–December 1995, pp. 704–710. Eliza Dresang's influence has been very important for the study of contemporary children's books and their intermediary role with digital technologies.

34. Jill McClay, "Wait a Second . . ." McClay's classic research is very revealing not only about this particular children's book, but also about the effects of postmodernism on children and adult readers.

35. Morag Styles and Evelyn Arizpe, "'A Gorilla with Grandpa's Eyes': How Children Interpret Visual Texts—A Study of Anthony Browne's *Zoo,*" *Children's Literature in Education,* 32(4), December 2001, pp. 261–281.

36. Margaret Meek, *How Texts Teach What Readers Learn* (Stroud, UK: The Thimble Press, 1988), p. 35. For a visionary but very readable short booklet, see Margaret Meek, "How Texts Teach What Readers Learn," 1988, available from www.thimblepress.co.uk.

37. Sylvia Pantaleo's research with postmodern picturebooks includes a thread for metafiction. A progression of this topic can be seen with the following publications:

    - Sylvia Pantaleo, "What Do Four Voices, a Shortcut and Three Pigs Have in Common? Metafiction!" *Bookbird: A Journal of International Children's Literature,* 42(1), 2004, pp. 4–12.
    - Sylvia Pantaleo, "Young Children Engage with the Metafictive in Picture Books," *Australian Journal of Language and Literacy,* 28(1), 2005, pp. 19–37.
    - Sylvia Pantaleo, "Postmodernism, Metafiction and *Who's Afraid of the Big Bad Book?*" *The Journal of Children's Literature Studies,* 3(1), 2006, pp. 26–39.
    - Sylvia Pantaleo, "Exploring the Metafictive in Elementary Students' Writing," *Changing English,* 14(1), 2007, pp. 61–76.

    Pantaleo sees the disruption in the narrative as one of the most important ways readers and writers can take advantage of seeing how texts work. Her most recent published work analyzes the narrative path of three recent children's books with postmodern tendencies: Sylvia Pantaleo, "Mutinous Fiction: Narrative and Illustrative Metalepsis in Three Postmodern Picturebooks," *Children's Literature in Education: An International Quarterly.* 41, 2010, pp. 12–27.

38. Lawrence Sipe and Caroline McGuire identify the six characteristics of postmodern picturebooks we will use in this segment. Sylvia Pantaleo's classroom research with children's responses to Wiesner's *The Three Pigs* reveals how savvy first-grade children were with this book: Sylvia Pantaleo, "Grade 1 Students Meet David Wiesner's *Three Pigs,*" *Journal of Children's Literature,* 28(2), 2002.

39. Bette Goldstone's work is very reader friendly, and she is frequently given credit for labeling books influenced by postmodern qualities as a subgenre. The resistance of the postmodern to classification makes this an unusual label worthy of discussion. Two of Goldstone's articles are recommended for their clear discussion of postmodern picturebooks:

   - Bette Goldstone, "Whaz Up with Our Picturebooks? Changing Picturebook Codes and Teaching Implications," *The Reading Teacher*, 55(4), 2001–2002, pp. 362–370.
   - Bette Goldstone, "The Postmodern Picture Book: A New Subgenre," *Language Arts*, 81(3), 2004, pp. 196–204.

40. Lawrence Sipe has done extensive research with picturebooks, including those identified as postmodern. See Lawrence Sipe and Sylvia Pantaleo, eds., *Postmodern Picturebooks: Play, Parody, and Self-Referentiality* (New York: Routledge, 2008). This resource is very valuable to teachers, parents, and librarians who want to examine the many facets of literature affected by postmodernism. Sipe discusses the idea of the continuum again in his recently published *Storytime: Young Children's Literary Understanding in the Classroom* (New York: Teachers College Press, 2007). This book is a comprehensive review of the literature related to books for children, especially the picturebook.

41. Kathleen O'Neil, "Once Upon Today: Teaching for Social Justice with Postmodern Picturebooks," *Children's Literature in Education,* 41, 2010, p. 42.

42. O'Neil, "Once Upon Today," p. 43.

43. Michele Anstey, "It's Not All Black and White: Postmodern Picture Books and New Literacies," *Journal of Adolescent & Adult Literacy*, 45(6), 2001, p. 445. Anstey's work with Geoffrey Bull is critical to the concepts of new literacies needed for the twenty-first century. These typically are about technology's impact on the learner and literacy learning. Anstey sees a role for the postmodern picturebook in providing a link between traditional literacy requirements and those for the digital world.

RECOMMENDED BOOKS

BAKER, JEANNIE. *Home.* Greenwillow, 2004.

BAKER, JEANNIE. *Window.* Greenwillow, 1991.

BANYAI, ISTVAN. *Re-Zoom.* Viking, 1998.

BANYAI, ISTVAN. *Zoom.* Viking, 1995.

BROWNE, ANTHONY. *Voices in the Park.* DK Children, 2001.

BRYANT, JEN. *The Trial.* Knopf, 2004.

BURG, ANN E. *All the Broken Places.* Scholastic, 2009.

CURTIS, CHRISTOPHER PAUL. *The Watsons Go to Birmingham, 1963.* Random House Children's Books, 1995.

GEORGE, JEAN CRAIGHEAD. *One Day in the Desert.* HarperCollins, 1996.

GEORGE, JEAN CRAIGHEAD. *One Day in the Tropical Rainforest.* HarperCollins, 1995.

DE HAAN, LINDA. *King and King.* Tricycle Press, 2003.

DEMATONS, CHARLOTTE. *The Yellow Balloon.* Handprint, 2004.

ENGLE, MARGARITA. *Tropical Secrets: Holocaust Refugees in Cuba.* Henry Holt, 2009.

HADDEN, MARK. *The Curious Incident of the Dog in the Nighttime.* Vintage, 2004.

HALE, SHANNON, AND DEAN HALE. *Rapunzel's Revenge.* Bloomsbury USA Children's Books, 2008.

HEIDE, FLORENCE PARRY, AND JUDITH HEIDE GILLILAND. *Sami and the Time of Troubles.* Sandpiper, 1995.

HESSE, KAREN. *Aleutian Sparrow.* Illustrated by Evon Zerbetz. McElderry, 2003.

HESSE, KAREN. *Out of the Dust.* Scholastic, 1997.

HEUER, PETER. *Lola & Fred & Tom.* 4N Publishing, 2007.

HUTCHINS, PAT. *Rosie's Walk.* Simon & Schuster, 1968.

JOHNSON, ANGELA. *Heaven.* Simon & Schuster, 2000.

KAMM, KATJA. *Invisible.* North-South Books, 2006.

LEE, SUZY. *Mirror.* Seven Footer Press, 2010.

LEE, SUZY. *Shadow.* Chronicle Books, 2010.

LESTER, JULIUS. *From Slave Ship to Freedom Road.* Puffin, 1999.

LEWIS, J. PATRICK. *Once upon a Tomb: Gravely Humorous Verses.* Candlewick, 2006.

LEZOTTE, ANN CLARE. *T4.* Houghton Mifflin, 2008.

MACAULAY, DAVID. *Black and White.* Houghton Mifflin, 1990.

MULLER, JORG. *The Changing Countryside.* Heryin Books, 2006.

PERKINS, MITALI. *First Daughter: Extreme American Makeover.* Dutton Juvenile, 2007.

PINKNEY, JERRY. *The Lion and the Mouse.* Little, Brown, 2009.

REISER, LYNNE. *Cherry Pies and Lullabies.* Greenwillow Books, 1998.

REISER, LYNNE, AND CORAZONES CALIENTE. *Tortillas and Lullabies.* Greenwillow Books, 1998.

ROHMANN, ERIC. *Time Flies.* Dragonfly Books, 1997.

RYAN, PAM MUÑOZ, AND PETER SÍS. *The Dreamer.* Scholastic, 2010.

SELZNICK, BRIAN. *The Invention of Hugo Cabret.* Scholastic, 2007.

SIEGEL, SIENA, AND MARK SIEGEL. *To Dance: A Ballerina's Graphic Novel.* Atheneum, 2006.

SÍS, PETER. *Starry Messenger: Galileo Galilei.* Farrar, Strauss, & Giroux, 2000.

SNICKET, LEMONY. *The Bad Beginning.* HarperCollins, 1999.

SONES, SONYA. *One of Those Hideous Books Where the Mother Dies.* Simon & Schuster Children's Publishing, 2005.

STAMATY, MARK ALAN. *Alia's Mission: Saving the Books of Iraq.* Knopf, 2004.

TAN, SHAUN. *The Arrival.* Arthur A. Levine Books, 2007.

THOMSON, BILL. *Chalk.* Marshall Cavendish, 2010.

TOWNSEND, SUE. *The Secret Diary of Adrian Mole, Aged 13¾.* HarperTeen, 2004.

VILLENEUVE, ANNE. *The Red Scarf ("L'escharpe rouge").* Tundra Books, 2010.

WABOOSE, JAN BOURDEAU. *Sky Sisters.* Kids Can Press, 2002.

WIESNER, DAVID. *Flotsam.* Clarion, 2006.

WIESNER, DAVID. *The Three Pigs.* Clarion, 2001.

WING, NATASHA. *Jalapeño Bagels.* Atheneum, 1996.

WINTER, JEANETTE. *The Librarian of Basra: A True Story from Iraq.* Harcourt Children's Books, 2005.

WOODSON, JACQUELINE. *Locomotion.* Penguin Group, 2003.

WOODSON, JACQUELINE. *Visiting Day.* Scholastic Press, 2002.

YANG, GENE LUEN. *American Born Chinese.* Macmillan, 2006.

MyEducationKit™

Go to the topic "Multicultural Literature" on the MyEducationKit for this text, where you can:

- Search the Children's Literature Database, housing more than 22,000 titles searchable in every genre by authors or illustrators, by awards won, by year published, and by topic and description.

- Explore genre-related Assignments and Activities, assignable exercises showing concepts in action through database use, video, cases, and student and teacher artifacts.

- Listen to podcasts and read interviews from some of the brightest and most enduring stars of children's literature in the Conversations.

- Discover web links that will lead you to sites representing the authors you learn about in these pages, classrooms with powerful children's literature connections, and literature awards.

ON THEIR LAST NIGHT TOGETHER,
BILL, PAM, JAMES, AND EAMON HAD A POPCORN PARTY.
JAMES AND EAMON SOON DISCOVERED THAT A PARTY WITH
BILL AND PAM COULD GET PRETTY NOISY.

SO, THEY WANDERED OUTSIDE
FOR SOME PEACE AND QUIET.
TOMORROW THEY HAD TO GO HOME.

A Couple of Boys Have the Best Week Ever
Marla Frazee

Contemporary picturebook illustrations
create humor when they show a story
different from the story told in the text.

CHAPTER THREE

Picturebooks

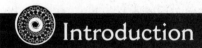

Introduction

Words or pictures:

Which are more

important?

Picturebooks hold a time-honored place in children's literature. When Randolph Caldecott introduced double-page full-color illustrations in the late 1800s, it set in motion a process of continual change and innovation in children's picturebooks. In his honor the Caldecott Medal was introduced in 1938 for the most distinguished American picturebook, institutionalizing the growing importance of illustration and encouraging the unique role picturebooks play in the literacy development of children. With their dual audience of both adults and children, picturebooks within every genre continue to innovate and present us with new styles, designs, and preferences.

Often referred to as **picture books** or *picture-books*, the term **picturebook** is currently used to recognize the union of text and art that results in something more when these elements are combined; it is the term we will use in this edition.[1] Although it is true that many popular picturebooks are fictional narratives, picturebooks include a range of styles and genres, which can be described as in the *picturebook format*.[2] As the guiding question to this chapter suggests, the importance of pictures, text, and their relationship permeate discussions of how these books should be classified and what their relative impact might be for readers and literary learning. More recently the questions related

Picturebooks are represented in every genre; they have a dual readership of adults and children.

to "words or pictures" swirl about what *effect* these two elements have for children's sense-making of contemporary picturebooks, whose design, content, and style often break with traditional expectations for children's books. Lawrence Sipe put it best when he described the actual reading event that creates a larger meaning from the pictures and words as *synergy*.[3] For this and other reasons, we discuss the picturebook format early in this edition; these wonderful creations are found in every genre and their qualities have important implications for today's readers.

Picturebooks mean "more" than the sum of the words and pictures.

 # Importance of Illustration and Text

Readers have traditionally assumed drawings are made to *accompany* verbal storytelling; the images are meant to complement the words. Perhaps because emphasis has historically been given to the text of any children's book, with illustration tied to text, illustration was often regarded as a lesser art. Today, however, technological improvements in printing have allowed publishers to employ art editors who encourage artistic creativity, appealing to successful artists such as Leo and Diane Dillon, Peter Sis, Jerry Pinkney, or David Weisner. Many others, such as Beckie Prange, Brian Selznick, Beth Krommes, or Bill Thomson, who illustrate children's books in collaboration with authors, also benefit from advancements in publishing technology and the creative opportunities of the picturebook format. Thanks to a more affluent society, an increased awareness of the importance of childhood, courses in children's literature and its critical evaluation, and the growing significance of children's book awards, picturebooks are increasingly well illustrated, and their artistic excellence is both apparent and appreciated. So much so that it is a rare contemporary picturebook in which illustration holds less than half the meaning.[4]

Pictures are at least one half of the meaning in a picturebook.

The proportion of illustration to text ranges from books that are primarily words, with illustration merely serving to confirm or illuminate the verbal text, to books that are essentially wordless, as discussed in Chapter 2. A book is typically referred to as "illustrated" when it includes a pictorial dust jacket, a cover picture, a frontispiece, and a few pictures scattered throughout. Examples might be *Just a Dream* by Chris Van Allsburg or *Frog and Toad Together* by Arnold Lobel, in which the text is much more prominent in telling the story, and the illustrations only serve to illuminate and enhance. These books primarily focus on the words, and the impact of the pictures on the reader's meaning making and the story itself is minimal. For this reason, we will not include discussion of illustrated books in this chapter (though they may be referred to throughout the handbook for the way they demonstrate other literary elements).

Contemporary picturebooks mirror the current cultural emphasis on visual communication; their meaning is dependent not only on the words but also the illustrations. Standard picturebooks, typically thirty-two pages infused with both text and pictures, will be the primary source for the examples throughout this chapter. Perry Nodelman, who has written extensively about this format, believes that children who come to understand the conventions and structures of picturebooks enjoy them with great enthusiasm and conscious appreciation, discovering how pictures and words work together.[5] He suggests that the two kinds of "texts" (visual and verbal, pictures and words) are read at different speeds, that one of their pleasures lies in grasping an element in one narrative that the other does not treat. Furthermore, a picturebook demands a different sense of pacing than text alone. The picturebook's short text requires a relatively short reading process, whereas reading the pictures that accompany the words involves close attention, searching for clues, putting together disparate pieces of information – a slower process. David Lewis suggests that numerous styles and text/picture combinations occur between and within picturebooks ensure an active process of stitching together the words and pictures to make meaning.[6] Whatever the style, reading a picturebook must allow for more time than it takes to read the words!

Pictures may take longer to "read" than the text.

Let's take a look at some classics whose balance is tipped toward the verbal text. In *The Snowy Day*, Ezra Jack Keats uses a significant number of words to elaborate upon the simple trek Peter makes through the fresh snow. He provides insights not shown in the illustration. This style has sometimes been referred to as *parallel storytelling;* both the text and illustration tell essentially the same story. However, the expectations for this style of storytelling have been complicated by influences in contemporary society. Even classic books like Robert McCloskey's *Blueberries for Sal* (in which a strong story line and two-page spreads feature events depicted both in words and excellent art) do something *more* in the illustration. The illustrator puts into visual form not only what the words say but also what they *imply*, such as the way the opening illustration establishes Sal as a child who is curious about her surroundings. More importantly in this wonderful story, the reader is aware of the mix-up between the mothers and their children—bear and human—during the berry hunt through illustration rather than the words.

A close look at an old favorite can be helpful.

Perry Nodelman[7] writes that "the pictures focus our attention on specific aspects of the words and cause us to interpret them in specific ways. As a result, a picturebook contains at least three stories: the one told by the words, the one implied by the pictures, and the one that results from the combination of the first two." In *Fish Is Fish*, author/illustrator Leo Lionni tells in pictures what would take a page of verbal description. When the frog returns to tell the fish of the wonders on land, they can picture only fish bodies: birds as fish with wings, people as fish in clothes, and fish-cows with horns, four legs, and "pink bags for milk." The illustrator has not only put into visual form what the words say, but he has also successfully added to the text, creating incongruous humor; in the process, the combination of the words and text comment on how we see others in terms of ourselves. Words and pictures interact to create a meaning that is more than the sum of their parts.

A picturebook contains at least three stories: words, pictures, and their union.

Some picturebooks are more complex, and the interactions between words and illustrations play a much more vital role, providing greater meaning than the verbal text alone. The story, in fact, does not fully exist without both pictures and words and the interpretations that can be made from their combination. In a classic case of this phenomenon, *Rosie's Walk* by Pat Hutchins, the verbal text contains one sentence, a string of prepositional phrases that takes Rosie on her path to supper over, around, under, and through the farm. A reader focusing on just the words would discover a humdrum story about a hen going home to eat. However, the illustrations reveal the additional character—a fox—whose efforts to catch Rosie are frustrated every step of the way, creating slapstick humor at Rosie's apparent obliviousness to the fox's efforts. The folksy, naïve art uses a bright but simple tricolor pallet, providing a light-hearted tone; the reader feels free to chuckle—and even interact with the story by attempting to warn Rosie or the fox of impending peril.

Occasionally pictures carry a second story.

The significance of this lies with the very strong traditions in our culture to assume the story line in a children's book is linear and told through words, regardless of the format. The short phrases of text in *Rosie's Walk* pull the reader in a straight line from start to finish, from beginning to middle to end. However, the illustrations tell a second story, simultaneously pulling the eye from the text, disrupting fluency as a new story is constructed from the interaction of the text and illustration. The combination of the two may provide readers with additional interpretations based on their individual personal responses to the text, the pictures, and their interactions. The role of the reader is essential in this process of "interanimating" the words and pictures as they work together at the semantic level where meanings are found. The reader is an active partner in creating meaning, depending on the experiences the reader brings to the reading.[8]

What the reader brings to their reading impacts the meaning they take from a picturebook story.

Contemporary Picturebooks

Contemporary picturebooks require a great deal of attention to the illustrations, and frequently more than one level of text and picture interaction can be identified in a single title. We will explore ideas about the complexities of contemporary picturebooks within a small cluster related to the common theme of childhood fears. Satoshi Kitamura's *Lily Takes a Walk* is reminiscent of *Rosie's Walk*: Two stories converge in the process of a young girl strolling home through the city with her dog, Nicky. Lily is thoroughly enjoying the familiar sights, oblivious to the monsters Nicky imagines in the commonplace items along their way. As Lily recounts the "events" of their walk, Nicky's version appears in "image balloons," suggesting that he remains worried about what may lie in wait. The text is linear, but the illustrations provide counterpoints and the simple irony of the turnabout of childhood fears, now located within the dog. Readers are empowered by knowing more than Lily and Nicky, allowing the consideration of alternate perspectives provided by the pictures. The urge to resolve the discrepant text/illustration relationship may lead readers to create their own closure for the story.

Successful picturebooks motivate new interpretations of their style.

Two different characters can tell two different stories.

The Little Bit Scary People by Emily Jenkins takes a different approach. Illustrations tell more than the text, which is a series of descriptions of people familiar to the protagonist, who shares her feelings of intimidation caused by the people she encounters every day, from policemen to teachers to her big sister. The expressive art reveals the characteristics that inspire "awe" as well as those that allay fears. The page design for Alexandra Boiger's illustrations, featuring a white background and a spooky font for the word *scary*, signals the child's fears, whereas corresponding pictures using traditional font and fully illustrated backgrounds represent the human qualities that defuse each frightening encounter. This book celebrates a child's capacity to resolve fears through firsthand knowledge of human nature and understanding that everyone has more than one persona.

In *Little Mouse's Big Book of Fears,* Emily Gravett creatively surveys the multitude of possible fears using Little Mouse's visual journaling technique for coming to terms with phobias such as a fear of clocks (chronomentrophobia) and the double childhood fears of going to bed (clinophobia) alongside the fear of monsters (teratophobia). Each concern couples a scientific definition with Little Mouse's response. Gravett creates an open ending with an imaginary term for the fear of getting lost (whereamiophobia) and a little reversal, alluding to the likelihood that the reader has a fear (of mice), too. Her creative mixed media is appropriate to the mixed phobias; the reader is invited to interact through Gravett's trademark cutouts, flaps, and clever childlike drawings. Gravett's *Wolves* also relies on illustrations that reveal much more than the brief story line about fears of storybook wolves. Rabbit attempts to put his own fears to rest by checking out some nonfiction from the library. He is too absorbed in the book (whose pages are visible to the reader) on his walk home to notice the wolf has left the confines of the book! Has rabbit met a bad end? Gravett interjects a note of reassurance and pieces together a hasty illustration showing a happy ending, but the endpages reveal a stack of unopened mail that leaves the reader with a different reality.

Neil Gaiman's *The Wolves in the Walls* sports a more eerie tone that leaves the reader chuckling at the plight of a family who discovers that the wolves they hear in the walls are real. Chased from home, they gather their courage and regain possession of the now damaged home. All is well until the young protagonist, Lucy, hears what sounds like an elephant suppressing a sneeze. The story ends with a visual foreshadowing of a new opportunity to overcome fear—a shadowy elephant footprint pressing a toast and jam sandwich. Dave McKean's blend of graphics and photography invites readers to reconsider the picturebook format and enjoy not only the stylized text–illustration relationship, but also the hint of subverting authority. Neil Gaimon pairs with the artistically talented Gris Grimley in *The Dangerous Alphabet*, a childhood adventure story in twenty-six alphabetic lines (thirteen rhyming couplets). The cartoon-style art is anything but humorous, as two children face and overcome mildly dangerous encounters within Gaiman's story, which is a hybrid interpretation of the traditional alphabet book. In both books the illustrations and words are tightly woven, each supporting and extending the other.

The relationship between verbal and visual texts (words and pictures) matters, and the ability to select an appropriate picturebook with multiple layers of meaning available for discovery in both text and illustration is important. Contemporary picturebooks are increasingly complex and examining them in light of their genre, artistic style, and the stories they tell takes time and energy.

Elements of the illustration and book design create mood in a picturebook.

Systems for Text and Illustration

By pinning pictures to words, pictures to one another, and words and pictures to ideas, the best picturebooks can enlarge the child's world in ways that even the most careful observation of either words or pictures cannot do. Several picturebook researchers have focused on these relationships in an attempt to highlight some of the elements to consider. Joanne M. Golden[9] has introduced a system to assist readers in differentiating the various interaction effects of text and illustration. Golden's model looks at text first, only considering the pictures *after* the text. Moreover, her system gives its greatest attention to the text-to-illustration ratio, from the illustrated book to the true picturebook. However, her categories do not include **wordless picturebooks,** in which the meaning lies completely with the illustration. In addition, focusing primarily on the ratio of text to illustration, which aspect has more power, ignores the dynamics between text and illustration and their impact on a reader's interpretation of a picturebook.

The elements of literature are important to text, but illustration impacts the literary elements, too, in complex picturebooks.

In *How Picturebooks Work,*[10] Maria Nikolajeva and Carole Scott recognize and systematically explore the wide array and diversity of the dynamics that picturebooks embody. We agree with their approach, and the terms they have developed are a useful way to analyze the ways picturebooks present literary features such as setting, characterization, and point of view, as well as the ways word-and-illustration interaction occurs. However, the terms are not absolute and a contemporary or complex picturebook will rarely fall neatly into any one category.

Nikolajeva and Scott have developed a spectrum of "**word/image interaction,**"[11] including a number of characteristic dynamics. For example, in *symmetrical interaction*, words and pictures tell the same story using different forms of communication. In *enhancing interaction*, pictures add to the meaning of the words, or the words elaborate the picture for a more complex dynamic. If there is significant enhancement the dynamic becomes truly *complementary*. A *counterpointing interaction* develops when words and images present differing information that together creates a new dynamic. In some cases the words and pictures seem to be in opposition to one another. This *contradictory interaction* challenges the reader to mediate between the words and pictures to understand what is being communicated.

Either classification system has value to inform readers about the text and picture interactions, but neither should be used to locate picturebooks along a strict continuum or to assign value according to how pictures and words are related or how they appear to interact in a particular book. A rigid process can distract from the fact that picturebooks are complex, adaptable, and flexible, and they can be interpreted variably. In particular, more complex contemporary picturebooks whose dynamics include contradiction or counterpoint are open to multiple interpretations.

This is important when we consider that picturebooks almost always have a dual reader audience, adult and child, sophisticated and unsophisticated, who will interpret both the text and illustrations in different ways. Teachers, parents, or caring adults need to consider both text and illustration and their combined effects as they select children's picturebooks. This consideration is important not only to effectively guide children's responses, but also to develop an attitude of inquiry that enhances the ways children can begin to communicate their aesthetic appreciation and literary understanding.

Complicating the reading and viewing process is the dual nature of reading verbal texts that are accompanied by or embedded within a visual text. In any composite of verbal and pictorial storytelling, the picture's contents appear all at once, but the verbal story is revealed a little at a time in linear progression. Joseph Schwarcz comments that we remember, assemble, and associate the elements of the verbal story, keeping them in mind as we simultaneously acquire new information. In a similar yet contrary way, we first look at a picture as a whole and then absorb the details little by little, noting how they compose the whole. Eyes wander over the picture, lingering here and skipping there, absorbing, assimilating, connecting details, colors, and shapes, until the picture is completely absorbed. As Schwarcz says, "Following an illustrated text is, then, a complex activity."[12] Despite complexities, however, and more likely because of them, children never weary of the intimately interwoven visual and verbal arts, demanding to see and hear new picturebooks as well as being excited by continuing discoveries in the familiar ones.

INQUIRY POINT

The Efferent Stance

Return to the notes you kept for the previous inquiry. Review the books you included in your inquiry. Using one or both of the picturebook classification systems (Joanne Golden or Nikolajeva and Scott), try classifying the books you chose accordingly. How did the system assist or hinder your choices? Compare your findings with a colleague.

The relationship between words and the pictures is complex and dynamic.

Literary Elements and the Picturebook

As Perry Nodelman comments, "The excitement of a good picture book is the constant tension between the moments isolated by the pictures and the flow of words that join these moments together. The jumpy rhythm of picture books is quite different from the gradually intensifying flow of stories told by words themselves."[13]

A good picturebook is just *not* as simple as it looks. The brevity of the text deceives us into thinking a good picturebook is much easier to create than a novel, for instance. Readers who look closely at recipients of an illustrative award, such as the Caldecott, Coretta Scott King, or Pura Belpré realize there is much more to a picturebook than the words. Appreciation for contemporary efforts grows as readers become acquainted with the wide array of picturebooks available across genres.

The complexity of a picturebook demands our close attention. As with any of the literary genres, the picturebook format will consider the literary elements of character, plot, setting, point of view, style and tone, and theme. The added impact of the illustrations means that the words alone will not fully develop any one of these areas. A story no longer needs to begin with the words "It was a dark and stormy night . . ." because this can be *shown* to the reader through the illustrations; dark tones can create the *feeling* someone might have in this setting. Authors can use their limited space to develop other elements of the story. It *is* possible to develop surprisingly full characters and create an engaging plot in this format; Maurice Sendak's *Where the Wild Things Are* is a classic example. Similarly, a vivid and realistic setting can be shown

Even the briefest of picturebook texts can show fully developed characters.

INQUIRY POINT

Visit a library where there is a large children's department. Browse through the picturebooks and take note of the wide variety in approaches. Notice the range in styles of book design, illustration, and how the words are placed on the page. Form categories to organize the picturebooks according to any features you have noted. What is their effect on how the picturebook would be enjoyed and interpreted? ◉

for historical topics through the illustration; this is very true of the World War II Holocaust story, *Rose Blanche*, by Roberto Innocenti.

The elements of literature matter in the picturebook format, where story is concerned. But illustrations matter in every genre, and the picturebook format spans all genres, with excellent examples in nonfiction information, poetry, and biography, to name just three. We will integrate representative picturebooks in every chapter to gradually develop a sense of the variations in this format. Words as well as pictures—fresh comparisons, vivid sensory appeals, and the writer and illustrator's intelligence and wit—make a successful story. We consider some ways picturebooks demonstrate various literary elements in the sections that follow, as well as within the subsequent literary chapters, to counter the traditional assumption that picturebooks are an uncomplicated literature form only for young children.

Character

Children enjoy plots of all kinds but they also want to hear their favorites again and again because of their interest in the **characters**. Good literature features heroes and heroines as well as other universal characters who pull readers back to read and re-read a book or to seek additional stories featuring appealing characters. Strong and believable characters (whether their actions are fanciful or realistic) are magnets that draw readers back to read again and again. Action that stems from the characters' personalities is just as important in a children's book as in adult literature.

Henry James's views on the interrelatedness of character and action apply to children's books; when we meet the protagonist in *17 Things I'm Not Allowed to Do Anymore*, written by Jenny Offill and illustrated by Nancy Carpenter, it is her *actions* that establish her as a creative and headstrong schoolgirl. She narrates her story of mock obedience in a matter-of-fact way, but the pen-and-ink and digitally enhanced illustrations advance the story, countering every verbal message with the character's actual sentiments. The reader knows for sure that this inventive girl will continue to subvert authority, such as saying "I'm sorry" at the story's end while holding a stapler behind her back with a knowing smile. Not only would the plot suffer, but also this spunky character would seem flat without Nancy Carpenter's well-designed illustrations, demonstrating the importance of each element in the picturebook format.

One of the surprising discoveries about character in fiction is that a **round character** can be created in a brief picturebook story. Ezra Jack Keats shows Peter in *The Snowy Day* as a real boy who is delighted at the snowfall, happy with his angel-making, sad at his snowball's melting, and wistful about joining the snowball fight; in short, Keats's Peter, with his childlike personality and behavior, is a character we could know and like. Keats's artwork is a blending of gouache with collage, making the tones bright and opaque and the shapes somewhat abstract. It seems to fit the childlike innocence of Peter's delight in the fresh snow.

Similarly, Eamon and James in Marla Frazee's *A Couple of Boys Have the Best Week Ever* are inseparably playful and appealing—so much so that they become "Jamon" as they spend a whirlwind week at the beach home of Eamon's grandparents. The boys are a bundle of energy as they attend camp, make crafts, watch TV, play digital games, eat, and romp. A round character, "Jamon" grows and changes as the boys absorb their identical experiences and culminate their week with a uniquely designed construction project—combining Grandpa's dreams of Antarctic exploration with found materials from the beach. The story comes full

INQUIRY POINT

Examine some of the titles mentioned in this section or other noteworthy picturebooks to note the approach to characterization. Then find a book from popular picturebook series, such as Marc Brown's *Arthur*. What is the difference? Do character-based picturebook series *show* growth and change, or do they provide a more static character? Why is this so? Would a steady diet of series characters impact a child's literary understanding? How might this happen?

circle and the boys resume their individual identities and return home. The gouache cartoon-style illustrations match the tongue-in-cheek humor of the dialogue in this delightful story.

Adults may find it difficult to attribute human traits to animals, but this is not so for most children. A child listening to *Officer Buckle and Gloria* by Peggy Rathmann would have no difficulty seeing Gloria as a developed, or round, character. When an animal in a children's story is a believable "human being," the **anthropomorphism** creates fantasy. If the fantastic but believable character is involved in action related to character, children feel very much at home with the whole idea. Character and incident in *Officer Buckle and Gloria* are so closely tied to each other that there is no separation. Gloria is mischievous from the start; throughout the story she misleads Officer Buckle into thinking his school safety presentations are dynamic and entertaining. Officer Buckle steadfastly delivers his talks while Gloria's personality is revealed through her comedic sidekick antics. *Continuous narrative* (a technique seen frequently in comics, in which action is depicted through the repeated picturing of the character in different places or motions all within the same illustration) quickly establishes the characters' personalities. When Gloria's tactics are revealed on the evening news, Officer Buckle's feelings of betrayal are visible, and the partnership seemingly doomed. Everyone loses, until a child intervenes, wounded egos are healed, and the duo is restored. Rathmann's cartoon artwork is filled with symbols that foreshadow upcoming events, but the best illustrative device is letting the reader know more than Officer Buckle, in on the secret with Gloria.

Young children have few problems with talking animals or objects.

Plot

The brevity of text in picturebooks does not eliminate the necessity for some kind of **plot**, some action or tension, the quality most likely to keep us reading. Even the straightforward story chronology and simple plot style of *The Snowy Day* has its quiet surprises. The wayward actions of the protagonist depicted in *17 Things I'm Not Allowed to Do Anymore* create a tension with the words that add interest to the plot and involve the reader in her story. Similarly, Gloria's subversive behaviors in *Officer Buckle and Gloria* complicate the basic story line and provide comic relief; her actions drive both

Some kind of tension is necessary to hold a reader's interest.

the tension and the resolution to the central problem. The carefully placed symbols add the sophistication of foreshadowing. Despite the compact nature of the picturebook, numerous plot structures are available from simple to more complex.

Maria, in *Too Many Tamales* by Gary Soto, reveals her character when she yields to temptation when kneading *masa* for tamales at her extended family's Christmas Eve observance. Without permission, she has worn her mother's diamond ring and, too late, Maria discovers the ring is gone from her finger. A frantic Maria convinces her cousins to join her in eating the large platter of tamales to find the ring, which turns up safe on her mother's finger after all. Children can relate to both the tension and to the negligent but remorseful Maria. Warmly colored oil illustrations by Ed Martinez add to the feeling of family unity and reveal the dismay not only of Maria, but also of the other children as they ponder eating a second batch of tamales! The story celebrates Mexican American traditions as it shows us how Maria's character drives the action of the familiar plot.

Picturebooks vary in the amount and degree of tension developed between the pictures and the words; they also vary in the degree to which the tension is resolved. Story endings in children's literature are traditionally happy; at the very least they leave the reader with a sense of satisfaction or closure. Quiet suspense permeates *The Wednesday Surprise* by Eve Bunting as we wonder about the birthday gift being prepared for Papa. Illustrations by Donald Carrick depict grandmother and granddaughter engaged in reading a book throughout the story. Readers' life experiences create the assumption that Anna, the seven-year-old narrator, is practicing reading with the help of her more experienced grandmother. Only at the end is it clear that Anna's grandmother, a European immigrant, has been learning to read. Despite the twist, the story concludes with a **closed ending**. *Erika-San* by Allen Say has a chronological plot that traces an American girl's romantic desire to live in Japan based on her grandfather's pre–World War II painting of a quaint home in rural Japan. Striving to reach her goal, Erika studies Japanese throughout her schooling and on graduating from college immigrates to Japan to accept a teaching position. After three moves, she eventually locates a teaching position where she not only finds the home of her dreams but also her husband. The plot is somewhat slow-moving and the tension is light with solid closure, but the realistic watercolor paintings, framed in white and signaling believability and idealism, carry much of the book's appeal.

Picturebooks for children are increasingly likely to have less resolution, with many gaps and uncertainties for readers to contemplate. A picturebook on any topic may have an **open ending**, such as that in *The Arrival* by Shaun Tan. This blend of graphic novel and picturebook creates a feeling of uncertainty that is revealed through the illustrations. Done in sepia tones and shades of charcoal, their style produces a somber tone. Yet elements of the story indicate hope that this new arrival will find his way. This continual tension between feelings of hope and despair, friendship and loneliness, familiarity and alienation, comfort and fear encourages the reader to share these emotions right along with the protagonist, immersed in the immigration experience. Recently separated from his family, he struggles with language, customs, rules, and finding work, but finds solace in the emotional sharing of stories of flight from oppression with other immigrants. New bonds are formed, and his family is able to join him, resolving his personal loneliness. But Tan leaves the ending open and the final illustration features the protagonist's young daughter pointing the way for another immigrant to open her new life's story. This amazing book is expertly

Picturebooks frequently leave gaps for the reader to fill, including unresolved or open endings.

Readers discover similar values in quite different cultures.

crafted with each thought-provoking panel inviting reader interpretation.

A bilingual memoir, *Calling the Doves* by Mexican poet Juan Felipe Herrera, unfolds in both English and Spanish with a sequential series of remembered events that reveal his early life within a migrant working family. Herrera recalls the pleasures of sitting under the starry night sky, hearing his father call the doves while relating stories of immigrating from Chihuahua, Mexico. The plot is his daily life, from eating breakfast in the open air to moving from farm to farm with other laborers picking crops. Juan's memories of his father playing the harmonica and his mother inspiring his love of poetry are pleasantly conveyed through simple language. Despite a humble lifestyle, the family is stable and happy. The serene title reflects the story's tone, and the illustrations support the textual storyline with bright, happy colors and stylized fabric designs that suggest an appreciation of family, the wonders of nature, and day-to-day growing and working. Despite the episodic structure, there is a sense of closure.

We can contrast Herrera's story with an examination of another children's book related to immigration that shows less complexity while combining resolution with a more straightforward plot. *From North to South/Del Norte al Sur* by Rene Colato Lainez combines hope and uncertainty in a story of family separation when one undocumented parent is returned to Tijuana, Mexico. Young protagonist José and his father face an uncertain future. Joe Cepeda's lively oil paintings in bright colors capture the essence of the family's Mexican heritage, while also revealing the emotions they share as they must separate and reunite across the border. Readers do not know what the eventual outcome will be for this family of immigrants, and the story inspires readers to think about the possibilities.

> ### INQUIRY POINT
>
> Stories in the picturebook format are increasingly complex. How do authors and illustrators take readers through a picturebook in contemporary books? *Interrupting Chicken* by David Ezra Stein and *A Sick Day for Amos McGee* by Phillip C. Stead were both honored by the 2011 Caldecott Awards. Both work in significantly different ways with plot. Examine these books and note the ways words and pictures create plot. ◉

Theme

The **theme** of a book is a message that creates an understanding about life, human nature, or elements of society. Identifying and appreciating the theme in a good book should avoid overt and preachy forms of didacticism. A theme *can* involve a lesson learned, but that should not become the only purpose for reading a children's book. Children should be *empowered* by recognizing and analyzing a theme that resonates with them, and the realization that a good book can have more than one central theme needs to be fostered.

Theme is not preachment.

Children's books contain a variety of important themes that may relate to culture, personal growth and development, the environment, or current social concerns. It is often assumed that a picturebook audience is composed of only younger children, for whom more serious themes may be less appealing or appropriate. However, valuable themes such as courage, perseverance, tolerance, and peace provide a great deal of satisfaction for both younger and older children (as well as adults). In the picturebook format, the illustrations can provide a space for these themes as well as

Themes may address current issues and a complex picturebook frequently has more than one central theme.

the text. Liz Garton Scanlon's *All the World* uses poetry to send a message of global interdependence. The illustrations by Marla Frazee make diversity and unity visibly available to the reader as they enhance the lines of poetry. The placement of each line within the expressionistic watercolor and colored pencil serves to interest the reader from start to finish. The concepts of hope, peace, love, and trust seem to be explicitly stated themes, but the final phrase suggests something more for the reader to consider.

Themes of all kinds occur in picturebooks, and the sense of identity or the process of discovering something about oneself is common in a format directed toward readers in the midst of their growing years. Names are important to our identity, and *The Name Jar* by Yangshook Choi explores this theme; ridicule of one's name creates concern, but approval can change self-image. In this story Unhei struggles with family pride and investment in her Korean name along with pressure to choose a name that reflects her new American identity. Unhei was selected with the advice of a name master and a golden stamp for a Korean name is a special treasure. A reader may consider this a "first day of school" story, but Unhei's name character stamped on the golden endpapers alongside the names classmates have suggested for her remind the reader of the story's larger identity theme. *My Name Is Yoon* by Helen Recorvits carries a similar theme as Yoon struggles to adjust to her new life in America. Gabi Swiatkowska's beautiful paintings, precise and slightly surreal, capture Yoon's feelings of displacement. As the illustrations gradually soften, they signal Yoon's increased feeling of being at home. The story is told in the first person, revealing Yoon's childlike emotions. The artist reveals the range of Yoon's emotions as she comes to terms with her identity through facial expressions revealed both visually and verbally.

Many picturebooks rely more heavily on the illustrations to reveal elements of a character's identity. *Emily's Art* by Peter Catalanotto reveals first-grader Emily's identity as a budding artist. This story of a school art contest and a careless judge's ruling that challenges Emily's confidence is told from a third-person perspective. Readers do not discover the depth of Emily's doubts about herself as she takes the judge's ruling to heart unless they analyze the illustrations. Catalanotto conveys Emily's emotional turmoil and her process of reconstructing her identity as a developing artist through the illustrations. When Emily is in doubt, her image becomes transparent, at times small in the background. When Emily is confident Catalanotto places her in the foreground, fully visible, and in many frames she is given an "aura." Themes in quality picturebooks will be revealed in some way through the illustration.

An increasing number of books for all ages explore the theme of restoration and care of the Earth. These are serious themes, of importance to everyone as we contemplate the kind of home we will have on Earth in the future. Children recognize and later internalize a particular theme when they can discover it within a number of selections. For example, oil spills are a reality in our environment, and (as with any theme or topic) a textset related to this problem would provide more support and open more possibilities than any single picturebook on the topic might. A classic picturebook on this topic that promotes consciousness without didacticism, Gloria Rand's *Prince William* gently embodies some of the tragic effects of the Juan Valdez oil spill on the creatures inhabiting Prince William Sound, as a young girl struggles to save a baby seal. The theme of the story is the community's volunteerism and individual dedication. Ted Rand's watercolor paintings focus on the beauty of the northern landscape juxtaposed with the thick oil and the harbor full of boats and planes bringing people dedicated to cleanup and wildlife rehabilitation. Readers will realize this environmental catastrophe is not an isolated event if they pair this story with the narrative of Sally Grindley's *Peter's Place*. In this story set along the Cornish coast, with a theme of man's impact on the Earth, a young boy works to rescue oil-covered eider ducks. Jacqueline Briggs Martin's *Birdwashing Song* provides a similar story. A tanker accident despoils Turtle Bay and a theme of collective and individual care and volunteerism are embodied in the meticulous and time-consuming process of saving a loon. Readers might also incorporate nonfiction information picturebooks to reinforce the themes of the other three picturebooks. For example, respected nonfiction writer Lawrence Pringle uses photography to show the clean-up, rehabilitation, and prevention in *Oil Spills*.

Setting

In literature for children, vivid descriptions and imagery through carefully chosen words give a reader an opportunity to create setting in his or her own mind, a special kind of experience that is one of the delights of literature. In some stories, such as folklore or stories in which character or another literary element is central, a setting may be purposely vague allowing for interpretation by the artist. Many illustrators enjoy working with the folklore genre for the opportunity they have to set the story according to the cultural milieu it portrays. This is especially useful for younger readers who do not have a well-developed sense of the past or familiarity with settings that are far from their base of experience. Illustration is critical to portraying cultural variants in folktales. For example, Barry Moser illustrates an Appalachian version of "Rumplestiltskin" set in a coal-mining town—*Tucker Pfeffercorn*. The realistic art in this picturebook feels authentic, and the reader will see a stark contrast to the illustrations created by Paul O. Zelinsky's fine interpretation of the European version of this tale in *Rumplestiltskin*. Though the words for these stories differ, the illustrations make the cultural differences specific for the reader.

We "see" setting through words as well as pictures.

Other stories depend on an accurately depicted setting. This is especially evident in historical stories whose young readers do not have images of life in the distant past to rely on when constructing the meaning of a story. For example, Michael O. Tunnel's historical fiction story, *Mailing May*, has a specific setting—rural Idaho in 1913. A young girl wants to visit her grandmother, but the family cannot afford the train fare; they resort to the creative interpretation of postal regulations to *mail* May to her grandmother. May rides in comfort with a chaperone in the form of a postal worker on the train all the way to Lewiston, Idaho. Ted Rand's illustrations need to depict this accurately, which he accomplishes with paintings of period photographs integrated into the watercolor scenes. The illustrations also reflect the story's nostalgic feel; the book jacket is the suitcase May carries on her trip, complete with postage. Emily Arnold McCully's artwork for *An Outlaw Thanksgiving* is similar in style—moderately impressionistic to give a nostalgic touch, yet realistic in the depictions. Readers of this story, set in 1896 Utah, encounter another young girl traveling on the rails. In this story, Clare is accompanied by her mother to California, with a stop in Utah to connect with her father. The train is stalled in a snowstorm and the pair end up spending Thanksgiving with strangers who turn out to be members of a famous

INQUIRY POINT

Setting is particularly important for historical fiction. Many comprehensive textbooks of children's literature are making it a separate genre, equal in status to contemporary fiction. Historical fiction is generally organized by the historical decade in which it is set (though picturebooks in this genre may still also be shelved with all fictional picturebooks). Find picturebooks that are set in three different decades—for instance, the 1960s, the 1920s, and the 1860s. What do you notice about the illustrations? Now, select a particular decade and choose four or five titles. What are the similarities and differences in the way events are depicted?

Why do you think setting is particularly important for this genre? Keep these thoughts in mind as you continue in this handbook. ●

gang of outlaws. Both stories have a basis in actual events, and readers will feel even more confident in the setting when they read the author's notes provided at the back of each story.

The action in Barbara McClintock's *Dahlia* takes place in a rural setting during the Victorian era, telling a story of a young girl torn between desires to play freely outside, getting soiled in the mud and racing her wagon downhill with the boys, and expectations for young girls' play at that time. Her dilemma is symbolized with the arrival of a new frilly doll, which she compares to her well-worn teddy bear; she finally decides there is room for both of them. The story *could* be set within a variety of locations or time periods; the themes are familiar to many young girls. The choice of the Victorian era is shown through McClintock's period illustrations in pen and ink with muted colors. Just enough detail is provided to give young readers an image of this time period—long ago. The same is not true for *Fannie in the Kitchen*, a nonfiction book about Fannie Farmer's start with recipe writing, set in a similar time and place. Despite similarities in the illustrations, which are also pen and ink with muted colors, the difference lies in the degree of detail Nancy Carpenter provides for Deborah Hopkinson's historical story. Because it is nonfiction, the details must be quite specific to the time and place in which the characters lived—the context of Fanny Farmer's actual life. Carpenter's well-researched illustrations reveal much about the clothing, utensils, and furnishings of the time.

These books are classic examples of **integral setting**; both author and illustrator integrate visual and word pictures for a setting that is closely interwoven with character, action, and theme.

Illustration is integral to revealing an accurate setting for historical fiction picturebooks.

Point of View

Point of view, or the mind through which the writer chooses to tell the story, varies in picturebooks, as it does in all literature. Although the objective or omniscient point of view can be successful in stories for the young child, first-person or "I" stories are an increasingly common way to present the text in picturebooks. There are even effective first-person stories among picturebooks for the youngest child. The "I" narrator of these stories, such as the young child anxious for the arrival of a new baby in Jacqueline Woodson's *Pecan Pie Baby,* is designed to provide a perspective young readers can relate to comfortably. This may require some mediation to help a young child determine who "I" represents in the story. Is it the self-centered reader? Is it the main character? Is it the author of a memoir or autobiographical story?

The Polar Express by Chris Van Allsburg, published in 1985, is a Christmas classic. The choice to write it from a **first-person point of view** perfectly fits the story itself. The main character does not wish to believe there is no Santa Claus, and a magical experience challenges his friends' skepticism. At midnight on Christmas Eve, he boards the Polar Express when it mysteriously arrives at his front yard to take him and a trainload of other children to the North Pole to meet Santa Claus and his elves. Selected to receive the first gift of Christmas, his wish for a single silver bell from Santa's sleigh is granted. But his joy turns to disappointment when the bell is lost. He returns home empty-handed only to discover the bell, wrapped and accompanied by a note from Santa, waiting for him under the tree. He and his sister joyously shake it, hearing its sweet sounds. Part of the story's authenticity for the reader stems from hearing the story from the believer himself through the first-person point of view.

However, picturebooks also provide a second perspective, often different from that of the verbal text. Van Allsburg's rich pastel illustrations complicate the point of view. The reader sees the main character in several illustrated scenes showing what the character could not possibly have seen. Readers have a perspective, for instance of Santa taking off in the sleigh, that *none* of the children in the story could have. Young readers are very aware of the illustrations, and providing opportunities for them to express their interpretations of the pictures is a critical step in analyzing the full meaning of a picturebook. Research into how adults and children view the same picturebooks indicates that they do not see illustrations in the same way. Adults have been trained to focus on the verbal text, the words, and to value them more. Children, whether hearing the story or reading it on their own, instinctively look first at the illustrations. Many times adults reject their interpretations based on the visual text (the story in pictures). This can present a dilemma for children just learning to express what they know about a picturebook's meaning.

> Picturebooks provide a second perspective, often different from that of the verbal text.

Truly **objective point-of-view** narration in picturebooks is complicated; the illustrations must be considered. Ezra Jack Keats's *The Snowy Day* seems at first glance to be objective. We know that Peter has a happy time in the snow because we *see* all his fun, and we remember our own similar pleasures. But a writer using **omniscient point of view** comments that Peter *thinks* it might be fun to play with the big boys, and he *knows* he isn't old enough. When Peter cannot find the vanished snowball he had tucked into his jacket pocket the night before, the omniscient narrator tells us that he *feels* sad. Even this simple and short story makes brief use of an interpretive omniscience.

In addition to the natural combination of first- and third-person narration in text and illustration, contemporary picturebooks may complicate point of view by design, telling a story (or aspects of it) from two perspectives. Jeannie Baker accomplishes this **dual point of view** with her wordless collage picturebook, *Mirror,* that compares the daily routines in two distinct places—Sydney, Australia, and a village in Morocco. The perspectives at first seem quite different, but readers looking closely will begin to notice similarities in the side-by-side illustrations. *Kapow!* also incorporates a dual point of view for younger readers, pairing scenes of everyday play and superhero fantasy. George O'Connor effectively frames the children's usual dress-up play activity within single white-bordered pages, whereas the corresponding superhero pictures fill their double-page spreads entirely with bold colors and larger-than-life action. Typical scenes of work and play around the household allow young readers to slip in and out of the characters' believable acts of play and their imagined roles as super heroes. The illustrations are essential to the story; the verbal text is confined to speech balloons befitting the cartoon format. The text's understated tone creates irony that enhances the dual perspective shown by the illustrations.

Words and pictures work seamlessly and in tandem revealing many perspectives.

Style and Tone

In this section style and tone will be considered somewhat separately only to emphasize the importance of design and style in picturebooks. The picturebook format includes illustrative styles and designs that awaken the interest of the reader to the story and match the genre. With picturebooks, style lies not only in the nuances of possible meanings and the pleasures of language, but also with the visual elements created through artistic styles and media and the elements of design. Contemporary picturebooks combine these elements, continually creating unique styles that resonate well with readers who are increasingly familiar with visual techniques, media, and digital technologies. Numerous possibilities exist, and we will focus on just a few we consider important to analyzing and interpreting picturebooks. Much of what we share here falls into the realm of **style** associated with elements of design.

Style can introduce us to the pleasures of language and illustration.

Contemporary picturebooks can also carry some of their meaning through design elements of the book. That is, the production of a picturebook includes many considerations that can impact the way the book is viewed and interpreted. Size, shape, materials, and dimension all enter into the form a book may take. *The Robot Book* by Heather Brown provides moveable nuts, bolts, and gears for curious readers to explore as they discover what makes up a robot. The choice of heavy cardstock, a compact square shape, and parts a child can manipulate are not accidental; each element combines to develop the concept of a working machine known as a robot.

Among of these specially designed books are the pop-up books, which are very much like toys to many readers. However, a quality pop-up book is conceptual, the elements of the book work together to create an idea, like Marion Bataille's award-winning *ABC3D*, a nonfiction alphabet book whose three-dimensional models of letters pop out at readers. Young readers are free to make their own verbal text—much like a wordless picturebook. The pop-up style creates a sense of exploration in this alphabet book. Illustrator Robert Sabuda is one of the premier engineers of the pop-up book well known for his 3-dimensional interpretations, including Clement C. Moore's *The Night Before Christmas* and poet Michael J. Rosen's *Chanuka Lights*.

Emily Gravett is known for the interactive designs of the picturebooks she creates. *The Rabbit Problem* is a delightful opportunity to understand and appreciate the Fibonacci sequence shown through a calendar year of a rapidly multiplying rabbit family. The design of the book mimics that of a hanging wall calendar, but the final vertical page opening takes this clever book into the realm of the pop-up book; readers can see first-hand how many rabbits come from one in the space of one calendar year. Gravett's *Spells* provides multiple story line possibilities for what the frog might become once the spell has been cast; the pages in the center of the story are cut in two halves, top and bottom. Each shows the top or bottom of one possible ending for the frog. It may be a convoluted route to the end of the story, but readers will be happy there is a handsome prince at the end.

Some books have a design that is representative of the book's overall theme. For example, Fani Marceau's *Panorama: A Foldout Book* is literally that. The story's poetic lines, which are printed on the bottoms of the cardstock pages, take the reader on a day trip around the world. Joelle Jolivet's illustrations are woodblock prints in black on white with yellow until readers reach the "end" page. There, they simply turn the book around, and the colors change to a blue backdrop as the trip is reversed. "What is different?" the author asks. Readers will have fun noticing the changes. The entire book opens out so that it could sit easily across a long counter or bookshelf, allowing readers to walk around the story to read in panoramic view.

The Changing Countryside by Jorg Muller is presented as an artist's portfolio. Inside, the reader finds a set of tri-fold paintings, each showing the change in the countryside surrounding a Victorian manse in Germany. The message, created only with the art, is one of regret for modern changes to the environment. Chris Van Allsburg's classic *The Mysteries of Harris Burdick* has been fittingly republished in a similar portfolio format. Readers who love to create stories from his surrealistic and mysterious illustrations and their suggestive captions will appreciate this change in style; it was, after all, an artist's portfolio that served as the basis for the original story. However, in 1984 picturebook fans were not quite ready to think of a picturebook as an artist's portfolio.

We see that a book doesn't always come in the form we've come to expect. Graphic artist Art Spiegelman's three-dimensional *Open Me . . . I'm a Dog* plays with the postmodern notion that things don't carry just one fixed meaning in this world. Here readers see a book purporting to be a dog, with warmly colored fuzzy endpapers and leash included. By playing with the notion of what a book can be, Spiegelman creates a positive connotation of books for the reader, and he creates a space for the reader's imagination to play with ideas about books.

Successful stories use many stylistic devices.

Although the **tone** varies in the picturebook format, just as it does in books of other genres, it is typically lighthearted, avoiding tones that might create unresolved emotions such as sadness or fear. Tone in a picturebook is generally an overall *feeling*, frequently an emotional response created through the story's resolution. Much of the tone is conveyed through the illustration. For example, the comforting tone of *The Moon Came Down on Milk Street* by Jean Gralley is created as the moon is set in its rightful place in the night sky, redirecting a young reader's fear to reassurance that cooperation can overcome catastrophe. The colors are cheerful, and the story characters wear satisfied expressions at the story's end. The tone of Virginia Lee Burton's classic *The Little House,* as it survives urban growth, encourages young readers to think about solutions to issues; the mock-serious tone of *The Extinct Files: My Science Project* (by Wallace Edwards) or the joyous appeal of *Roller Coaster* (by Marla Frazee) are each appropriate to the topics and themes of their stories. The illustrations are vital to the messages they convey.

Similar to elements of character and point of view, tone can be the choice of the author, illustrator, or both. Some author/illustrators who

INQUIRY POINT

Pop-up books are increasingly popular in children's picturebooks. Their styles are unique and include a variety of topics. Find several pop-up books or other books having elements that encourage interaction with the book and its story. Strive for a diverse collection. What do you notice? Are these books necessarily just for the very young child?

have control over both text and pictures, like Chris Van Allsburg, are capable of creating a variety of sophisticated picturebooks ranging in tone from eerie mystery in *The Garden of Abdul Gasazi* to wonderment in *The Polar Express* to humorous puzzlement in *Bad Day at Riverbend*. Molly Bang created a classic example of an author/illustrator's creation of tone in the picturebook format with *When Sophie Gets Angry . . . Really, Really Angry*.[14] The main character, Sophie, battles the emotions of childhood. Her surroundings, brilliant yellows, oranges and red as Sophie becomes angry with her sibling change to cooler grays, greens and blues when she goes outside and comes to terms with her feelings.

Humor—an important quality that assists the development of perspective on life and promotes good health—is essential in the life of a young child. Many writers and illustrators respond to that need, or perhaps they respond to their own need to see things through the sound of laughter. Humor is a popular feature of children's books, from nonfiction to fantasy, and often stems from the interaction of a book's text with the illustrations, becoming a large part of a picturebook's tone. For instance, years ago, a nonfiction series about the lives of the presidents would stress only the accomplishments of each president. Occasionally, a writer would use a touch of humor to bring a president to life, complete with quirks and whims. But Judith St. George's *So You Want to Be President* deliberately includes interesting traits, personality quirks, or distinctive personal characteristics of U.S. Presidents to demonstrate their individuality and bring them to life. In each case, illustrator David Small correlates the information in the text with his trademark cartoon illustrations. The selection of cartoon art creates the tone of this book: political humor. The particular humorous tone of the art may remind readers of political cartoons within commentary on current events in editorials and news magazines.

Caralyn Buehner's simple but effective presentation in *Snowmen at Night* could assume a tone of regret and loss for a child who awakens to find yesterday's snowman has lost its shape and come undone overnight. Instead the story shares an alternative to the reality of melting and settling snow—the possibility of snowmen coming to life in the night and having a great time while everyone is asleep. The oil and acrylic paintings show off the actions and emotions of the snowmen as they frolic throughout the night, returning home bedraggled and tired by morning's light. The illustrations contain enough realism to suspend a child's disbelief, with enough expressionism to reveal the gaiety and hilarity of the imagined snowmen antics. The illustrations provide a very humorous and satisfying interpretation for the story's text.

We close here with a brief note about nostalgia in picturebooks, a tone of longing for something past. Many children's books rely on a nostalgic tone, such as Susan Swanson's *The House in the Night*. The black-and-white scratchboard illustrations by Beth Krommes are stunning as they remind adult readers of the time when they were very young, and such illustrations were commonplace. There is nothing frightening in this nighttime story's rustic appeal. But nostalgia isn't necessarily going to be what young readers with little experience feel; that's not a familiar emotion yet. The appeal of this book for them will be finding the embedded objects identified in the rhyming text; they will respond to the cumulative story pattern as something new, rather than a pattern from the past. Similarly, the response to *A Sick Day for Amos McGee* may have nostalgic overtones for adult readers, who may connect elements of the story with books from their own reading histories. But children will relate

Tone, the attitude of writer and artist toward reader and story, is often humorous.

to being comforted by loved ones and being tucked into bed when they are sick. Children fortunate enough to have experienced numerous classic picturebooks like *Goodnight Moon* by Margaret Wise Brown or other bedtime stories may find other connections and even have experiences of youthful nostalgia.

A nostalgic tone is often missed by children.

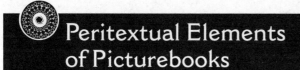

Peritextual Elements of Picturebooks

In this edition we rely on broader theories to account for the interconnected nature of texts, to explain how texts carry many possible meanings that range across many texts. The concept of *intertextuality*, how books relate to one another, forms the basis of our textsets, but the concept has grown, along with an appreciation for its many possibilities. Gerard Genette is associated with the concept of intertextuality as it pertains to children's literature.[15] Genette organized intertexuality into categories grouped under the more encompassing term of *transtextuality*—the connections within and across texts. For picturebooks, Genette's work with *paratexts* has become valuable as one of many ways to work with their increasingly visual nature. Studies of visual literacy lie outside of the scope of this handbook, but the paratextual features of picturebooks need some mention.[16]

The paratext of a picturebook, sometimes referred to as the **peritext**, includes features such as the dust jacket, casings, and endpapers.[17] In addition, information at the front and at the end is making an increasingly important contribution to the meaning of a picturebook. The picturebook's thirty-two-page format is restrictive; authors, illustrators, and book designers make use of available spaces to foreshadow elements of plot, introduce the traits of a character, or provide background information that illuminates a story. The messages contained in the peritext are frequently more valuable than decorative, more than providing credits; every inch of space has potential for meaning making. Teachers, librarians, and others in a position to mediate a picturebook with a child will find these features another of the many ways to assist a reader's access to a book. As is important to our approach with this handbook, we would advocate visiting a picturebook's peritext (i.e., covers, endpapers,

text continues on page 69

TABLE 3.1 Artistic Styles in Children's Picturebooks

ARTISTIC STYLE	ARTISTS	DEFINITION	EXAMPLES
SURREALISM	Anthony Browne David Wiesner Chris Van Allsburg Bill Thomson Rob Gansalves Shaun Tan	Surrealist paintings are generally based on dreams. Filled with familiar objects painted to look strange or mysterious, surrealism forces viewers to look at things in a different way, change their feelings about things, or stir up emotions in people's minds. The artwork is disturbingly realistic and fantastic at the same time.	*The Water Tower* by Gary Crew, Illus. Steve Woolman *Chalk* by Bill Thomson *The Piggy Book* by Anthony Browne *Voices in the Park* by Anthony Browne *Flotsam* by David Wiesner *Sector 7* by David Wiesner *Imagine a Place* by Sarah Thomson, Illus. Rob Gonsalves *Imagine a Day* by Sarah Thomson, Illus. Rob Gonsalves
PRIMITIVISM/ NAÏVE/FOLK	Faith Ringgold Giselle Potter Tomie dePaola Lois Ehlert Terry Widener Patricia Polacco David Diaz Rachel Isadora Jeanette Winter	Primitive Art is a technique of painting very simply, often with "flat", or two-dimensional, subjects. However, this understates the many rich illustrations done in this style, often associated with regional art or folk art.	*Tortillas and Lullabies/Tortillas y Cancioncitas* by Lynn Reiser, Illus. Corazones Valientes *Tar Beach* by Faith Ringgold *Ghost Wings* by Barbara Joose, Illus. Giselle Potter *Strega Nona* by Tomie DePaolo *Biblioburro: A True Story from Columbia* by Jeanette Winter *Me, Frida* by Amy Novesky, Illus. David Diaz
REALISM	Terry Widener Kadir Nelson Brian Selznick Ted Rand Stephen Johnson Bill Thomson Bryan Collier Paul O. Zelinsky John Thompson	Realism is a type of art that shows things exactly as they appear in life. It began in the 1700s, but the greatest Realist era was in the 1800s. Postimpressionism is similar, but mainly still life and landscape. The postimpressionists like to use lots of colors and shadows.	*Christmas in the Big House, Christmas in the Quarters* by Patricia & Fredrick McKissack, Illus. John Thompson *Soccer Hour* by Carol Nevius, Illus. Bill Thomson *The Invention of Hugo Cabret* by Brian Selznick *Henry's Freedom Box* by Ellen Levine, Illus. Kadir Nelson *The House* by J. Patrick Lewis, Illus. Robert Innocenti *Tricycle* by Elisa Amado, Illus. Alfonso Ruano *City by the Numbers* by Stephen Johnson *Alphabet City* by Stephen Johnson *Dave the Potter: Artist, Poet, Slave* by Laban Carrick Hill, Illus. Bryan Collier

Style	Artists	Description	Examples
IMPRESSIONISM	E. B. Lewis Jerry Pinkney Emily Arnold McCully Carol Byard Jerome Lagarrigue	Impressionism was developed in France during the late 1800s and early 1900s; it is painted as if someone just took a quick look at the subject of the painting. The paintings are often bold in color but without a lot of detail. This style is often outdoor scenes and background (like landscapes) and look like they are shimmering. A specific kind of impressionism is **pointillism**. Here the artist uses small dots or strokes of paint to make up the pictures. From far away, these dots blend together to form the picture and give the impression of different colors as they blend together.	*The Negro Speaks of Rivers* by Langston Hughes, Illus. E. B. Lewis *Working Cotton* by Shirley Anne Williams, Illus. Carole Byard *The Secret Cave: Discoverion Lascaux* by Emily Arnold McCully *Freedom on the Menu: The Greensboro Sit-Ins* by Carole Boston Weatherford, Illus. Jerome Lagarrigue *Charlotte in Giverny* by Joan McPhail Knight, Illus. Melissa Sweet *Virgie Goes to School with Us Boys* by Elizabeth Fitzgerald Howard, Illus. E. B. Lewis
CARTOON/POP ART	David Small Scott McCleod Mini Grey Marla Frazee George O'Connor	Pop art is short for Popular Art; it can be any every day item drawn in a brash, colorful way. It is inspired by comic strips, advertising, and popular entertainment. Is becoming more widely used for children's books from all genres, including graphic novels and manga.	*So You Want to Be President?* by Judith St. George, Illus. David Small *Into the Volcano* by Don Wood *Super Hero ABC* by Scott McLeod *The Adventures of Sparrowboy* by Brian Pinkney *Kapow!* by George O'Connor *Traction Man Is Here!* by Mini Grey *A Couple of Boys Have the Best Week Ever* by Marla Frazee
ABSTRACT	Lois Ehlert Michelle Berg Leo & Diane Dillon Eric Carle Leo Lionni Chris Raschka	Abstract art does not try to show people, animals, or places exactly as they appear in the real world. It mainly uses color and shape to show emotions and suggest an actual object. The viewer does not see specific objects, rather shapes that represent what is being depicted.	*Traffic Jam* by Blexbolex, Enchanted Lion, 2010. *Big Blue and Little Yellow* by Leo Lionni, Demco Media, 1987. *Gone Wild: An Endangered Animal Alphabet* by David McLimans *Rap-A-Tap-Tap!* by Leo and Diane Dillon *The Very Hungry Caterpillar* by Eric Carle *Meow, Ruff: A Story in Concrete Poetry* by Joyce Sidman, Illus. Michelle Berg *R-R-Ralph!* by Lois Ehlert

TABLE 3.1 *(Continued)*

ARTISTIC STYLE	ARTISTS	DEFINITION	EXAMPLES
EXPRESSIONISM	Terry Widener Scott Goto Patricia Polacco Stephen Gammel Matt Tavares Marla Frazee	In Expressionist Art, the artist tries to express certain feelings about some thing. Artists that paint in this style are more concerned with having their paintings express a feeling, emotion, or personality trait than in making the painting look exactly like what they are painting.	*Wilfrid Gordon McDonald Partridge* by Mem Fox, Illus. Julie Vivas *Roller Coaster* by Marla Frazee *Shooting Star: Annie Oakley, The Legend* by Debbie Dadey, Illus. Scott Goto *Thunder Cake* by Patricia Polacco *Casey at the Bat: A Ballad of the Republic Sung in the Year 1888* by Ernest L. Thayer, Illus. C. F. Payne *Mudball* by Matt Tavares *The Relatives Came* by Cynthia Rylant, Illus. Stephen Gammel *America's Champion Swimmer: Gertrude Ederle* by David Adler, Illus. T. Widener
PHOTOGRAPHY AND COMPUTER-GENERATED/MIXED MEDIA	DiTerlizzi Devin Asch Melissa Sweet Pamela Zagarenski David Diaz	Realism through images captured through camera lens, mixed styles increasingly using digital tools. Frequently a collage of styles and media.	*The Spider and the Fly* by Mary Howett, Illus. Tony DiTerlizzi *This Is Just to Say: Poems of Apology and Forgiveness,* by Joyce Sidman, Illus. Pamela Zagarenski. *My People* by Langston Hughes; Illus. Charles R. Smith *Children of the Dustbowl: The True Story of the School at Weedbatch Camp* by Jerry Stanley *The Brothers' War: Civil War Voices in Verse* by J. Patrick Lewis *A River of Words* by Jen Bryant, Illus. Melissa Sweet *Mr. Maxwell's Mouse* by Frank Asch, Illus. Devin Asch *Red Sings from Treetops: A Year in Color* by Joyce Sidman, Illus. Pamela Zagarenski *Art and Max* by David Wiesner

title pages) before, during, or after reading to show the possibilities for interpretation and appreciation of the text.

For example, the embossed snowflake on the casings of Jacqueline Briggs Martin's *Snowflake Bentley* is symbolic of the central passion in Wilson Bentley's life. Young readers aware of this feature might predict snow as a main idea for the story; returning to this peritextual feature allows the stamping to acquire a deeper meaning based on Martin's fine biography. Additional information and photographs of Bentley and his snowflakes at the back of the book further authenticate this nonfiction work.

The front matter for Chris Van Allsburg's classic *The Mysteries of Harris Burdick* is more than an introduction, it fabricates the story that hooks the reader and suspends their disbelief for the mysterious episodes depicted in the book. Readers of all ages take the story of the abandoned portfolio in earnest, until a revisit uncovers Van Allsburg's technique, producing a laugh at the author's trick. The dedication opening Jean Gralley's *The Moon Came Down on Milk Street* is more than a gentle quote about helping out when something is going wrong. A return look ties the story to Mr. Rogers, an icon of childhood culture in the United States.

Dust jackets and **endpapers** in contemporary picturebooks may be coded with meaning through color, design, or a sample illustration to foreground the action to come in the story or the personality of a central character. The sunny yellow endpapers of Donna Jo Napoli's *Mama Miti: Maathai and the Trees of Kenya* feature authentic African cloth designs, as does the background for the dust jacket's back cover, lending additional authenticity. Joyce Sidman and Rick Allen's *Dark Emperor and Other Poems of the Night*, a 2011 Newbery Honor book, uses color to show the onset of night (deep blue) and the arrival of the dawn (sherbet orange) on its endpapers. Younger readers—even adults—might miss the symbolism, but a thoughtful return to the text makes it a noticeable feature of the peritext, in addition to the color-coded table of contents and glossary of terms. *Mailing May*'s dust jacket surrounds the book in a style that mimics the suitcase May carries on her trip in a train's mail car, and the author's note is back matter that grounds the story; this informative background would bog down historical fiction in a picturebook format.

Every element or feature in contemporary picturebooks has the potential to carry a portion of a story's message, or provide a theme to a nonfiction information book. Every genre is represented in the picturebook format, and each is taking advantage of the peritext to create a unified whole, filled with potential significance for readers of all ages. Our view is that picturebooks are not in Section E of the library because they are "easy." Many are for every reader at some point in time, giving picturebooks a special place in children's literature.

> Peritextual features such as dust jackets, casings, and endpapers contribute to the meaning of a picturebook.

SUMMARY

Picturebooks are dependent on illustration; some contain text and others are wordless. The design of the whole—the entire book, including size, shape, whether there are single pictures or double-page spreads, endpapers, title page, cover, dust jacket, and the placement of the gutter—all are important. The illustrator puts into visual form what the words say and in the process the text is amplified, conveying more than what the words say. The decision-making process in what is illustrated and in what style and medium impacts the picturebook in significant ways.

TEXTSET

Picturebook Peritext

The following textset is a quick list of some picturebooks associated with particular peritextual elements. As you explore the titles with others, discuss *how* you think the book represents the category. Look closely. What other element might it represent that is not included? Consider book jackets, endpapers, casings, title pages, glossary, dedication, and author or illustrator's notes. Even elements such as color and the use of borders or frames are design features to consider.

Special Styles and Formats

Cotton, Menino. *The Black Book of Colors*. Elisa Amado, Illus. Groundwork Books, 2008.

Marceau, Fani. *Panorama: A Foldout Book*. Joelle Jolivet, Illus. Abrams, 2009.

Reibstein, Mark. *Wabi Sabi*. Ed Young, Illus. Little Brown, 2008.

Young, Ed. *Beyond the Great Mountains*. Chronicle, 2005.

Dust Jackets

Anholt, Laurence. *Seven for a Secret*. Jim Coplestone, Illus. Frances Lincoln, 2006.

Edwards, Wallace. *The Extinct Files: My Science Project*. Kids Can Press, 2006.

Tunnel, Michael. *Mailing May.* Ted Rand, Illus. Perfection, 2000.

Winter, Jonah. *Here Comes the Garbage Barge!* Red Nose Studio, Illus., Schwartz & Wade, 2010.

Casings

Lehman, Barbara. *Rainstorm*. Houghton Mifflin, 2007.

Martin, Jacqueline Briggs. *Snowflake Bentley*. Houghton Mifflin, 1998.

Van Allsburg, Chris. *Queen of the Falls*. Houghton Mifflin, 2011.

Wiesner, David. *Flotsam*. Clarion, 2006.

Woodson, Jacqueline. *Show Way*. Hudson Talbott, Illus. Putnam, 2005.

Endpapers

Bryant, Jen. *A River of Words*. Melissa Sweet, Illus. Eerdmans, 2008.

Foreman, Michael. *Mia's Story*. Candlewick, 2007.

Gravett, Emily. *The Rabbit Problem*. Simon & Schuster, 2010.

Guarnaccia, Steven. *The Three Little Pigs: An Architectural Tale*. Abrams, 2010.

Front Matter/Back Matter

Bildner, Phil. *The Hallelujah Flight*. John Holyfiled, Illus. Putnam, 2010.

Crowl, Janice. *Pulelehua and Mamaki*. Bishop Museum Press, 2009.

Hopkinson, Deborah. *A Packet of Seeds*. Bethanne Andersen, Illus. Greenwillow, 2004.

Moss, Marissa. *Nurse, Soldier, Spy: The Story of Sarah Edmonds, a Civil War Hero*. John Hendrix, Illus. Abrams, 2011.

Color

Browne, Anthony. *Me and You*. Farrar, Straus & Giroux, 2010.

Browne, Anthony. *Voices in the Park.* Turtleback, 2001.

Burningham, John. *It's a Secret!* Candlewick, 2009.

Lee, Suzy. *Mirror.* Kane/Miller, 2010.

Lee, Suzy. *The Zoo.* Kane/Miller, 2007.

Lehman, Barbara. *The Red Book.* Scholastic, 2004.

Sis, Peter. *The Wall: Growing Up Behind the Iron Curtain.* Farrar, Straus & Giroux, 2007.

Borders or Frames

Brett, Jan. *The Mitten: 20th Anniversary Edition.* Putnam, 2009.

La Prise, Larry. *The Hokey Pokey.* Sheila Hamanaka, Illus. Simon & Schuster, 1997.

Martin, Jacqueline Briggs. *Snowflake Bentley.* Houghton Mifflin, 1998.

Sidman, Joyce. *Song of the Water Boatman & Other Pond Poems.* Beckie Prange, Illus. Houghton Mifflin, 2005.

Van Allsburg, Chris. *The Garden of Abdul Gasazi.* Houghton Mifflin, 1979.

Like other stories for children, a picturebook is judged by standards of literary excellence in plot, character, theme, setting, point of view, style, and tone. Illustrations impact each of these literary elements in varying degrees, depending on the relationship of the words and pictures.

Children's taste, like that of most adults, is dependent largely on exposure. Although it is important to learn what children like or dislike, we remember that children have had only limited exposure to literature and art. Their uninformed responses cannot be the only criterion for judging which picturebooks are acceptable, suitable, or desirable. However, children appreciate a good picturebook in ways adults focused on the words may not. Understanding the ways picturebooks work will give all readers the tools they need to communicate their appreciation and understanding of picturebooks effectively. Parents, librarians, and teachers with an understanding of the many ways picturebooks develop the arts as well as literature are a valuable resource for young readers. As we contemplate illustration, we see it as an extension of experience, an additional source of pleasure but also an integral part of constructing the meaning of increasingly savvy picturebooks.

NOTES

1. David Lewis first coined this term in his very complete discussion of this format in *Reading Contemporary Picturebooks: Picturing Text* (New York: Routledge/Falmer, 2001). He opened the door to a new way to think about "picture books" and how they can be "read" and what they "mean." Lewis uses *"picturebook"* as the term for contemporary children's books in which illustration and words combine in ways that produce a larger meaning than either would convey individually. He was especially interested in this term for books for which the author and illustrator were the same person, but picturebook researchers such as Sylvia Pantaleo and Lawrence Sipe have adopted this term for the complex picturebooks being published for today's readers to indicate the combined meaning of words and pictures.

2. Carol Driggs Wolfenbarger and Lawrence Sipe confirm picturebooks' status as a *format* in their literature review: "A Unique Visual and Literary Art Form: Recent Research on Picturebooks," *Language Arts*, 3(84), January 2007. This is a very readable article and a good companion to this chapter.

3. Lawrence Sipe described the effect of reading picturebooks as *synergetic:* "How Picture Books Work: A Semiotically Framed Theory of Text–Picture Relationships," *Children's Literature in Education,* 29, 1998, pp. 97–108). A thorough treatment of

the picturebook format can be found in Lawrence Sipe, *Storytime: Young Children's Literary Understanding in the Classroom* (New York: Teacher's College Press, 2007).

4. Anne Hoppe shares the importance of words and images in the modern picturebook and alludes to the reality that the whole meaning of the words and pictures is greater than the sum of these two parts in "Half the Story: Text and Illustration in Picture Books," *The Horn Book Magazine*, January/February 2004, pp. 41–50.

5. Perry Nodelman, *Words about Pictures: The Narrative Art of Children's Picture Books* (Athens: University of Georgia, 1988). See an excellent review of Nodelman's book: "Close Encounters of A Pictorial Kind," by Jane Doonan in *Children's Literature*, vol. 20 (New Haven, CT: Yale University Press, 1992), pp. 204–210.

6. The uneven rhythm created by the ways readers process text and pictures is thoroughly described in "The Rhythm of Picture-Book Narrative" in Perry Nodelman, *Words about Pictures: The Narrative Art of Children's Picture Books* (Athens: University of Georgia, 1988). Jane Doonan introduced the uneven nature of reading text and illustration as a 'tension' in her 1993 classic *Looking at Pictures in Picture Books* (Stroud, Glos., UK: The Thimble Press). David Lewis further illuminates text/picture dynamics (creating the term 'picturebook') in his important book: *Reading Contemporary picturebooks: Picturing Text* (London: RoutledgeFalmer, 2001).

7. Perry Nodelman, *Words about Pictures: The Narrative Art of Children's Picture Books* (Athens: University of Georgia, 1988), p. 153.

8. Denise Agosto describes some of the useful categories and subcategories of interdependent storytelling and some of the effects of interdependent storytelling for the reader in "One and Inseparable: Interdependent Storytelling in Picture Storybooks," *Children's Literature in Education*, 8(4), 1999, pp. 267–280.

9. See Joanne M. Golden and Annyce Gerber, "A Semiotic Perspective of Text: The Picture Story Book Event," *Journal of Literacy Research*, 22(3), 1990, pp. 203–219. Golden introduced five effects of the relationship between words and pictures:

- Text and picture are symmetrical—simplest and most basic (*Hondo and Fabian* by Peter McCarty)
- Text depends on picture for clarification (*The Snowy Day* by Ezra Jack Keats)

- Illustration enhances and elaborates text (*Emily's Art* by Peter Catalanotto)
- Text carries primary narrative and illustration is selective (*Frog and Toad Together* by Arnold Lobel)
- Illustration carries primary narrative and text is selective (*The Zoo* by Suzy Lee)

To this we would suggest

- Illustration carries virtually all of the narrative (*The Red Book* by Barbara Lehman)
- Illustration provides a story that counters or tells a story that differs from the text (*The Three Pigs* by David Wiesner)

10. Maria Nikolajeva and Carole Scott, *How Picturebooks Work* (New York: Garland, 2001). An abbreviated discussion of the basic findings from this book can be found in Maria Nikolajeva and C. Scott, "The Dynamics of Picturebook Communication," *Children's Literature in Education*, 31(4), 2000.

11. Maria Nikolajeva and Carole Scott "The Dynamics of Picturebook Communication," *Children's Literature in Education*, 31(4), 2000, p. 226. Five categories of interaction included in their work are:

- *Symmetrical interaction*: words and pictures tell the same story, essentially repeating information in pictures and text
- *Enhancing interaction*: pictures amplify the meaning of the words, or the words expand the meaning of the pictures (*Kitten's First Full Moon* by Kevin Henkes; *Little Beauty* by Anthony Browne).
- *Complementary interaction*: when enhancing becomes very significant, telling more than the meaning of the words (*Emily's Art* by Peter Catalanotto).
- *Counterpointing*: words and images collaborate to communicate meanings beyond the scope of either one alone (*Rosie's Walk* by Pat Hutchins).
- *Contradictory interaction*: extreme counterpointing in which words and pictures seem to be in opposition to one another. This ambiguity challenges the reader to mediate between the words and pictures to establish a true understanding of what is being depicted (*The Three Pigs* by David Wiesner).

12. Joseph Schwarcz. *Ways of the Illustrator: Visual Communication in Children's Literature* (Chicago: American Library Association, 1982).

13. See Perry Nodelman, "How a Picture Book Works," in *Image and Maker*, edited by Harold Dar-

ling and Peter Neumeyer (New York: Greenwillow, 1984).

14. Molly Bang's *Picture This: How Pictures Work* (SeaStar Books, 1991) describes in words and shows in pictures how elements of shape, position in space, and color can create tone.

15. The work of Gerard Genette with intertextuality comes from *Palimpsests: Literature in the Second Degree*, translated by Channa Newman and Claude Doubinsky (Lincoln: University of Nebraska Press, 1998). His discussions of the ways books are connected across texts has increased in popularity, motivating classification systems for organizing texts of all kinds for many kinds of studies.

16. Gerard Genette, *Paratexts: The Thresholds of Textuality* (Literature, Culture, Theory. Ser., No. 20), translated by J. E. Lewin (New York: Cambridge University Press, 1997).

17. Lawrence Sipe and Caroline McGuire explore peritextual features of picturebooks in "Picturebook Endpapers: Resources for Literary and Aesthetic Interpretation," *Children's Literature in Education*, 37, 2006, pp. 291–304. This study reveals young children's effective interpretation of the peritext and ways these features contribute to the "whole" message of a picturebook.

RECOMMENDED BOOKS

AMADO, ELISA. *Tricycle.* Illustrated by Alfonso Ruano. Groundwood Books, 2007.

BAKER, JEANNIE. *Mirror.* Candlewick Press, 2010.

BANG, MOLLY. *When Sophie Gets Angry . . . Really, Really Angry.* Blue Sky Press, 1999.

BATAILLE, MARION. *ABC3D.* Roaring Book Press, 2008.

BLEXBOLEX. *Traffic Jam.* Enchanted Lion, 2010.

BROWN, HEATHER. *The Robot Book.* Accord Publishing, 2010.

BROWN, MARGARET WISE. *Goodnight Moon.* Illustrated by Clement Hurd. HarperCollins, 2005.

BROWNE, ANTHONY. *Little Beauty.* Candlewick Press, 2008.

BRYANT, JEN. *A River of Words.* Illustrated by Melissa Sweet. Eerdmans, 2008.

BUEHNER, CARALYN. *Snowmen at Night.* Harcourt, 2005.

BUNTING, EVE. *The Wednesday Surprise.* Illustrated by Donald Carrick. Clarion, 1989.

BURTON, VIRGINIA LEE. *The Little House.* Houghton Mifflin, 1942.

CARLE, ERIC. *The Very Hungry Caterpillar.* Philomel, 1986.

CATALANOTTO, PETER. *Emily's Art.* Atheneum, 2001.

CHOI, YANGSHOOK. *The Name Jar.* Knopf, 2001.

DEPAOLA, TOMIE. *Strega Nona.* Simon & Schuster, 2010.

EDWARDS, WALLACE. *The Extinct Files: My Science Project.* Kids Can Press, 2006.

EHLERT, LOIS. *Boo to You!* Beach Lane, 2009.

FLOURNOY, VALERIE. *The Patchwork Quilt.* Illustrated by Jerry Pinkney. Little, Brown, 1992.

FOX, MEM. *Wilfrid Gordon McDonald Partridge.* Illustrated by Julie Vivas. Kane/Miller, 1989.

FRAZEE, MARLA. *A Couple of Boys Have the Best Week Ever.* Harcourt. 2008.

FRAZEE, MARLA. *Roller Coaster.* Harcourt Children's Books, 2003.

GAIMAN, NEIL. *The Dangerous Alphabet.* Illustrated by Gris Grimley. HarperCollins, 2008.

GAIMAN, NEIL. *The Wolves in the Walls.* Illustrated by Dave McKean. HarperCollins, 2003.

GEISERT, ARTHUR. *Hogwash!* Houghton Mifflin, 2008.

GERSTEIN, MORDICAI. *The Man Who Walked Between the Towers.* Roaring Brook Press, 2003.

GRALLEY, JEAN. *The Moon Came Down on Milk Street.* Henry Holt, 2004.

GRAVETT, EMILY. *Little Mouse's Big Book of Fears.* Simon & Schuster, 2007.

GRAVETT, EMILY. *The Rabbit Problem.* Simon & Schuster, 2010.

GRAVETT, EMILY. *Spells.* Simon & Schuster, 2009.

GRAVETT, EMILY. *Wolves.* Simon & Schuster, 2005.

GRINDLEY, SALLY. *Peter's Place.* Illustrated by Michael Foreman. Anderson, 1995.

HENKES, KEVIN. *Kitten's First Full Moon.* Greenwillow, 2004.

HERRERA, JUAN FELIPE. *Calling the Doves.* 74Elly Simmons. Children's Book Press, 1995.

HILL, LABAN CARRICK. *Dave the Potter: Artist, Poet, Slave.* Illustrated by Bryan Collier. Little, Brown, 2010.

HOPKINSON, DEBORAH. *Fannie in the Kitchen.* Illustrated by Nancy Carpenter. Atheneum, 2001.

HUTCHINS, PAT. *Rosie's Walk.* Macmillan, 1968.

ISADORA, RACHEL. *At the Crossroads.* Greenwillow, 1991.

JENKINS, EMILY. *The Little Bit Scary People.* Illustrated by Alexandra Boiger. Hyperion, 2008.

JOHNSON, STEPHEN. *Alphabet City.* Viking, 1995.

KEATS, EZRA JACK. *The Snowy Day.* Viking, 1962.

KITAMURA, SATOSHI. *Lily Takes a Walk.* Dutton, 1987.

KNIGHT, JOAN MCPHAIL. *Charlotte in Giverny.* Illustrated by Melissa Sweet. Chronicle Books, 2000.

LAINEZ, RENE COLATO. *From North to South/Del Norte al Sur.* Illustrated by Joe Cepeda. Children's Book Press, 2010

LEE, SUZY. *The Zoo.* Kane/Miller Book Publishers, 2007.

LEHMAN, BARBARA. *The Red Book.* Houghton Mifflin, 2004.

LEWIS, J. PATRICK. *The House.* Illustrated by Robert Innocenti. Creative Editions, 2009.

LIONNI, LEO. *Big Blue and Little Yellow.* Demco Media, 1987.

LIONNI, LEO. *Fish Is Fish.* Random House, 1970.

LOBEL, ARNOLD. *Frog and Toad Together.* Harper & Row, 1972.

MARCEAU, FANI. *Panorama: A Foldout Book.* Illustrated by Joelle Jolivet. Abrams, 2007.

MARTIN, JACQUELINE BRIGGS. *Birdwashing Song: The Willow Tree Loon.* Illustrated by Nancy Carpenter. Simon & Schuster, 1995.

MARTIN, JACQUELINE BRIGGS. *Snowflake Bentley.* Illustrated by Mary Azarian. Houghton Mifflin, 1998.

MCCARTY, PETER. *Hondo and Fabian.* Henry Holt, 2002.

MCCLINTOCK, BARBARA. *Dahlia.* Farrar, Straus & Giroux, 2002.

MCCLOSKEY, ROBERT. *Blueberries for Sal.* Viking, 1969.

MCCULLEY, EMILY ARNOLD. *An Outlaw Thanksgiving.* Dial, 1998.

MOORE, CLEMENT C. *The Night Before Christmas.* Illustrated by Robert Sabuda. Little Simon, 2002.

MOSER, BARRY. *Tucker Pfeffercorn.* Little Brown, 1994.

MULLER, JORG. *The Changing Countryside.* Heryin Books, 2006.

NAPOLI, DONNA JO. *Mama Miti: Maathai and the Trees of Kenya.* Illustrated by Kadir Nelson. Simon & Schuster, 2010.

NEVIUS, CAROL. *Karate Hour.* Illustrated by Bill Thomson. Marshall Cavendish, 2004.

NOVESKY, AMY. *Me, Frida.* Illustrated by David Diaz. Abrams, 2010.

O'CONNOR, GEORGE. *Kapow!* Aladin, 2007.

OFFIL, JENNY. *17 Things I'm Not Allowed to Do Anymore.* Illustrated by Nancy Carpenter. Schwartz & Wade, 2007.

O'MALLEY, KEVIN. *Once upon a Cool Motorcycle Dude.* Walker & Company, 2005.

PINKNEY, BRIAN. *The Adventures of Sparrowboy.* Simon & Schuster, 2000.

PRINGLE, LAWRENCE. *Oil Spills: Damage, Recovery, and Prevention.* William Morrow, 1993.

RAND, GLORIA. *Prince William.* Illustrated by Ted Rand. Henry Holt, 1992.

RATHMANN, PEGGY. *Officer Buckle and Gloria.* Putnam, 1995.

RECORVITS, HELEN. *My Name Is Yoon.* Illustrated by Gabi Swiatkowska. Farrar, Straus and Giroux, 2003.

REISER, LYNN. *Tortillas and Lullabies/Tortillas y Cancioncitas.* Illustrated by Corazones Valientes. HarperCollins, 1998.

ROHMANN, ERIC. *My Friend Rabbit.* Roaring Brook Press, 2002.

ROSEN, MICHAEL J. *Chanuka Lights.* Illustrated by Robert Sabuda. Candlewick, 2011.

RYLANT, CYNTHIA. *The Relatives Came.* Illustrated by Stephen Gammel. Atheneum, 2001.

SAY, ALLEN. *Erika-San.* Houghton Mifflin, 2009.

SENDAK, MAURICE. *Where the Wild Things Are.* Harper & Row, 1963.

SIDMAN, JOYCE. *Dark Emperor and Other Poems of the Night.* Illustrated by Rick Allen. Houghton Mifflin, 2010.

SOTO, GARY. *Too Many Tamales.* Illustrated by Ed Martinez. Putnam, 1993.

SPIEGELMAN, ART. *Open Me . . . I'm a Dog!* HarperCollins, 1997.

STEAD, PHILIP C. *A Sick Day for Amos McGee.* Illustrated by Erin Stead. New York: Roaring Book Press, 2010.

STEIN, DAVID EZRA. *Interrupting Chicken.* Candlewick, 2010.

ST. GEORGE, JUDITH. *So You Want to Be President.* Illustrated by David Small. Philomel, 2004.

SWANSON, SUSAN MARIE. *The House in the Night.* Illustrated by Beth Krommes. Houghton Mifflin, 2008.

TAN, SHAUN. *The Arrival.* Arthur A. Levine, 2006.

TUNNEL, MICHAEL O. *Mailing May.* Illustrated by Ted Rand. Perfection, 2000.

VAN ALLSBURG, CHRIS. *Bad Day at Riverbend.* Houghton Mifflin, 2000.

VAN ALLSBURG, CHRIS. *The Garden of Abdul Gasazi.* Houghton Mifflin, 1979.

VAN ALLSBURG, CHRIS. *Just a Dream.* Scholastic, 1992.

VAN ALLSBURG, CHRIS. *The Mysteries of Harris Burdick.* Houghton Mifflin, 1984.

VAN ALLSBURG, CHRIS. *The Polar Express.* Houghton Mifflin, 1985.

WIESNER, DAVID. *Art and Max.* Clarion, 2010.

WIESNER, DAVID. *The Three Pigs.* Clarion, 2001.

WILLIAMS, KAREN LYNN. *Four Feet, Two Sandals.* Illustrated by Doug Chayka. Eerdmans, 2007.

WOOD, DON. *Into the Volcano.* Blue Sky Press, 2008.

WOODSON, JACQUELINE. *Pecan Pie Baby.* Illustrated by Sophie Blackall. Putnam, 2010.

ZELINSKY, PAUL O. *Rumpelstiltskin.* Dutton, 1986.

MyEducationKit™

Go to the topic "Picture Books" on the MyEducationKit for this text, where you can:

- Search the Children's Literature Database, housing more than 22,000 titles searchable in every genre by authors or illustrators, by awards won, by year published, and by topic and description.
- Explore genre-related Assignments and Activities, assignable exercises showing concepts in action through database use, video, cases, and student and teacher artifacts.
- Listen to podcasts and read interviews from some of the brightest and most enduring stars of children's literature in the Conversations.
- Discover web links that will lead you to sites representing the authors you learn about in these pages, classrooms with powerful children's literature connections, and literature awards.

The Storyteller's Candle: La velita de los cuentos

Lucia Gonzalez / Illustrated by Lulu Delacre

Historical fiction is a genre that should have
a strong basis in fact. Stories help young
readers acquire a sense of the past.

CHAPTER FOUR

Genre in Children's Literature

Why know about genres? What does each of the genres contribute to the child reader? How?

A **genre** is a type of literature that has a common set of characteristics. Fairy tale, biography, fiction, memoir, science fiction, fantasy, and mystery can all be considered different genres of literature. In this chapter we will list characteristics common to each of these most well-known genres. Within each genre there are further subcategories—such as traditional literature's inclusion of fables, folktales, myths, and legends.

Genres are not always clear-cut. As you will recall from Chapter 2, a new category called the "genre-blend" book has been added to the world of children's literature. A genre-blend book could, for example, combine a fictional mystery story with true biography, as we see in *Zora and Me*; it could also be a graphic novel working in the manner of a silent film, as we see in *The Invention of Hugo Cabret*. The information genre might blend with fantasy the way it does in *The Magic School Bus* series. A genre-blend book might combine the fantastic of magical realism with simple biography, as in *The Dreamer,* or it might combine folklore, realism, and fantasy in the way of the graphic novel *American Born Chinese*. Despite the prevalence of these new, blurred genres in children's and young adult literature, we must be as clear as we can about the characteristics that each separate genre of literature contains.

It is important to understand the concept of genre and to know the differences between genres, for many reasons. First, the term can be useful in organizing discussions of children's literature and their intertex-

"Genre" describes a group with similar characteristics.

tual relationships. Second, understanding the concept of genre clarifies the ways literary elements such as character, setting, and theme function differently in different genres. Knowing these different genres can help readers fully understand how these elements function, as we will demonstrate later in the handbook. Third, sensitivity to the broad and rich variety in literature available to children can allow teachers to help students sample many different genres.

As readers, we tend to become familiar and comfortable with particular genres and less familiar and comfortable with others. Using the term *genre* helps us be aware that there is more literature for children than only the genres we love most. Finally, and most importantly, children need to be taught—in some cases overtly—what their expectations should be for each of the genres of literature they read. They need to be taught, for example, that in a folktale the characters will be simple and flat and that the plot will move quickly, but that in quality realistic fiction the characters should be more complex and the plot more intricate. Learning genre conventions is an important part of becoming a competent and confident reader.[1]

> Learning genre conventions is an important part of becoming a competent and confident reader.

For our purposes we will try to use the term *genre* in a way that is clear and useful. In this chapter we first discuss traditional or folkloric literature because of the foundational role it plays in the structures of other fictional genres. Next we discuss fantasy and its subgenres of high fantasy, fantastic stories, and science fiction. Then we discuss contemporary fiction, including mysteries and thrillers and animal stories. Finally we provide information about contemporary realism, which is another type of contemporary fiction. This genre includes coming-of-age stories, romance, and problem-centered stories. We will conclude with a thorough discussion of historical realism, a genre of growing importance whose dependence on developing conceptions of time and place can make it difficult for inexperienced readers.

Descriptions of poetry, biography, and information books are not included since these genres will be fully discussed in separate chapters.

Traditional Literature

The term *traditional* (or *folk*) literature implies that the form comes to us from the ordinary person and exists orally rather than in writing—at least until some collector finds, records, and publishes the stories or rhymes. There is no final and definitive version of a piece of folk literature. Folktales have been called the "spiritual history" of humankind, the "cement of society" binding a culture together. They seem to express the universality of human wishes and needs. Hundreds of versions of the same story, such as "Cinderella," occur in countless cultures and show almost infinite variations, but are similar in their focus on human yearning for social acceptance and material comfort. We are now fortunate that, because of scholarly collecting, folktales that once flourished only in communities where people did not read or write have become the property of all people.

Perhaps it is a need to maintain a sense of wonderment or to keep alive a hope that we can seize opportunities for transforming and improving our world that sends us back to traditional literature. Regardless, storytellers continue to collect original tales from cultures around the world. The **literary lore** that mimics characteristics of traditional literature of all kinds has been written since Hans Christian Andersen created his original fairy tales. His nineteenth century works continue to be celebrated, parodied, and illustrated in many styles to this day. The subgenres of traditional literature serve as the backbone of children's stories across genres. For this reason, we begin this chapter with traditional literature.

Fables

The **fable** is a very brief story, usually with animal characters, that points clearly to a moral or lesson. The moral, an explicit and didactic theme, is usually given at the end of the story and is the reason for the existence of the fable. The fable makes visible an objective lesson, like the one in "The Tortoise and the Hare": "Slow but steady wins the race." Janet Stevens successfully illustrated this fable for younger children, but Aesop's fables are most fully appreciated by older children. In a fable, each character exemplifies a single trait, and conflict is sharp and clear, as it is in "The Tortoise and the Hare." The fable has no interpretive narrator telling extra details of characters' thoughts or feelings. Style is crisp and straightforward. Everything in the fable exists to make a lesson clear—as clear as the moral in the story of the milkmaid who dreamily drops her basket of eggs on the way to market: "Don't count your chickens before they hatch." Arnold Lobel's 1981 Caldecott Award–winning *Fables* plays with this genre in twenty one-page, witty, concise, and fanciful fables Lobel invented himself.

The picturebook format complicates the traditional fable formula in the beautifully illustrated wordless version of *The Lion and the Mouse* by Jerry Pinkney. The typically explicit verbal moral statement is no longer the centerpiece of the tale; the illustrations must do this work and the formula of the crisp, clear lesson is blurred. Susan Gaber's almost surreal illustrations for Heather Forest's version of *The Contest Between the Sun and the Wind* add layers of possibility to the sparse verbal text. The illustrations, rather than providing the typical one-to-one correspondence with the verbal text, encourage the reader to interpret the story according to the tone in the illustrations. The dark greys of the wind's efforts are replaced by lemon tones when the sun begins to win the contest. The repeating figure of a man traveling along a road adds the sense of action sometimes missing in more traditional fables. Well-illustrated versions of old fables add new interpretive possibilities; fables are open to adaptation in the same ways other folklore genres are.

> The fable is a very brief story, usually with animal characters, that points clearly to a moral or lesson.

Folktales

The **folktale** relies on flat characters, both bad and good, easily recognized. Since folktales were heard by the teller and then retold in the teller's own words, there was hardly time for subtle character development. A brief phrase, which may be repeated often, serves to draw character, since the teller cannot risk losing the audience by departing from the fast-paced narration of action.

Stock characters, like the fairy godmother and the wicked stepmother in "Cinderella," frequently appear. Conflicts are often between people or personified animals, as when, for example, Jack battles the giant in "Jack and the Beanstalk." Plots are simple and strictly chronological, with the climax coming at the very end and the closing as brief as "They lived happily ever after." In European tales, incidents often

> Stock characters, like the fairy godmother and the wicked stepmother in "Cinderella," frequently appear in folktales.

occur in threes as they do in "The Billy-Goats Gruff"; in stories from other traditions, the numbers vary. The setting is usually a background that creates universality by its vaguely recognizable appeal. Point of view is rarely first person. The tone of folktales varies; it may be sentimental, as in "Beauty and the Beast," or somewhat dark, as in "Little Red Riding Hood." Themes also vary but there is usually commentary on human needs and wishes, such as the theme in "The Fisherman's Wife": "People are never satisfied."

For years children in the United States read and heard few tales other than those from western European traditions. Now, children have access to folktales from various cultural traditions: Virginia Hamilton's *Her Stories: African American Folktales, Fairy Tales, and True Tales*; versions of tales from Africa, like those found in *Nelson Mandela's Favorite African Folktales*; Jewish folk tales such as *Golem*, a picturebook by David Wisniewski; or Abenaki Indian tales, like those gathered in *Keepers of the Earth* by Joseph Bruchac. Throughout the world, folktales tell and retell similar stories. Versions of the Cinderella story have been found in countries as diverse as Turkey, Ireland, Laos, and India, and made into beautiful and popular picturebooks. Caldecott Award–winner *Lon Po Po* by Ed Young tells a Little Red Riding Hood story from China; *Pretty Salma* by Niki Daly is a similar story from Africa; *Petite Rouge* by Mike Artell is a Cajun Red Riding Hood tale from the Bayou. These folktale variants often have identical themes, reinforcing that certain ideas are often universal.

The style of the folktale often relies on recurring images and phrases like "Not by the hair of my chinny-chin-chin." These often include short rhyming patterns such as those in "Snow White": "Mirror, mirror, on the wall/Who is fairest of us all?" From the South American collection *Tales from Silver Lands* comes "A Tale of Three Tails," where "They sing and they play/For half of the day"; from "The Calabash Man" comes "From forest to hill/We come at your will/Call, Aura, call." The cadenced prose and repetition fit the needs of oral traditions that rely on memory and retelling.

Though all folktales have similarities, they can be subdivided into many types. Possibly the most well-loved tales for children are **fairy tales,** which typically feature folkloric characters such as fairies, wicked stepmothers, princesses, princes, goblins, elves, and fairy godmothers. Magic, spells, and enchantment are hallmark elements of the fairy tale, as is the typically happy ending. Oral versions of fairy tales have been collected and written by the Brothers Grimm (German) and Perrault (French), but additional versions of these tales exist in some form all over the world. We have already alluded to "Cinderella," but other favorite fairy tales such as "Rumplestiltskin," "Beauty and the Beast," and "Rapunzel" have variations.

There are **noodlehead stories,** tales of good-hearted people who make lots of mistakes, as in David Adler's gently silly *Chanukah in Chelm*, or Coleen Salley's *Epossumondas*, a variation on an archetypal noodlehead tale based on the time-honored Southern legend of Epaminondas. **Tall tales** come primarily from the United States and include exaggerated stories of folk heroes and heroines, as in Julius Lester and Jerry Pinkney's award-winning *John Henry* or Anne Isaacs and Paul O. Zelinsky's *Swamp Angel*. These subcategories often overlap; they serve to emphasize the richness and variety of the genre. **Cumulative tales** are based on a series of additions like those in "The House That Jack Built" or "The Gingerbread Man." However, in *Why Mosquitoes Buzz in People's Ears*, Verna Aardema boldly reverses the cumulative pattern to unravel the question of how the owlet was killed, answering a question about nature as many **pourquoi stories** do. **Talking beast tales** employ folkloric

Folktales from many different cultures are now available in picturebook format.

devices as other folktales do, but they primarily feature animals as characters with little, if any, interaction with human characters. Though animals behave like people in these stories, there is not an emphasis on magic; examples include "The Three Pigs" and "Goldilocks and the Three Bears."

We would be remiss, in this section on folktales, not to mention the many other ways that folktales and fairy tales are being used in children's literature today. Cultural variants are many, such as Pat Mora's *Dona Flora*, a Mexican tall tale with a female leading the action. Barry Moses tells an Appalachian version of "Rumplestiltskin" in *Tucker Pfeffercorn*. Modern variants of folktales include Frances Minters's *Sleepless Beauty*, a jazz-age version in which the beauty outwits the witch. Fiona French's art deco *Snow White in New York* is suave and witty, and *Cinder Edna* by Ellen Jackson plays with gender expectations. Each one takes the original tale and turns it on its head to provide a message for modern times. The folktale is being developed and revised for older children as well: Donna Jo Napoli, Jane Yolen, and Gail Carson Levine have each written series of young adult novels based on fairy tales. Finally, of course, there are many folktales updated and revised, available in graphic format, such as the wacky collection called *Rabbi Harvey Rides Again: A Graphic Novel of Jewish Folktales Let Loose in the Wild West* by Steve Sheinkin or Will Eisner's graphic version of *The Princess and the Frog*.

Myths

Myths are stories that originate in the beliefs of nations and present episodes in which supernatural forces operate. Because they are handed down by word of mouth, their forms vary. Some myths, like the Norse myth about the god Thor and his hammer of thunder, are stories that interpret the world, including involvement of the gods and mortals in stories explaining natural phenomena. Other myths try to make visible and concrete the ways that humans see nature, such as the explanation of the seasons in the story of Ceres and her daughter Proserpina. The girl is abducted and kept for part of the year in the underworld of Pluto, explaining the disappearance of summer's warmth and growth. Still other myths may describe human nature, such as the generosity demonstrated in the myth of Baucis and Philemon. This myth shows that hospitality is valued; its reward the promise of abundance.

Myths are stories that originate in the beliefs of nations and present episodes in which supernatural forces operate.

Myths show the ways that humans see the forces that control them, such as the separation of day and night caused by Apollo's crossing the sky in his sun chariot. Myths explain creation, religion, and divinities; they suggest the meanings of life and death, or the cause of good and evil, as made clear in the myth of Pandora's box. As Virginia Hamilton says in an introductory note to *In the Beginning: Creation Stories from Around the World*, although "fairy tales take place *within* the time of human experience . . . myths take place before the 'once upon a time'. . . [and] go *back beyond anything that ever was,* and begin *before* anything has happened."

Myths are important for children to know about because, like folktales, they are the basis for many stories, allusions, and well-known phrases. For many years the *D'Aulaire's Book of Greek Myths* was a staple in the elementary classroom. Today, however, children can read myths that have origins from many cultures. One of the benefits to readers of myths is the reinforcement of the idea that all peoples value similar human traits. The plot of a myth is often a single incident or a few incidents linked by characters. An opening phrase such as "Long ago in ancient China" is sufficient for setting. Since the abstract issues or themes that myths explore are broad and universal, their tone is dignified and somewhat mystical. The effective telling of a myth has dignity and simplicity.

Legends and Hero Tales

Legends are similar to myths because both are traditional narratives of a people; sometimes the two subgenres are interwoven. Legends, however, often have more historical truth and less reliance on the supernatural. When, for example, we read the legends of the Knights of the Round Table, we are aware of the actual physical castle as well as of legendary heroes and actions. Readers are also immersed in the history and culture of the Middle Ages in Europe. Although there was a King Arthur, most stories about him are not historical truth but legend. The grandeur of the legend is maintained in *The Legend of the King*, retold by Gerald Morris. This story caps off his well-received series, beginning with Arthur's pulling the sword from the stone and setting up the Round Table, to his love and loss of Guinevere, and his final departure for the magic isle of Avalon. There are multiple ways the legends of King Arthur can be brought to life with books from other genres, including tales of the heroes who inhabit and perform brave deeds within these action-packed stories. Like other traditional literature, legends and hero tales provide strong patterns for stories in other genres.

The historical backdrop to legends is an important consideration for children who sometimes wonder about the truth of their favorite heroes from the past. Heroic figures like George Washington, John Chapman, or Abraham Lincoln accumulate many stories about their lives. Some of these, like "Johnny Appleseed," become legends rooted in authenticity, but exaggerated and fictional in the specific details. Legends, tall tales, and biographical fiction can be difficult for children to separate.

INQUIRY POINT

Find three stories of John Chapman, also known as Johnny Appleseed. Find a biography, a fictionalized biography, a legend, or a tall tale version. How can readers tell the difference? Do illustrations play a role? You might also do the same procedure with a different person from history. ✷

Folk Epics

The **folk epic** is a long narrative poem of unknown authorship about an outstanding or royal character in a series of adventures related to that heroic central figure. Ezra Pound has called the **epic** "a poem including history." This character or hero is, like Beowulf, larger than life, grand in all proportions, and superhuman in physical and moral qualities. The action may involve journeys and quests, and it may show deeds of great courage and valor coupled with superhuman strength; the forces of the supernatural intervene from time to time. The setting is vast, including a nation, a continent, or even the universe. The point of view is often objective, the tone is dignified, and the style is elevated. Often the story is told in vivid detail so the reader will become invested in it. The language might include extended comparisons called "epic similes." Like the best retellings of myth, epics show the values of the society and awe the reader with the possibility of great courage and moral strength. This genre is best suited to older children, but the hero cycle in an epic is a popular one, and readers who love high fantasy, legends, and hero tales are possible candidates for this genre.

Fantasy

In the years since Harry Potter flew into town on his Nimbus 2000, the genre of **fantasy** has enjoyed a rebirth. Perry Nodelman writes that "the best definition [of fantasy] is the vaguest: fantasy depicts a world unlike the one we usually call real."[2] For readers to accept this other world, a writer has to make the reader trust the narrator's voice, and to make the imaginary universe so credible, "so solidly grounded in reality," as Madeleine L'Engle wrote, that we wish it were all true; for sheer pleasure, we believe. High fantasy, fantastic stories, and science fiction are identifiable subgenres of fantasy; often they overlap.

High Fantasy

The **high fantasy** subgenre is primarily characterized by its focus on the conflict between good and evil. It is very often closely related to themes from folklore featuring a quest and sometimes a courageous hero or heroine. If it is successful, it captures our belief in two major ways. First, by the internal consistency of the new world, as we believe in, for example, the classes of small nonhumans in *The Lord of the Rings* by J. R. R. Tolkien. Second, by our belief in the protagonist's experience. High fantasy portrays full and complete humans. The Harry Potter series can be considered an example of this subgenre, since much of the books' plot is centered about an ongoing battle with the evil Voldemort. The wizard world in which Harry lives—complete with strange and grumpy teachers, friends, school sports, and fantastic objects like the Marauder's Map, the invisibility cloak, and the Weasleys' clock—is a consistent one, and one in which many children have consistently wanted to live. The wild success of the seven novels in the Harry Potter series has generated movies, websites, video games, and fan fiction, in addition to publishers' new interest in the fantasy genre.

> The high fantasy subgenre is primarily characterized by its focus on the conflict between good and evil.

Deep and complicated novels of high fantasy are everywhere these days: Phillip Pullman's *The Golden Compass*, *The Subtle Knife*, and *The Amber Spyglass* are serious and thoughtful novels in which each human has an animal "familiar," bears can talk, children can step into different worlds by cutting holes in the air, and what looks good may truly be evil. Jonathan Stroud created a very sarcastic genie for his apprentice magician to battle in the award-winning and witty Bartimaeus series; Ursula LeGuin's elegant Earthsea series begins with the story of a young apprentice wizard who must ask himself questions "that have to do with shadow and substance, good and evil, light and dark."[3] The second book in the Earthsea series, *Tombs of Atuan*, told of a young woman's coming of age; with this book, LeGuin began a tradition of fantasies that wrestled with questions of gender, influencing a generation of feminist fantasy writers such as Tamora Pierce, Diana Wynne Jones, and Susan Cooper.

All of these novels address problems of good and evil, time and memory, growth and sex, and the strangeness of the world. In some, like Madeleine L'Engle's *A Wrinkle in Time*, time itself becomes flexible; in others, like *Alice in Wonderland*, the body grows or shrinks; in still others, such as C. S. Lewis's *Narnia* series, children become heroes and heroines as they fight for what they believe is right in a world very different from this one. Because of the nature of high fantasy, picturebooks are less likely to represent it. However, Jeff Smith's heroic graphic novel epic, *Bone*, tells of a courageous creature who battles dragons and evil forces bent on conquering mankind. The nine books of Bone's adventures create a kind of high fantasy saga.

Fantastic Stories

We might call one subgenre of fantasy *fantastic stories,* stories realistic in most details but still requiring us to willingly suspend our disbelief. The beautifully written novel *Tuck Everlasting* by Natalie Babbitt is a classic example of the fantastic story. Realistic in every detail but one, this is the story of ten-year-old Winnie Foster, who discovers a spring that provides those who drink from it eternal life. It is a carefully presented, beautifully thought-out argument for the value of time, of growing old, and even of experiencing death. Other examples of this type of fantastic story include Mary Norton's *The Borrowers*, a classic and much-loved series about a tiny family living in a normal-sized family's house. Roald Dahl's *The BFG* is a story of a gentle giant with magnificent ears who kidnaps, and then delights, an orphan girl named Sophie as they join forces to defeat the terrible flesh-eating giants and save the world from their ravenous nightly raids. Children of all ages delight in Dahl's inventive language and earthy descriptions.

Some fantastic stories are about characters that are not people but talk or live in houses like ours, have feelings like ours, or lead lives similar to ours; these we might call fantastic stories of personification. **Talking animal stories** personify animals; successful examples like *Charlotte's Web* and *Stuart Little* feature well-rounded characters and avoid fuzzy cuteness. In Beverly Cleary's series about Ralph S. Mouse, we meet a mouse who wants his own motorcycle; in Kenneth Oppel's *Silverwing* series, we watch the small bat, Shade, journey toward home, millions of wingbeats away; in Dick King-Smith's *Harry's Mad,* we root for a parrot who is also a linguist, a chess champion, and a gourmet. Ted Hughes's classic *The Iron Giant* features a giant robot from another world.

Other kinds of fantastic stories abound. Kathi Appelt has expertly crafted *The Underneath,* a blend of both realism and fantasy. Readers sit on the edge of their seats with worry about a dog and cat as they raise kittens together under a porch in constant peril from the very real danger of violence from both humans and supernatural creatures. Ingrid Law creates a contemporary story where the imaginative and supernatural are found somewhere within each of the characters and in the everyday communities in which they live. Her *Savvy* plays on a reader's desire to imagine their own special talents, or savvy, outside of the magic associated with traditional literature.

Fantastic stories in picturebook format, of course, provide readers with visual as well as written fantasy. In *StellaLuna,* Janell Cannon adapts the talking animal subgenre by successfully creating a parallel story of a small batlet who falls from his

Fantastic stories are realistic in most details.

I N Q U I R Y   P O I N T

Allusions to traditional stories are frequent in children's fantasy. Some are explicit, in the form of a parody, but others require a solid background of the original tale to be truly appreciated. Look closely at these stories for the connection they have with other stories.

Me and You by Anthony Browne

Into the Forest by Anthony Browne

The Tunnel by Anthony Browne

The Jolly Postman or Other People's Letters by Allan Ahlberg, Illus. Janet Ahlberg

Can you find all of the allusions to classic folktales in both the text and the illustrations? What is their significance, if any?

The allusions are more subtly included in *Into the Forest* and *The Tunnel.* What do you see? What is the significance of the choices Browne has included?

mother's grasp and is raised by a family of birds. The readers follow the plight of the batlet, all the while the mother's story appears as an inset on each two-page spread. Realistic illustrations encourage readers to suspend disbelief. This story (and other stories by Cannon) also features back matter to inform readers about bats after the story has been enjoyed.

Chris Van Allsburg is a master of the picturebook format and of the fantasy subgenre. Van Allsburg's picturebook *The Widow's Broom* tells of a witch whose broom has lost its magic until a widow finds it and the magic begins; *Bad Day at Riverbend* features unsuspecting coloring book characters who grapple with the mysterious waxy scribbles intruding on their space. Readers will chuckle at the perplexed antics of the story's cowboy characters and at the source of the characters' trouble—Van Allsburg's daughter is also a character in this story. It's "lights out" at the end as the story "blacks out." David Wiesner's *Tuesday* takes the reader on a journey in which time is of the essence when frogs take flight on their lily pads across the countryside at precisely 8:00 p.m. But a bit of visual foreshadowing at the story's end makes the reader aware that the thrill of flight is not reserved for frogs when a pig is shadowed against the barn wall. Readers familiar with Wiesner's techniques may wonder if pigs will fly in this story or another!

Science Fiction

Science fiction may be seen as a type of fantasy, since the events of the stories could not or have not occurred as they do in our world as we know it. William Sleator, author of the award-winning young adult science fiction novel *House of Stairs*, writes that, "Science fiction is literature about something that hasn't happened yet, but might be possible someday. That it might be possible is the important part; that's what separates science fiction from fantasy."[4] When they read science fiction, readers are immersed in a world that wills them to suspend their disbelief and contains possibilities that resonate with them in some way.

In recent years there has been a boom in science fiction writing for children and teens.

In recent years there has been a boom in science fiction writing for children and teens. There has particularly been a rise in the subgenre of science fiction called **dystopian literature,** in which the writer envisions a dark future world. Many readers of this handbook will remember the power of Lois Lowry's 1994 Newbery Award–winning masterpiece *The Giver*. Frequently challenged, this is a book that can sustain many readings, each reading providing new insights. At first the place in which eleven-year-old Jonas lives *seems* to be a utopia, an ideal future society in which everyone is equal and there is no poverty or war. Slowly readers sense what Jonas and his fellow citizens have had to give up for this equality—color and emotion, sexual feeling, and memory. Readers are gradually immersed in the reality of a dystopian society, in this case, one where a community runs smoothly, but in accordance with laws and daily practices that run counter to dominant views in many ways.

Though this finely crafted novel is perhaps one of the best known, there are many other works of science fiction for this age group that exemplify the concept of the dystopia. The *Hunger Games* series by Suzanne Collins, one of the most popular young adult series of late, shows us a world in which teenagers fight to the death on national television. Many other young adult science fiction novels are dark in similar ways; including the *Uglies* series by Scott Westerfeld, in which every sixteen-year-old citizen takes a pill that makes them beautiful; the British writer Malorie Blackman's *Naughts and Crosses* series, which envisions a society in which apartheid is law; and Phillip Reeve's Nestle Smarties Book Prize winner *The Hungry City Chronicles*, in which the city of London moves through the world consuming other cities.

Science fiction for younger students abounds as well. In the fifth and sixth grades students are just beginning to grapple with large ideas, and to think about a world beyond their own families, so, developmentally speaking, the science fiction genre may be perfect for this age group. This genre has been particularly attractive to boys. Science fiction has many thought-provoking titles to offer young readers, among them Orson Scott Card's *Ender's Game*, Margaret Peterson Haddix's *Running Out of Time*, and Nancy Farmer's story of mutant detectives in an Africa of the future, *The Ear, the Eye, and the Arm*.

Very young readers do not have the world experiences to enjoy many of the science fiction selections older readers love. For this reason, adults (teachers, librarians, and parents) find it a genre that is rich with opportunities to introduce readers to its possibilities in more mediated settings. Often themes of outer space are a good introduction since children have some understanding of this from modern life. Jane Yolen's *Commander Toad in Space*, Pinkwater's humorous *Fat Men from Outer Space*, and Gordon Korman's *Nosepickers from Outer Space* are good science fiction books for younger readers. All of these titles have absurd and optimistic elements that science fiction for older students does not.

As with any genre, science fiction works come in varied formats. Shaun Tan's surprising and poetic *Tales from Outer Suburbia* can be considered a collection of science fiction short stories told through a graphic format. *Woolvs in the Sitee*, written by Margaret Wild and illustrated by Anne Spudvilas, successfully depicts a dark, off-kilter world where fear confines the young protagonist. Similarly, *The Lost Thing* by Shaun Tan creates a dark world that is stark and unfamiliar. The eerie world is open to interpretation, but the surreal illustrations create the sense of possibility as they keep the reader wondering. Paul Fleischman's *Weslandia* features a young protagonist who doesn't accept traditional cultural expectations for summer fun. During summer vacation he decides to create a self-sufficient civilization in his backyard. The ordinary story is illustrated by Kevin Hawkes's paintings for a delightful science fantasy picturebook for younger children, who are encouraged to imagine a better world in the future. The illustrations in science fiction picturebooks need to be thoughtfully examined; they can add great sophistication to an otherwise simple and straightforward storyline. The picturebook format is particularly inviting to many artists, such as the accomplished David Wiesner, who artistically creates a fantastic imaginary world amongst the clouds in his wordless *Sector 7*. Children on a field trip to the top of the city discover the place where clouds are manufactured—a place where imagination begins. The young boy protagonist never sees clouds in quite the same way again. Wiesner's trademark embossed casing previews the underwater shapes that dominate the imagination of the unnamed protagonist. At the same time, the ocean life foreshadows a future Wiesner picturebook, *Flotsam*.

Science fiction for younger children blends imagination and impossibility along with a world based on what is known. This blend makes the picturebook format, with its exciting mix of techniques and styles, a delightful adventure for both adults and children.

INQUIRY POINT

Science fiction and science fantasy are sometimes criticized because they encourage imaginative flights that have no grounding in reality. By pairing books, a teacher can provide children with both an imaginative take on a problem and a more realistic one. Here are some pairings that offer examples of grounding fantasy stories in reality. In each pairing you select, read the fantasy picturebook first. Note your impressions. Then read the realistic fiction or nonfiction selection. Note the points and counterpoints. Think about how you might mediate fantasy with realism to encourage students to think about how writers' imaginative worlds might become real.

Pair Paul Fleischman's *Weslandia* with Jim LaMarche's serene summer adventure of self-discovery, family relationships, and appreciation for nature, *The Raft*.

Pair Paul Fleischman's *Weslandia* with *The Gardener*, written by Sarah Stewart and illustrated by David Small. What are the most striking similarities? What points of difference might motivate younger readers to take action and change their worlds as the children in these books do? Pair David Weisner's *Flotsam* with the Orbis Pictus and Boston Globe honor book, *Tracking Trash: Flotsam, Jetsam, and the Science of Ocean Motion*, by Loree Griffin Burns. The comparisons for these two books are very rich. What do you see? What actions might a reader take when leaving the realm of fantasy for parallels in our own world?

Pair the Wiesner picturebook, *Sector 7*, with young readers' *The Kids' Book of Clouds and Sky* by Frank Staub or Anne Rockwell's *Clouds* for younger readers. Or pair it with the biography *The Man Who Named the Clouds*, by Julie Hanna and Joan Holub.

Can you find other fantasy, science fantasy, and science fiction picturebooks that might be paired? ◉

Contemporary Fiction

Contemporary fiction
includes any work
of fiction that takes
place in modern
times.

Contemporary fiction includes any work of fiction that takes place in modern times. There are many kinds of contemporary fiction: mystery novels, novels centered on the lives of people involved in the animal world, novels in which there is a central problem to be solved, coming-of-age stories, and romances are the few subgenres we will focus on. These stories can center on contemporary topics such as sports, school, conservation, sibling rivalry, romance, or even world crises. Contemporary fiction includes fantasies as well, therefore the major category of realistic fiction will be considered separately from the category of contemporary fiction. What this means is that there will be some crossover between the subgenres. For the purposes of this handbook we will first look at two categories of contemporary fiction that have quite a bit of range in the degree to which they adhere to the conventions of fantasy or realism: mysteries and thrillers, and animal fiction.

Mysteries and Thrillers

Though mysteries, even adult mysteries, were once looked down on as a lower form of fiction, today's mystery writers are improving the genre, infusing it with playful, particular language, wit, and serious ideas. This genre includes the detective story and novels of crime, suspense, and espionage. It includes the thriller and the Gothic novel, with its connections to the ghost story and to horror. As for mysteries written for children, we have come quite a distance from the days when the only ones available were those about Nate the Great and Cam Jansen—child-as-detective series that are still being written, and are still much loved. Carl Hiassen's eco-mystery *Hoot*, in which Ray Eberhart finds friendship and mystery when he discovers a building company is threatening a group of owls, will appeal to many readers who enjoy a mystery that includes contemporary problems. Hiassen also wrote *Flush*, in which teenaged Noah Underwood discovers a sewage-spilling ship. In both, readers will be satisfied with a resolution that bodes well for the environment.

Neil Gaiman is a writer who has pushed the boundaries of the genre. His picturebook, *The Wolves in the Walls*, illustrated by Dave McKean, is truly creepy in the way it plays on normal fears of "things that go bump in the night" and the possibility of truth in strange noises in the walls. The popularity of his chapter book, *Coraline* (now both a film and a graphic novel), shows that children still thrill at being a little bit frightened by what they read. *The Graveyard Book* is a more complex thriller taking on not only the possibility of ghosts, but also of true interaction between the living and the dead in a graveyard setting. Unlike the other two Gaiman selections that leave the reader hanging a bit, this story leaves the reader surprisingly more satisfied if they prefer an upbeat resolution. *The Graveyard Book* is really a book about life, and the reader's qualms about the cast of characters are allayed.

Another writer who pushed the boundaries of the mystery genre is Virginia Hamilton. In her magnificent *Sweet Whispers, Brother Rush*, Teresa is a grieving girl with many responsibilities who meets and learns from a ghost. In Hamilton's *The*

House of Dies Drear, ghostly happenings encourage children to learn about the slave history of the house into which their family has moved. This example is important because books like this, though fictional (bordering on fantasy), can encourage readers not only to explore historical events but also to try new genres.

Plot carries most mysteries and thrillers, but Gaiman, Hiassen, Hamilton, and others have brought wit, humor, full characterization, and social commentary to the genre as well. The mood in mysteries is usually suspenseful, and the settings may include large houses with empty rooms, abandoned buildings, even graveyards. One of the literary elements mysteries traditionally use is **foreshadowing**—hints at what is to come—which those who read many mysteries use to help them predict possible outcomes.

Plot carries most mysteries and thrillers.

Animal Stories

Light fantasy is filled with animal characters that behave, think, and feel as humans do. These stories do work that is similar to the work done by traditional folktales of the talking beast variety. Animals stand in place of human characters in stories like "The Three Pigs" or "The Bremen Town Musicians." This technique assists the reader in internalizing the story's themes and coping with more serious issues underlying the story. When young children read *Charlotte's Web,* they enter into a world where they must confront the losses involved in growing up, the dangers of greed, and the inevitability of death. Confronting those issues is easier, perhaps, when animals stand in for human characters the young reader might identify too closely with.

However, some fiction for children focuses directly on real animal life: Farley Mowat is a master of realistic, animal-centered fiction; his *Owls in the Family* is a delightful read for adults as well as children. When reading this subgenre of realistic fiction, children can empathize with animals and learn about some of the difficult experiences and decisions people must make about the animals in their lives. In Bill Wallace's classic, *A Dog Called Kitty*, a frightened boy learns to love a scared dog; he later learns how to mourn for his dog as well. In her now classic *Shiloh* series, Phyllis Reynolds Naylor provides a moral drama about one boy's compassionate response to animal abuse. In the course of an adventure in **animal realism,** readers' transactions range freely between the aesthetic and the efferent—that is, the "lived through" experience of reading and the information-receiving experience of reading—when they identify with characters that care for pets as they do. Those same readers make discoveries about animals and their relationships to humans as they consider the story more closely.

In this subgenre it is essential that authors do not fall into anthropomorphism. The animals must behave as animals would in real life, without human thoughts and emotions being attributed to their actions in the story. In the previously mentioned *The Underneath* by Kathi Appelt, readers fully identify with the characters that are primarily animals in dire need. However, because the animals' thoughts and interactions drive the plot, they may need to remind themselves that the characters with whom they are identifying are animals. This should not be the case with animal realism. Theodore Taylor's classic *The Trouble with Tuck* features a dog whose blindness requires assistance from a guide dog. The book is all about Tuck, but the reader never doubts for a moment that this protagonist is an actual dog.

Jean Craighead George is a master of this genre: the animals she includes in her stories are believable, and the characters interact with them in believable ways. Known for the classic *My Side of the Mountain* (and its sequels), George has ventured into the picturebook format. *Cliff Hanger* is a great example of successfully integrating action and suspense into thirty-two pages of dramatic adventure. Grits, the dog, has wandered off and is stranded on a mountain trail as a dangerous summer storm approaches. Axel, a young boy, must use his rock climbing skills to execute the daring rescue. The illustrations are realistic and enhance the sense of danger for Axel and his dog. In this picturebook George succeeds in creating a dramatic look at rock climbing and the love of a boy for his dog.

Contemporary Realism

"With the exception of picturebooks," Shelia Egoff and Wendy Sutton wrote in 1996, "realistic fiction makes up the largest group of modern publications for the young."[5] In 2011, this still seems to be true, despite the increased publication of fantasy and science fiction works for children. **Contemporary realism** is the kind of fiction most of us are very familiar with—it is a fictional story set in a possible, believable world. There is no magic and there are no supernatural effects; the outcomes of the novel or picturebook are reasonable; the story is a representation of action that seems truthful. The picturebook format would be supported by a variety of illustrative styles and techniques, but they would reveal characters and actions that are possible. Realistic stories have in common several characteristics: they are fictional narratives with characters that are involved in some kind of realistic action that holds our interest, set in a place that is plausible for readers in today's world. Once again, keep in mind that by dividing realistic fiction into subgenres, the divisions frequently overlap.

> Realistic fiction is set in a possible, believable world.

Romance

The romance continues as a thriving subgenre of contemporary realistic fiction. If we define this genre broadly to mean any semi-realistic novel in which a central aspect is the romantic relationship of a young couple, we find many interesting examples of the romance in young adult literature. The genre contains quite a few series that could be called something other than literature—for example, the much loved and very influential *Twilight* series, the lively *Hotlanta* series, and the series interesting primarily for having been written entirely in instant-messaging shorthand, beginning with the novel *ttyl*.

However, thoughtful writers of the genre are creating complicated characters who confront the many difficulties of being a girl in our contemporary society. Sarah Dessen is one of the best of our contemporary young adult romance novelists. Her many novels describe young women facing realistic and nuanced problems with parents and friends and, sometimes, finding love: in *The Truth about Forever*, Macy Queen recovers from her father's sudden death and finds an artistic and insightful boyfriend along with a group of kooky friends; in *Just Listen*, a teen model meets an anger-management class dropout and gains insight about herself; in *Lock and Key*, Ruby, abandoned by both of her parents, learns to live with her wealthy sister and tries to help a neighbor who has big problems of his own; in *Dreamland,* Caitlin begins to understand why she allowed herself to be abused by her moody boyfriend Rogerson.

Three interesting young adult romance novels include Ellen Wittinger's *Hard Love* (which has a companion novel, *Love and Lies: Marisol's Story*), Gayle Forman's *If I Stay* (which has a sequel, *Where She Went*), and Nancy Werlin's ballad-based *Impossible.* Both *If I Stay* and *Impossible* can be considered blends of romance and fantasy. In *If I Stay* the main character hovers in a place between death and life for much of the novel; in *Impossible,* the main character must complete three impossible tasks in order to end the curse that has plunged all the women in her family into madness. In addition to introducing readers to a complex, counter-culture lesbian character and a thoughtful, J. D. Salinger–loving boy, *Hard Love* has graphic and intertextual elements that are unusual; it uses the phenomenon of teen zines as an important part of its plot.

Coming-of-Age Stories

Other realistic stories for children fall into the subgenre of the coming-of-age story. In this subgenre, as well, it is necessary for the writer to create a believable character who has enough awareness of self to learn about who he or she is and enough complexity to change and grow over the course of the story. In this kind of story character and its development are particularly important; we must see a movement in the understanding, courage, or sensitivity of the character. A few examples of coming-of-age stories may help readers see just how well written such a story can be.

A light, structurally complex example of a coming-of-age story is the delicate, whimsical, quietly humorous Newbery Award–winner *Criss-Cross* by Lynne Rae Perkins. This novel, set in the small town of Seldem, somewhere during the 1970s, is told from the perspectives of four friends who meet every week to sit in an old truck and listen to a funny radio show. It's the story of Hector, who wonders how he can show the girl he likes—is her name really Metal?—something new in this dull old town; Lenny, who understands mechanical objects like nobody else does and once read encyclopedias just for fun, but now chews tobacco; Patty, who helps Debbie write haikus, like "Jeff White is handsome/but his hair is so greasy/If he would wash it"; and most of all Debbie, who wishes something would happen.

For older readers, the masterful and highly acclaimed 1999 National Book Award Finalist, Laurie Halse Anderson's *Speak,* serves as a kind of coming-of-age story. In this young adult novel, the troubled character Melinda shares a sardonic take on high school life—its cliques and cruelties—that is funny, sad, and dead-on. Melinda has become an outcast, and as readers slowly learn why, they watch her take hold and wait with excitement and a sense of triumph as Melinda finally decides to speak. This is an excellent example of adult themes—the idea of female voice and silence is plentiful in adult feminist novels—trickling down into young adult and children's literature.

Laurie Halse Anderson's *Speak* can be considered a coming-of-age story.

An example of a coming-of-age story for younger readers is Susan Patron's thoughtful, cleverly written, and moving novel, *The Higher Power of Lucky.* In this novel Lucky Trimble, age ten, is trying to find her Higher Power. She learns about the Higher Power by listening to the "anonymous people" at Hard Pan's Found Object Wind Chime Museum and Visitor Center, where they tell their stories of hitting rock bottom. As Lucky thinks about these things, rides the bus with her friends Lincoln and Miles, and worries that her Guardian, the French Brigitte, will leave her, she grows in character—especially when a dust storm hits Hard Pan, she discovers how to accept the loss of her mother, and she gains inner strength as she saves the life of her young friend.

Two other young girls who come of age are the first-person narrator of Jacqueline Woodson's *After Tupac and D Foster* and her friend, Neeka, who lives across the street in a busy, churchy family. These two eleven-year-old best friends ache to be allowed to go off the street, but when they meet the new girl, D, whose mother allows her to "roam," they begin to change their minds. All of these girls love the music of Tupac Shakur, whose lyrics describe a life they know well, where one girl sees a relative sent to jail for doing something stupid and another watches a relative dream of becoming a basketball star. Delicately rendered and carefully nuanced, this short novel shows two young girls coming of age in a modern, urban environment

In some cases coming-of-age stories overlap with what we might call *family stories,* such as the long-loved tales of Ramona by Beverly Cleary, or novels like *Walk Two Moons* by Sharon Creech and *The Year Money Grew on Trees* by Aaron Hawkins. In cases in which these genres overlap, as in *The Higher Power of Lucky,* part of coming of age is learning to accept the family you have instead of worrying and dreaming about the family you once had or wish you had.

The characteristics of this subgenre make it difficult to accomplish within the confines of the picturebook format, but *Emily's Art* does so nicely. It is a wonderful example of a young child who grapples with her budding identity as an artist when her cherished picture is carelessly overlooked during the school art contest. In the space of thirty-two pages, Emily comes full circle as she moves from loss to introspection to a satisfying resolution that resonates fully. The illustrations provide the information necessary for the development of a round and evolving character and reveal aspects associated with coming-of-age fiction. Peter Catalanotto's watercolor illustrations enhance the plot by showing how Emily loses her aura of confidence, becomes small and transparent with a sense of loss, and is placed in the foreground, opaque and bright, as she regains her confidence.

Problem-Centered Stories

One subgenre of realistic fiction can be called problem-centered stories. Children in some problem-centered stories have troubles that are personal and particular: In *Eleven* by Patricia Reilly Giff, Sam has difficulty reading and needs to solve a mystery, the problem of his past; in Sharon Draper's *Out of My Mind* we see the development of a strong character who struggles from her wheelchair to be heard. Children in novels about personal and social issues show the character—usually the **protagonist,** or central character—encountering a problem shared by others. The central theme or issue is frequently related to societal injustices such as discrimination because of race, gender, disability, or social position. In these stories it is the protagonist's problem that is the source of plot and conflict, which may be with self, society, or another person. In the best realistic fiction, character and conflict are both well developed and interrelated.

While all elements are important in **realism,** we notice particularly the elements of theme, character, and conflict. In order to succeed, such fiction must assist readers to understand themselves as well as other children, the characters must be fully real- <span></span> ized, and conflicts must be believable.

Problem-centered stories are found more often in the young adult area than in books for younger children, and while some of these novels can be thin, with a too-clear focus on dramatic problems and simple solutions, there are many stand-out examples of this category of realistic fiction. Winner of a Printz Award, Carolyn Mackler's *The Earth, My Butt, and Other Big Round Things* centers about a young teen's struggle to solve problems stemming from her relationship with her mother, her weight, and the accusation of date rape attributed to her highly esteemed brother. Recent young adult novels like Adam Rapp's gritty tale of a boy's escape from a military school, *Punkzilla;* Francisco X. Stork's complex story about a boy with an Asperger-like condition, *Marcelo in the Real World*; and Laurie Halse Anderson's stark tale of a girl with an eating disorder, *Wintergirls*, all deepen and complicate the more traditional young adult problem-centered novel.

The Disreputable History of Frankie Landau-Banks was a National Book Award finalist in 2009, and with good reason. A problem-centered story of a completely different sort, this tale of suddenly beautiful Frankie's attempt to learn how to fall in love without losing herself will have female readers asking good questions about gender, power, and privilege. At her elite private school Alabaster Prep, Frankie is sought out by the popular and gorgeous senior Matthew, who belongs to the all-male Loyal Order of the Basset Hounds, of which her father once was a member. Forbidden to join or even discuss the club, Frankie joins by creating a fake identity and conducts a series of pranks against the group. Frankie is a fan of the humorist P. G. Wodehouse and revels in the wordplay of his novels; *The Disreputable History of Frankie Landau-Banks* is a satire of the lives and habits of the wealthy of the sort Wodehouse himself would approve.

Though this subgenre is typically associated with young adult readers, children can be introduced gently to contemporary problems. For example, Jacqueline Woodson's picturebook *Visiting Day* and Maria Testa's *Nine Candles* feature young characters facing the incarceration of a parent. Vera Williams's *Amber Was Brave, Essie Was Smart* develops the character of two young girls who face caring for themselves on a daily basis as a result of their father's incarceration for check forgery. This verse novel extends both the format and the problem subgenre into the realm of contemporary realism for younger readers. Similarly, Jacqueline Woodson's *Our Gracie Aunt* introduces young readers to the reality that many children care for themselves when a parent is unable to do so. In this story two children find a safe haven in family-based foster care with their loving Aunt Gracie. Mediated experiences with this subgenre prepare readers for more sophisticated stories on problems like incarceration, such as Walter Dean Myers's *Lockdown*.

In order to succeed, realistic fiction must help readers understand themselves and conflicts must be believable.

Historical Realism

Fictionalized stories of the past are considered somewhat differently from contemporary fiction. We will not separate historical fiction and historical realism; rather, we will consider this genre historical realism. This choice is based on the expectations for what can happen in a fictional story, and what can be expected from a story referred to as *realistic*. Historical fiction has always been a part of children's literature, but its importance has increased significantly in recent years. In 2008 the Newbery Medal, Caldecott Medal, and Coretta Scott King Awards were all awarded to historical fiction books. Excellent historical fiction perfects the art of combining an exciting story with historical fact.[6] The defining difference lies with the responsibility for historical accuracy and authenticity for the time and place.

Historical realism is placed in the past; the time and place determine setting. Details about transportation, technology, clothing, furnishings, and food preparation, for example, must fit the time and place of the story being told. Historical realism requires the same elements of a good story as contemporary realism, except much more attention must be given to the setting. Stories set in contemporary times feel more familiar to their readers; a great deal of description relating to the particulars of time and place may not be necessary for readers to appreciate the theme, plot, or characters. But this is not so with historical fiction.

Historical fiction is placed in the past; details fit time and place.

Distant in Time and Place

Historical realism contains a broad spectrum of topics; it is frequently organized around historical eras or important events from history. Stories from the earliest recorded histories to those very close to the present are found in this genre. Readers will benefit from exploring historical stories set in times and places we know little about. For example, *A Single Shard* by Linda Sue Park is a survival story from twelfth century Korea. A homeless boy struggles in his apprenticeship to a master potter at the same time as he strives to find a place for himself within a rigid social system. This Newbery Award–winning story features conflicts of self against others and self against society; it succeeds as a story at the same time it reveals details of attitudes and societal norms in ancient Korea.

Readers may be familiar with the more recent World War II era, but unaware of less well-known events such as the relationship between Japan and Korea at that time. A second example of a historical novel set in a distant time and place is *When My Name Was Keoko,* also by Linda Sue Park. This novel reveals aspects of Japan's harsh occupation of Korea through the eyes of ten-year-old Sun-Hee and her thirteen-year-old brother, Tae-Yul. The story's alternating first-person narration effectively tells this family's story from two perspectives and reveals the importance of gender in Korean society. The characters' responses to the occupation range from courage and resistance to strategic compliance necessary not only for survival, but also for preservation of their Korean identity. Keoko's story opens a door to aspects of World War II little known by children in the United States.

A third example of a historical novel set in a distant time and place is a powerful story told from a perspective not frequently heard in stories of the Vietnam War. Newbery Award–winner Cynthia Kadohata's simply written novel of Vietnam, *A Million Shades of Gray,* carefully introduces the reader to thirteen-year-old Y'Tin, a member of the Montgnard Rhade tribe, living with his family in his village in 1975 South Vietnam. All he has ever wanted to do with his life is to become an elephant handler and care for his elephant Lady until she is old. But when the North Vietnamese burn his village and he must hide in the jungle, he begins to question the foundations upon which his life was built. His father's wisdom, his loyalty to his friends—everything but his love of elephants—seems unclear. He makes courageous, but painful, decisions that he knows are right in a world where there is no black and white, only a million shades of gray. In the back of the novel, Cynthia Kadohata provides notes that help readers set this story in history.

Historical Eras and Settings

Historical realism is generally organized by historical eras; World War II, for example, represents an event that affected an entire decade and the years surrounding it. From events in the Pacific, to the European theatre, to stories set in the United States, children can learn about World War II through historical fiction. Younger readers may gain a better sense of this time period if it is set closer to the world they know. Multiple stories from this era that are set in the same region can provide a clearer historical and geographical understanding. For example, the Appalachian Mountain region has been a rich source of traditional stories of all kinds. Some readers might not associate this region as the setting for stories from the World War II era, but they can benefit from an introduction with the stories we share here.

Regional author Gloria Houston's picturebook, *But No Candy,* features the home front sacrifices associated with war-related rationing. In a region all too familiar with sharing scant resources, the shortages associated with war shape the growth of this story's main character. The illustrations authenticate the setting and create a mood that correlates well with both the story events and the historical setting. The wartime years in this region also featured bookmobiles traveling the remote rural roads to encourage reading, as depicted in *Miss Dorothy and Her Bookmobile.* Susan Condie Lamb's illustrations provide details that are not included in the short story of a librarian's dedication to the region. Ruth White's Appalachian story is set in Way Down Deep, West Virginia, at the close of World War II. *Way Down Deep* centers around an abandoned baby who is rescued and raised in a small mountain town whose traditions and the setting influence Ruby June as she decides what makes up a family. Another book by Ruth White, *Little Audrey,* is also set in post–World War II Appalachia, but this event does not drive its plot. Rather, the effects of poverty and illness associated with life in a Virginia coal mining camp determine the development of the main character and her actions. These stories exemplify the importance of setting the time and place: World War II was experienced uniquely in Appalachia, and many times regional concerns played a more important role than the era in which the stories were set. None of the historical stories would be exactly the same if they were set in another time or place; setting matters in historical fiction.

The integral setting in particular is important to historical fiction; in the case of stories from the era of the Great Depression it would show how the characters lived and how families supported themselves in difficult times. A 1930s era textset with varied geographical settings helps readers get a sense of the way the same historical event affected varied places both similarly and differently.

In the short but effective chapterbook *Wingwalker* by Rosemary Wells, the young narrator, Reuben, is afraid to fly on the Oklahoma Champion airplane, but he conquers his fears and flies. With people losing jobs all over the country, Reuben's father, a dance instructor, takes a job as a wingwalker at a Minnesota-based circus. Reuben enjoys meeting the people of the circus—Josephine the tattooed lady, Otto the fat man, and Dixie Belle herself, who flies the plane whose wings Reuben's father will walk on. At the end of the book, Reuben needs to conquer his fear again as his father

Themes of optimism, adaptability, and resilience are often associated with the Depression era. They are shared in Pam Muñoz Ryan's *Esperanza Rising* and Karen Hesse's verse novel *Out of the Dust*.

There are many other parallels between these two novels. Read each one with a partner or on your own. What connections do you see with elements of the setting?

Keep these two books in mind as you consider the other literary elements and genres in this handbook. ◉

*The historical accuracy of this story is more evident through pairing with other texts.[7]

invites him to come stand on the plane's wing as it flies over the Cumberland River, Tennessee, and the Great Smoky Mountains. The difficult times of this era forced many to do what they never considered possible. The sepia tones of Selznick's illustrations in *Wingwalker* reinforce the somber mood of the Dust Bowl years.

In picturebooks, the illustrations and design elements help set the story in time and place. In the simply told story *Potato: A Tale from the Great Depression* by Kate Lied, younger readers also discover how setting can be integral to the rest of the story. Lisa Ernst Campbell's brown tones achieve the effect of the constant grit endured during the Dust Bowl as a family travels from Iowa to Idaho for migrant work on a potato farm. The burlap border on the jacket ties the story to the potato farm so crucial to their survival; the family album style signals authenticity to younger readers.

Floyd Cooper's warm, textured artwork in *Tree of Hope,* by Amy Littlesugar, shows the changes the Depression brought to Harlem. Soft yellow and gold colors are used when Florrie thinks about the olden days, before the Depression, when her father was a full-time actor, working hard and with joy. Pages are painted in rich shades of brown when Florrie thinks about the times the Depression shadows her life. Famous director Orson Welles comes to create an all–African American production of Shakespeare's play *Macbeth* and Florrie's father is able to revive his love of acting alongside his job as a baker. Both time and place are integral to this powerful story.

Though *The Storyteller's Candle* by Lucia Gonzalez is set in 1929 New York, the effects of the Depression are not integral to the story. This story focuses on the dedicated work of librarian and storyteller Pura Belpre as she welcomes new Puerto Rican immigrants and shows them the importance of the library to their community. Here the setting but not time is integral to the story.

Format and Historical Fiction

Format is as varied with historical fiction as it is with other genres. *Out of the Dust* by Karen Hesse, from our inquiry point, successfully uses verse and white space to mimic the spare times of the Depression era in which it is set. The brevity of each chapter allows the reader time and space to handle the emotionally charged events in this story. The reader's flow is disrupted visually, so the changes in place do not really interrupt the reader's appreciation of this down-to-earth story. Matt Phelan's historical fiction graphic novel, *The Storm in the Barn*, blends a bit of folklore and thriller as it deals with a very real illness associated with the Dust Bowl: "dust dementia." The illustrations in *The Storm in the Barn* visually mimic the dust and wind, and the rise and fall of the story's tensions are revealed by the size and placement of the graphic panels.[8] Graphic novels are a recent addition to the historical fiction genre, but the idea of mixing genres is not. Some historical fiction involves the protagonist traveling back into history, as in Jane Yolen's classic

The Devil's Arithmetic, in which the main character moves back and forth through time and space to Nazi Germany. Patricia Polacco relies on this technique in a time-travel story of two boys transported during a trip to a Civil War museum to the battlefield at Antietam and back to learn about a time that is critical to United States history. The illustrations are critical to alerting the reader to the change in time and space.

The picturebook format allows younger readers to more fully understand the setting from history. The style and tone affect young readers' interpretations of time and place. *Finding Daddy,* by Jo and Josephine Harper and illustrated by Ron Mazellan, succeeds in depicting how the Great Depression affected one family; its design is more important than its qualities as a story. The paratextual features provide factual information about the Depression: its endpapers include a timeline, a glossary, and photographs from the era. It is the time rather than the specific place that matters in this story. These historical facts provide authenticity, but do not distract from the story. Well-written historical fiction often raises within the reader a question that begs to be answered: How much of this is true? Looking for information in paratextual features reassures readers.

"Telling a good story is the essence of historical fiction"[9] and varied paratextual features work together to create the possibility of a much better story than the verbal text could accomplish on its own. Talking with students about the relationship between the parts of a picturebook can be just as important as pairing books.

Authenticity in Historical Realism

Historical fiction requires authenticity, and that includes stories about the real problems people have faced throughout history. Realism and problem-centered stories now reflect societal problems previously considered "too risky" for younger readers. Recent trends toward more problem-centered historical stories are based on the interests and expectations of today's readers.

Similar to contemporary realism, historical realism can open the door to critical conversations about complicated topics, social issues, and traumatic events from history. James Damico and Laura Apol refer to these texts as "risky historical texts."[10] By risky texts, they mean historical fiction books that grapple with problems authentic to their historical contexts. Readers of all ages benefit from not being completely shielded from historical events that reveal, for example, injustice and inequity, violence, poverty, or catastrophe. Mildred Taylor's *Roll of Thunder, Hear My Cry* is a classic example of such a text set in the 1930s. This story of the Logan family opened the door for thoughtful discussions and introduced a full range of children's books that form a more complete picture of the Depression era through the eyes of people living in the segregated south. Another of Taylor's stories of the Logans from this era, *Mississippi Bridge,* is a powerful, disturbing tale of racism in segregated Mississippi told through the eyes of a ten-year-old boy who aspires to befriend the Logan children. The tenet that historical fiction stories should be written so realistically that readers feel they have traveled to a place of long ago should sometimes be met with caution when immersion into the authentic historical detail of "risky historical texts" is considered. As with other genres, older readers may be better suited for these stories.

We may not be aware of the horseback riders throughout isolated areas of Appalachian region during the Great Depression. *That Book Woman,* by Heather

Historical fiction today is more problem-centered than it was in the past.

Henson and illustrated by David Small, presents an episode from the work of the courageous Pack Horse Librarians during the Great Depression. *When the Whippoorwill Calls* by Candice F. Ransom shares one story of families displaced from their homes in Appalachia during Roosevelt's creation of the Shenandoah National Park during the Depression era. Both stories provide a solid author's note that creates realism through authenticity.

Because language should be appropriate to the time, current slang or contemporary terms would be out of place in historical realism. Readers would expect stories from Appalachia to include dialect appropriate to that setting. The language may be revealed through characters' speech patterns, through the narrator, or through the language of cultural elements such as the song lyrics included in *Finding Daddy*. Mildred Taylor considers the importance of language in *The Friendship* when the characters' dialogue harshly reveals the racism in parts of the South in the 1930s. The tone of courage, resistance, and peer pressure can stand up to strong language in this tale, but it would be less fitting to the tone of Taylor's *Song of the Trees*, which features a younger girl's efforts to save the family's grove. Pairing Taylor's *The Friendship* and *Song of the Trees* would encourage discussion and perhaps encourage additional reading about the civil rights movement that gained momentum in the 1950s and 1960s.

What can be confusing for both adult and younger readers is determining whether certain stories should be considered historical or contemporary realism. Tunnell and Jacobs discuss whether a contemporary novel becomes historical fiction with the passage of time.[11] We feel the tenet for historical facts to be correct and true can override the importance of a good story in historical fiction. Stories written as contemporary fiction would not be written with the same detail for setting, for example, emphasizing the story instead. Expectations for paratextual features such as author's notes, glossaries, or back matter that provide historical background would be missing. A story written in the 1950s for readers of that time, such as Eleanor Estes's *The Hundred Dresses*, would reflect the language and cultural attitudes of the time, but those same cultural beliefs may make the story less inviting for modern readers without some kind of mediation. This story can still spark excellent discussions of attitudes toward immigration, social class, and gender roles, and we believe that this classic story has merit for this reason. It is a good story, but its historical merit would be revealed in combination with other books of related theme, setting, and issues. A good story written in an earlier time does not become historical realism, but it can inform readers about history from the genre it represented originally.

Matters that not long ago were recent events become the materials of a historical period. For example, Mildred Taylor could show with increased objectivity the events of the Great Depression as she did with *Roll of Thunder, Hear My Cry* in 1976.

text continues on page 101

INQUIRY POINT

Select a decade or an era from history. Identify an event or topic associated with that time period that is of importance to you or of particular current interest. Find recently published historical fiction children's books. Try to include novels, picturebooks, verse novels, and graphic novels if possible. How well were you able to fully represent your topic? Which other genres would help you create a more complete picture? ◉

TEXTSET

The Holocaust Across Genres

This textset is a collection of books on a topic of importance. Its value is best realized by creating a solid context of children's books across genres. There are many combinations that would work for this textset, but we find these titles to be particularly worthy. You will encounter each genre within this handbook. Certain texts are marked with an asterisk* to emphasize new formats: picturebooks that were created for a specific audience, genre blends, verse novels, and graphic formats.

This textset suggests books that tell some of the many stories that have come out of the period of genocide we now call the Holocaust. Many middle schoolers read *The Diary of Anne Frank* or Elie Wiesel's classic *Night*. Perhaps because of the success of these classics, and because they provide only a limited view of the reverberations caused by Hitler's attempted extermination of the Jews, many writers and artists have created books that look at the events in different ways. First, in the textset below, we list books related to Anne Frank. From there we list children's books focusing on different aspects of the Holocaust.

Anne Frank

*Jacobson, Sid, and Earnie Colón. *The Anne Frank House Authorized Graphic Biography*. Hill and Wang, 2010.

Traces the history of Anne Frank's immediate family. Graphics and narrative are intermixed with historical background and details about the Franks and their household. An important graphic novel.

*Johnson, Phyllis. *Being Frank with Anne*. Community Press, 2007.

Poetic reflections in the voice of Anne Frank provide a useful text for students to read alongside the diary.

*Suzuki, Etsuo, and Yoko Miyawaki. *Anne Frank*. Digital Manga Publishing, 2006.

In this mixed-genre graphic novel, Astro Boy and his sister Uran visit Kobe, Japan, with their friend the professor, who tells them the story of the life of Anne Frank and shows them Nishinomiya Anne's Rose Church, which has been built in her memory.

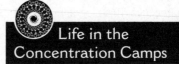

Life in the Concentration Camps

Both before and after children learn about Anne Frank, they may have questions about the concentration camps. Many people wonder if it is appropriate to try to explain the story of Hitler and the Holocaust to children, but others say that if children don't hear about this time period early in their lives, or only read the abridged version of Frank's diary that can be found in most textbooks, they will never understand the whole story. Others worry that the stories will be lost as survivors and soldiers of World War II die. One way people can more comfortably share stories of the Holocaust with children is to focus on the experiences of children who lived through that time.

*Rubin, Susan Goldman. *The Cat with the Yellow Star*. Holiday House, 2006.

This mixed-genre book tells the story of one girl, Ela Weissberger, who played the cat in the Terezin opera of *Brundibar*. Full of photographs of the people and paintings by the children of Terezin as well as health records, postcards, and other documents, this book provides good context for the picturebook *Brundibar*.

(continued)

*Sendak, Maurice, and Tony Kushner. *Brundibar*. Hyperion Books for Children, 2003.

In 2003, Maurice Sendak and the playwright Tony Kushner together created a picturebook, not necessarily for children, telling the story of the opera performed by Jewish children at Terezin.

 People Who Helped

Adler, David A. *A Hero and the Holocaust*. Holiday House, 2002.

The story of Janusz Korczak, a doctor and orphanage director who cared for thousands of children before dying in Treblinka. This biography can be paired with Bogadaki's *The Champion of the Children*, also about Korczak.

*Frederick, Luba Tryszynska. *Luba: The Angel of Bergen-Belsen*. Triangle Press, 2003.

The true tale of a woman in the German death camps who hid and helped fifty-two children survive the war. This picturebook biography includes luminous oil and collage art.

*Hesse, Karen. *The Cats in Krasinski Square*. Scholastic, 2004.

A simple tale of Jewish resistance in Poland, in poetry and pictures.

*Rubin, Susan Goldman. *The Flag with Fifty Six Stars: A Gift from the Survivors of Mauthausen*. Holiday House, 2006.

The nonfiction picturebook story of inmates of Mauthausen, an Austrian camp, who created an American flag to present to the soldiers who freed them.

*Vander Zee, Ruth. *Erika's Story*. Creative Education, 2003.

A picturebook of historical fiction in which the pictures tell much more than the story told by the text. Note that the star on the cover is not a Star of David.

 Others Who Helped

*Innocenti, Roberto, and Christophe Gallas. *Rose Blanche*. Creative Edition, 1985.

Tender fiction story of a young girl in a Nazi-occupied town in Europe. Illustrations gradually darken as the Nazis gain control. Colors brighten with the arrival of liberation forces, but the ending might be too powerful for younger readers.

*Mochizuki, Ken. *Passage to Freedom: The Sugihara Story*. Lee and Low, 2003.

The true tale of a Japanese diplomat who saved hundreds of Jewish lives.

*Ruelle, Karen Gray, and Deborah Desaix. *The Grand Mosque of Paris: A Story of How Muslims Rescued Jews During the Holocaust*. New York: Holiday House, 2010.

"Save one life and it as if you have saved all of humanity." Many Jewish lives were saved when Muslims encouraged adults and children about to be taken by the Nazis to hide in the grand mosque of Paris; this nonfiction picturebook tells the tale.

*Yolen, Jane. *Briar Rose*. Tor, 1992.

This book tells two stories—one fiction, of Becca's search for the truth behind her grandmother's telling of the Briar Rose story and one nonfiction, the true tale of a Polish nobleman who fought the Nazis.

*Zusak, Mark. *The Book Thief*. Knopf, 2006.

This unforgettable young adult novel about two thirteen-year-olds living in Germany during Hitler's rise to power is a multiple award winner. The book is told from the perspective of Death (personified), who reveals empathy as "he" narrates this story.

 Hiding and Surviving

*Engle, Margarita. *Tropical Secrets: Holocaust Refugees in Cuba*. Henry Holt, 2009.

This beautiful verse novel is told in poetry and in two voices: the voice of thirteen-year-old

Jewish Daniel, who has migrated to Cuba after Kristallnacht, and Cuban Paloma, who helps him hide a Jew suspected of spying.

*Krinitz, Esther, and Bernice Steinhardt. *Memories of Survival.* **Hyperion, 2005.**

Through beautiful embroidery artwork this survivor of the camps tells the story of her life to her daughter, who provides more details alongside the notes her mother wrote. This memoir of how fifteen-year-old Esther and her thirteen-year-old sister hid themselves in forests and homes is told in through the daughter's voice, the mother's voice, and art.

*LeZotte, Ann Clair. *T-4: A Novel in Verse.* **Houghton Mifflin, 2008.**

This novel in verse tells the story of Paula, a thirteen-year-old deaf girl who must hide because all people with disabilities are slated for death by the Nazis.

*Ruby, Lois. *Shanghai Shadows.* **Holiday House, 2006.**

Novel in which Austrian Ilsa spends her teen years as a Jewish refugee in Japanese-occupied Shanghai.

*Wiviott, Meg. *Benno and the Night of Broken Glass.* **Kar-Ben Publishing, 2010.**

Beautiful picturebook about a cat hiding during the night of broken glass.

It can be difficult to see the times and places of our past as historical. Adults growing up in the 1970s might respond to stories like Jacqueline Woodson's *Feathers* as problem-centered contemporary realism! However, contemporary children will clearly view the same novel as historical, set in the 1970s. Some current adult readers will resist considering stories centering about 9/11 as historical fiction. The actual event has passed, but the aftereffects still surround us daily. The line is not always clear when issues in a historical fiction story have not yet been fully resolved.

SUMMARY

Awareness of the similarities and differences in the genres of children's literature can be useful. Perhaps the most obvious and important thing to realize is that not all books or all genres appeal to all children. However, a child hooked on one genre—science fiction, for example—may find the craving for adventure is further satisfied through sports or other realistic stories. Curiosity about imaginatively created worlds may lead the reader to find pleasure in another closely related genre, such as high fantasy. Expansion of the young reader's world results as the reader finds new styles of writing, broader themes, and other motivations in characters with varied experiences. Greater appreciation of self and of other humans and their societies results as such vicarious experiences grow in number.

Table 4.1 summarizes similarities and differences in the genres. It may prove helpful, but only if we keep in mind the dangers of generalizing. Literature, since it is not so easily classified as the chemical elements, will often be elusive, refusing to fit neatly into a genre. The table may, however, serve as a reminder of the tremendous breadth of literature available to children for their joy, pleasure, and increased understanding.

TABLE 4.1 Genre in Children's Literature

FICTIONAL GENRES

GENRE	EXAMPLES	CHARACTER	PLOT	SETTING	THEME	POINT OF VIEW	STYLE	TONE
CONTEMPORARY FICTION/ REALISM	*Hatchet* *After Tupac and D Foster* *Locomotion* *A Couple of Boys Have the Best Week Ever* *Visiting Day* *The Tricycle*	Best novels have round central characters; poor ones load protagonist with problems or have flat or stereotyped characters	Any kind of conflict, but if problem is solved too easily, story is flawed Increased use of nonlinear plots	Any: Integral is most effective, but background can be used with character stories such as *Mirror* or *Shadow*	Any, but sentimentality, sensationalism, didacticism are flaws[1]	Any: Increasing use of first-person point of view; multiple points of view as in *The Misfits*	Uses all devices: May use interesting ways to narrate, such as tape recordings in *Thirteen Reasons Why*	Any, but sentimentality or sensationalism are flaws[1]
ANIMAL FICTION/ REALISM	*The Underneath* *Me and You* *Wabi Sabi* *The Trouble with Tuck* *Cliff Hanger*	Realistic portrayal of animals, without personification Fantasy stories can blend fiction and fact, as with *Wabi Sabi*, or be personified	Conflict is usually animal versus nature Fantasy animal stories can have any plot style	Usually integral[1]	Usually related to some discovery about animals or their relationships to humans	Objective in respect to the animal character; human characters may be shown in other points of view[1]	Uses all devices	Any, but if point of view falters, tone may become sentimental[1]
MYSTERIES	*Coraline* *Hoot* *Nate the Great* *Woolvs in the Sitee*	Well developed, but storyline is more important	Usually carries story, some coincidence	Any; often spooky but must be believable	Any	Any; can involve flashback	Uses all devices but dropping clues and foreshadowing are important	Mysterious or questioning
COMING-OF-AGE/ FAMILY STORIES	*Wringer* *The Higher Power of Lucky* *Amber Was Brave, Essie Was Smart* *The Pecan Pie Baby*	Realistic	Any conflict, often self against others or self against self or society	Any, but should be in recognizable place Needs less description if in familiar place	Often personal growth and family relationshps	Any: Likely to be in first person	Uses all devices: Dramatic point of view might include camera, such as with *Monster*	Any, but should match the story being told Can be humorous

	Titles	Characters	Conflict	Setting	Theme	Point of View	Style/Devices	Tone
ROMANTIC STORIES	Just Listen Along for the Ride If I Stay	Realistic	Boy-meets-girl	Any	Sometimes "Love conquers all"; sometimes "Be yourself"	Any	Uses all devices	Any
HISTORICAL REALISM	The Evolution of Calpurnia Tate A Million Shades of Gray The Storyteller's Candle Henry's Freedom Box	Protagonist has universal human traits, but is a product of the time and place[1]	Any, but conflict more often person versus society or self, as well as another person	Integral setting with focus on particular time and place, often time of stress, crisis, or of social, political change In picturebook format, illustrations will reveal setting	Any universal theme, but matches historical period; for example, hopeful during Depression or patriotic during war	Any, but first person is less likely unless it is autobiographical	Uses all devices: Relies on accurate descriptions of place, cultural artifacts, and activities for credibility	Avoids presenting past sentimentally or sensationally[1]
FANTASY								
HIGH FANTASY	Harry Potter and the Sorcerer's Stone A Wrinkle in Time When You Reach Me	Realistically portrayed	Any, but underlying conflict is good versus evil	Often special worlds and integral settings where time and place have qualities of expansion or limitation	Universal, important themes of good and evil in conflict	Any	Usually highly sensory; may be series format	Serious, awed
FANTASTIC STORIES	Charlotte's Web Savvy; The Underneath Imagine a Day Imagine a Night	Like or unlike humans; includes magical qualities and personified toys, animals, or objects	Any kind of conflict, but must be detailed enough to suspend disbelief	Believable world with some fantastic qualities	Any	Any	Any: May combine with other genres	Any: Often humorous but can soften serious tones or issues for younger readers
SCIENCE FICTION	The Hunger Games The Giver Feed The Water Tower Westlandia	Well-developed central characters[1]	Any: Often mechanical or natural forces are antagonists Plots usually progressive and suspenseful	Setting is detailed and believable; distinctive; set in future societies or in unexplored worlds	May be subtle, implicit	Any	All devices: Often much description in concrete forms	Often objective, but flawed story may be heavily didactic

(continued)

TABLE 4.1 *(continued)*

TRADITIONAL TALES

GENRE	EXAMPLES	CHARACTER	PLOT	SETTING	THEME	POINT OF VIEW	STYLE	TONE
FABLE	"The Boy Who Cried Wolf" "The Sun and the Wind"	Flat and stock; often personified animals with single traits	Person-versus-person conflict; extremely brief; usually a single incident[1]	Backdrop	Explicit and didactic	Objective or dramatic	Terse, lacking imagery or connotative language	Straightforward, didactic, and moralizing
FOLKTALE	"Cinderella" "Jack and the Beanstalk"	Flat protagonist; bad and good characters easily identified; stock characters like the wicked stepmother or fairy godmother	Person-versus-person or person-versus-nature conflicts personified Action moves rapidly to a climax and stock closing	Backdrop setting: "Long ago and far away . . ."	Either implicit or explicit Often strongly focused on justice	Usually omniscient or limited omniscient	A few recurring images; often short verses and cadenced prose[1]	Varied: May be sentimental, humorous, objective, but is not often didactic
MYTH	"Apollo's Sun Chariot" "How Fire Came to Earth People"	Gods and heroes with traits linked to supernatural powers	An incident or incidents linked by character	Backdrop: "Long ago in ancient China . . ."	Explanations of natural phenomena or human relationships	Usually objective	Significant symbols, abstract terms, little or no dialogue, brief descriptions of action	Dignified, perhaps mystical Sentimentality is a flaw
LEGEND OR HERO TALE	"King Arthur" "Robin Hood"	Historical figures with fictional traits and situations	Any conflict featuring protagonists	Backdrop: "When Arthur was King . . ."	Fictional glorification of historical figures	Usually objective	Significant symbols, abstract terms, little or no dialogue, brief descriptions of action	Often objective Sentimentality is a flaw

FOLK EPIC	Beowulf Finn MacCool	Protagonist is heroic, superhuman	Begins in the middle of conflict, which is person versus person, society, or nature Often three incidents Hero is victorious against supreme odds[1]	Undefined long-ago, but set in the vast world or universe	Good victorious over evil, after great struggle against superhuman odds and with assistance from gods[1]	Objective or dramatic	Long, cadenced lines of oral language; symbols and images; grandeur and simplicity; epic similes; elaborate comparisons; extended formal speeches	Dignified, grand, awesome

RHYME TO POETRY

GENRE	EXAMPLES	FORM OR FOCUS	RHYTHM	RHYME	DEVICES
NURSERY RHYMES	Mother Goose	Topics open to young children; usually brief; any tone; folk in origin	Regular	Regular	Personification, simile, metaphor, and others
VERSE	Once Upon a Tomb; Gravely Humorous Verses Out of the Dust Love That Dog	Easily understood; for specific purpose; meaning less important than form; often trite, banal in form; phrasing	Highly rhythmic; rhythm often more important than meaning	Usually regular in scheme but can be free verse Any form; novel can be written in verse	Often ordinary images, predictable; less emotion, imagination, intensity than poetry
NARRATIVE POETRY	The Night Before Christmas Dark Emperor and Other Poems of the Night	Storytelling, long or short	Suited to story		Any, though fewer than in lyrics

(continued)

TABLE 4.1 *(continued)*

RHYME TO POETRY

GENRE	EXAMPLES	FORM OR FOCUS	RHYTHM	RHYME	DEVICES
BALLAD OR FOLK BALLAD (UNKNOWN AUTHOR)	"John Henry"	Narrative of physical courage; incidents in lives of common people; supernatural; largely dialogue; little characterization; great simplicity; refrains, often incremental; abrupt transitions; single dramatic episode	Great variation, but usually lines 1 and 3 have four accented syllables, lines 2 and 4, three unaccented syllables; variations in number of unstressed syllables	Refrain often used; usually *abcb* rhyme; approximate rhyme very common	Any (See "Form or Focus")
LYRIC OR PERSONAL POETRY	*Morning Has Broken*	Brief, subjective; personal emotional response; single unified impression; "An end in itself"; intense, compact	Suited to topic and emotion evoked	Rhymed or unrhymed	All figurative and sound devices used to produce compactness
SPECIAL POETRY FORMS	*Meow, Ruff! Doodle Dandies*	Concrete poetry, shape poetry, list poetry	Rhythm less important than concept	Generally unrhymed	Integrates graphics: Words become pictures and vice versa

NONFICTION

GENRE	EXAMPLES	ESSENTIAL QUALITIES	ORGANIZATION AND SCOPE	STYLE	TONE	ILLUSTRATIONS
INFORMATIONAL BOOKS	*Christmas in the Big House, Christmas in the Quarters*	Gives information and facts; relates facts to concept; stimulates curiosity; "starter," not "stopper"	From simplest to most complex; from known to unknown; from familiar to unfamiliar; from early developments to later; chronological; may be narrative for younger reader	Imagery, figurative language, all devices; comparisons very useful	Wonder, not mystery; respect; objectivity, occasional humor; fostering scientific attitude of inquiry Flaws include condescension, anthropomorphism, oversimplification, and facts not separated from opinions[1]	Diagrams and drawings often clearer than photographs
BIOGRAPHY	*Charles and Emma* *The Wall* *A River of Words;* *Eleanor: Quiet No More*	Gives accurate, verifiable facts and authentic picture of period; subject worthy of attention; sources of information shown or listed	Assumes no omniscience; shows individual, not stereotype; does not ignore negative qualities of subject; focuses not only on events, but also on nature of person, can be chronological or episodic	Storytelling permissible for youngest readers; too much fictionalizing destroys credibility	Interest; enthusiasm; objectivity Some interpretation is present but should be made transparent	Authentic, any style but frequently incorporates photography, realistic artistic styles

[1]Represents elements that have special importance in a genre, or elements that are frequently sources of inadequacy in a work.

NOTES

1. Lawrence Sipe, *Storytime: Young Children's Literary Understanding in the Classroom* (New York: Teachers College Press, 2008), p. 81.

2. Perry Nodelman, "Some Presumptuous Generalizations about Fantasy," in *Only Connect: Readings on Children's Literature* (New York: Oxford University Press, 1996), p. 175.

3. Jane Yolen, "Turtles All the Way Down," in *Only Connect* (New York: Oxford University Press, 1996), pp. 164–178.

4. William Sleater, "What Is It about Science Fiction?" in *Only Connect* (New York: Oxford University Press, 1996), pp. 206–213.

5. Sheila Egoff and Wendy Sutton, "Some Thoughts on Connecting," *Only Connect: Readings on Children's Literature,* edited by Sheila Egoff, Gordon Stubbs, and Ralph Ashley (New York: Oxford University Press, 1996), p. 378.

6. Mary Taylor Rycik and Brenda Rosler, "The Return of Historical Fiction," *The Reading Teacher,* 63(2), 2009, pp. 163–166.

7. In this section, we do not share the nonfiction selections for children that would ground these fictional stories. Some of the award winning nonfiction we recommend are Jerry Stanley, *Children of the Dust Bowl: The True Story of the School at Weedpatch Camp* (Knopf, 1992); Russell Freedman, *Children of the Great Depression* (Clarion, 2005); Martin W. Sander, *The Dust Bowl Through the Lens: How Photography Revealed and Helped Solve a National Disaster* (Walker Books, 2009); Sara Goodman Zimet, *Hannah and the Perfect Picture Pony: A Story of the Great Depression,* illustrated by Sandy Ferguson Fuller (Denver, CO: Discovery Press Publications, 2005).

8. Margaret Rudiger Hollis, "Reading Lessons: Graphic Novels 101," *Horn Book Magazine,* March/April 2006, pp. 126–134. This very readable article provides a clear and concise description of the way graphic novels reveal the plot and the importance of particular events as well as the tempo of the story.

9. An additional source for the qualities associated with good historical fiction is Michael O. Tunnell and James S. Jacobs, *Children's Literature, Briefly* (Upper Saddle River, NJ: Merrill, 2000). We rely on some of their comments in this section.

10. James Damico and Laura Apol, "Using Testimonial Response to Frame the Challenges and Possibilities of Risky Historical Texts," *Children's Literature in Education,* 39, 2008, pp. 141–158. These authors advocate not only the use of "risky historical texts" but also stories that have been framed as personal testimonials to encourage readers to relate to stories set in the past and to respond with a problem-solving stance.

11. Michael O. Tunnell and James S. Jacobs, *Children's Literature, Briefly* (Upper Saddle River, NJ: Merrill, 2000).

RECOMMENDED BOOKS

AARDEMA, VERNA. *Why Mosquitoes Buzz in People's Ears.* Puffin/Dial, 2004.

ADLER, DAVID. *Chanukah in Chelm.* HarperCollins Publishers, 1997.

AESOP. *The Tortoise and the Hare.* Illustrated by Janet Stevens. Holiday House, 1884.

AHLBERG, ALLAN. *The Jolly Postman or Other People's Letters.* Illustrated by Janet Ahlberg. LB Kids, 2001.

ANDERSON, LAURIE HALSE. *Speak.* Penguin, 1999.

ANDERSON, LAURIE HALSE. *Wintergirls.* Speak, 2010.

APPELT, KATHI. *The Underneath.* Atheneum, 2009.

ARTELL, MIKE. *Petite Rouge: A Cajun Red Riding Hood.* Dial, 1997.

BABBITT, NATALIE. *Tuck Everlasting.* Farrar, Straus & Giroux, 1988.

BLACKMAN, MALORIE. *Naughts and Crosses.* Nick Hern Books, 2008.

BLOOR, EDWARD. *Tangerine.* Harcourt Children's Books, 2007.

BOND, VICTORIA & T. R. SIMON. *Zora and Me.* Candlewick Press, 2010.

BROWNE, ANTHONY. *Into the Forest.* Walker Children's Paperbacks, 2005.

BROWNE, ANTHONY. *Me and You.* Farrar, Straus & Giroux, 2010.

BROWNE, ANTHONY. *The Tunnel.* Walker Children's Books, 2008.

BRUCHAC, JOSEPH. *Keepers of the Earth.* Fulcrum Publishing, 1997.

BURNS, LOREE GRIFFIN. *Tracking Trash: Flotsam, Jetsam, and the Science of Ocean Motion.* Sandpiper, 2010.

CANNON, JANELL. *StellaLuna.* Harcourt Children's Books, 1993.

CATALONOTTO, PETER. *Emily's Art.* Atheneum, 2001.

CLEARY, BEVERLY. *The Mouse and the Motorcycle.* HarperCollins Children's Books, 1990.

COLLINS, SUZANNE. *The Hunger Games.* Scholastic, 2008.

COOPER, MICHAEL. *Dust to Eat.* Clarion, 2004.

CREECH, SHARON. *Walk Two Moons.* HarperTeen, 2003.

DAHL, ROALD. *The BFG.* Puffin, 2007.

DALY, NIKI. *Pretty Salma: A Little Red Riding Hood Story from Africa.* Clarion, 2007.

DAVIS, AMANDA. *Wonder When You'll Miss Me.* HarperCollins, 2003.

DESSEN, SARAH. *Dreamland.* Speak, 2004.

DESSEN, SARAH. *Just Listen.* Speak, 2008.

DESSEN, SARAH. *Lock and Key.* Speak, 2009.

DESSEN, SARAH. *The Truth about Forever.* Speak, 2006.

DICAMILLO, KATE. *The Tale of Despereaux.* Candlewick, 2006.

DRAPER, SHARON. *Out of My Mind.* Atheneum, 2010.

EISNER, WILL. *The Princess and the Frog.* Nantier Beall Minoustchine, 2003.

ESTES, ELEANOR. *The Hundred Dresses.* Sandpiper, 2004.

FARMER, NANCY. *The Ear, the Eye, and the Arm.* Firebird, 2006.

FLEISCHMAN, PAUL. *Weslandia,* Candlewick, 2002.

FOREST, HEATHER. *The Contest Between the Sun and the Wind.* Illustrated by Susan Gaber. August House, 2008.

FORMAN, GAYLE. *If I Stay.* Speak, 2010.

FORMAN, GAYLE. *Where She Went.* Dutton, 2011.

FRANK, ANNE. *The Diary of Anne Frank.* Doubleday, 1991.

FRENCH, FIONA. *Snow White in New York.* Oxford University Press, 1990.

GAIMAN, NEIL. *Coraline.* HarperCollins, 2002.

GAIMAN, NEIL. *The Graveyard Book.* HarperCollins, 2010.

GAIMAN, NEIL. *The Wolves in the Walls.* Illustrated by Dave McKean. HarperCollins, 2005.

GEORGE, JEAN CRAIGHEAD. *Cliff Hanger.* Illustrated by Wendall Minor. HarperCollins, 2002.

GEORGE, JEAN CRAIGHEAD. *My Side of the Mountain.* Puffin, 2004.

GIFF, PATRICIA REILLY. *Eleven.* Yearling, 2009.

GIFF, PATRICIA REILLY. *Pictures of Hollis Woods.* Yearling, 2004.

GONZALEZ, LUCIA. *The Storyteller's Candle.* Illustrated by Lulu Delacre. Children's Book Press, 2008.

HAMILTON, VIRGINIA. *Her Stories: African American Folktales, Fairy Tales, and True Tales.* Blue Sky Press, 1995.

HAMILTON, VIRGINIA. *The House of Dies Drear.* Aladdin, 2006.

HAMILTON, VIRGINIA. *In the Beginning: Creation Stories from Around the World.* Harcourt, 1988.

HAMILTON, VIRGINIA. *Sweet Whispers, Brother Rush.* Putnam, 1982.

HARPER, JO AND JOSEPHINE. *Finding Daddy.* Illustrated by Ron Mazellan. Turtle Press, 2005.

HAWKINS, AARON. *The Year Money Grew on Trees.* Houghton Mifflin, 2010.

HENSON, HEATHER. *That Book Woman.* Illustrated by David Small. Simon & Schuster, 2008.

HESSE, KAREN. *Out of the Dust.* Scholastic, 1997.

HIASSEN, CARL. *Flush.* Yearling, 2010.

HIASSEN, CARL. *Hoot.* Yearling, 2005.

HOUSTON, GLORIA. *But No Candy.* Illustrated by Lloyd Bloom. Philomel, 1992.

HOUSTON, GLORIA. *Miss Dorothy and Her Bookmobile.* Illustrated by Susan Condie Lamb. HarperCollins, 2010.

HUGHES, TED. *The Iron Giant.* Harper & Row, 1988.

ISAACS, ANNE. *Swamp Angel.* Illustrated by Paul O. Zelinsky. Dutton, 1994.

JACKSON, ELLEN. *Cinder Edna.* HarperCollins, 1998.

KADOHATA, CYNTHIA. *A Million Shades of Gray.* Atheneum, 2010.

KING-SMITH, DICK. *Harry's Mad.* Yearling, 1997.

KORMAN, GORDON. *Nosepickers from Outer Space.* Hyperion, 1990.

LAMARCHE, JIM. *The Raft.* HarperCollins, 2002.

LAW, INGRID. *Savvy.* Puffin, 2010.

LEGUIN, URSULA. *Tombs of Atuan.* Pocket, 1970.

L'ENGLE, MADELEINE. *A Wrinkle in Time.* Farrar, 1962.

LESTER, JULIUS. *John Henry.* Illustrated by Jerry Pinkney. Dial, 1994.

LIED, KATE. *Potato: A Tale from the Great Depression.* Illustrated by Lisa Ernst Campbell. National Geographic, 1997.

LITTLESUGAR, AMY. *Tree of Hope.* Illustrated by Floyd Cooper. Philomel Books, 1999.

LOBEL, ARNOLD. *Fables.* HarperCollins, 1980.

LOCKHART, E. *The Disreputable History of Frankie Landau-Banks.* Hyperion, 2009.

LOWRY, LOIS. *The Giver.* Delacort, 2006.

MACKLER, CAROLYN. *The Earth, My Butt, and Other Big Round Things.* Candlewick, 2005.

MANDELA, NELSON. *Nelson Mandela's Favorite African Folktales.* WW Norton, 2007.

MINTERS, FRANCES. *Sleepless Beauty.* Scholastic, 2001.

MORA, PAT. *Dona Flor: A Tall Tale about a Giant Woman with a Great Big Heart.* Knopf, 2005.

MORRIS, GERALD. *The Legend of the King.* Houghton Mifflin, 2010.

MOSES, BARRY. *Tucker Pfeffercorn.* Little, Brown, 1994.

MOWAT, FARLEY. *Owls in the Family.* Yearling, 1996.

MYERS, WALTER DEAN. *Lockdown.* Amistad, 2010.

NAYLOR, PHYLLIS REYNOLDS. *Shiloh*. Atheneum, 2000.

NORTON, MARY. *The Borrowers*. Harcourt, 1965.

OPPEL, KENNETH. *Silverwing*. Simon &Schuster, 1997.

PARK, LINDA SUE. *A Single Shard*. Sandpiper, 2011.

PARK, LINDA SUE. *When My Name Was Keoko*. Yearling, 2004.

PATRON, SUSAN. *The Higher Power of Lucky*. Atheneum Book for Young Readers, 2006.

PETERSON, MARGARET HADDIX. *The Shadow Children*. Simon & Schuster's Children's Publishing, 2004.

PERKINS, LYNNE RAE. *Criss-Cross*. Greenwillow, 2007.

PHELAN, MATT. *The Storm in the Barn*. Candlewick, 2009.

PINKNEY, JERRY. *The Lion and the Mouse*. Little Brown, 2009.

PINKWATER, DANIEL. *Fat Men from Space*. Yearling, 1980.

POLACCO, PATRICIA. *Just in Time, Abraham Lincoln*. Putnam, 2011.

PULLMAN, PHILLIP. *His Dark Materials*. Knopf Books for Young Readers, 2007.

RANSOM, CANDICE F. *When the Whippoorwill Calls*. Illustrated by Kimberly Bulcken Root. HarperCollins, 1995.

RAPP, ADAM. *Punkzilla*. Candlewick, 2009.

REEVE, PHILLIP. *The Hungry City Chronicles*. HarperTeen, 2004.

ROCKWELL, ANNE. *Clouds*. Collins, 2008.

RYAN, PAM MUÑOZ. *The Dreamer*. Scholastic, 2010.

RYAN, PAM MUÑOZ. *Esperanza Rising*. Scholastic, 2000.

SALLEY, COLEEN. *Epossumondas*. Illustrated by Janet Stevens. Harcourt, 2002.

SELZNICK, BRIAN. *The Invention of Hugo Cabret*. Scholastic, 2007.

SLEATOR, WILLIAM. *House of Stairs*. Puffin, 1991.

SMITH, JEFF. *Bone: The Complete Cartoon Epic in One Volume*. Cartoon Books, 2004.

STAUB, FRANK. *The Kids' Book of Clouds and Sky*. Sterling, 2005.

STEWART, SARAH. *The Gardener*. Illustrated by David Small. Square Fish, 2007.

STORK, FRANCISCO X. *Marcelo in the Real World*. Scholastic, 2011.

STROUD, JONATHAN. *The Bartimaeus Trilogy: 3-Book Boxed Set*. Hyperion, 2010.

TAN, SHAUN. *The Lost Thing*. Lothian, 2010.

TAN, SHAUN. *Tales from Outer Suburbia*. Arthur A. Levine Books, 2009.

TAYLOR, MILDRED. *The Friendship*. Perfection, 1998.

TAYLOR, MILDRED. *Mississippi Bridge*. Puffin, 2000.

TAYLOR, MILDRED. *Roll of Thunder, Hear My Cry*. Puffin, 1976.

TAYLOR, MILDRED. *Song of the Trees*. Perfection, 2003.

TAYLOR, THEODORE. *The Trouble with Tuck*. Yearling, 2000.

TESTA, MARIA. *Nine Candles*. Carolrhoda, 1996.

TOLKIEN, J. R. R. *The Lord of the Rings*. Houghton Mifflin, 1974.

VAN ALLSBURG, CHRIS. *Bad Day at Riverbend*. Houghton Mifflin, 1995.

VAN ALLSBURG, CHRIS. *The Widow's Broom*. Houghton Mifflin, 1992.

WALLACE, BILL. *A Dog Called Kitty*. Aladdin, 1994.

WELLS, ROSEMARY. *Wingwalker*. Illustrated by Brian Selznick. Hyperion, 2002.

WERLIN, NANCY. *Impossible*. Speak, 2009.

WESTERFELD, SCOTT. *Uglies*. Simon & Schuster Children's Publishing, 2008.

WHITE, E. B. *Charlotte's Web*. HarperCollins, 2004.

WHITE, E. B. *Stuart Little*. Harper & Row, 1974.

WHITE, RUTH. *Little Audrey*. Farrar, Straus and Giroux, 2008.

WHITE, RUTH. *Way Down Deep*. Farrar, Straus and Giroux, 2007.

WIESEL, ELIE. *Night*. Hill & Wang, 2006.

WIESNER, DAVID. *Flotsam*. Clarion, 2006.

WIESNER, DAVID. *The Three Pigs*. Clarion, 2001.

WIESNER, DAVID. *Tuesday*. Clarion, 1991.

WIESNER, DAVID. *Sector 7*. Clarion Books, 1997.

WILD, MARGARET. *Woolvs in the Sitee*. Illustrated by Anne Spudvilas. Boyd Mills Press, 2007.

WILLIAMS, VERA B. *Amber Was Brave, Essie Was Smart*. Perfection, 2004.

WISNIEWSKI, DAVID. *Golem*. Sandpiper, 2007.

WITTINGER, ELLEN. *Hard Love*. Simon & Schuster, 2001.

WITTINGER, ELLEN. *Love and Lies: Marisol's Story*. Simon & Schuster, 2009.

WOODSON, JACQUELINE. *After Tupac and D Foster*. Speak, 2010.

WOODSON, JACQUELINE. *Feathers*. Speak, 2010.

WOODSON, JACQUELINE. *Our Gracie Aunt*. Illustrated by John J. Muth. Hyperion, 2002.

WOODSON, JACQUELINE. *Visiting Day*. Illustrated by James Ransome. Scholastic, 2002.

YANG, GENE LUEN. *American Born Chinese*. Square Fish, 2008.

YOLEN, JANE. *Commander Toad in Space*. Puffin, 1996.

YOLEN, JANE. *The Devil's Arithmetic*. Puffin, 2004.

YOUNG, ED. *Lon Po Po*. Philomel, 1989.

MyEducationKit™

Go to the topics "Traditional Literature," "Modern Fantasy," "Contemporary Realistic Fiction," and "Historical Fiction" on the MyEducationKit for this text, where you can:

- Search the Children's Literature Database, housing more than 22,000 titles searchable in every genre by authors or illustrators, by awards won, by year published, and by topic and description.
- Explore genre-related Assignments and Activities, assignable exercises showing concepts in action through database use, video, cases, and student and teacher artifacts.
- Listen to podcasts and read interviews from some of the brightest and most enduring stars of children's literature in the Conversations.
- Discover web links that will lead you to sites representing the authors you learn about in these pages, classrooms with powerful children's literature connections, and literature awards.

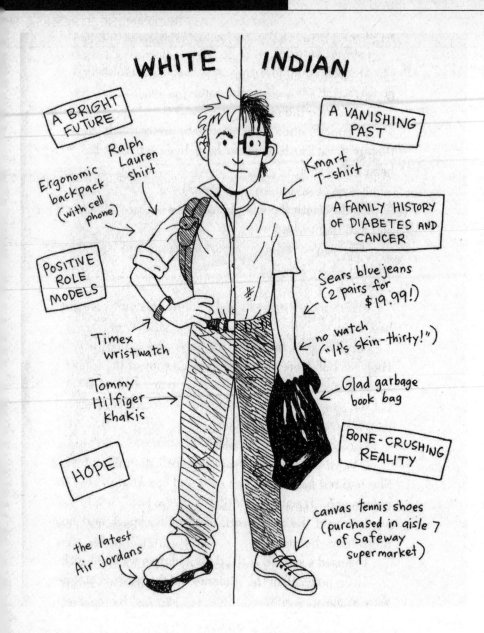

The Absolutely True Diary of a Part-Time Indian: A Novel

Sherman Alexie / Illustrated by Ellen Forney

In fiction, the focus is frequently a character's construction of a personal identity.

CHAPTER FIVE

Character

Why begin with character? Suppose there are no characters in a story, no characters you know very well, or who live in your heart?

Children are aware of the many subtleties of human nature; they respond to variations in people and in their surroundings. Even the youngest children are aware of personality in the people around them and can detect their differences. They care about and are attuned to people and human interactions in their world. It is not surprising, then, that children recognize the personalities of characters in stories they hear and read; they respond to these story characters and are sensitive to consistency in their actions.

One of the functions of literature, aside from pleasure, is to discover people and how they interact *with* the world around them. Character development in children's books supports this function: *Character*, as the term is generally used, means the aggregate of mental, emotional, and social qualities that distinguish a person. In literature, the term **character** is used to mean a person, or in the case of children's literature, sometimes a personified animal or object. Each of the living beings in a story, play, or poem is a character. These characters have an important role in the telling of the story.

When we add the word *development*, we have a literary term, **character development**. In life the development of a person's character or personality is a matter of growth and change over time. In literature, however, there is rarely the time or space for that to fully occur. But there is the promise of change, even within the brief space of the picturebook format.

The child who responds to real people will respond to characters in books.

Character development means showing the character—whether a person, animal, or object—with the complexity of a living being. Each of us in real life is three-dimensional; that is, we are a mixture of qualities. None of us is completely generous—we have our limits—or completely selfish. We all like to laugh; some of us like to provoke laughter. In the full development of character in the literary sense, the writer shows the whole, composed of a variety of human traits like those of real people.

Writers and illustrators have both privileges and responsibilities in this matter of character development. Since the reader frequently follows either a central character or a set of characters in a story, the writer and illustrator have an obligation to make this character's thoughts and actions believable. However, if the character is less important, the writer and illustrator have the privilege of making the character two-dimensional or even representative of a class—for example, the bossy older sister or the impish little brother. The importance of a character in a story—primary, secondary, or minor—determines how fully the character is developed and understood. The closer the character comes to the center of the conflict, the more important the character is, and the greater is the reader's need to know the complexity of the character's personality. Conversely, the more the character functions merely as background, the less the character needs to be developed. For example, Templeton is not a main character in *Charlotte's Web*, but he is in many ways very close to the pivotal points of the story. Let's look at this member of the cast of characters in our mentor text, *Charlotte's Web*.

> The importance of a character determines how fully the character is developed and understood.

 # Revelation of Character

We are acquainted with people in our lives in many ways. Imagine new neighbors have just moved in. Watching from a distance, you make tentative conclusions about age, occupation, and social status. As you observe further, patterns of speech and dress are revealed; style and quantity of personal belongings, make of car, and family make-up become apparent. From the public aspects of their move, we begin to decide whether we want to become further acquainted. As we observe their day-to-day actions and their decisions about taking care of their property, going to work, perhaps minding a pet or tending a garden, we begin to notice if there are other ways we might connect with our neighbors, such as their occupation, social connections, or recreational interests. At each level, if we can relate to the new neighbors, we increase feelings of closeness and willingness to listen to their opinions and consider their actions. We come to know these neighbors by their appearance, how they speak and what they say, their actions, the work, play, and social connections they have with us, and perhaps what other friends say of them.

> We come to know character by several means.

The process of coming to know a literary character is comparable. In literature, however, the writer and illustrator have an additional alternative: Each or both may choose to reveal what the characters are thinking and fill in details about the characters' appearance, innermost anxieties and dreams, patterns of behavior, and varied cultural attributes. We will turn to our mentor text, *Charlotte's Web* by E. B. White, where we are most familiar with Wilbur and Charlotte; the other characters and actions revolve around them in various ways. Templeton is a supporting character, yet White gives Templeton a great deal of interest, which serves to illuminate the traits of Charlotte and Wilbur. How does White do this?

By Appearance

Gluttony is one of Templeton's most obvious traits, and his appearance shows it. He returns after his night of gorging at the fair, swollen to double his usual size. Only an appeal to appetite will tempt Templeton to fetch the egg sac, and as he eats first at Wilbur's trough every day, he grows fatter and bigger than any other known rat. Templeton's appearance verifies and supplements what we know of his character: gluttony and self-interest are the essence of Templeton. Templeton's greed not only allows the reader to know *him*, but it also serves to magnify the more selfless and generous natures of Charlotte and Wilbur.

By Speech and Language

Accompanying Templeton's gluttonous appearance are his predictable sarcasm and ill-tempered outbursts as he gripes to Wilbur in sneering tones. He crawls into Wilbur's crate as a stowaway and grumbles: "Kindly remember that I am hiding down here in this crate and I don't want to be stepped on, or kicked in the face, or pummeled, or crushed in any way, or squashed, or buffeted about, or bruised, or lacerated, or scarred, or biffed. Just watch what you're doing, Mr. Radiant."

At the fair, when Wilbur is optimistic about his chances of avoiding a future as bacon, Templeton cannot resist commenting that when Zuckerman hankers for smoked ham, he will take the butcher knife to Wilbur. Templeton boasts about every grudging action and every carefully bought favor; he even pretends his motives are kind when he bites Wilbur's tail or saves the rotten egg. Complaining, "What do you think I am, anyway, a rat-of-all-work?" Templeton resentfully orders the directors' meeting to break up because meetings bore him. He grumbles at his commission to find words for the web, insisting he is not spending all his time rushing over to the dump after "advertising material." Templeton is characterized by what he says as well as by the way in which he speaks, showing himself to be cynical and selfish, resentful of any intrusion on his own pursuits. By contrast, Wilbur is naïve and optimistic, and Charlotte is patient and wise.

By Actions

Templeton's actions also help to define his nature. We first meet Templeton after Wilbur moves to the barn, as he creeps up cautiously to the goslings, keeping close to the wall. Templeton's furtive manner arouses our curiosity and suspicions; we are as wary as the barn animals. Twice in the story Templeton grins, first when Wilbur lands with a thud, hurt, crushed, and tearful after his unsuccessful web-spinning efforts. Templeton grins a second time as he takes Wilbur's tail and bites it as hard as he possibly can. Gleefully savage, Templeton delights in slinking about and nipping at his friend; he is surly, sneaky, and ill-tempered, pleased at others' discomfort. He is self-centered and gluttonous, going to the fair only to scavenge in the garbage and litter. Templeton's actions create a picture of Templeton's character, and we can imagine something much gentler for Charlotte and childish for Wilbur in the process.

By Connections and Relationships

Templeton is characterized by what he does, what he says, and by the way he looks. However, there is more to be learned from others' comments about him. The animals carefully watch his furtive actions, since they neither like nor trust Templeton. The old sheep enlists Templeton's help in finding words, and reports that the rat can be persuaded only by appeals to "his baser instincts, of which he has plenty." Since the sheep is on our side, the side of saving Wilbur, we trust his judgment. Conversely, we distrust the characters on the wrong side of our sympathies and are less accepting of their judgments: we would doubt Templeton's opinions on any character because we know how duplicitous he is. The comments of the other characters and Templeton's relationships and connections with others help to show character. Intuitive Charlotte reminds the barnyard inhabitants and the reader (lest they think Templeton can be reformed), "A rat is a rat."

By Author and Illustrator Revelations

White's verbal portraits also add to the picture we have of Templeton's character. He calls Templeton a crafty rat who does as he pleases; even his tunnel shows his cunning. White's thoroughly negative description of Templeton verifies the goose's and gander's feelings about the rat who "had no morals, no conscience, no scruples, no consideration, no decency, no milk of rodent kindness, no compunctions, no higher feeling, no friendliness, no anything. He would kill a gosling if he could get away with it." Templeton becomes a character we know so well that we know what to expect of him in almost any situation; he is consistent. By the same token, readers can predict the actions of other characters through Templeton's choices.

Garth Williams's pen-and-ink illustrations confirm and extend White's verbal descriptions. When Wilbur is readying for his attempt at making a web, Templeton fetches some string from his stash and proceeds to attach it to Wilbur's tail. Looking at the illustration, the reader can see the detail in Templeton's face, the intent look as he carefully ties two half hitches. Readers can also see Templeton's gleeful grin when Wilbur's attempt fails; Templeton cooperates, but doesn't reveal essential information that might have avoided Wilbur's calamitous fall.

Unity of Character and Action

Writers create a whole cast of characters for a story—some important, some minor, some complex, some relatively simple—through the use of the previous techniques. In the case of the picturebook format, the illustrator has an influence as well, showing readers more than the words tell. As we come to know these characters, we respond to them.

Most of us respond to others as we see similarity to ourselves—or if not similarity, recognizable traits, qualities, or actions. We may say we "identify with" someone, or that someone is credible. While reading a story, we make the same demands of character—that the character has been made credible by the author.

In real life we know that changes occur in ourselves and in those we know well. We recognize the changes best if we see a person before and after the change. The need for a *before* and *after* to see growth applies to a character's change as well. If the impact of events shapes or reshapes the personality of the character, the author must show how that change has come about. In *Charlotte's Web* Wilbur gains confidence through Charlotte's orchestrated actions. Her words cast a positive aura around Wilbur: a self-fulfilling prophecy.

The acceptance of an event depends on understanding its cause; cause involves the story's action. A complex character and plausible events in a believable context are the combination that should propel the reader through the story. The phrase "unity of character and action" is not an empty phrase; it expresses one of the most important ideas in understanding any fiction.

Writer Henry James's quote "What is character but the determination of incident? What is incident but the illustration of character?"[1] implies that the traits of a particular character affect that character's actions. A character's actions reveal his or her nature.

Donald Graves, much admired for making the writing process transparent for authors of any age, tells us that though fiction writers can and do start anywhere, it is perhaps best to focus on character, for it is the actions and reactions of characters that shape the plot of a story. In literature for children, the skillful writer shows characters by means of actions and speech so that character, incident, and outcome seem interwoven—and, in the end, inevitable.[2] Think about Brian Robeson in Gary Paulsen's *Hatchet,* or the Logan family in Mildred Taylor's *Roll of Thunder, Hear My Cry.* Can you think of these characters apart from the actions in which they take part? Three examples that follow show us the relationship between character and action.

Let's consider Koly, the central character in Gloria Whelan's *Homeless Bird,* a story set in India, where Hinduism, the principal religion, has certain customs of marriage and family as well as those surrounding funerals and the role of widows and daughters-in-law. Koly, an impoverished thirteen-year-old, must be married for the sake of the family's survival. Without funds for a dowry, Koly's father must make the best marriage arrangement he can, and Koly is soon the bride of a young man she has never met—and who soon dies, leaving Koly a widow. A docile daughter-in-law, she is thus enslaved. "I also knew that I could not crawl about like a beaten dog. I had heard about families that had murdered the widows of their sons to get rid of them." As Koly's resentment grows, she becomes mischievous, like the god Krishna. Meanwhile her quiet resistance and her meticulous artistry in embroidery save her spirit, and ultimately her life. The change in Koly shows her to be a **dynamic character;** her change is credible.

In the early chapters of *The Watsons Go to Birmingham—1963* by Christopher Paul Curtis, Byron is a troublesome boy who grows steadily more defiant of parents and teachers. His parents, thinking he needs to see what may be ahead for an African American in the United States, take him to Birmingham, Alabama. There, younger brother Kenny takes a risk and almost drowns in a whirlpool. To Kenny's surprise, Byron rescues him, but is angry that Kenny has been so foolish. Little by little, Byron (By) pays more attention to his family, and when someone sets fire to the church where their younger sister, Joetta, is attending Sunday school, he, like Kenny, is deeply concerned. By's next act is significant evidence of change:

"What is character but the determination of incident? What is incident but the illustration of character?"

Henry James

It is the actions and reactions of characters that shape the plot of a story.

persuading Kenny—depressed by such acts of hatred—that he has not been negligent. By helps Kenny out of his deep depression and encourages him to see his
strengths. Byron has changed from a self-absorbed and destructive adolescent to
a caring brother. Just as people change slowly, this change develops slowly.

In another book by Curtis, *Bud, Not Buddy,* the main character wants it known
that he is self-reliant, resourceful, determined, and able to be recognized as Bud (not
Buddy). To this end he leaves the abusive foster home; consoles a younger foster
child, Jerry, about the home he's to be placed in; worries about revealing himself;
protects the cardboard suitcase containing all he knows of his past; feels awestruck
about restaurants and their varieties of food; is intrigued by a flush toilet; worries
about Mr. Calloway's health; and is delighted with his gift from the band—a recorder
soon replaced by a saxophone. Bud is whole, interesting, and convincing—a boy we
care about, just as the members of Calloway's band care about, shelter, and guide
him.

> One of the biggest disappointments for a perceptive reader may be inadequate character portrayal.

Types of Characters

There are terms that describe the degree of character development and that refer to
change or lack of it in a character in the course of a story. Briefly, a **round character** is
one that we know well and who has a variety of traits that make him or her believable. A **flat character** is less developed and has fewer traits. A **dynamic character** is
generally a round character who changes, while a **static character**, despite credibility,
does not change over the course of the story.

> Flat or little-known characters are the least important to plot.

Flat Characters

Flat characters are less important, but essential to a story's action. They are not fully
developed, but in most stories, these flat characters help carry the action by showing how the central character behaves or relates to others. Flat characters make the
setting a believable place because they are a part of a community of characters.
Flat characters are quickly made known to the reader, then assume their necessary
places in the narrative so that the story can then focus on the central characters. In
Charlotte's Web, Dr. Dorian and Mr. Arable are clearly flat characters.

Fern is a *relatively* flat character in this story, a child with an intense interest that
absorbs her for a time. She treats Wilbur like a doll, and listens to the animals' conversations and reports them to her incredulous parents. She plays and quarrels, and
she loves the Ferris wheel and the freedom of the fair. However, Fern has few traits
that distinguish her from other little girls of her day; she remains a believable little
girl but not a special one. Wilbur's relationships and worries are the focus of the
story, and the conflict goes on without Fern being totally aware of all that Charlotte
and Wilbur mean to each other. Because this is Wilbur's story, not Fern's, she needs
no greater development.

When characters are given very few individual traits, readers may have a difficult time viewing them as unique human beings. When characters seem to have
just a few of the traits associated with a class or of a group of people, the character is

called a **stereotype**. Each of us has a few mental stereotypes—of politicians, fathers, athletes, or poets. When we examine these mental pictures and compare them to individuals we know well, we generally find the stereotype inaccurate in some way. The stereotype may be inadequate, a glorification, or even an injustice to the actual person. In literature stereotypic characters function somewhat differently, depending on the genre. The literary stereotype is one whose traits are understood, and whose actions combine to fulfill the theme or moral of the story.

> Flat or stereotyped protagonists do not contribute to understanding.

In *Charlotte's Web*, Lurvy is an example of a stereotype—in this case of a hired man. Lurvy has only the expected traits and performs only the actions expected of him in the story. He nails down the loose board on Wilbur's pen, he slops Wilbur, he discovers the exploded dud egg. Lurvy is confined to agreeing with those in a position of authority, relying on their words:

> "You notice how solid he is around the shoulders, Lurvy?"
> "Sure. Sure I do," said Lurvy. "I've always noticed that pig. He's quite a pig."
> "He's long, and he's smooth," said Zuckerman.
> "That's right," agreed Lurvy. "He's as smooth as they come. He's some pig."

As Lurvy's speech shows, flat and stereotypic characters are portrayed by what they say as well as how they say it. Many stories contain flat characters that function as stereotypes, as White included Lurvy. As these stories become dated, views of these flat characters may change, seeming out of sync with the world as it currently is. Readers may be curious to know more about or express concern for a particular stereotypic character, someone they identify with, but with whose portrayal they feel unsatisfied. Beyond explaining these kinds of characterizations, teachers, parents, and librarians should be prepared to suggest additional titles to fill gaps stereotypic portrayals often create for readers. Workers portrayed as simple and without any complexity might not resonate well with children whose families have made their living through manual work.

We have noted the necessity for character and action to be unified. However, flat and stereotyped characters do not truly grow out of action, and action cannot grow out of their less-than-full human natures. It seems more descriptive of flat characters and action to say that they coexist; flat characters and stereotypes move over the surface of the action, rather than being integrated with the action. Flat characters, furthermore, make little contribution to our understanding of human nature. In fact, if we read only about underdeveloped characters, our perceptions about people may be narrowed rather than expanded. Younger readers do not typically have the breadth and depth of experience to justify reading only stories that make their points by careful stereotyping. Nevertheless, many popular children's stories make use of flat characterization.

It is a somewhat different case when the concept of a flat character is parodied, as it is in the recent series by Lemony Snicket. Easy to categorize, the characters in *A Series of Unfortunate Events* are essentially flat, with few traits. Three of the best-known characters are orphaned children constantly pursued by the villainous Count Olaf. Violet Baudelaire is the inventor who steers the orphaned children out of danger; Klaus is the bespectacled reader and researcher who finds necessary information; and Sunny is the tagalong little sister whose unusual baby talk masks her intelligence and problem-solving abilities. In each of the thirteen installments, the plot carries the story without significant new insight into the characters. Because the series parodies

TEXTSET

Developing Dimension to a Story Character

Many families are justifiably proud of the role work plays in their lives. How might these stories provide an additional dimension to the flat presentation of Lurvy in *Charlotte's Web*?

Hesse, Karen. *Brooklyn Bridge*. Chris Sheban, Illus. Feiwel & Friends, 2008.

Early twentieth century Russian immigrants produce the first teddy bears in New York City while vagrant kids survive under the Brooklyn Bridge, told from a dual perspective.

Hopkinson, Deborah. *Sky Boys: How They Built the Empire State Building*. James Ransome, Illus. Schwartz & Wade, 2006.

Proud portrayal of brave workers who constructed this building during the Depression, with an interesting use of perspective.

Krull, Kathleen. *Harvesting Hope: The Story of Cesar Chavez*. Yuyi Morales, Illus. Harcourt, 2003.

Story of farm worker activist detailing his struggle to improve working conditions, containing beautiful illustrations.

Paterson, Katherine. *Lyddie*. Puffin, 1991.

Classic story of family struggling to save their farm through child labor in the fields and in the factory in mid-nineteenth-century Vermont.

---

melodrama and perhaps series literature itself, these flat protagonists serve a particular purpose.

Stereotyping, or compressing people into flat caricatures that eliminate individual differences, is most suitable in literature for particular background figures that fill narrow roles. Flat and stereotyped characters, however, are not generally appropriate protagonists; we should be particularly watchful for cultural stereotypes that glorify or denigrate particular ethnic or racial groups, religious beliefs, or personal lifestyle choices. In multicultural literature, it is especially important that characters are nuanced in ways that realistically and fairly represent the culture portrayed.

Stereotypes in literature about cultures other than the dominant one are unfair and misleading.

Round Characters

A **round character** is one that is fully developed; we know this character well, because many traits are demonstrated in the action of the story. We know appearance and actions, speech and opinions, what others say and think about the character, and often what the writer thinks about him or her. The character is so fully developed that we may even be able to predict actions and reactions. Yet, like a real person, the character may surprise us or respond impetuously on occasion. It is as though we know the character so well that the character has become a real person, one we wish we could meet or might enjoy knowing.

Children's literature has a great many round characters that we may feel we know. David Almond's outstanding story, *Skellig*, features two round characters: Michael and Mina. But this story is Michael's; readers follow his path of self-discovery primarily through his actions in response to those around him. Readers recognize his curiosity about the more delicate aspects of the world as he navigates the unfamiliar surroundings of a new neighborhood. The questions he poses to his teachers at school, his parents, and his new neighbor, Mina, reveal his inquisitive nature. His inquiry into the origins of human shoulder blades, for example, foreshadows the encounter on Falconer Road with the winged Skellig. The nurture he provides this fading owl-man he discovers in the family's ramshackle garage, as well as the gentle concern he shows as he caresses his fragile baby sister, reveal his sensitivity toward others as well as hope for the future. Michael finds satisfaction in the hands-on work of renovating the new family home, and he demonstrates strength and athleticism through his skill at football (soccer). Michael is multi-faceted, balancing action with friends and family with the pursuit of art, writing, and nature.

The challenge of creating a round character is greater for the artist and writer of picturebooks, but the combination of words and illustration in quality picturebooks can be very successful. In *17 Things I'm Not Allowed to Do Anymore*, readers understand the main character; she is believable. As the protagonist narrates the story, we learn that she is a mischievous young girl through her running commentary of the privileges her mother, the necessary flat character, is withdrawing. She reveals the consequence, then tells us "just because I . . ." to remove herself of responsibility; illustrations show what *really* happened and reveal her false remorse. The action of the plot, a simple form of flashback to deeds already done, is pushed forward by illustrations of lively action sequences and facial expressions that reveal the human nature of each character.

In order to see the meaning of a round character more clearly, return to *Charlotte's Web* and compare the many traits of Wilbur to the few traits of Mr. Arable, or the stereotype Lurvy. From the first words of the first page, when Fern asks where her father is going with the ax, we are anxious about Wilbur's fate. We soon discover that Wilbur's struggle is the conflict, and that he is therefore the **protagonist**, or central character. Tiny, dependent Wilbur has almost no life of his own at the opening of the story, except to amuse himself like a toddler, finding the mud moist and warm and pleasantly oozy. When he goes to live in the barn, he is bored, unable to dream up anything exciting to do. Friends must introduce themselves to him. When he squeezes through the fence and is pursued, he has no idea what to do with freedom, and his appetite makes him captive again. Since Lurvy's pail of slops is irresistible, Wilbur plans his day around his body: sleeping, eating, scratching, digging, eating, watching flies, eating, napping, standing still, eating.

He wonders uncertainly about friendship; it seems such a gamble. Once Wilbur finds friendship in Charlotte, life becomes more exciting and he becomes confident enough to try spinning a web. Cheerfully, he tries and fails; he humbly admits that Charlotte is more clever and brighter than he is. Wilbur's innocence and dependence are clear when he pleads for a story or a song, for a last bedtime bite or a last drink of milk, and calls out the series of quiet "good-nights" to Charlotte. Panic is Wilbur's reaction to the news of his destiny—the Arables' dinner table. But once he is assured that Charlotte can perform miracles, he calms down, becoming patient, trusting, and humble. The congratulatory words in Charlotte's web make Wilbur an exemplary pig; he decides that if he is called "radiant," he must act radiantly, and

A character is not only affected by events; the character's nature may cause the events.

in his way he becomes radiant. Despite all the admiration Wilbur attracts, he remains modest. Happy and confident, he honestly admires Charlotte's peach-colored egg sac and gazes lovingly into the faces of the crowd. He looks both grateful and humble. On the day that Wilbur wants love more than comfort and food, he has grown. Wilbur has enough traits to classify him as a round character and a suitable protagonist.

Concepts of Change in Character

Consistency

It is not necessary that a story have a dynamic or changing character. In one story the round central character may change, and in another, like *17 Things I'm Not Allowed to Do Anymore*, the round central character may not. The change or lack of it does not constitute a judgment about the quality of characterization. However, the static or dynamic nature of the protagonist does help the reader to see the action and to understand the idea behind it.

Change is not always necessary.

Since less important characters do not receive as much close focus and may remain on the fringes of a story's action, their change is unlikely to be important or to grow out of the events of the plot. Furthermore, their changing could even be distracting. A **static character** is one who does not change in the course of the story. The conflict does not influence the character by making any impact on personality or outlook. Flat characters—including stereotypes and foils—will not change because they are not known well enough for us to recognize or care about changes, but a round character, too, may be unchanged by the conflict. In fact, even the protagonist may be unchanged by the action. Although Charlotte is a round character who is central to the story, she does not change. We know her consistent nature very well. Charlotte is not only motherly, but hardworking as well, and her web words prove it. She is the same wise and selfless character at the end of the story that she was at the beginning, and we therefore call her a static character.

In *Skellig*, Michael's mother is also a static character, steadfastly nurturing of both Michael and the new baby, though in different ways. Her responses to the demands of moving, renovation, and a sick child are predictable; they range fully from frustrated outbursts to gentle lullabies that serve to make her more believable. Her vision of Skellig at the baby's hospital bedside reveals a spiritual dimension, but does not unbalance the story for readers. Her role as a static character does not lessen her importance for this story.

Characters on the fringe of action are unlikely to change.

Often children become fascinated with a particular series of books, as we discussed in Chapter 2. The success of a particular series may actually depend on a character such as Gooney Bird Green, Clementine, or Olivia remaining relatively unchanged or static. Many adults consider this trait to be a drawback of some series books for children where plot alone carries the story. But readers of these stories are seeking action or suspense, often accompanying the character to new places to meet new people. Not only does it not always matter that the characters are static and predictable, it might even be an unwelcome distraction if the character has changed

I N Q U I R Y   P O I N T

Second- and third-grade protagonists are well represented in the following series. The first installments provide an opportunity to analyze these series stars as characters. Are they round, flat, stereotypic, static, or dynamic? Are these characters essentially very much alike or different? What might be the advantages and disadvantages of reading one series after another? Do the illustrations have a significant impact?

Harper, Cherise Mericle. *Just Grace.* Houghton Mifflin, 2007.

Look, Lenore. *Alvin Ho: Allergic to Girls, School and Other Scary Things.* LeUyen Pham, Illus. Schwartz & Wade, 2008.

Lowry, Lois. *Gooney Bird Green.* Thomas Middy Chilman, Illus. Perfection, 2004.

McDonald, Megan. *Stink: The Incredible Shrinking Kid.* Peter H. Reynolds, Illus. Perfection, 2005.

Naylor, Phyllis Reynolds. *Roxie and the Hooligans.* Alexandra Boiger, Illus. Ginee Seo, 2006.

Pennypacker, Sara. *Clementine.* Marla Frazee, Illus. Hyperion, 2006.

Sachar, Louis. *Why Pick on Me?* Perfection, 1993.

in too many ways from story to story. Although these books may not be desirable as the only stories a child accesses, their impact can be greater if teachers, parents, and librarians suggest titles that thoughtfully juxtapose other books with varied perspectives and more rounded characters.

Dynamics

If there is a unity of character and action, as we mentioned earlier, then the character is not only affected by events, but his or her nature may also bring about various events. This interaction of character and action in the story may change a character; as is the case when Michael evolves from lonely and worried to confident and involved following the chain of events surrounding his discovery and subsequent nurturing of the mystical creature in *Skellig*.

When the word *dynamic* is used in ordinary conversation, it may mean influential or exciting. The descriptor could easily apply to a character that has a strong impact within the story and on a reader. However, in the context of literature, the word has special meaning: a **dynamic character** is one who changes over the course of the action. He or she may change from being shy to possessing poise, from being cowardly to displaying bravery, or from selfish indulgence to performing selfless acts. The character may demonstrate a new realization about himself or herself, or about his or her personal values. He may show that he is now able to take care of himself, or she may show that she has become able to care for others as well as herself. Somehow, the events of the story and qualities of the character have effected some basic character change. The variety of possibilities for change is impressive.

A character may grow older by an hour or by a decade in the course of a novel's action. However, the mere passage of time is not always a sufficient ingredient for character change. Some people are changed significantly by a single event, whether traumatic or joyous, that brings a realization of some kind. Beyond the passage of time, it is the impact of events on the character—the unity of character and action—that creates new traits to supplant or alter the old. The character may not necessarily be conscious of the change, but the reader is.

Big Red Lollipop is an excellent example of dynamic change in a young character. Rubina is humiliated when her mother adheres to Pakistani traditions and requires that her younger sister, Sana, tag along on a birthday party invitation. The passage of time is expertly depicted through pictures as the two girls experience typical incidences of sibling rivalry and their baby sister grows old enough to enter the action. When Sana's turn comes for a birthday party invitation, Rubina has matured enough to persuade their mother, Ami, to allow Sana to attend without taking *her* younger sibling. In this fine picturebook we see a character change as a result of cultural change and a traumatic experience. This time, it's not only Rubina who changes, but also her mother, Ami.

In *Surviving the Applewhites* by Stephanie Tolan, Jake is a dynamic character, changing throughout the story from a belligerent cynic who has been in trouble with the law to a caring family member. When he meets kindness at the Applewhites', he begins to change as Winston the Bassett hound adopts him, as little Destiny adores him, as Jake helps E. D. with her butterfly science project, and as he discovers he can sing as the goatherd in the musical *The Sound of Music*. Character and action are intricately entwined in a believable character change.

The struggle to find out who we are is paramount to growing up; it may resemble a dialogue between differing views of or future possibilities for ourselves. Such a technique is central to *If I Stay* by Gayle Forman. As Forman tells the story, high school senior and gifted cellist Mia's story unfolds in the aftermath of a horrific car accident in which her parents are killed. Her lively younger brother is gravely injured, while Mia remains in a comatose state. This allows Mia to alternate between out-of-body experiences and recollections of the past, as she tells the stories that will help her visualize her choices and decide whether to stay or go with her family. In twenty-four hours, Mia gradually changes from a watcher to a participant in her future. The characters, from her alt-rock boyfriend to her friends and remaining family are so believable that a reader will easily suspend disbelief with the slightly supernatural elements of the telling. Mia is both physically and emotionally changed as the story is resolved.

Wilbur is a character in *Charlotte's Web* who shows change. He is a believable character early in the story, although he is young and immature. The experience of receiving selfless friendship makes him able to give selfless friendship. Slowly, as we watch this change occurring, Wilbur is altered by his part in the action, by his receiving so much; he is the same Wilbur, and yet not the same. To his early qualities of humility and naiveté are added dependability and steadfastness, sacrifice and purpose. Even Wilbur's vocabulary matures. When first he hears the bad news, he is a panicky child: "'I can't be quiet,' screamed Wilbur, racing up and down. 'I don't want to die. Is it true . . . Charlotte? Is it true they are going to kill me when the cold weather comes?'"

By the end of a summer of maturing, Wilbur responds to news that his dearest friend will die, and knows that he must save the egg sac. Notice how his vocabulary has changed to adult words, and his tone has changed to reasonable persuasion: "Listen to me! . . . Charlotte . . . has only a short time to live. She cannot accompany

Trauma may cause sudden character change.

us home, because of her condition. Therefore, it is absolutely necessary that I take her egg sac with me. I can't reach it, and I can't climb. You are the only one that can get it. There's not a second to be lost. . . . Please, please, please, Templeton, climb up and get the egg sac."

Wilbur does not scream; he uses "please" liberally. His desperation does not arise from his own need, but from the need of another. Charlotte had once said to the screaming Wilbur that he was carrying on childishly; the new Wilbur tells Templeton to "stop acting like a spoiled child." Wilbur—who once planned his day around his slops—can now, out of deep concern for Charlotte, promise solemnly that Templeton may eat first and take his choice of all the goodies in the trough.

During winter Wilbur warms the egg sac with his breath in the cold barn. By the end of the story, it is Wilbur who offers the first mature greeting, a cheerful "Hello!" to the baby spiders. The change is significant, and it occurs slowly. It is convincing. Little by little, events have molded a self-centered child into responsible maturity; we believe in Wilbur's maturity just as we believed in his childishness.

Additional Thoughts on Characterization

The number of round characters depends on the complexity of the plot. There is no firm rule about the number of round characters, but it is not feasible for every character to be round; a large number of fully developed characters could be highly distracting in a story for children. Even *Charlotte's Web*, which has three round characters, focuses more fully on Charlotte and Wilbur than on Templeton, important as he is to the story. Some writers, when speaking of their writing process, say that a too fully developed minor character can take over the story, changing the plot. For the sake of unity in the story, it then becomes the writer's choice to either flatten out that character once again, or give that character new importance in what must now be an altered plot.

A complex plot may require more round characters.

In *Skellig* Michael's mother enters and leaves the story; Almond flattens her character following the episodes where she has a more prominent voice. But Mina, a round but static character, is a different case. Almond increases her importance at story's end where the reader sees her interacting with Michael's family; there is a sense that she may be featured in a future installment. Almond discusses the feelings he developed for Mina's character in an author's note in the *10th Anniversary Edition* of *Skellig* (2010). In fact, he composes a short story creating the seed of Mina's fascination with archaeopteryx and the connectedness of living things.

Rounding Out Flat Characters

During the process of writing a story and following the response of readers, an author may decide a flat character is worth a story of his or her own and create a spin-off novel in which the character can be more fully developed. Louis Sachar's *Holes* featured protagonists Stanley Yelnats and Zero, but its companion, *Small Steps*, brings to life two minor characters, Armpit and X-Ray. Armpit is a foil to Zero:

both are African American, but in contrast to Zero's resolved and positive outcome, Armpit leaves Camp Green Lake to an uncertain fate, with his struggle to set goals and resolve the issues that landed him at the camp in the first place still ahead of him. Armpit is making progress when X-Ray, the unofficial head of the boys from the camp, arrives on the scene and manipulates Armpit into funding a money-making scheme. Sachar elevates the status of Armpit's character from flat to round, and from static to dynamic. X-Ray remains very much the same. Regardless of the believability of the story, readers who wondered about the numerous characters in *Holes* will find some answers in the more straightforward action in *Small Steps*.

Similarly, James Howe's *The Misfits* features four characters with a relatively equal status, but limited opportunity to fully develop any of the four. Howe was compelled to resolve this by developing the character of Joe Bunch in a companion book, *Totally Joe*, where Joe resolves his gender identity and his relationship with Colin through self-reflexive writing. Howe succeeds with this through a unique writing format: the "alphabiography," short narratives describing significant events, people, possessions, or emotions Joe associated with each letter of the alphabet.

Characters as Foils

Occasionally the writer may use a **foil**, a minor character whose traits are in direct contrast to those of a principal character in order to highlight them. The snobbish lamb is as young and naive as Wilbur, but she is smug instead of humble. Pigs are little or nothing to her. Since the lamb is consistently disdainful, her behavior contrasts sharply with Wilbur's humility, thus acting as a foil. In *Skellig* we meet Michael's two school buddies and football mates from his former neighborhood. Together Leakey and Coot represent Michael's formerly "guys only," sports-centered friendship as well as the two sides of Michael's personality: the active athlete and the inquisitive artist. They highlight the conflict Michael experiences with his change in neighborhoods and his increasingly important relationship with Mina.

Satoshi Kitamura demonstrates the concept of the foil creatively in his classic picturebook, *Lily Takes a Walk*. He introduces the comic function as the young protagonist, Lily, takes her dog on a routine walk in the neighborhood. The narrated story is about Lily's routine and somewhat humdrum walk with her dog at her side; the cartoon style illustrations show a second story as her dog is terrified by every encounter, from the mailbox to the trees in the park. The monsters and frightening images arising as they encounter the typical urban landmarks are visible to him

---

INQUIRY POINT

Some novels employ techniques with characterization as a central feature. This is the case with *One Crazy Summer* by Rita Williams-Garcia. This award-winning novel features several characters, including three young sisters on a quest to reconnect with their mother, who left home to play an active role in the civil rights movement in 1968 Oakland, California. What kind of characterization would you assign to each of the characters? Explain.

Delphine	Cecile Johnson
Vonetta	Sister Mukumbu
Fern	Hirohito Woods
Big Ma	

alone. At story's end, Lily recounts the events of their walk for her parents; the dog is simultaneously visualizing each of the frightening experiences. Only the reader can see this and appreciate his fearful walk. For many readers, the dog is the foil, the comic relief for Lily's character. However, looking at the story again, other readers may decide that Lily is the foil; despite the narration, the illustrations place him as the protagonist. Lily is just there for the walk in this comic routine. We learn more about the dog through the story's action than we can about Lily.

A foil often helps to reveal the full nature of a main character.

Similar to a foil is the frequent introduction of comical characters into children's stories. Sometimes this comic is the protagonist, but more often a minor character, one whose sole function is to provide comic relief. A clear example for younger children is the relationship between Officer Buckle and his service dog Gloria in *Officer Buckle and Gloria* by Peggy Rathmann. Readers can't avoid chuckling as Gloria and her comic antics carry the day during Officer Buckle's safety assemblies. When he realizes what is going on, his relationship with Gloria is damaged, but the children intercede on her behalf; Officer Buckle forgives Gloria and accepts that they are a unique team sharing the spotlight as they advance safety for children. The interactions between Officer Buckle and Gloria are just as important as Gloria playing the comic to Officer Buckle's dull safety presentations. Through their relationship children see trust, timing, and forgiveness.

 ## Learning about Characters

An important way to learn about characters is to examine how they relate or compare to other characters. Many stories feature groups of characters, such as *Holes*. Sachar compared the boys at Camp Green Lake to each other; he showed us how characters from the past related to each other as well. In the end, readers discover the way characters, past and present, are also related to one another. James Howe's story, *The Misfits*, depends on the relationship between the four main characters as much as it does on any single character. It is the combination of the characters and their effect on one another that is important for their development and for the story.[3] Juxtaposing characters with similar attributes, those who share a historical time and place, or even those who are sharply contrasted can help readers understand a character more fully. Textsets or text pairings can illuminate a character, allowing us to see them more clearly or in different ways.

For example, late elementary or middle level students might be invited to imagine the kind of conversations eleven-year-old Lonnie Collins Motion, of Jacqueline Woodson's 2003 verse novel *Locomotion*, might have with Matt Pin, the twelve-year-old Vietnamese boy of Ann Burg's 2009 verse novel *All the Broken Pieces*.

The boys have some experiences in common: Neither boy lives with his original family. Both boys have experienced personal tragedy: Matt, the loss of his mother when he was airlifted out of Vietnam; and Lonnie, the death of his parents in a house fire. Both boys live with adoptive parents; both struggle with the effects of living in a racist society; both are trying to define themselves within new homes. Both boys find solace in art—Lonnie in writing the poems that make up the book we read; Matt in the piano lessons he takes from his father's friend Jeff, a Vietnam veteran.

We expect memorable round characters to be known through their actions, feelings, speech, what others in the story say about them, and what the author tells us about them. A powerful way for readers to learn about characters is to see how they relate or compare to other characters. These Depression era stories have protagonists that are similar in age. Though all of their stories unravel during the 1930s, the protagonists are not all affected in the same way, and they live in many different settings. Select a protagonist and note his or her traits: appearance, actions, speech, other characters' comments, or author's descriptions. Which characters might be friends? What might they tell each other? How might they assist each other?

Bud, Not Buddy by Christopher Paul Curtis
Esperanza Rising by Pam Muñoz Ryan
Out of the Dust by Karen Hesse
Roll of Thunder, Hear My Cry by Mildred Taylor
The Storm in the Barn by Matt Phelan
The Trial by Jen Bryant
A Year Down Yonder by Richard Peck ●

Traditional Literature and Literary Lore

Folktales typically succeed without rounded or dynamic main characters; the actions and the attributes of the characters must still work together logically to create the story. Look at Hans Christian Andersen's "The Ugly Duckling" as an example of Henry James's view on the unity of character and action. In this literary folktale we can clearly see how a reader comes to know the central character. The Duckling's appearance seems of primary importance, since that is the basis for his exclusion. He is big and ugly, clumsy and grayish black throughout the story. However, at the end of the story his strong wings, white ruffled feathers, and slender neck have replaced his earlier awkwardness with beauty and grace. As for the dejected Duckling's actions, he does not look up when he is bitten and ridiculed in the duck yard. In the old woman's cottage, his panic sends him into the milk dish, the butter trough, and the flour barrel. But at the end of the story he floats gracefully on the water, his head tucked modestly under his wing. What the Duckling says is equally revealing of his character: several times he says sadly, "I'm so ugly," or "Even the dogs won't bite me." The Duckling is sure that he is an inferior nothing, and he never resists his enemies. At the end of the story, the Duckling shows by his speech that he is still modest when he says joyously, "I never dreamed of so much happiness when I was the ugly duckling."

As for what others say about the Ugly Duckling, his mother says he is not pretty, his brothers and sisters that they will not put up with him, for he is too big, and some wish that the cat would get him. The old woman's hen calls him a fool and finds him no fun. However, at the end of the story, the children call him the prettiest, "so young and lovely!" Finally, Andersen the writer has kept us informed about the Duckling not only by describing appearance and actions and reporting speeches, but also by his writer's comments, the result of his knowing everything. Andersen, the author, calls him a poor duckling and tells us he is miserable, exhausted, unhappy, terrified, a laughingstock. He calls the Duckling "poor thing!" and informs us of the Duckling's strange desire to float on the water, of his mysterious yearning to join the migrating swans. Finally, at the end of the story, Andersen tells us of the Ugly Duckling's beauty, which combines with his shyness, his happiness without pride as the Duckling speaks "from the depths of his heart."

Through all the means at his disposal, Andersen has shown us the character of the Ugly Duckling. The result is that we know this character well, and know that the story is the result of the character's traits combined with the actions that occur. The two are inextricably intertwined; together they demonstrate the unity of character and action. The character of the Ugly Duckling lives because the trials and harassments he endures in the course of growing up determine his personal change and his character; the story identifies the reality of maturing. Family rivalry, rejection, fear of failure, inability to find friends or to relate to others, even the feeling of ugliness and wishing one were dead are included in Andersen's story of the self-doubt of childhood.

Stock Characters in Traditional Literature

Traditional literature has been handed down orally from generation to generation and finally been set into print. Perhaps because of the necessity to keep the spoken story moving with suspense or action, the folktale relies on **stock characters.** A jealous fairy, a foolish youngest son, or the "girl as good as she is beautiful" are all useful stock characters. Since suspense and action carry the tale and the usually optimistic ending makes a comment on life, characters need only be briefly described to be easily understood. In a sense, this is one of the pleasures of traditional literature; we enjoy meeting character types we have met before, whose actions are thoroughly predictable. The reader can then concentrate on action and ideas, moving along quickly. Discovery of human nature comes, then, from the relationship of *theme to action*, often a discovery about universal human yearnings. Teachers, librarians, and parents can assist readers to understand not only the concept and literary purpose of flat characters, but also their role in a particular culture. Providing multiple examples of a particular tale and multiple portrayals of a particular character can avoid stereotyping or creating misconceptions.

Stock characters behave predictably.

We will make a case in point with the **trickster,** a popular folktale character who teaches and learns lessons the hard way, making up for physical weakness by making subversive jokes and playing underhanded tricks on his unsuspecting victims. Tricksters can be alternatively clever and stupid, kind and mean, deceived and deceitful; they play an important role in the folklore and culture of the United States. Readers will enjoy the wide variety of individual Native American trickster tales, but they will benefit more from seeing and hearing several trickster stories. This is so with *Trickster: Native American Tales: A Graphic Collection* by Matt Dembicki. In this collection the trickster character appears variously as a rabbit, raccoon, coyote, raven, and other guises. Numerous Native American storytellers present these authentic trickster tales through graphic art. Each tale's graphics are created in a style that matches both the tone and the telling style of the story. This is a unique collection and the visual comparisons highlight the diversity within Native American trickster folktales.

Lazy but tricky characters often appear in folktales.

INQUIRY POINT

There are many forms of trickster tales. There is generally a foil—another "foolish" character or a character whose role is to reveal the fool in the trickster. Here are several trickster tales and tales that follow the trickster pattern. See if you can decide who is the trickster, the fool, and what human characteristic or cultural belief is being subverted. You may see that the trickster is sometimes quite irreverent. How do the illustrations change the way you know the trickster?

Aardema, Vera. *Anansi Does the Impossible: An Ashanti Tale*. Lisa Desimini, Illus. Perfection, 2000.

Lester, Julius. *The Tales of Uncle Remus*. Jerry Pinkney, Illus. Puffin, 2006.

McDermott, Gerald. *Jabuti the Tortoise: A Trickster Tale from the Amazon*. Sandpiper, 2005.

McKissack, Patricia. *Flossie and the Fox*. Rachel Isadora, Illus. Dial, 1986.

Nelson, S. D. *Coyote Christmas: A Lakota Story*. Abrams, 2007.

Van Allsburg, Chris. *The Widow's Broom*. Houghton, 1992.

Wooldridge, Connie Nordhielm. *Wicked Jack*. Holiday House, 1995.

Fantasy

A discussion of character in children's literature needs to address the various kinds of protagonists. This is especially possible within the fantasy genre, where characters are not only people or animals, but may also be inanimate objects. Hans Christian Andersen characterized the inanimate long ago, endowing these characters with various traits, depending on the length of his story and the theme he was exploring. The tin soldier in "The Steadfast Tin Soldier," although an inanimate object, is a convincing character. In the many still frequently read tales Andersen wrote, it is the unity of character and action that makes each story live. Contemporary children still find pleasure in stories with either animals or inanimate objects as characters, so we will mention a few current examples here.

We loved *Harold and the Purple Crayon*, but *The Pencil* by Allan Ahlberg adds a new spin; the pencil itself is the main character, drawing itself in and out of adventures. In this case the suspense hangs on its ability to escape his own creation: an eraser gone amok. *Traction Man is Here* by Mini Grey involves an action figure come to life, engaging in a never-ending battle of good versus evil that incorporates every household item available to him. Mini Grey appreciates the inventive nature of children who can repurpose the most common objects during creative play.

Contemporary children's books include characterizations neither human nor inanimate: plants, too, can participate in a story. *The Little Yellow Leaf* features a solitary yellow leaf that fears the unknown and clings to its home on the branch of a great oak tree. Encouragement from another leaf provides the little leaf with the courage to let go just as the snow begins to flurry. Though the little leaf is an object dependent on nature for its course through the seasons, readers can sense its feelings of indecision about the choices life holds for us all. Carin Berger's beautiful collage illustrations provide a glimpse of nature's texture and a sense of the seasons as we follow the Little Yellow Leaf along a looping path of growth and change.

Inanimate objects of all kinds can become acceptable characters for younger readers.

Interesting possibilities for characters exist when writers blend plant and animal, nonfiction and fantasy, as is the case with *Pulelehua and Mamaki* by Janice Crowl. The story is organized around the life cycle and metamorphosis of the Kamehameha butterfly through both the voice of the narrator and the dialogue between the host mamaki tree and the Kamehameha butterfly, Pulelehua. Their conversation enlivens the narrative of the relationship between the endemic Hawaiian tree and butterfly. Each double page spread includes bright painted collage illustrations of the lush vegetation of Hawaiian rainforest. The illustrations reveal the personification of the tree; an expressive face appears on the trunk. The butterfly is realistically illustrated in all of its life phases, as is the rest of the setting. Aside from their conversation, the tree and butterfly behave as the living things they are. Extensive back matter provides authentic information for this story of endemic Hawaiian species. The plant and animal dialogue belongs in the realm of fantasy, but it also intimates a Hawaiian cultural belief in the interdependence of nature—the technique is not solely for purposes of characterization in an otherwise nonfiction narrative.

Fantasy, Realism, and the Supernatural

When writers permit animal characters to talk with one another in human speech, realism becomes fantasy. Our mentor text, *Charlotte's Web,* includes animals that are, in essence, people. But E. B. White's writing is so skilled in the portrayal of each animal that many children engaged with the characters could easily forget that the story is fantasy! Similarly, the picturebook *Hook* by Ed Young has a realistic human protagonist—a young boy who finds an abandoned egg and places it in a chicken's nest to incubate. Upon hatching, it is clear that Hook is no chicken. Fantasy begins as the animals and protagonist work together to steer the eaglet in the right direction: up, as he he soars away. Along with the dialogue, there is a slight change in the illustrations; the expression of the chicken signals personification and fantasy. Mark Reibstein and Ed Young's *Wabi Sabi* is a cat's quest to find the meaning of her name, Wabi Sabi. Though the cat talks to all she meets on her journey, the combination of beautiful collage art, haiku, a well-paced story, and top-to-bottom format has the effect of harmony among all the elements to make something beautiful. Her dialogue is just one of the elements that make this book so much more than a talking animal story in the traditional sense, where animals are stand-ins for people. Animal stories remain an important category that children can explore in their quest to discover how their world works.

Realistic animals must be true to their species; fantasy is more believable if the animals are realistic.

Categories such as contemporary realism and historical fiction do this work through characters that could or did exist. For years children have enjoyed fiction focused on or including animals as central characters. The historical fiction stories *Hachiko Waits* by Leslie Newman and *Hachiko: The True Story of a Loyal Dog* by Pamela S. Turner are both based on a true story. Their storied accounts focus on a real dog, Hachi, and realistic human characters either as narrators or as a part of the fictionalized story from history. Because of the complications in creating an engaging and rounded animal character that is also believable, most realistic animal fiction places these characters in a secondary role, or a shared primary character role with humans. In a realistic story animal characters must behave like real animals. These books, despite some elements of anthropomorphism, can increase understanding of the natural world and of animal and human bonds, and can assist many readers in viewing animals in a different light.

Contemporary books are frequently hybrids; they create interesting results through blending genres. Realistic portrayals of animal characters appear in elements of Kathi Appelt's enchanting animal adventure *The Underneath*. The nonhuman characters are a unique mix of anthropomorphized animals and shape shifters; their actions reveal their "human" qualities, both good and evil. Though some human thoughts and characteristics are ascribed to them, the animals carry the story. We don't hear them speak; rather, their thoughts and actions are in keeping with the dogs and cats they are, despite the feats they undertake to survive and help one another. We believe in Calico Cat and gasp with disbelief when she and her kitten are thrown into the river; our disgust flares when Gar Face shoots Ranger, his loyal dog, and chains him under the porch to suffer alone; later Ranger is tied along the river bank as alligator bait. The antagonist in this hybrid novel is wholly human; Gar Face is so despicable, readers will cheer when he loses the battle with the Alligator King. Amazingly, the actions of the characters from one level of this parallel story affect the characters in the other, but all are oblivious to one another's existence. The stories intertwine and characters interconnect in unusual ways, resulting is an exciting story that gives readers an emotion-packed experience. Teachers, parents, and librarians will have many opportunities to guide readers in analyzing these unique characters once they've enjoyed this novel.

Shape shifters like those in the southern Gothic novel *The Underneath* are but one of a host of supernatural characters populating children's books. Ghosts, witches, and vampires are incorporated into stories, not necessarily as an evil force to contend with as in traditional literature portrayals; these beings are characters that intermingle freely with humans. Readers empathize with them and recognize their human qualities much as they do human characters. For example, the supernatural characters who rescue and raise young Bod (Nobody) from a certain death in Neil Gaiman's *The Graveyard Book* display more human characteristics than the chillingly evil "man named Jack."

Readers of WWII historical fiction embrace the dramatized narrator of *The Book Thief*, who is Death personified. Though he is a flat character, the reader has a sense of his humanity and the tireless work he is required to do, delivering souls to their final destination. It is through Death's voice that we come to know the cast of characters living in a small town outside of Munich. His storytelling includes foreshadowing that prepares readers for the story's unhappy ending, yet readers will find it moving just the same. This story bends the expectations for the historical fiction genre, and the unique characterizations communicated through the all-seeing eyes of Death are not only believable, but also mesmerizing.

Science Fiction

Examining literature by genre sets up a collective set of expectations derived from our experiences with a particular genre. Science fiction has been called the fiction of change, "future history." Many readers can't get enough of the rich and imaginative visions for the future; many others avoid this genre. A number of reasons, from reading experiences to the complexity of requirements for good science fiction, may explain this. In years past, topics related to space travel and colonization could be highly speculative, but technological advancements have made good science fiction that suspends our disbelief quite difficult for both writers and readers.

Once written with an adult audience in mind, with attention to the effects of science and technology on a future society, science fiction's greater concern for character is now reaching a larger audience. There is now a home for science fiction writers in the young adult literature market; authors write not only for the genre, but also for an audience with a desire for connectivity with strong characters. Science fiction's growth to encompass character as well as social and political problems has extended its audience; however, it has also caused regret among some writers and critics because they see science fiction as growing virtually indistinguishable from mainstream contemporary fiction.[4]

Science fiction's original focus was on plot and action. However, as science fiction gains popularity with younger readers, it now emphasizes character in addition to plot. The protagonists of *The Ear, the Eye, and the Arm* by Nancy Farmer are three pampered children confined to their home by their father (prominent military figure Amadeus Matsika) for security reasons. They even attend "Scouts" by holophone in 2194 Zimbabwe. Toxic waste threatens their world; many species are extinct and most characters are mutants of some kind—they have gardener robots, house robots, even an automatic Doberman. This story follows them on a journey across the city of Harare without bodyguards in order to earn a scout badge. Tendai, Rita, and Kuda overcome numerous obstacles and encounter fantastic futuristic beings before being kidnapped and later defeating the Masks (evil men trying to destroy Mwari, the Heart of Zimbabwe). Three detectives who pursue the children are men who grew up near a nuclear reactor: Arm can outreach anyone; Ear can fold his ears in "like morning glories"; and Eye has no whites, only pupils. Following a series of dangerous encounters and with the assistance of the detectives, the children are reunited with their family. With the help and praise of a walking communicator, Mellower, everyone in the family relaxes, even the harsh militaristic father. This story is filled with fantastic characters and lots of action; it focuses on issues of a society gone awry and environmental devastation. True to traditional science fiction stories, there is a satisfying ending.

Science fiction relies on extrapolation from known scientific principles, as well as the expectation of an optimistic future where characters overcome obstacles. Contemporary science fiction increasingly features characters who live with darker possible futures in technologically contrived worlds affected by medical and scientific advancements and political strife, mind control, and dystopian societies. Titles considered most successful retain some sense of possibility for the characters. The intriguing, award-winning young adult novel *The Adoration of Jenna Fox* by Mary E. Pearson introduces us to a complicated teenage character who is trying to understand the mystery of her existence in a world where technological advances in healthcare are beyond our wildest imaginations. Are Jenna's memories really her own? Why do her parents, apparently loving, keep her from doing what she wants? Teens reading this book will find many similarities between their own real-life questions about who they are and the questions Jenna asks in her science fiction world. Margaret Haddix Peterson's series *The Shadow Children* and *The Missing* are also examples of science fiction for teens and "tweens" that develop unified and believable characters, although in these novels readers will be more focused on fast, exciting plots that cause us to wonder about the directions in which scientific advances are taking society.

Similarly, Margaret Wild and Anne Spudvilas successfully create characters who are realistic and believable. In their sophisticated picturebook, *Woolvs in the Sitee,* a young boy lives alone in fear in a post-apocalyptic world where survivors hide from

Fully developed characters are expected in today's science fiction.

Unless plot grows out of character, it seems contrived.

"woolvs" in the outside world. Mrs. Radinski, an elderly friend, is his touchstone; it is her disappearance that motivates him to overcome his crippling fear and go out into the hostile environment to try to find her. The story is saturated with a feeling of gloom and the suggestion that society is no longer functional; still the young man leaves on his quest with a sense of optimism, inviting the reader to "joyn" him. The style of the illustrations, dark with bold charcoal lines and strategic patches of color, reinforce the stark setting and the bravery of the main character's final action.

Our world is changing so fast, children are bombarded by various electronic media, and it has become so easy to settle into an unthinking acceptance of the world's fast pace. For these reasons, it is more important than ever for children's literature to depict protagonists who are not afraid to fight for what they believe in, even when—sometimes especially when— their beliefs run counter to those accepted by the authorities. Teachers, parents, and other adults may find that science fiction offers characters whose actions create a sense of autonomy and model ways to be proactive in a complex world. Lois Lowry's *The Giver* and M. T. Anderson's *Feed* are two novels that provide readers with opportunities to not only think about the world as it could become, but also to examine and test accepted truths around them. Both stories' protagonists struggle when what they know to be right in their heart goes against what they've been taught.

Readers enter Jonas's world in *The Giver,* and like its residents, accept what appears to be a harmonious, egalitarian society. However, like Jonas, readers sense that things are not as they seem. Jonas, through the narrator's descriptions, his actions, and his relationships with other characters, is credible; readers cheer for his safety when he escapes the community with Gabe at the end of the story. Violet from *Feed* pushes the limits of her world, where technology is advanced enough that information is fed directly into the minds of the citizens, guiding their every choice in accordance with corporate agendas. Violet has escaped the continuous "feed" of propaganda and mind control because she is home schooled. Her friend Titus, having been raised with constant media input through implanted wires, much of it at school, is thoroughly influenced by the corporate feed. Through his friendship with Violet he sees the possibility for something different. At story's end, Titus gives the impression that he may follow Violet's example and attempt to break free from the system, or at least start to question it. Characters like these affect young readers who are figuring out their place in the world.

If we apply the axioms of character development, we realize that believing in the reality of character makes us believe in the experience. A believable character can make us feel that the discoveries within the story have significance and assist in our discovery of ourselves.

Picturebooks

We have integrated picturebooks throughout this chapter, but we will provide a reminder that the characterization in the picturebook format is unique. The expectation for characters we love is that they are developed enough to make us believe in them through the combination of pictures and the story's action. The compact nature of the picturebook makes it virtually impossible to create a fully rounded and dynamic character through words alone. Therefore, a significant portion of what a reader knows about a character will be provided by the illustrations. *A Couple of Boys Have the Best Week Ever* relies almost completely on the cartoon style art of Marla Frazee to visually show the reader the personalities of James and Eamon as they experience summertime with Eamon's grandparents. Frazee shows us just what it means to be a kid, as well as just what it means to be a grandparent!

Illustrations are essential in rounding out picturebook characters, providing the nuanced emotions, the settings in which they interact, and details surrounding their actions. The autobiographical *Little Cliff* books by Clifton Taulbert are three stories about a young boy growing up in the South during the 1950s. The illustrations by E. B. Lewis support the range of emotions the character has about the first day of school in *Little Cliff's First Day of School.* His great-grandparents cheerfully lay out the clothes for his first day of school, but Cliff feels differently. As his smiling grandparents make preparations, we see Cliff in the background, small and apprehensive. Later, the pictures show his bowed head, downcast eyes, and slumped posture as he is firmly guided toward this important day. In each episode, the words tell the story and describe the setting, but the illustrations provide the depth readers want in a main character; they make Cliff believable.

Interesting possibilities for character exist with wordless picturebooks. A stellar example of this is Suzy Lee's *Mirror*. Done in shades of gray and black on a white background, a lonely girl discovers her image in the mirror. Her personality blooms as she interacts with her image; warm colors verify the brightening mood. The young girl's self-conscious realization that the image is the effect of a mirror, thereby in her control, leads to an unfortunate ending. There is a visual reminder of actions and consequence, but readers will know there is much more to this very intriguing story. They will want to return and re-examine each two-page spread to speculate about this character—and understand themselves a little better.

Classic Characters

In our intertextual model, we must also consider how characterization plays an important role in the ways children's books grow and change. Different from the notion of a character motivating the creation of a series, as did *Eloise,* a classic character can be one that influences a variety of authors to create a similarly rich character. Or a classic character may be so convincing that an additional inquiry ensues; a search for actual people whose lives would inform our appreciation of a character. Take, for example, a textset inspired by Christopher Paul Curtis's now classic, *Bud, Not Buddy.*

SUMMARY

In life and in books, children can sense differences in people and are capable of recognizing and responding to well-developed characters. In even the simplest stories it is possible to find characters that reveal various aspects of human nature. We meet these characters in actions that seem to be part of their natures, and know them— whether they be personified objects, real or personified animals, or humans—by their appearance, words, actions, thoughts, and the opinions of others about them.

Illuminating Characters: Bud, Not Buddy

Bud searches for his father and finds a surrogate family with jazz musicians surrounding Herman F. Calloway, who he believed was his real father, beginning his own jazz career. Herman Calloway and the Dusky Devastators played jazz. Who are other story characters, fictional and nonfictional, that might have interacted with Bud as peers or mentors? What might Bud learn from them? What are their similarities with and differences from Bud? Could you create another character who might have interacted with Bud?

Christensen, Bonnie. *Django: World's Greatest Jazz Guitarist.* **Roaring Brook Press, 2011.**

How might Bud have been able to interact with Django Reinhardt, who would have been several years older?

Dillon, Leo, & Diane Dillon. *Jazz on a Saturday Night.* **Blue Sky Press, 2007.**

Beautifully illustrated story of jazz musicians, including a CD to guide budding jazz lovers, like Bud.

Ehrhardt, Karen. *This Jazz Man.* **Harcourt, 2006.**

A picturebook collection of biographies of jazz legends.

Isadora, Rachel. *Ben's Trumpet.* **Greenwillow, 1979.**

Boy growing up in the 1920s aspires to be a jazz musician.

Miller, William. *Rent Party Jazz.* **Charlotte Riley-Webb, Illus. Lee & Low, 2001.**

Story of how the tradition of "rent parties" started to help those in need and their link to the development of jazz in New Orleans; young protagonist could be a contemporary of Bud.

Orgill, Roxanne. *If I Only Had a Horn: Young Louis Armstrong.* **Houghton Mifflin, 1997.**

A boy overcoming incredible odds to achieve his dream; contemporary of Cab Calloway musicians.

Pinkney, Andrea. *Duke Ellington: The Piano Prince and His Orchestra.* **Brian Pinkney, Illus. Hyperion, 2006.**

Contemporary of Cab Calloway.

Pinkney, Andrea. *Ella Fitzgerald: The Tale of a Vocal Virtuoso.* **Brian Pinkney, Illus. Hyperion, 2002.**

Companion book to the biography of Duke Ellington; a female figure for Bud.

Raschka, Christopher. *Charlie Parker Played Be Bop.* **Scholastic, 1992.**

Could have been a contemporary of Bud at the time of the story.

Raschka, Christopher. *Thelonious Monk.* **Orchard Books, 1997.**

Could have been a contemporary of Bud.

Weatherford, Carole Boston. *Before John Was a Jazz Giant: A Song of John Coltrane.* **Sean Qualls, Illus. Henry Holt, 2008.**

Could have been a contemporary of Bud.

Winter, Jonah. *Dizzy.* **Sean Qualls, Illus. Arthur A. Levine, 2006.**

Winter recognizes that if he can get readers interested in a character—in this case, revolutionary trumpet player, Dizzy Gillespie—they may want to learn more about his music. Just as knowing Bud's character can motivate interest in the jazz world – then and now. Contemporary of Charlie Parker, would have been a peer of Bud.

Round characters have many traits, while flat characters have limited development. Two kinds of characters that serve as background figures or contrasts are stereotypes and foils. Central characters in the action are round, so that by believing in their reality we are led to discover something about humanity, and we are thereby convinced that the conflict in the story, like conflict in life, is significant. The round characters may or may not change, but if they do, we expect those changes to be convincing.

Great pleasure results from reading about people like ourselves, or people we know from all walks of life, from varied cultural backgrounds, with different life experiences. This pleasure of recognition can lead to understanding. Children, as much as adults—or even more than adults—need to view themselves and others as part of a larger social system, a culture. If literature helps children understand the nature of humans, we need reality in the portrayal of character. Nothing—not style, or conflict, or adventure, or suspense, or vivid setting, or even laughter or tears—nothing can substitute for solid character development in creating pleasurable and lasting literature for children as well as adults.

NOTES

1. Henry James, *The Art of Fiction and Other Essays* (New York: Oxford University Press, 1948), p. 13.
2. For further information, read Donald Graves's "Help Children Read and Write Fiction," a chapter in his *A Fresh Look at Writing* (Portsmouth, NH: Heinemann, 1994), pp. 287–304. Educators owe a great debt of gratitude to Donald Graves's stellar contributions to literacy. Those interested in character development will find great strategies for any setting in this seminal book.
3. Though the authors address primarily secondary teachers, the suggestions of Michael W. Smith and Jeffrey D. Wilhelm in *Literary Elements: How to Teach What Really Matters about Character, Setting, Point of View and Theme* (Urbana, IL: National Council of Teachers of English, 2010) have great promise for anyone interested in accessing fiction, adult or children's. This handbook for teaching literary elements provides the "so what" of looking closely at literature—it's not only knowledge of the book, but also of the reader and their context that matters in reading critically.
4. Farah Mendlesohn, "The Campaign for Shiny Futures," *The Horn Book Magazine,* 85(2), 2009, pp. 155–161. This article is very readable; it touches upon some difficulties that plague the science fiction genre for children and the reasons the style and tone of science fiction has changed since the 1970s. She cites Roger Sutton; this article introduces the findings in her book, *The Inter-Galactic Playground: A Critical Study of Children's and Teens' Science Fiction: (Critical Explorations in Science Fiction and Fantasy).*

RECOMMENDED BOOKS

ACKERMAN, KAREN. *Song and Dance Man.* Illustrated by Stephen Gammell. Knopf, 1988.

AHLBERG, ALLAN. *The Pencil.* Illustrated by Robert Ingman. Candlewick, 2008.

ALCOTT, LOUISA MAY. *Little Women, 1868–1869.* Reprint. Dutton, 1948.

ALMOND, DAVID. *Skellig*: 10th Anniversary Edition. Delacorte, 2009.

ANDERSEN, HANS CHRISTIAN. *The Steadfast Tin Soldier.* Atheneum, 1971.

ANDERSON, M. T. *Feed.* Walker Books, 2003.

ANDERSON, M. T. *The Ugly Duckling.* Macmillan, 1967.

APPELT, KATHI. *The Underneath.* Illustrated by David Small. Atheneum, 2009.

BERGER, CARIN. *The Little Yellow Leaf.* Greenwillow, 2008.

BURG, ANN. *All the Broken Pieces.* Scholastic, 2009.

CROWL, JANICE. *Pulelehua and Mamaki.* Illustrated by Harinani Orme. Bishop Museum Press, 2009.

CURTIS, CHRISTOPHER PAUL. *Bud, Not Buddy.* Delacorte, 1999.

CURTIS, CHRISTOPHER PAUL. *The Watsons Go to Birmingham—1963.* Delacorte, 1995.

DEMBICKI, MATT. *Trickster: Native American Tales: A Graphic Collection.* Fulcrum, 2010.

FARMER, NANCY. *The Ear, the Eye, and the Arm.* Orchard Books, 1994.

FORMAN, GAYLE. *If I Stay.* Dutton, 2009.

FOX, MEM. *Wilfrid Gordon McDonald Partridge.* Illustrated by Julie Vivas. Kane/Miller, 1990.

FRAZEE, MARLA. *A Couple of Boys Have the Best Weekend Ever.* Harcourt, 2008.

GAIMAN, NEIL. *The Graveyard Book.* HarperCollins, 2008.

GREY, MINI. *Traction Man Is Here.* Knopf, 2005.

HOWE, JAMES. *The Misfits.* Atheneum, 2003.

HOWE, JAMES. *Totally Joe.* Ginee Seo, 2005.

KAHN, RUKHSANA. *Big Red Lollipop.* Illustrated by Sophie Blackall. Viking, 2010.

KITAMURA, SATOSHI. *Lily Takes a Walk.* Sunburst, 1998.

LEE, SUZY. *Mirror.* Seven Footer Press, 2010.

L'ENGLE, MADELEINE. *A Wrinkle in Time.* Farrar, Straus & Giroux, 1962.

LOWRY, LOIS. *The Giver.* Houghton Mifflin, 1993.

NEWMAN, LESLIE. *Hachiko Waits.* Illustrated by Machiyo Kodaira. Henry Holt, 2004.

OFFILL, JENNY. *17 Things I'm Not Allowed to Do Anymore.* Illustrated by Nancy Carpenter. Schwartz & Wade, 2006.

PAULSEN, GARY. *Hatchet.* Bradbury, 1987.

PEARSON, MARY E. *The Adoration of Jenna Fox.* Henry Holt, 2008.

PETERSON, MARGARET HADDIX. *Among the Hidden: The Shadow Children. Book One.* Simon & Schuster, 2000.

PETERSON, MARGARET HADDIX. *Found: The Missing Book One.* Simon & Schuster, 2008.

RATHMANN, PEGGY. *Officer Buckle and Gloria.* Putnam, 1995.

REIBSTEIN, MARK. *Wabi Sabi.* Illustrated by Ed Young. Little Brown, 2008.

SACHAR, LOUIS. *Holes.* Farrar, Straus & Giroux, 2008.

SACHAR, LOUIS. *Small Steps.* Turtleback, 2008.

SLEATOR, WILLIAM. *Interstellar Pig.* Dutton, 1984.

STEVENS, JANET. *From Pictures to Words: A Book about Making a Book.* Holiday House, 1995.

TAULBERT, CLIFTON L. *Little Cliff's First Day of School.* Illustrated by E. B. Lewis. Dial, 2001.

TAYLOR, MILDRED. *Roll of Thunder, Hear My Cry.* Dial, 2001.

TOLAN, STEPHANIE S., *Surviving the Applewhites.* HarperCollins, 2002.

TURNER, PAMELA S. *Hachiko: The True Story of a Loyal Dog.* Illustrated by Yan Nascimbene. Sandpiper, 2009.

WHELAN, GLORIA. *Homeless Bird.* HarperCollins, 2000.

WHITE, E. B. *Charlotte's Web.* Illustrated by Garth Williams. Harper & Row, 1952.

WILLIAMS-GARCIA, RITA. *One Crazy Summer.* Amistad, 2010.

WILD, MARGARET. *Woolvs in the Sitee.* Illustrated by Anne Spudvilas. Boyds Mills Press, 2007.

WOODSON, JACQUELINE. *Locomotion.* Putnam, 2003.

YOUNG, ED. *Hook.* Roaring Book Press, 2009.

ZUSAK, MARKUS. *The Book Thief.* New York: Knopf, 2007.

MyEducationKit™

Go to the topics "Traditional Literature" and "Modern Fantasy" on the MyEducationKit for this text, where you can:

- Search the Children's Literature Database, housing more than 22,000 titles searchable in every genre by authors or illustrators, by awards won, by year published, and by topic and description.

- Explore genre-related Assignments and Activities, assignable exercises showing concepts in action through database use, video, cases, and student and teacher artifacts.

- Listen to podcasts and read interviews from some of the brightest and most enduring stars of children's literature in the Conversations.

- Discover web links that will lead you to sites representing the authors you learn about in these pages, classrooms with powerful children's literature connections, and literature awards.

I hear a sound in
known. That's whe
I shove aside the
Quick as a rat, sl
around and around
kitchen, yelling, "A

Big Red Lollipop

Rukhsana Khan / Illustrated by Sophie Blackall

Developing the plot and revealing a series
of events across time can be done effectively through illustration in the picturebook format.

Plot

Without some plot
in a story, will the
reader continue to
turn the pages?

While some adult readers may be more interested in character than in any other element in the story, most of us—and most children—cannot get involved with stories that are only character studies. We want things to move and happen; we call this order **plot**. Plot is the sequence of events showing characters in conflict. This sequence is not accidental but is chosen by the author as the best way of telling his or her story. If the writer has chosen well, the plot will produce conflict, tension, and action that will arouse and hold our interest.

Children want what most adults want in literature: action, happenings, questions that need answers, answers that fit questions, glimpses of happy and unhappy outcomes, discovery of how events grow and turn. Younger children find pleasure in recognizing daily routine within the pages of a book, but many people think that *all* a child needs in a narrative is the recognition of an everyday happening—an action as prosaic as going to bed at night or waking up in the morning. It is surprising that adults who would never find pleasure in a literal, hour-by-hour account of their own daily routines expect such accounts to satisfy children. No matter how content children of any age are with daily order, children very soon expect that they should find life more exciting in a story than in their own experience. Look, for example, at John Burningham's *Time to Get Out of the Bath, Shirley*. In this marvelous picturebook, Shirley is not content simply to take an ordinary bath. As her mother

> Plot is the sequence of events showing characters in conflict.

chastises her about leaving the soap in the bathtub, says she should take a bath more often, and picks her clothes up from the bathroom floor, Shirley, in the bathtub, is having adventures: escaping from the bathtub on her spotted duck, meeting up with a knight, racing across the field on the back of the knight's horse, and jousting with knights and ladies in a lake. In *Time to Get Out of the Bath, Shirley,* as in most books children and adults love, readers lose themselves in possibility as they pose the big question of all literature: What if? This element of possibility, of possible action and reaction, builds the plot.

Types of Narrative Order

One of the writer's privileges is to reorder existence, rearrange events, or, in other words, create plot. The writer may focus on one moment of a day and ignore all others; he or she may charge one hour with significance that influences the months or years of a life. The writer may ignore the segments of time that have little significance or simply summarize those moments. The writer makes alterations and deletions that our memories are unable to make for us in our own lives. The writer's selectivity and purposeful reordering and highlighting create plot.

Children learn about narrative order very early in their lives, as C. W. Sullivan III reminds us.[1] The earliest play with babies in "This Little Piggy" and "Patty Cake" follows simple narrative form. Soon children hear "Little Red Riding Hood" and "The Three Little Pigs." As they listen to and tell other tales, they learn about situation and sequence and come to expect the "beginning, middle, and end" order. **Narrative order** in fiction, the order in which events are related, may follow several patterns, but the most common pattern in young children's literature is the chronological arrangement.

Chronological Order

Our lives are one twenty-four-hour period after another. This time order is simple chronology. If a story relates events in the order of their happening, the story is in **chronological order**.

To say the plot order is chronological does not tell us a lot about the book itself. For example, Arthur Dorros's picturebook *Papa and Me* and Jeanette Winter's *Nasreen's Secret School: A True Story from Afghanistan* both progress in chronological order, but they are very different books.

Papa and Me begins when the narrator wakes his father: "Good morning!" "*Buenos dias!*" The narrator describes his day with his father: breakfast; a trip to the park to splash in *agua,* climb trees, and draw in the sand; and then, in the evening (as we see from the darkened skies in the swirling illustrations), taking the number forty-three bus back home to see *abuela* and *abuelo,* the narrator's grandparents. The structure of the book is chronological, from beginning to end, describing the simple pleasures of a single day father and son share together.

Nasreen's Secret School, a picturebook for slightly older children, is also structured chronologically. This book is illustrated in Jeannette Winter's signature style of naïve art—drawings that express simplicity and innocence and use bright colors and sometimes folkloric motifs. The story is told in the voice of Nasreen's grandmother, with whom Nasreen lives in Herat, Afghanistan. The book begins by explaining how the music and art—the cultural expressions of learning—have been taken from the city, now that the Taliban occupy it. The Taliban has forbidden girls to go to school. When the soldiers take Nasreen's father away, she sinks into a depression. Worried about her, Nasreen's grandmother takes her to a school that must be kept secret from the Taliban leaders. Nasreen's grandmother watches as, at the school, Nasreen slowly comes alive again, making a friend and beginning to talk. At the end of this short book, Nasreen's grandmother says she knows that Nasreen will hold what she learns at the school inside her heart forever; she says that she knows that the knowledge Nasreen learns at the school will keep her company. This story may take place over weeks or months, but it is ordered chronologically, just as in *Papa and Me*.

Variations in Narrative Form

Chronological plot structures may vary in the amount of time they cover, as we see above, but they can vary in other ways as well. Four novels for children and young adults that are all chronologically structured are: *Pictures of Hollis Woods*, *Stowaway*, *Jumped!*, and *The Surrender Tree: Poems of Cuba's Struggle for Freedom*. Yet each has a narrative form distinctly different from the others.

For example, *Pictures of Hollis Woods* by Patricia Reilly Giff moves from the past to the present in alternating chapters. Hollis, a foster child who thinks of herself only as "trouble," has lived in several foster homes, feeling sure each one is the wrong place for her. In some she resents rigidity or condescension, and in others feels unwanted, not part of a "real family." When Old Man Regan, his wife Izzy, and their son Steven take her in for the summer, everyone is happy with the arrangement—until Hollis is lost on a dangerous hike in the mountains. Steven, underage, takes his father's truck to find her and is hurt in an accident. Hollis, who has done a bad thing, feels she must leave this home, too. Her next placement is with a forgetful old woman named Josie, an artist who encourages Hollis's artistic talent and whom Hollis cares for lovingly. Chapters are alternating memories of her love for the Regan family, where she felt like a daughter, and her life with Josie.

Karen Hesse's *Stowaway* provides a fictional daily journal of Captain Cook's voyage around the world, describing not only crises of the voyage, but also friendships and animosities on shipboard. The journal form may seem less immediate, but it shows effects of events on the young journalist. The *Endeavor* sailed for three years, between 1768 and 1771, and endured being becalmed for days and weeks at a time and losing most of the seamen to unknown fevers. Nicolas begins by scrubbing decks, scraping the hull, standing watch, and imitating birdcalls. When he concludes his voyage he is an essential seaman who helps collect specimens, nurses the sick, discovers unknown insects and animals, and meets cannibals while fighting the force of a hostile sea.

Jumped! is a National Book Award Finalist about girl-on-girl violence by Rita Williams-Garcia told from three different perspectives. In short alternating first-person chapters, each of three girls—Leticia, Dominique, and Trina—tells the story of one day in high school, a day that begins when Leticia overhears tomboyish and aggressive Dominique telling her friends that she is going to beat up artistic, girly, flakey Trina, just because she walked by her with a flippant attitude. The main conflict in the book is internal, as Leticia tries to ignore friends who tell her she must warn Trina that she is going to be jumped by Dominique outside of the school at 2:45. The tension rises through the day as we read about it from each girl's first-person perspective. We hear Dominique's thoughts about basketball; Trina's excitement about her art; and

Leticia's concern over a broken fingernail as well as her occasional worry about the upcoming fight. At the climax of the novel we see the fight occur. The story's resolution shows Leticia watching the news about the fight on television.

Another variation can be seen in Margarita Engle's verse novel *The Surrender Tree: Poems of Cuba's Struggle for Freedom*. Like the narratives listed above, this award-winning historical novel is structured chronologically, but it covers a very long swath of time, the years of Cuba's wars for independence from Spain—from 1850 to 1899. The narrative, in one-page blank verse poems, alternates among four voices: the voice of Rosa, a runaway slave who became a great and famous healer of the rebel soldiers; her husband, José; a slave catcher nicknamed Lieutenant Death; and Silvia, an eleven-year-old boy who comes to live with Rosa and José after his parents are killed. We see Rosa grow from a child to a woman, hiding in caves, learning about medicinal herbs, marrying, saving the sick, and riding on her horse between two hospitals, taking care of the Cubans fighting the Spanish. We see how José protects Rosa and helps her hide, and we see how Lieutenant Death hunts and tries to murder Rosa, whom he calls "the witch." This novel, which is very closely based on history, shows the great poet José Marti murdered in his first battle, Rosa meeting the nurse Clara Barton, and the U.S. battleship *Maine* exploding in Havana harbor. In the end, Lieutenant Death dies in the jungles and we hear in three voices that Cuba is independent from Spain and at peace.

Variations in Representations of Time

A flashback may juggle time to show how things began.

In fiction for mature readers, narrative order may involve a **flashback**. Many readers can recall their first experience with a flashback: it was puzzling. "What happened? How come?" The writer disrupts normal time sequence to recount some episode out of the character's past, showing how that event influences the character's response to an event in the present. Or the writer shows in flashback a past event that has brought on the present one. In either case, the writer chooses to juggle time to make a point about the character and the story. The young child, however, may find it difficult to follow such movement back and forth in time.[2]

The child relies on his or her own experience of time to understand when and how events occur. Since the child knows from experience, for instance, that one falls asleep and dreams, he or she understands Maurice Sendak's *In the Night Kitchen*. The child knows that such a marvelous adventure could happen to Max while he sleeps or daydreams, since the child has had dreams. As the child grows in sophistication, he or she comes to comprehend the possibility in literature of mixing memory, imagination, dream, daydream, and flashback. Television probably increases children's exposure to flashback and dream techniques, and this experience could help them to recognize them in literature.

An example of a traditional flashback can be seen in Cynthia DeFelice's fine historical novel for elementary school students, *The Apprenticeship of Lucas Whitaker*. As the book opens it is 1848, and young Lucas has just dug a grave and hammered his mother's initials onto the top of her coffin lid. He looks over the graves of his infant brother and sister, his Uncle Asa, and his sister Lizy. Then Lucas recalls: "When they'd buried Lizy, Lucas and his father had worked together in stunned silence, afraid to think about, much less speak about, the mysterious way in which the sickness could sweep through a household, taking one family member after another. . . ."

In a flashback, then, Lucas sees his father turn into a "thin, pale stranger" before he dies; his mother's cheeks grow "flushed and red, then gray and gaunt." He sees himself coaxing his mother to take spoonfuls of tea and porridge, and wishing helplessly he could do something to save her. Finally, there is nothing he can do, and "a mixture of terror and anger" rises in his throat, but he pushes that feeling down "until he'd felt the way he did now, his insides as numb and cold as the rough-red hands that grasped the shovel. Quickly, he finished the job."

This elegant glimpse back in time, occurring as Lucas buries his last remaining relative, tells us a lot about our protagonist, serves as helpful exposition, and sets the stage for the tensions to come.

As literature for children has become increasingly sophisticated, representations of time have become more nuanced as well. Many picturebooks represent a change in time through use of color. For example, Louise Borden's wonderful *A. Lincoln and Me* shows us a boy whose birthday falls on February twelfth. The boy is tall, gangly, and awkward, with unusually big hands and feet. When his classmates tease him, his teacher tells them that Abraham Lincoln had unusually big hands and feet, too. Behind the color sketches of the boy, and on separate pages, we see A. Lincoln, looming large in black and white. The color and black and white pictures parallel each other, showing us two different time periods at once.

Another very different text that shows two different time periods running in parallel plots is the best-selling *Holes* by Louis Sachar. Sachar tells the story of Stanley Yelnats, a young teen who is arrested for stealing sneakers and sent to Green Lake Juvenile Detention Facility. At Green Lake, Stanley and the other boys are forced to dig holes in the blinding heat all day. Stanley slowly makes friends with an African American fellow inmate named Zero, and the two run away together, climbing through holes dug by other inmates, subsisting on onions they find buried in the ground, discovering occasional strange treasures. Parallel to this story of the present day, we read a story about Stanley's ancestors, and about the former inhabitants of Green Lake, Kate Barlow and her lover, Sam the onion man. Whether this second story is fantasy or realism is hard to tell, but the two stories intertwine and resonate with each other; the old story provides some answers to questions raised by the present-day story. The point may be that the events of the past often influence the present in ways we can never really know.

Some picturebooks show parallel plot not through stark differences in time in the story narrative, but through a second story suggested through the artwork. *The Storyteller's Candle (La velita de los cuentos)* by Lucia Gonzalez and Lulu Delacre is the story of the librarian Pura Belpré and the difference she made to the Puerto Rican children of New York City during the Great Depression, when she let them know that the library is for everyone. In that library, she told stories in Spanish and English and created special festivities to remind the children of their Puerto Rican home far away. Lulu Delacre makes statements about time in this story through art, showing that it takes place in the past by using washes of sepia tones. She also inserts clippings from a *New York Times* newspaper from 1930 to make collages, providing a sense of the many other stories taking place during this time: readers can see words on the newspapers that relate to topics running parallel with this story.

In *Harry Potter and the Prisoner of Azkaban*, the character Hermoine is given a time turner, a dangerous necklace which she can use to change time so that she can take three classes which all begin at 9:00. Other writers of children's literature play, or have their characters play, with time in different ways. *When You Reach Me* is another

> As literature for children has become increasingly sophisticated, representations of time have become more nuanced as well.

book for elementary school students that plays with representations of time. It might be considered a **time slip** novel, although it's very different from Peg Kehret's *Disaster* series or Mary Pope Osborne's *Magic Treehouse* series, in which children suddenly find themselves running from an exploding Mount St. Helens or living in the time of the dinosaurs. Still, in *When You Reach Me,* time does some very strange things.

A realistic novel on the face of it, one in a long tradition of books about growing up in New York City (for example, *Harriet the Spy, From the Mixed Up Files of Mrs. Basil E. Frankweiler,* and *All of a Kind Family*), *When You Reach Me* is the story of Miranda, a sixth grader who lives with her mother, a secretary at a law firm. As her mother prepares to become a contestant on the television show *The 20,000 Dollar Pyramid*, Miranda mourns the loss of her best friend Sal, who has been acting strange lately; works with two new friends at Jimmy's store; reads her favorite book, *A Wrinkle in Time*; and tries to avoid the scary laughing man who sleeps under the mailbox near her house. But Miranda has been receiving mysterious messages from someone who seems to know what is going to happen in the future. He also seems to have found a way of entering her house unseen. Just like Meg's father in *A Wrinkle in Time,* that same person has learned how to *tesser,* that is, "ride a wrinkle" in time. Past, present, and future all come together in one bold action in this book—one tragic accident averted, one friend regained and another understood, on one amazing day.

Types of Conflict

Plot is a more inclusive concept than narrative order or its synonym, story line, since it involves not only sequence of events, but also **conflict**. In this discussion of books for the young, tension, friction, force, alternatives, excitement, suspense, discovery, and resolution are parts of conflict. Conflict occurs when the protagonist struggles against an **antagonist**, or opposing force. In short, it is conflict that, added to narrative order, makes plot.

A conflict is struggle against opposing forces.

The following subsections discuss four kinds of conflict in literature: person-against-self, person-against-person, person-against-society, and person-against-nature.

Person-Against-Self

Though in some ways Paul Volponi's *Hurricane Song: A Novel of New Orleans* is about a group of people working to remain human in a society that shows no concern for their lives, the core of the novel is the internal conflict within the protagonist, a young football-loving teen named Miles. The main conflict in the book can thus be considered **person-against-self**. Miles has been living with his jazz-musician father in New Orleans for only two months when Hurricane Katrina hits. Holed up with his father and his father's friend in the increasingly dangerous Superdome, Miles must decide whether to forgive his father for putting his music before everything else in his life. As we see Miles decide whether to join classmates who roam the building, taking money from others; as we see him decide to join his father and help heal some of the sorrow inside the Superdome by playing a jazz funeral for a man who has committed suicide; and as we see him slip by a brutal white National Guardsman and follow his father back into the city, we watch and learn from the healing ways that Miles solves his internal conflicts, and learns to understand and forgive.

A protagonist may face two possible choices, thus causing an internal conflict.

Internal conflict is also at the core of Katherine Paterson's *Lyddie,* a story set in New England in the mid-nineteenth century. When a bear enters the family's tiny house, Lyddie, determined to save her family, stares him down, and he turns tail and runs. Although Lyddie would like to go on to college, she leaves for Lowell, Massachusetts, to earn money working eighteen-hour days at the cotton mills to pay off a loan made to the family earlier. Ignoring the recruiting union members pushing for shorter workdays and better pay and working conditions, she instead suffers the long hours and constant airborne lint, despite its inevitable effect on health. When a young woman Lyddie has coached is a victim of the supervisor, she confronts him— just as she had confronted the bear. She will sign the petition and take charge of her life. " 'I'm off . . .' she said, and knew as she spoke what it was she was off to. To stare down the bear! The bear she had thought all these years was outside herself, but now, truly, knew was in her own narrow spirit. She would stare down all the bears." And she goes off to Ohio to be a student at the only college that admits women. Lyddie's conflict is internal, person-against-self.

Grace Founier in Elizabeth Winthrop's *Counting on Grace* feels internal conflict as well, though some of her conflict is with the mores of the society she lives in. Still, as a girl growing up in a mill-working family in the largely French-Canadian town of North Pownal, Vermont, in the first years of the twentieth century, she would have much to say to Patterson's Lyddie. Like Lyddie, Grace works long hours in the cotton textile mill, and like her, at first she cannot imagine any other life. Still, when the lively, curious, plainspoken girl who tells us her story meets the photographer and reformer Lewis Hine, she befriends him right away. She helps him take photographs and learns about the almost-magical process of developing film: she sees herself for what is perhaps the first time, captured in the glass, and is not entirely happy with what she sees. Influenced by Hines and others, she is full of internal conflict: should she accept the mill ways, as her mother wants her to, or try to find a different kind of life, as her teacher Miss Lesley and her friend Arthur want her to? Like Lyddie, Grace learns that education is a way out.

In Margot Theis Raven's picturebook *Night Boat to Freedom,* beautifully illustrated by E. B. Lewis, one of the conflicts is person-against-self. Christmas John's beloved Granny Judith tells him one night that because he is young, he can move about without being suspected by their master. She tells him he is the one who needs to row the cook's child across the river to a station for escaping slaves in the free state of Ohio. Christmas John is frightened to do this, but works against his fear, reminding himself of what Granny Judith told him to do with his heart what his mind told him to fear. E. B. Lewis's watercolor washes—black rowboat against dark blue water and sky; rounded gray figures against night water—create a sense of the tension of the night journeys Christmas John takes as he brings fellow slaves to freedom. At the end of the book Raven provides information about how she learned the stories that influenced the book, and provides readers with the words of an old slave blessing.

Person-Against-Person

The terms used to describe these conflicts are not so important. What does matter is that we see clearly the protagonist and the antagonist. The strain between the two forces is what holds our continuing interest and our intense curiosity about the outcome. Children's literature is filled with suspenseful examples of one kind of tension, **person-against-person** conflict.

Tiphanie is a ninth grader in 1975 when her parents move from the part of Denver where she has grown up to a wealthier, whiter suburb called Brent Hills. Tiphanie is anxious about being one of the very few black students at her new school. She worries that she won't find any friends, and she worries that she'll lose her sense of her black identity. She meets students and teachers who make dismaying assumptions about her—that she must be poor, that she cannot test out of her honors math class, that she must be in love with the only other black student in school. But it is Clay, a white boy whose father owns a trailer park, who causes Tiphanie trouble in the engaging novel *Finding My Place* by Traci L. Jones. Whenever Clay's name is on the page, the reader's tension picks up. Clay keeps Tiphanie from her best friend, Jackie Sue, who lives in the trailer park that Clay's father owns. Clay also calls Tiphanie a pickaninny, tells her to go back to Africa, and harasses her in other ways. Tiphanie is sent to the principal for yelling at Clay when he provides her with a racist interpretation of history. Tiphanie's need to respect herself causes her to take action in this person-against-person conflict.

In Sharon Flake's novel *The Skin I'm In*, Maleeka is in almost constant conflict with Charlese, the fellow student she depends on for help, excitement, and trouble. Maleeka's problems are that her skin is dark black, which her classmates tease her about; she's poor and wears ugly clothes; and she's too smart for her classes, maybe too smart for her school. As Maleeka tells the story of her seventh-grade year we see her torn between becoming a studious girl and running with Charlese's crowd. Charlese tempts and troubles Maleeka and loans her snappy clothes that make her look and feel good. Over the course of the novel, with prodding from a new teacher and a friend who loves her, Maleeka takes two steps forward and one step back, finally standing up to her nemesis, Charlese.

In Molly Bang's wordless picturebook, *The Gray Lady and the Strawberry Snatcher*, the person-against-person conflict is clear. The gray lady has bought some luscious strawberries that she carries toward home. A creepy blue creature follows her, reaching his long arms out to snatch her basket of strawberries. The gray lady evades him, catching a bus, running through swamps, hiding behind and at the top of a tree, finally fading into the gray background. When we last see him the blue strawberry snatcher has been distracted by strawberries on a bush and the gray lady has made it home safely, to share her berries with her cheerful gray family.

Person-against-person conflict is seen often in children's literature, perhaps not as the main conflict, but as one of many in a longer novel. In *90 Miles to Havana*, Julian and other children in the refugee camp are in person-against-person conflict with Caraballo, the bully; in *Harriet the Spy*, Harriet is in a conflict with her classmates; in *Where the Wild Things Are*, Max is in conflict with his mother; and in Madeleine L'Engle's *A Wrinkle in Time*, Meg is in conflict with IT, the disembodied brain.

Person-Against-Society

Conflict and an unknown outcome keep us reading *Charlotte's Web*. Wilbur's struggle is serious: life and death. Although we may define the struggle as a **person-against-society** conflict, the child knows it simply as "Will Wilbur live? Will Charlotte save him from being made into bacon?" In this case we may regard society as the farming business, which, after all, is based on profit. A runt pig is not worth keeping. Although the child reading *Charlotte's Web* gets involved in the conflict of Wilbur-versus-dinner-table, the conflict is actually Wilbur against good business. The conflict begins immediately, page 1, line one: "Where's Papa going with the ax?" Whether Wilbur will be saved from death commands our interest. This conflict of Wilbur against the business of farming keeps our interest from start to finish.

There are many other examples of person-against-society conflict in recent children's literature: here we will examine three, all showing women struggling against a society that does not respect them. *Tofu Quilt* by Ching Yeung Russell is a subtle example. This delicate verse novel is narrated by Yeung Ying, a young girl growing up in 1960s Hong Kong. Yeung Ying tells us that although she loves books and wants to become a writer, and although she's the only one in her family who can write letters for Pau Pau to Uncle Five, no one she knows, except her mother, believes that girls can do much of anything. "How I wish I were a boy," she writes, as she tells us of daily occurrences, her first taste of *dan lai*, her first cup of coffee, her first trip to Jade Street. Finally, after struggling with teachers and classmates who make fun of her imitations of Mark Twain, she sells a story about the tofu quilts her father makes, and then she can call herself a new name—writer.

An equally short novel, also written for and about an eight- or nine-year-old girl, *Rickshaw Girl* by Mitali Perkins is the story of Naima, who is the best artist in her Bangaladeshi village, and who, like Yeung Ying, wishes she had been born a boy. These books could be paired to provide children with interesting conversations: What do they think Naima and Yeung Ying might say to each other, if they met? Naima might talk to Yeung Ying about how she changed into boy's clothes and snuck away from home to try to find work to help her father pay the bills. She might tell Yeung Ying that, like her, she persevered, and found she had talent. Like Yeung Ying, she learned she could use that talent to make money, even though her parents and her friends told her girls could not. Naima, who gets a job painting rickshaws for a female entrepreneur, might tell Yeung Ying that she learned that girls know some things boys don't. Both girls in these two stories are in conflict with their societies, which tell them that girls have only limited roles.

A Woman for President: The Story of Victoria Woodhull by Kathleen Krull is a picturebook biography about a woman who fought against a patriarchal society her whole life. Victoria Woodhull grew up in a time when women were not allowed to go to college, vote, testify in court, serve on juries, earn money of their own, or divorce their husbands. Male doctors wouldn't examine women, and laws spelled out just how big an object a man could use to beat his wife. Yet Victoria Woodhull became wealthy through her own skills, then set up the first female-owned U.S. company that bought and sold stocks. After that success, she started the Equal Rights Party and, in 1872, became the first woman in the United States to run for President. She didn't become president, of course: She spent Election Day in jail. She continued to fight against society, demanding that women deserved to lead lives as full of ambition and glory as men, until she died at eighty-nine.

> Person-versus-society conflict appears in many children's books.

Person-Against-Nature

Master of suspense Gary Paulsen has written several books with a conflict of **person-against-nature**, *Hatchet* and its sequel, *The River,* among them. Brian Robeson, whose plane goes down in the northern wilderness while he is on his way to see his father, struggles and survives for fifty-four days because he has one tool: a small hatchet. Breathlessly we follow his defeat of the natural forces that seem insurmountable. In *The River,* the government wants Brian to repeat the survival process so that a representative can follow and record his experiences in order to train others. Thinking it could be helpful, Brian reluctantly agrees. Once in the wild, however, Brian sees that this trip will not be a true test because he is provided with life-sustaining supplies. Without a real struggle, nothing will be proven and his senses will be dulled to what must be done in crisis after crisis. He sends back the entire load of equipment, keeping only a radio. When lightning strikes Derek, leaving him unconscious, the radio is useless. With nothing but his own wits, this experience is totally different: he has nothing, and is not only responsible for his own survival but also for the unconscious Derek. Without tools, Brian must build a raft, move Derek, and tie him to it. Then he must maneuver the unwieldy raft down the winding river, survive the rapids, and, when thrown into the turbulent water, swim until he finds the rapids-tossed raft with Derek's inert body. Can Brian's strength last? Seeing him tempted, in an internal conflict, to lose Derek's body in the wild river so that he can move more easily, we wonder if he has the courage to continue in his rescue. Person-against-nature is not the only tension holding us to the final page.

Don Wood's full-color graphic novel *Into the Volcano* is an adventure story for younger students also containing a person-against-nature conflict. In this beautifully illustrated book, two brothers, Duffy and Sumo, must defeat their enemies and tangle with a volcano. Duffy, more adventurous, and Sumo, a suspicious worrier, are sent to visit their mysterious Aunt Lulu on the island nation of Kocalaha. Lulu won't let them call their dad, which is strange, but just as they are settling in, having met their cousin Mister Come-and-Go and the beautiful Pulina, they are whisked off on an expedition across the seas and into the middle of a volcano, accompanied by suspiciously behaving strangers. The artwork in this graphic novel is luscious: Don Wood's pictures show golden orange lava spewing, lush Hawaiian yards, and dark, wet, shadowy caves. The paintings, as in all graphic novels, are integral to the story: one frame shows the characters in the boat, waves pounding, the next frame provides a bird's eye view of the tiny boat in the huge ocean. After revelations of some family secrets, the boys find themselves deep in dark caves, facing death, and forced to use resources they didn't know they had. Information about volcanoes is woven into this fast-paced adventure story, in which person-against-nature is only one of the many conflicts that cause us to turn the pages. Conflict in this graphic novel grows in part out of character—in this case the characters of Duffy and Sumo—as conflict of any kind should in a piece of literature.

With person-against-nature conflict patterns, classic stories set the plot to represent people overcoming nature and defeating it. The resolution is one where humans win out over adversity presented by nature. This is still the case when disaster strikes; we want to see the protagonist safely home or rescued in the end, as is the case with Ivy Ruckman's *Night of the Twisters* and *Eight Days: A Story of Haiti* by Edwidge Danticat. In stories where disease is the force to be overcome, readers hope to see protagonists have the possibility of recovery, as in Laurie Halse Anderson's *Fever: 1793* or *Our Shadow Garden* by Cherie Foster Colburn.

While many stories succeed with an adversarial relationship, others succeed in creating a story where the protagonist works *with* nature, to protect and preserve the environment, or to assist nature when disaster strikes.

Inadequately developed conflict, like flat characterization, leaves us unconcerned about the outcome of a story. Conflict holds our attention if it presents some semblance of a fair fight, and if the outcome is uncertain. Inadequate conflict occurs in poor science fiction, when the protagonist combats an irresistible natural force, or if, in person-against-person conflict, the ingenuity of two intellects without emotions becomes a dry, academic struggle. When pure intellect does battle with itself in person-against-self conflict, the struggle is merely a problem with a rational answer. The reader who is uninvolved in either characters or conflict becomes apathetic: "I cannot conceive of it; I therefore cannot care."

A variety of conflicts may exist in a single story.

 ## Patterns of Action

Plot is more than the sequence of actions or conflict. It is also the pattern of those actions. If we oversimplify plot patterns by diagrams, we might describe one of the most common as an upward slanting line followed by a peak and a downward slide, then a short straight line. Another plot structure can be seen as an almost straight horizontal line.

The first, and most common, of these patterns, is complex. The story moves from one incident to another related incident, rises to a peak or climax, then clearly concludes. **Rising action** begins with a situation that must be shown and explained. What has happened before the story opens, what has created the current situation? This explanation of the situation and the characters' condition is called **exposition**. In most stories for children, it is woven into early action so that attention is caught immediately and held.

One plot pattern is complex.

Such a pattern is clearly demonstrated in both Cynthia Kadohata's *Weedflower* and Flores-Gallis's *90 Miles to Havana*, a pair of books that could be interestingly taught together because of their similar themes. In both of these historical fiction books, the main character is taken from his or her home and sent to live in a government camp. In *Weedflower*, Sumiko is a *Nisei*, or an American whose parents were born in Japan. In the first chapter, we learn about Sumiko, and how she lives in California on her aunt and uncle's flower farm. We learn that Sumiko is a thoughtful, responsible, and sensitive girl who loves and takes care of her little brother, works on the farm, and sells flowers. This exposition helps ground us in the story as we learn a little about the girl we will be following throughout the book. We learn that she's very like her readers: excited to go to a sixth-grade classmate's birthday party. In the very next chapter tension begins to rise as we hear her family worry about the war in Germany, and about recent reprisals against Japanese people living in California. Sumiko is treated rudely by the white mother of the girl who invited her to the birthday party in one chapter, and in the next chapter, the sixth of thirty-three chapters, even more **complications** begin: the Japanese bomb Pearl Harbor, and some of the friends of Sumiko's family are rounded up and put into relocation camps by the government. We wonder if Sumiko's family will be next.

Similarly, the first chapter of *90 Miles to Havana* grounds us: we learn about young Julian as he tries to catch a fish and, losing it, is embarrassed in front of his two older brothers. And, as in *Weedflower*, complications begin very quickly: in the second chapter of the book, we watch the family drive through an eerie chaos, hear gunshots in the distance, and see cars turned over, people throwing a piano out of a second story window onto the street, and men pulling parking meters out of the ground with their bare hands. We hear Julian's mother tell him, "Don't look away. I don't want you to ever forget what a revolution looks like." The exposition is over and the novel continues with tension upon rising tension, question upon question: Will ten-year-old Julian get out of Cuba in time? Where will his parents go? How will he survive in the camp? The book has an exciting climax and a satisfying resolution.

In the picturebook *Crossing Bok Chitto: A Choctaw Tale of Friendship and Freedom*, Tim Tingle uses this same plot structure. In the exposition, a Choctaw girl named Martha Tom is supposed to be finding blackberries for a wedding feast. But she disobeys her mother and crosses the Bok Chitto River that cuts through Mississippi. She crosses the way the Choctaw always do, walking on an invisible stone path hidden just below the water. On the other side of the river she hears a black slave preacher mysteriously telling people hidden in the trees that they will find the promised land one day. Their singing moves Martha Tom and she befriends Little Mo, a slave boy who takes her back across the river to her family. The two children become friends. When Little Mo learns that his slave mother is to be sold, the story becomes more complex. Little Mo crosses the river and asks Martha Tom's mother for help. In the **climax** of the story we watch the entire slave family walking across the hidden stones in the river, guided by Choctaw women in white wedding clothes. A quick **resolution** tells us of how this story was told over and over by white people and Choctaw alike, and how Little Mo and his family were never seen on the slave side of the river again. It is unusual to see this more complex plot structure in picturebooks.

The second of these patterns of action, a straight horizontal line, is seen often in stories for younger children. We see one example of this structure in Sara Varon's graphic novel *Robot Dreams*. Dog needs a friend and builds himself a Robot, but when Dog takes Robot to the beach and they go in the waves together, Robot rusts. Dog leaves Robot there and tries to find other friends to satisfy him, but none does—the anteaters expect him to eat ants, the duck leaves for the winter. Tension does not mount to a breaking point, but there is enough to keep us interested in Dog's search for a new friend and in Robot's dreams and memories about his old friend Dog. This practically

A second plot pattern looks more like a straight horizontal line.

wordless book, drawn in muted colors, quietly tells us about friendship and loss.

The straight line plot is much more likely in stories for younger children, though the illustrations may either work with the story or counter it in some way. The narrative text in Colin Thompson's *Looking for Atlantis* is a descriptive but sequential story of a young boy's search for the magical land of Atlantis. The ten-year-old boy examines the many treasures in his grandfather's trunk without success; his grandfather had said all he had to do was "learn how to look for it." The young boy, with the help of his grandfather's parrot, at last realizes that finding Atlantis is within his power, if he uses his imagination. This realization happens at the end of the story, so readers will be pulled back through the book to find all that was right under the young boy's nose! Illustrations are terrific, filled with allusions and quirky details. Readers suspect the young boy is not seeing all of what his grandfather promised, but the illustrations *show* this. As this creative picturebook reveals, there are many different ways a writer can use plot.

INQUIRY POINT

In the library find two chapterbooks for emerging readers, such as Cynthia Rylant's *Harry and Mudge and the Starry Night* and Arnold Lobel's *Uncle Elephant*. Draw a graphic, or story map, that expresses the plot in each of these simple books. Does the plot consist of a sharp line rising upwards after a bit of flat-line exposition? Where does the climax occur, if at all? Is there a resolution in any of these stories?

Now create a story map for a story for third or fourth graders, such as Ivy Ruckman's *Night of the Twisters* or Peg Kehret's *Flood Disaster*. How are these plot graphics different from the ones for younger children?

The elements of a story that deal with action are suspense, the cliffhanger, foreshadowing, sensationalism, the climax, and denouement. Each of these terms will be treated separately in the following subsections.

Suspense

From the first line in the first chapter of *Charlotte's Web*—"Where's Papa going with the ax?"—we know that Wilbur's fate is uncertain, and from that initial moment White holds us in **suspense**, a state that makes us read on. By tears, sobs, cries, and yells, Fern wins temporary reprieve for Wilbur, who becomes Fern's baby. Wilbur's brothers and sisters are all sold, and it is Wilbur's turn. But then Uncle Homer Zuckerman buys Wilbur so Fern can visit him at the nearby farm. Wilbur is lonely, finding his life boring without Fern as constant companion. When he finds a friend, loneliness vanishes. Then, electrifying news comes: An old sheep spitefully tells Wilbur he is being fattened for Christmas slaughter. Charlotte comes to the rescue. She weaves the words "Some Pig" into her web; people come from miles around to see Wilbur. Mr. Zuckerman now admires him, and no celebrity has ever been made into sausage.

As the excitement wears off, our worries revive. Charlotte, however, sends Templeton to the dump for more words. When each of the woven words miraculously appears, we have new hope. Then Wilbur's protector announces regretfully that she cannot accompany Wilbur to the fair. Catastrophe looms again, but a ray of hope glimmers: "We'll leave it this way: I'll come to the Fair if I possibly can." Our security lasts only until we overhear Arable and Zuckerman talking about the fine ham and bacon he'll make. A huge pig called Uncle is stiff competition: "He's going to be a hard pig to beat." Wilbur's doom is sealed. Suddenly, an unprecedented award, but Wilbur faints and "We can't give a prize to a *dead* pig. . . . It's never been done before." No prize. Then Templeton bites Wilbur's tail, and Wilbur revives and wins the prize.

But Charlotte is languishing. Can Wilbur survive without Charlotte? Charlotte spins her final magnum opus and dies, and Wilbur, now mature, takes responsibility for Charlotte's egg sac. When spring comes, Wilbur is still alive and hearty, and life continues.

Suspense, the emotional pull that keeps us wanting to read on, involves us in conflict up to the climax in the final pages. These moments of suspense, however, are not panic points in the story, nor at any time do we know the outcome with certainty. White controls the suspense to keep it peaking and leveling. At every point we remain not only curious but concerned for the outcome, because either success or failure looms, and we cannot be completely certain which will prevail.[3]

Suspense has kept us reading, but White has carefully led us with optimism, never despair. The author skillfully builds the story so that nowhere is the ending too predictable, lest we lose interest, or too frightful, lest we give up. At the end of the book, the reader feels that the ups and downs of "perhaps he'll win, perhaps he'll lose" are finally settled. Suspense does not go beyond the story's ending. White, as he pulls us to the satisfactory end of the story, makes us heave a final, relieved sigh. The feeling that all will be well, even after the final page, results from White's skill in handling suspense. Our optimism has been justified.

Suspense is held throughout *A Single Shard* by Linda Sue Park, a Korean story of Tree-ear, orphan helper to the skilled potter Min. Tree-ear, who admires Min's skills, waits patiently and works long days, hoping that the master potter will teach him to throw pots. Tradition and law, however, demand that an apprentice be the potter's son. Nonetheless, devoted Tree-ear carries and cuts wood for the kiln and digs and prepares special clays for innovative inlaid vases. When the king's emissary admires Min's beautiful work, Tree-ear offers to walk for weeks through the mountains, carrying the best of Min's vases to the king for his approval. When Tree-ear is threatened by two thieves, there is a nearly fatal fight; he struggles at the canyon edge to save the vases, but the robbers throw them into the abyss. Tree-ear searches frantically but finds only a single shard to carry to the capital. That single colorful shard, inlaid with chrysanthemums, is so stunning that Min is awarded the commission at the story's **climax**. During Tree-ear's eighteen months with Min, he has been learning only to mold the clay. Now a grateful Min calls him "son" and will teach him to throw pots. These final events provide **resolution** for the story.

Cliffhangers

A form of suspense that E. B. White does not use is the **cliffhanger,** which is an exciting chapter ending that makes it hard to lay the book aside. Unlike the chapters in *Charlotte's Web*, wherein each contributes to the central conflict in the total plot, each moving to its own peak and yet managing to end quietly, the cliffhanging chapter ends with so much suspense that a listening child may insist, "Please, just one more chapter!" The cliffhanger is most obvious in the classic *Goosebumps* series. Each chapter of the series ends with a suspenseful moment, as in *My Hairiest Adventure*, when Larry Boyd is chased by a pack of dogs and moans, "They've got me this time. They've got me." Readers of the series will quickly come to expect scenes like this—and scarier ones—at the end of every chapter.

Cliffhangers enhance the suspense of *Harry Potter and the Sorcerer's Stone*, the first book of J. K. Rowling's enormously successful series. One chapter concludes with gigantic Hagrid knocking on the castle door, suggesting ominous possibilities. A second ends with a question about Hagrid and Snape. And a third suggests disaster because the cloak that makes Harry invisible has been left behind. Another moment of high suspense leaves us hanging: Why is Hagrid looking so furious?

Jean Craighead George's picturebook *Cliff Hanger* uses this same technique as she takes us through a boy's terrifying climb in Wyoming's Teton mountain range. In this book, a young boy, Axel, learns that his dog, Grits, is at the top of Cathedral Wall; he is determined to rescue him before a storm comes. Axel starts up the sheer, treacherous cliff with his rock-climbing gear. The realistic illustrations make us feel we are right there with Axel, climbing into the sky. *Cliff Hanger* literally contains the suspenseful ending, the literary technique, called a cliffhanger.

Foreshadowing

Children's authors must decide how much suspense the child can sustain and how much reassurance is necessary to balance suspense. To relieve the reader's anxiety and to produce a satisfying sense of the inevitable, the writer must drop clues about the outcome—without destroying suspense. These clues are called **foreshadowing**. Such clues must be planted artfully and unobtrusively within the action. Not all readers will be alert to all dropped hints, it is true, but White in *Charlotte's Web* uses them to hint at Wilbur's ultimate safety and Charlotte's death, and to reassure us that all will be well in the end.

In Wilbur's first conversation with Charlotte, he learns that gentle Charlotte lives by eating living things; friendship looks questionable. Seeing a need to reassure, White adds that "she had a kind heart, and she was to prove loyal and true to the very end." The first clue suggests friendship; the second, "to the very end," has a prophetic ring.

Foreshadowing and suspense balance throughout the narrative. When in the chapter "Bad News" Wilbur hears he is being fattened for slaughter, he wails. However, his safety is foreshadowed when Charlotte says calmly, "I am going to save you."

Another event for which we must be prepared is Charlotte's death. If her death had been unforeseen, we might accuse White of playing with our emotions. But Charlotte's acceptance of her life span foreshadows her approaching death and prepares Wilbur and the readers. The song of the crickets foreshadows death of all kinds. "Summer is over and gone . . . Over and gone . . . Summer is dying, dying," they sing. Charlotte, whose life, like the crickets and the seasons, has a predictable cycle, "heard it and knew that she hadn't much time left." Of the word "humble," she says, "It is the last word I shall ever write." When she says that she is "languishing," she is peaceful and contented, and we are as resigned as she. *Charlotte's Web* concludes with a sense of inevitability, and, because of the 514 baby spiders, with optimism.

Inadequate foreshadowing leaves readers surprised or even shocked.

In Laurie Halse Anderson's historical novel *Chains*, foreshadowing is used often to hint at something important. One instance occurs when the protagonist, the slave girl Isabel, first sees the woman who will be her mistress in New York City during the American Revolution. Anderson writes that the thin woman who is interested in buying Isabel and her sister is about forty-five years old, with small eyes "like apple seeds. A fading yellow bruise circled her right wrist like a bracelet." Alert readers know the writer would not add that detail without having a good reason. They find out that Anne Lockton has been beaten by her husband, a wealthy Tory named Elihu Lockston. The domestic violence between the couple is an important part of what moves the plot.

Foreshadowing can also appear in the picturebook format. *Officer Buckle and Gloria* does this well in the illustrations. Several pages show a small picture of, for instance, a banana peel in the lower corner of the recto. Readers who see this will realize that slipping on a banana peel is the next incident earning a safety message from Officer Buckle. To the adult reader this can seem more like "telegraphing" than foreshadowing, but any reader inexperienced at noticing illustration might miss the visual symbols in this book that foreshadow Officer Buckle's next safety point.

Sensationalism

If the reader is to feel satisfaction as the story unfolds, the author must drop reassuring hints about what is ahead. In the strong life-and-death conflict of *Charlotte's Web*, unrelieved suspense might be too much for the young child. The skill of the writer lies in balancing two elements—suspense over the action and hints at the outcome.

Unrelieved suspense, however, makes a story *sensational*; it plays us like instruments, keeping us holding our breaths in crescendos of anxiety. The writer for adults has greater latitude in the creation of anxiety, since adults can tolerate it. With persistent enthusiasm, some adults read **sensationalism**: mystery stories, murder thrillers, spy stories, and survival adventures. The suspense absorbs them; they breathe terror with the protagonist. However, they are never deceived, since they never forget that it's just a story. Other adults are bored with the unrelieved suspense because they, too, know that it's just a story; wanting more than sensationalism, they seek some discovery of real people in suspenseful action. They demand the significance of well-developed character in a conflict that reveals something about humans.

Some recent movies have turned children's stories into sensational presentations. Among other things, such presentations teach children that life is a constantly heightened experience, with one frightening thrill after another, unlike real life, which consists of a series of small anxieties, quiet pleasures, and little successes. The flatter characterization of these sensational stories isn't useful for children, either: characters depicted realistically serve to teach children about the complexity of character in ways more sensational books and movies do not. [4]

Climax

The peak and turning point of the conflict, the point at which we know the outcome of the action, is called the climax. Throughout the development of plot, from initial recognition of the conflict through the critical turns and irregular progress, past reversals and discoveries, up to the point where we know who wins the conflict, we follow the plot to the climax. While we speak of the climax as the turning point in the conflict, children call it "the most exciting part," or "where I knew how the book would end." No matter which term is used, the climax is inextricably related to conflict.

Whether intense or quiet, the climax comes when we know the outcome of the conflict.

The climax of *90 Miles to Havana* occurs when the protagonist and narrator, Julian, goes with his older friend Tomas across the ocean on a dangerous mission from Miami to Havana to bring fourteen neighbors—Tomas' family and friends—out of Castro's new revolutionary Cuba to a freer life in the United States. Tension has been building throughout the book as Julian fights with bullies in the refugee camp in South Florida, then runs away from the camp; as he is chased by the policeman, Captain Rodriguez; as Tomas's friends steal the money he has been saving for the trip; and as Tomas is increasingly uncertain that the ship he has built is safe for the journey. The skill with engines that Julian learned from his old friend Bebe back in Cuba saves their lives as Julian and Tomas cross the open ocean, seeing freighters and whales and watching the little ship dip in the night waves, until they see the pink- and gold-shadowed buildings of Havana. At the harbor in Havana, they must load people onto their little boat in such a way that the police don't recognize what they are doing. They succeed in that task, and, with the help of friends, succeed in bringing Tomas' family across the ocean again and back to Miami. This is a dynamic, exciting climax; after it is over, there is little tension, and we read a quiet resolution.

In comparison, look at the quiet climax of *Charlotte's Web*. Here, in the conflict of person-against-society, Wilbur is in a life-and-death struggle. The climax logically comes when we know that he will live. Checking on suspense, we find that the high point, brought on by frequent minor crises and excitement peaks, finally comes when Wilbur revives and wins the prize—the handsome bronze medal for "attracting so many visitors to our great County Fair." The runt pig has defeated good business, since Wilbur has taken the final round of the contest. His additional award, the special prize of twenty-five dollars, proves that Wilbur is a good business investment after all; this is the climax. From here on Wilbur has nothing to worry about; the conflict is resolved.

When we look back over these examples of climax, we note that each involves the final battle of the protagonist with an antagonist. Though children's literature increasingly shows us heroes who are not perfect, it generally still introduces us to a protagonist who wins. However, the winning has not happened without a struggle. There is a difference between the climax that says with sticky sweetness, "The world is good, since right always wins," and one that says, "The forces of evil are powerful, but courage and justice together can defeat them." A conflict brought to a climax makes the idea of the story clear through a plot that has tension and resolution.

Denouement

Children who are following an exciting story may have trouble pinning down the climax. Agreeing on that, however, is not as important to the success of the story as agreeing that the story ends with a sense of completeness, or resolution.

The **denouement** begins at the climax, at the point where we feel that the protagonist's fate is known. From here the action of the plot is also called the **falling action**. In the denouement of *Charlotte's Web*, Templeton and Wilbur, the two survivors of the original trio, reach a bargain about who eats first at Wilbur's trough. Wilbur returns the egg sac to the barn, and its presence sustains the feeling that Charlotte is still there. Finally, warmed and protected by Wilbur's breath, the eggs hatch. Joy, Aranea, and Nellie, three of Charlotte's tiny progeny, stay on in the barn to keep Wilbur company and learn the ways of barn life. The seasonal cycle continues; everything is resolved. There is no question left unanswered. There is a resolution.

When the reader is assured that all is well and will continue to be, we say that the denouement is closed, or that the plot has a **closed ending**. In this case, the tying of the loose ends is thoroughly optimistic and satisfactory, a good conclusion for a young child's story. There is no anxiety for the reader or listener on the last page of *Charlotte's Web*. The sigh is not a breath of anxiety, but of regret that so good a story is over.

Denouement is called either the unknotting of ends, or the tying up of loose ends.

With a highly suspenseful plot filled with intricacies and turnabouts, Carl Hiaasen's *Hoot* holds the reader to the denouement. Roy is new in his Florida school; he is victimized by Curt, an aggressive troublemaker who rides the bus with him. Meanwhile, Curly, the construction supervisor for a building project, is infuriated by nightly vandalism. Stakes that define the territory to be cleared are pulled and the holes filled so the bulldozer crew cannot clear the area. Alligators appear in the portable toilets, snakes intimidate vicious guard dogs, and Curly may soon lose his supervisory job. Police are baffled. False names, strangers hiding in odd places, various injuries—there is no let-up in the destructive actions. The solution to the mystery finally rests with Roy, the fearless environmentalist whose suspicions of Curt prove correct.

In an **open ending**, an occasional device of fiction, we are left to draw our own conclusions about final plot resolution. Sometimes a novel will end at the climax, with the outcome of the climax being untold; other times the novel might end with a question for the reader. Such endings represent the real experience of life, which is not neatly organized into tidy resolutions, as many novels are.

Perhaps the most popular example of one kind of open ending are those in the series *Choose Your Own Adventure*, which was popular in the 1980s and 1990s and is now being republished. In these books, the reader assumes the role of the protagonist and at various points along the way must make choices about how to proceed. If he makes one choice, his instructions are to turn to page 6. If she makes a different choice, she turns to page 14. So, depending on the choices the reader makes, each reader can be reading a slightly different story. All of the many, many books in this series allowed readers a choice among two or three endings.

The Watertower by Gary Crew and Steven Woolman is a marvelous example of a picturebook with an open ending that will intrigue older children and make them wonder. In this eerie book, two boys, the braver Spike and more hesitant Bubba, climb to the top of an old watertower on a hot summer day. When he climbs down into the tank to swim, Bubba is frightened by the strange sounds and smells and the swirling eddies of the water. He comes back up without swimming, but can't find his pants where he left them. Spike offers to run home and find a new pair of shorts for Bubba. Bubba waits for Spike for a long time. When Spike comes back, Bubba climbs up from inside the tank and tells Spike that the water was great, which is worrisome to friend and reader alike, as it is unlike the Bubba we have come to know. Children will speculate about what happened to Bubba. Why are the faces of the people in town so strange, and why do all the men have water tower symbols on their hats?

Wolves by Emily Gravett is a picturebook for younger children. Its open ending is less potentially unsettling than the ending of *The Watertower*, partly because, in a lighthearted fashion, Gravett provides alternative endings to choose from. This simply, sparely drawn award winner shows a rabbit who takes a book about wolves out from the "Public Burrowing Library." As he walks home reading the book he recedes into its narrative, getting smaller as the wolf in the book gets bigger and closer. A page then shows a partially eaten book and no rabbit. Then the author slyly reassures readers that no rabbits were eaten during the making of this book and shows a somewhat saccharine picture of the (vegetarian) wolf and the rabbit happily eating a jam sandwich together. And yet if a reader turns the next page, he might imagine another possible ending to the book. Gravett's mixed-media art and her postmodern, open, ambiguous ending will give children much to talk about.

Types of Plots

The plots of *Charlotte's Web, Weedflower,* and *90 Miles to Havana,* with their central climaxes followed quickly by denouement, are called **progressive plots**. Apparently people have always liked suspense and climax because the progressive plot is common in traditional European tales. In "The Shoemaker and the Elves," for example, we move directly into the action from a few short phrases—"once upon a time" and "the couple was very poor." The first short paragraph also includes the elves' first visit and the work they leave behind. By the end of the second paragraph, the shoemaker is rich and we are halfway through the story. The couple hides to watch; their grateful gift of clothes for the elves brings on the climax—the dance of the delighted elves, who then disappear. The teller of oral tales knows that once the climax comes, he may lose his audience; he must end the story quickly and conclusively.

Some book-length stories for children have another type of plot, an **episodic plot**, in which one incident or short episode is linked to another by common characters or by a unified theme. Rodman Philbrick's newest novel, *The Mostly True Adventures of Homer P. Figg,* provides us with an example of a rollicking episodic plot. Homer leaves the farm in Pine Swamp, Maine, where his Uncle Squint has sold his brother as a substitute soldier in the Civil War. Homer, an indefatigable liar, takes off to find his brother and rescue him from the war. Along the way, Homer is kidnapped by slave catchers, Stink and Smelt; meets up with a kindly Quaker landowner and helps slaves escape to the Underground Railroad; is bamboozled out of money by a pair of professional con artists; joins Professor Fleabottom's traveling medicine show and plays the Amazing Pig Boy in the Caravan of Miracles; and floats in a hot air balloon by himself, straight into the Battle of Gettysburg. None of the episodes is told in more detail or is presented as more important than any of the others. Each of these stories is complete and separate from the next, and some of the same characters appear throughout. This is what an episodic plot can do: present one interesting or comic or familiar episode after another, linked in loose ways.

Older books, like Beverly Cleary's Henry Huggins and Ramona books, show their mischief in a series of episodes, too. New stories in episodic form, both fantasy and realism, are continually written for children, stories that rely on character, theme, humor, or nonsense to sustain the reader's interest.

In addition to these basic types of plots there are many others. This section of this chapter will briefly describe a few other plot structures, using quality picturebooks as examples.[5]

Beyond the chronological structure, there are cumulative structures, such as in *This Is the House That Jack Built,* Randolph Caldecott's first book. More and more objects, events, and players are added to the story as we read along—this is the cat that killed the rat that ate the malt that lay in the house that Jack built. The plot of *Bark, George!,* Jules Feiffer's picturebook about a mother dog whose baby, George, does not bark but meows, oinks, and moos, can be seen as an increasing plot structure. The vet solves George's problem by finding increasingly large animals—from a cat to a cow—inside of George. Finally, without all of those animals inside him, George can make the sounds he's supposed to.

The House in the Meadow, by Shutta Crum, can be seen as having a simultaneously increasing and decreasing plot: it is the story of people who come to help build a house. It is a modern version of the old song, "Over in the Meadow," and like it, is a numbers song. As the house becomes more complete (increasingly featured), fewer and fewer tradespeople come to do the work (decreasing tradespeople), beginning with ten friends, moving on through seven carpenters, and ending with "Inspector Number One." Don and Audrey Wood also use a simultaneously increasing and decreasing plot in their comforting classic, *The Napping House.*

Picturebooks do have different ways of showing plot than chapterbooks do: Some picturebooks have parallel structures, or two plots going on at the same time—one story told in words, and a very different one told by the pictures. John Burningham's delightful *Time to Get Out of the Bath, Shirley,* and his *Come Away from the Water, Shirley,* both use this structure. As her mother and father snooze in their deck chairs and warn Shirley about the dangers she might find on the beach, we see Shirley going off on an imaginary pirate ship and courting danger—in her imagination. The juxtaposition of the oblivious parents' practical concerns and Shirley's wild imagination has us smiling in recognition.

Another type of plot is the **story within a story**, as we see clearly in Alan Say's wonderful picturebook *Kamishibai Man.* The first, or frame story, shows us an old couple. The husband of the couple, Jichan, decides to go back to the place where he once told stories, or did "paper theatre," *kamishibai.* When the old man stands in his spot, readying his candies and clacking his wooden blocks together for the children to come and hear his stories, he recalls how he used to be a *kamishibai* man when he was young. Similar to but longer and more detailed than a flashback, the story about Jichan's time as a *kamishibai* man is a story within a larger story. After the story of his youthful storytelling is over, readers are returned to the present day, and the old man discovers that some of his faithful listeners, grown up now, recall and appreciate his old tales. The present-day frame story is a satisfying completion of the story within the story.

My Life with the Wave by Catherine Cowan can be considered an around-the-clock or full-circle plot. In this picturebook, the narrator falls in love with waves at the seashore and begs his parents to let him take one home. Getting the wave home on the train is a bit of a struggle (she hides herself in the water cooler), and when she comes home, the wave breaks into many waves and "flooded our rooms with light and air . . ." The boy plays with the wave as it becomes like a liquid tree and sings "sweet songs" to him at night. Finally, since it is driving the boy's mother "crazy," the family leaves the house and only comes back when the wave has frozen. The parents wrap the wave in a quilt and take her back to the sea, ending the story where it began, in a full circle.

As you see, there is great possibility for variation and combination in plot structure. To provide just one more example of that variation, we'll describe Trent Stuart's *The Mysterious Benedict Society,* which combines a progressive with an episodic plot. There is a sense of unity and progress as the four child geniuses—Reynie, Kate, Sticky, and Constance—gather, pass their various tests, learn about each other and about Mr. Benedict, then move into spy mode and infiltrate the mysterious school for gifted children. Many small episodes occur along the way, though: Reynie meets Rhonda and passes her test, the children meet Mr. Benedict, Constance gets lost, Sticky tells about his life before the Society, and Kate describes her experiences in the circus. In many of these stories, order is not so important. The plot continues in this progressive, episodic way throughout all the books of this humorous, exciting, best-selling series.

Other Considerations about Plot

Coincidence

The concurrence of events apparently by mere chance is **coincidence**. In real life, we know that coincidence does occur. In literature, however, where the truths of human nature and human existence are explored, reliance on coincidence to resolve conflict weakens plot. White might easily have fallen into the coincidence trap in *Charlotte's Web*. For example, had the enormous and healthy Uncle, the obvious choice for first prize, happened to take sick at the fair—*that* would have been coincidence. Had Wilbur won the blue ribbon by mere default, our pleasure in the outcome would then have been a mixed pleasure over a far less satisfying victory. Furthermore, if Charlotte had by incredible coincidence eventually lived as long as Wilbur, she would have defied the natural laws of a spider's life cycle. Charlotte may talk and write words in her web, but she is a spider leading a spider life. White, by using fore-shadowing and by rejecting coincidence, has given *Charlotte's Web* an inevitable and satisfying conclusion.

Sentimentality

Nor should another negative element, called **sentimentality**, mar a well-constructed plot. We term *sentiment* a natural concern or emotion for another person. If, for instance, our parents are hurt in a painful accident, our natural sentiment causes an emotional response. However, when our sentiments are used or played on as they are in soap opera, we have what we call a *tearjerker situation*, or sentimentality.

We have all at some time left a movie theater surreptitiously wiping our eyes, knowing the movie wasn't worth tears. At other times we have been unashamed of our tears, perhaps even proud. It is the legitimacy of our emotional reaction that makes us feel honest. When we are honestly moved by art, we may weep because we suffer with the character empathically, taking his or her sorrow on ourselves. But sometimes the writer may cause us to weep or to exult and we are uncomfortable because we are asked for an emotional response in excess of what the situation requires.

Sentimentality takes varied forms. A character may be sentimentally drawn. For instance, a saintly, sweet woman who never raises her voice, who is patient, kind, loyal, and true, and who keeps a full cookie jar and a spotless kitchen is no reality. She is a cardboard, two-dimensional figure, a highly sentimentalized picture of Mother.

Charlotte's Web does not resort to sentimentality. Lingering sobs and whimpers from Charlotte at her own death would have destroyed credibility. Charlotte is a spider and knows it. Her spider-defined life prepares Wilbur and readers for her dignified and inevitable death. Or Wilbur's fainting might easily have become sentimental panic, but is instead humorous. Or Templeton might have broken down, become a reformed rat, and committed some unselfish or heroic act. Such an incredible change would have been sentimentality. Our response to each situation in White's story is legitimately roused, never exaggerated or superficial, and therefore unsentimental.

What is wrong with sentimentality? A good cry never hurt anyone. However, there are dangers inherent in a steady diet of forced emotion. We are manipulated by the dramatic occurrences, crises, and tragedies of some television show and movies. We are pumps primed to spout tears and then, just as we have settled down, primed again.

By contrast to such texts—whether movie, television show, or novel—notice the wide range of emotions that readers wrestle with in Katherine Paterson's story, *Bridge to Terabithia*. They follow Jess from his shyness with other children to his rivalry with his sister, Brenda, to pleasure over the secret bridge to the hideaway island, to numbness and grief at his friend Leslie's drowning. Or chart the genuine sentiment that a young child, reading or being read to, experiences over the relationship between Charlotte and Wilbur. Here he or she comes to know loneliness, friendship, sacrifice, tact, patience, loyalty, and maternity; negative traits as selfishness, avarice, and gluttony; and finally death and continuity. Furthermore, among the more surprising discoveries is the way in which such significant human traits and experiences are explored in both books—not with bathos or sentimentality, but with seriousness and deft humor. The total impact of White's book embodies respect for animals, yes, but more important, respect for people, as Wilbur and Charlotte personify humans.

TEXTSET

Books with Exciting Plots

Much research shows that boys lag behind girls in their literacy learning. There are many reasons why this may be so. First, boys may see their mothers, female teachers, and female librarians reading. They may rarely see other boys or men reading; they may be encouraged to play outside or on computers, rather than read a book.

It may also be that boys are interested in reading different kinds of fiction than teachers usually select for their classrooms. Based on her research, Elaine Millard suggests that teachers should select literature boys like, which includes "narratives which emphasized action and plot rather than 'knowledge of the human heart.'"[6] She writes that boys are attracted to nonfiction as well, particularly expository text formats that allow multiple entry points and the opportunity to "browse" rather than be immersed in a book.

Even in fiction, the topics boys are interested in may differ from topics that attract girls. Boys may like gross humor, sports, and action, including military themes. Boys may prefer a male protagonist, but if the topic and plot resonate, they are not averse to reading books with strong female protagonists. Research shows that young boys like stories that have action, animals, or icky humor.

With these points in mind, we include narratives that are boy-friendly. That is, they emphasize the aspect of children's books that has been the focus of this chapter: plot. Take a look at a few books we think boys may enjoy, beginning with fiction for the youngest boys and moving on through teen years, ending with nonfiction.

Lawson, Robert. *Mr. Revere and I.* Little, Brown, 1988.

Paul Revere's revolution-beginning midnight ride, as told by his horse.

Murphy, Frank. *George Washington and the General's Dog.* Random House, 2002.

A book about how General George Washington took care of the dog that belonged to General Howe, his enemy during the revolution. A Step-into-Reading book.

Pilky, Dav. *The Adventures of Captain Underpants.* Scholastic, 1997.

Graphic novel series about two naughty boys.

Some research suggests that even when they read fiction, boys are interested in the information they learn from a book rather than in character or emotion. The novels below—loved by generations of late elementary and middle school boys—contain information about philosophy, computers, wars, weapons, and history.

Card, Orson Scott. *Ender's Game.* Tor Science Fiction, 1994.

A young genius learns to become a warrior in a computerized future world. Winner of multiple awards.

Jacques, Brian. *Redwall.* Puffin/Philomel Books, 2002.

A young mouse tries to save Redwall Abbey from an evil rat. First of a series.

Kochalka, James. *Monkey vs. Robot.* Top Shelf Productions, 2000.

Graphic novel about a battle between a monkey community and a self-run robot factory. First of a series.

Sutcliffe, Rosemary. *The Eagle of the Ninth.* Square Fish, 2010.

Young Marcus takes off to discover the whereabouts of the lost Ninth Legion, in ancient Rome.

Older boys will like the books listed below, which are about boys at war, in the past and in the future. We include a nonfiction expository text selection as well.

Marsden, John. *Tomorrow when the War Began.* Scholastic, 2006.

Australian teenagers come back from a camping trip to find their country occupied by a foreign military force. The seven teens must decide how to survive and make plans to fight the occupying force. First of a series.

Mazer, Harry. *A Boy at War: A Novel of Pearl Harbor.* Simon & Schuster, 2002.

Adam Pelko, whose father is stationed on the USS *Arizona,* witnesses the horrific air attack on Pearl Harbor with his Japanese American friend Davi.

Mazer, Harry. *The Last Mission.* Laurel Leaf, 1981.

In 1944, 15-year old Jack Rabb enlists in the U.S. Air Force. After flying 24 bombing missions over Europe, Jack's plane is shot down and he becomes a prisoner of war.

Philbrick, Rodman. *The Last Book In the Universe.* Blue Sky Press, 2002.

Life with Spaz and Ryter after the Big Shake.

The research of Millard and others shows that boys like nonfiction. Below are some good nonfiction texts we think boys will like.

Doedon, Matt. *Weapons of the Revolutionary War.* Blazers, 2008.

Expository text describing firearms and artillery used in the war. Part of a series about weapons in history.

Hickam, Homer. *Rocket Boys.* Delta, 2000.

Best-selling memoir of a miner's kid who grew up to be a NASA engineer.

Nelson, Vaunda Micheaux. *Bad News for Outlaws.* Carolrhoda Books, 2009.

The story of Bass Reeves, first African American U.S. deputy marshal and the most successful one in American history.

Note:

Jon Sciescka started an exciting movement to increase boys' interest in reading. Read his book *Guys Write for Guys Read* (Viking, 2005) and visit his very informative website at www.guysread.com.

SUMMARY

Character study alone rarely carries a child's interest, but character becomes inextricably woven into plot by the very nature of the protagonist and the antagonist in the conflict. Order is easier for the child to follow if it is within his or her experience; chronological order is therefore more frequent, while flashback is more common in stories for older children. In a progressive plot, suspense pulls the reader through the rising action to the central climax, where conflict is resolved in a manner foreshadowed and thus inevitable; the last questions are usually answered in a denouement with a closed ending.

By contrast, each chapter in an episodic plot may have its own small tensions and be joined to the others by theme and character. Finally, a well-plotted story relies on neither sentimentality nor coincidence for action and resolution.

There is no right plot structure in a story for children. There are only variations of the principal forms. The understanding of the reader or listener may determine the length or structure of the story, whether that story is a single progressively arranged unit or an episode in a longer work. However, what *does* matter is that literature sustain interest and give pleasure.

In considering the plot development, we are most aware that without sufficient conflict or tension accompanied by suspense and foreshadowing, a story is just plain dull. Few adults want to read a dull story, and certainly no young people will.

Pleasure comes in all kinds of forms. A good story can provide them all.

NOTES

1. C. W. Sullivan III, "Narrative Expectations: The Folklore Connection," *Children's Literature Quarterly*, 15, Summer 1990, pp. 52–55.
2. For a discussion of time in time fantasy, a subject in itself, see Eleanor Cameron, *The Green and Burning Tree* (Boston: Little, Brown, 1985).
3. Perry Nodelman, writing of tension in "Pleasure and Genre," notes perfectly: "I want to know, I need to know, I don't know quite . . ." (Perry Nodelman, "Pleasure and Genre, *Children's Literature*, 28, 2000, pp. 1–14).
4. Walt Disney's early films for children, his retelling of folk and fairy tales, have been criticized for their

graphic portrayal of frightening characters and episodes. Imagined scenes and characters in a storybook can be as scary as the child wishes, but can be absolutely terrifying when seen in vivid color.
5. This discussion of plots in picturebooks was influenced by Shutta Crum's article "Story Skeletons: Teaching Plot Structure with Picturebooks," first published in *Book Links* in May 2005, and retrieved from http://shutta.com/storyskeletons.pdf on October 16, 2005.
6. Elaine Millard, *Differently Literate: Boys, Girls, and the Schooling of Literacy* (London: Routledge Falmer, 1997), p. 161.

RECOMMENDED BOOKS

ANDERSON, LAURIE HALSE. *Chains*. Atheneum, 2010.

ANDERSON, LAURIE HALSE. *Fever: 1793*. Simon & Schuster, 2002.

BANG, MOLLY. *The Gray Lady and the Strawberry Snatcher*. Four Winds Press, 1980.

BORDEN, LOUISE A. *Lincoln and Me*. Scholastic, 2009.

BURNINGHAM, JOHN. *Come Away from the Water, Shirley*. Red Fox, 1992.

BURNINGHAM, JOHN. *Time to Get Out of the Bath, Shirley*. Random House, 1978.

CALDECOTT, RANDOLPH. *This Is the House That Jack Built*. Dodo Press, 1992.

COLBURN, CHERIE FOSTER. *Our Shadow Garden*. Bright Sky Press, 2010.

COWAN, CATHERINE. *My Life with the Wave*. Lothrop, Lee, & Shepard Books, 1997.

CREW, GARY, AND STEVEN WOOLMAN. *The Watertower*. Crocodile Books, 1998.

CRUM, SHUTTA. *The House in the Meadow*. Albert Whitman & Co., 2003.

DANTICAT, EDWIDGE. *Eight Days: A Story of Haiti*. Orchard Books, 2010.

DEFELICE, CYNTHIA. *The Apprenticeship of Lucas Whitaker*. Farrar, Straus & Giroux, 1996.

DORROS, ARTHUR. *Papa and Me*. HarperCollins, 2008.

ENGLE, MARGARITA. *The Surrender Tree: Poems of Cuba's Struggle for Freedom*. Henry Holt, 2008.

FEIFFER, JULES. *Bark, George*. HarperCollins, 1999.

FITZHUGH, LOUISE. *Harriet the Spy*. Yearling, 2001.

FLAKE, SHARON. *The Skin I'm In*. Perfection Learning, 2007.

FLORES-GALLIS, ENRIQUE. *90 Miles to Havana*. Roaring Brook Press, 2010.

GEORGE, JEAN CRAIGHEAD. *Cliff Hanger*. Illustrated by Wendell Minor. Harpercollins, 2002.

GIFF, PATRICIA REILLY. *Pictures of Hollis Woods*. Random House, 2002.

GONZALEZ, LUCIA. *The Storyteller's Candle*. Illustrated by Lulu Delacre. Children's Book Press, 2008.

GRAVETT, EMILY. *Wolves*. Simon & Schuster, 2006.

HESSE, KAREN. *Stowaway*. Simon and Schuster, 2000.

HIAASEN, CARL. *Hoot*. Knopf, 2002.

JONES, TRACI L. *Finding My Place*. Farrar, Straus & Giroux, 2010.

KADOHATA, CYNTHIA. *Weedflower*. Atheneum, 2007.

KEHRET, PEG. *Flood Disaster*. Aladdin, 2008.

KONIGSBURG, E. L. *From the Mixed Up Files of Mrs. Basil E. Frankweiler*. Atheneum, 2007.

KRULL, KATHLEEN. *A Woman for President: The Story of Victoria Woodhull*. Walker and Co., 2004.

L'ENGLE, MADELEINE. *A Wrinkle in Time*. Square Fish, 2007.

LOBEL, ARNOLD. *Uncle Elephant*. HarperCollins, 1986.

OSBORNE, MARY POPE. *Magic Treehouse*. Random House Books for Young Readers, 2008.

PARK, LINDA SUE. *A Single Shard*. Clarion Books, 2001.

PATERSON, KATHERINE. *Bridge to Terabithia*. HarperTeen, 2004.

PATERSON, KATHERINE. *Lyddie*. Dutton, 1991.

PAULSEN, GARY. *Hatchet*. Bradbury, 1987.

PAULSEN, GARY. *The River*. Delacorte, 1991.

PERKINS, MITALI. *Rickshaw Girl*. Charlesbridge, 2007.

PHILBRICK, RODMAN. *The Mostly True Adventures of Homer P. Figg*. Scholastic, 2009.

RATHMANN, PEGGY. *Officer Buckle and Gloria*. Putnam Juvenile, 2004.

RAVEN, MARGOT THEIS. *Night Boat to Freedom*. Illustrated by E. B. Lewis. Farrar, Straus & Giroux, 2006.

ROWLING, J. K. *Harry Potter and the Prizoner of Azkaban*. Scholastic, 2001.

ROWLING, J. K. *Harry Potter and the Sorcerer's Stone*. Arthur A. Levine, 1997.

RUCKMAN, IVY. *Night of the Twisters*. HarperCollins, 1986.

RUSSELL, CHING YEUNG. *Tofu Quilt*. Lee & Low, 2009.

RYLANT, CYNTHIA. *Harry and Mudge and the Starry Night*. Live Oak Media, 2002.

SACHAR, LOUIS. *Holes*. Farrar, Straus, & Giroux, 2008.

SAY, ALAN. *Kamishibai Man*. Houghton Mifflin, 2005.

SENDAK, MAURICE. *In the Night Kitchen*. Harper, 1963.

SENDAK, MAURICE. *Where the Wild Things Are*. HarperCollins, 1988.

STEAD, REBECCA. *When You Reach Me*. Random House, 2009.

STEWART, TRENTON LEE. *The Mysterious Benedict Society*. Illustrated by Carson Ellis. Little, Brown, 2007.

TAYLOR, SYDNEY. *All of a Kind Family*. Yearling, 1984.

THOMPSON, COLIN. *Looking for Atlantis*. State Street Press, 1993.

TINGLE, TIM. *Crossing Bok Chitto: Choctaw Tale of Friendship and Freedom*. Cincto Puntos Press, 2006.

VARAN, SARA. *Robot Dreams*. First Second, 2007.

VOLPONI, PAUL. *Hurricane Song: A Novel of New Orleans*. Penguin, 2008.

WELLS, ROSEMARY. *Wingwalker*. Hyperion, 2002.

WHITE, E. B. *Charlotte's Web*. Harper, 1952.

WILLIAMS-GARCIA, RITA. *Jumped!* HarperCollins, 2009.

WINTER, JEANETTE. *Nasreen's Secret School: A True Story from Afghanistan*. Beach Lane Books, 2009.

WINTHROP, ELIZABETH. *Counting on Grace*. Random House, 2006.

WOOD, DON. *Into the Volcano*. Blue Sky Press, 2008.

WOOD, DON, AND AUDREY WOOD. *The Napping House*. Harcourt, 1991.

MyEducationKit™

Go to the topic "Picture Books" on the MyEducationKit for this text, where you can:

- Search the Children's Literature Database, housing more than 22,000 titles searchable in every genre by authors or illustrators, by awards won, by year published, and by topic and description.

- Explore genre-related Assignments and Activities, assignable exercises showing concepts in action through database use, video, cases, and student and teacher artifacts.

- Listen to podcasts and read interviews from some of the brightest and most enduring stars of children's literature in the Conversations.

- Discover web links that will lead you to sites representing the authors you learn about in these pages, classrooms with powerful children's literature connections, and literature awards.

Museum Trip

Barbara Lehman

In many stories the setting is a backdrop,
but some stories have a specialized setting
that is integral to the story.

CHAPTER SEVEN

Setting

Does setting have to

be important?

Change the setting

and see.

What happens to

the story?

Both depiction of character and unfolding of plot and theme occur in time and place. These elements of time and place are called **setting**. In an adult novel, action may occur anywhere, even in the mind of the protagonist, and may need little delineation of place or time. However, stories for children are frequently set in a time and place described in some detail. When we consider all the times and places known to us, and add to them all those we are capable of imagining, the possibilities are limitless.

Sometimes the writer wishes to make setting clear because the story depends on understanding and envisioning the particular setting. At other times, the writer deliberately refrains from closely examining and describing setting—making it too specific, for example, might limit the universality of conflict, characters, or ideas the writer is exploring. It is the writer who determines the nature of the story and thereby determines the setting.

It is frequently important to know the physical description of the setting, the details of what is present, how it all looks, smells, feels, and sounds. These relevant details will directly influence character, conflict, and theme. Such details may also set the mood of the time and place and so create the atmosphere for the characters and the conflict.

In *A Corner of the Universe* by Ann M. Martin, a small town, a boarding house, and a traveling carnival and its "freak show" are the setting. Hattie Owen is happy just to stay at home in a familiar world interrupted only by the traveling carnival with a few actual

Sometimes understanding a story depends on awareness of setting.

Setting may influence character, conflict, and theme.

"Setting . . . by confining charac-ter . . . defines it."

Eudora Welty

167

"freaks" ("How else are they going to support themselves?") and others who merely pretend to be freaks. Into this world comes an uncle never mentioned by her parents or grandparents, a young man who is mentally ill. Uncle Adam's behavior is unpredictable, sometimes laughable, sometimes frightening, but nonetheless happy and loving. "Adam's moods are like a deck of playing cards with someone riffling through them—dozens of cards, one after the other in a blur." The boarders, each one odd in individual ways, comfortably accept Adam's strange behavior. "Most of the performers in the sideshow are putting on an act, the ones who have learned how to do tricks or to wear special makeup and costumes. . . . People stare at them because of the way they were born." The small town, however, has insensitive citizens who call Uncle Adam a freak. Finally being called a "freak" is more than Adam can take. Here setting has a strong impact on a theme that suggests acceptance of everyone, each one a "corner of the universe."

Types of Settings

In any piece of literature, whether for children or adults, there are essentially two types of setting: (1) the essential, or **integral setting**, and (2) the relatively unimportant, or **backdrop setting**.

The importance of setting—whether integral or backdrop—depends on the writer's purpose. For example, in a story of internal conflict, the first-person narrator may tell the progress of the plot in narrative, dialogue, action, or diary form. The reader may not need to know where or when the character lives, since understanding depends on interest in character and in the character's internal conflict—time and place are merely a backdrop. This kind of setting contrasts sharply with the significant integral setting in a nonfiction book such as *Anne Frank: The Diary of a Young Girl*. Although this autobiographical account, too, has internal conflict, where and when the action occurs is essential information if we are to understand conflict and character. In fact, the setting's effect on character is the essence of conflict in this book.

The writer makes the setting clear in descriptions. Each reader may have a personal catalogue of mentally pictured settings—a beach, a farm, or a cabin—but the writer does not depend on the reader's experience or recollection of settings. If the writer wants to make the setting integral to a story, the writer must describe it in concrete details, relying on sensory pictures and vivid comparisons to make the setting so clear that the reader understands how this story is closely related to this particular place.

By contrast, if a writer insists that setting is significant, yet creates a setting superficial in concept and shallow in depiction, the reader may then reject all of the story's reality, from character through action and unifying idea. A one-dimensional setting cannot be integral; little that happens would be believable. Children's literature at every level of sophistication can provide settings that convince readers the story is possible. These kinds of settings make fiction "work" for readers of all ages.

The writer is responsible for making the setting clear for the purposes of the story he or she is creating.

Integral Setting

A story has an integral setting when action, character, or theme are influenced by the time and place. As writer Eudora Welty says, setting has "the most delicate control over character . . . by confining character, it defines it."[1] These characters, given these circumstances, in this time and place, behave in this way.

A Beach Tail by Karen Williams suggests that the setting is an integral part of the action. The seashore is so interesting that Gregory becomes engrossed in what he is doing; his adventure would not be the same in a different place. At the beach, Gregory meanders from one discovery to another. He is interested in his surroundings to the degree that he loses sight of the landmark his father has set as the parameters for his play. This basic conflict occurs because of his involvement in the activities the setting suggests—creating a tail for the lion he has drawn in the sand. The setting comes alive and involves Gregory in the plot; he is amazed by his discoveries of a jellyfish, ghost crab, and sand castle. The grainy impressionistic illustrations by Floyd Cooper and the "swish-swoosh" waves reinforce the sandy setting. The wide-open backdrop of sky and shoreline show the reader how he lost sight of his father's towel and umbrella. The relevance of the book's title becomes apparent; Gregory follows his lion's tail, retracing his steps to safety. The setting is an integral part of the story, because it influences character, conflict, and idea. This picturebook design reinforces this importance with the sandy tone of the endpapers; the impressionistic illustrations are done in pastels with a "grainy" finish that visually locates this story on a sandy beach. Even books designed for the very young are best when their setting is convincing.

Chapter 1 of Patricia MacLachlan's classic *Sarah, Plain and Tall* immediately draws the reader into the integral setting. Caleb sits close to the fire, the dogs "beside him on the warm hearthstones"—a pioneer home. Anna looks out the window to the prairie that reaches out and touches "the places where the sky came down. Though winter was nearly over, there were patches of snow and ice everywhere." A dirt road "crawls" across the plains, and there are "fields and grass and sky and not much else." The wind seems to blow Papa into the house. When Sarah responds to Papa's ad for a wife, the family is relieved to find that she enjoys farm life, even climbing up the ladder on "the mound of hay for bedding, nearly half as tall as the barn, covered with canvas to keep the rain from rotting it." Because the issue is whether Sarah, who loves the dunes and sea of Maine, can be happy as a prairie wife and mother, readers must see her involved with and enjoying the prairie farm. The setting is integral.

Knowing the nature of the river in which Tony dares Joel to swim is essential to plot and theme in *On My Honor* by Marion Dane Bauer. The red-brown water is "slithering" under the bridge. Chemicals and sewage are not visible, but Joel knows they are there. Although the water flows past like "a refreshing massage," Joel doesn't want to put his face in it; "the river smelled of decaying fish," the current dividing in a sharp V at the boys' waists. There is also a strong current, a threat to an inexperienced swimmer like Tony. The river and its qualities are an essential element in this contemporary story's presentation of a moral dilemma; it is symbolic of the current of suspense that runs through this thought-provoking novel.

Brian, the protagonist in *Hatchet* by Gary Paulsen, is the sole survivor of the crash of a single-engine plane in Alaska; his only survival tool is his hatchet. To believe in his struggle with isolation in the rugged surroundings he must make habitable, we must see the setting clearly. A stone ridge near the lake that the plane has crashed into yields a cave-like shelter:

> At one time in the far past it had been scooped by something, probably a glacier, and this scooping had left a kind of sideways bowl, back in under a ledge. It wasn't very deep, not a cave, but it was smooth and made a perfect roof and he could almost stand

in under the ledge. . . . Some of the rock . . . had . . . been pulverized by the glacial action, turned into sand, and now made a small sand beach that went down to the edge of the water in front.

Here, once he can build a fire, Brian finds protection from the black flies and mosquitoes that blanket his body.

Setting is also clearly shown in Mordecai Gerstein's *The Man Who Walked Between the Towers*, the story of Philippe Petit's fantastic tightrope walk between the twin towers of the World Trade Center in Manhattan in 1974. This French aerialist carefully planned his death-defying feat that would take him a quarter of a mile over the city. The paint-and-ink drawings detail the setting, revealing the cityscape from Petit's perspective as he skillfully places his foot on the wire stretched across 140 feet of open space. With a crossbar balancing the space, readers also experience what pedestrians would have seen from below; both views are presented on either side of a tri-fold panel. The passage of time is shown by views of the skyline in starlight as well as sunlight. The final pages reveal the somber effects of 9/11, in sharp contrast to the illegal prank of Phillipe Petit. The illustrations create the larger-than-life setting where larger-than-life events occurred. This story could only happen this way in this place and time.

Backdrop Setting

The term *backdrop setting* comes from the theater. For example, some of the action in scenes from Shakespeare and from many musicals takes place on the stage in front of a featureless curtain, or before a flat, painted scene of an unidentified street or forest. Soliloquy, dialogue, action, or character confrontation concerns us; where the characters are positioned matters, but seeing and hearing them, and following them in the developing conflict is most important. While the street or forest is unidentified, it may have importance. It may have some subtle meaning that suggests the forest as a place of physical or spiritual darkness, or the busy street is a reminder of society.

Backdrop settings may also have symbolic meaning.

A clear example of a children's story with a backdrop setting is the classic *Winnie-the-Pooh*. A. A. Milne's Christopher Robin might live anywhere at all—from Land's End to Lancashire, from Bangor to Sacramento. Action occurs on the bank of a stream, or by a big oak tree with a honeybee hive. While time and place are not specific, they may suggest something about the action or characters when Pooh, Eeyore, Rabbit, and his assorted friends and relations set off on an "expotition" to the North Pole. The Forest—with a capital *F*—is of course the proper place for Pooh and Piglet to track the fearful Woozle/Wizzle, but there is minimal description of the beech tree beyond its being in the middle of the Forest. It is the tension among the characters that matters.

In backdrop settings, time and place do not necessarily influence action or character.

In *Winnie-the-Pooh*, setting is generalized and universal; its vividness exists in our minds merely as the place where the interesting action occurs. We do not know, for example, what Rabbit's house looks like; what matters is the memorable view of Pooh's legs serving as towel racks. Although time and place have importance, they do not influence the character and plot in the same ways that an integral setting does.

Picturebooks employ a similar technique when time and place are not as important as the central concept or character. Suzy Lee's *Mirror* uses complete white space to emphasize the main character's antics with her mirror image. The symmetrical black and grey on white highlight her expressions, moving the visual plot from loneliness to interaction and back to to isolation. A splash of color indicates the high point of the plot, but the concept of the story does not rely on an integrated setting. Similarly, *Not a Box* by Antoinette Portis is all about action and the concept of imaginative childhood play. Small Rabbit and a cardboard box are simple line drawings reminiscent of *Harold and the Purple Crayon* by Crockett Johnson; each page shows Small Rabbit engaged with the "box." The narrator questions Rabbit's actions with the box, encouraging a description of Rabbit's play. But, Small Rabbit always replies, "It's Not a Box." Turn the page and a red outline overlays Small Rabbit, showing the rocket the box has become in the game of make-believe. Brown paper endpapers, casings, and verso pages remind the reader that the box—and its changing functions—is central to this story. The setting highlights the character.

Setting in *Charlotte's Web*

Our mentor text, *Charlotte's Web,* is an excellent example of integral setting literally described.[2] This story could have occurred nowhere but on a farm—in fact, only on a traditional farm. This is not a sprawling ranch or a grain-growing industry, because such farms have concerns other than pigs and their barnyard friends. The Arable farm is near a country road, since Fern catches the school bus at her front door. There is a brook for playing in, with wonderfully oozy, sticky mud. This farm has a dump where Templeton can find essential words for the web. It has meadows that show seasonal changes, maples that redden with anxiety, and a big pasture that frightens a timid piglet. This farm, with an orchard where apples fall and the gander's family feasts, is no generalized farm; there is no other farm quite like it, where fog and rain, crickets and song sparrows are all parts of the setting. However, most important of all, this farm has a barn that houses a variety of animals—or how could sheep, pigs, and geese become acquainted, advising, consoling, and taunting one another? White shows the Zuckerman barn as soon as Wilbur sees it. The reader, too, knows its smells, its sights, and its warmth:

> The barn was very large. It was very old. It smelled of hay and it smelled of manure. It smelled of the perspiration of tired horses and the wonderful sweet breath of patient cows. It often had a sort of peaceful smell—as though nothing bad could happen ever again in the world. It smelled of grain and of harness dressing and of axle grease and of rubber boots and of new rope. And whenever the cat was given a fish-head to eat, the barn would smell of fish. But mostly it smelled of hay, for there was always hay in the great loft overhead. And there was always hay being pitched down to the cows and the horses and the sheep.

Readers would not likely confuse this setting with any generalized backdrop, since each item in the description shows the singularity of this setting, home of Wilbur, Charlotte, and Templeton. We know this place as well as Wilbur does, and because its description is so vivid, we are alerted to its importance in the total story. To know the exciting fairgrounds, we must

> hear music and see the Ferris wheel turning in the sky . . . smell the dust of the race track where the sprinkling car had moistened it . . . smell hamburgers frying and see balloons aloft . . . hear sheep blatting in their pens.

At night the lighted Ferris wheel revolves in the sky, the gambling machines crackle, the merry-go-round makes music, and a voice calls numbers from the beano

---

INQUIRY POINT

Charlotte's Web has an integral setting. Select a scene you find central to the story. Change an element of the setting. How does the story change? How does the change affect the action?

Now select *Not a Box*, or a member of Antoinette Portis's series honoring free play. Provide different settings. Does it change the central idea of the story?

---

booth. In the morning we hear sparrows stirring, roosters crowing, cows rattling chains, and cars whispering on the roadway.

The fair is an essential part of the story, and it is therefore necessary that the reader see, hear, smell, and even touch and taste it. Wilbur's character is fully revealed at the fair, where, experiencing threatened failure and final success, he remains humble but radiant. Wilbur's conflict, furthermore, cannot be resolved without the fair. Wilbur must have time to grow and then prove himself worthy of being saved; the fall fair is a traditional proving time for farm animals. Charlotte's efforts to prolong Wilbur's life produce no certainty of success until the fair, where he wins the prize for attracting so many visitors.

White must also show temporal change, since character growth and conflict, as well as several of the story's thematic discoveries, depend on the passing of time. White must make us see the seasons as they exist, merge, and change. As we hear, see, and smell, we are aware of time passing, and of weather and landscape changing.

Spring is the time for pigs to be born; rain drips from the eaves, runs crookedly through the pigweed, and gushes from the rainspouts. Summer is everyone's holiday; lilacs are blooming, bees are dropping in on the apple blossoms, horses are pulling the noisy mower, and birds sing and nest. However, since summer cannot last forever, the crickets' song prepares us for fall and the important fair. Uneasy sheep break out of their pasture and the gander's family invades the orchard. Although little of the story's action occurs in winter, it is not slighted. The pasture is frozen, the cows are standing in the sun beside the straw pile, the sheep are eating snow, and the geese are just hanging about. Then, to complete the year's cycle and to prove that Wilbur has survived butchering time and that Charlotte's eggs have hatched, White returns to spring, with its strengthening light, new lambs, nine goose eggs, and Charlotte's old web floating away.

In *Charlotte's Web*, the passing of a full year makes clear both outcome and theme.

The time element is important here. As the year passes, Wilbur matures from panicky child to responsible adult. In the passing of a full year we know that his victory over society is complete. We have had time to see the truth of such themes as the growth of friendship and of maturity, and the inevitability and acceptance of death. The integral setting has helped to make all this clear.

Functions of Setting

Not every setting has the same function in a story. Even in a story where a certain level of agreement exists about the setting and its function, there can be varied interpretations according to the interests and background of the reader. We are reminded again of Louise Rosenblatt's views of reading literature as a transaction between the reader, the text, and the context. A reader's interpretation of setting, then, is flexible instead of being pre-determined and fixed. The text influences the reader's interpretation, and the reader's interpretation in turn influences the meaning of the text.[3]

All readers have lived and grown up in a variety of contexts or environments, encompassing family, friendships, community, school, perhaps a place of worship. In addition, readers of all ages will be gradually influenced by various cultural experiences—people and places beyond those immediate ones. Readers also touched by international experiences, global concerns, and abstract elements of culture will be more and differently able to make sense of their world. All of this will affect the background information available to them, influencing how a reader interprets a story, in particular the setting. Stories for younger readers are more likely to be set in contexts that relate to their most immediate influences, closer in time and space to what is familiar and recognizable. Settings also have a human element; stories have events that influence the characters. Those characters will have feelings about what has occurred and feelings toward elements of the setting. This gives the story setting an emotional dimension as well.[4]

The setting, and all it entails, provides the guidelines and sets the parameters for what can logically occur in a good story. Characters who are experiencing fear may impel a reader to have the same emotion; a setting that includes humorous events may evoke laughter from the reader; unfair or unjust events in the setting may spark indignation or urge a reader to action.

Setting That Clarifies Conflict

An integral setting plays an important part in conflict. Setting for a story can be any time, past, present, or future. Where and when a story takes place can define the kind of conflict that is likely or even possible to occur within a story. Authors have a responsibility to make an integral setting possible and probable.

In *Lizzie Bright and the Buckminster Boy* by Gary Schmidt, Turner finds life in a small town in Maine quite different from that in Boston; the differences in attitudes toward African Americans become clear in the description of setting. Lizzie, Turner's African American friend, lives on a rocky island so wild it looks uninhabitable. Self-righteous and greedy townspeople exhibit racial attitudes congruent with the setting's time period, working to destroy the community and turn the island into a money-making resort. The writer's description of the rugged island clarifies both its natural beauty and symbolizes the town's wish to exclude the inhabitants from their lives.

> Turner felt as if he was on the brink of a discovery. Ahead of him, the beach was covered with stones, their hard outsides rubbed off and smoothed so that they glowed as the waves gathered them up and down. The granite ledges were streaked by a thousand shades of gray and silver, separated by slices of pink quartz that glowed like happiness. . . . The pines threw their roots around the shore's boulders, grappling with the living rocks and wrestling them into position. And out of those rocks they thrust themselves into the air as if they might scratch the blue dome of heaven.

When action is affected by setting, the author must adequately detail the time and place. For example, turn to *The Witch of Blackbird Pond,* in which Kit Tyler is transported from her West Indies birthplace to an austere Puritan New England setting. Author Elizabeth Speare does not rely merely on our history book knowledge of that time and place when witchcraft was feared; she clarifies setting by her description of the austerity of life among the Puritans: the house with hand-rubbed copper, indicative of hard work; the heavy, fortress-like door; the dim little mirror; and the severe wooden bench. Speare weaves description of the house itself into a description of Kit's tasks in a typical day. Meat must be chopped, vegetables prepared, and the pewter mugs polished with fine sand and reeds. Throughout the day Kit stirs the kettle of boiling soap with a stick, the heavy stirring tiring her muscles. Even the easiest task, making corn pudding, keeps her leaning over the smoky fire that burns her watering eyes. As Kit walks through the little town to church, we see severity in the straight, cold lines of functional buildings with punitive devices. The unpainted Meeting House, the whipping post, the pillory, and the stocks are frightening evidence that Kit is now in a rigid and uncompromising environment, one for which her carefree Barbados upbringing has not prepared her.

The Evolution of Calpurnia Tate identifies the integral role setting plays in the story's conflict right away; the actions of the characters and the plot build on this throughout the novel. The physical environment significantly affects the characters' daily routine, requiring the day's work to be done by noon: "By 1899, we had learned to tame the darkness but not the Texas heat. We arose in the dark, hours before Sunrise, when there was barely a smudge of indigo across the eastern sky . . . We lit our kerosene lamps and carried them before us . . . like our own tiny wavering suns."

However, in keeping with the social expectations of the time, the heat affects some more than others: "it was the women who suffered the most in their corsets and petticoats." Jacqueline Kelly shows the evolution of the protagonist, eleven-year-old Callie Vee, who is sandwiched midway between six brothers and wants to be a scientist despite the existing societal expectations for girls and women. The five-acre patch of wilderness between her family's large cotton and pecan farm and the river becomes the site of her inquiry into the region's flora and fauna. Callie's passion for scientific investigation is supported by her enlightened grandfather, whose insight into her nature leads to her introduction to the new scientific theory of times: *The Origin of Species* by Charles Darwin.

Emily Arnold McCully's *The Ballot Box Battle* is a story featuring a young girl in the 1880s similarly challenged by the conflict between social norms and personal goals. Cordelia is also mentored by an enlightened older person, this time Elizabeth Cady Stanton, who encourages Cordelia's determination, courage and desire to learn as she fights to cast a vote on Election Day in Tenafly, New Jersey. The historical illustrations use muted tones and impressionistic style to evoke a feeling of the past; McCully also uses a technique for Stanton's flashbacks that makes the pictures appear to be viewed from a telescope. In these illustrations we see Stanton sharing the parallels of her girlhood and Cordelia's. Pairing this book and others set in the late nineteenth century creates an opportunity to see a time period or a social movement like women's rights more broadly than any one story can accomplish.

Setting as Historical Background

Historical fiction can make the past come alive so that the reader can better understand life in another time. The wide range of current historical fiction books focus on events from the past where politics, social movements, environmental concerns, or economics have affected human lives. The setting is a critical element for this genre because readers, especially younger readers, will have limited experience with contexts surrounding historical events. Descriptions of language, dress, and lifestyle must be accurately portrayed so readers can differentiate between the story's setting and their own life setting. The longer ago the event, the greater the responsibility there is to provide a setting that informs the reader about a story's place and time with not only intrigue, but also accuracy.

Like adults, children will accept as much or as little setting as the story demands. Similar to adults, younger readers expect that when a setting is important to understanding a story, the author will allow them to see, to hear, perhaps even to smell the setting—to sense the setting in any way relevant to the mood, conflict, and characters in the story. However, younger children will be less likely to sit still for long descriptions that take them away from the conflict and characters. For them, and for many adults as well, setting interwoven with action is the most interesting and readable. Once this setting is established, a reader of any age expects the writer to be consistent.

Setting in historical fiction is very important.

Much of the history we read is associated with conflict; stories associated with war and violence from history are becoming common for readers of all ages, not just adults or readers of young adult fiction. Similarly, stories of conflict in the picture-book format are no longer associated solely with very young readers. *Rose Blanche* by Roberto Innocenti is a perfect example. The realism in the illustrations clarifies and extends the historical story told in the narrative. Readers can see the change in the town and the demeanor of its citizens through the darkening tones as Nazi officials take control of the European town. The lighter palette at the end shows the liberation of the prison camp and the promise of a brighter future, but the death of the young protagonist creates a sharp contrast better understood by older readers.

A dark event in U.S. history is the incarceration of Japanese Americans in camps during World War II—a wrongful event many citizens want to see remembered to avoid its repetition. Although Japanese immigrants had lived for many years in the United States, the bombing of Pearl Harbor awakened suspicions about their loyalty. *Journey to Topaz* by Yoshiko Uchida shows the educated and assimilated Sukanes, and it is heartbreaking to read how the family of four is divided, forced to live in a horse stall for a time, and shipped off to the Topaz camp in Utah. The parents' sorrow and the children's anger are understandable. The camp is "white powdery dust, covering everyone in a smothering blanket . . . flour-dusted cookies that had escaped from a bakery":

> There wasn't a single tree or a blade of grass to break the monotony of the sun-bleached desert. It was like the carcass of a chicken stripped clean of any meat and left all dry, brittle bone. . . . They sank into with each step as though they were plowing through a snow bank.

Allen Say presents a more poignant treatment of this time in history in *Music for Alice*. This picturebook is based on the true story of Alice Sumida's life. Alice grew up on a farm and dancing was her passion. She married and operated a seed store, but their business came to a halt with the bombing of Pearl Harbor and their subsequent forced labor on a farm in the Oregon desert. Alice and Mark combined skill and hard work to become the largest gladiola bulb growers in the country. Allen Say's watercolor paintings boost the historical elements of this story, showing in detail the clothing they wore, the landscape in which they struggled, the satisfaction as Alice dances again. This picturebook is deceptively complex, and readers with additional knowledge of this time and place in America's history will appreciate the role setting plays in this story.

Setting is increasingly important for nonfiction selections that have a story to tell; authors like Jim Murphy create outstanding nonfiction narratives like *The Great Fire*. This suspense-filled story of the 1871 Chicago fire is skillfully told through the eyes of several survivors; the setting is fortified through selected documents, personal accounts, photographs, and illustrations reproduced in sepia tones. Murphy's telling of this event includes political conditions underlying the rapid onset and spread of the fire throughout the city. The myth of Mrs. O'Leary's cow's responsibility for the fire is debunked by the well-researched account that builds a solid setting. The specificity of Murphy's account frees him to create a well-developed and true story from history.

Our nonfiction mentor text, *Christmas in the Big House, Christmas in the Quarters* is an illustrated book whose setting is achieved primarily through carefully crafted factual accounts of a yuletide celebration on an 1859 Virginia plantation—the last "before the Southern Rebellion." The McKissacks meticulously researched plantation records, and this composite account is based on actual "Big House" and "Quarters" settings. Though this book is set in a particular season, one that heightens the disparity between the plentitude of the plantation family and the bleakness of those living in the "Quarters," the findings underlying this account should be applied more broadly. It is not only a local, but also a regional representation of life on a southern plantation prior to the Civil War. The compare-and-contrast design of this award-winning nonfiction selection is an apt choice. Readers will view the comfort and material wealth, rich tones, and bright accents of the plantation celebration; turn the page and they will see the bleak backdrop of the same celebration for the slaves. Readers will also note that though the colors are muted, there is still a warm tone, a celebratory mood. The setting comes alive through John Thompson's beautifully realized representational paintings.

The picturebook format has a very important role in developing setting, and careful research is just as important in the illustrations as it is in the narrative text. *Fanny in the Kitchen* by Deborah Hopkinson is the story of the first cookbook of Fanny Farmer. It is a stellar example of a well-researched visual setting that illuminates the story and enriches the reader about the clothing, furnishings, and utensils of a Victorian household. Nancy Carpenter's drawings, along with etchings and engravings, help young readers visualize the time period accurately; at the same time they sense the spirit of fun. Superb detail and additional author's notes about Fanny Farmer come together to make this setting noteworthy. In nonfiction picturebooks, it is important that both the author and illustrator make readers aware of the accuracy in the elements of the setting. An outstanding example of this is the biography *Nurse, Soldier, Spy: The Story of Sarah Edmonds, a Civil War Hero* by Marissa Moss. This inspirational story of a very daring young woman is meticulously illustrated by John Hendrix who provides an illustrator's note that complements the author's note, source material, and index. Readers should expect with quality nonfiction books for children. Hendrix succeeds in portraying the character of Sarah Edmonds and her brave actions, but not at the expense of creating a historically accurate setting.

Setting as Antagonist

Sometimes setting itself is the antagonist, as it is for Sheila Burnford's classic *The Incredible Journey*. An essential part of the story, the Canadian wilderness, is not only setting but also antagonist. Without clear descriptions of the dense brush, forest, and river, such a novel would have no believable conflict to hold the reader. However, on the opening page of the novel, Burnford prepares the reader for the conflict; the rugged country of northwestern Ontario is introduced, and the description continues for a page and a half:

> [A] vast area of deeply wooded wilderness—of endless chains of lonely lakes and rushing rivers. Thousands of miles of country roads, rough timberlanes, overgrown tracks leading to abandoned mines, and unmapped trails snake across its length and breadth. It is a country of far-flung, lonely farms and a few widely scattered small towns and villages, of lonely trappers' shacks and logging camps.

Not all settings rely on this kind of thick verbal description. For example, Matt Phelan's graphic novel, *The Storm in the Barn*, effectively creates the feeling of dust permeating every corner of a midwestern town during the Dust Bowl. Sepia tones and swirling lines show the movement of the clouds of dust engulfing the Kansas countryside, choking the existence of every living thing, parching plant life, and bringing on dust dementia. Young Jack struggles to win the admiration of his family and the community as he enlists the help of nature, in the Storm King, to bring back the rain and restore the parched earth. Setting is antagonistic, but it is also integral to the resolution—it is both foe and ally.

Sometimes there is neither training nor tactics for survival when natural disasters devastate the environment, as is the case in *Eight Days: A Story of Haiti*. Edwidge Danticat's story is told through the first-person narration of seven-year-old Junior, who was trapped beneath his house as a result of the Port-au-Prince earthquake. The setting is the antagonist, but in this story, the memory of that setting and Junior's imagination counter the negative effects of his eight-day ordeal. The pastel and acrylic paintings signal time elements and the conditions on the surface, the bright blue sky over Haiti as the backdrop when Junior is free. Both words and illustrations build the setting; it is not only the specificity of the time and place that make this picturebook setting noteworthy, but also the dual role of the Haitian setting as antagonist and refuge.

Picturebooks frequently provide minimal text to evoke setting, but the illustrations can provide a sharp contrast, almost telling another story. An eerie picturebook for older readers, *The Watertower*, tells a disquieting story with an antagonistic setting. Two friends disobey rules to sneak a swim in the town's watertower, and Bubba, a timid swimmer, mysteriously loses his shorts. Spike, the duo's leader, sneaks to Bubba's house for a fresh pair. He returns to find Bubba crawling from the tank, boastful about his skill in the water and oddly changed. Gary Crew spins a simple enough story, but Woolman's surreal illustrations create the setting, featuring a looming watertower decorated with a logo oddly similar to the iris of an eye. The town's residents wear dazed expressions and sport clothing bearing the tower's logo; they are depicted staring blankly toward the tower when Bubba is being seduced to take a dip in the dark, slimy water. This story's antagonistic setting provides a subtle conflict that leaves readers unsettled; the book design increases this effect by shifting the viewing orientation.

Setting can heighten suspense.

Picturebooks present a unique opportunity to think about setting as antagonist in a special way. In Virginia Lee Burton's classic *The Little House*, the impact of man on the neighborhood is the antagonist, but also the solution when the Little House is relocated to the countryside; this is established in both the narrative text and illustration. But a wordless picturebook, *Window*, provides a special opportunity to see this same device without specific written messages from the author. The illustrations alone show the impact of encroaching suburbia on the character, a family's home. Readers see the problem resolution much differently not only because illustration alone tells the story, but also because the complete story spans two books, published years apart, in Jeannie Baker's *Window* and sequel, *Home*. In addition, the resolution does not include the implicit expectation that "progress" will again antagonize, as it certainly will for the *Little House*. In Baker's *Home* there is no personification of the house, though it is the focal point of both the story and the character's actions. Moving the house is not the solution to the problem already established in *Window*; rather a change in what is considered "progress." Readers see the landscape lose its natural habitat over time in *Window*; they see the revival in *Home*. The three-dimensional collage art provides realism to the setting. The antagonist is "progress," and 'progress' creates the refuge.

Setting That Illuminates Character

In many examples, setting influences character. Notice the effect of isolation and crowding on the protagonist's fear in that unusual autobiography *Anne Frank: The Diary of a Young Girl*. We must see the stiflingly cramped atmosphere of the secret annex or we cannot experience the yearning for freedom and privacy that Anne expresses during the twenty-five months her family hides from the Nazi soldiers who are rounding up Jews for imprisonment. We must see Anne's surroundings as we follow her tensions with her parents and fellow prisoners, her awakening sense of self, and her curiosity about growing up. Just two days after the family crowds into the annex, Anne writes as though it is an adventure, the tone of her entries are upbeat. But thirteen months later even the approach of bedtime requires effort:

> *Nine o-clock in the evening.* The bustle of going to bed in the "Secret Annexe" begins. . . . Chairs are shoved about, beds are pulled down, blankets unfolded, nothing remains where it is during the day. I sleep on the little divan . . . chairs have to be used to lengthen it. A quilt, sheets, pillows, blankets, are all fetched from Dussel's bed where they remain during the day . . . creaking in the next room: Margot's concertina-bed being pulled out! Again, divan, blankets, and pillows, everything is done to make the wooden slats a bit more comfortable. It sounds like thunder above, but it is only Mrs. Van Daan's bed . . . shifted to the window.

The setting becomes overwhelming in its effect on every aspect of the characters' lives. Bickering, quarrels, arguments, and rages result from the pressures of close confinement.

Confinement in one room for two years, with extremely rare opportunities to walk outside, surely has impact on a character. That is also the case in Johanna Reiss's *The Upstairs Room*, the autobiographical account of the author's life during the Holocaust. Annie at first does not understand and is resentful that she cannot go to school, to the shops, or outside to play. As her confinement continues in the home of a Dutch farm family, she grows in understanding, but at the age of eleven is still resentful. She does not realize the life-and-death danger to her host family should she and her sister Sisi be found, nor does she see why twenty-year-old Sisi has more privileges than she does. Her resentment and frustration are like those of most children and are therefore believable.

Setting affects character.

The title alone of *Olive's Ocean* implies that setting is important to the story. In Kevin Henkes's story, Martha learns that Olive, who has just been killed in an accident, admired her and that like Martha she wanted to be a writer who wrote about the sea. During her dreamy summer vacation by the sea, Martha, thinking about Olive, writes of loving the sea, the sand, the waves, and the rocks. This summer's experience is also the first thrill of liking a boy. Picnics on the shore, hand-holding walks, sharing secrets and memories, and building a sand castle together seem to be the stuff from which romance is made. But when Jimmy ruthlessly wrecks the castle, that action seems to metaphorically signify the destruction of their closeness; his kiss captured on tape is merely a response to a challenge. As Martha sits close beside Jimmy on the couch, she hears a voice. "'The world is not what you think it is,' a voice repeated. Martha guessed it was Jimmy's voice, altered somehow, making him sound mechanical, roboticized." Setting helps to reveal character.

The autobiographical picturebook and graphic narrative, *The Wall: Growing Up Behind the Iron Curtain*, creates a political setting that most assuredly influenced the main character, author and artist Peter Sís. Black-and-white illustrations are increasingly tainted with red, signifying communism overtaking Czechoslovakia under Soviet rule. From infancy to young adulthood, Sís resists the constraints of the restrictive cultural climate; this is shown through the patches of colorful illustration that represent his passion for creativity, art, and freedom. The setting is critical to developing his talent that readers in a free political climate can now appreciate. This picturebook is an important example of this format's importance for young adult audiences; the setting of Peter Sís's formative years clearly affected the autobiographical character in this powerful memoir.

Setting That Creates Mood

As several of the preceding examples demonstrate, setting affects mood. The mood a setting evokes can range from frightening to sentimental in any genre. Setting is sometimes sentimentalized, as it is in Lois Lowry's *Crow Call*. Here Lowry creates a pastoral setting for her post-WWII story based on a childhood memoir of bonding with her father, who has just returned from his service in the war. The narrative and realistic illustrations work together to show Liz's shyness in reconnecting with her father for a long-awaited day of hunting crows; their head-to-head interactions create a feeling of emotional connection. The decision to allow Liz's successful crow call finish their day indicates that her father's attentiveness is genuine; he understands her desire for a hunting shirt and the hunting trip for what it is. The earth-toned watercolor paintings are perfect for the fall setting, creating a subdued mood. There are moments of laughter, but the overall tone is one of tenderness and consideration.

Settings can be effectively portrayed in the picturebook format—often in ways that cannot be similarly accomplished by the words alone. Two stories about the same person can be set in a similar time and place, but the illustrations create a very different mood that affects the way the reader interprets the story and the character. *Snowflake Bentley* by Jacqueline Briggs Martin is an excellent picturebook biography that narrates Wilson Bentley's story in a straightforward manner that is interesting to readers. To supplement the story, Briggs Martin provides additional factual information in the sidebars of each two-page spread. The setting is expertly depicted by Mary Azarian's woodcuts, providing a historical mood appropriate to the time in which Bentley lived. The tones are blues, white, and earth tones connotative of the cold, snowy New England winter critical to Wilson Bentley's life and work.

By contrast, another biography of Wilson Bentley by Mary Bahr tells his story from the perspective of his older brother, Charlie. The story emphasizes the emotional side of Bentley's life, creating a different mood in the text. But the significant way Bahr's *My Brother Loved Snowflakes: The Story of Wilson A. Bentley, The Snowflake Man* creates mood is through the illustration of the setting. Illustrator Laura Jacobsen's warm color palette that emphasizes the warmth in the relationship between the characters. However, the impact of the colors is the creation of a *feeling* of the sunny southwest for the snowy New England setting in which Bentley lived and worked. The choice of color can affect the reader's response to and acceptance of the character as well.

Setting, too, can be sentimentalized.

Setting as Symbol

Symbols may operate in setting as they may in other elements of literature. A **symbol** is a person, object, situation, or action that operates on two levels of meaning: the literal and the figurative or suggestive. Once aware of the existence of symbols, it is easy to read into stories and assign meanings not legitimately supported by the text. The important point here is that symbols in literature understood by most children are relatively straightforward; they may be in the narrative or embedded in the illustrations.

A symbol operates on two levels of meaning.

For example, a simple symbolic setting is the forest, which can be both a literal setting as well as a symbol for the unknown. Some folktale settings share this symbolic meaning: Hansel and Gretel, as well as Snow White, are lost in the fearful and unknown—the forest. The forest is also the domain of ogres and giants, mysteriously frightening creatures. Despite their backdrop qualities, these symbolic settings often set the mood in traditional tales. Modern fantasy stories that incorporate folkloric elements, like Anthony Browne's *Into the Forest*, rely on readers who have internalized this symbol. In contrast, *Winnie-the-Pooh*'s Forest is a natural place for Pooh and Piglet to hunt a Woozle/Wizzle; extending the symbolic meaning of a forest to the point of calling it a dark symbol would be misleading.

The same idea would apply to Hannah, the supposed Quaker witch in *The Witch of Blackbird Pond;* she does not live in the dark forest. A kind and harmless woman, she lives in the benign and sunny meadows. Just as she chose the forest because of the place where the story is set, Speare chooses this sunny meadow for Hannah's home to assist in creating conflict. Calling the setting symbolic would be inaccurate.

Symbols may be combined to create **allegory**, as they are in some stories for children. According to Northrop Frye, allegory translates into images.[5] Qualifying as a true symbol requires the object to be emphasized or repeated and supported throughout the entire story; the symbolic object represents something quite different from its literal meaning. But stories for children operate on a fairly literal level. Ideas of good and evil may be translated into characters, actions, or setting, which then become symbols for ideas.

In this sense the Narnia series by C. S. Lewis is allegory. However, the Narnia books are also highly successful when read on a literal level; the young reader may or may not see the ideas symbolized by characters or setting. A reader may enjoy the series for the adventures they provide, gradually recognize the struggle of good and evil, and then reread them all, this time on an allegorical or symbolic level.[6]

Setting in these stories functions as more than escape. Once again, the principle is that the essential setting should be integrated with character and conflict, and not a mere digression. Since folk literature and fantasy are more common in literature for children than for adults, their special considerations bear closer examination.

A true symbol is emphasized, repeated, and supported.

 # Setting in Traditional Literature

In most folktales, action and theme are the focus of interest and the setting is backdrop. The action is usually brisk and little time is spent describing time and place. The setting is a vague long ago and far away that avoids pinning down time and place. Such a setting anticipates the pleasurable possibility that perhaps the tale could happen again, perhaps here! We have noted in discussion of character that in a folktale the protagonists are so general and universal that what happens to them might happen to anyone. Similar vagueness in setting reinforces the possibility of adventures.

Folktale settings are often vague.

Folktale settings often follow the "once upon a time" formula. A random sampling of tales from Grimm—the tales best known in Western culture—reveals the following settings in their opening lines:

> Once upon a time there lived an old man and his wife who for a long time . . .
>
> Once upon a time there was a king who had twelve daughters. . . .
>
> Once upon a time in deep winter, when the snowflakes were falling like feathers . . . [7]

Occasionally a simple variation occurs: "At the edge of a great forest lived a woodcutter and his wife." Folktale settings from other cultures seem to vary little from the patterns of Grimm, with little more specific definition of time and place than the Native American "My grandfather told me. . . ." It is the nature of the folktale—originally told to a mixed audience that understood the setting of their own tales or imagined others—to plunge into conflict and action. Such generalized settings can demonstrate more clearly a universal theme: The kindness of the daughter is rewarded; she lives happily ever after in the palace of the prince.

Some tales come from a common heritage, their setting is shared by a number of stories, but others are associated with a particular geographic region. A folktale type frequently associated with various regions of the United States and North America is the tall tale. These tales feature larger than life characters whose basis may be the actions of a person who performed brave feats in life, such as stories of John Henry, who is associated with the mining regions.

Julius Lester and Jerry Pinkney have collaborated on a retelling of John Henry based on several versions of an African American folk ballad. Their version focuses on creating a down-to-earth character; the strength and wit of this man with West Virginia origins is a fit with the rugged mountain terrain. The earth tones of the illustrations capture the earth's warmth and beauty; woodland animals play the role of bystanders throughout the story. John Henry almost *is* the setting, so the story can move ahead with the action.

Similarly brave and strong, pioneer Angelica Longrider harkens from the Great Smoky Mountains. Her story is an original tall tale whose dialect is in keeping with the Tennessee woods setting where Angelica Longrider earned the name *Swamp*

Garden Settings for Children's Books

Anholt, Lawrence. *The Magical Garden of Claude Monet*. Barron's, 2003.

Features an imaginary visit to Monet's garden at Giverny. Paintings based on Monet's popular impressionistic works overlayed with Anholt's cartoon show characters enjoying the day. (Integral, historical setting)

Bjork, Cristina. *Linnea in Monet's Garden*. Lena Anderson, Illus. Joan Sandin, Trans. R & S Books, 1987.

Classic picturebook that juxtaposes period photos of Monet, his art, and scenes from Monet's garden in Giverny. (Integral, historical setting)

Coburn, Cherie Foster. *Our Shadow Garden*. Children's Cancer Hospital at M. D. Anderson Cancer Center, Illus. Bright Sky Press, 2010.

Child empathizes with grandparent undergoing treatment for cancer who can no longer garden during the day. Night blooming garden that attracts nocturnal animals is created. (Integral, mood setting)

Fleischman, Paul. *Seedfolks*. Harper, 2004.

An empty lot in a troubled Cleveland, Ohio, neighborhood becomes the site of a community garden and a revival of community spirit. (Integral setting)

Hahn, Mary Downing. *A Doll in the Garden*. Clarion, 1987.

Classic ghost mystery writer for older children chooses a setting popular with adult murder mysteries: the garden. Young girl moves to a new town and lives in the upstairs apartment of an old house. The discovery of an antique doll half buried in the garden means a mystery to be solved. (Background, symbolic, mood setting)

Havill, Juanita. *Grow: A Verse Novel*. Stanislawa Kodman, Illus. Peachtree, 2008.

Popular theme of urban garden as the focal point for bringing a diverse neighborhood together spiritually and physically; includes illustrations. (Integral, symbolic setting)

Havill, Juanita. *I Heard It from Alice Zuccini: Poems about the Garden*. Christine Davenier, Illus. Chronicle, 2006.

Havill shares her love of gardening in verse and with whimsical illustrations, including a fairy who visits the garden. (Integral, mood setting)

Reynolds, Peter. *Rose's Garden*. Candlewick, 2009.

Brief, imaginative picturebook in Reynolds trademark small books about the power of planting a garden in the city. (Background, symbolic setting)

Stevens, Janet. *Tops and Bottoms*. Harcourt, 1995.

Trickster story of a clever rabbit that devises ways to keep all of the garden produce for himself. (Integral, symbolic setting)

Stewart, Sarah. *The Gardener*. Farrar, Straus & Giroux, 1997.

A young girl sent to live with her uncle during the Depression finds a way to brighten the urban landscape with a garden. (Integral, historical, mood setting)

Van Allsburg, Chris. *The Garden of Abdul Gasazi*. Houghton Mifflin, 1979.

Strange events fill this story of a boy who chases his dog onto the property of his mysterious neighbor. (Background, mood setting)

Angel when she pulled a stuck wagon from a muddy swamp. She is resourceful, helpful, and strong; she is unafraid of the hardships that defeat even the strongest woodsmen of the day. The naïve folk art illustrations by Paul O. Zelinski perfectly depict the rural mountain setting, each oil painting is done on wood from trees indigenous to the Appalachian region, including cherry, birch, and maple. The setting in a regional tale should mesh with the character and make sense with the actions that are the tall tale. This is now a classic tall tale—one of the first to feature an extraordinary female. Isaacs and Zelinsky have teamed up for a sequel, *Dust Devil*, placing "Angel" Longrider in Montana where she has more space for her larger-than-life feats. Once again Zelinsky uses oil on native Montana woods to paint a slightly expressionistic setting; young readers know this is a tall tale.

Doña Flor by Pat Mora is a gentle larger-than-life female heroine who performs her peacemaking feats through kindness and language in and around Southwestern Pueblo. She is comfortable surrounded with lots of people and communicates with nature to bring harmony to the setting—along with a few fanciful feats, like providing tortilla roofs and rafts. The scratchboard-and-pencil drawings have warm earth tones that are a fit with the southwestern environment; the Spanish language alludes to her roots in Mexico. Her story needs to be told in a way that provides readers, especially those with limited personal experience with Southwestern culture, a sense of place.

Johnny Chapman, like John Henry, existed first in history. Known to folklore as Johnny Appleseed, his travels really did change the landscape of the countryside where he did his planting. Stories about Appleseed John abound, but Jane Yolen's version is illustrated in American folk art. The setting features quilted hillsides that are symbolic of the culture associated with his early frontier life in the hills of western Pennsylvania and the Ohio Valley. The paintings feature yellowed paper for an antiqued effect; they combine realism and folk art to match this mixture of biography, tall tale, and legend. This version is set in the time and place appropriate to the time in which Johnny Chapman lived and worked.

Legends are unauthenticated stories handed down from local and regional traditions. Readers regard them as only figuratively possible. They are by their definition related to historical events or people. As with regional tall tales, their connection to actual historical people and events narrows the time and place of their setting somewhat. For example, Robin Hood's adventures occur in Sherwood Forest since, according to history, that is where Robin Hood lived.

Kathryn Lasky provides readers with an untold story that is filled with the romance and bravery readers expect in a legend. She tells the story of Maid Marian, formerly Matty, the daughter of Nottingham's most famous falconer. She becomes the falcons' champion after an attack on the castle leaves her mother dead and her father poverty stricken. Set during the power struggle between Richard the Lionhearted and his brother John of England, *Hawksmaid: The Untold Story of Robin Hood and Maid Marian* is set in the depleted English castle. Matty and her father lead the villagers and peasants to survival with the help of their hawks. Early in the story Lasky establishes the hawks as their allies:

> Matty streaked out the kitchen's back door. She was running toward a small tower between the dog kennels and the stables in the bailey. . . . Matty had but one thought: she must get to the tower mews where the hawks were kept. If she could get to them, the birds would keep her safe. She felt this in the deepest part of her being.

Legends place setting in a historical time.

Matty and her childhood friend Fynn reinvent themselves as Maid Marian and Robin Hood. With their gang of boys, now the Merry Men, she leads escapades throughout the countryside to help the starving neighbors. As is the case with many legends, elements of magic occur; when the falcons exchange dialogue with one another they signal their importance to this story.

Other folk literature seems to return us to the traditional vague setting. The fable, in fact, omits setting altogether, going immediately into action and its didactic point:

> A certain Wolf, being very hungry, disguised himself in a sheep's skin.
> A mischievous Shepherd's Boy used to amuse himself by calling "Wolf! Wolf!"

Many of the fables are only a few sentences long, and since they exist to point to a moral, setting is quite logically unimportant. The lesson is universal, unlimited by time or place. Illustrators, again, have the opportunity to place these stories, changing their universality to a more specific setting that has other connotations for the message it provides. For example, this is the case between interpretations of Aesop's fables by David Davis and illustrated by Susan Ward in *Texas Aesop's Fables* and the fine collection adapted and illustrated by Jerry Pinkney. Modern adaptations closely following the criteria for a particular folklore category are literary lore and fall into the genre of fantasy.

In fables, setting exists as a backdrop for the stated moral.

 ## Setting in Fantasy

Setting in fantasy is a special consideration since fantasy often begins in a setting of reality and moves to a fantasy realm, then back again. Time, particularly in fantasy, has a way of lengthening or shortening, depending on the make-believe world the writer creates. Time is relative: when we're entertained, time goes quickly; when we're bored, time drags endlessly. But the writer of fantasy takes other liberties with time, perhaps by making one event, or one life, last through centuries or be over in seconds. At times we not only desire, but also accept settings as escapes; fantasy can fulfill this.

In fantasy, time may take any form.

In the classic and well-loved fantasy, *Alice's Adventures in Wonderland*, readers move easily from the real to the fantastic by the device of a dream. Lewis Carroll sets all logic awry, including the logic of setting. A rabbit hole extends deep into a strange, unbounded world, and time moves in all directions to create a setting essential to our experience of the story. To us as well as to Alice, time and place are illogical and confusing; they influence nonsensical behavior that defies every rule. In defiance of time and the related laws of growth, Alice grows and shrinks; the Mock Turtle's lessons lessen; the tea party murders time by going on forever; the White Rabbit tries fruitlessly to catch up with time. As for place, nothing seems to be where it is expected to be, and nothing can be counted on to be in the same place at another moment. The great hall with the glass table and tiny door vanishes, and Alice finds her way into a tidy little room. Turning her back on the tea party, Alice walks through a door into a tree—only to discover she is back in the long hall with the glass table and the tiny door. Finally, cause and effect—which occur in that order and are logically related to time—defy time to appear in nonsensically reversed order: sentence first, verdict later.

Other transitions are more complex. In Susan Cooper's *The Dark Is Rising,* the world that Will enters is filled with the mysterious and the supernatural—the setting is integral and essential to the story. The castle where Will meets the Old Ones, who for centuries have been battling evil, is the setting for Will's discovery that by exercising willpower he can actually bring change. Reluctantly, he learns that he must accept his power in order to use it for good:

> [He looked] across the room at the light and shadow dancing side by side across the rich tapestries on the stone walls, and he thought hard, in furious concentration, of the image of the blazing log fire in the huge fireplace behind him. He felt the warmth of it on the back of his neck, and thought of the glowing heart of the big pile of logs and the leaping yellow tongues of flame. *Go out, fire,* he said to it in his mind, feeling suddenly safe and free from the dangers of power, because of course no fire as big as that could possibly go out.

The fire goes out. Next Will sees that each of the many tapestries on the castle walls has its own frightening image, some as terrifying as "the empty-eyed grinning white skull of a horse, with a single stubby broken horn in the bony forehead and red ribbons wreathing the long jaws." Threatened by the rising of evil, the Dark, Will sees clearly his responsibility to use the special power given him.

Neil Gaiman expertly chills readers with an ultra-realistic setting in the opening pages of *The Graveyard Book.* The comfort and safety of home are disrupted when "the man Jack" ruthlessly murders a sleeping family and subsequently pursues the baby, who has awakened and toddled from the nursery and out the front door. The child inadvertently finds a safe haven when he wanders through the threshold of a cemetery and is rescued by an assortment of ghosts and vampires who become his family, naming him Bod. Readers are taken back and forth between the real world and the fantasy world of the cemetery as Bod finds his unique place between the two. The dual setting is critical to the suspension of disbelief, and beyond the opening scene, the creative setting and characters interact to promote living and caring.

Setting may move between reality and fantasy.

Techniques for moving back and forth from realistic settings to a fantasy setting exist with the picturebook format as well. For example, two children and their pet cat escape into the "place cats go at night" using the pet door in John Burningham's *It's a Secret*; it is the literal and figurative portal to another world frequently found in fantasy. Similarly, a brother and sister crawl through a tunnel to reach a magical world in Anthony Browne's *The Tunnel.* Barbara Lehman's *Rainstorm* features a lonely boy who discovers the key to a trunk one rainy afternoon. The open lid of the trunk leads him through a tunnel to a lighthouse where he finds friends. Younger readers who discover these devices for setting change in a visual format may generalize the technique when they read more sophisticated stories.

Borders and frames are another popular device for moving characters from one setting to another in fantasy. For example, "breaking frame" occurs when a character escapes from a setting by somehow leaving a framed page. Illustrators frequently confine characters using a frame or border as the visual boundary that restricts their movement. Arthur Yorinks's *Hey, Al* features a dejected caretaker and his dog escaping their drab apartment life to a brightly colored tropical paradise. The illustrations allow this adventure by "breaking frame," going from reality to fantasy and back.

In the classic *Where the Wild Things Are*, Max escapes the confines of his bedroom to let the wild rumpus begin as the frame on the page becomes thinner, making room for a new lush setting. Max is transported to a setting different from the bedroom where his options are restricted. As his temper tantrum subsides, Max returns "home" to the safety of those boundaries, to discover supper awaiting his return.

John Burningham is an expert at using illustrative techniques to signify the change in setting from everyday reality to childhood fantasy adventure through the

INQUIRY POINT

This setting inquiry point incorporates a textset to provide a series of explorations into the qualities of setting with the books included.

First: The compact nature of picturebooks makes them good choices to examine literary elements for all ages. They are particularly suited to examining setting.[8] Because it is not always easy to determine whether a setting is integral or a backdrop, it is often useful to take another look and try to step away from the actual story you have read. Browse through these books. Choose three or four to examine more carefully. Which type of setting is used?

Next: Try changing the setting. Does it make a difference to the story? How?

Finally: Is the setting primarily revealed by the words or the illustrations?

Amado, Elisa. *Tricycle.* Alfonso Ruano, Illus. Groundwood Books, 2007.

*Anzaldua, Gloria. *Friends from the Other Side: Amigos del Otro Lado.* Consuelo Mendez, Illus. Children's Book Press, 1997.

*Bunting, Eve. *One Green Apple.* Ted Lewin, Illus. Clarion, 2006.

Crew, Gary. *The Viewer.* Shaun Tan, Illus. Simply Read Books, 2003.

Davis, Aubrey. *Bagels from Benny.* Dusan Petricic, Illus. Kids Can Press, 2005.

*Harjo, Joy. *The Good Luck Cat.* Paul Lee, Illus. Harcourt, 2000.

*Lainez, Rene Colato. *From North to South: Del Norte al Sur.* Joe Cepeda, Illus. Children's Book Press, 2010.

Lehman, Barbara. *Museum Trip.* Houghton Mifflin, 2006.

*Myers, Walter Dean. *Patrol: An American Soldier in Vietnam.* Ann Grifalconi, Illus. Turtleback, 2005.

*Reibstein, Mark. *Wabi Sabi.* Ed Young, Illus. Little, Brown, 2008.

Rumford, James. *Silent Music.* Roaring Book Press, 2008.

*Say, Allen. *Erika San.* Houghton Mifflin, 2009.

*Say, Allen. *Tea with Milk.* Houghton Mifflin, 1999.

Smith, Cynthia Leitich. *Jingle Dancer.* Cornelius Van Wright, Illus. HarperCollins, 2000.

Tunnell, Michael O. *Mailing May.* Ted Rand, Illus. Greenwillow, 1997.

Willems, Mo. *Knuffle Bunny.* Hyperion, 2004.

*Williams, Karen Lynn, and Khadra Mohammad. *Four Feet, Two Sandals.* Doug Chayka, Illus. Eerdmans Books, 2007.

Woodson, Jacqueline. *Pecan Baby.* Sophie Blackall, Illus. Putnam, 2010.

*Zee, Ruth Vander. *Always with You.* Ron Himler, Illus. Eerdmans, 2008.

After: What other considerations for setting do you find in these books? Does it matter more if the author and illustrator are the same person, or if a different person provides the illustrations?

Titles with asterisks (*) are related to each other in some way. Explore the relationships and the way setting plays a part in this. ◉

use of color, detail, and borders. For example, his classic *Come Away from the Water, Shirley* features a set of distracted parents administering nonchalant warnings for their daughter to stay away from the water as they relax on the beach. These framed illustrations feature the parents in their lounging chairs, reading the paper and napping, bound by the concerns of everyday life. Their inaction is cleverly countered with detailed illustrations on a borderless page; the setting of Shirley's imaginary adventures from encounters with pirates to buried treasure. Children can relate to the stories as they learn about illustrative devices for creating setting.

Setting can be realized through many techniques; it is an essential element to a successful story, whether it assists in suspending disbelief in fantasy or if it grounds a historical story.

SUMMARY

Setting is of two principal types. First, it may be a backdrop for the plot, like the generalized backdrop of a city, street, or forest against which we see some of the action of a play. In traditional literature, setting is usually backdrop, so generalized that it becomes universal. Or setting may be an integral part of the story, so essential to our understanding of this plot, these characters, and these themes that we must experience it with our senses. The integral setting may not only clarify the conflict; it may also help the reader understand character, be cast as the antagonist, influence mood, or act as symbol. Often the sense of place prepares the reader to accept the story and the writer's personal view of life and its significance.

Whether setting is integral or backdrop does not constitute a judgment about the quality of a piece of writing. What is important, however, is that understanding may develop only when we realize that this particular setting is essential to this story. And if setting is essential to our understanding, the writer must make the reader see, hear, touch, and perhaps even smell the setting. It is the writer's task to evoke setting, described either in paragraphs or in phrases woven into action, including details of color, sound, figurative comparisons, and other stylistics.

NOTES

1. Eudora Welty, *Place in Fiction* (New York: House of Books, 1957), p. 22.
2. Roger Angell, "For E. B. White's Readers and Family, a Sense of Trust Came Easily," *New Yorker*, February 14, 2005, p. 143. Writing of his stepfather, E. B. White, Angell notes that White waited to write *Charlotte's Web* "until he had the country stuff in it down by heart. He knew how geese sounded when they were upset, and on what day in the fall the squashes and pumpkins needed to be brought in and put on the barn floor—which is to say that he'd still be himself in writing about it, and would not put in a word that might patronize his audience." Angell comments further that he probably knew that his story of seasons and farm life would be his masterpiece. "[It] would not occur to him to feel uneasy that his best book was for children."
3. Louise Rosenblatt, *The Reader, the Text, the Poem* (Carbondale: Southern Illinois University Press, 1978).
4. M. W. Smith and J. D. Wilhelm, *Fresh Takes on Teaching Literary Elements: How to Teach What Really Matters about Character, Setting, Point of View, and Theme* (New York: Scholastic, 2010). The authors discuss setting to include a psychological dimension in their work with teachers of secondary students. These same dimensions of time, space, and emotion apply to younger children as well.

5. Northrop Frye, "Theory of Symbol," in *Anatomy of Criticism* (Princeton, NJ: Princeton University Press, 1957), pp. 71–128.

6. C. S. Lewis and the *Chronicles of Narnia* series are closely associated with Lewis's Christian beliefs, though Lewis would regularly comment that they were first and foremost good stories. Their purpose was not to teach lessons. A nice synopsis and discussion of the most well-known novel in the *Chronicle of Narnia* series is Jeanne Murray Walker, "The Lion, the Witch, and The Wardrobe as Rite of Passage," *Children's Literature in Education*, 3(16), 1985, pp. 177–188.

7. Alfred David and Mary Elizabeth Meek, eds., *The Twelve Dancing Princesses* (Bloomington: Indiana University Press, 1974).

8. M. W. Smith and J. D. Wilhelm, *Fresh Takes on Teaching Literary Elements: How to Teach What Really Matters about Character, Setting, Point of View, and Theme* (New York: Scholastic, 2010).

RECOMMENDED BOOKS

BAHR, MARY. *My Brother Loved Snowflakes: The Story of Wilson A. Bentley, the Snowflake Man*. Illustrated by Laura Jacobsen. Boyds Mills Press, 2002.

BAKER, JEANNIE. *Home*. Greenwillow, 2004.

BAKER, JEANNIE. *Window*. Greenwillow, 1991.

BAUER, MARION DANE. *On My Honor*. Houghton Mifflin, 1986.

BROOKS, BRUCE. *Everywhere*. Harper & Row, 1990.

BROWNE, ANTHONY. *Into the Forest*. Candlewick, 2004.

BROWNE, ANTHONY. *The Tunnel*. Knopf, 1990.

BURNFORD, SHEILA. *The Incredible Journey*. Little, Brown, 1961.

BURNINGHAM, JOHN. *Come Away from the Water, Shirley*. Crowell, 1977.

BURNINGHAM, JOHN. *It's a Secret*. Candlewick, 2009.

BURTON, VIRGINIA LEE. *The Little House*. Houghton Mifflin, 1942.

CARROLL, LEWIS. *Alice's Adventures in Wonderland*. 1865. Reprint. Macmillan, 1963.

CHOLDENKO, GENNIFER. *Al Capone Does My Shirts*. Putnam, 2004.

COOPER, SUSAN. *The Dark Is Rising*. Atheneum, 1973.

CREW, GARY. *The Watertower*. Illustrated by Steven Woolman. Crocodile Books, 1999.

DANTICAT, EDWIDGE. *Eight Days: A Story of Haiti*. Illustrated by Alix Delinois. Orchard Books, 2010.

DAVIS, DAVID. *Texas Aesop's Fables*. Illustrated by Susan Ward. Pelican, 2008.

FRANK, ANNE. *Anne Frank: The Diary of a Young Girl*. Doubleday, 1967.

GAIMAN, NEIL. *The Graveyard Book*. HarperCollins, 2008.

GEORGE, JEAN. *The Talking Earth*. HarperCollins, 1993.

GERSTEIN, MORDECAI. *The Man Who Walked Between the Towers*. Roaring Book Press, 2003.

HENKES, KEVIN. *Olive's Ocean*. Greenwillow, 2003.

HOPKINSON, DEBORAH. *Fanny in the Kitchen*. Illustrated by Nancy Carpenter. Simon & Schuster, 2001.

INNOCENTI, ROBERTO. *Rose Blanche*. Creative Editions, 1985.

ISAACS, ANNE. *Dust Devil*. Illustrated by Paul O. Zelinsky. Schwartz & Wade, 2010.

ISAACS, ANNE. *Swamp Angel*. Illustrated by Paul O. Zelinsky. Dutton, 1994.

JOHNSON, CROCKETT. *Harold and the Purple Crayon*. HarperCollins, 1998.

KELLY, JACQUELINE. *The Evolution of Calpurnia Tate*. Henry Holt Company, 2009.

LASKY, KATHRYN. *Hawksmaid: The Untold Story of Robin Hood and Maid Marian*. HarperCollins, 2010.

LEE, SUZY. *Mirror*. Seven Footer Press, 2010.

LEHMAN, BARBARA. *Rainstorm*. Houghton Mifflin, 2007.

LESTER, JULIUS. *John Henry*. Illustrated by Jerry Pinkney. Dial, 1994.

LEWIS, C. S. *The Chronicles of Narnia*. Macmillan, 1951–1956.

LOWRY, LOIS. *Crow Call*. Illustrated by Bagram Ibatoulline. Scholastic, 2009.

MACLACHLAN, PATRICIA. *Sarah, Plain and Tall*. Harper & Row, 1985.

MARTIN, ANN M. *A Corner of the Universe*. Scholastic, 2002.

MARTIN, JACQUELINE BRIGGS. *Snowflake Bentley*. Illustrated by Mary Azarian. Houghton Mifflin, 1998.

McCULLY, EMILY ARNOLD. *The Ballot Box Battle*. Knopf, 1996.

McKISSACK, PATRICIA C., AND FREDRICK L. McKISSACK. *Christmas in the Big House, Christmas in the Quarters*. Illustrated by John Thompson. Scholastic, 1994.

MILNE, A. A. *Winnie-the-Pooh*. Dutton, 1926.

MORA, PAT. *Dona Flor: A Tall Tale about a Giant Woman with a Big Heart*. Illustrated by Raul Colon. Knopf, 2005.

MOSS, MARISSA. *Nurse, Soldier, Spy: The Story of Sarah Edmonds, a Civil War Hero*. Illustrated by John Hendrix. Abrams, 2011.

MURPHY, JIM. *The Great Fire*. Scholastic, 1995.

PAULSEN, GARY. *Hatchet*. Bradbury, 1987.

PHELAN, MATT. *The Storm in the Barn*. Candlewick, 2009.

PORTIS, ANTOINETTE. *Not a Box*. HarperCollins, 2006.

REISS, JOHANNA. *The Upstairs Room*. Harper & Row, 1987.

SAY, ALLEN. *Music for Alice*. Houghton Mifflin, 2004.

SCHMIDT, GARY D. *Lizzie Bright and the Buckminster Boy*. Clarion, 2004.

SENDAK, MAURICE. *Where the Wild Things Are*. Harper-Collins, 1988.

SÍS, PETER. *The Wall: Growing Up Behind the Iron Curtain*. Farrar, Straus & Giroux, 2007.

SPEARE, ELIZABETH. *The Witch of Blackbird Pond*. Houghton Mifflin, 1958.

UCHIDA, YOSHIKO. *Journey to Topaz*. Scribner's, 1971.

WABOOSE, JAN BOURDEAU. *Sky Sisters*. Illustrated by Brian Deines. Kids Can Press, 2002.

WHITE, E. B. *Charlotte's Web*. Harper, 1952.

WILES, DEBORAH. *Countdown*. Scholastic, 2010.

WILLIAMS, KAREN. *A Beach Tail*. Illustrated by Floyd Cooper. Boyds Mills, 2010.

YOLEN, JANE. *Johnny Appleseed: The Legend and the Truth*. Illustrated by Jim Burke. HarperCollins, 2008.

YORINKS, ARTHUR. *Hey, Al*. Illustrated by Richard Egielski. Perfection, 1989.

MyEducationKit™

Go to the topics "Traditional Literature" and "Modern Fantasy" on the MyEducationKit for this text, where you can:

- Search the Children's Literature Database, housing more than 22,000 titles searchable in every genre by authors or illustrators, by awards won, by year published, and by topic and description.

- Explore genre-related Assignments and Activities, assignable exercises showing concepts in action through database use, video, cases, and student and teacher artifacts.

- Listen to podcasts and read interviews from some of the brightest and most enduring stars of children's literature in the Conversations.

- Discover web links that will lead you to sites representing the authors you learn about in these pages, classrooms with powerful children's literature connections, and literature awards.

I, Vivaldi

Janice Schefelman / Illustrated by Tom Schefelman

Biographies for young children increasingly include episodes from the life of a famous person in his or her youth. *I, Vivaldi* adds another technique: the biography is told from the first person perspective. Vivaldi's speech is fictionalized from existing accounts of Vivaldi's life.

CHAPTER EIGHT

Point of View

Whose story is this, anyway? Try changing the point of view in a story. What happens?

When we hear the term **point of view**, we commonly think of opinion or attitude. But point of view has a special meaning for literature. As we read a story, we may see the events through the eyes—and mind—of one character. Or we may feel that we are objective observers watching the events unfold before our eyes. The writer wants to tell us this story, but whose point of view the writer uses to tell it determines how the story will develop.

When two people experience the same incident simultaneously, they can tell different versions of the story. Each responds out of past experience, the place from where he or she observed the incident, or from beliefs about appropriate behavior, as well as from the more obvious differences in the physical and emotional effects of the incident. Each version of the facts is a personal truth.

A similar situation exists in literature. As readers, we describe point of view depending on who sees and tells about the action. The same story can be different depending on which version of the story we see. In the case of Anthony Browne's contemporary picturebook *Voices in the Park,* the story depends on four perspectives of one visit to the park. The story is told visually and verbally through the distinct voices of four characters. The first voice is that of a wealthy, controlling

Point of view determines how we see the story.

woman who shows more affection toward her pedigreed dog, Victoria, than her son, Charles. The second voice is that of an unemployed and dejected man whose circumstance has left him emotionally distant from his daughter, Smudge. The third voice is that of Charles, a boy who is lonely until he meets Smudge in the park; his world visibly brightens as they play with the dogs and connect with one another. Smudge provides the fourth voice; full of life, her imagination and warmth affect the mood of the story. Each perspective is presented in a distinct font; the first-person perspectives are shared within a symbolic seasonal setting. Readers will respond individually to the multiple visual symbols embedded within the surreal illustrations. Though readers will generally have a sense that there are social inequities in this world, their individual interpretation will vary with background and experience at any age.[1]

In literature, interpreting a story is often a matter of point of view—whose thoughts we know, whose view of the action we follow. Increasingly, stories not only reveal multiple points of view, but also include the voices of people traditionally unheard in children's literature.

Types of Point of View

Point of view is determined when the writer chooses the narrator and decides how much the narrator knows about the action in the story and the thoughts of the characters. The first possibility a writer might consider is the **first-person point of view**, used when a story is told in first person "I." In such storytelling, the reader lives, acts, feels, and thinks the conflict as the protagonist experiences and tells it, just as Franny does as she navigates the days surrounding the 1962 Cuban Missile Crisis in *Countdown* by Deborah Wiles. Occasionally the first-person narrator is not the protagonist, but instead a minor character observing the action. Or it might be an unseen character, as it is with Markus Zusak's innovative story, *The Book Thief*, where the story is told from the point of view of Death.

A second possibility is the **omniscient point of view**. Here the writer, telling the story in third person (using "he," "she," and "they"), is all-knowing or omniscient about any and every detail of action, thought, and feeling—conscious or unconscious—in the past, present, or future. If the writer chooses, he may recount any and all details. When he wrote *Charlotte's Web*, E. B. White chose to tell the story from the omniscient point of view rather than, for example, only from Wilbur's limited perspective.

A third possibility is the **limited omniscient point of view**, in which the writer, again telling the story in third person, concentrates on the thoughts, feelings, and significant past experiences of only one character, usually the central character or protagonist. In Louis Sachar's *Holes*, for example, we understand the story purely through Stanley Yelnats's eyes. No one tells us why Zero acts the way he does; we have to infer from his behavior along with Stanley. We can't see into the mind of Mr. Sir, either, to understand what he thinks about his life at Green Lake Camp. Occasionally the writer may choose to be omniscient about several—though not all—characters; this choice, too, is sometimes called limited omniscient.

The fourth possibility is the **objective (dramatic) point of view**. It again uses the third person, as in Burnford's classic animal story, *The Incredible Journey*. The meaning of this term becomes clear when we refer to the fictional reality of drama or motion picture. A camera seems to record—it cannot comment or interpret. There is no one there to explain to the reader what is going on or what the characters think or feel. The camera selects and we see and draw our own conclusions. This is expertly portrayed in *Monster* by Walter Dean Myers, where readers are both a witness and juror in the trial of a young man accused in the murder of a convenience store owner.

First-Person Point of View

The first-person narrator is limited; like the reader, he or she cannot tell what another character thinks unless explicitly told. Although the narrator sees the action of another character, the narrator, again like the reader, can speculate only about what the other is thinking. A hasty tucking in of a shirt or a nervous shaking of the head gives evidence from which the narrator may draw conclusions, just as we draw conclusions. However, unless the second character says aloud what he or she thinks, the first-person narrator, again like us, can only guess.

The first-person narrator who tells the story may be the protagonist or a minor character observing the action. For example, in Angela Johnson's *Toning the Sweep*, we see everything through fourteen-year-old Emily's eyes: she is the story's first-person narrator. She can only guess what her mother thinks and feels; she can't see into her mind: "I didn't know that Mama believed in God until I heard her in the bathroom in the airport praying," she tells us as she travels into the California desert to see her grandmother Ola. Emily can only try to understand her grandmother, too: "I have always loved my grandmother," she says, "But I know she is a strange woman." Early in the book, Emily learns that Ola has cancer, and as she and her mother help Ola say goodbye to her beloved desert, she listens to these two women's stories about family, love, and mourning. She cannot feel exactly what is in their hearts; like the rest of us, she can only infer who they are by watching their actions, hearing their stories, and telling us about their love.

One of the strongest assets of first-person **narration** is its great potential for pulling the reader into what appears to be autobiographical truth. Because Johnson has drawn a lively and thoughtful character in Emily, the reader sympathizes with her. Because what she claims to know is believably limited, she is consistent. Because Emily tells her own realistic story, her experience of loss and love is a powerful reality, convincingly immediate to the reader. If the story had been filtered through an omniscient writer, the immediacy of the experience would be less intense. The story would then be more remote, and less intensely real.

> First-person point of view creates a sense of autobiographical truth.

The semiautobiographical novel *The Absolutely True Diary of a Part-Time Indian* is a prime example of the first-person narrative. Sherman Alexie tells the story from the perspective of Arnold Spirit, a Spokane Indian from Wellpinit, Washington, who is torn between loyalty to the tribe and life on the reservation and his realization that in order to see more of the world he will need to not only learn the rules of operating within the white culture, but also leave his family, friends, and connected community on the reservation. This story tells how he began to split his identity by enrolling in a well-to-do small-town high school twenty-two miles from the reservation for his freshman year. The graphic art by Ellen Forney shows how torn Arnold is; the panels inform the reader visually about Arnold's growth as a cartoonist and as a maturing adolescent. His continual socio-political commentary on the events of his freshman year—both at home and school—reveal his ambivalence toward the choice he has made. The clever graphic elements weave in and out of the verbal text, providing multiple clues about Arnold's identity.

Alexie is authentic both in the language he uses to tell his story and in the life situations he portrays. When providing the first-person narration, he stays true to the limitations and possibilities available to the main character. This story is told primarily through dialogue between Arnold and his friends, family, and members of both communities. Thoughts and actions attributed to Arnold are reasonable in this story, allowing readers to laugh and cry over his insider comments. The assumptions he makes are appropriate to Arnold's age and life experiences, living in poverty and splitting time between home and school. It is the language of a bright fourteen-year-old overcoming physical and emotional hardship, speaking his feelings and sharing his thoughts, without presuming to know more than what he can know.

> Speech and language are compatible with the age and personality of the narrator.

In first-person narration, matters of vocabulary and word use are restrictions; the person telling the story is limited to diction compatible with age, experience, and personality. In a time when the topic of childhood disorders are frequently discussed we increasingly meet characters whose lives are impacted by autism spectrum disorder (ASD) or attention deficit hyperactivity disorder (ADHD); or stories may be told through the perspective of characters with physical disabilities or special abilities. These perspectives broaden horizons for readers who experience these first person stories, like Sharon Draper's *Out of My Mind*. Eleven-year-old Melody is locked inside her own mind by severe cerebral palsy, her brilliant photographic memory unrecognized by those around her. We learn of her special awareness of language through her words: "I have no idea how I untangled the complicated process of words and thought. . . . By the time I was two, all my memories had words and all my words had meanings. But only in my head. I have never spoken one single word. I am almost eleven years old." Melody's eventual access to adaptive technology gives her the voice she needs to share her personal story of overcoming obstacles.

Katherine Erskine's *Mockingbird* is told from the perspective of Caitlyn, a bright fifth grader with Asperger's syndrome. Readers will experience Caitlyn's story through her perceptions of how her world is organized, and how she learns to socialize, communicate, and understand emotions with people around her. Erskine masterfully integrates symptoms of Caitlyn's form of Asperger's within her first person narrative; her voice is authentic and believable. For example Caitlyn's guidance counselor reinforces her skills with identifying human emotion by setting up a facial expressions chart: "I have looked at that chart about a million times to try to figure out which emotion goes with each face. I'm not very good at it. I have to use the chart because when I look at real faces I don't Get It."

Readers can get a rare glimpse of what it is like to live with ADHD in *Joey Pigza Swallowed the Key* by Jack Gantos. In a first-person account, Joey explains how it feels: "I must have looked pretty calm on the outside, like I was really normal . . . But inside my body I felt like a big bottle of warm Coke when you drop it in the grocery store and it begins to fizz out the top like a bomb about to blow."

Joey's narrative shows his inability to control his actions, and it suggests that he is aware of the ways he is different from others. In this story, he realizes how his behavior makes life difficult for his mother; he is sad for her, but he cannot control the fluctuations in his attention span. The doctor gives Joey a patch: "The goal is to give you a fighting chance to maintain a normal attention span." Joey's need for the patch influences the plot in each of the books in this series.

Varied Ways to Present First-Person Perspectives

Writers are increasingly presenting characters' perspectives in varied ways. For instance, in *Letters from Rifka* by Karen Hesse we come to know the first-person narrator through letters the main character, Rifka, writes. Set in 1919, this epistolary novel recounts the difficult immigration experience of a twelve-year-old Russian girl named Rifka, who is repeatedly detained as she reaches Ellis Island. Rifka records her impressions of her journey, the immigration process, and finally of the United States in imaginary letters to her Russian friend in the margins of a volume of Pushkin's poems. Her gift for languages convinces stubborn officials that she will not become a ward of the state; Hesse uses this character trait in the vocabulary and style attributed to Rifka. The first-person point of view creates a convincing personal account.

Similarly, the same story can be told from a first-person perspective through the travel logs written by two different characters, each presenting their own perspective. In Sharon Creech's *The Wanderer*, cousins Sophie and Cody tell alternating stories of a life-threatening sailing voyage across the Atlantic to Ireland. At first each thirteen-year-old is uncertain about the other, but over the voyage, they become strong and appreciative friends, and readers learn about Sophie's three-sided personality. The author's careful use of first-person point of view provides a sense of intimacy. The first chapters of the book focus on Sophie's views, but readers gradually learn more of Sophie through Cody's entries as well; both write in believable ways. The book shows the differences between the two girls visually as well as verbally: each character's pages are presented in a different font.

Letter or diary form uses first person comfortably.

In *Bronx Masquerade* Nikki Grimes uses an unusual variation on first-person point of view. The novel's structure is a series of first-person comments from a group of students, all describing in prose how they see themselves. Each prose comment is followed by a revealing poetic or rap selection about him- or herself. Mr. Ward, the teacher, holds Open Mic Fridays, when students read their personal descriptions. One dislikes her name, another her Jewish heritage in a predominantly African American class, another wishes she were darker like the others, and still another reveals a truly personal but hidden skill. Race, skill, and interest differences no longer matter. Each now sees something new in the others, a reason for lack of confidence, a self-conscious wish not to seem different, or something common to all. As one poem says, "Is your heart/like an onion, too? . . . Your turn/Peel away." "It don't matter what your skin color is, or what name you call yourself. Everybody is different inside. We're all trying to fit in. Ain't nothing new about that." As the weeks go by, the class discovers what each person is truly like; pictures of self, spoken aloud, help the class to become an accepting family.

Avi's use of first-person narrator in *Nothing but the Truth* presents an interesting situation, that of the "unreliable narrator." Although the jacket blurb suggests that the issue confronted is the importance of communication, a more important idea is that false communication can wreak havoc. Bent on squeezing an unearned grade from his teacher so he can run track, Phillip, the narrator, is totally rebellious. He blames his poor grades not on neglected homework, but on a popular teacher; to annoy her in class, he hums the national anthem under his breath. When she reprimands him, Phillip claims patriotic motives. Phillip's parents believe him, his story is publicized, his teacher humiliated, and his classmates angered. No one hears "nothing but the truth," and only Phillip knows what he has done—told *anything but* the truth to serve his own purposes.

First-Person Perspective and Younger Readers

At one time it was thought that small children found stories written in first person difficult to follow, but in recent years many books written for younger children use this narrative style. Making the voice of a young narrator easy to recognize is important for these stories; they are often set in familiar places and with characters younger children can connect with. For example, the first-person perspective of *Thunder Cake* by Patricia Polacco resonates with readers who remember being afraid of approaching thunderstorms, or who have had a special adult to mediate childhood fears. Polacco bases this story on her own childhood memories of overcoming a fear of thunderstorms on visits to her grandmother's farm. Polacco integrates traditional ways of determining when a storm will hit—counting the seconds from a bolt of lightning to the crack of thunder and multiplying by six minutes. The suspense built into the story's plot is derived from the continual countdowns, starting with the initial ten-second count, or one hour to prepare the thunder cake and place it in the oven. Babuska and Patricia ("I") scurry around the farm collecting necessary ingredients as time runs out; thankfully all of this purposeful activity provides the necessary distraction from the storm's approach; a thunder cake is successfully baked to soothe the main character.

Story illustrations matter in *Thunder Cake*. The story is told from the first-person perspective, but the illustrations provide a broader view than Patricia would be able to see. As she reaches for the flour in the dry shed, readers see her face—eyes wide with nervous energy. The expressionistic art reveals the emotions of all characters in the story, adding a feel of exaggeration when this extends to the farm animals. For instance, illustrations on the cover and opening pages foretell the coming storm before the story begins: the farm animals are gazing at the sky, anticipation on their faces. The goslings are scurrying to their mother for safety; though the animals do not talk, they are subtly personified in the illustrations.

The skillful writer recognizes and presents a child's views.

Jacqueline Woodson's *Pecan Pie Baby* tells the story of a young girl who, along with her mother and extended family, is preparing for the arrival of a new baby. Through Gia's point of view readers are primarily treated to her emotions, thoughts, actions, and speech. They see her mother's response to Gia's worries through Gia's words, as well. The focus of Gia's entire world seems to be centering on the excitement family and friends are feeling over that "ding-dang baby!" The repeated use of "I" shows Gia as the self-centered child she still is, until the last two-page spread when she refers to her mother, the baby, and herself as "we." The illustrations extend the story, showing the passing seasons as Gia and her family await the arrival of the "ding-dang" pecan pie baby.

INQUIRY POINT

These companion books present the boarding school experience of two Native American children who leave home for Residential School in Canada, written from their perspective.[2] How does the point of view influence how readers would receive the stories?

Campbell, Nicola I. *Shi-shi-etko*. Kim LaFave, Illus. Groundwood Books, 2005.

Campbell, Nicola I. *Shin-chi's Canoe*. Kim LaFave, Illus. Groundwood Books, 2008. ✵

Omniscient Point of View

A distinct change from the limitations of the first-person point of view occurs when the writer chooses the freedom of the omniscient point of view. The writer in this case may recount relevant information about any and every character—their thoughts, ideas, and feelings about themselves as well as others. The writer may flash back into past experiences, feelings, and thoughts, or forward into what will happen in the future. The omniscient writer may relate anything he or she believes is relevant to the story, moving around, in, and through the characters, knowing everything, explaining motives, and giving the reader helpful information. In adult fiction, details may be more subtly and less obviously related to the conflict and characters, but in children's stories, the writer concentrates on what is essential to the reader's understanding. In William Armstrong's *Sounder,* for example, how the boy feels when his father has been taken to jail becomes clear: "The loneliness that was always in the cabin . . . was heavier than ever now. It made the boy's tongue heavy. It pressed against his eyes, and they burned. It rolled against his ears. His head seemed to be squeezed inward, and it hurt."

E. B. White considered the omniscient point of view best for *Charlotte's Web.* The objective, third-person statement that Fern wore a very pretty dress to the fair has little significance until the young reader has the omniscient writer's interpretation: she thought she'd see boys there. When Wilbur learns of Charlotte's bloodthirsty appetite, he thinks that although Charlotte is pretty and clever, she is everything he doesn't like—scheming and fierce. The reader is as uncertain as Wilbur until White adds that fears and doubts go with new friendships. We know why Templeton likes the dirty junkyard: he thinks it's a good place to hide. If we had merely heard speeches and seen actions, we might have interpreted the details quite differently. White knows and tells what is in the minds of all his characters: Fern thinks the world is blissful; Lurvy feels weak at the sight of the dew-covered words in the miraculous web; Wilbur can't bear loneliness; Templeton is miserable when his rotten egg breaks. And when Wilbur tries to spin a web, Charlotte watches him delightedly, pleased that he is no quitter. White is truly the omniscient narrator. The reader knows everything because of the point of view.

Charlotte's Web effectively uses omniscience.

Louise Erdrich's *The Birchbark House* begins in the summer of 1847 on Madeline Island in Lake Superior; the story follows an Ojibwa family in a third-person narrative set in four seasons. The story focuses on young Omakayas and her loving family; Erdrich gives voice to each well-developed character with varied styles of speech and rich description of their thoughts and actions. Omakayas, a survivor of a deadly smallpox outbreak as a baby, is consistently developed as an active child: "Omakayas was skinny, wiry, and tough for seven winters." Erdrich's well-grounded historical fiction novel details everyday life from rice harvest to smallpox threat to making maple syrup. The combination of dialogue and description reveal both cultural traditions and universal characteristics such as reluctance to do chores, the love of a pet, and mixed emotions about siblings. The characters and setting come alive through the omniscient narrator.

Picturebooks necessarily create the omniscient point of view through both the limited text and the much more revealing illustrations. In a very straightforward way, John Burningham's *It's a Secret* employs the omniscient point of view. The tone of this imaginative tale of what cats *really* do when they go outside for the night reports the story in an understated way. "They went quietly past the dogs" shows the children,

Marie Elaine and Norman, being "shushed" by Malcolm, their cat, as they walk past the sleeping street dogs at dawn. Nowhere in the text does the reader know these details—they are revealed in the cartoon style illustration. The last sentence tells that they traveled quickly home, and the next page shows them clustered more tightly as they cross the street in the emerging light of morning.

Limited Omniscient Point of View

Inexperienced in drawing conclusions from action, children may find limited omniscience helpful.

Often a story is told from a limited omniscient point of view. Here the writer chooses to see action usually through the eyes of one character—occasionally several characters—and to report that character's thoughts. In children's literature, this character is usually the protagonist. The writer shows not only what the character sees and hears, but also what the character feels and believes. The writer is inside as well as alongside the character.

When Dicey of *Dicey's Song* by Cynthia Voigt is asked in her classroom if her portrait-essay of a person she knows is really her relative, Dicey stands accused of showing fiction as fact, and even of plagiarism. She lifts her chin and deliberately concentrates on something else—the sailboat Gram has let her refinish:

> She didn't answer. There was no way anybody could make her answer. In her mind, she made a picture: the little boat, she'd have painted it white by then, or maybe yellow—it was out on the Bay beyond Gram's dock and the wind pulled at the sails. Dicey could feel the smooth tiller under her hand; she could feel the way the wooden hull flowed through the water.

This is Dicey's story, her mind and feelings.

Yolanda of *Yolanda's Genius* by Carol Fenner is smart, tough, and a new arrival in Grand River; she defends and cares for her younger brother Andrew, and finally persuades the great B. B. King of Andrew's musical genius. Yolanda, whose thoughts are always on one of two things—Andrew or food—arranges for Andrew to fake being lost at Chicago's big blues concert weekend, and, when "found," to be seen onstage with celebrities. There Andrew plays his harmonica and his pipe, imitating the sounds of the city, from the wind off Lake Michigan and the shushing or roaring of the crowd, to the strength and queenliness of oversized Yolanda. Andrew's musical genius is recognized. Because the point of view is limited omniscient, we know the thoughts and feelings of both Andrew and Yolanda. Six-year-old Andrew closes his eyes through it all and finally decides to learn to read—so he can read music. For Yolanda, being both smart and independent are good, but finding a new best friend with whom to share things is wonderful.

When Van, the boyfriend of Jamie's mother in Carolyn Conan's *What Jamie Saw*, tries to throw baby Nin against the wall, Jamie catches her, and the family escapes to live in friend Earl's tiny trailer in the woods. Jamie's "nosey" teacher finds help for the three cold, hungry people, and slowly they begin their painful efforts for a normal life. The story is told in limited omniscient point of view: Jamie worries about Nin's safety, and while the baby sleeps in a drawer, he wonders if she'd fit if he pushed the drawer in when he was in a hurry. Perhaps he could punch holes in the drawer, as he had when he kept bugs in a jar. When Van shows up, Jamie lifts infant Nin from the drawer, then hides under the bed, crawling in first, then pulling her in after him. Characters are few in this short novel, but its effectiveness is largely due to knowing Jamie's fears as we live within his body.

Ellen Levine's *Henry's Freedom Box* is a powerful example of the limited omniscient point of view in the picturebook format. This historical fiction story is based on a segment in the life of Henry Brown, a slave in Virginia during the mid 1800s. The focus is on Henry's unusual route to freedom on the Underground Railroad, but the narrator is in control of reporting his story, which is supported with additional back matter. True to quality picturebooks for this genre, the illustrations reveal much of the emotional content of this story. Kadir Nelson's rich paintings reinforce the straightforward story; after Henry is curled into the box that will carry him to Philadelphia and to freedom, it is placed upside down on the wagon. Levine's text simply states that Henry's face is hot, his eyes hurt, and he thinks his head might burst. The words tell what happened, but the illustrations that dominate the two-page spread provide a close up of Henry's face, one hand placed protectively in front. Readers see the anguish Henry must endure to achieve his goal of freedom.

INQUIRY POINT

The omniscient view in a picturebook is difficult to accomplish in the limited space this format requires. Illustrations generally tell more than the words in contemporary picturebooks. Allen Say is a master with this point of view in the picturebook format. Choose from the titles below. Is the story third-person omniscient? Limited omniscient? Describe how the illustrations help to create a more complete point of view, such as the emotional aspects of the story:

Allison. Sandpiper, 2004.

Erika San. Houghton Mifflin, 2009.

The Kamishibai Man. Houghton Mifflin, 2005.

The Sign Painter. Houghton Mifflin, 2000.

Tea with Milk. Sandpiper, 2009. ●

Objective (Dramatic) Point of View

In the objective or dramatic point of view, the writer does not enter the minds of any of the characters. The action speaks for itself. The term *dramatic* comes from *drama*, where characters reveal themselves by what they say, what they do, and what others say about them. Inner thoughts or feelings must be revealed by visible action; in most plays there is no interpreter standing at stage left to tell the audience what thoughts run through the speakers' minds. The audience must usually figure out for itself the meaning of the actions and speeches, deciding from a character's voice inflections or actions what—beneath or in spite of the words—may lie in that character's mind.

The objective or nearly objective point of view in some stories makes heavier demands on the imagination and understanding of the reader. Adults guess that when a character looks at the floor, scuffs the dust with a toe, or twists a lock of hair, that person is shy or embarrassed, but the ability to interpret body language is a skill few children have. It is the writer's responsibility when using the objective or dramatic point of view to describe and report action that, since it is without interpretation, must be within the child's understanding.

> The objective point of view makes heavier demands on the reader's imagination and understanding.

Monster by Walter Dean Myers opens with a first-person prologue by the protagonist, Steve Harmon, who is incarcerated pending trial for his alleged role in a convenience store murder. Steve is trying to figure out how he can possibly fit in with what he sees of prison—just what is he? A monster? Myers removes all judgment using the dramatic point of view. This is beautifully accomplished by having the protagonist use a video camera to record each conversation with lawyers and the dialogue from his trial. What the reader sees are the film transcripts in the form of a screenplay of the trial, interspersed with diary entries of Steve's incarceration. This approach leaves the account of the trial and decisions about just who Steve is—an innocent bystander or a guilty teen—open to readers' interpretations, actively involving them in predicting a verdict . . . and delivering one about Steve. Steve is not an entirely trustworthy narrator; the story ends with a first-person epilogue, "5 months later." When Steve tells us about the way his father and his defense attorney responded to the trial, readers' uncertainty is only reinforced: "When Miss O'Brien looked at me, after we had won the case, what did she see that caused her to turn away? What did she see?"

The picturebook format provides an example; children and parents looking for an updated tooth fairy story will love the coming-of-age version, *April and Esme: Tooth Fairies*. Two young tooth fairies convince their parents they are ready for their first lost tooth mission. In straightforward narration and dialogue, with just the right amount of description, readers follow April and Esme's successful trip—the only moment of panic happens when the young boy who is the object of their quest awakens as they take his tooth. Fortunately, they have a cell phone to text their parents for advice. Bob Graham's illustrations follow the storyline and provide a lighthearted dramatization of the story; readers see the details and can make their own interpretation of this winged contemporary family working to preserve the tooth fairy tradition for future generations.

The picturebook format provides yet another opportunity for the objective (dramatic) point of view through wordless picturebooks. These works of art can provide the entire story for the reader. Though elements of emotional content might be provided in facial expressions, or through the style and tone of the illustration, readers are provided an opportunity to capitalize on the information, creating their own interpretation of the story. For example, Barbara Lehman's *Museum Trip* shows the adventure a young boy has in the museum when he separates from his classmate, creating the opportunity to discover a closed door and some magical exhibits beyond. He returns to his class just in time to go home, wearing a special badge; observant readers of pictures are sure to see this same medallion on the uniform of the museum guard as the children make their exit. The cartoon art is easy for children to follow, and a field trip to the museum is a setting familiar enough for many readers to engage with a story from the sequence of illustrations.

INQUIRY POINT

Choose one of the following wordless picture-books and write a simple story. Consider the illustrations; they can provide an omniscient point of view. What perspective did you choose for the story you wrote? Explain. How might the story change if a different point of view was used? If you are using a partner, try telling the story instead of writing.

Barbara Lehman

Rainstorm. Houghton Mifflin, 2007.
The Red Book. Houghton Mifflin, 2004.
Trainstop. Houghton Mifflin, 2008.

Suzy Lee

Mirror. Seven Footer Press, 2010.
Shadow. Chronicle Books, 2010.
The Wave. Chronicle Books, 2008.

David Wiesner

Flotsam. Houghton Mifflin, 2006.
Sector 7. Houghton Mifflin, 1999.
Tuesday. Houghton Mifflin, 1991.

Bill Thomson

Chalk. Marshall Cavendish, 2010.

Variations in Point of View

Authors can create variations in point of view, as they do with all facets of children's literature. For example, Alice Childress presents varied perspectives with great skill in her classic *A Hero Ain't Nothin' but a Sandwich.* Using first-person point of view, this story explores thirteen-year-old Benjie's difficulties with drug addiction through his thoughts as well as the perspectives of those associated with him. The combination of their narratives creates a complex story; we see events, characters, plot, and theme, as well as setting. To be convincing, each of the speakers needs to reveal self through distinctively personal speech and language; readers see each voice as believable and as belonging to a character that matters to the development of the protagonist.

E. L. Konigsburg in *The View from Saturday* uses a combination of omniscient and first-person points of view in her story about four students, their teacher, and an academic bowl. The omniscient author tells how Mrs. Olinski appointed the team representing the school; each seemed to be a loner. The four students—Ethan, Nadia, Julian, and Noah—each reveal family history and personal fears and insecurities in alternating chapters. Nadia: "Dividing my time was part of the divorce settlement. I was to spend Thanksgiving, spring vacation, and one month over the summer with Dad." Noah is visiting his grandparents and helps with wedding plans: "On the day of the wedding I was in great demand to take things over to the clubhouse in my wagon . . . Fact: I did a wonderful job." Julian invites the three others for a mystery meeting that soon evolves into "The Souls," a compatible group of students who develop a kinship and who act together for the benefit of both school and teacher.

The nonfiction picturebook *The Lamp, the Ice, and the Boat Called Fish: Based on a True Story* by Jacqueline Briggs Martin details a survival story of an Inupiaq family stranded on an Arctic fishing boat, the *Karluk,* during an early onset of winter in 1913. Despite abandonment and starvation, the intelligent and courageous eight-month survival of this family, the ship's captain and crew, and their sled dogs and cat is poetically detailed. Martin successfully varies the omniscient point of view with a sprinkle of authorial interjections throughout the story. In this way she provides information that would not otherwise be available in this nonfiction story. For instance, rather than supply the feelings of the family when it is clear the leader will not return, she integrates into a stanza: "I do not think Pagnasuk and Makpii worried about the boat. . . . And they trusted their father and mother to keep them safe." Beth Krommes's scratchboard illustrations are well chosen for the Arctic setting; the tan seal skin clothing, wooden ship's hull, crates and barrels, and the fur of the dogs and cats, outlined in black lines, stand out clearly against the surrounding white space. The vantage point keeps readers at a distance, reinforcing the omniscient view. Emotions on the faces of the characters are somewhat similar to authorial interjection: they are implied.

A skillful writer and illustrator can make this variation in point of view easily understood in the picturebook format. In fact, as with other literary techniques, the picturebook format can introduce readers of any age to how books "work." David Wiesner's *The Three Pigs* is an excellent example; in this case it is illustrator intervention when the lead pig turns his attention to the reader. He makes eye contact and addresses the reader, commenting that he thinks there is someone "out there." At last, he invites the reader to join the pigs and other characters in constructing their own story.

Brian Selznick's Caldecott-winning *The Invention of Hugo Cabret: A Novel in Words and Pictures* is a blend of literary formats: historical fiction novel, flipbook, graphic novel, even a movie. We previously discussed this book in Chapter 2, but it is worth mentioning again; the variation in format is accompanied by a variation in the point of view. Selznick's narrative text is told from the limited omniscient point of view; the protagonist Hugo is the primary focus of the story. Selznick reinforces this with his black-and-white pencil drawings where Hugo is either the subject or it is his view we see on the sequential full and two-page panels. This novel works like a picture-book in the way the illustrations are half the story; in addition they enhance and extend the point of view in this story.

A skillful writer may vary the point of view.

Why Consider Point of View?

Why bother with point of view? Authors and illustrators want their readers to accept what they write and create artistically; credibility of the story often depends on a successfully maintained point of view. If we didn't know what Wilbur was thinking in *Charlotte's Web,* we'd wonder why he runs madly about once he gains his freedom. Or how would a spider and a pig forge a friendship? And what motivates that rat, anyway? The three pets of *The Incredible Journey,* who wander across the Canadian wilderness, would be characters from fantasy if we knew what they thought. The resulting destruction of realism would mar the story. *Black Beauty* gains interest when the author attributes some human characteristics along with the objective third-person perspective. We'll share a few additional considerations valuable for teachers, librarians, and parents as they look closely at children's books.

Maturity of the Reader

It is not possible, or even relevant, to make authoritative statements about the best or most successful point of view for children's literature. Many of the points we share here have been shared in previous sections of this chapter, but deserve a quick review since point of view can develop not only with experience, but also with guided opportunities with books written from various perspectives.

The choice of point of view affects acceptance of a story.

The first-person point of view may present difficulties for the youngest readers just learning their own "I" identity; they may have trouble identifying with the abstract "I" of a story. Older children, however, may find first-person stories exciting proof of understanding, and of the capacity to project self into another "I."

First person is an increasingly popular choice in stories for children. As we shared earlier in the chapter, a first-person perspective has not always been a choice for children's books; but it is becoming increasingly popular with stories for younger readers, and is now a well-respected choice for older readers as they explore the issues of growing up. Contemporary nonfiction children's books that rely on the narrative structure are also gaining popularity. Using the first-person perspective with an autobiographical story or a memoir makes sense.

The objective point of view can be problematic for children who are are inexperienced in drawing conclusions from descriptions of actions; they may find the dramatic point of view hard to understand. The necessity for objectivity with this perspective presents a challenge to an author who writes for an audience of young children. If the story incorporates illustration that reveals the characters' feelings through facial expressions—as they may in picturebooks—the interpretive words about emotions and thoughts can be clarified; picturebooks can provide an important segue to reading books that rely solely on verbal text for the point of view.

A story written from the perspective of two narrators is appropriate for older readers. Jay Asher's *Thirteen Reasons Why* is a story told from two alternating perspectives. This young adult realistic contemporary fiction novel tells of a teen suicide through a series of thirteen tapes containing the reasons sixteen-year-old Hannah has taken her own life. The tapes are to be delivered to the responsible person, one after another—beginning with Clay Jensen. This part of the story is told in Hannah's voice from the first-person perspective, counterbalanced by Jay's thoughts through his first-person perspective. Keeping track of the narrators is eased by Asher's choice of two different fonts, but many younger readers may need guidance with the style of this book, as well as experience with others using a similar style. In addition to the double narrative, teachers and parents may find the topic of suicide better suited to more mature readers. Stories based on emotional issues using a first-person perspective might overwhelm some readers.

Younger readers or those with little experience with point of view might enjoy gaining experience with a book like Kevin O'Malley's *Once Upon a Cool Motorcycle Dude*. This book features a girl and a boy assigned to partner in creating a story. The story is begun by the girl with ponies and a princess; countered by the boy's warrior who battles giants and relegates the princess to spinning golden thread. The dual plot thickens as the story's plot and characters continue to change along typical gender expectations. The cartoon-style art incorporates the humorous perspective switches, visually showing the gender differences at the heart of this story. The style of this book provides a humorous tone as the two children create a story from an omniscient point of view. Appropriate to younger readers and writers, compromise rules on both sides of the story as the characters incorporate mixed gender traits—and the princess is relieved from her thread-making duties.

There is no "best" point of view in a story for children.

Animal Fantasy and Realism

We have discussed animal fantasy at several points in this edition, sharing ways stories featuring animals as significant characters present special problems. This holds true in point of view; look again at *Charlotte's Web*, a story in which the characters are animals. White's story is animal fantasy about pigs and spiders and rats that live in barns; we know that. If it were animal realism, the book would show these characters living and moving like the animals they are. It would have to be told from an objective omniscient point of view that does not imagine or report the thoughts of nonhumans acting human.

Creative Animal Perspectives and Points of View

This inquiry point includes a textset of picture-books employing both a realistic and fantasy perspective. How do the illustrations and other features assist with creating the perspectives? Can you find other picturebooks with creative ways to reveal points of view?

Barracca, Debra and Sal Barracca. *The Adventures of Taxi Dog*. Mark Buehner, Illus. Dial, 1990.

The story of a homeless dog that is adopted by a taxi driver who allows the dog to join him on his routes; readers learn about New York City from the dog's perspective. This is one of a series of "travelogues" featuring Maxi, the taxi dog.

Edwards, Wallace. *The Extinct Files: My Science Project*. Kids Can Press, 2006.

The story of a young boy's science project that is eaten by the dinosaurs he is studying in his urban environment. The story opens in the first person, but switches to omniscient for the nonfiction style of his journal. The "dinosaur" perspective is shown in the illustrations.

Reibstein, Mark. *Wabi Sabi*. Ed Young, Illus. Little Brown, 2008.

The concept of Japanese Wabi Sabi is developed beautifully through the perspective of a cat and everyone she meets on her quest to understand her very special name. Haiku is an important feature. ◉

A realistic animal story needs an objective or dramatic point of view.

Since White needed to suspend disbelief, he chose to portray his animals living as animals and yet similar to people. So successful is White that readers have a distinct feeling that the characters *are* people. In fact, since they all think and worry and love and hurt and laugh and needle one another as people do, White's animal story reveals human attitudes about friendship and continuity, death and maturity. His careful control of what is animal and what is human in each character, never confusing the two, is a source of his success with animal fantasy.

The objective or dramatic point of view is a logical choice for a realistic animal story, in our view. However, this technique does not engage younger readers in the same way fantasy might, or the way personified animals can. In contrast, the classic *Black Beauty* by Anna Sewell, overcomes this drawback. The book gives the impression of being a realistic story because the horses lead "horse lives." But *Black Beauty*'s first-person narrator is a horse that shares his emotions and thoughts using human language. Sewell mixes Black Beauty's animal and human natures, which has made this story very appealing to readers who enjoy animal fiction; a relatively objective point of view is important, whether the story is for children or adults.

Vantage Points

If fantasy is to be successful, a reader must willingly suspend disbelief. If the story's characters, conflict, and theme *seem* believable, it is plausible and even natural to know the thoughts and feelings of animal characters or tiny people. In fact, the story may be so good that we wish it *were* true. This persuasion that the writer wishes to bring about—persuasion that "what if" is really "it's true"—is most successful when the writer is consistent about point of view.

Point of view is an essential part of Mary Norton's *The Borrowers*, in which most of the action is seen through the eyes of young Arrietty. The Clock family is only six inches tall, and everything in the story, from postage stamps to primroses, is seen in relationship to the characters' size. To believe that Arrietty is so tiny, the reader must enter the dimensions and scale of her world. Pushing through the grass, she is startled by something glittering and discovers "It was an eye. Or it looked like an eye. Clear and bright like the color of the sky. An eye like her own but enormous." While "human beans" find a walk across the carpet easy, to tiny Arrietty it is like pushing through a dense field of grain. The grassy yard is huge from Arrietty's vantage point as she moves "in amongst the green blades. As she parted them gently with her bare hands, drops of water plopped on her skirt . . . pulling herself up now and again by rooty stems into this jungle. . . ."

Disbelief is suspended to convince readers that the Clock family lives. Not only do safety pins and postage stamps come in handy, but also everything from furniture to flowers is from the point of view of Arrietty, who sees everything from a six-inch height. The scale is relative to a tiny borrower, and point of view is omniscient and thoroughly consistent.

Other stories for children work with consistency in point of view and vantage point differently when the story's intent is more like a fable—and didactic. In *Two Bad Ants*, author and illustrator Chris Van Allsburg tells the story of two greedy worker ants who are following the lead of their scout and fellow worker ants on a mission to obtain mysterious crystals for the queen. They decide to stay behind to enjoy as much of the crystals as they can; a harrowing adventure ensues, and they narrowly escape a cup of coffee, the garbage disposal, and an electric socket. When their comrades return the next night, the two bad ants are grateful to return home. An omniscient point of view is consistently used for narrating the story, and the illustrations show the ants in scale; they can only carry one sugar crystal at a time, and a drop of dew from the grass along their way to the kitchen creates quite a splash. The illustrations provide an ant's perspective; but they, too, are omniscient, showing more than the characters can know. Van Allsburg provides vantage points that are above (bird's-eye), below, and parallel with the ants.

The picturebook format has a great deal of potential for variation with the vantage point it presents, not only in fantasy stories, but also for creative interpretations. Readers can expect illustrations to collaborate with the narrative text: confirming it, enhancing it, or even running counter to it. The story is just as likely to occur through the illustrations as it is in the text.

A story's credibility may depend on a consistent point of view, particularly with fantasy.

Illustration can assist with or even counter the point of view in the words.

Cultural Considerations

Writing stories with characters from cultures that differ from that of the author and illustrator requires special consideration. Well into the twentieth century, stories featuring children outside of the dominant culture were filled with misrepresentations; the characters might be flat, even stereotypical, with a condescending tone. Quality stories need to be as authentic as possible in their portrayal of characters from any cultural background.

Our nonfiction mentor text, *Christmas in the Big House, Christmas in the Quarters*, is a perfect example of the power of presenting a narrative to show different points of view. This Coretta Scott King Award–winning book illustrates the discrepancy in lifestyles between a wealthy southern plantation owner and a family living as slaves on the property. The comparison/contrast nonfiction structure is perfectly implemented as readers learn about the customs and preparations surrounding a Christmas season in 1859. The story of the two families is from the limited omniscient point of view, told from an objective third-person voice; dialogue reveals the emotional content of the families' conversations. The stunning realism of the illustrations provides a visual glimpse that makes the comparisons much more intense. Readers see the sharp contrasts between two cultures in this illustrated book, existing side-by-side. Readers will bring their own emotional response to this very clear portrayal of difference, inequity, and injustice from U.S. history.

Writers and illustrators can describe various cultures accurately, make the story credible, and at the same time present truths of human nature through careful use of point of view. The objective point of view in this story set in the Antebellum South, for example, might leave readers curious about the uninterpreted facts, creating a space for significant inquiry to find companion books that fill in the gaps. The limited

TEXTSET

Vantage Points Across Genres

These picturebooks provide creative vantage points for the reader. Look for the vantage point they provide. What are possible effects for the reader? How do the words and pictures work together?

Dematons, Charlotte. *The Yellow Balloon.* Lemniscaat, 2003.

This is the story of a global adventure by an escaped yellow balloon. From a bird's-eye perspective, readers must find the tiny balloon amidst diverse settings filled with everyday, supernatural, imaginative activities from various historical periods, geographic locations, and times of day. Following recurring characters (a blue car, fakir on a flying carpet, and a prisoner).

Gerstein, Mordecai. *A Book.* Roaring Book Press, 2009.

This story shows how characters come alive through a reader's eyes; they are central to creating a story. The illustrations are from the perspective of the reader in this light fantasy.

Jenkins, Steve. *Looking Down.* Houghton Mifflin, 1995.

Steve Jenkins uses his wonderful collage art to zoom in from an asteroid in space to a ladybug. The wordless nonfiction picturebook is from the bird's-eye perspective. Readers are taken closer and closer to the final scene, similar to zooming in on a Google Map.

Nevius, Carol. *Building with Dad.* Bill Thomson, Illus. Marshall Cavendish, 2006.

Photorealism shows the construction of a school, with full-color illustrations that flow down each page rather than follow a left-to-right progression. The process is viewed through a variety of vantage points in the contemporary realism story.

TEXTSET

Different Perspectives

A book collection should include representation from various cultural settings, providing different perspectives to assist readers in becoming global citizens. First-person narratives are increasingly accepted in stories for children; hearing authentic voices within a variety of cultural settings and genres is important for children. They can relate to the characters whose personal stories resonate with their own experiences. From what perspective are these stories told? How did the point of view influence the way you read the story? How might that perspective enrich the views of a less experienced reader? If the point of view changed, how would the story be affected?

Amado, Elisa. *Tricycle.* Alfonso Ruano, Illus. Groundwood, 2007.

Guatemala; contemporary realism; moral dilemma; social class

Bunting, Eve. *One Green Apple.* Ted Lewin, Illus. Clarion, 2006.

U.S./Muslim immigration; contemporary realism; inculturation

Danticat, Edwidge. *Eight Days: A Story of Haiti.* Alix Delinois, Illus. Scholastic, 2010.

Haiti; contemporary fiction; response to disaster

Henson, Heather. *That Book Woman.* David Small, Illus. Atheneum, 2008.

Appalachia; historical realism; Depression era; rural poverty

Innocenti, Roberto. *Rose Blanche.* Creative Editions, 1985.

Germany; WWII; first-person to omniscient perspective change; historical realism

Kahn, Rukhsana. *Big Red Lollipop.* Sophie Blackall, Illus. Viking, 2010.

Pakistani/U.S.; sibling rivalry; first-person perspective

Lainez, Rene Colato. *From North to South: Del Norte al Sur.* Joe Cepeda, Illus. Children's Book Press, 2010.

California/Tijuana, Mexico; contemporary realism; illegal immigration

Mortenson, Greg and Susan L. Roth. *Listen to the Wind: The Story of Dr. Greg & Three Cups of Tea.* Susan L. Roth, Illus. Dial, 2009.

Pakistan; contemporary nonfiction; collective first-person perspective: "we"

Say, Allen. *Music for Alice.* Houghton Mifflin, 2004.

Japanese-American; WWII; historical; flashback

Tunnel, Michael O. *Mailing May.* Ted Rand, Illus. Greenwillow, 1997.

Rocky Mountains; historical realism

Waboose, Jan Bourdeau. *Sky Sisters.* Brian Deines, Illus. Kids Can Press, 2000.

Ojibwa; Canadian; contemporary realism

---

omniscient point of view creates a more personal approach by revealing thoughts of the story's characters; readers can relate to them and find some universal connections. The first-person point of view has a great deal of power for younger readers learning to connect with characters in a story; they can show a character relating their personal view of their culture, a significant event, or a setting that differs in time, place, or perspective from the reader's. When first-person perspective is used,

Various cultures can and should be presented authentically through any point of view.

a young reader is no longer reading *about* another child; he or she is reading *with* another child.

Point of view can help readers discover many interesting correlations between literary depictions of various cultures; readers can see cultural difference as well as similarity across time and place through a variety of books.

SUMMARY

Point of view, an integral part of storytelling, determines the view the reader gets of events, character motivation, suspense and climax, and theme. There are four major kinds of point of view: first person with an "I" narrator; omniscient with an all-knowing writer; limited omniscient with focus on one or a few characters; and objective or dramatic with a report only of what can be seen and heard. Each one, when suited to story and reader, accomplishes a significant task.

Since the limited experience of children makes it hard for them to draw their own inferences from objective description of action and speech, the writer often clarifies the story by use of some degree of omniscience. The pleasure of literature comes from style, character, or plot—all the literary elements. In literature for children, understanding of character and the other elements is aided by a sensitive choice of point of view adapted to subject matter, type of conflict, and expected maturity level of readers.

NOTES

1. Louise Rosenblatt, *The Reader, The Text, The Poem: The Transactional Theory of the Literary Work* (Carbondale, IL: Southern Illinois University Press, 1978/1994).
2. Doris Seale and Beverly Slapin, eds, *A Broken Flute* (New York: AltaMira Press; Berkeley, CA: Oyate, 2006). This resource critically evaluates books related to Native Americans; it is an excellent resource for librarians, teachers, parents, and anyone interested in solid criteria for selecting books. This resource does not go beyond books published in 2003, but commentary can be applied to newer books. The Oyate website (www.oyate.org) continually lists highly recommended books about Native Americans and provides quick lists of criteria.

RECOMMENDED BOOKS

ALEXIE, SHERMAN. *The Absolutely True Diary of a Part-Time Indian*. Illustrated by Ellen Forney. Little, Brown, 2007.

ARMSTRONG, WILLIAM. *Sounder*. Harper & Row, 1969.

ASHER, JAY. *Thirteen Reasons Why*. Penguin, 2007.

AVI. *Nothing but the Truth*. Orchard, 1991.

BROWNE, ANTHONY. *Voices in the Park*. DK Children, 1998.

BURNFORD, SHEILA. *The Incredible Journey*. Perfection, 1995.

BURNINGHAM, JOHN. *It's a Secret*. Candlewick, 2009.

CHILDRESS, ALICE. *A Hero Ain't Nothin' but a Sandwich*. Coward, 1973.

CONAN, CAROLYN. *What Jamie Saw*. Front Street Press, 1995.

CREECH, SHARON. *The Wanderer*. HarperCollins, 2000.

DRAPER, SHARON. *Out of My Mind*. Atheneum, 2010.

ERDRICH, LOUISE. *The Birchbark House*. Hyperion, 1999.

ERSKINE, KATHERINE. *Mockingbird*. Kindle Edition Puffin, 2010.

FENNER, CAROL. *Yolanda's Genius*. McElderry, 1995.

GANTOS, JACK. *Joey Pigza Swallowed the Key*. Harper Trophy, 1998.

GRAHAM, BOB. *April and Esme: Tooth Fairies*. Candlewick, 2010.

GRIMES, NIKKI. *Bronx Masquerade*. Dial, 2002.

HESSE, KAREN. *Letters from Rifka*. Henry Holt, 1992.

JOHNSON, ANGELA. *Toning the Sweep*. Orchard, 1993.

KONIGSBURG, E. L. *The View from Saturday*. Atheneum, 1996.

LEHMAN, BARBARA. *Museum Trip*. Houghton Mifflin, 2006.

LEVINE, ELLEN. *Henry's Freedom Box*. Illustrated by Kadir Nelson. Scholastic, 2007.

LOWRY, LOIS. *Anastasia at This Address*. Houghton Mifflin, 1991.

MARTIN, JACQUELIN BRIGGS. *The Lamp, the Ice, and the Boat Called Fish: Based on a True Story*. Illustrated by Beth Krommes. Houghton Mifflin, 2001.

McKISSACK, PATRICIA AND FREDRICK McKISSACK. *Christmas in the Big House, Christmas in the Quarters*. Illustrated by John Thompson. New York: Frontline Books, 1994.

MYERS, WALTER DEAN. *Monster*. HarperCollins, 1999.

NORTON, MARY. *The Borrowers*. Harcourt, 1965.

O'MALLEY, KEVIN. *Once Upon a Cool Motorcycle Dude*. Illustrated by Scott Goto and Carol Heyer. Walker, 2005.

POLACCO, PATRICIA. *Thunder Cake*. Putnam, 1990.

SACHAR, LOUIS. *Holes*. Farrar, Straus and Giroux, 2008.

SELZNICK, BRIAN. *The Invention of Hugo Cabret: A Novel in Words and Pictures*. Scholastic Press, 2007.

SEWELL, ANNA. *Black Beauty*. Sterling, 2004.

VAN ALLSBURG, CHRIS. *Two Bad Ants*. Houghton Mifflin, 1988.

VOIGT, CYNTHIA. *Dicey's Song*. Random House, 1982.

WHITE, E. B. *Charlotte's Web*. Harper, 1952.

WIESNER, DAVID. *The Three Pigs*. Clarion, 2001.

WILES, DEBORAH. *Countdown*. Scholastic, 2010.

WOODSON, JACQUELINE. *Pecan Pie Baby*. Sophie Blackall, Illus. Putnam, 2010.

ZUSAK, MARKUS. *The Book Thief*. Knopf, 2006.

MyEducationKit™

Go to the topic "Contemporary Realistic Fiction" on the MyEducationKit for this text, where you can:

- Search the Children's Literature Database, housing more than 22,000 titles searchable in every genre by authors or illustrators, by awards won, by year published, and by topic and description.

- Explore genre-related Assignments and Activities, assignable exercises showing concepts in action through database use, video, cases, and student and teacher artifacts.

- Listen to podcasts and read interviews from some of the brightest and most enduring stars of children's literature in the Conversations.

- Discover web links that will lead you to sites representing the authors you learn about in these pages, classrooms with powerful children's literature connections, and literature awards.

Roller Coaster

Marla Frazee

CHAPTER NINE

Style and Tone

Is it possible to
identify the sources
of distinctive style?
In what ways does
style influence
tone?

Consider now two literary elements that make stories memorable—style and tone. Frequently someone asks, "But does the writer know what he or she is doing with words?" Yes. The author has added, subtracted, experimented, and substituted, creating the style and tone that best tell the story. The skilled writer chooses words that become the setting, plot, character, and theme, together making a piece of literature.

 ## Style

Style refers to *how* an author says something as opposed to *what* he or she says. From an infinite number of words available, the writer chooses the best words and their best arrangement to create a particular story. For example, Rita Williams-Garcia's *One Crazy Summer* begins:

> Good thing the plane had seat belts and we'd been strapped in tight before takeoff. Without them, that last jolt would have been enough to throw Vonetta into orbit and Fern across the aisle. Still, I anchored myself and my sisters as best I could to brace us for whatever came next. Those clouds weren't through with us yet and dealt another Cassius Clay-left-and-a-right-jab to the body of our Boeing 727.

This is eleven-year-old Delphine, telling us about her first experience in an airplane. But Williams-Garcia

Style refers to how an author says something as opposed to what he or she says.

has chosen the words for Delphine to say, of course, and the rhythmic, vernacular, direct style in which Delphine says it tells us a lot about the girl we will get to know.

By contrast, Polly Horvath's nostalgic and formal style in *My One Hundred Adventures* is suited to the setting, conflict, and character of this book. The protagonist remembers her twelve-year-old self, living with her mother and siblings in a house by the sea:

> All summers take me back to the sea. There in the long eelgrass, like birds' eggs waiting to be hatched, my brothers and sister and I sit, grasses higher than our heads, arms and legs like thicker versions of the grass waving in the wind, looking up at the blue washed sky.

Horvath's longest sentence is forty-four words, whereas Williams-Garcia's longest sentence uses only twenty-three words. Horvath's introductory phrase "there in the long eelgrass" adds a lyricism to her sentence, whereas Williams-Garcia's shorter, more simple sentences provide a jerkier rhythm. Horvath's longest sentence, with clause building on clause, provides a slow musicality that expresses a sense of nostalgia and perhaps longing; Williams-Garcia has chosen to use short sentences because they provide a sense of the urgency that her character Delphine, who has many responsibilities, feels. Horvath's two sentences include three similes or metaphors, mostly comparisons to aspects of nature; Williams-Garcia's four include only one comparison—to Cassius Clay, a boxer from the 1960s. And compare the verbs these two writers use: Williams-Garcia's are active, vivid, unusual—*strapped*, *brace*, *anchored*; Horvath's are quieter, more common—*take*, *waiting*, *hatched*, *sit*. The styles of *One Crazy Summer* and *My One Hundred Adventures* could not be interchanged. In each case the style is right for that particular story.

Similarly, the style of *The Mostly True Adventures of Homer P. Figg* is suited to the Civil War period in which it is set. Rodman Philbrick has his main character, Homer, use words and phrases that are no longer as common as they were during the war between the states. The word *scalawag*, for example, is an old-fashioned word, originally meaning *rascal*; if it is used today, it has that meaning. During the Civil War, however, the word referred to Southern whites who supported reconstruction. See if you can find other words or phrases in the following quotation that seem similarly old-fashioned:

> My name is Homer P. Figg and these are my true adventures. I mean to write them down, every one, including all the heroes and cowards, and the saints and scalawags, and them stained with the blood of innocents, and them touched by glory, and them that was lifted into Heaven, and them that went to the Other Place!

In fiction, style at its best increases not only our pleasure in words and sounds, but also our belief in the characters' reality. We come to know characters through the words they say and the words that describe how they look and how they act. Eager to believe in the characters' experiences, we follow the plot and visualize the action described in the chosen words. Through these words, we see, hear, and even smell the setting, realizing its effect on characters and conflict. Style is the product of all the choices the writer makes.

These choices are, of course, an entirely personal matter, since style and writer are inextricable. Kathi Appelt's style is no more David Almond's style than Appelt is Almond. Each writer expresses his or her vision of reality or fantasy in his or her own way. A writer does, of course, vary style. Since one story differs from another,

A writer's style is a personal choice dependent on setting, plot, and characters.

styles will differ as the writer suits style to story. Notice how Williams-Garcia's style in *One Crazy Summer* differs from her style in her National Book Award–winning novel, *Jumped!* In *Jumped!* the reader can tell right away the narrator is not Delphine. Williams-Garcia chooses to write in present tense this time:

> Zero period. You got that right. Fail one math test and you're up before the first chirp of day. Up before street lamps turn off and sun rays shoot through the blinds. Fail one math test and you're stepping over a snow-covered homeless lump to get to the stop, shiver, and wait for the city bus to pull up to your boots.

Style is not something applied to a finished piece of writing; rather, it *is* the writing, conveying both the idea and the writer's view of the idea. The writer Henry James said that each word and every punctuation mark directly contribute to meaning; the content of a story and how it is told are inseparable.[1] Tone, word choice, grammatical structure, devices of comparison, sound, and rhythm—all are style. All these elements vary with the author's purpose, as the idea, the incidents, and the characters vary. Style gives the whole work its distinction and makes the story memorable.

> Style is not *applied* to writing. It *is* the writing.

Even in picturebooks, in which the reader often interacts with the art at least as much as with the words, readers can immediately tell the difference between the styles of two good writers. In the 1986 Caldecott Medal–winning *Hey Al!* by Arthur Yorinks and Richard Egielski, Yorinks uses repetition and parallel structure in his first three sentences, which makes the slightly Yiddish syntax of his last sentence, a question, stand out: "What could be bad?"

In *Gorky Rises,* William Steig uses language and a cadence that only he would choose. His character, Gorky, saunters through white clover on a beautiful, light-filled morning. Steig uses the word "gracious" to describe the light. The word has religious connotations; coming at the end of Steig's sequence of rhythmic clauses, the word is surprising and exactly the right one to express Steig's vision.

Originality and style are not the same, but they are related in the sense that a good writer is original. If the writer's way of telling the story and its truth is distinctively the writer's own, then that expression has a personal mark, and the style should become the best possible one for a particular work. Reading a work aloud is a pleasurable way to discover style as senses awaken, rhythms appear, and comparisons become vivid.

The most easily identified element of style is the writer's use of certain specific devices of language. Many stylistic devices are listed in dictionaries of literary terms; our concern here is to provide examples of the ways these elements are

INQUIRY POINT

Compare the styles of two children's writers whose work you like. Take one paragraph of each writer's work and count the number of words in all the sentences of each writer's paragraph. Who tends to write longer sentences? Who uses more clauses in their sentences? Speculate about the reasons each author chose to write in longer or shorter sentences, and what difference those choices make to the reader's sense of the story.

Next, single out all the metaphors and similes. Who uses more of them? Read each paragraph aloud. Whose sentences are more lyrical, whose more rhythmic? Then look at the syntax of the writers' sentences, that is, the way the words are arranged. Does one writer use parallel structure or repetitive sentence structures more often than the other? Finally, are there particular words that one writer uses that you can surely say the other writer would never use? Write up your findings and report them to a classmate.

used in literature for children. Many of the examples we list will be, as they were previously, from *Charlotte's Web*.

Connotation

Connotation is the associative or emotional meaning of a word. Connotation adds significance and impact to a term's **denotation**, or dictionary meaning. Charlotte, for example, is not as big as a thimble, or as small as a fingernail, or as round as a button—all comparisons that might convey her proper size and shape but that have no emotional impact. Charlotte is, instead, "about the size of a gumdrop." Now there's a reassuring comparison for a bloodthirsty spider. The stomach of gluttonous Templeton is not bulbous, or enlarged, or even like a ball. Instead, "as big around as a jelly jar" expresses comparative size and shape, but adds pleasant connotations. No spider egg sac ever had the appeal of Charlotte's; it is neither orange nor pink but peach-colored, and looks like cotton candy. Cotton candy, jelly jar, and gumdrop are all favorites with children; each of these comparisons describes size, color, and shape, but adds pleasant and positive emotional meaning.

Words often have emotional meaning.

Imagery

By far the most frequently used device, and the most essential, is imagery. **Imagery** is the appeal to any of the senses; it helps create setting, establish a mood, or show a character. We use imagery in our everyday conversations to describe sounds, smells, and sights. We say the sky is sapphire blue, the carpet is celery green, and a jacket is fire-engine red; we describe the nature of a sound as clanging, buzzing, humming, or thundering. We say that tastes are bitter, sweet, or salty, that smells are acrid or musty, and that texture is scaly or slimy.

Imagery is the appeal to any of the senses.

The writer relies on imagery to give the reader impressions of what the writer wishes to depict. But verisimilitude, or description to duplicate reality, is not the writer's only goal. The writer, by the choice of details and of the words used to describe them, stirs the reader's imagination; the impact may be recognition or delight.

Charlotte's Web demonstrates the use and effectiveness of imagery. In the opening pages of the third chapter, Wilbur has just come to live in the manure pile of the Zuckerman barn, and we explore the building with him. No barn was ever more real, more suggestive of security and activity. The imagery convinces us as we smell the variety of odors, feel the warmth and coolness, and see the clutter of equipment. We may not settle down snugly in the manure pile, but we are as much at home in the barn as Wilbur is.

White describes the silence of the barn, but by sound imagery of a negative kind. The quiet itself is described by White's noting the absence of the customary noises; animals are so quiet that we hear only the weather vane:

> The sheep lay motionless. Even the goose was quiet. Overhead, on the main floor, nothing stirred: the cows were resting, the horses dozed. Templeton had quit work. . . . The only sound was a slight scraping noise from the rooftop, where the weather-vane swung back and forth.

When Wilbur first arrives at the fairgrounds, that setting is created for the reader by imagery. As White lists the senses one by one, a specific image appeals to each:

> They could hear music and see the Ferris wheel turning in the sky. They could smell the dust of the race track where the sprinkling cart had moistened it; and they could smell hamburgers frying and see balloons aloft. They could hear sheep blatting in their pens. An enormous voice over the loudspeaker . . .

White relies on imagery to make the reader aware not only of setting, but also of character and action. When Wilbur gets his buttermilk bath, we see him; he stands with closed eyes, feeling the buttermilk trickling over his sides. When he greedily opens his mouth and tastes the delicious buttermilk, Wilbur's childlike character is revealed. He stands in the pig trough and drools with hunger, while White itemizes the slops, each particle a distinctly visual image with a taste of its own:

> It was a delicious meal—skim milk, wheat middlings, leftover pancakes, half a dough-nut, the rind of a summer squash, two pieces of stale toast, a third of a gingersnap, a fish tail, one orange peel . . . the scum off a cup of cocoa, an ancient jelly roll, a strip of paper from the lining of the garbage pail, and a spoonful of raspberry jello.

As we visualize slops, each item has color and shape in our minds. At the same time, White appeals to taste by listing foods a child knows and likes. And finally, the variety has the distinct quality of slops, since it is punctuated by a fish tail and a bit of garbage pail liner. Imagery not only helps create setting, but action and character as well.

Figurative Language

Another device of style is **figurative language**, in which the writer uses words in a nonliteral way, giving them an extra dimension of meaning beyond their usual, everyday definitions. Personification, simile, and metaphor are the most common kinds of figurative language in stories for children.

Children's stories often make use of **personification**, the giving of human traits to nonhumans or inanimate objects. In *Charlotte's Web* a large cast of nonhuman characters is personified, from Wilbur to the maple trees and even crickets:

> The crickets sang in the grasses. They sang the song of summer's ending. . . .
> The sheep . . . felt so uneasy they broke a hole in the pasture fence. . . . The gander discovered the hole and led his family through. . . . A little maple tree . . . heard the cricket song and turned bright red with anxiety.

We hear the crickets singing, rather than chirping. The sheep are "uneasy," the goose "family" eats apples, and nearby the "anxious" maple turns autumn colors. Human qualities are given to everything.

One of the simplest figurative devices is the **simile**, a stated comparison between unlike things using *as, like,* or occasionally *than.* Straw fluttered down "like confetti" at the exciting news from the fair loudspeaker. When Charlotte is weary, she is swollen and listless and feels "like the end of a long day." These very specific comparisons are easy to see, since they are directly stated. Their combination of imagery and comparison makes them distinctive enough to stir the reader's imagination.

An implied comparison, such as the sapphire sky or the celery green carpet, is called a **metaphor**. They are sometimes so neatly put, so recognizably clear that we scarcely notice them—like the familiar "beads" of water decorating Charlotte's web. Templeton hears the fair is a figurative "paradise," where he'll find a "veritable treasure" of leftovers, enough for "a whole army of rats." Paradise is great happiness, treasure great wealth, and army a vast number; all are metaphors.

Hyperbole

We are so accustomed to exaggeration as humor that we scarcely recognize it as a figure of speech; we often stretch a comparison to create **hyperbole**. When, for example, Mrs. Zuckerman is scared to death, or Wilbur threatens to die of a broken heart, the author uses hyperbole that has become part of our daily conversation. But when Templeton grouses that he did not come to the fair to be a newsboy and refuses to "spend all my time chasing down to the dump after advertising material. . . . Next thing you'll want . . . is a dictionary," his grumbling and sarcasm are hyperbole. Wilbur uses self-pitying hyperbole when he says, "I'm less than two months old and I'm tired of living." But we may laugh at the words of the sheep whose hyperbole is sheer imaginative extremism. He speaks to Templeton: "If Wilbur is killed and his trough stands empty day after day, you'll grow so thin we can look right through your stomach and see objects on the other side."

Note the combination of similes and metaphors, personification, hyperbole, and imagery or appeals to the senses in a short paragraph from Gary Schmidt's *Lizzie Bright and the Buckminster Boy*. Turner has just heard that a developer wants to destroy the island homes in the African American settlement to build a resort.

> The afternoon had become as hot as meanness, and since the shirt he was wearing had enough starch in it to mummify two, maybe three, pharaohs, he began to feel he could hardly breathe. The only thing that saved him from absolute suffocation was the sea breeze somersaulting and fooling, first ahead, then behind, running and panting like a dog ready to play. And he followed it, pulling at his collar, trying not to wish what a minister's son should not wish.

Hyperbole adds interest to the way of speaking captured by Susan Patron in *The Higher Power of Lucky*. Lucky's guardian, the French Brigitte, has just found a snake in the dryer. Lucky thinks Brigitte says the word *snake* "like most people would say 'rotting dead pus-filled rat.'" Later, when Lucky calmly asks her what kind of snake it is, Brigitte replies, "I am sure she is a viper—a rattlesnake! Imagine to live in a place where just by doing the laundry you can be killed!"

Understatement

The reverse of exaggeration is **understatement**, or playing down. Like hyperbole, it may be used for comic effect. When Fern bites into a raspberry with a concealed "bad-tasting bug" and gets "discouraged," discouragement seems minimal. When Avery removes from his pocket the frog that has traveled back and forth on the barn swing all morning, scrunched and dried in a tight pants pocket, we read that the frog seems tired from a morning of swinging. Merely tired?

Understatement can be a way of avoiding sentimentality when writing of hard times. There are many instances in which the young narrator of Karen Hesse's award-winning *Out of the Dust*, describes difficult times—such as her mother's death in childbirth—using simple, factual, restrained language. The matter-of-fact telling of painful experiences makes the reader's experience more powerful than it would be had the writer chosen to use florid or emotional language.

Similarly, Cynthia Kadohata uses understatement in *Kira-Kira* to describe Katie's sadness and her parents' exhaustion as the family watches Lynn's death approach.

Exaggeration or hyperbole often adds humor.

Sometimes understatement can be more effective than hyperbole.

I cried and cried. For a while as I cried I hated my parents, as if it were their fault that Lynn was sick. Then I cried because I loved my parents so much.

Then I didn't feel like crying anymore. I just felt barren, my eyes felt dry. The sky was still gray. Everything was gray, the sky and the store and even my hand when I held it in front of myself.

And yet I knew Lynn was dead. I could feel the place inside me where she had. This place was empty.

Katie describes with simple vividness the love sweet Auntie and volatile Uncle Katsuhisa share.

Uncle's face got wistful as he stared into the sky. Auntie kissed his face. He put his arm around her, and they leaned against each other.

Allusion

One figure of speech, **allusion**, is a reference to a past event or piece of literature. For someone who knows Paul Lawrence Dunbar's poem about the experience of being black in a white society, "We Wear the Mask," the fact that the McKissacks call one chapter of *Christmas in the Big House, Christmas in the Quarters* "We Wear the Mask on New Year's Eve," is very moving. One of the pleasures—for adults, at least—of reading Lemony Snicket's books is in identifying the many allusions the series contains—from the more obvious Mr. Poe (an allusion to the writer Edgar Allan Poe) and Sunny and Klaus (an allusion to Sunny and Claus Von Bulow, of the famous murder case) to the more obscure allusion to the work of J. D. Salinger, when, later on in the series, Jerome and Esme Squalor are introduced. Not all allusions are to literary titles—the main character in Angela Johnson's novel *Heaven* is named Marley, after the singer Bob Marley; the title of Ellen Wittinger's *Hard Love* alludes to a song by folk singer Bob Franke.

Symbol

As stated in Chapter 7, a symbol is a person, object, situation, or action that operates on two levels of meaning: the literal and the figurative or suggestive. Certain symbols are universal: the dove is the symbol for peace; a flag symbolizes a certain country. Other symbols are particular to a story. In Jacqueline Woodson's Newbery Honor–winning *Feathers*, the protagonist Frannie has scars from chicken pox—two little scars on the palms of her hands. The scars are only mentioned one or two times throughout the book but toward the end, after learning a few things about the "Jesus boy," the white boy with black parents who has come to their school, Frannie remembers that her religious friend Samantha was "one of the few people outside of my family who knew about the pock scars on my hand. When I'd showed them to her, all those years ago, she was the one who'd said, 'Those could be nail holes.'" The scars are like stigmata, Samantha suggests, the nail holes created in the real Jesus' hands when he was killed on the cross. This image of the chicken pox scars, when surrounded by all the other religious ideas in the book (the boy named Jesus, the importance of hope, Samantha's thoughts about God), accrues a deeper meaning. The scars become a symbol of the idea that Frannie puts into words at the end of the book: "Maybe there's a little bit of Jesus inside of all of us."

To be a symbol, a term needs meaning beyond its literal meaning.

TEXTSET

Intertextuality and Allusion

Students can make many intertextual connections when they read Jacqueline Kelly's award-winning novel *The Evolution of Calpurnia Tate*, which is rich in allusions. Understanding what these allusions refer to will add to a student's depth of understanding of the book.

Charles Darwin

The title of the book alludes to Charles Darwin's classic *The Origin of the Species,* which was published in 1859 and in libraries during the time of Calpurnia Tate. Calpurnia finds the book in her grandfather's library and begins to read it. Each chapter of *The Evolution* begins with an epigraph from *The Origin of the Species*, which often comments on or foretells action that will occur in the chapter. Students who read *The Evolution of Calpurnia Tate* may not want to read Darwin's original text, but providing them with more recent books about Darwin and his work will add depth to their understanding of Kelly's novel.

Heiligman, Deborah. *Charles and Emma: The Darwins' Leap of Faith.* Henry Holt and Co., 2009.
Ages 12 and up.

Lasky, Kathryn. *One Beetle Too Many: The Extraordinary Adventures of Charles Darwin.* Candlewick, 2009.
Ages 4–6.

McGinty, Alice. *Darwin: With Glimpses into His Journals and Letters.* Houghton Mifflin, 2009.
Ages 8 and up.

Plato

When Callie tells her grandfather of her surprise at her first glimpse of microscopic creatures, he tells her of Plato's phrase: "all science begins with astonishment." (p. 105). Students might want to learn more about Plato in order to understand more about Callie and her grandfather.

Whiting, Jim. *Plato (Biography from Ancient Civilizations).* New York: Mitchell Lane Publishers, 2006.
Ages 9–12.

Rumplestiltskin

When Calpurnia is trying to learn to knit, she fancies that "a malevolent Rumplestiltskin crept into my room at night and undid my best work, turning the gold of my efforts into pathetic dross on a wheel perversely spinning backward."

Zelinsky, Paul O. *Rumplestiltskin.* Puffin, 1996.

Marie Curie

When Calpurnia tells her grandfather she doesn't know of any women who are scientists, he rattles off a few names, any of which a student could research. Marie Curie is the most familiar of these.

McClafferty, Carla. *Something Out of Nothing: Marie Curie and Radium.* Farrar, Straus and Giroux, 2006.

In a picturebook, a symbol can help readers understand a thematic point. *Fly Away Home* by Eve Bunting tells of a homeless father and his small son who live at the airport, moving constantly so as not to call attention to themselves. When a bird flies in, the boy watches it dash itself repeatedly against windows, trying to be free. Wounded, then rested, it finally manages to "fly away home," symbolic of the boy's hopes that he and his father will also be able to fly away to a home.

Many times readers assume that picturebooks are designed for an audience too young to appreciate symbolic thinking, so they overlook symbols used there. Yet picturebook artists do use this kind of representation of ideas: Chris Van Allsburg opens each picturebook with an embossed symbol on the casing. In his classic *The Polar Express,* the symbol is a small bell. This small bell is literally, physically, the first gift of this particular Christmas experience, but it can be seen to mean more: we could say the bell represents a child's capacity to believe in something that cannot exist in the world of logic.

INQUIRY POINT

Go to a library and read one or two picturebooks that employ a symbol on the casing. What does each image represent within the story? Is there another significance to the symbol outside of the story?

For example, David Wiesner's *Sector 7* has a stylized underwater fish embossed on the casing. The fish appears as an amazing cloud formation within *Sector 7,* but is also featured in his later book *Flotsam.*

Lehman, Barbara. *Rainstorm.* Houghton Mifflin Books for Children, 2007.

Martin, Jacqueline Briggs. *Snowflake Bentley.* Sandpiper, 2009.

Van Allsburg, Chris. *Queen of the Falls.* Houghton Mifflin Books for Children, 2011.

Wiesner, David. *Tuesday.* Sandpiper, 1997.

Do these author/illustrators have other books that use this technique? ✸

Puns and Wordplay

An imaginative writer who enjoys the pleasure of words is tempted to echo words of other literary works. When White says that Templeton has no "milk of rodent kindness," we may recognize an echo from *Macbeth.* Wilbur is lured back to his pen by the promise of slops and the goose warns, "It's the old pail trick, Wilbur. Don't fall for it!" Here are echoes of "the old shell game."

White plays with words in still other ways. Naïve Wilbur uses faultless logic when he argues with the lamb that he is not less than nothing: "I don't think there is any such thing as less than nothing. Nothing is absolutely the limit of nothingness. It's the lowest you can go. . . . If there were something that was less than nothing, then nothing would not be nothing."

Devices of Sound

Onomatopoeia

One sound device called **onomatopoeia,** or words that sound like their meanings, dominates an occasional paragraph of *Charlotte's Web.* For example, as White describes Wilbur eating his slops, he uses the onomatopoeic words "swishing and swooshing," which suggest Wilbur's happy gluttony. While these slushy sounds suggest one kind of eating, the explosive sounds of "gulping and sucking" describe another.

Alliteration

Another easily recognized sound device is **alliteration**, repetition of initial consonants, as in, "They *s*ang the *s*ong of *s*ummer's ending." The effect of the sentence is musical, but its movement is slow and the music sad and final. By contrast, the Zuckerman dump becomes exciting as visual imagery rhythmically piles up interesting debris, layer upon layer. Alliteration then adds to the pleasure of the passage: "*b*roken *b*ottles . . . *d*iscarded *d*ishmops . . . last *m*onth's *m*agazines."

Assonance

A device that enhances meaning by the repetition of similar vowel sounds within a phrase is called **assonance**. When we hear the crickets' song, "*a* sad, m*o*n*o*t*o*n*ou*s s*o*ng," the neutral *a* and the similarly sounded *o*'s suggest the feeling of sorrow and sameness. Reading the passage aloud shows how sadness and monotony are extended by assonance.

Consonance

The close repetition of consonant sounds is called **consonance**. In the phrase "emp*t*y *t*in cans and dir*t*y rags and bi*t*s of me*t*al and broken bo*tt*les," repetition of the abrupt *t*'s in varying positions in the words emphasizes the idea of ragged remains of unrelated items—junk. The title of Dorie Thurston's *Thank You for the Thistle* is another example of consonance. Reading the sentence aloud is the best test for sound devices, since sound rather than spelling shows how meaning is affected.

Rhythm

So closely is rhythm—from the Greek word *rhythmos,* meaning flow—associated with poetry and verse that we often forget that it is also part of prose. Stories that are read aloud to children can make particularly effective use of **rhythm**, which in prose is sometimes called **cadence**. White uses the word *and* to create rhythm as he shows the Zuckerman dump, an accumulation of one item after another, each joined to the others by *and*. Reading aloud is the test for rhythm as it is for other sound devices. Here is:

> . . . an astonishing pile of old bottles and empty tin cans and dirty rags and bits of metal and broken bottles and broken hinges and broken springs and dead batteries and last month's magazines and old discarded dishmops and tattered overalls . . . and useless junk of all kinds, including a wrong-size crank for a broken ice-cream freezer.

Rhythm or cadence suits meaning.

The rhythmic list slows to a halt with the last comma, followed by the final, jerking phrase filled with abrupt and explosive consonants: "a wrong size cran*k* for a *b*ro*k*en ice-cream freezer." The changed rhythm brings the astonishing pile to an end.

An unusually effective example of cadence occurs in White's description of the rope swing as it flies back and forth. The first phrases of the passage anticipate "and jumped," and then the swinging begins. Again, by reading aloud, we hear each of the phrases shorten as the arc of the swing shortens. Abruptly the words bring the swing to a halt, and the swinger jumps to the ground:

Then you got up all your nerve, took a deep breath, and jumped. . . . The rope would twist and you would twist and turn with the rope. Then you would drop down, down, down out of the sky and come sailing back into the barn almost into the hayloft, then sail out again (not quite so far this time), then in again (not quite so high), then out again, then in again, then out, then in; and then you'd jump off and fall down and let somebody else try it.

Rhythm ceases completely with the series of short, explosive words and phrases at the end of the paragraph. As the successive phrases shorten, there is pleasure in the description of action as well as in the understanding of the experience. Rhythm is the key.

 Diction

Word choice, or **diction**, is an aspect of style that should give the reader the flavor of the time and place in which the story is set, as Rodman Philbrick did when he had his Civil War era character Homer P. Figg use the word "scalawag." Below are some examples of different ways writers use style to help us believe in their characters from other times and places.

Eloise McGraw maintains her fantasy world in *The Moorchild* not only by using folktale elements such as the changeling traded for a human being, but also by the rich cadences and unusual figurative language:

> Eavesdropping on the activities of the "Folk": . . . they boasted of their pranks around the cookfires; one had stripped a farmer's honeycombs, another emptied a fisherman's basket as fast as he filled it. . . . as it was meant to be . . . went on, seamlessly, until she and the other younglings had finished their nighttime learning and began to go abroad by day—to find out about dogs and iron and crosses, and humans who were not safely asleep but awake and wary.

Here fantasy creates another world or society that uses its own vocabulary. An argument becomes an argle-bargle, a trundle bed a truckle bed, a fool a lackbrain, disciplinary detention a tether, and to hurry is to skimble-skamble. When the moorchild is angry, she "vents her baffled spleen," and when meaning is clear, it is "clear as a shout." Flavor and color are appropriate in *The Moorchild*; they apply to time, place, characters, and genre.

Similarly, in writing his young adult science fiction novel *Feed*, M. T. Anderson made up new words so that readers could feel the different world in which the characters live. On the first page of *Feed* Anderson's protagonist tells us,

> Everything at home was so boring. Link Arkwaker was like, "I'm so null," and Marty was all, "I'm null, too, unit," but I mean we were all pretty null, because for the last like hour we'd been playing with three uninsulated wires that were coming out of the wall. We were trying to ride shocks off of them.

In this novel, M. T. Anderson manages the astonishing feat of showing his readers how inarticulate his characters are, while having his main character articulate, sometimes in language we don't fully understand, exactly what the problem with this new society is.

In *Sweetgrass Basket*, Marlene Carvell's prose-and-poetry novel about Mohawk sisters removed from their home in New York and sent to the infamous Carlisle Indian Boarding School in Pennsylvania, the words we notice are those of a different, but real, culture: "He'en," Mattie says to her father as he puts her on to the train to go to the boarding school, "Yes, I will take care of my sister." Later, Mattie's little sister can't find her: "Aktsi:'a/My older sister/Where is my older sister?"

And in Gary Blackwood's wonderful novel *Shakespeare's Scribe*, we can tell from the earliest sentences that we are in a very different time and place:

> I was an admirable liar. I had even lied myself into the most successful company of players in London, the Lord Chamberlain's Men. It stood to reason that I would be an admirable actor as well. But I had since discovered that there is far more to performing than merely mouthing words in a lifelike fashion. A lad who aspires to be a player must be able to sing as sweetly as a nightingale, dance as gracefully as the Queen, change garments as swiftly as the wind changes, swordfight as skillfully as a soldier, die as satisfyingly as a martyr, and learn an astonishingly large number of lines in a distressingly short time.

Actors are no longer called *players*, boys rarely called *lads*, clothing never called *garments*, and boys who want to act don't have to know how to dance like the Queen anymore, as they did in Shakespeare's time. The diction of Shakespeare's scribe, a boy called Widge, helps readers fully believe in him and in the times he is describing.

Stories of other cultures and times make special demands on the writer. Before we can accept them as believable, we must first believe that the characters are human like ourselves. To understand the new culture, we must see the particular differences between our own lives and those of other people. Style makes the difference.

 Tone

Just as tone of voice reveals how a speaker feels about a subject, **tone** in literature tells us how the author feels about his or her subject and about the audience to whom the literary work is directed. In literature, readers cannot rely on inflection in a writer's voice, so they rely entirely on words. Without vocal inflection to help convey tone, the writer must choose her words with great care.

The writer's **style** conveys the tone in literature. The writer's choice of images, details, and cadence, as well as the arrangement of words, or sentence **syntax**, all influence style. The writer chooses metaphors and similes for their sounds as well as for their meanings. All these choices reveal the attitude of the writer toward both the subject and the reader. Tone is not exactly point of view. The literary meaning of point of view is the mind or minds through which we see the story—the voice telling the story, whether it is a character's first-person presentation or the presentation of an all-seeing narrator. Tone is different. It is the writer's *attitude* toward the story and its readers. By the writer's choice of materials, the writer almost inevitably reveals something about his or her own personality. If the writer told the story orally, voice tone would reveal attitude and self; since the writer is telling the story in print, the choice of words must be the means of showing attitude.

Tone in *Charlotte's Web*

How do we discover tone? Sometimes it's easier to describe a writer's tone than it is to be aware of how it is discovered. Tone seems to creep into our consciousness without our awareness. But tone, like the showing of action, depiction of character, and description of setting, is created by the writer's choice of words. If we look carefully at a few passages from *Charlotte's Web*, we may see how White's tone is revealed.

The first pages of the book are filled with kindness and affection: Mr. Arable looks at Fern "with love" and speaks to her "gently." Fern kisses her father and mother, pleased that the runt pig is safe. White describes the setting and the characters in the same kinds of affectionate terms. The action—Wilbur spinning a web, for example, or fainting at his honors—is humorous and yet affectionate.

The chapter "Summer Days" begins with a description of setting:

> The early summer days on a farm are the happiest and fairest days of the year. Lilacs bloom and make the air sweet, and then fade. Apple blossoms come with the lilacs, and the bees visit around among the apple trees. The days grow warm and soft. School ends, and children have time to play and to fish for trouts in the brook. . . .
>
> All morning you could hear the rattle of the machine as it went round and round, while the tall grass fell down behind the cutter bar in long green swathes. Next day . . . the hay would be hauled to the barn in the high hay wagon, with Fern and Avery riding at the top of the load. Then the hay would be hoisted, sweet and warm, into the big loft, until the whole barn seemed like a wonderful bed of timothy and clover. It was fine to jump in, and perfect to hide in.

In this selection, there are none but pleasant sensory images—fragrant lilacs, apple blossoms visited by friendly bees, children fishing for trout. Summer work goes on, but the sights and sounds are pleasant; work is another kind of sensory pleasure—rhythmic "round and round," colorful "long green swathes," sweet-smelling clover, a soft timothy bed for playing in. The abstract terms "happiest," "fairest," "warm," and "soft" describe the days, while "wonderful," "fine," and "perfect" describe the fun the days bring. Both the abstract words and the vivid appeals to the senses have pleasant connotations. Summertime is not marred by a single unpleasant image or connotation. Summer fun is also humorous; Avery carries in his pocket a stiff, warm trout to be fried for dinner, or finds a slender grass snake and pockets it. Like the rest of the story, this chapter is filled with descriptions of a serene and pleasant world. White loves the summertime, the farm, the children, and the animals. Although White later builds suspense to a strong climax, his affectionate descriptions of all that summer brings have assured us that he will not permit disaster to come. While his emphasis on the cycle of seasons prepares for change, he never suggests in his choice of words that the change will bring tragedy or despair. Summing up White's attitude toward his story, we can best characterize it as humorous affection. As White goes on to compare a gray spider to a gumdrop, equate the contours of a gluttonous rat to a jelly jar, and describe a pig as terrific, radiant, and humble, affection and humor are apparent in all that happens in the story. White's word choices—style—have determined tone.

Tone and Subject Matter

Any kind of tone can be found in any genre of children's literature, but writers choose tone carefully, depending on the attitude they most want to convey about their material. A piece of historical fiction, for example, may be matter-of-fact in tone, as is *The Evolution of Calpurnia Tate,* or humorous and full of exaggeration, as is *The Mostly True Adventures of Homer P. Figg.* Most novels present a combination of tones, based on the situation that is being described. *The Watsons Go to Birmingham—1963* by Christopher Paul Curtis is a good example of a writer's shift in tone. The first part of the book is a simple family story told in a humorous tone. Ten-year-old Kenny is taunted by his teasing older brother, Byron, who calls himself "King Cool" and continually works at being a bad boy. When Kenny and his sister Joetta complain about wearing piles of the warm clothes that their Southern mother insists on, lest they "freeze solid," Byron claims it's true; they really will freeze solid. Furthermore, they mustn't ever look inside the garbage trucks with the huge mouths because early each morning the workers pick up all the bodies so frozen they "won't bend in the middle" and dispose of them. The tone becomes serious, however, once the family reaches Birmingham. After a church is bombed and four little girls are found dead—and Kenny sees one of them—Byron becomes tender and strong, comforting his little brother with some serious talk. Tone changes as the situation changes.

Science fiction and high fantasy need carefully controlled tone to persuade us to suspend disbelief willingly. Throughout the high fantasy *A Wizard of Earthsea* by Ursula Le Guin, the elevated language, often with long and sonorous line, emphasizes the seriousness of the struggle between good and evil in the soul of Ged. Le Guin preserves such departure from ordinary language when she describes the otak, a small animal Ged carries with him on his travels. Using inverted word order, she sets the otak apart from earthly animals. "They are small and sleek, with . . . fur dark brown or brindle. . . . Their teeth are cruel and their temper fierce, so they are not made pets of. They have no call or cry or any voice." Not every high fantasy story is written in such a formal tone, but Le Guin's word choice seems highly appropriate.

One of the reasons Jane Yolen's *Owl Moon* is compelling as a picturebook is that the tone of the paintings by John Schoenherr and the tone of Jane Yolen's words fit together so well. As the narrator and her Pa trudge slowly through the snow-covered fields, they are quiet; Yolen describes the silence, and the way the night world is hushed around them. The narrator and her Pa watch for an owl; Pa turns on his big flashlight and there, suddenly, in the bright snow, is a huge owl, his wings wide and his eyes yellow on the page.

Joseph Bruchac's *Hidden Roots* is an example of a coming-of-age story in which a serious, anxious tone is appropriate to the subject matter and adds suspense to the plot. Howie is a sixth grader, an Abenaki boy growing up near the Adirondack Mountains, and there is some mystery about his father, his Uncle Louis, and his mother. Readers first meet Howie in the middle of a frightening dream; on the second page we learn what his mother has taught him about life:

> I was surprised, though, that my mother had been able to come into my room without waking me up. I was a light sleeper. I'd been taught that it was good to not sleep too heavily. Otherwise you might get "crept up on." My mother had told me that for as long as I could remember. It wasn't the kind of reassuring thing that most kids would expect a mother to say. Most mothers tell their children that everything is going to be all right, no matter what. But most mothers weren't like mine.

The flat, matter-of-fact style of the short sentences; the words "crept up on" and "as long as I could remember"; the idea that even when he should feel comforted and calm, asleep in a room with his mother, he still can't sleep deeply; and the idea that his mother doesn't tell him that everything will be all right create an anxious, almost threatening tone.

Parody

The tone of Lemony Snicket's *The Bad Beginning* is not hard to find. Here is one scene from the novel:

> Their home destroyed, the Baudelaires had to recuperate from their terrible loss in the Poe household, which was not at all agreeable. Mr. Poe was scarcely at home, because he was very busy attending to the Baudelaire's affairs, and when he was home he was often coughing so much he could barely have a conversation. Mrs. Poe purchased clothing for the orphans that was in grotesque colors, and itched. And the two Poe children—Edgar and Albert—were loud and obnoxious boys with whom the Baudelaires had to share a tiny room that smelled of some sort of ghastly flower.

The tone of this passage is serious, even grim. The words "destroyed," "terrible," and "scarcely"; the details that their new clothes are "grotesque" and that they itch; that the other children are loud and obnoxious, and that their room smells of a "ghastly" flower, along with the straightforward sentence structure with few active verbs create a creepy, sober tone.[2]

Of course *The Bad Beginning* is a **parody**, a subgenre of comic writing, so we would expect its tone to be somewhat snide or sarcastic and Snicket's description of this scene is so negative that it's over the top. Parody is like this—it's an imitation intended to spoof and amuse. Parody is usually a device for older readers, because it relies on the reader's memory of a known piece of writing or of a way of talking. It retains the form of the original but changes the words and the tone for humorous effect.

Along with the increasing sophistication in children's literature that we described in Chapter 2 comes an increase in the use of this more sophisticated literary device. Lemony Snicket's *A Series of Unfortunate Events* is a parody of certain kinds of old-fashioned melodramas, and a reader can see that Lois Lowry's parody, *The Willoughbys,* has been influenced by Snicket's work. In a review of *The Willoughbys,* Snicket himself writes that Lowry's book is "a short novel mocking the conventions of old-fashioned children's books stuffed with orphans, nannies, and long-lost heirs."[3]

In *The Willoughbys* (an allusion to Joan Aiken's classic Gothic children's novel *The Wolves of Willoughby Chase*), two wicked parents can't wait to get rid of their children, and the children—Tim, Jane, and Barnabys A and B—ask each other "Shouldn't we be orphans?" Behaving very much like the old-fashioned

---

INQUIRY POINT

Mark Twain may seem like an old-fashioned, out-of-date writer, but he is one of the great American writers just the same. To see just how much his work has influenced children's books, read aloud the first page of Christopher Paul Curtis's *Elijah of Buxton*, a pre-Civil War historical fiction story of an escaped slave living free in a settlement in Canada, and of Rodman Philbrick's *The Mostly True Adventures of Homer P. Figg*, the story of a white boy looking for his brother who is fighting in the Civil War. Then read the first page of Mark Twain's *The Adventures of Huckleberry Finn.* What similarities do you see? What writing skills do you think these two children's writers learned from Mark Twain? Look especially at the type of humor all three authors use. ◉

family they insist they are, the children march into and out of situations that will be familiar to readers of old-fashioned children's literature. They meet a wealthy candy-maker, rescue a baby ("Oh, my goodness, we don't want a baby!" says their mother), find a sweet and somewhat magical nanny, and discover a fortune. At the end of the book Lowry provides an idiosyncratic glossary—a kind of parody of a glossary—and lists all the classic children's books—*Mary Poppins, The Bobbsey Twins, Heidi,* and many more—to which *The Willoughbys* refers. This parody is intertextuality at its best.

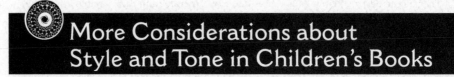

More Considerations about Style and Tone in Children's Books

Trite versus Fresh Style

Some writers think writing for children is an easy task; they use the simplest, most familiar words; their language often becomes wooden and full of **clichés**. The books these writers create, which may be tied to television shows or movie characters and may receive much advertising, need not be bought. There are so many great children's writers at work creating styles that are fresh and meaningful that there is no need for children to read books in which the writer does not do his or her best writing. The following examples of three different writers' styles show how fresh and original writing for children can be.

In this scene from *A Step from Heaven,* An Na's story of the life of a Korean immigrant family in California, Young Ju has just won an award for having the highest GPA in her ninth-grade class. Though her parents are working and cannot attend the awards ceremony, when Young Ju shows the award to her mother, she holds it in the light, questions her, and then tells her how proud she is. Young Ju's mother leaves the award in the middle of the coffee table, next to the Korea Times newspaper, so that Young Ju's Apa will see it when he gets home from work. But when her father comes home, he does not notice the award, and when Young Ju wakes the next day she finds it hidden underneath his newspapers. Young Ju picks up the award later and thinks, it's only a piece of paper. She tells the reader how she feels using fresh and vivid sensory images.

> I look down at my name and begin to crumple the entire certificate, but a tiny black smudge catches my eye. For some reason, before I can think, I lift the certificate to my nose. Ammonia and bleach. An ache deep and wide as the sea threatens to drown my heart.

The style of Gary Paulsen's *The Winter Room* is unlike that in his adventure stories, but perfectly suited to the storytelling skills of Eldon, an eleven-year-old living on a farm in northern Minnesota. His father and Uncle David give only puzzling answers to many of his questions, "with words around the edges." "And sometimes Uncle David is never wrong so that might be the way of it." Time to thrash is Father's favorite time "if there's been good rain and the oats and wheat are good, and his sad time if it's been dry and the oats and wheat didn't make right." Fall is the time when "all the grain is up and the barn is full of hay and the fields are tucked in with haystacks waiting to be used and everything is done." Eldon describes arguing with his brother:

> Wayne says there aren't any divisions in things. We had a big fight one time over whether or not there was a place between days when it wasn't the day before and it wasn't tomorrow yet. I said there were places, divisions in things so you could tell one from the next but he said no there wasn't and we set to it. By the time we were done I had a bloody nose.

In his survival story *Hatchet*, Paulsen's style is very different. Brian finds seventeen leathery turtle eggs and knows that to survive he must eat them raw. He sharpens a stick to poke a hole in the shell, widens it with a finger and looks inside to see a yolk of dark yellow. We watch him as he brings the egg to his lips, closes his eyes, squeezes the flexible shell, and swallows as fast as possible. Despite its oily taste, it was an egg. "His throat tried to throw it back up, his whole body seemed to convulse with it, but his stomach took it, held it, and demanded more." The vivid sensory images show Brian's struggle to do what he must to survive.

Pacing is an aspect of style that Jon Scieszka controls particularly well. He also uses fresh, interesting words. In *Summer Reading Is Killing Me*, one of Scieszka's Time Warp Trio books, Sam, Fred, and Joe suddenly realize they might be in a book themselves, or in the summer reading list their teacher has handed out. When Sam asks if story characters have a life that we don't know about, Joe says that would explain everything. Fred chimes in that it would explain *almost* everything.

> "Everything except that frog in a suit coat and pants over there."
>
> I looked around. "There's no frog in a suit in *The Hoboken Chicken Emergency*. Where?"
>
> "Right there," pointed Fred. "Next to the toad in the plaid jacket."
>
> "Frog?" I said.
>
> "Toad?" Sam said.
>
> We looked at each other in horror.
>
> "Frog and Toad?" we said.
>
> And we knew then and there that something had gone terribly, mixed-uply, summer-reading-listly wrong.

Condescension

In *Criticism, Theory, & Children's Literature*, Peter Hunt provides us with a fine example of **condescension** in children's literature when he quotes from the work of British children's writer Enid Blyton. This is from Blyton's book *Tricky the Goblin*:

> Well, think of that! Janey could hardly believe her ears! She took the mother's hand and they ran across the road. In a few minutes Janey's mother had heard all about how Janey had saved the Christmas tree from falling onto the tea-table, and Janey was putting on her pink party frock and bushing her hair in the greatest excitement!
>
> Robin stood and watched. How he wished he had been as kind as Janey![4]

Yes, this is a didactic passage, and an old-fashioned one, too, but Hunt draws us to the stylistic flaws, not just the flaws of content, in this piece of writing. He points out what he calls "the blend of cliché, spoken idiom, and simplification" in writing like this example from Blyton. He quotes another writer who points out Blyton's excessive use of exclamation points and clichés ("could hardly believe her ears," "ran across the road"). Hunt calls this "less-than-thoughtful writing"; the writer's tone betrays a condescending belief that children need to be hit over the head to understand a point, and that that point needs to be explained in the simplest way.

"Cute" stories are often condescending.

For a different perspective on writing for children, a perspective we endorse, let's listen to E. B. White in "On Writing for Children":

> Anyone who writes down to children is simply wasting his time. . . . Some writers deliberately avoid using words they think the child doesn't know. This emasculates the prose, and, I suspect, bores the reader. Children are game for anything. They love words that give them a hard time, provided they are in a context that absorbs their attention.[5]

For an example of words used in thoughtful, not condescending, writing, look at George Ella Lyon's language in her 2009 picturebook *You and Me and Home Sweet Home.* Lyon's main character Sharonda doesn't believe at first that the church people are actually going to build her a house, and she speaks about the possibility in a sarcastic way. Later, after she has watched people actually building the house, she teaches her third-grade class about roof trusses and learns about insulation, inspecting, drilling, and measuring and laying pipes. There is no shortage of grown-up, fresh words and unusual images in this short book. When Sharonda and the church people have finished building her house, they brush the sawdust off the pizza and dig in.

Sentimentality

Sentimentality is a kind of condescension. Thornton W. Burgess's *Mother West Wind's Animal Friends,* still in print and on some library shelves after many years, uses trite language as well as a sentimental tone. Burgess creates talking animals that have few traits to convince us either of their likeness to people or of their animal natures—except that those with wings fly, and those without, walk. Open a Burgess story and find this:

> Then old Mr. Toad picked up his cane and started down the Crooked Little Path to the Green Meadows. There he found the Merry Little Breezes stealing kisses from the bashful little wind flowers. Old Mr. Toad puffed out his throat and pretended that he disapproved, disapproved very much indeed, but at the same time he rolled one eye up at jolly, round, red Mr. Sun and winked.
> "Haven't you anything better to do than make bashful little flowers hang their heads?" asked old Mr. Toad gruffly.

The many capitalized nouns and adjectives; the personification of breezes, flowers, and sun; the repetition of words and phrases ("disapproved, disapproved very much indeed") and the clichés ("anything better to do") do little to convey conflict or to make the story move. Peter Rabbit (a nod to Beatrix Potter) and the "little meadow people and forest folk" are organizing an Easter Egg Rolling for everyone in the Green Meadows, the Purple Hills, and the Green Forest. The long-winded combination of sentimentality and the omniscient point of view create a coy tone and fail to reveal character or to describe actions. Burgess lacks respect for his readers as well as his characters; his condescension makes a shallow story.

The Land, the story of Paul Edward, who is of mixed race and is mistreated by both whites and African Americans, might easily have become sentimental. But author Mildred Taylor successfully promotes understanding by a sympathetic rather than sentimental tone. A prequel to *Roll of Thunder, Hear My Cry*, this is Paul Edward's story; he is the son of a Southern farmer and his African American slave. Just after the Civil War, Paul Edward grows up in a close family of five children: Cassie, his true sister, and three older half-brothers born to a white farmer and his white wife. Paul's fair skin and hair result in his being ostracized by both the white people, who regard him as black, and the African Americans, who distrust him as part of the white world. In his struggle to be himself and be in control of his life, Paul encounters cruelty on every side. An argument with his close white brother Robert opens for him a realization that follows him through adulthood.

> I thought on my brother Robert. "If you're colored, that white man's going to always think of you with your color in mind, and I don't care how close you think you are, if that white man figures it's in his interest to turn his back on you, that's just what he's going to do."

When Paul Edward's valuable palomino horse—won fairly in a competition—is killed by a white man his friend does not understand. Paul does.

> Digger was a little man who had nothing. Out of his own meanness he had killed that magnificent animal because he had belonged to me, a man of color. He had killed my horse and he had killed my friend.

In his effort to save enough money for the land he loves, Paul says, "I worked with fever and I worked with pain. . . . I pushed myself until I could push no further." But white landowners do not believe he has the money, and bankers cannot believe he will repay a loan.

Nor is there sentimentality in Katherine Paterson's portrayal of Jess's grief at the death of his friend in *Bridge to Terabithia*. After Leslie drowns in the floodwaters Jess's stomach "felt so odd." And yet, the morning after the news, pancakes doused in syrup taste "marvelous." Jess's sister accuses him of not caring, and he is puzzled: "The coldness curled up inside of him and flopped over." As Jess's mother and sister talk, he "could hear them talking and they were farther away than the memory of a dream." He cannot leave the table, but he doesn't know what to do. Then, his mind a blank, he mumbles, "What little girl?" Paterson's depiction is not sentimental, filled with sighs and tears and sobs; we nonetheless see that Jess is shocked and grief-stricken.

Even the death of a loved one can be described without sentimentality.

Sensationalism

Sensationalism, as noted in the discussion of plot, is another kind of tone. An Na's *A Step from Heaven* or Marlene Carvell's *Sweetgrass Basket*, for example, could easily have been sensational stories, as the main characters in both have to confront horrible circumstances. The writers, however, have carefully chosen words that convey meaning and control tone but avoid sensationalism.

A sensational tone occurs in some books published for children. Writing can be called sensational when it plays to our lowest, most quickly satisfied interests—violence that has no purpose other than to thrill the reader, sexuality that is gratuitous. When the subject is delicate—child abuse, incest, family violence, young sexuality—and the writing is sloppy, the book is likely to have a sensational tone. The topics of the book are there to sell the book, not to enlighten the reader.

It is not necessarily what happens in the book that causes it to be called sensational; it is the writer's attitude towards it. Some books that are currently considered classics were called sensational when they first appeared. Robert Cormier's *The Chocolate War* was criticized in 1974, when it was first published, because the final boxing match that punished Jerry Renault for his refusal to join in the Vigils' behavior seemed unnecessarily violent. Later readers have seen that that section of the novel is an integral part of the whole and not added for sensational reasons; we know that unfortunately such behavior is not uncommon among the young. Cormier, who wrote *The Chocolate War* for an adult audience, was persuaded to make some changes for a younger audience. Judy Blume's *Forever* was much castigated for what by today's standards seems tame sexual allusion. The writing of Blume's book is not sensational in tone, although many years ago its subject seemed to be.

So standards change. Just as in the 1960s a married couple couldn't be shown sleeping in the same bed on television, even good writing for children that had violence or admitted to sexuality between teens was considered sensational. Now, both in television and in books for children, mores have changed somewhat. Still, the standards are there: most any subject can be addressed in a children's book, if the writer is careful, writes delicately, and respects the reader.

When Dad Killed Mom by Julius Lester can be seen as sensational; it is Lester's only failure in a long line of thoughtful, carefully written books for children. This book addresses many delicate subjects: told from the point of view of two children, twelve-year-old Jeremy and fourteen-year-old Jenna, it is the story of what happens to two children when their father shoots their mother in broad daylight. This book covers many sensational topics: incest, the accidental death of a child, possible lesbianism, and other sexual topics. The problem is that the voices of the children, the daughter in particular, are not believable; the daughter is a little more articulate about her problems than most fourteen-year-olds would be. Furthermore, the courtroom scene becomes melodramatic, with the twelve-year-old pulling from his knapsack a diary that exonerates the mother and condemns the father, the fourteen-year-old yelling obscenities at her father, and the judge looking from daughter to lawyer, asking, "Is what she said true?" It seems far too unsophisticated a question for a judge to ask in such a trial. A reader can tell Lester didn't imagine this work fully and rushed in the writing.

Readers who misunderstand folktales and nursery rhymes, considering them too violent for children, are put off by the **distanced tone** of these works. This dispassionate view of the people,

INQUIRY POINT

In order to think about what a distanced tone might be like, compare the narrative and visual tones of four different versions of the folktale "Little Red Riding Hood." Find the following texts at a library:

Hyman, Trina Schart. *Little Red Riding Hood.* Holiday House, 1987.

Perrault, Charles. *Little Red Riding Hood.* Sarah Moon, Illus. Creative Publications, 2002.

Pinkney, Jerry. *Little Red Riding Hood.* Little Brown, 2007.

Spirin, Gennadii. *Little Red Riding Hood.* Marshall Cavendish, 2010.

What is the tone of the narrative of each text? What is the tone of the artwork of each text? Does the tone of the writing and the tone of the art differ? Which is more powerful in conveying the tone of the folktale, the artwork or the written tale? How is the tone of Sarah Moon's photography different from the tone of the illustrations of Trina Schart Hyman's version of *Little Red Riding Hood?* How does setting impact the tone of the book?

places, and events in a literary work can complicate a reader's understanding; reading this dispassionate view well depends on the reader's ability to recognize the separateness of art and reality. Form, as noted earlier, is strong in folktales, in their plotting as well as their characters, and because they are unlike anything known to them, readers do not identify with the characters or situation.

Didacticism

Didacticism, or preaching, is expected of sermons that point to moral lessons, and teaching from textbooks that spread before us the truths of concept or fact. In folk literature, the fable exists only to make visible or tangible a moral lesson. In fact, that may be one of the pleasures of the fable: Once heard, a reader can say, "I know what that story means." Fable form requires didacticism, but in other imaginative literature it is often considered a negative quality.

Still, different readers have different levels of tolerance for writing that is aimed at providing information in a fictionalized setting. Some readers are more interested in the ideas that reading brings them than they are in descriptions of nuanced emotional relationships. This is often the case in science fiction, which can present readers with positive didacticism. The much-loved science fiction novel *Ender's Game*, for example, can be considered didactic in that it discusses math, philosophy, and Nietzschean ideas about morality. In defending this book and science fiction devoted more to ideas than to character development in general, Farah Mendlesohn writes that "the comment that a book is didactic is often rather prejudiced: we ignore the didactic we like but hit on the didactic we don't." She writes that, like much of science fiction, *Ender's Game* is a book "in which information is prized over emotional response."[6]

Blindsided by Patricia Cummings is another example of a careful, sophisticated didacticism. In this book, fourteen-year old Nat is slowly going blind from juvenile glaucoma. Very well-researched and convincing in its discussion of a farm girl going to a school for blind children, meeting others with different disabilities, learning how to walk with a cane and read Braille, and slowly accepting herself as being fully blind, this novel is one that does well in serving its didactic purpose. A reader comes away from the novel knowing much more about the technology, tools, and psychological complexities that come with being a blind teenager. But the characters are flat and the plot seems overtaken by the writer's desire to teach her audience about her subject. Though this book provides interesting insights into a little-known world and is not condescending to its reader as some books with didactic purposes are, it cannot be considered literature because its intent to teach outweighs its intent to create a fully believable world.

Didacticism will always be with us. The degree of acceptance varies with the reader, but the pleasure is diminished for many when the teaching purpose seems more important than the complexity of the characters and their significant experiences.

Changing Values in Style and Tone

Styles in writing change for children as they do for adults. Sometimes tone forces the retirement of a onetime classic. Beverly Cleary's *Ramona Quimby, Age 8* is far from being retired, but aspects of its style and tone are old fashioned compared, say, to the more contemporary *The Higher Power of Lucky*. Both are in some sense family stories, and both present the reader with a child's sense of wonder at ordinary, everyday life. Still, when she listens in on a family conversation, what Ramona hears and how she reacts is very different from what Lucky hears and how she reacts:

> Beezus silently cleared the table. Mrs. Quimby served applesauce and oatmeal cookies while Mr. Quimby talked about his work as Santa's Little Helper in the frozen-food warehouse. He told how snow fell inside the warehouse door when someone opened it and let in warm air. He told about a man who had to break icicles from his moustache when he left the warehouse.
>
> Snow indoors, icicles on a moustache—Ramona was full of questions that she would not let herself ask. Maybe working as Santa's Little Helper wasn't as much fun as she had thought.

Susan Patron's *The Higher Power of Lucky* has a style that is far more contemporary. Here is Lucky listening in on an Alcoholics Anonymous meeting:

> But Short Sammy didn't head right to the good part. To stretch it out and get more suspense going for the big ending he veered off and told about the old days when he was broke and couldn't afford to buy rum, so he made home made liquor from cereal box raisins and any kind of fruit he could scrounge up. This was the usual roundabout way he talked, and Lucky had noticed that it made people stay interested, even if the story got quite a bit bigger than it would have if someone else had been telling it.

Although both stories are humorously common, *Lucky* shows us a ten-year-old girl who knows the stories of an Alcoholics Anonymous meeting well enough that she can critique the style of their telling, whereas Ramona Quimby is an eight-year-old girl who imagines working as Santa's Helper might be fun for her father. Aside from the relative experiences these two girls have, the tone of each of these tales is somewhat different.

Retellings

Retelling does not always improve a story, but may instead make the story drab.

When stories are no longer protected by copyright laws, publishers may ask other writers to retell the story in "simple" language. *The Velveteen Rabbit*, for example, has been retold countless times, sometimes with didactic messages for children or with new and trite illustrations.

Tom Sawyer is an example of a young adult book so well known that even people who have never read it or seen any of its innumerable film or cartoon versions know many of its scenes. Most know the story about how Tom tricked his friends into whitewashing a fence for him, how Tom swung a dead cat around in a graveyard in the moonlight, or how Tom and Becky got lost in a cave dripping with stalactites. These scenes have imprinted themselves on our national memory not because the scenes themselves are so interesting—although Twain did manage to say things about the American character that remain true to this day—but because of Twain's witty, vivid style of writing, his use of the right word in the right place.

Twain meticulously describes Tom's mischief with Peter the cat. Notice the imagery and action, wit and empathy with the cat, in this short description:

> Peter was agreeable. So Tom pried his mouth open and poured down the Painkiller. Peter sprang a couple of yards in the air, and then delivered a war whoop and set off round and round the room, banging against furniture, upsetting flowerpots, and

making general havoc. Next he rose on his hind feet and pranced around, in a frenzy of enjoyment, with his head over his shoulder and his voice proclaiming his unappeasable happiness. Then he went tearing around the house again spreading chaos and destruction in his path.

A reteller of *Tom Sawyer*, Monica Kulling, adapting the book for less patient readers, substitutes short sentences and simpler language when she tells the same scene:

> The next morning Tom decided to stop moping around. He was itching for an adventure. He took the Pain-killer off the shelf and gave a dose to Peter the cat. Peter leaped into the air. He screamed and ran around and around the room. He upset flowerpots. He stood on his back legs and pranced around![7]

Twain has Tom "pry" Peter's mouth open, as one would have to when feeding a cat; Kulling's Tom simply gives the cat a dose. Twain's long sentences have cadences and rhythms that provide the reader with a dizzying sense of the cat's activities; Kulling substitutes an exclamation point for the words she thinks might give kids a hard time: "unappeasable," "proclaiming," and "destruction." E. B. White would have told her to leave those words in. Twain creates a more complete picture of Tom's prank, using rhythm and specific language.

The two stories are vastly different, even though the same events are reported in the retelling. The reason for the difference is not what happens, but how the writer selects and uses words to show what happens. This is style.

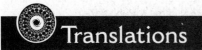 Translations

Translations may present other problems. In an otherwise beautifully translated story, *The Island on Bird Street* by Israeli author Uri Orlev, translator Hillel Halkin occasionally lapses from informal language into U.S. slang. Polish Alex, the first-person narrator who is hiding in the ruins of the Warsaw ghetto of Holocaust days, is "bushed" (exhausted); feels "like a dope"; and is told to "shut up." Although these lapses seem trivial, in an otherwise seamless narrative that is totally convincing—rooted as it clearly is in the reality of Orlev's experience—they call attention to the story as a translation from another language. Lest these brief comments detract too much from an excellent and engrossing narrative, notice the convincing language describing Alex's scavenging efforts:

> I decided to make just one bundle of clothes. Into it went a few things that fit me, the suits for father, the coat, and some towels and sheets. I found a beat-up Polish army hat, the kind tough Polish kids like to wear, and stuck it happily on my head. Then I filled a second blanket with books and dragged the two bundles to the entrance to the cellar, where I took them apart and carried in a few things at a time. Before it got dark I went back again and took a mattress. I picked a nice soft one. And then I made one last trip for a folding chair that I managed to fit through the opening too.

INQUIRY POINT

At the library find three or four versions of *The Velveteen Rabbit* by Margery Williams. Compare the language, the style and tone, and the illustrations. What are the similarities and differences? Which aspect was most prominent in the retelling or revised versions? Why do you think the variations were made?

TEXTSET

Style and Tone

This annotated textset lists picturebooks that provide examples of various aspects of style and tone.

Connotation

Browne, Anthony. *Zoo*. Red Fox, 1994.

Visitors to the zoo resemble its inhabitants; what do the zoo and its visitors mean to the reader? This book is filled with images that have more than one meaning.

Marceau, Fani. *Panorama: A Foldout Book*. Joelle Jolivet, Illus. Abrams, 2009.

Beautiful picturebook that can be flipped through like a traditional picturebook, but as the title suggests, the book may be opened out to see the whole picture. Excellent visual and tactile demonstration of this concept.

Imagery

Mannis, Celeste Davidson. *One Leaf Rides the Wind*. Susan Kathleen Hartung, Illus. Viking, 2002.

Despite the fact that this is a counting book, the haiku poetry is exquisite in the imagery it creates of a Japanese garden.

Myers, Walter Dean. *Harlem*. Christopher Myers, Illus. Scholastic Press, 1997.

This songlike poem paints a vibrant picture of the area and its residents for a more sophisticated audience; the imagery is subtle, but vibrant. The collages and computerized illustrations create the total image of Harlem.

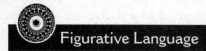

Figurative Language

Personification

Bianco, Margery Williams. *The Velveteen Rabbit*. Monique Felix, Illus. Creative Editions, 2010.

An illustrated version of this classic 1922 story. Beautifully illustrated in appropriately realistic style, this version reveals the passion of the author and her original rich language and an illustrator who clearly loves this story.

Burton, Virginia. *The Little House*. Houghton Mifflin, 1946.

Story of a house affected by the changing neighborhood shown in illustrations and described by a narrator who attributes feelings to the house as it suffers, is relocated, and finds new life; a classic picturebook with current themes. Other "house" books such as *The Changing Countryside* work with similar dilemmas, but without personifying the house.

Snicket, Lemony. *The Lump of Coal*. Brett Helquist, Illus. HarperCollins, 2008.

Parody of holiday traditions and miracle stories, cloaked in a quest story and pourquoi tale of how the lump of coal came into his own; the protagonist is a lump of coal.

Simile

Isadora, Rachel. *The Night Before Christmas*. Putnam, 2009.

Set in Africa with cultural cut-paper collage illustrations; and African traditions are juxtaposed with the traditional poem.

Piven, Hanoch. *My Best Friend Is as Sharp as a Pencil*. Schwartz and Wade, 2010.

Wonderful descriptions of people with representative objects turned into portrait collages; a very clever realization of Piven's trademark three-dimensional collage.

Metaphor

Beamer, Nona. *Naupaka*. Bishop Museum Press, 2008.

Sophisticated folklore that is a metaphor for the pre-contact social hierarchy of Hawaii.

Young, Ed. *Seven Blind Mice*. Philomel, 1992.

A classic collage version of this East Asian fable in which several metaphors individually create a misconception; collectively they reveal the truth.

Hyperbole

Isaacs, Anne. *Swamp Angel*. Paul O. Zelinsky, Illus. Puffin, 2000.

Anne Isaacs and Paul Zelinsky expertly tell this Appalachian tall tale; readers see and hear the exaggeration that describes not only the defeat of a pesky bear but also the formation of the Big Dipper and the Great Smoky Mountains.

Morris, Carla. *The Boy Who Was Raised by Librarians*. Brad Sneed, Illus. Peachtree Publishers, 2007.

Glorifies the attributes of libraries and librarians; illustrations are stylized to show the exaggeration that librarians will love!

Understatement

Frazee, Marla. *A Couple of Boys Have the Best Week Ever*. Harcourt Children's Books, 2008.

Straightforward text tells astory that is countered by the actions portrayed in the illustrations.

Wiesner, David. *June 29, 1999*. Clarion, 1992.

This book's dry humor, with sophisticated, minimal text combined with surreal illustrations, works for all ages; includes deadpan descriptions of a schoolgirl's science experiment with surreal results and alliterative language.

Allusion

Palatini, Margie. *Piggie Pie*. Howard Fine, Illus. Sandpiper, 1997.

The Piggies are threatened by a message written in the sky: "Surrender Piggies!" which alludes through illustration to *The Wizard of Oz*.

Stein, David Ezra. *Interrupting Chicken*. Candlewick, 2010.

Parent and child perform their bedtime story routine, but Little Red Chicken cannot help revealing the end of the story—changing the ending every time.

Wiesner, David. *Art and Max*. Clarion, 2010.

Cleverly introduces two new characters and makes allusions to various artistic styles and media in honor of budding artists of all ages.

Wiesner, David. *The Three Pigs*. Clarion, 2000.

Wiesner makes allusions to his own illustrations as the pigs escape their obligations to the traditional tale and borrow from other stories through illustrations.

Symbol

Rathmann, Peggy. *Officer Buckle and Gloria*. Putnam, 1995.

Small illustrations in the lower righthand corner serve to foreshadow upcoming story events with humor.

Puns and Wordplay

Browne, Anthony. *Changes!* Walker Books, 1991.

Double meanings for everyday changes; includes sly allusions to popular culture and famous works of art.

Browne, Anthony. *Look What I've Got!* Knopf, 2010.

This book is filled with visual jokes and puns.

Lester, Julius. *Ackamarackus*. Emilie Chollat, Illus. Scholastic Press, 2001.

Six highly alliterative modern fables with silly imaginative characters are filled with verbal puns.

 Using Sound

Onomatopoeia

Frazee, Marla. *Roller Coaster*. Sandpiper, 2006.

A realistic interpretation of a familiar experience, including words that express the sounds of a roller coaster: Whoosh, zoom; Clickity, clackity; Clickity, clackity.

Gollub, Matthew. *The Jazz Fly*. Tortuga Press, 2000.

Includes scat refrains like "ZA-baza, BOO-zaba, ZEE-zah RO-ni," as animal sounds are put to a jazz beat.

Alliteration

Deedy, Carmen Agra. *Martina the Beautiful Cockroach*. Peachtree Publishers, 2007.

A sweet and sly retelling of an old Cuban folktale in which a cockroach uses café cubano to help her find a husband. Gorgeous acrylic illustrations.

Gerstein, Mordecai. *The Absolutely Awful Alphabet*. Sandpiper, 2001.

Each letter of the alphabet is something vile, putrid, or arrogant, with luscious vocabulary and right on characterization through illustrations.

(continued)

Assonance

Fleming, Denise. *Where Once There Was a Wood*. Henry Holt, 1996.

Descriptive language describes changes readers will recognize as natural environment is replaced with modern landscapes of suburban homes.

Moss, Lloyd. *Zin! Zin! Zin! A Violin*. Marjorie Priceman, Illus. Simon and Schuster, 1995.

Musical portraits of instruments (in quatrains) filled with well-chosen alliterative sounds.

Shaw, Nancy. *Raccoon Tune*. Howard Fine, Illus. Holt and Company, 2005.

Nighttime illustrations show raccoon capers: "Ash cans. / Trash cans. / How we love to crash cans, / Mash and smash and bash cans."

Consonance

Lester, Helen. *Hooway for Wodney Wat*. Sandpiper, 2002.

Seeger, Laura Vaccaro. *Walter Was Worried*. Neal Porter Books, 2006.

These books incorporate consonance as they build an effective picturebook character.

SUMMARY

Any good story is words, many words, selected and arranged in a manner that best creates character, draws setting, recounts conflict, builds suspense to a climax, and ties it all together with some significance.

Style involves the use of figurative language appropriate to the story; imagery that describes for the senses what is happening or how things look; exaggeration or understatement to entertain or to heighten feelings; allusions to people or events already known; wordplay with puns or echoes; and sound devices to give pleasure and to heighten meaning.

Tone, which is the author's attitude toward subject and readers, is an integral part of a story, and dependent on style, since both are created by the writer's choice of words. Tone is not created by any single, obvious decision of the author; instead it is the result of all the choices made in telling the story. Tone can make the same story—one of heroes and valiant deeds, for example—either a series of trivial anecdotes or a monument to human valor. Tone can fill us with affection and acceptance, or rouse us to examine ourselves and even to laugh with delight at the frailties we find. Appropriateness and freshness—the sense that these words are the best possible words for this particular story—are not only the style of the story and do not only contribute to the tone of the story, they *are* the story.

NOTES

1. Henry James, *The Art of Fiction and Other Essays* (New York: Oxford University Press, 1948).
2. This parsing of the Snicket quotation, and the inquiry point that goes with it, were suggested by Nancy Dean's book that helps junior high and high school students understand style, tone, and voice in writing, *Discovering Voice: Voice Lessons for Middle and High School* (Gainesville, FL: Maupin House, 2006).
3. This review by Lemony Snicket first appeared in *Publisher's Weekly* but was retrieved from amazon.com on September 5, 2010. Also available online at http://www.publishersweekly.com/978-0-618-97974-5
4. Peter Hunt, *Criticism, Theory, & Children's Literature* (Cambridge, MA: Basil Blackwell, 1991). This quotation from Enid Blyton's *Tricky the Goblin* is taken from page 106 of Hunt's book. Some of the criticisms of the Blyton story have been taken from page 107 of that same chapter, "Style and Stylistics."
5. Peter Hunt, 'The Importance of Language," in *Criticism, Theory, & Children's Literature* (Cambridge, MA: Basil Blackwell, Inc. 1991), p. 104. Originally in E. B. White, "On Writing for Children," in *Children's Literature: Views and Reviews*, edited by Virginia Haviland (London: Bodley Head, 1974).
6. These quotations were taken from a fascinating article about science fiction for children. Farah Mendlesohn, "The Campaign for Shiny Futures," *The Horn Book Magazine*, March/April 2009.

Available online at www.hbook.com/magazine/
articles/2009/mar09_mendlesohn.asp

7. Mark Twain, *The Adventures of Tom Sawyer*, adapted by
Monica Kulling (New York: Random House, 1995).

RECOMMENDED BOOKS

AIKEN, JOAN. *The Wolves of Willoughby Chase*. Yearling, 1987.

ANDERSON, M. T. *Feed*. Candlewick, 2004.

BLACKWOOD, GARY. *Shakespeare's Scribe*. Scholastic. 2000.

BRUCHAC, JOSEPH. *Hidden Roots*. Scholastic. 2004.

BUNTING, EVE. *Fly Away Home*. Sandpiper, 1993.

CARD, ORSON SCOTT. *Ender's Game*. Tor Science Fiction, 1994.

CARVELL, MARLENE. *Sweetgrass Basket*. Dutton's
Children's Books, 2005.

CLEARY, BEVERLY. *Ramona Quimby, Age 8*. HarperCollins, 1992.

CURTIS, CHRISTOPHER PAUL. *The Watsons Go to Birmingham—1963*. Random House Children's Books, 1995.

HESSE, KAREN. *Out of the Dust*. Scholastic, 1997.

HORVATH, POLLY. *My One Hundred Adventures*.
Schwartz and Wade, 2008.

JOHNSON, ANGELA. *Heaven*. Simon & Schuster, 2010.

KADOHATA, CYNTHIA. *Kira-Kira*. Atheneum, 2004.

KELLY, JACQUELINE. *The Evolution of Calpurnia Tate*.
Henry Holt, 2009.

KULLING, MONICA. *Tom Sawyer*. Random House Books
for Young Readers, 1995.

LE GUIN, URSULA. *A Wizard of Earthsea*. Spectra, 2004.

LOWRY, LOIS. *The Willoughbys*. Houghton Mifflin Books
for Children, 2008.

LYON, GEORGE ELLA. *You and Me and Home Sweet Home*.
Atheneum, 2009.

MCGRAW, ELOISE. *The Moorchild*. Simon and Schuster,
1996.

MCKISSACK, PATRICIA, AND FREDERICK MCKISSACK.
Christmas in the Big House, Christmas in the Quarters.
Scholastic, 1994.

NA, AN. *A Step from Heaven*. Front Street, 2001.

ORLEV, URI. *The Island on Bird Street*. Translated by
Hillel Halkin. Houghton Mifflin, 1984.

PATERSON, KATHERINE. *Bridge to Terabithia*. Harper
Teen, 2004.

PATRON, SUSAN. *The Higher Power of Lucky*. Atheneum
Books for Young Readers, 2006.

PAULSEN, GARY. *Hatchet*. Bradbury, 1987.

PAULSEN, GARY. *The Winter Room*. Orchard Press, 1989.

PHILBRICK, RODMAN. *The Mostly True Adventures of
Homer P. Figg*. Scholastic, 2009.

PINKNEY, ANDREA DAVIS. *Duke Ellington*. Scholastic, 1998.

SCHMIDT, GARY D. *Lizzie Bright and the Buckminster Boy*.
Clarion Books, 2004.

SCIESZKA, JON. *Summer Reading Is Killing Me*. Puffin
Books, 1998.

SNICKET, LEMONY. *The Bad Beginning*. HarperCollins, 1999.

STEIG, WILLIAM. *Gorky Rises*. Farrar, Straus, and
Giroux, 1986.

TAYLOR, MILDRED. *The Land*. Speak, 2003.

TAYLOR, MILDRED. *Roll of Thunder, Hear My Cry*. Puffin, 2004.

TWAIN, MARK. *Tom Sawyer*. Dover Publications, 2011.

VAN ALLSBURG, CHRIS. *The Polar Express*. Houghton
Mifflin, 2009.

WHITE, E. B. *Charlotte's Web*. Harper, 1952.

WILLIAMS-GARCIA, RITA. *Jumped!* HarperCollins, 2009.

WILLIAMS-GARCIA, RITA. *One Crazy Summer*.
HarperCollins, 2010.

WITTINGER, ELLEN. *Hard Love*. Simon & Schuster
Children's Publishing, 2001.

WOODSON, JACQUELINE. *Feathers*. G.P. Putnam's Sons, 2007.

YOLEN, JANE. *Owl Moon*. Illustrated by John Schoenherr.
Philomel, 1987.

YORINKS, ARTHUR. *Hey Al!* Illustrated by Richard
Egielski. Farrar, Straus & Giroux, 1989.

MyEducationKit™

Go to the topic "Modern Fantasy" on the MyEducationKit for this text, where you can:

- Search the Children's Literature Database, housing more than 22,000 titles searchable in every genre by authors or illustrators, by awards won, by year published, and by topic and description.

- Explore genre-related Assignments and Activities, assignable exercises showing concepts in action through database use, video, cases, and student and teacher artifacts.

- Listen to podcasts and read interviews from some of the brightest and most enduring stars of children's literature in the Conversations.

- Discover web links that will lead you to sites representing the authors you learn about in these pages, class-rooms with powerful children's literature connections, and literature awards.

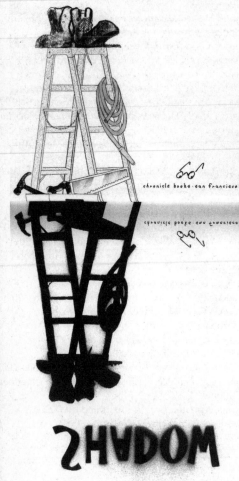

Shadow

Suzy Lee

Readers enjoy stories where a theme is one of encouraging imaginative play.

CHAPTER TEN

Theme

We have all had opportunities to discuss a story with someone younger than we are—perhaps a child. The child may have seen a television show or movie with a particularly interesting story; he or she may have read the story in a book. In response to the simple question, "What was the story about?" that child might respond by telling us each and every event of the story; he or she might provide a single word summing up the movie's topic. Another child might describe the underlying meaning behind the movie or story instead. In many cases a group of children, seeing the same movie or reading the same story, might describe that story quite differently in both their style and substance. Our point here is that readers and viewers respond differently to the same text based on their prior knowledge, the text, and the context in which the text was read or viewed. Different readers or viewers can construct fairly different themes from the same text, depending on the experiences they have had. "Theme" is a somewhat elusive concept.

In storytelling, "What happened next?" is a question about chronology and narrative order. "Why did it happen?" is a question about character and conflict. "How did it happen?" may be revealed through the style and tone. But when we ask, "What does it all mean?" we begin to discover theme. In a well-written piece of literature, all elements (setting, characters, plot, point of view, style and tone) combine to suggest its theme.

Theme: Significant Insight

Theme in literature is the idea that holds the story together, such as a comment about society, human nature, or the human condition based on the intersection of the text, the reader, and the context. It is the main idea or central meaning of a piece of writing *constructed by the reader*, which means there will generally be a range of plausible themes within a particular story.

Ask a woman about the plot of *Little Women*, the story she loved as a child, and she may look baffled and perhaps chagrined that she cannot remember all of it. Setting, however, is not merely "in the past." It is the image, perhaps, of Jo's room, candlelight glowing during stolen moments for writing. Character too is still with her, because restless Jo, who has difficulty fitting into traditional female roles, seems to be "Everywoman"—or at least "Manywomen." And chances are the adult's memory of the ideas or themes of the novel are still strong; she can confidently say, "It's about a close family of varied but accepting people," or "People find time for their passions." The characters and actions of Louisa May Alcott's story come together to convince readers of one of its themes—the love of family members for one another is real and enduring.[1] The theme comes alive and becomes memorable as the characters act out the plot in a time gone by.

Look back at our definition of literature: Literature provides a reader with significant insights into the human condition through use of memorable language. The "significant insights" go beyond the specifics of the story and comment on what it means to be human in this complicated world. A work that we consider literature often requires multiple readings and the company of other stories so that the reader can construct different and increasingly deep insights with each read.

The "significant insights" are essential to turning a simple narrative into literature; they exceed the story and comment on our humanity. The discovery holds the story together so that long after details of plot, character, or setting are forgotten, the themes remain.

Themes unify and illuminate a story as they give the reader enjoyment. The reader gains one pleasure from the discovery of the simplest of insights, and another from the discovery that these insights are not simple. Theme provides this discovery, this understanding, this pleasure in recognizing, "Yes, that's the way it is!"

Stating theme in a sentence clarifies its focus.

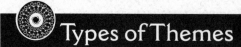

Types of Themes

Explicit

Sometimes writers state the theme openly and clearly—an **explicit theme**. Once again, we look to *Charlotte's Web* for examples. The devotion between Charlotte and Wilbur suggests many ideas that make the reader say, "It's true"; their relationship reveals and defines friendship and other themes.

Charlotte has encouraged, protected, and mothered Wilbur, bargained and sacrificed for him, and Wilbur, the grateful receiver, realizes that "friendship is one of the most satisfying things in the world." And Charlotte says later, "By helping you perhaps I was trying to lift my life a little. Anyone's life can stand a little of that." Because these quoted sentences are exact statements from the text, they are called *explicit themes*.

Explicit themes are easily understood.

The theme in *Miracle's Boys* by Jacqueline Woodson is stated explicitly. This is the story of inner-city boys, each of whom feels responsible for a death. Despite being completely innocent, each one feels guilty for failing to intervene success-fully. Ty'ree begs his dad to save a dog drowning in a frozen pond and feels responsible for his father's death from hypothermia; Lafayette, who finds his mother in a diabetic coma, somehow feels guilty for not having revived her; and Charles holds himself responsible for the death of a dog hit by a car. When each reveals his feeling of guilt, the others insist that he could not have saved the vic-tim. Freed of guilt, each is able to free the other. The function of freedom may be to free someone else.

Ruth White's novel, *Belle Prater's Boy*, presents a theme that appearances are less important than what is inside. Arbutus, called Beauty by her father, dis-likes the focus on her appearance, and calls herself Gypsy instead. When Cousin Woodrow (who hates his crossed eyes) moves in next door, Gypsy comes to love him dearly. She learns that his mother was a loving but unattractive woman, and that her own gentle father killed himself because, following his heroic rescue of a child in a fire, he could not accept his disfigurement. Gypsy's mother tells her that "appearances were too important to your father," and he became deeply de-pressed. The outside didn't matter; inside, each was worthy of love. This is not the only theme, but the connection with a specific statement makes it explicit.

Throughout Karen Cushman's *The Midwife's Apprentice*, Alyce's life changes. At first she must sleep in a warm dung heap; then she is praised for delivering twin calves. Later she delivers a healthy infant for the bailiff's wife. After a failure, she goes away to become an "inn girl" and there her curiosity about the Magister's writing helps her learn to read. Her "miraculous" delivery of the young squire's infant fol-lows. With successes behind her and a strong will to learn all she can, Alyce returns to become an apprentice to the midwife. In the last lines of the story, Alyce states an explicit theme concerning the real source of success: "I know how to try and risk and fail and try again and not give up."

As immigration and population numbers alter the makeup of U.S. and Canada, multicultural themes are justifiably critical in contemporary books for children. In an early example, *Class President*, Johanna Hurwitz makes an explicit point about ethnic pride when a new teacher, Mr. Flores, gives Julio's name its proper Spanish pronunciation: *Hulio*. "It's a good Spanish name and you should be proud of it. . . . Your name is a very important part of you." He tells the class that electing the class president should be based on leadership qualities: "A good leader is . . . fair and . . . stands up for what he or she thinks is right." Julio begins to stand up for what he believes in, first of all his ethnic heritage.

Circle of Fire shows the impact of the Ku Klux Klan's hatred on society. In an explicit thematic statement, author William H. Hooks replies to Harrison's question "Why?" by having Pa explain human frailty:

> "Your Grandma would tell you that they're just poor white trash and that quality folks would never resort to such meanness . . . But there's more to it than that. There's some-thing in all of us that wants to be top dog that wants to keep *our kind* in control. Human decency doesn't seem to be a God-given gift. It's a precious thing you have to learn early and keep working at."

Hooks does not leave it at that: an author's note following the story reminds readers of the KKK's prevalence everywhere, and warns, "These same events could happen today." Hooks avoids didacticism by keeping this comment out of the story itself. Its truth is sufficiently clear in Pa's statement. Such explicit themes are common in children's literature because writers may want readers find the unifying insights, some of which can serve as a "truth" on a personal level.

Theme is a unifying idea that holds a story together.

Implicit

Underlying *Charlotte's Web* are certain implied or **implicit themes**, as important and at times as apparent as are explicit themes. If two such different characters as a runt pig and a carnivorous spider can find friendship, others can; even a self-centered rat can be a friend of sorts. White thereby implies that friendship can be found in unexpected places.

Charlotte's selflessness—working late at night to finish a new word, expending her last energies for her friend—is evidence that friendship is giving of oneself. Wilbur's protection of Charlotte's egg sac, his sacrifice of first turn at the slops, and his devotion to Charlotte's babies—giving without any need to stay even or to pay back—leads us to another theme: True friendship is naturally reciprocal. As the two become fond of each other, still another theme emerges: One's best friend can do no wrong. In fact, a best friend is sensational! Both Charlotte and Wilbur believe in these ideas; their experiences verify them. These themes are all developed through the characters, their actions, and their thoughts as we see them throughout the story's conflict—they are story-driven.

An important purpose of a good story is to entertain through its action and characters; at the same time, it gives us insight into people—how they think and feel—and enlarges our understanding. In order to hold our interest, a story must give us some kind of pleasure, but the theme of a story is often part of what enlarges our understanding.

Virginia Hamilton's *Cousins* is a story in which the protagonist dreads the death of her aged Gram Tut and is haunted by the memory of seeing her cousin, Patty Ann, drown. Absorbed in both her grief at Patty's death and her own guilt at being jealous of her pretty cousin, Cammy cannot face death but buries the experience, then remembers it over and over until she is helped by Gram Tut to recognize that death happens to us all. Some wait for it, like Gram; for others it comes too early, as it does for Patty. Because this theme is suggested but not stated precisely at any point, it is implicit.

Implicit themes, such as "friendship knows no ethnic barriers," also underlie *Circle of Fire*. Harrison values his African American friends and adds another friend, Liam Cafferty, from among the migrant Irish gypsies traveling the East Coast. Harrison's fear that his father might be a Klan member dissolves when he learns that Pa is responsible for the eviction of the Klan from the area. The implicit theme remains: "When we don't know the facts, we may doubt even those we love."

In our view, readers are more likely to discover important themes, whether explicitly or implicitly stated, when the story is connected to significantly related stories. Using many stories whose meanings resonate with each other can help students confirm their initial ideas about the theme of one of the stories in the group; using multiple stories can also provide students opportunities to rethink an initial response.

Themes can often be clarified within clusters of related stories.

For example, Karen Hesse's fine verse novel *Witness* uses eleven unique voices to present the varied perspectives of people in a small Vermont town in 1924. Members of the Ku Klux Klan have settled in the community, deeply affecting the people's experiences and values. Learning about and listening to the members of this community, each victimized by the KKK, could provide readers with opportunities for introspection and a confirmation of the theme: "Everyone is affected by intolerance." As we have shown in Chapter 2, topics from adult and young adult fiction are making their way into stories for younger children, including potentially risky topics like the impact of the KKK. *Bessie Smith and the Night Riders*, a historical fiction picture-book whose colorful paintings match the colorful personality of blues singer, presents children with an idea of what courage looks like. During a 1927 performance, the jazz legend was alerted to the presence of the KKK. But Bessie Smith was a brave woman: in the story she tells them off rather than allowing them to chase her away. Readers may or may not be ready to hear the full story behind this account—it may be too much for the youngest readers—but the theme that "individuals can stand up to threats" illuminates the narrative.

Primary and Secondary

Each reader brings to a story a personal past, a present, and plans for the future. These elements shape the reader's responses to the story. It seems unreasonable, then, to expect that diverse humans must agree that exactly the same ideas are the most important and unrealistic to expect every reader to take exactly the same themes from a story. A story speaks to us out of our own individual and varying experiences; it speaks a particular truth to us, but it's our own truth, a personal transaction with the text and context. It may not be correct to say that an aspect of a text that speaks to one person's experience deeply is only a secondary theme. Aside from the most explicitly stated or purposeful themes, whether a theme is primary or secondary is more closely related to the meaning the story holds for the reader.

> The best stories have a thematic idea or point; they likely have more than one.

Although complexity and variety in themes may be one of the strongest proofs of a work's excellence, most literature for children has until recently centered on a **primary theme**. As we have indicated, children's literature has become increasingly sophisticated; we frequently see multiple themes in texts for children. Often, in these stories, some ideas presented seem less important than others. These less important themes are **secondary themes**.

In *Charlotte's Web*, almost as important as the themes about the nature of friendship is a secondary theme about death. It is the possibility of Wilbur's death that disturbs us; we would feel differently if he were an old boar that had lived long and well. We recognize, just the same, that "death is inevitable and not to be feared." Charlotte, knowing her life cycle, foresees her own death, but neither dreads it nor asks for pity. Others accept death, too. Seasons die when they have run their terms. Maple trees, crickets, lilacs, baby spiders, and the Harvest Fair all celebrate the inevitable cycle of birth, life, and death. There is no grief, only acceptance.

Many other minor themes also emerge in *Charlotte's Web*: "People are gullible"; "people don't give credit where credit is due"; "the meek may inherit the earth"; "youth and innocence have unique value." Each character accepts and maintains the simplicity of his or her own particular style of living, so "be what you are." As for nature, "beauty and wonder exist in all things, even the simplest," "life in nature is constant and continuous," and finally, "nature is a miracle," from the silver forest of asparagus to the waterproof egg sac.

The now classic award-winning story *Skellig* by David Almond is an excellent example of a book with multiple primary and secondary themes. Following his family's move to a rundown house in a different neighborhood, Michael, the main character, discovers a new friend, Mina. Quirky but insightful, Mina is fond of William Blake's poetry; she chooses lines from his work to serve as her personal motto, and that motto carries through the entire book: "How can a bird that is born for joy/Sit in a cage and sing?" Some readers would take this as an explicit theme; others less familiar with Blake's work might overlook these poetic lines. However, the numerous instances of its realization would likely mark the image of a caged bird born for joy as an indicator of a primary theme. The reader might not choose to relate Blake's words to Mina's tawny owl and blackbird chicks, to Michael's baby sister confined to the incubator, to winged Skellig fading in the garage, or even to Michael's growth as a figurative spreading of his wings. Almond, a skilled writer who believes in his readers' intelligence, does not provide the answer, but allows his readers to wonder and debate. In the original edition of *Skellig*, Almond does not reveal much about the creature Skellig, where it came from, or where it goes in the end.

But authors do provide clues to the meanings of their work, and Almond's author's note in the tenth anniversary edition of the book reveals his preference for Mina as his most intriguing character. In his author's note, Almond describes Mina's interest in natural science and provides an excerpt from her journal that she wrote on a trip to the museum of natural history before she met Michael and the winged creature Skellig. Mina's journal entry reveals her reverence for the *archaeopteryx* (meaning "ancient wing"). Mina provides several different responses and understandings of this word, responses that could serve as hints toward the primary or secondary themes of *Skellig*. For example, the word *archaeopteryx* suggests to Mina that "evolution will never end," or "that we, just like the archaeopteryx, may one day be extraordinary." These very different responses to the meaning of an image or a word suggest the different kinds of responses today's diverse readers might have to any reading. Some, like Mina, would gravitate toward the natural explanation; for others the magical would become a primary meaning. An ancient wing links this preamble with what is to come, and perhaps with what has gone before. When a story contains a variety of themes, they are often linked.

Jacqueline Woodson's Newbery Honor winner, *Feathers*, has a primary theme: People can find hope in this world in numerous ways. As in *Skellig*, feathers are symbolic in this novel; readers might find other parallels between these two novels. Frannie, the narrator of *Feathers*, loves a poem by Emily Dickinson, and wonders about its first lines: "Hope is the thing with feathers/that perches in the soul." A skilled reader can see how this idea of hope as a fragile thing, like a feather, carries through the story. Readers may also see secondary themes that link to the concept of hope: Frannie's brother, Sean, hopes for acceptance in the hearing world; "Jesus Boy" hopes for interracial acceptance; and Frannie's mother hopes for the life of her unborn baby. Woodson opens the door to serious questions about religion, racial segregation, and deafness, but she creates possibilities rather than providing a simple moral.

In Virginia Hamilton's *Cousins*, the return of Cammy's divorced father when she is suffering from grief and shock suggests an optimistic secondary theme about

Themes are often linked when a story has more than one.

change: "Even in difficult times, things may change and good things happen." In her brief novel *Journey*, Patricia MacLachlan suggests related themes. Journey and Cat are left to live with their grandparents when their mother, grieving over a husband who has abandoned the family, in turn abandons her two children. "Try though we may, we cannot always understand the behavior of others" comes through. "A family need not be the traditional parents and children, but may be a different form" is a second theme.

Helping Readers Think about Theme

We believe that pairing related books from a variety of genres assists students in reading literature in meaningful ways. This approach extends to the ways literary elements and related stories can combine to reveal theme. In the previous section we described a trio of books in which the Ku Klux Klan are visible—*Witness, Circle of Fire,* and *Bessie Smith and the Night Riders.* We might similarly cluster Karen Cushman's *The Midwife's Apprentice* with Cushman's other stories in which strong female protagonists confront life in medieval times: reading *Catherine, Called Birdy; Matilda Bone;* and *Alchemy and Meggy Swann* together can provide readers with a larger context and a better understanding of the times in which the stories are set. This larger context can help students more readily understand the courage and confidence that the characters develop with each obstacle they overcome. Reading all four books can help students develop the language necessary to express their ideas about a theme and provide justification for their understanding of it.

Whether an implied theme is primary or secondary, the reader must state it for him- or herself. The first reading of a good story usually reveals one or even a few thematic ideas, both explicit and implicit. More possibilities are discovered, perhaps, on second or third readings. But thematic wealth in a book for children often creates continuous discovery, well into readings of other stories.

Children may know concepts they are unable to express in words.

INQUIRY POINT

Authors who write children's books often place a quote within a story that either explicitly states the theme or suggests an important idea for the reader to internalize. Sometimes writers develop themes in their works based on their own life experiences. *Alchemy and Meggy Swann* by Karen Cushman features a protagonist struggling with mobility just as the author did at the time of the writing. The novel *T4* features a deaf protagonist; the author, Ann Clare LeZotte, is also deaf.

Select and read a children's book such as *Out of My Mind* by Sharon Draper or *Mockingbird*

by Katherine Erskine. Decide on some of the themes (explicit or implicit; primary or secondary) that were important for you. Research the author (or illustrator) or locate an interview or article about him or her. How did the author's life or background influence the story and its themes?

For example, read the short novel *Little Audrey* by Ruth White and note its themes. Read an interview by Ruth White.[2] What aspects of Ruth White's life influenced the book? How did her experience influence the ideas or themes in the story?

Children differ, and the variety of their capacities for discovery, as well as for phrasing that discovery, is almost infinite. We might expect that a younger child would be less likely to state a theme clearly; small children's understanding of abstraction often exceeds their capacity to articulate it. We believe that readers of any age might have this experience when the sophistication of a story is greater than the background of the reader, or when a fresh approach is presented for the first time. Although a reader at a particular point may not be able to define or express a theme, they may understand it perfectly well: Understanding an abstraction often precedes the capacity to express it clearly.

Topic, Theme, or Moral

It may seem unnecessary or even unwise to state theme in sentence form. Why not say, "The theme of *Charlotte's Web* is friendship"? Notice what happens if we do state the theme this simply. *Friendship* is too broad a term. "Friendship is fraudulent" or "friendship is a useless luxury" or "friendship is all giving and no receiving" are all statements concerning friendship that might reasonably be explored in literature, but none is the central insight of E. B. White's story. Forcing ourselves to make a specific statement based on the facts of the story defines the theme more carefully.

Lists of popular themes are readily available: hope, justice, evil, cooperation. But these are in actuality topics or concepts. The theme of a book entails something more, and that "so what" in a book often needs time to emerge. Constructing themes from a good story is not always as easy at may seem. For example, *Lizzie Bright and the Buckminster Boy* by Gary D. Schmidt is a powerful story set in 1912 based on a historical event along the coast of Maine. Possible theme words could be *friendship*, *coming-of-age*, or *coastal environment*. But these concept or topic words could have the effect of missing the ideas the story presents about the injustice in this community's desire for progress. Simply listing these words would not describe the ways Schmidt weaves many subplots together in this complex story, either.

> A theme has a much richer set of connotations than a single topic or concept.

In our view the process of thinking in complicated and nuanced ways about a book's themes can be encouraged. One way to encourage more specific thinking about the theme of a story is to ensure that students write it out as a complete sentence—this helps students express the particularity and nuance of the theme. Another way we recommend is to arrange a group of books around an important topic or subject, such as the civil rights movement of the 1950s and 1960s. Textsets like the one we describe can help readers see ideas or themes that recur throughout many of the books. Many books about the civil rights movement describe the importance of having the courage to speak out against injustice, or the pain and exhilaration of putting yourself in danger in order to right one of society's wrongs; or the complex development of friendships between black and white children. The fact that these themes recur in many stories written about one period can help students see those themes more clearly and with more confidence. Reading a collection of stories with similar concepts, characters, issues, and settings can help a reader make clearer sense of the meanings of one book, and develop a sense of a theme for him- or herself, without an adult telling him or her the theme as if it were a correct answer on a test.

Textsets arranged this way are purposely grouped in a more open-ended fashion to encourage readers to compare books, to pull history from one and an imaginative story from another or an overview from one and an individual's story from another. From a synthesis of two or three stories, a theme or main idea that fits all can be discerned. A more authoritarian approach of assigning possible themes to each book in a set does not allow students' minds to follow curiosities and encourage the kinds of intuitions that promote understanding. A child reading *T4* by Ann Clare LeZotte within the context of other books in a Holocaust textset would have a stronger likelihood of developing a primary theme related to the Holocaust, such as "atrocities

---

INQUIRY POINT

Select a book from among the titles presented here, or choose one of your own. Read the book all the way through, marking places of particular interest to you. When you have finished, make a three-column chart with these headings: Topic/Theme/Moral. Think about single-word topics or concepts that might describe a main idea you see in the book. List these words. Consider the "so what" statement for each topic or concept. Now change the single word or topic into a complete sentence in the middle column.

Think about those ideas as a lesson to be learned, an idea to take with you. Provide information from the story to support your theme. Write this in the third column. Look at the result. What kind of thought processes did you use with each column? Which was easiest to write? How did the process differ for each? Which is most valuable for a reader as they bring their background, the book, and the context together to construct their own interpretation of the story?

Crew, Gary. *The Watertower*. Steven Woolman, Illus. Crocodile Books, 1999.

Hole, Stian. *Garmann's Street*. Eerdmans, 2008.

Hole, Stian. *Garmann's Summer*. Eerdmans, 2006.

Kroll, Virginia L. *Especially Heroes*. Tim Ladwig, Illus. Eerdman's, 2003.

Schotter, Roni. *The Boy Who Loved Words*. Giselle Potter, Illus. Schwartz & Wade, 2006.

Soto, Gary. *The Skirt*. Eric Velasquez, Illus. Delacorte, 1992.

Tan, Shaun. *The Lost Thing: Three by Shaun Tan*. Arthur Levine, 2011.

Winter, Jonah. *Here Comes the Garbage Barge!* Red Nose Studio, Illus. Schwartz & Wade, 2010.

Example: Estes, Eleanor. *The Hundred Dresses*. Louis Slobodkin, Illus. Harcourt, 1944. ◉

TOPIC	THEME	EVIDENCE	MORAL
Gender	Children's behaviors and actions reflect the dominant cultural values that surround them	New immigrant Wanda Petronski is an outcast because of her unfamiliar name, her strange language, and her shabby clothing; this changes to cruel teasing by other girls	Teasing is like bullying; children should treat others the same way they would like to be treated

"Sad but true"
themes are often
only implied.

during the Holocaust brutalized many innocent people." If *T4* were grouped with other books in which major characters were deaf or hearing impaired, the same reader might construct a different theme.

In the same way that equating theme with concept or topic words diffuses and flattens a theme's nuanced meaning, reducing the theme to a moral or lesson promotes the idea that reading is purely for instruction, not for pleasure, that we must learn how or how *not* to behave from what we read. But a good story is not meant to instruct in this way; its value lies in the nondidactic statements of theme.

Didacticism

We often wish to help children by telling them what they ought or ought not do—often in the form of little mottoes or short, preachy verses. From our own past experience we tell them stories that really are instruction disguised as reminiscence. Or we reduce more complex stories to a single message, generally the one we want them to hear. Just as adults do, children tire of this kind of treatment. They yearn for the opportunity to read and think for themselves about the themes within a story. Even if there is a poignant message to be found, the tone should avoid being overly inclined to teach or to take a moralistic stance.

We advocate reading and teaching literature that informs as it focuses on the issues we face in the world without letting a "teacherly" quality of the book take over from a suspenseful and exciting plot or from well-developed characters. Details about a historical period, a geographical area, a social inequity, or a physical disability can be expanded with a rich supporting context so that conflict, character, and theme are not lost in "what the reader ought to know or do." If the information displaces the understanding, then didacticism may be overtaking story. Literature not only teaches; it helps us understand.

Adults who select stories that force a moral on children may think that a story is good only if it contains obvious lessons. However, knowing our own adult dislike for literature that preaches, we can scarcely expect children to enjoy similar preaching. Book selection should encourage a child to make personal discoveries that foster growth. When a book *does* contain a valuable lesson or moral, it should be surrounded with a story that is also rich in plot, character portrayal, and style. Children who come to a story excited by the promise of some pleasure but are provided an experience with the didactic are at risk of not only rejecting a message that has value, but also of choosing not to read important stories, closing off great joys and vast discoveries about society available to them.

Stories with an obvious purpose show little imagination on the part of the writer and awaken little response from the reader; they may even stimulate resistance. A selfish, tit-for-tat approach to friendship that says, "Be nice to your friends and they will be nice to you" would be shallow and unrealistic. This is hardly the story *Charlotte's Web* reveals to readers. Wilbur has no assurances that Templeton can overcome selfishness, and he frequently does not. Throughout this story, the understanding of many kinds of friendship grows.

That ordinary experiences may also be imaginative is one theme of the classic *Harold and the Purple Crayon* and of the more recent story *Not a Box*. But the stories are far more than these messages; they are the wit and imagination with which the messages are presented. The stories should not be reduced to an exhortation for children to "take out their crayons and imagine." Similarly, Bill Thomson's magically surreal artwork in *Chalk* will connect with readers who have had the pleasure to sketch imaginatively on a sidewalk or playground surface more than a message about graffiti.

Young people question and even resist expectations from adults. But stories revealing this reality can do so without a scolding tone or explicit reminders about behavior. Gary Soto's story, *The Skirt,* is about a Mexican American girl in Los Angeles whose family retains their Mexican *folklorica* dance traditions. Miata is preparing her dance for the school recital; she longs for a new skirt for this event. She receives a new and vividly colored skirt to replace her mother's old and now drab one; she proudly (yet secretly) takes it to school but leaves the skirt on the bus. Her adventures in breaking rules to recover it from the bus are the story, but the theme concerns the pride one feels in one's heritage: "Moving to another country does not necessitate leaving all tradition behind."

In the almost surreal illustrations of Anthony Browne's classic *Piggybook*, a reader can see plenty of messages about the selfish and chauvinistic behaviors of the father and sons in a traditional family. Rather than explicitly describing the self-centered actions, Browne reverses the mother's role so the reader can see how expectations of the different genders change. The main ideas of this book could be "everyone can help around the house" or "fathers aren't the only ones who can fix a car," but these themes are revealed in the illustrations, not told.

Contemporary stories often deal with realistic concerns of today's readers. They can show us believable characters; they can explore the problems of today's youth. However, what is true for other literature is true here as well: When we believe in the character, we believe in the experience, and are then prepared to accept the theme. When, however, theme seems to have been the first motive for writing, the stories become didactic. If we look beneath the surface of many realistic stories for young people, we find didacticism and sentimentality. The well-written stories, however, will convince us of the truth of the theme and thus contribute to the reader's growth and discovery. Mature themes can be explored in children's literature; they contribute to understanding when they meet the requirements of excellence.

> When we believe in the character, we believe in the experience and can accept the theme.

Theme and Traditional Literature

Didacticism isn't prized in good fiction, but it is somewhat expected in traditional literature, such as folklore. One of the original functions of folklore was to instruct the audience about acceptable ways of behaving and the consequences of disregarding cultural expectations. In contemporary publications for children, even this genre is seeking ways of moving beyond a single moral to a story from which multiple themes can be constructed.

> Didacticism is the function of textbooks; pleasure and understanding those of literature.

Folklore is a genre in which themes are often explicit. The fable, a particular category of folklore, provides the reader with a statement stronger and more explicitly stated than even an explicit theme—a moral, which tells the reader something about how to live well. Even if the story is far-fetched or humorous, the moral hits the mark.

Collections of the fables by Aesop are an important part of western literary heritage. These brief tales were originally told and later written in many languages. Aesop's fables contain morals that often make abstract, conceptually difficult points, which are not suited for younger children. But variations on the original fables offer features that allow readers of this genre to go beyond a single reading or moral. Consider *The Tortoise and the Hare* and its reminder that "slow and steady wins the race." Janet Stevens creates cartoon–style illustrations to give a humorous touch to her rendition of the well-known *The Tortoise and the Hare*, expanding the possibilities for the circumstances of this famous race. Eric Carle shares his updated version of this fable within a collection of ten other fables: Carle's *The Rabbit and the Turtle* is presented with Carle's trademark collage art; this version uses limited language yet manages to retain the original moral.

Comparing Carle's version of the story with Ranjit Bolt's contemporary English translation of poet Jean La Fontaine's clever rhymes can provide students much to consider. Such a comparison can help students rethink their interpretations of the original "Tortoise and the Hare" fable as well. Ranjit Bolt's collection of updated fables is very upbeat; the informative author's note details the Sanskrit origins of the stories. Giselle Potter's naïve art folk art flattened perspective is childlike, and a good match for the style of the fables. Another version of the fables, by Angela McAllister, reminds the reader that this story has appeal beyond the English-speaking world with its dual Polish and English presentation. Each of these versions holds to the storyline that finds the tortoise surprisingly victorious in the end: Slow and steady wins the race. But Toni Morrison and her son, Slade, provide a twist on the traditional outcome. Their version breaks with the fable formula, and allows the reader to enter into the decision making about the outcome of the race; this provides the old moral with a nuance and complexity that makes it more like a theme than a hard-hitting, simple moral.

Like the conflicts in plots of folktales that so obviously set protagonist against antagonist, the themes in folktales are straightforward and easily seen. Although themes are often implicit, the conflict and the characters make them so evident that explicit statements are unnecessary. Hard work can bring success; intelligence is more valuable than physical strength; kindness brings rewards—these are basic issues that the vigorous action of the folktale makes clear. Their prominence in traditional stories seems to verify the human wish to know not only what happened and how it happened, but also why it happened and what it means. According to critic Wayne Booth, one of the strongest of human interests is the "desire for causal completion." He states, "Not only do we believe that certain causes do in life produce certain effects; in literature we believe that they should." This interest is distinct from the "pleasure of learning, of satisfaction of intellectual curiosity."[3]

> One of the strongest of human interests is "the desire for causal completion."

These short, traditional stories are not designed for complexity, and their certainty may provide comfort. But the expectation of certainty in a changing world also spurs authors and illustrators to alter even the simplest tales. As we have seen in previous chapters, changes in literature sometimes occur through the narrative, but sometimes they are presented in the design of the book and its illustrations. The creators of these new kinds of folktales allow readers space to create themes of their own devise.

> Even simple stories for early readers can have themes.

The story of "The Little Red Hen" is a nice example. The original tale finds the long-suffering hen continually doing the work of others, typically resulting in those who did not help being denied the rewards; other versions find the hen sharing the results of her work anyway. But Alma Flor Ada has created a version where the traditional storyline is complicated by the actions of Goldilocks and Red Riding Hood who, through letter writing, conspire to help Little Red Hen with her tasks. In the communication process, however, two wolves plan to make short work of the Red Hen. The story has the familiar resolution, but the spaces opened in the plot allow readers to construct a new moral.

Jerry Pinkney's version uses his trademark watercolor art to illuminate Red Hen's importance to the story yet realistically depict the remaining farmyard animals. The work ethic and initiative of Red Hen and the natural consequence for those shunning the work remain a part of this story. But Red Hen adds a little flattery to her requests and is rewarded with a pot of jam by the miller. Pinkney also lets the reader know this is an author's version: Red Hen signals the reader into the story, and we see Pinkney pictured as the miller—metafiction in its simplest form.

Fabulist Heather Forest joins with Susan Gaber for an original ending to Red Hen's story. Different from most versions, the twist is that the lazy animals learn their lesson; they are given a chance to redeem themselves. Readers learn that working together makes working fun. The illustrations provide interest as well as an opportunity for readers to think through the ideas they see expressed there.

Traditional literature's morals have been translated in ways that erase the original forms of didacticism, such as their grim endings and violent punishments. Contemporary adaptations frequently soften harsh responses to evil and even reveal the good that certainly must reside in the evil witch or jealous stepmother. In selecting folklore the version of the tale and its cultural origins affect the themes the reader constructs. All writers choose style and tone to influence the statement they are trying to make about life; writers of folklore—whether new versions or old—do the same. Perrault's "Little Red Riding Hood" has been adapted many times, but the version illustrated by Sarah Moon replaces a sense of innocence and gentle caution with a very dark tone and a theme of more imminent danger.

Hans Christian Andersen's nineteenth century literary lore mimics the attributes of the fairy tale, and like the earliest tales he avoids constant optimism and preaching about what people ought to be. He prefers to show what people *are*. Many of his stories of humble people, animals, and inanimate objects demonstrate one of his most personal and optimistic themes, that of the Ugly Duckling: "Humble beginnings and painful trials can end in happiness." But Andersen's themes also frequently remind us that people are foolish; they value the artificial and the trivial more than the real, as "The Nightingale" and "The Princess and the Pea" tell us. People will do anything for vanity, as we see in "The Emperor's New

---

INQUIRY POINT

Look at these versions (or find some of your own) of the popular tale, *Little Red Riding Hood.* How does the style of writing and illustration affect the theme you assign to this story? Express your themes in a sentence and tell how the version affected your view.

Brothers Grimm. *The Story of Little Red Riding Hood.* Christopher Bing, Illus. Chronicle, 2010.

Brothers Grimm. *Little Red Riding Hood.* Daniel Egneus, Illus. Harper Design, 2011.

Hyman, Trina Schart. *Little Red Riding Hood.* Holiday House, 1982.

Perrault, Charles. *Little Red Riding Hood.* Sarah Moon, Illus. Creative Editions, 2002.

Wisnewski, Andrea. *Little Red Riding Hood.* David Godine, 2006.

Stories can clarify where explanations fail; illustrations assist with this.

Clothes." Whether we like it or not, the rogue sometimes wins the prize, as he does in "The Tinder Box." Andersen explores serious themes and develops them into individualized and realistic comments on humankind. His stories show that literature for children as well as for adults can make sad or even negative comments and still give both pleasure and discovery as well as provide material for important themes.[4]

Mature Themes in Children's Stories

As we shared in Chapter 2 and have reinforced throughout this handbook, stories for younger readers have been changing. With today's society more open in its discussion of the many problems confronting our world, contemporary children's books have confronted subjects that were once taboo. Although there are boy-meets-girl romances, novels now explore sexuality and its effects. What has been called the perfect-parent syndrome has been broken, and books for young people can show parents as imperfect, unreliable, even apathetic. Stories carry themes related to death, divorce, incarceration, drugs, and disease. These subjects attract readers because these matters concern today's youth, who expect their books to reflect the themes they see in the world around them.

Topics once taboo are now a part of children's literature; folklore and literary lore can explore these in less threatening ways.

Quality children's literature deals with important issues with sensitivity and skill, writing about the problems that confront the young through good stories that invite the reader to recognize and construct themes that resonate with their lives. Style and characterization show skill and perception, while the themes show universal insights into conflicts past, present, and future. Every genre, including nonfiction, can have theme as an important element.

Christmas in the Big House, Christmas in the Quarters is an illustrated nonfiction book that shows life on a pre–Civil War plantation in the South. The compare/contrast format would naturally inspire theme statements such as, "Life was bleak in the quarters compared to the big house." But a response to the final scenes' ironic foreshadowing when the master tells his young daughter that she'll be old enough to have her own slave in 1865 might provoke a statement that "Parents are important to the values of their children." Nonfiction is not value-free.

Graham Salisbury addresses issues of integrity in his highly suspenseful *Lord of the Deep*. Mikey's soon-to-be stepfather Bill is the captain of a deep-sea charter boat, and it has been a slow season. Two demanding passengers are willing to spend any amount of money and ignore regulations to bring in a fish of prize-winning size. According to the rules, the catch must have been played and landed, start to finish, by the fisherman who claims victory. But Captain Bill helped and knows that Ernie does not qualify. Bill's reputation for honesty is at stake, and twice he refuses to attest to Ernie and Cal's claim. The two men offer Mikey a bribe to keep silent, and Bill a triple fee and a promise to throw more business his way. To Mikey's disappointment, Bill finally agrees to the deal. Mikey's rejection of him does not change Bill's troubling decision. Bill takes time to explain, in an effort to bridge the breach of trust: "'Believe it or not, Mikey, I was thirteen years old myself once. I believed something was either right or it was wrong, and there was no in-between.' Bill paused, then looked down and said, 'Well, there is an in-between, Mikey.'" The theme of a trusted adult modeling the gray areas of situational ethics is unusual for children's literature, but a child vocalizing a theme that "it's okay to lie when it suits our needs" might be even more questionable.

Problems of growing up can be explored with skill and sensitivity.

True Believer, by Virginia Euwer Wolff, is concerned with another significant issue: "What should I believe?" LaVaughn is entering high school with goals to go to college and escape the urban setting and a lifestyle she has come to reject. LaVaughn ignores the boys, studies hard, makes new friends, and discovers that with the support of her teachers and her mother she can attend college. But the path to reaching her goal is filled with difficult choices. She must find the strength to stand up to the religious intolerance of her two best friends, who have joined the Cross Your Legs for Jesus Club as a way to avoid getting pregnant. Her childhood friend has returned to the projects, but he is attracted to another boy. Her mother, though supportive of her goal to attend college, is distracted by her own struggles with work and a new boyfriend. LaVaughn gradually becomes part of a new and accepting group. She discovers how to make religion a part of her life. "Religion must be for trusting. And trusting, what is that for? I figured it out: It helps you go on when you can't go on." Religion has been a part of children's books for some time, but stories where a young protagonist grapples openly with faith are more recent.

Complex and important ideas may appear in stories for the young.

Shabanu by Suzanne Fisher Staples is a coming-of-age story of a twelve-year-old girl living a nomadic life in the desert of Cholistan, Pakistan. Shabanu's close-knit family successfully raises fine camels in the desert extremes, carrying on cultural traditions dictating that, at the age of thirteen, a girl must leave her home and move to the home of her husband. Shabanu and her older sister are fortunate to have their marriages arranged with brothers from a good family because their father has accumulated, through hard work, sufficient wealth for a dowry. Carefully breeding camels for their strength and ability to dance, the family works together, following the cycle of moisture from their desert water hole and into the village to survive. Safety is never guaranteed for women in Shabanu's world, and an incident of attempted rape by a powerful landowner changes her fortunes forever. We follow the growth of her pet, an orphaned camel, and realize the animal's adjustment to a new life parallels Shabanu's as she accepts the necessity of marrying the powerful landowner's brother in order to save her family. As with most stories where new experiences are portrayed, this story offers opportunities for multiple themes, such as "Childhood lasts much longer in our culture"; "males have a great deal of power over women"; or "life in the Pakistani desert is harsh."

Similar themes seem to surface across cultures or specific historical events.

A book focusing on contemporary issues and cultural concerns has a good chance of eliciting thoughtful themes, but mature topics and multicultural influences do not guarantee a book will serve as a source for rich and important themes. As with all good literature, the combination of literary elements and genre or format criteria determines the overall quality of the book. A quality book's intersection with the background of the reader and their context affect which themes will be identified and how they will be articulated. In addition, themes are more likely to evolve and be internalized when a reader finds their initial views confirmed or even contradicted through additional reading experiences. At any point in the process of articulating a theme, readers should be able to return to the text and support their theme.

How readers express theme varies.

TEXTSET

Themes in Picturebooks

Although two readers may experience the same theme, the words they use to state it may be somewhat different. In the picturebook format, the reader considers the illustrations as well as the design of the book when determining how to express what the theme of the book is for them. That is, the style of the illustrations and the way they work with the text will influence the meaning of the book. For this reason, readers should be expected to include evidence from the illustrations. Many readers unfamiliar with the complexity of the picturebook format take their impact for granted unless they are guided by a more experienced reader to articulate their influence—in this case their role in the theme of the book. Readers of all ages are finding the picturebook format important for discovering and appreciating literary elements and how they work in literature.

The sets are best appreciated if you consider the general theme statement we have provided for each cluster of books. They are organized this way not to predetermine or provide a theme for the reader. Rather, they are a loosely organized for the purposes of an adult learner's exploration. Imagine the role of the text and the pictures in the way you articulate the theme.

Artistic Imagination and Creativity Are Important in Children's Lives

Browne, Anthony. *The Shape Game*. Farrar, Straus and Giroux, 2003.

Catalanotto, Peter. *Emily's Art*. Atheneum, 2001.

Reynolds, Peter H. *The Dot*. Candlewick Press, 2003.

Reynolds, Peter H. *Ish*. Candlewick Press, 2004.

Say, Allen. *The Sign Painter*. Houghton Mifflin, 2000.

Shulevitz, Uri. *How I Learned Geography*. Farrar, Straus and Giroux, 2008.

Thomson, Bill. *Chalk*. Marshall Cavendish, 2010.

Wiesner, David. *Art & Max*. Clarion, 2010.

Winter, Jonah. *Frida*. Ana Juan, Illus. Arthur A. Levine, 2002.

People Bring Changes to Neighborhoods

Baker, Jeannie. *Home*. Greenwillow Books, 2004.

Baker, Jeannie. *Window*. Greenwillow Books, 1991.

Burton, Virginia. *The Little House*. Houghton Mifflin, 1942.

Lewis, J. Patrick. *The House*. Creative Editions, 2009.

Muller, Jorg. *The Changing Countryside*. Heryin Books, 2006.

Stewart, Sarah. *The Gardener*. David Small, Illus. Farrar, Straus and Giroux, 1997.

Imagination Makes Fanciful Things Become Magically Real

Burningham, John. *It's a Secret*. Candlewick Press, 2009.

Lee, Suzy. *Mirror*. Seven Footer Kids, 2010.

Lehman, Barbara. *Museum Trip*. Houghton Mifflin, 2006.

Lehman, Barbara. *Rainstorm*. Houghton Mifflin, 2007.

McLerran, Alice. *Roxaboxen*. Barbara Cooney, Illus. HarperCollins, 1991.

Thomson, Sarah L. *Imagine a Day*. Rob Gonsalves, Illus. Atheneum, 2005.

Thomson, Sarah L. *Imagine a Place*. Rob Gonsalves, Illus. Atheneum, 2008.

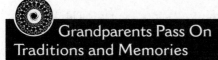 Grandparents Pass On Traditions and Memories

Bahr, Mary. *The Memory Box*. Albert Whitman, 1992.

DiSalvo-Ryan, DyAnne. *Grandpa's Corner Store*. HarperCollins, 2000.

Erdrich, Louise. *Grandmother's Pigeon*. Hyperion, 1996.

Fox, Mem. *Wilfrid Gordon McDonald Partridge*. Kane/Miller, 1985.

Fraustino, Lisa. *The Hickory Chair*. Benny Andrews, Illus. Arthur E. Levine, 2001.

Hamanaka, Sheila. *Grandparents Song*. HarperCollins, 2003.

Howe, James. *Kaddish for Grandpa in Jesus' Name Amen*. Catherine Stock, Illus. Atheneum, 2004.

Lindbergh, Reeve. *My Hippie Grandmother*. Candlewick Press, 2003.

SUMMARY

Theme, whether stated explicitly or implicitly, is essential to a children's story if it is to merit the name of literature. A narrative with action and characters, but without theme, is a story without meaning that leaves the reader wondering at the end: "So what?" A piece of literature for children—that collection of words with plot, character, setting, style and tone, and frequently illustration—carries the same expectations for quality as it does for adults. The theme we take to become part of ourselves is the one that enlarges our understanding and the one we ourselves discover, not the one delivered didactically by the author or a teacher, librarian, or parent who has selected a book for a child.

NOTES

1. Social historian Stephanie Coontz comments on such themes in *The Way We Never Were: American Families and the Nostalgia Trip* (New York: Basic Books, 1992).
2. A brief but thoughtful interview by Ruth White related to her work and its connection with conditions in coal mining communities in Appalachia is Jane Stimmen, "An Interview with Author Ruth White, Author of *Little Audrey*," March 6, 2009, retrieved from www.wsws.org/articles/2009/mar2009/whit-m06.shtml.
3. Wayne Booth, *The Rhetoric of Fiction*, p. 126 (Chicago: University of Chicago Press, 1961). The satisfaction of knowing causality in children's literature is most obviously demonstrated in cumulative tales like the humorous "Old Woman and the Pig" or the verse story "This Is the House That Jack Built."
4. Jack Zipes, in *Fairy Tales and the Art of Subversion* (London: Heineman Educational Books, 1983), discusses the tales of Grimm and Andersen. The former shows girls and women their subordinate roles; the latter, though commonly thought to show a triumph over misfortune by the poor and lowly, actually admires the hierarchy.

RECOMMENDED BOOKS

ADA, ALMA FLOR. *With Love, Little Red Hen*. Atheneum, 2004.

ALCOTT, LOUISA MAY. *Little Women*. 1868–1869. Reprint. Dutton, 1948.

ALMOND, DAVID. *Skellig*. Delacorte, 2009.

ANDERSEN, HANS CHRISTIAN. *The Twelve Dancing Princesses*. Edited by Alfred David and Mary Elizabeth Meek. Indiana University Press, 1974.

BABBITT, NATALIE. *Tuck Everlasting*. Farrar, Straus and Giroux, 1975.

BOLT, RANJIT. *The Hare and the Tortoise: and Other Fables of La Fontaine*. Illustrated by Giselle Potter. Barefoot Books, 2006.

BROTHERS GRIMM. *Little Red Riding Hood*. Illustrated by Daniel Egneus. Harper Design, 2011.

BROTHERS GRIMM. *The Story of Little Red Riding Hood*. Illustrated by Christopher Bing. Chronicle, 2010.

BROWNE, ANTHONY. *Piggybook*. Dragonfly, 1990.

CARLE, ERIC. *The Rabbit and the Turtle*. Orchard Books, 2008.

CREW, GARY. *The Watertower*. Illustrated by Steven Woolman. Crocodile Books, 1999.

CURTIS, CHRISTOPHER PAUL. *The Watsons Go to Birmingham—1963*. Perfection, 1997.

CUSHMAN, KAREN. *Alchemy and Meggy Swann*. Clarion, 2010.

CUSHMAN, KAREN. *Catherine, Called Birdy*. Perfection, 1995.

CUSHMAN, KAREN. *Matilda Bone*. Clarion, 2000.

CUSHMAN, KAREN. *The Midwife's Apprentice*. Clarion, 1995.

ESTES, ELEANOR. *The Hundred Dresses*. Illustrated by Louis Slobodkin. Harcourt, 1944.

FOREST, HEATHER. *The Little Red Hen: An Old Fable*. Illustrated by Susan Gaber. August House, 2006.

HAMILTON, VIRGINIA. *Cousins*. Putnam, 1990.

HESSE, KAREN. *Witness*. Perfection Learning, 2003.

HOOKS, WILLIAM H. *Circle of Fire*. Macmillan, 1982.

HURWITZ, JOHANNA. *Class President*. Morrow, 1990.

HYMAN, TRINA SCHART. *Little Red Riding Hood*. Holiday House, 1982.

JOHNSON, CROCKETT. *Harold and the Purple Crayon*. HarperCollins, 1998.

KROLL, VIRGINIA L. *Especially Heroes*. Illustrated by Tim Ladwig. Eerdman's, 2003.

LEZOTTE, ANN CLARE. *T4: A Novel*. Houghton Mifflin, 2008.

MACLACHLAN, PATRICIA. *Journey*. Doubleday, 1991.

McALLISTER, ANGELA. *La Lievre it la Tortue/The Tortoise and the Hare: Une fable d'Esope/An Aesop's Fable*. Illustrated by Jonathan Heale. Frances Lincoln Children's Books, 2010.

McKISSACK, PATRICIA C., AND FREDRICK L. McKISSACK. *Christmas in the Big House, Christmas in the Quarters*. Illustrated by John Thompson. Frontline, 1994.

MORRISON, TONI, AND SLADE MORRISON. *The Tortoise or the Hare*. Illustrated by Joe Cepeda. Simon and Schuster, 2010.

PERRAULT, CHARLES. *Little Red Riding Hood*. Sarah Moon. Creative Editions, 2002.

PINKNEY, JERRY. *The Little Red Hen*. Dial Books, 2006.

PORTIS, ANTOINETTE. *Not a Box*. HarperFestival, 2011.

SALISBURY, GRAHAM. *Lord of the Deep*. Delacorte, 2001.

SCHMIDT, GARY D. *Lizzie Bright and the Buckminster Boy*. Clarion, 2004.

SOTO, GARY. *The Skirt*. Illustrated by Eric Velasquez. Delacorte, 1992.

STAPLES, SUZANNE FISHER. *Shabanu*. Knopf, 1989.

STAUFFACHER, SUE. *Bessie Smith and the Night Riders*. Illustrated by John Holyfield. Putnam, 2006.

STEVENS, JANET. *The Tortoise and the Hare*. Holiday House, 1984.

TAYLOR, MILDRED. *Roll of Thunder, Hear My Cry*. Dial, 1976.

THOMSON, BILL. *Chalk*. Marshall Cavendish, 2010.

WHITE, E. B. *Charlotte's Web*. Harper, 1952.

WHITE, RUTH. *Belle Prater's Boy*. Threshold Books, 1996.

WHITE, RUTH. *Little Audrey*. Farrar, Straus and Giroux, 2010.

WISNEWSKI, ANDREA. *Little Red Riding Hood*. Illustrated by David Godine. 2006.

WOLFF, VIRGINIA EUWER. *True Believer*. Atheneum, 2001.

WOODSON, JACQUELINE. *Feathers*. Putnam, 2007.

WOODSON, JACQUELINE. *Miracle's Boys*. Putnam, 2004.

MyEducationKit™

Go to the topic "Traditional Literature" on the MyEducationKit for this text, where you can:

- Search the Children's Literature Database, housing more than 22,000 titles searchable in every genre by authors or illustrators, by awards won, by year published, and by topic and description.
- Explore genre-related Assignments and Activities, assignable exercises showing concepts in action through database use, video, cases, and student and teacher artifacts.
- Listen to podcasts and read interviews from some of the brightest and most enduring stars of children's literature in the Conversations.
- Discover web links that will lead you to sites representing the authors you learn about in these pages, classrooms with powerful children's literature connections, and literature awards.

This Is Just to Say: Poems of Apology and Forgiveness

Joyce Sidman / Illustrated by Pamela Zagarenski

Contemporary poets for children explore themes that appeal to contemporary readers, motivating them to explore this genre. Illustrators can play an important role with poetry's appeal.

CHAPTER ELEVEN

From Rhyme to Poetry

Children naturally respond to the rhythms and rhymes of verse, but some never move on to poetry. Are these children missing anything you can describe?

Many people are nervous around **poetry**. They believe that it can't be understood without special knowledge or written without an Ivy League degree. At the beginning of *Love That Dog* by Sharon Creech, Jack, the young narrator, has a distaste for and confusion about poetry with which many readers will identify. Jack believes that only girls, not boys, write poetry. He tells his teacher Miss Stretchberry that he can't write a poem because there is nothing in his brain. Over the course of the short novel in verse, readers listen to Jack's side of the conversation as he talks to his teacher, complaining, asking questions, practicing, and finally imitating the poets whose work Miss Stretchberry introduces to him. *Love That Dog* is an example of the principle of intertextuality at work. Creech weaves into her novel about a young boy gaining voice the work of excellent poets—William Carlos Williams, Robert Frost, William Blake, Valerie Worth, Arnold Adoff, S. C. Rigg, and, most importantly, Walter Dean Myers. The novel shows—among many other things—how writers old and new build on the work of those who came before them. Jack, a boy who loves his dog, learns to articulate that love through poetry with the help of his teacher and immersion in the works of great poets.

Kenneth Koch's *Rose, Where Did You Get That Red?*, shares ways children learn how to write poetry using the experiences Koch had when he taught in an

INQUIRY POINT

Just as Jack did, try your hand at writing your own version of one of the poems from a book of poems for children. For example:

A set of poems written by children or youth:

Pauline Johnson Public School. *Hatching Hope: Poems Written in Gold by the Elementary Students of Pauline Johnson Public School.* Book in a Day, 2011.

A book of poems that work with the concept of varied perspectives:

Janeczko, Paul B. *Dirty Laundry Pile: Poems in Different Voices.* Melissa Sweet, Illus. HarperCollins, 2001.

Rex, Adam. *Frankenstein Makes a Sandwich.* Harcourt, 2006.

Zimmer, Tracie Vaughn. *Cousins of Clouds: Elephant Poems.* Megan Halsey and Sean Addy, Illus. Clarion, 2011.

A set of poems using a special format, such as list poetry or reversible verse:

Heard, Georgia, ed. *Falling Down the Page,* Roaring Book Press, 2009.

Singer, Marilyn. *Mirror, Mirror: A Book of Reversible Verse.* Josee Massee, Illus. Dutton, 2010.

elementary school in New York City. Koch had students imitate poems written by the greatest writers of poetry, as Miss Stretchberry has Jack do in *Love That Dog.*

Jack learns to read and write poems as he decides that anyone can be a poet, as long as they write lines that are short. He overstates the simplicity of the writing of poetry, of course. Still, the poetry children come to first tends to be simple, like the poems Jack learns from and eventually writes—short, strong in rhythm, and creating clear pictures in words, almost like songs. Some children first learn about something like poetry when a parent or teacher at the daycare center flips through the bright pink-and-orange pages of Bill Martin's *Chicka Chicka Boom Boom* and other children chant the unstoppable rhymes. Bill Martin's rhymes are not poetry, of course; not everything that rhymes is poetry, in the same way that not all poems need to rhyme. Yet the rhythms of a chant like "chicka chicka boom boom" introduce children to some of the sound-and-sense play that they will come to associate with poetry. Other children first hear poetry in Mother Goose rhymes, or some of the many modern variations on Mother Goose rhymes. Because nursery rhymes use the elements of literature and the devices of style, and because the rhymes are sources of pleasure, they can legitimately be called the earliest literature for the youngest child. These **rhymes** are brief stories that have been passed orally from generation to generation, and are the beginning of poetry for many children.

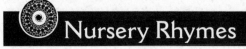 Nursery Rhymes

Nursery rhymes are some of the most economic narratives. "Sing a song of sixpence, a pocketful of rye" tells a complete tale in three short verses. "Three wise men of Gotham" could hardly be more condensed:

Three wise men of Gotham
Went to sea in a bowl.
If the bowl had been stronger,
My story had been longer.

Nursery rhymes are good for small children, who have short attention spans. They provide children with an introduction to the concept of rhyme.

Nursery rhymes introduce children to rhyme.

Literary Elements

Many Mother Goose or nursery rhymes are brief stories. The characters are the Queen of Hearts who made some tarts, the old woman tossed up in a basket, and Old Mother Hubbard whose cupboard is bare. Setting, too, is quickly sketched in some rhymes—the Old Woman lives in a shoe and Peter Pumpkin Eater's wife lives in a pumpkin shell. The rhymes have simple plots: The crooked man uses his crooked sixpence to buy a crooked cat that "caught a crooked mouse/And they all lived together in a little crooked house" for a satisfying closed ending. Action in these stories varies from the simplest of tumbles taken by Humpty Dumpty to the more complex involvements of "The House That Jack Built" and "Who Killed Cock Robin?"

Ideas also occur in Mother Goose rhymes. Some of the rhymes are surprisingly clear in their insights, and oftentimes the short verse-stories have slight themes. In a modern-day Mother Goose—Clyde and Wendy Watson's collection of rhymes, *Catch Me and Kiss Me and Say It Again*—a mother teaches her child about a thunderstorm. In the Watsons' brief rhyme, a reader can see one theme, which is that although nature can be frightening, it can also be beautiful and exciting.

Rhymes increase a child's understanding in other ways as well. Curiosity about the world is roused when the commonplace is made exciting. The trip to the gas station is no longer ordinary when the driver chants a new tongue-twisting rhyme (from, for example, *Orangatan Tongs* by Jon Agee) about how the car is climbing a steep hill to buy some cheap gas. Nursery rhyme books like Alma Flor Ada and F. Isabel Campoy's *¡Muu, Moo!*, a collection of rhymes with the original Spanish on one page and the English translation on the next, provide children with the expansive sense that their world is known by other children who speak a different language. They learn that those children have fanciful relationships with the creatures—cicada, owls, ducks—that they themselves see every day.

Style

Thinking, speaking, and talking in rhythm is one of our oldest tendencies, and the rhythm in rhymes may correspond to this heartbeat within us. Rhythm is an aspect of the writer's style, and it is a way into poetry:

Hickory, dickory, dock.
The mouse ran up the clock.
The clock struck one,
And down he run,
Hickory, dickory, dock.

Children clap their hands to "The Farmer in the Dell" and swing their arms to "London Bridge." Rhythm, which is determined by patterns of accented and unaccented syllables and by long or short vowels, moves the lines quickly.

The variety of **sound effects** in nursery rhymes, although simple, acquaints children with poetic devices that give pleasure and make rhymes memorable. Assonance, the sound created when a vowel sound is repeated but consonant sounds are changed, can be heard in the off-rhyme of the repeated *i* sound in "Twinkle twinkle little star" or in the old song about the mulberry bush: "a penny for a spool of thread, a penny for a needle/that's the way the money goes, pop goes the weasel." Consonance is easy to find in these old rhymes, too. Consonance is in some ways the opposite of assonance: It provides a repetition of a consonant as the vowel changes. Examples include the nursery rhyme "a tisket, a tasket, a green and yellow basket," the description of "a misty moisty morning," and the tongue twister "Betty Botter bought some butter, but, she said, the batter's bitter!" These last examples have alliteration, too, the repetition of consonants at the beginning of a word, as do "Daffy-down-dilly," and "Baa, baa black sheep." Children can learn about onomatopoeia—though they don't need to learn that big word—when they memorize "Hark, hark, the dogs do bark!" and "Bow-wow-wow, whose dog art thou?" And of course **end rhyme** in nursery rhymes is always pleasing, confirming that all is right with the world:

> Little Boy Blue, come blow your horn!
> The sheep's in the meadow, the cow's in the corn.
> Where's the boy who looks after the sheep?
> Under the haystack fast asleep!

Figurative language is another stylistic trait of Mother Goose rhymes. Dishes, which run off with spoons, are given human qualities—personified—as are a "robin and a robin's son/who went to town to buy a bun." Jack Sprat and his wife figuratively—or literally if we prefer—"lick the platter clean." "Twinkle, twinkle, little star" introduces children to similes when it tells them that a star is "like a diamond in the sky."

As for **tone**, humor is prevalent in nursery rhymes.

> Barber, barber, shave a pig.
> How many hairs will make a wig?
> Four and twenty, that's enough.
> Give the barber a pinch of snuff.

Verbal **irony** can be found in:

> A diller, a dollar,
> A ten o'clock scholar,
> What makes you come so soon?
> You used to come at ten o'clock,
> And now you come at noon.

In addition to the rhymes we commonly call Mother Goose, children are made ready for poetry by jumping rope and patty-cake rhymes, like the one with the refrain:

> Here comes the doctor,
>   Here comes the nurse,

Here comes the lady
    With the alligator purse.

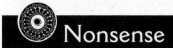 # Nonsense

Nonsense takes a cue from nursery rhymes and plays on our pleasure in the illogical and the incongruous, our enjoyment of words cleverly used or misused, on some secret yearning to see the immutable laws of nature overturned. The best nonsense can do all these things. In his 1894 introduction to Edward Lear's *Nonsense Omnibus*, Edward Strachey wrote that nonsense is not "a mere putting forward of incongruities and absurdities, but the bringing out of a new and deeper harmony of life in and through its contradictions."

One example of such nonsense can be seen in Gerda Rovetch's poems, which are about absurd characters—sardines who wear jeans, men who chew the lizards in their shoes, and others who love lima beans, carried carefully in little velvet bags.

Children—and most adults, too!—love this kind of silliness. Children make up and invert words or make illogical comparisons; one child tells another "It's cold as a bumblebee out!" and both children roll on the floor, laughing. They repeat nonsense words in series, just for the pleasure of tasting and hearing their sounds: "Eenie-beenie-pepsi-deenie." Nonsense relies on rhythm, sound patterns, figurativeness, compactness, and emotional intensity—the intensity of laughter that may be repeated, stored in the memory, then shared again and again.

Rhythm and Sound

The **limerick** form, first popularized by Edward Lear in the nineteenth century, is the most traditionally structured nonsense verse. It clearly shows how important rhythm and sound are to such verse:

    There was an old lady named Crockett
    Who put a new plug in a socket
        But her hands were so wet
        She flew up like a jet
    And came roaring back down like a rocket.

Suitable to the tone, the rhythm is quick, with the syllables more frequently unaccented than accented. The sounds are short, which suggests a happy, quick mood.

Compactness and Surprise

Much of the humor in nonsense verse comes from the surprise of names, events, or words. Shel Silverstein's poetry, for example, is tightly put together with surprising rhymes. Silverstein often chooses unusual settings for his verse. In one poem the narrator speaks from the inside of a lion; in another he's being swallowed by a boa constrictor. Though teachers will want to encourage students to move toward more sophisticated types of poetry, Shel Silverstein's silly, simple, and delightful verse is certainly a way to entice children, and to help them see that poetry is not just dreary, serious, moony stuff.

Another place to look for compact and surprising rhymes is in the work of Jack Prelutsky, children's poet laureate. He and the great children's artist Paul O. Zelinsky have created a book about the travails of an ogre:

Awful Ogre Speaks of Toast
My toaster's out of order
But I'm no knucklehead . . .
Until it's properly repaired
A dragon toasts my bread.

The funny-sounding word "knucklehead" is part of what gives the poem its humor—in addition, of course, to the idea of an ogre having such a mundane problem. The surprise is the dragon.

Lewis Carroll wrote some of the most compact and intense nonsense, so witty that not a word is wasted, not a sound out of place. "The Jabberwocky," a mysterious tale of valor from *Through the Looking-Glass*, uses made-up words in such familiar syntactical positions that we can almost understand what the words mean. Indeed, some of the words Carroll made up, like "galumphing," are used by other writers today. Along with Prelutsky and Carroll, Ogden Nash is a poet to introduce children to. His nonsense combines silly rhythms and made-up words. Children might be encouraged to imitate Nash's silly language when they write their own nonsense poems.

Children might be encouraged to write nonsense poems.

 Poetry

So we see that poetry need not be serious. In *Love That Dog*, Jack learned something like that, too—that while his own and other people's poetry can address serious, sad subjects, it can be playful, too, as well as enjoyable to write. In *Love That Dog*, Jack is in elementary school. If readers were to see him move into junior high and high school, they would see him learn about other aspects of poetry as well. He might learn some of the things we discuss below.

Prose and Poetry

Poetry is not all that different from prose—both usually use complete sentences, as well as rhythm and metaphor. The cadences of rhythm are perhaps more marked in poetry and sound patterns such as alliteration and onomatopoeia exist in poetry to a greater degree than they do in prose. Connotative meaning in prose acquires heightened significance in poetry. Figurative language that compares unlike things exists in prose, but occurs more frequently in poetry. But what is it that makes readers feel that the two forms are totally different from each other?

The main difference is this: Poetry is much more compact than prose is. A single word in poetry says far more than a single word in prose; the connotations and images hint at, imply, and suggest other meanings. A poet distills meaning in

Poetry is much more compact than prose is.

brief and vivid images. A poet suggests in three words what a prose writer explains in ten.

The characteristics of poetry that set it apart from prose are essentially rhythm, sound patterns, figurativeness, compactness, and emotional intensity. Compactness is to a large extent the result of effective use of the first three characteristics to produce compressed expression in words. This compactness results in emotional intensity.

Readers can probably guess what we will say the difference between poetry for children and poetry for adults is: not much. Poetry for children tends to be about the things children do and think about each day, which is a little different from what adults do and think about each day. There are children's poems about school, fairy tales, teeth, parents, mud, boa constrictors, bridges, rain, and chocolate milk. Poems for adults are more likely to be about work, fairy tales, teeth, children, mud, bridges, rain, and chocolate milk. Poetry that adults read may use more complicated syntax and bigger words than poetry for children does, but the standards for poetry for both adults and children should be high.

Many have tried to define poetry, and most have failed. Robert Frost famously said that poetry is "what gets lost in translation."[1] Another poet said that "the poet is the professor of the five bodily senses."[2] In her essay asking whether poetry written exclusively for children can be called real poetry (answer: it can), children's literature critic Glenna Sloan "risks" a definition of poetry, and hers is the one we like best: "While there are many aspects of poetry, many givens—such as rhythm, musicality of sound, and the like—a true poem, whatever its form, ought to express a keen, an incisive insight, one that is fresh and memorable, astonishing the reader with its rightness."[3] We think Glenna Sloan would agree with others that a good poem is concrete, not abstract. A good poem is full of *things*—sharp, specific images—bread, violet, sunlight, skin, lima beans, thunderstorms, ogres, toasters. And like every other piece of reading material, a poem is constructed, built, made. A poet has an idea, or, more likely, sees or remembers an image. Then she writes a few lines, crosses out words, rewrites, grows frustrated, pulls down and reads the work of a poet she loves, goes back to the desk, writes some more, changes some words, crosses out, rewrites, and reads her draft aloud. A poet is a *maker*, and a good poem is made so that every word counts.

Verse and Poetry

Verse is not quite the same as poetry, distinguished mainly by its lower level of intensity. (It is a little confusing: We say a poem has *verses*, meaning stanzas. Those verses are not the same as the kind of verse we describe here.) We want to say here that verse has its place, but it is not poetry, which is, by one definition, the most imaginative and intense perceptions humans can express about themselves, others, and their relationships to the world. Verse tends to emphasize strong rhythm over sharpness of language. T. S. Eliot, for example, describes poetry by contrasting it to verse. He says that while feeling and imaginative power are found in real poetry, verse is merely a matter of structure, formal metrical order, and rhyme pattern. Its structure, furthermore, may seem more important than its meaning. Proverbial wisdom occurs in verses like "A stitch in time / saves nine." The purpose of other verses is to sell diet drinks and chewing gum; still others convey traditional sentiments: "Just stopping by / with a friendly hi!" We know what greeting card verse is, and, perhaps without knowing why, have a feeling that it is not quite poetry. Some

According to T. S. Eliot, the structure of verse often seems more important than its meaning.

of such verse is humorous, some sentimental, and some so incongruous that it may provoke a condescending smile: "To love a father is no fad/When he's a father like my dad." Verse is not poetry as T. S. Eliot has described it—the distilled and imaginative expression of feeling.

We have a tendency to see the name of a poet, like Robert Frost or John Ciardi, and assume that everything that person writes is fine poetry. That is not the case. Both Frost and Ciardi, as well as many, many other poets, have written both great poems for adults and lighter verse mainly for children. Ciardi's *The Man Who Sang the Sillies* is one such case—a book of fine and silly verse that is clever and fun for children to read but that no one, not even Ciardi himself, would call poetry. Robert Louis Stevenson's *A Child's Garden of Verses* and A. A. Milne's *When We Were Very Young* are also examples of fine verse for children. The division may sometimes be difficult to distinguish, but the difference between verse and poetry lies in intensification of feeling and in distillation of language, not in regular end rhymes and predictable figures of speech.

Large quantities of both verse and poetry are available to children. With exposure, children grow in awareness of the pleasure that artful poetry can bring. Greater experience with imaginative poetry can lead children to an awareness and appreciation of Walter de la Mare's "rarest of the best." But children enjoy verse as well; each has its place.

Kinds of Poetry

There are many different kinds of poetry, but a simple way of classifying most of those forms is to say that there are only two kinds: **narrative poetry,** which is situational or storytelling poetry; and **lyric poetry,** or song poetry. One of the most well-known examples of narrative poems is Henry Wadsworth Longfellow's "The Midnight Ride of Paul Revere," which children should hear at some point in their schooling lives, because it is so deeply ingrained in our culture.

Narrative poems for children can be of any length; surprisingly, even in eight short lines, a story comes alive. In "New Friends Talking," Kristine O'Connell George captures the experience of finding a new friend.

> Talking all the way, we're suddenly at my house.
> We're not done, so much more to talk about,
> so we turn around, keep on walking and talking
> all the way back to Kori's house, but we're *still* not
> finished, so we walk around the park (twice), then we
> keep walking and talking halfway back to my house.
>
> Then
>
> > We run straight home
> > To phone.

One type of narrative, the **ballad**, started as part of traditional or folk literature. Other ballads are of known authorship; both may show supernatural intervention, themes of physical courage and love, and incidents common to ordinary people. Ernest Thayer's 1888 poem, "Casey at the Bat," is an example of a ballad that has been made into numerous fine picturebooks, such as Caldecott Award–winner Christopher Bing's fake scrapbook complete with tickets to the game, postcards, and advertisements and clippings from the Mudville Monitor; one with textured, cartoonlike illustrations by C. F. Payne decorating each scene of the old ballad; and Dan Gutman's *Casey Back at Bat*, with its modern update of the poem. All present the poem as it originally flowed, with songlike cadence and the rousing story of a hero.

Some other fine ballads that have been passed through time are those by the poet of the Yukon, Robert Service. These may not be categorized as poetry, exactly, but they tell exciting stories in strong rhythm that boys, especially, may enjoy.

> A bunch of the boys were whooping it up in the Malamute saloon;
> The kid that handles the music-box was hitting a jag-time tune;
> Back of the bar, in a solo game, sat Dangerous Dan McGrew,
> And watching his luck was his light-o'-love, the lady that's known as Lou.
>
> When out of the night, which was fifty below, and into the din and the glare,
> There stumbled a miner fresh from the creeks, dog-dirty, and loaded for bear.
> He looked like a man with a foot in the grave and scarcely the strength
>   of a louse,
> Yet he tilted a poke of dust on the bar, and he called for drinks for the house.
> There was none could place the stranger's face, though we searched ourselves
>   for a clue;
> But we drank his health, and the last to drink was Dangerous Dan McGrew.

One of Services's other rollicking ballads, *The Cremation of Sam McGee*, has been made into a vibrant picturebook with paintings by Ted Harrison.

The other major type of poem is the lyric, a songlike poem that uses sounds, rhythms, and figurative devices to express emotional response to some brief moment of experience, as does Carl Sandburg's familiar "Fog." The classic "Morning has Broken" by Eleanor Farjeon is likely more recognizable in its musical version than the picturebook format so beautifully illustrated by Tim Ladwig. Gordon Titcomb's *The Last Train*, illustrated by Wendell Minor, provides sentimental lyrics that paint a nostalgic account of the role steam locomotives played in the growth of the United States. The Pulitzer-Prize winning Mary Oliver is one of the great lyric poets of our time, and there's no reason to keep her tender nature poems from children; read "The Summer Day" to your class in June.

Many of Langston Hughes' poems are lyrics, and *Poetry for Young People: Langston Hughes,* provides children with an excellent introduction to this writer. Pair the book with *The Block*, published by the Metropolitan Museum of Art, which places 12 of Hughes' poems next to the jazzy, multi-layered artwork of Romare Bearden, and then add the biography–in–poems *Love to Langston* by Tony Medina for a nuanced sense of the life and work of this powerful poet.

Poetry provides a rich source of songs and reading or listening experiences for all ages. Learn to enjoy all kinds of poems, and then share that pleasure.

Rhythm

Look now at the characteristics of poetry, several of which will be known to young children who have become acquainted with rhymes and nonsense. Rhythm, one of the more important characteristics of poetry, can be considered the recurrence of stressed beats in language. In prose, rhythm is described by the word *cadence,* but when rhythm is set into a more regular pattern as it is in verse or poetry, it is called **meter**. The writer uses rhythm to enhance the feeling that his or her words express. In choosing the rhythm for a poem, whether it is an unvarying metrical form or more freely flowing lines, the writer makes several commonsense choices. When people are happy, they speak quickly; when they are sad, or serious, or matter-of-fact, words come more slowly. In the same way, the writer of poetry uses a quickly moving line with many unaccented syllables and short vowels to express lightheartedness. When the writer wants to express serious thoughts, the rhythm moves more slowly, with longer vowels and a higher proportion of accented syllables. Within the line, rhythm may also vary as the writer wishes to stress an idea or a single word. And within the poem, the rhythm slows or quickens to vary the mood or shift the tone.

Abstract terms do not appeal to our senses. Concrete ones do.

The best poetry uses rhythm to add meaning to words.

The abrupt and halting rhythm and frequent accented syllables in Myra Cohn Livingston's "74th Street" create the sense of a beginner on roller skates, struggling to get and maintain balance, then to take another jerky stroke:

> Hey, this little kid gets roller skates.
> She puts them on.
> She stands up and almost
> flops over backwards.
> She sticks out a foot like
> she's going somewhere and
> falls down and
> smacks her hand. She
> grabs hold of a step to get up and
> sticks out the other foot and
> slides about six inches and
> falls and
> skins her knee.
>
> And then, you know what?
>
> She brushes off the dirt and the
> blood and puts some
> spit on it and then
> sticks out the other foot
>
> *again.*

When reading aloud a poem like this one, remember that a writer starts and stops lines of poetry in units of meaning; this requires readers to make a tiny pause at the end of the line. Lines that end with a conjunction or adverb, like "and" and "almost," force the rhythm into even more abrupt pauses, just like the jerkiness of the skater's strenuous efforts and continuous failures.[4]

As Eve Merriam says in "Inside a Poem," rhythm is important:

> It doesn't always have to rhyme, ˘/˘/˘/˘/
> but there's the repeat of a beat, somewhere ˘/˘˘/˘˘/˘/
> an inner chime that makes you want to ˘/˘/˘/˘

tap your feet or swerve in a curve; /ˇ/ˇ/ˇˇ/
a lilt, a leap, a lightning split:— ˇ/ˇ/ˇ/ˇ/

Merriam's quick, changeable beat contributes to meaning. The first line of her poem is a serious statement about rhyme, and her rhythm enforces the factual meaning of the line with regularity and uniformity. The first line has four accented syllables. The second line has the same number of accented syllables, but the line's rhythm picks up speed with the use of two additional unaccented syllables, a ratio of six light to four heavier syllables. The more unaccented syllables, the more quickly the line runs, and the more lightness the meaning acquires. Line 3 includes five unaccented syllables; in line 4 the final anapestic foot (two unaccented syllables followed by one accented syllable) also adds to the lightness and the unexpected quality of the rhythm. Again in line 5, there are four accented syllables, but this time the internal punctuation interrupts the rhythm. The scansion looks the same as that of the first line (ˇ/ˇ/ˇ/ˇ/), but the commas cause readers to stop and start, stop and start. The surprise caused by the pause for the final *t*'s of "lilt" and "split" and the final *p* of "leap," when added to the short vowels and the plosive consonants, is all part of what Merriam is saying about rhythm: rhythm need not be absolutely regular, but it should suit meaning. The idea of "Inside a Poem"—while a poem need not rhyme, its rhythm exists to clarify meaning—is clear. Merriam uses rhythm not as an end in itself as the versifier does, but as a way to enforce meaning.

Sound Patterns

Patterns of sound are an important part of poetry, too, and a part that often distinguishes poetry from prose. Read this poem aloud for full appreciation:

Patty Tacket
Patty Tackett
held a racket
right beside my head.
"Move it once and,
boy, I'll whack it
Patty Tackett said."

So I stood there
very still—
(stillness is a kind of skill)—
till, motionless,
I broke the will

Of crazy Patty Tackett.

This poem is clearly influenced by the limerick in its end rhymes, its quick sounds, its **internal rhymes** (*still* and *stillness* and *skill* and *till* and *will*) and its general silliness. Words with *ks* and *ts* can often be funny words, like the onomonopoetic word, *whack*.

In *Come with Me: Poems for a Journey*, poet Naomi Shihab Nye also uses sound patterns to convey more completely the meanings of her poems. Nye uses a wonderful **extended metaphor** (that is, a comparison developed at great length, occurring throughout the whole work) when she compares the sky to a letter in her poem "Envelope." Pictures in the book show you that in the first section of the poem the girl is looking up at the sky; in the second, she's in her very messy room, frustrated:

> The sky sends a letter to the ground.
> Down, down from that high place
> The giant page keeps shifting shapes,
> Moving around, thick waves of cloud
> Sent off to the edge of everywhere.
>
> If you stare hard enough, you read
> Mountains, messages, feathers.
> The story of roads
> Rolling in, drifting away.
> Ripples and bits of song.
>
> What did I do wrong?
> Forget to say?
> The sky erases it.
>
> 2
> Mixed-up messy mush of stuff . . .
> I get lost, looking.
> Find my mother's silver scissors,
> Brother's twine.
> Homework, birthday cards,
>
> Stones from an island,
> Stuffed bumblebee . . .
> Go outside for relief.
> Stare up to read my mail.
>
> No other letter
> Is better.

Though this poem doesn't have consistent end rhymes, it does have **off rhymes** (imperfect rhymes, sometimes called "slant" rhymes) that use assonance: "ground" and "cloud" as well as "place" and "shape" repeat similar vowel sounds. These sounds in the first section of the poem are long and deep and suggest a lazy gaze. In the next section of the poem, the repeated sounds of *s* in "silver scissors," combined with "mixed-up messy mush of stuff"—the repeated *m* sound—make the poem move swiftly. Later in the poem, the long sounds of the words "stones from an island" and "stuffed bumblebee" slow the sound patterns of the poem down (as the girl is feeling sad and frustrated by her room); the long vowels give added duration to the words.

Nye ends the poem with a simple, quick rhyme, which makes us feel, like the girl in the poem, that everything is once more all right when she is outside with the sky again.

Figurative Language

Figurative language is as important in poetry as rhythm and sound patterns. When a poem makes either implied comparisons, often called metaphors, or explicit comparisons, often called similes, the images called up may acquire connotative meaning.

In Joyce Sidman's *This Is Just to Say: Poems of Apology and Forgiveness*, children write poems based on William Carlos Williams's great small poem, "This is Just to Say," just as the students in Miss Stretchberry's class did. In this book about children writing poetry, the sixth graders of Florence Scribner School write poems of apology and receive poems of forgiveness in response. In "Brownies—Oops!" a fictional child named Maria uses sensory details, internal rhymes, personification, and a simile or two as she asks for forgiveness from her mom:

> I smelled them from my room
> A wafting wave of chocolate-ness.
>
> I listened for a moment,
> Ears pricked like a bat's.
>
> I crept down, stepped
> Over the sleeping dog.
>
> I felt the cold linoleum
> On my bare toes.
>
> I saw the warm, thick
> Brick of brownies.
>
> I slashed a huge chunk
> Right out of the middle.
>
> The gooey hunks of chocolate
> Winked at me as I gobbled them.
>
> Afterwards, the pan gaped
> Like an accusing eye.
>
> My head said, Oops!
> But my stomach said, Heavenly.

The figurative language and sensory details in this poem help the reader experience Maria's temptation and understand why she gave in. Describing her ears pricking up "like a bat's" gives us an unusual visual comparison, and the pan of brownies is personified, made into something like a gaping, accusatory eye; the chocolate itself

In the best poems, rhythm does not distract from, but reinforces meaning.

winks. The strong verbs this writer uses are important, too: she *slashed* a chunk of brownie—she didn't just cut it.

Some poems aren't as simple as Sidman's; sometimes readers may be puzzled by the figurative language in a poem. The more complex the poem, the more subtle the metaphors may be. The simplest way to check the meaning and suitability of comparisons is by means of simple "this = that" equations. The similes and metaphors in Lillian Moore's "Bike Ride" form a series of figurative comparisons:

Look at us!

We ride a
road
the sun has paved with   sun = paving machines
shadows   shadows = pavement

We glide
on leaf lace   leaf lace = shadow pattern

across tree
spires over   spires = steeplelike shadows of tree tops

shadow ropes of
droopy wires.   ropes = telephone wire shadows

We roll
through a shade tunnel   tunnel = overhanging branches
into light.

Look!
Our bikes
spin black-and-white   pinwheels = shadows of whirling
shadow pinwheels.   bicycle wheels

Simply saying, "we ride through the road on our bikes" tells the same story as the poem, but these words are not the same as the poem. The rightness of Moore's figurative comparisons has made a fresh experience from what might have been an ordinary one.

Imagery, the appeal to our senses, makes the figurative comparisons additionally vivid. In her collection of poems called *Hailstones and Halibut Bones*, Mary O'Neill uses

---

INQUIRY POINT

There are many kinds of poetry, using many different kinds of poetic devices, that are finding their way into anthologies for children of all ages. The anthologies of Lee Bennett Hopkins (the world's most prolific anthologist of poetry for children, as of July, 2011, Guinness World Records, Ltd.) provide a good place to start. Find current anthologies of poetry selected by Bennett Hopkins. Find examples of various styles and devices, in, for instance, his *Sharing the Seasons: A Book of Poems*, David Diaz, Illustrator, McElderry, 2010 or his celebration of the book and reading, *I Am the Book,* Yayo, Illus. Holiday House, 2011.

There's plenty of poetry to be found on the Internet, too. Go to the Poetry Foundation at http://www.poetryfoundation.org, and then find the collection of 179 poems for children. Find one you like and share it. ●

another figurative device called **synesthesia**, in which stimulation of one sense such as colors or sight results in our seeing concrete images of smells and sounds as well.

Compactness and Varied Poetic Forms

One of the pleasures of reading poetry is to see just how compactly the writer was able to say something; one of the pleasures of writing it is to see how quickly you can say it. A poem is best said in few and artfully chosen words; it follows that if we change a word, we change the poem.

There are many forms of poetry that require the writer to make his or her point in a few short lines. **Concrete poetry** can be considered one of these forms, and it is one that children will find pleasure in. Joyce Sidman's charming picturebook *Meow Ruff: A Story in Concrete Poetry* can provide an enjoyable introduction to the concrete poem.

Sound words are used throughout Sidman's book: on the first page, a little red butterfly says "flutter flutter," the white word "wisp" in the sky represents a cloud, and the word "caw" comes out of a black crow's yellow beak. Later, the puppy (who says "must run run run don't want leash want speed want Freedom!") sees a cat by a green tree with a brown trunk. The shape of the tree is made from these words:

Each/leaf/a map of/branches/each twig/
a branch/of leaves/each branch/a tree of twigs/
each tree/a green/haired/
Slim
great
hearted
gnarl-armed
strong
legged
deep-rooted
one.

And you can see how, on this page, the words have made something like the shape you will see more clearly in the book—the shape of a tree and its trunk.

Korean **sijo** and Japanese **haiku** are also very compact forms of poetry, so compact that they must be counted in syllables, rather than lines. In *Tap Dancing on the Roof*, Linda Sue Park explains that the little-known Korean sijo, as it is translated into English, has three lines, each with fourteen to sixteen syllables. Each line has a special purpose: the first introduces the topic, the second carries the topic a bit further, and the third contains some kind of surprise. All of the sijo in her book relate to common children's experiences. For example, "Bedtime Snacks":

Good: Cookies and one glass of milk
For two dunkers—me and my dad.

Better: Popcorn, a video,
And sleeping bags stuffed with friends.

Best: Blanket pulled up over my head—
book, flashlight, and chocolate bar.

Mark Reibstein's award-winning *Wabi Sabi* tells the story of a cat in Kyoto who is searching for the meaning of his name. As the cat, whose name is Wabi Sabi, asks

Concrete poetry, haiku, and sijo are three forms of poetry that are often compact.

I N Q U I R Y   P O I N T

Look at some compact poetic forms in the following texts. Share your findings through reading aloud or viewing.

Franco, Betsy. *A Curious Collection of Cats: Concrete Poems*. Michael Wertz, Illus. Tricycle Press, 2009.

Concrete poems blend poetry forms and pictures.

McGhee, Alison. *Only a Witch Can Fly*. Taeeun Yoo, Illus. New York: Feiwel & Friends, 2009.

Sestina about following one's heart.

Mora, Pat. *Yum! Mmmm! Qué Rico! America's Sproutings*. Rafael Lopez, Illus. Lee and Low, 2007.

Celebration of food through haiku.

Prelutsky, Jack. *If Not for the Cat.* Ted Rand, Illus. Greenwillow, 2004.

Quiet-toned haiku about animals from their perspectives.

Raczka, Bob. *Lemonade & Other Poems Squeezed from a Single Word*. Nancy Doniger, Illus. Roaring Brook Press, 2011.

Poetry and puzzles unite.

Werner, Sharon. *Bugs by the Numbers*. Blue Apple Books, 2011.

Unique blend of number, word, shape, and poetry. ◉

various characters the meaning of his name they each reply that it's hard to explain. But along the pages there begin to be haiku, placed against the gorgeous paper-cut collages by the Caldecott Award–winning artist Ed Young. On a page with a pink-eyed, black-handed monkey holding a bowl whose steam rises in white strips upward, there is a haiku about a monkey offering someone tea.

Along the sides of some pages, decoratively, are haiku written in Japanese characters. The English haiku are written by Reibstein, the ones in Japanese (translated at the end of the book) were written by Basho, the greatest haiku writer of all time. This book's form and content work together to create a mood and an idea about how to live and how to find beauty in simple things, which is the meaning, perhaps, of the phrase *wabi sabi*. Both Reibstein and Parks's books contain information about the short poetic forms and some suggestions about how to help students write them.

Emotional Intensity

A poem is not a description, but an experience in itself.

Like fiction at its best, poetry at its best lets readers understand a new experience, or enjoy an old experience with new insight. However, unlike the writer of fiction, the poet condenses the experience. Poetry attempts to capture the reader where he or she is, and to involve the reader briefly but intensely.

The successful poem is an intense emotional experience. We have noted how rhythm, sound, and figurative language contribute to compactness, and compactness to emotional intensity. But it is true that response to poetry is very personal. What one person finds emotionally intense may leave another cold. As with all reading, what touches a reader depends in part on the experiences they have had. A poem can't tell a reader how to feel, it can only be a map that suggests responses.[5] Still, if the writing has been done well, a poem, with its combination of sensory imagery, sound, rhythm, richly connotative words, and meaning, should move the reader. Here's a lyric poem that children may learn to love as they grow older. The poet imaginatively describes a particular instance of yearning for love—using internal rhyme, imagery, metaphor, rhythm, and end rhymes—in a way most who have been sad in love can understand.

He Wishes for the Clothes of Heaven
Had I the heavens' embroidered cloths,
Enwrought with golden and silver light,
The blue and the dim and the dark cloths
Of night and light and the half-light,
I would spread the cloths under your feet:
But I, being poor, have only my dreams;
I have spread my dreams under your feet;
Tread softly because you tread on my dreams.

Poetic Styles to Avoid

There have been very funny books of collected bad poetry (for example, the anthology called *Very Bad Poetry*). There are also contests to see who can write the worst poem (type "bad poetry contests" into your Internet browser for a sampling). These very bad poems take the worst qualities of bad writing—didacticism, sentimentality, and condescension—to a new height . . . or, perhaps, a new low. These very bad poems use distracting connotations, trite comparisons, odd or impossible metaphors, repetitious and unvaried beat, or sound or rhythm unsuited to meaning and tone. Children are often subjected to bad poetry, of which this preaching verse is one example.

A Music Box
I am a little Music Box
Wound up and made to go,
And play my little living-tune
The best way that I know.

If I am naughty, cross, or rude
The music will go wrong,
My little works be tangled up,
And spoil the pretty song.

I must be very sweet and good
And happy all the day,
And then the little Music Box
In tune will always play.

If you were a child today, wouldn't you be irritated by this poem? We hope so.

The best poetry is made with care and artistry. Sometimes, in fact, poetry can be found in paragraph form; the writer has chosen each word for its imagery and connotative power, asking of the reader concentration and imagination to discover meaning. And sometimes prose and prosaic writing are put into the form usually reserved for poetry—irregular, short lines and stanza arrangement. But by failing to use words rich in connotative meaning, to make figurative comparisons or to use rhythm to enhance meaning, or to provide the reader with a fresh, memorable insight, the writer has written bad poetry. It is not completely true, then, that to make poetry you just have to write lines that are short.

SUMMARY

Nursery rhymes and sidewalk chants are many children's first experience with literature, and surely their first introduction to verse and poetry. The rhymes' simple stylistic devices of rhythm, sound, and comparison, their colorful characters involved in elementary tensions, and their occasional themes about the lives of humans are sufficient reasons for including them as literature for the youngest child.

Nonsense rhymes contain many of the elements of poetry and its style. These inventive and surprising rhymes give pleasure through story and sounds. With its rapid rhythms and unexpected rhymes, its topsy-turvy, silly way of looking at the logic of life, nonsense, too, is a way into poetry.

Poetry stands as an aesthetic experience in itself. Rhythm, sound, and connotation expand meaning; imagery heightens our sensory awareness; and apt figurative comparisons tempt our imaginations. A distilled representation of an experience, poetry at its best permits the reader to participate, but without the burden of didacticism or sentimentality.

Introduce children to all the different forms of poetry that you have available. The experience of the best efforts of skillful poets is enlarging; it gives pleasure and promotes understanding. To keep that pleasure forever, children should be allowed to memorize what they choose—because we are all different.

At the end of his rousing book of poetry, *Please Bury Me in the Library*, J. P. Lewis' acknowledgements state

> Whose book this is I hardly know,
> Considering the debt I owe
>
> To Lewis Carroll and Edward Lear
> To X.J.K.—a toast (root beer)!
>
> To Shel, and Jack, and Myra Cohn,
> Who always gave this pup a bone.
>
> To those word wizards I've left out,
> The only thing to do is shout:
>
> Whose book is this? The bottom line . . .
> It's partly theirs. It's partly mine.

In this poem, the poet J. P. Lewis is referring to other writers of children's poetry: X. J. Kennedy, Shel Silverstein, Jack Prelutsky, and Myra Livingston Cohn, many of whom have written poetry we've quoted in this chapter. J. P. Lewis's poem is a very clear statement of intertextuality, of how, as Jane Yolen wrote, "each book stands on the back of story"[6] or, in this case, on the back of other people's poems. And, as Jack from *Love That Dog* would say after his experiences in Ms. Stretchberry's class, the first line of J. P. Lewis's poem, "whose book this is I hardly know" is an imitation of the first line of "Stopping by Woods on a Snowy Evening," by Robert Frost.

TEXTSET

Love That Dog

Creech, Sharon. *Love That Dog*. Joanna Cotler Books, 2001.

We've shared this original verse novel as a mentor text that shows a young boy's growth and change as a person and a poet. Jack's inspiration could be the inspiration for others. Some of the book's themes and topics motivated this textset. There are many possibilities for stretching this exemplary verse novel. We share a few ideas here.

Books for You, Jack!

These books are ones that the main character, Jack might enjoy reading to stretch his appreciation for some of the poets Miss Stretchberry encouraged him to enjoy. For that reason, they are written to Jack!

Bryant, Jennifer. *A River of Words*. Melissa Sweet, Illus. Eerdmans Books for Young Readers, 2008.

Jack, you made allusions to the work of William Carlos Williams as you grappled with the loss of your dog and your identity as a poet. Melissa Sweet's fantastic mixed-media illustrations create a great biography of one of your favorite poets. You'll love seeing that "The Red Wheelbarrow" is included, along with other well-known poems by Williams.

Frost, Robert. *Birches*. Ed Young, Illus. Henry Holt, 1988.

This book was illustrated by Ed Young. I like the way that this book is a whole poem by Robert Frost, but it was made into a picturebook, which makes a poem a little easier to read for beginning poets like you. I also like how this picturebook has "Birches" in the back of the book so the reader can see how the poem looks without the picture format.

Frost, Robert. *Stopping by Woods on a Snowy Evening*. Susan Jeffers, Illus. Dutton, 2001.

This picturebook format of one of Robert Frost's poems is illustrated by Susan Jeffers, which adds a little extra touch. All of the effective illustrations are black and white, giving the book a frosty feel. Slight coloring on clothes and other elements in each scene provide a little warmth. You saw this poem and talked about it, but you never saw the full version.

Holdridge, Barbara, ed. *Swinger of Birches: Poems of Robert Frost for Young People*. Peter Koeppen, Illus. Stemmer, 1982.

Jack, here is a book of thirty-eight poems by Robert Frost. The illustrations are a little old fashioned, but they look like the natural style of New England that this poet would have created.

Schmidt, Gary D., ed. *Poetry for Young People: Robert Frost*. Sterling, 1994.

Author Gary D. Schmidt has chosen twenty-five of Frost's poems and organized them by seasons. You might like that he provides some tips on how to go about reading the poems, and there is some biographical information on Frost, too. Jack, you and your classmates might explore some of Frost's poetry to know his work better.

Sidman, Joyce. *This Is Just to Say: Poems of Apology and Forgiveness*. Pamela Zagarenski, Illus. Houghton Mifflin, 2007.

Jack, another classroom is putting poetry in action in this great collection. These sixth graders liked William Carlos Williams's poem, "This Is Just to Say," and they wrote their own poems of apology. You'll see that they are budding poets, just like you. They've learned that it's not so bad to publish their work. And they inspired others to write poetry, too.

(continued)

Verse Novels

Here are some verse novels that explore young protagonists who grow and change, overcoming personal difficulty.

Havill, Juanita. *Grow.* **Stanislawa Kodman, Illus. Peachtree, 2008.**

This verse novel is narrated by a twelve-year old who leads her urban neighborhood in planting a garden on a vacant city lot in downtown Minneapolis. The challenges are many as the community transforms trash into treasure. Abundant illustrations show the cooperative spirit of building the garden.

Hesse, Karen. *Out of the Dust.* **Scholastic Press, 1997.**

This Newbery Medal novel set in Oklahoma during the Dust Bowl is written in a journal-poem format like *Love That Dog.* This book covers the hardships that a young girl, Billy Jo, must face with her family as they struggle to survive poverty and the drought-stricken landscape.

Williams, Vera. *Amber Was Brave, Essie Was Smart.* **Greenwillow Books, 2004.**

You might know Vera Williams best for her picture-books (*A Chair for My Mother*). This time she has written a story about two sisters who take care of one another day-to-day as their mother works to provide for them while their father is incarcerated. This story has Williams's colored pencil drawings and a hopeful ending.

Woodson, Jacqueline. *Locomotion.* **Putnam, 2003.**

A story of struggle and hope, this verse novel features a fifth-grade boy whose teacher assigns different forms of poetry. Lonnie learns to use poetry as a vehicle for his grief. This story has many parallels with Jack's story in *Love That Dog.* An excellent companion book is Jacqueline Woodsen's *Peace Locomotion* (Putnam, 2009). In this sequel, Lonnie has reached sixth grade and this story is told through his letters to his sister while they are living in foster homes following the death of their parents. The sequel

is not a verse novel, though the language is lyrical. Like Jack's, Lonnie's story deserved this sequel.

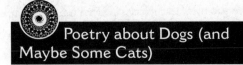

Poetry about Dogs (and Maybe Some Cats)

These selections relate to Jack's love of his dog. (He doesn't like cats, but he will soon need to find a way to resolve this!)

Cook, Ferris, ed. *Bark: Selected Poems about Dogs.* **Bullfinch Press, 2000.**

Jack loved his dog, and he grew to love poetry by reading selected works by famous poets. These uplifting poems will appeal to Jack and introduce him to poets he knows (Robert Frost) and many he may want to find out about (Ogden Nash, Langston Hughes, Pablo Neruda). Ferris Cook illustrates each of the collected poems.

Cook, Ferris, ed. *Yowl: Selected Poems about Cats.* **Bullfinch Press, 2000.**

Jack had trouble finding room in his heart for a cat! Readers who enjoy Ferris Cook's collection of dog poems by famous poets may want to try this book. The black-and-white drawings are realistic, and some of Jack's favorite poets also find cats to be a worthy subject.

Florian, Douglas. *Bow Wow Meow Meow: It's Rhyming Cats and Dogs.* **Houghton Mifflin, 2003.**

Jack found out that poetry doesn't have to rhyme, but some poets have fun working with rhyme. Doug Florian is one, and he has lots of fun creating impressionistic art to reveal the special traits of animals—dogs as well as cats. Some think this is a fun book for experimenting with rhyme.

Johnston, Tony. *It's about Dogs!* **Ted Rand, Illus. Harcourt, 2000.**

Forty-three poems about dogs of all kinds, in all states of emotion, illustrated with watercolor paintings by Ted Rand. Tony Johnston loves dogs, and these poems might comfort children who love their dogs!

Fabulous Forms and Formats

 Walter Dean Myers

Jack experimented with concrete poetry. Who else has done that? Each of these could be read by Jack as he becomes more adept with poetry.

Heard, Georgia, ed. *Falling Down the Page: A Book of List Poems.* **Roaring Brook Press, 2009.**

Georgia Heard selects a rich collection of list poems, a format that will feel new and fun for readers interested in an imaginative format. Contemporary poets such as Naomi Shihab Nye and Jane Yolen are included. There are no illustrations—the poems do that work themselves!

Janeczko, Paul. *A Kick in the Head: An Everyday Guide to Poetic Forms.* **Chris Raschke, Illus. Candlewick, 2005.**

This duo really hits the nail on the head with many poetic forms that might mentor a novice. Here are examples of all kinds of poems by well-known poets on all kinds of topics, in poetic formats that suit each one well. You will hear from Georgia Heard about lives lost in 9/11 and fun couplets from Ogden Nash. There is even a little Blake and Shakespeare! Chris Raschke provides perfect variety in the illustrations for each style of poetry.

Janeczko, Paul. *A Poke in the I: A Collection of Concrete Poems.* **Chris Raschke, Illus. Candlewick, 2001.**

Paul Janeczko really provides some fun models for concrete poetry here. Chris Raschke's abstract and expressionistic art in calligraphy and torn paper are a good combination. It's concrete poetry, but readers will still find plenty of space to think and read between the lines.

Sidman, Joyce. *Meow Ruff: A Story in Concrete Poetry.* **Michelle Berg, Illus. Houghton Mifflin, 2006.**

Poet Joyce Sidman takes the verse novel and concrete poetry to a new level in a concrete verse storybook! This book is filled with word images that give readers a look into the possible thought processes of a dog, an abandoned cat, and a few blackbirds and ladybugs as a friendship forms.

This prolific and successful author writes poetry— and he's teaming up with his son as illustrator in these poetry selections. Jack admires Walter Dean Myers, and he'll be excited to learn that Myers has a son who is teaming up with him on some of his books. These are picturebooks, but they are sophisticated in their topics and themes.

Myers, Walter Dean. *Blues Journey.* **Christopher Myers, Illus. Holiday House, 2003.**

This poem explores the blues by showing them with "call and response" verse. Walter Dean Myers's front matter introduces the reader to the history of the blues and explains the rhyme scheme. There is also a glossary to provide additional background information about the blues. It's a sophisticated book with very striking illustrations in dark blue and brown highlighted in white. This book is a little tougher to read, so it's one readers will want to revisit.

Myers, Walter Dean. *Harlem.* **Christopher Myers, Illus. Scholastic, 1997.**

Myers celebrates a city that is very special to him using a style that is as much song as it is poetry, which fits Harlem! The illustrations make this a visual treat as well. It's an oversized book—why do you think they chose this design?

Myers, Walter Dean. *Jazz.* **Christopher Myers, Illus. Holiday House, 2006.**

Another father-and-son book was written by Walter Dean Myers and illustrated by his son Christopher Myers, this book includes illustrations that are black ink on acetate overlays on acrylics. A brief introduction explains the importance of jazz in African American history. Each two-page spread is a poem about jazz. The back matter provides a timeline of historic times for jazz musicians and a glossary of jazz terminology. Important concept words are highlighted with color.

Myers, Walter Dean. *Looking Like Me.* **Christopher Myers, Illus. Egmont, 2009.**

This jazzy and joyful picturebook poetry was made in a unique way: Usually the illustrator works with

(continued)

the text, but Christopher Myers created these experimental, even surreal, cut-paper and photographic collages. Walter Dean Myers created the text for a different project. Though the two projects were uniquely different, the decision to combine the two resulted in a surprise—this wonderful, rhythmic celebration of self.

INQUIRY POINT

Anyone who has read *Love That Dog* needs to read the sequel: *Hate That Cat!* Readers will want to know what has happened between Jack and Miss Stretchberry, and if he continues to develop as a poet.

What are key elements of this novel written in free verse that could be illuminated by a textset? Are there poets introduced? Does Jack learn more about Walter Dean Myers? What poetic devices could be explored? After examining the book, create a textset of your own for *Hate That Cat*.

Creech, Sharon. *Hate That Cat*. Joanna Cotler Books, 2008. ●

NOTES

1. This saying, attributed to Robert Frost, is apocryphal. Apparently there is no record of his having said or written it anywhere. Joseph Brodsky, the Nobel Prize–winning Russian poet, is said to have responded that "Poetry is what is gained in translation."
2. The great twentieth-century Spanish poet Federico Garcia Lorca, author of "Green, how much I want you green," among many other great poems, is the one who said this.
3. Glenna Sloan, "But Is It Poetry?" *Children's Literature in Education*, 1(32), 2009, pp. 45–55.
4. Listen to a recording of a poet reading his or her own poetry. Line breaks are recognized by the poet.
5. This metaphor for what a book does for a reader was suggested by a reading of Dennis Sumara, *Why Reading Literature in School Still Matters: Imagination, Interpretation, Insight* (Mahwah, NJ: Lawrence Erlbaum Associates, 2002).
6. This quotation is from Jane Yolen's essay "Turtles All the Way Down," in *Only Connect* (New York: Oxford University Press, 1996), pp. 166–174.

RECOMMENDED BOOKS

ADA, ALMA FLOR, AND F. ISABEL CAMPOY. *¡Muu, Moo!: Animal Nursery Rhymes*, Rayo, 2010.

AGEE, JON. *Orangutan Tongs: Poems to Tangle Your Tongue*. Hyperion Books. 2009.

BING, CHRISTOPHER. *Casey at the Bat: A Ballad of the Republic Sung in the Year 1888*. Chronicle Books, 2000.

CARROLL, LEWIS. *Through the Looking-Glass*. Create Space, 2010.

CIARDI, JOHN. *The Man Who Sang the Sillies*. J.B. Lippincott, 1961.

CREECH, SHARON. *Love That Dog: A Novel*. HarperCollins Publishers, 2001.

FARJEON, ELEANOR. *Morning Has Broken*. Illustrated by Tim Ladwig. Eerdmans, 1996.

FISHER, AILEEN. *Out in the Dark and Daylight*. Harper & Row, 1980.

GEORGE, KRISTINE O'CONNELL. *Swimming Upstream: Middle School Poems*. Clarion, 2002.

GIOVANNI, NIKKI. *Spin a Soft Black Song*. Illustrated by George Martins. Collins Publishers, 1985.

Gutman, Dan. *Casey Back at Bat*. Illustrated by Steve Johnson and Lou Fancher. HarperCollins, 2009.

Hughes, Langston. *The Block*. Illustrated by Romare Beardon. Metropolitan Museum of Art, 1995.

Janeczko, Paul, ed. *Looking for Your Name*. Orchard Books, 1993.

Lawson, Jon Arno. *Black Stars in a White Sky*. Illustrated by Sherman Tjia. Wordsong, 2006.

Lear, Edward. *Nonsense Omnibus*. Frederick Warne, 1943.

Lewis, J. Patrick. *Please Bury Me in the Library*. Illustrated by Kyle M. Stone. Harcourt, 2005.

Livingston, Myra Cohn. *Whispers and Other Poems*. Harcourt Brace Jovanovich, 1958.

Martin, Bill. *Chicka Chicka Boom Boom*. Little Simon, 2006.

Medina, Tony. *Love to Langston*. Illustrated by R. Gregory Christie. Lee & Low Books, 2006.

Milne, A. A. *When We Were Very Young*. Puffin, 1992.

Nash, Ogden. *The Face Is Familiar*. Garden City Publishers, 1941.

Nye, Naomi Shihab. *Come with Me: Poems for a Journey*. Illustrated by Dan Yaccarino. Greenwillow Books, 2000.

Oliver, Mary. *Dream Work*. Grove/Atlantic, 1986.

O'Neill, Mary. *Hailstones and Halibut Bones*. Illustrated by John Wallner. Doubleday, 1989.

Park, Linda Sue. *Tap Dancing on the Roof*. Illustrated by Istvan Banyai. Houghton Mifflin, 2007.

Prelutsky, Jack. *Awful Ogre Running Wild*. Illustrated by Paul O. Zelinsky. Greenwillow Books, 2008.

Reibstein, Mark. *Wabi Sabi*. Illustrated by Ed Young. Little, Brown, 2008.

Roessel, David, and Arnold Rampersan, ed. *Poetry for Young People: Langston Hughes*. Illustrated by Benny Andrews. Sterling, 2006.

Rorvetch, Gerda. *There Was a Man Who Loved a Rat and Other Vile Little Poems*. Illustrated by Lissa Rovetch. Philomel, 2008.

Service, Robert. *The Cremation of Sam McGee*. Illustrated by Ted Harrison. Kids Can Press, 2006.

Service, Robert. *The Shooting of Dan McGrew*. Kids Can Press, 1986.

Sidman, Joyce. *Meow Ruff: A Story in Concrete Poetry*. Illustrated by Michelle Berg. Houghton Mifflin, Co. 2006.

Sidman, Joyce. *This Is Just to Say: Poems of Apology and Forgiveness*. Illustrated by Pamela Zagarenski. Houghton Mifflin, 2007.

Silverstein, Shel. *Where the Sidewalk Ends*. Evil Eye Music, 1974.

Stevenson, Robert Louis. *A Child's Garden of Verses*. Star Bright Books, 2008.

Thayer, Ernest, *Casey at the Bat: A Ballad of the Republic Sung in the Year 1888*. Simon & Schuster, 2003.

Titcomb, Gordon M. *The Last Train*. Illustrated by Wendell Minor. Roaring Book Press, 2010.

Watson, Clyde, and Wendy Watson. *Catch Me and Kiss Me and Say It Again*. Philomel, 1993.

MyEducationKit™

Go to the topic "Poetry" on the MyEducationKit for this text, where you can:

- Search the Children's Literature Database, housing more than 22,000 titles searchable in every genre by authors or illustrators, by awards won, by year published, and by topic and description.
- Explore genre-related Assignments and Activities, assignable exercises showing concepts in action through database use, video, cases, and student and teacher artifacts.
- Listen to podcasts and read interviews from some of the brightest and most enduring stars of children's literature in the Conversations.
- Discover web links that will lead you to sites representing the authors you learn about in these pages, classrooms with powerful children's literature connections, and literature awards.

A River of Words: The Story of William Carlos Williams

Jen Bryant / Illustrated by Melissa Sweet

Biography is increasingly accessible to readers of all ages. They can understand the contributions of people from many walks of life through well-designed biographies that include inviting illustrative styles in the picturebook format.

CHAPTER TWELVE

Biography

Some children get hooked on biography, and others may never discover it. What reasons are there for leading children to biography?

Sometimes curiosity leads children to wonder about people. How did this writer start writing? Who explored the moon? Who led millions of people to resist racism? What kinds of careers have women had?

Biography Defined

Biography is a story of the life of an individual told by a different author. The story is more than a series of life's events; it is also how the subject experienced those events. It includes three essentials: facts, a concept or theme that the facts relate to, and an attitude toward the subject and the reader. The facts are expected to be accurate, up-to-date, and authentic in their depiction of the subject for the time and culture in which they lived. A biographer must decide which events and details to include to match the interests and age level of the readers for whom the biography is intended. When considering the concept or central theme, biographers seek subjects worth reading, writing, and thinking about. The subject for biography has accomplished something that makes her or his life significant—perhaps in the field of science, politics, global peace, the arts, or sports; they may have overcome obstacles in pursuit of a goal. The attitude of the writer reflects interest and enthusiasm, even delight in the person in a successful biography. If the writer finds the subject worth writing about, he or she finds the subject worth writing about with style. The skillful biographer uses words imaginatively, even in the simplest biographies for the youngest readers.

Autobiography, written by its subject or in conjunction with its subject, cannot be totally objective because the narrated events are filtered through the writer's own consciousness. An autobiography can be as rigorously researched as a biography, but it may also be based entirely on the subject's memory, and is sometimes referred to as a memoir. A particularly moving series of personal accounts can be found in Julius Lester's collected slave narratives, *To Be a Slave.* The insights Lester shares are clearly the views of those experiencing the institution of slavery.

A subgenre closely related to autobiography and difficult to distinguish is the **memoir**. A memoir is slightly different in character from an autobiography; it has a narrower focus and more intimate tone of memories, feelings, and emotions. Many authors choose to write memoirs, which frequently provide valuable insights into their books. For example, fanciful as they are, many of Roald Dahl's stories contain allusions to his childhood. Reading *Boy: Tales of Childhood* would provide a Dahl fan with many clues to the themes in his imaginative stories.

Readers often turn to the lives of significant people because they want to discover more about what it was like to be alive and contributing to a period of history they have just discovered. Or readers may be curious about the "what if" of being a hero or heroine—"What if it could be *me*?" The true story of a winning athlete, an activist for social justice, or the inventor of life-saving technology may inspire a reader to pursue a personal goal important to the future of our world. Curiosity, wonder, the possibility of discovery, or increased appreciation—a number of related motives may lead us to read about the lives of individuals.

In this chapter we will strive to share a variety of children's books that demonstrate not only a range of subjects addressed in biographies, but also the many possibilities for style and form within contemporary biographies, autobiographies, and memoirs. As has been our approach throughout this handbook, we will show ways biographies can be clustered to enhance understanding of both the genre and the subjects being portrayed.

Facts, concept, and attitude are essential to biography.

Autobiography and memoir are becoming increasingly popular.

Curiosity may lead the reader into a subject and beyond it.

The Writer's Obligation

Within the definition of biography—the truthful story of the life of an individual—are three terms, *truthful, story,* and *individual*; each term presents a separate obligation for the writer. We will elaborate on each of these terms since they will apply regardless of the type, style, tone, subject, or theme of the biography.

The first term, *truthful,* implies facts. Like all nonfiction, biography should be based on accurate information about the life and times of the subject. Authentic information should come from primary source material such as letters, journals, diaries, court records, interviews, newspaper accounts, recorded conversations, and interviews. Although not all biographies for children include a bibliography, it is a useful addition that is often included as back matter or in an author's note. A foreword or acknowledgments page that tells something about the writer's research process and perhaps suggests other readings for further inquiry is also valuable. A closer look at the text itself should reveal dates, quotations, places, and names as they fit into the narrative. Often the last pages of a biography list in detail the sources the biographer examined. Increasingly, the illustrator will also provide information about their choices with the visual elements of the book. Convincing the reader of authenticity is important; the number of these elements and quantity of details depend on the type of biography, its length, and the age of the intended readers. We expect an **authentic biography** to be truthful and to provide us with accuracy, facts, and information about the research process.

Bibliographies and other sources certify authenticity.

Accuracy, Authenticity, and Facts

Many of the facts in Russell Freedman's *Eleanor Roosevelt: A Life of Discovery* are taken from Eleanor Roosevelt's own writings—her letters, newspaper columns, and autobiography—along with transcriptions of interviews and conversations with those she knew, as well as from a variety of other carefully researched sources. The unifying concept or theme comes from one of her own statements, used as an epigraph: "You gain strength, courage and confidence by every experience in which you really stop to look fear in the face. . . . You must do the thing you think you cannot do." Roosevelt's early years and the first years of her marriage to Franklin were filled with experiences during which she looked fear in the face, doing what she felt she could not do—but did. In 1946, the plain and awkward child once demeaned by her beautiful mother was a grown woman given a standing ovation in the United Nations. Freedman's biography concludes convincingly with a return to the concept expressed in the words of the epigraph: "And having learned to stare down fear, I long ago reached the point where there is no living person whom I fear, and few challenges I am not willing to face."

Freedman's impeccable research is thoroughly documented in this biography, as young adult readers would expect. Some biographies are more openly concept-oriented; portions of their research may be documented within a picturebook for younger readers. *Eleanor, Quiet No More* provides a timeline to reinforce the chronology of the story, as well as source and resource lists for readers interested in doing personal inquiry. But the strength of this biography is the way it presents the story of Eleanor Roosevelt: readers see her progress from a shy, quiet young girl to the confident activist and speaker she became. Well-chosen narrative text capped off with select quotes, reveal the complex person she was. A significant part of each two-page spread is a Gary Kelley illustration done in muted pastels that expertly convey mood. For example, when Rappaport tells of the criticism Eleanor received as a child, the quote "I wanted to sink through the floor in shame" follows. The illustration shows young Eleanor, unsmiling, but highlights on her hair bow create an angelic effect. She is in front of an empty staircase; her mother stands watchfully in the darkened hallway, distant. Each double page is just this way—insightful text paired with illustrations that enhance and connote something deeper about Roosevelt. The biography's theme is revealed by Rappaport's trademark book jacket style, featuring a portrait on the front, and the concept-based title on the back. A story is told.

Illustrations can support and extend the facts of a good biography as well as interpret the subject.

Story

The term *story* implies another obligation on the part of the writer: A true story, properly written, not only has a basis in fact, but also needs to be an engaging account. The story is frequently told objectively, from a third-person perspective; additional data supplied by the author will place a responsibility on the reader to synthesize the information and the narrative to construct the actual story. Whether the subject is no longer living or still alive, a biography will include some history of the subject's life and of the context of their time and place. A biographer must be a historian of sorts, avoiding personal bias and assuming an omniscient stance. Biographers can only assign thoughts and feelings to historical figures based on evidence. A conscientious biographer, despite interest in and knowledge of the subject, has limitations. They cannot presume to know the mind of the subject; this information should be closely tied to verifiable emotions, speech, or thoughts. The more contemporary the times in which a person lived, the more resources there will be to support the subject's personal thoughts and feelings. The more historically distant the life of a subject, the fewer will be such resources.

> The more historically distant and lesser known the subject of a biography, the more likely resources will be missing.

Susanna Reich creates the story of Clara Schumann, a piano virtuoso during the 1800s, for young adult readers. Letters, journals, newspapers, concert reviews, books, and music manuscripts in libraries and universities were available sources for Reich as she worked on the biography *Clara Schumann: Piano Virtuoso*. Clara, the daughter of a demanding piano teacher who brutalized her brothers when they performed poorly, was identified early as a musical genius. Reich speculates that perhaps the chaotic fury in her home led her to express herself only through music, which kept her content and happy by the hour as she lost herself in beautiful sound. She was a virtuoso at the age of nine who played a heavy schedule of concerts; as a young woman she was forbidden to see fellow musician Robert Schumann, whom she loved. Only through her acts of youthful rebellion could she gain control of her career, take her father to court over her rightful earnings, and marry Robert. But Clara's musician husband Robert was less in demand than she, and he tragically attempted to take his own life. In order to support their eight children, Clara carried her heavy concert schedule for most of her life, traveling and performing even during pregnancies. One of the elements that make this life of an artist an interesting, even fascinating, story is the evidence of conflict, the struggles of a vibrant and resourceful woman for whom "art is life."

Shorter biographies of musicians who began their careers as child prodigies can be valuable for readers interested in music or in the experiences of others whose young lives were orchestrated around a particular talent. Another gifted musician and composer, Wolfgang Amadeus Mozart, comes to mind; we will share two Mozart biographies for younger readers. In *Mozart: The Wonder Child: A Puppet Play in Three Acts*, biographer Diane Stanley creates a story of Mozart that relies not only on verbal narrative, but also on the book's design and visual elements. Younger readers will see the chronology of his life—childhood, adolescence, and adulthood—through a three-act puppet play modeled after the Salzburg Marionette Theatre, whose opening performance featured Mozart. The illustrative style stages a setting appropriate to the time period in which Mozart composed and played, and the media is fitting: Stanley uses gesso over wood panels, then egg tempera paint (an effect similar to oil, but water-based). The scenes are adorned with cherubs holding additional facts, musical stanzas from Mozart's masterpieces, and characters attached to marionette strings. Back matter includes information about the evolution of his name, the Salzburg Marionette Theatre, and a timeline. Stanley also provides quotes throughout the "performance" of Mozart's life, with its triumphs and tragedies.

Peter Sís provides another, this time **episodic biography** of Mozart, focusing on his childhood. The brief, simple story is illustrated so that the very young can see the subject—the figure of Mozart is accented in bright red. They can see his restrictive childhood through the appearance of his father as a dark silhouette in the background. His life was filled with concert tours from a young age, giving Sís the opportunity to both draw the cities in miniature and to show the royalty for whom Mozart played, displayed on the opened hand fans associated with upper class women of the period. Young readers will enjoy the depictions of Mozart's musical dreams, hinting at the double meaning in the title, *Play, Mozart, Play!* A brief, biographical sketch serves as back matter.

One biography, on its own, presents part of the picture of a biographical subject. In most cases, younger readers will benefit from seeing a shorter picturebook biography, then accessing other versions that meet their needs and interests. Any reader can benefit from the wide range of styles picturebooks provide. A fan of Mozart might select Hugh Brewster's *The Other Mozart: The Life of the Famous Chevalier de St. George* to discover a violin virtuoso, composer, athlete, and soldier. Joseph Bologne was the son of a West Indian slave and French plantation owner who overcame prejudice to become one of the most famous men in eighteenth century France; he was a contemporary of Mozart. Readers gain a broader sense of the individuality of a subject by clustering biographies.

> Several picturebook biographies can combine to form a unified view of the subject.

Individuality of Subjects

By definition, a biography is about an *individual;* the third responsibility of a biographer is to convey the individuality of that subject. Children who become interested in the lives of presidents, for example, may have difficulty separating the life of one president from another. In addition to living in different historical periods, if the presidents portrayed in children's biographies do not reveal individual qualities, readers may lump them together as one. When a biography constructs identity around a single trait—Washington is honest, Lincoln compassionate, Woodrow Wilson scholarly, Theodore Roosevelt nonconforming but commanding—the biographies may lack the full humanity of their subjects. In an episodic biography, or an authentic biography that is shorter in length, there are limits to how many individual traits can be developed; combining biographies into textsets becomes a valuable strategy. Our textset for this chapter focuses on Abraham Lincoln, a favorite choice of many biographers; therefore, it is possible to construct a fairly complete view of Lincoln as an individual.

The process of writing biography, like that of writing nonfiction informational books, is a process of constant decision-making: what to select and what to omit in order to create a realistic, well-rounded portrayal. Avoiding flat subject portrayal is an important consideration. Readers of any age should expect a biography to provide a well-rounded view of the subject, including multiple sides to his or her life and personality—appropriate to the reader—to avoid creating an uninteresting story.

Portraying an individual requires thoughtful choices; the intended reader is a necessary consideration. Three very different biographies about individuals with a love of ballet show these choices.

While he narrates the story of her remarkable life in *Martha Graham: A Dancer's Life,* accomplished biographer Russell Freedman does not hesitate to tell of Martha Graham's weaknesses: her furious temper and her exploitation of the competitiveness in her dance troupe in order to heighten tension for a spirited performance. As she aged, she worked through her arthritis, choreographing as well as performing, but with far fewer accolades. Nor does Freedman neglect the fact that Graham frequently reeked of alcohol when she appeared in public. This detail, however, does not negate the dancer's great artistry. Young adults would relate to this portrayal, but younger readers interested in the life of this accomplished dancer and choreographer would find *Ballet for Martha: Making Appalachian Spring,* an episodic view of Martha Graham's life, one that reveals not only her innovations in the world of modern ballet, but also the importance of teamwork with set innovations of artist Isamu Noguchi and the musical genius of composer Aaron Copland. The story of this loved ballet is well-told, but also well-documented; Floca's variation in perspectives for the illustrations matches the theatrical nature of this story.

To Dance: A Ballerina's Graphic Novel would be another very rewarding biography of an accomplished dancer. This memoir by dancer Siena Cherson Siegel shows how a young girl realized her dream of becoming a prima ballerina, from her childhood beach home in Puerto Rico to her debut with the New York City Ballet. Siegel's memoir is not a simplistic chronicling of her accomplishment; she interjects the realities of physical pain, personal injury, competition, and long hours of study and practice. The panels of graphic art show her emotion over the disharmony between her parents, her awe of Maya Plisetskaya during the Bolshoi's performance of *Swan Lake,* and her sadness over the death of George Balanchine.

The picturebook *Dancing to Freedom: The True Story of Mao's Last Dancer* is the memoir of Li Cunxin's rise from his impoverished village life in Maoist China to stardom with the Houston Ballet. Its focus on theme—the willingness to make the most of one's opportunities, even when it entails tremendous personal sacrifice, and his defection to America are downplayed in this version for young readers. Anne Spudvilas creates the bleak tone of Li's early life with muted gray and blue tones; she incorporates bursts of color to represent the time of his defection to America. The portrayal of Li is selective, but the choices do not create a flat character.

A well-researched biography strives for authenticity. It paints a picture that avoids stereotypes. Biographies written for children years ago tended to treat this genre as an opportunity to glorify the subject, providing only their virtuous side. Although there is a trend toward showing the less admirable character traits of the subject in biographies, writers usually temper the inclusion of socially disapproved behavior in biographies for younger readers. Quality biographies, however, cannot completely ignore negative qualities and present only the good. The biographer needs to show the individual as a believable human, which may include flaws such as self-interest, faulty judgment, or human frailty. An example of a historical figure traditionally portrayed as infallible, based on his very admirable qualities as a statesman, and scholar, is Thomas Jefferson. These accounts may not portray his many talents as a scientist, master gardener, or architect, or the inconsistencies in his views on equality. Exploring a variety of books will help provide a more complete portrait of this president and the times in which he lived.

INQUIRY POINT

Find the books listed below, or select additional ones. Begin with a biography of Thomas Jefferson (Cheryl Harness provides a basic one that considers more than one trait). Write down the individual traits you notice about Jefferson. Form some questions you still have about him. Look through the other sources to confirm, disconfirm or ignore the traits you found. What's missing to make Jefferson more fully rounded? Who were his contemporaries? What might paint a more complete picture of the context in which he lived, wrote, discovered, and governed?

Giblin, James Cross. *Thomas Jefferson: A Picture Book Biography.* Michael Dooling, Illus. Scholastic, 1994.

Harness, Cheryl. *Thomas Jefferson.* National Geographic, 2004.

Pinkney, Andrea Davis. *Dear Benjamin Banneker.* Brian Pinkney, Illus. Harcourt, 1994.

Piven, Hanoch. *What Presidents Are Made Of.* Atheneum, 2004.

St. George, Judith. *So You Want to Be President?* David Small, Illus. Philomel, 2004.

 # Who Gets a Biography?

Not every unique individual who contributed to society earns a biography, but there are many diverse personalities who have earned at least one. The question of which individuals should become the subject of a biography is important. Young girls finding a library shelf filled with biographies about scientific discoveries contributed by men and boys may think that a career in science is not meant for them. Restricting biographies of African Americans to those set in the years of slavery cannot develop an understanding of the multiple important accomplishments of African Americans throughout American history. Younger children who do not see the childhood years of interesting people many not see themselves as readers of this genre. Increasingly varied subjects whose contributions are unique and interesting to contemporary children can encourage a broader readership for biography in the future.

Sandy's Circus by Tanya Lee Stone is told from a third-person perspective; it does not pretend to have mobile artist Sandy Calder speak directly to young readers. The illustrations by Boris Kulikov provide the introduction to his art: the wire sculpture circus. There is no simple way to capture the movement of his trademark mobiles, and this short biography leaves this to the end, which may seem to shortchange this art. However, it represents the way young readers might have a jumping-off point to self-discovery of mobiles through the kind of hands-on inquiry Calder delighted in throughout his life.

Jen Bryant and Melissa Sweet team up to make poet William Carlos Williams accessible to younger readers (and probably many young adult readers). Sweet's intricate collage art complements this biography of an extraordinary man whose poems were at once sparse and complex in their observation of the everyday. This biography is truly a work of art, supported with a timeline that places Williams in the context of his times, an author and illustrator's note, and suggestions for further reading. Sweet creatively embeds some of Williams's poetry into the collage backdrops; they reappear on the endpapers. The illustrations and Bryant's free verse are bordered and strategically placed on and beside the collages to show Williams's work as a family doctor and author. Sweet indicates in the illustrator's note that "this book was a true gift," and we agree. *A River of Words* may motivate aspiring poets to enjoy young poets' work in *River of Words: Young Poets and Authors on the Nature of Things* by Pamela Michael and Robert Haas.

When selecting these unique, almost stand-alone biographies, authenticity is especially important. Master storyteller James Rumford has created an award-winning biography, *Sequoyah: The Cherokee Man Who Gave His People Writing*.[1] This bilingual story, whose cadence matches the oral storytelling tradition, owes the Cherokee translation to Anna Sixkiller Huckaby. Readers will be inspired by the perseverance and genius of an ordinary man with an idea that surprised not only the Cherokee Nation, but also the world of the 1820s: a system to give the Cherokee language a written form. The tall, slim design suggests the tree that is the namesake of the biography; the woodblock paintings add authenticity to the historical setting. Back matter includes a timeline of Sequoyah's life, biographical information, and a chart of the Cherokee syllabary. A model of authenticity, this biography does not rely on fictionalizing for its story and representation of individuality.

> Biographies must arrange facts so as not to create or perpetuate stereotypes.

Carmen Agra Deedy, in collaboration with Wilson Kimeli Naiyomah, has created a unique biographical work with *14 Cows for America*. It is an episodic story of the work of Kimeli Naiyomah after he shared the news of 9/11 with his Maasai village in Kenya. The Maasai people are filled with compassion and respond with a most generous gift of fourteen sacred cows, blessed by village elders to take away some of the sadness "from American hearts." The unexpected gift was graciously accepted by the American ambassador some nine months following the attack on New York City; the cows cannot be slaughtered and remain in the care of the Kenyans. The herd numbered over thirty at the time of this story's publishing. Gonzalez has beautifully captured the brilliant hues of the Kenyan landscape. The final page leaves readers with a concept about the stark difference in world power between the two nations. Naiyomah provides an important appendix that helps readers appreciate the magnitude of the gift and the importance of this emotional story. Young readers also realize that biographies are written for subjects still living and contributing to society.

> The number of interesting and accomplished individuals who earn a biography has grown.

Biography and Fiction

We see the terms **biographical fiction** and **fictionalized biography** and wonder what they mean. Both admit that the writer has dramatized or invented parts of the story that perhaps cannot be verified, or that the writer wishes to make facts into a story to show how the subject might have behaved, given his or her character. This fictionalizing should be acknowledged; the more fictionalizing included, the more likely a biographical story will be classified as fiction. The problem for the writer of biography for children lies to a great extent in the answers to two basic questions: How much fact shall I include? How much narrative may I invent? Three of the stories from our textset for this chapter on Abraham Lincoln will be used to show levels of fictionalizing.

For younger children some fictionalizing is acceptable.

Jen Bryant, for example, used a quote Abraham Lincoln made about the War of 1812 along with fictional storytelling in *Abe's Fish: A Boyhood Tale of Abraham Lincoln*. She weaves Lincoln's known traits and factual information about his childhood to tell a story of generosity and compassion when six-year-old Abe gives away the fish he spent the afternoon catching to a passing soldier in need of a meal. Bryant provides extensive back matter—an author's note organized around inquiry questions and a selective bibliography. But readers' interest will be held by not only the imaginative narrative, but also Amy June Bates's superb paintings. This biographical fiction is valuable because it motivates readers to become more interested in both the subject and the genre of biography.

As we have shown previously, biography in picturebook format can also be effective nonfiction, telling only the most significant events. It is possible to stick to the facts and write an interesting book. If the writer does dramatize, these inventions should be historically true to the times and not merely possible, but probable. Such dramatization can occur when the subject of the biography is long dead and where few written records remain, which is the case for many aspects of Lincoln's youth. A fictionalized biography becomes the best solution to this lack of resources, and this is the strategy Kay Winters takes in her *Abe Lincoln: The Boy Who Loved Books*. This narrative in free verse is a brief chronology showing the path from his birth to the White House, accompanied by oil paintings and an appendix filling in some of the gaps from the story. This fictionalized biography could have happened this way, and is a good motivator to search other, more detailed biographies for younger readers.

Biography for the older child may fall closer to the factual end of the spectrum, and exemplify an authentic full-length style of biography. The older child can absorb more facts and may require less story; they can construct the story from the narrative and supporting factual information provided as back matter, preface, or interspersed within the narrative itself. Too much factual detail, however, makes the page dense with dates, events, photographs, and quotes; the appearance can be similar to that of an encyclopedia. The response to this style of biography may be, "This is more than I really want to know." Yet too much dramatization or inclusion of probable dialogue prompts the response, "What can I really believe?" The carefully researched *Lincoln: A Photobiography* by Russell Freedman is very convincing, largely because Freedman quotes from Lincoln's handwritten notes and occasional journals. He catches the tone of Lincoln's writing, interpreting what happens in light of the insights gained from personal glimpses. Lincoln's last day, for example, rings true to what we know of his compassion. After lunch he "revoked the death sentence of a Confederate spy." He also pardoned a deserter, signing his name with the comment, "Well, I think this boy can do us more good above ground than under ground!" Members at the last Cabinet meeting heard his wish that no retaliatory "bloody work" be carried out, adding that blood enough had been lost.[2]

Invention, a biographer's compromise, should be acknowledged.

In his collection of critical essays about children's literature, *Should We Burn Babar?*[3] Herbert Kohl critically examined textbooks that mention the part Rosa Parks played in the 1955 Montgomery bus boycott. Kohl concluded that some texts suggest that Mrs. Parks, a seamstress, refused to move to the back of the bus simply

---

INQUIRY POINT

Look at three biographies of Charles Darwin, or substitute a set of books on another subject, such as Muhammud Ali or Amelia Earhart for whom there are a variety of biographies.

   Which is most fictionalized? Least? In what ways did the author and illustrator fictionalize the story? Why? Who will be the intended reader for each of the biographies?

Heiligman, Deborah. *Charles and Emma: The Darwins' Leap of Faith.* Henry Holt, 2009.

Hopkinson, Deborah. *Humblebee Hunter: Inspired by the Life & Experiments of Charles Darwin.* Jen Corace, Illus. Hyperion, 2010.

Hopkinson, Deborah. *Who Was Charles Darwin?* Nancy Harrison, Illus. Perfection, 2005.

Keller, Michael. *Charles Darwin's On the Origin of Species: A Graphic Adaptation.* Nicole Rager Fuller, Illus. Rodale Books, 2009.

Krull, Kathleen. *Charles Darwin.* Boris Kulikov, Illus. Viking, 2010.

McGinty, Alice B. *Darwin.* Mary Azarian, Illus. Houghton Mifflin, 2009.

Sís, Peter. *The Tree of Life: Charles Darwin.* Farrar, Straus and Giroux, 2003.

Anniversaries can spark publication of relevant biographies and provide opportunities to show the multi-faceted nature of famous individuals.

because she was tired. This gives the false impression that her unjust arrest was instigated by an emotional moment she had that brought on a spontaneous boycott and was quickly resolved. This kind of fictionalizing misrepresents the carefully planned movement for social change, ignoring Rosa's long service to the cause as well as her willingness to submit to arrest. It ignores as well that the bus boycott was carried out by many people who thought and worked long and hard to bring about change. Multiple biographies of Rosa Parks, such as Faith Ringgold's *If a Bus Could Talk,* or *Rosa* by Nikki Grimes are a good way to counter misrepresentations like this. The recently lauded young adult biography *Claudette Colvin: Twice Toward Justice* by Phillip Hoose provides a lesser-known story that preceded Rosa Parks's actions in Montgomery. As a high school student, Claudette Colvin took a stand, independent of the official, organized civil rights movement. This was exceedingly brave during a time when children her age were murdered for less, as was the case with fourteen-year old Emmet Till in Mississippi. This very complete biography includes a narrative by Colvin from her public talk to high school students at her (now integrated) former high school.

The same individuals may be portrayed differently in different books. This is not the same as fictionalizing.

Tweaking a Biography

Fictionalizing is not identical to what we will call *tweaking,* which can take the form of emphasizing particular aspects of a person's character or organizing stories around a theme to gain interest and unity, or to make a statement one biography cannot do on its own. It's not a matter of inserting probable events, dialogue, or actions; rather, it is emphasizing particular elements of the person's life story to create an **interpretive biography**. Children enjoy realizing that famous people also had personality quirks and frequently made human mistakes, shared recognizable fears, or were simply amazing. Authors and illustrators have the opportunity to choose which facets they make evident to the reader.

Biographies of philosophers, poets, artists, or musicians who lived quiet lives or before modern media techniques highlighted the small drama in their lives could be difficult to make interesting to readers, particularly younger readers. The obligation remains, however, for the biographer to focus on the nature of the person as well as on the exciting events of their life. When the subject's achievement is less filled with action or adventure, the writer must hold interest in the subject and yet keep invented action to a minimum. This dual responsibility is not easy to fulfill, particularly when the subject has left few recorded statements. Invention is sometimes the biographer's compromise, but should be acknowledged, as it is with *The Dinosaurs of Waterhouse Hawkins* by Barbara Kerley.

Waterhouse Hawkins was immersed in his art from the time he was a boy, spending hours sketching outside; animals were his passion. Illustrator Brian Selznick shows that he brought dinosaurs to life by providing colored three-dimensional versions next to the sepia drawings Waterhouse drew as a boy. With this technique, he foreshadows the real work that consumed Hawkins's adult career: the creation of life-sized models of dinosaurs the public could enjoy. The iguanodon was his crowning glory in England; the model turned into the site of a scholarly dinner party, a fabulous exhibit at the famed Crystal Palace, and an invitation to create models of American dinosaurs for the planned Paleozoic Museum in New York City. The politics of William "Boss" Tweed led to the devastation of his work and his artistic spirit: Selznick shows Waterhouse walking dejectedly away from the ruined work, gray skies pouring down, though Hawkins eventually built American dinosaur models at Princeton University and for the Smithsonian in Washington, D.C. His story finally comes full circle with the discovery of more iguanodon remains; he returns to drawing and creates a mural that remains on display (along with his models) in England. A little-known artist was brought to life with the careful selection and depiction of the facts of his life.

People who live active lives are more easily made interesting for children; when adventure is part of the subject's life, the narrative pulls the reader along. Few people have led more active lives than Babe Didrikson Zaharias, named by the Associated Press as the Woman Athlete of the Year six times, in an era when "nice girls" just didn't become competitive athletes. Freedman's biography is highly entertaining, in large part because Babe herself was entertainment. Starting in high school as a basketball player, she became an American Athletic Union All American, went on to track and field wins in javelin throw, baseball throw, shot put, high jump, and broad (or long) jump. "And then she began to train." She made a bracelet of her first ten golf medals. When Babe began playing golf, she entered a world dominated by socially elite women; she was called "Muscle Moll" by reporters and subjected to insulting comment, but she played to the crowd successfully. When she flubbed a shot, she grinned and said, "All that work and a dead baby!"—a comment unlikely to be made by her sophisticated competitors.

Lives of the Artists: Masterpieces, Messes (and What the Neighbors Thought) is a complex title for any book. But Kathleen Krull's collection of brief biographies of nineteen artists does what her title implies. The life and work of each artist is described, but each

INQUIRY POINT

Biographies can be truthful at the same time they create interest in not only the subject of the biography, but also in the genre of biography itself. See how Kathleen Krull interests readers in the subjects of her effective biographies. Notice the diversity in subjects and think about the effect the various illustrators have on the feel of Krull's biographies.

Albert Einstein. Boris Kulikov, Illus. Viking Juvenile, 2009.

The Boy Who Invented TV: The Story of Philo Farnsworth. Greg Couch, Illus. Knopf Books for Young Readers, 2009.

Harvesting Hope: The Story of Caesar Chevaz. Yuyi Morales, Illus. Harcourt Children's Books, 2003.

Kubla Khan: The Emperor of Everything. Robert Byrd, Illus. Viking Juvenile, 2010.

Lincoln Tells a Joke: How Laughter Saved the President (and the Country). Paul Brewer, Coauthor. Stacy Innerst, Illus. Harcourt Children's Books, 2010.

Lives of Pirates: Swashbucklers, Scoundrels (Neighbors Beware!). Kathryn Hewitt, Illus. Harcourt Children's Books, 2010.

Pocahontas: Princess of the New World. David Diaz, Illus. Walker Books for Young Readers, 2007.

The Road to Oz: Twists, Turns, Bumps and Triumphs in the Life of L. Frank Baum. Kevin Hawkes, Illus. Knopf Books for Young Readers, 2008.

has a wondrous quirk that holds interest. Chagall threw paintings out the window; van Gogh was run out of town by his neighbors; Michelangelo rarely bathed and so rarely took off his dog-skin boots; Anguissola was so old that she had to get a document saying she was alive; Rembrandt painted a family who owned no monkey but whose picture included one, so the family refused to pay; Hokusai drew pictures on a grain of rice; Andy Warhol had 175 cookie jars; Kathe Kollwitz's empathetic art was so disliked by the Nazis that she carried a vial of poison so she could kill herself rather than be taken alive. Each short account is not merely odd information about an artist, but is complete with descriptions of an artist's life and work.

The tone of some biographies can be highly personal, even humorous.

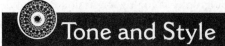 ## Tone and Style

The reader of biography should expect suitable style and tone appropriate to the subject, just as they would with other genres. The growing number of picturebook biographies can make style and tone even more evident for readers of all ages.

Three biographies of Martin Luther King exemplify how style and tone can affect readers differently. The first, *Happy Birthday, Martin Luther King,* is a bare-bones account of his life centered on his birthday, something young readers can relate to with ease. A racist society is briefly described in a few sentences about drinking fountains, restaurants, and segregated schools; King's philosophy of nonviolent protest is simplified into phrases young children can understand: "Love one another in peace." Brian Pinkney's scratchboard illustrations show strength through their dark outlines, but warmth with the pastel colors beneath. Children are not bogged down by details in this true story.

A number of picturebooks also tell King's story. Faith Ringgold's *My Dream of Martin Luther King* is unique. In the narrator's dream, great crowds of diverse people are gathered, each with a paper bag containing ignorance, fear, and hatred. The essential facts of King's life and times—his family, the country's racism, nonviolent protest, Rosa Parks—all are there in the narrator's illustrated dream, but the crack of an assassin's gun ends King's life. When the dream crowd gathers to mourn his death, they empty their bags of hatred and racism, which go up in a burst of flame. Words are seen by the crowd "emblazoned across the sky": "Every good thing starts with a dream." The biography is an effective, personal, and artistic response to King's life and work. Though it is a picturebook, more experienced readers will appreciate the time sequence created by the dream metaphor. Ringgold's folk art paintings are muted to provide a more somber tone than is customary with her art.

Martin Luther King by Rosemary L. Bray, with paintings by Malcah Zeldis, has an unusual combination of dense and lengthy text on a full ten-by-twelve-inch page across from a full-size illustration. It tells of the bus strike initiated by Rosa Parks, organized by King and encouraged by the NAACP. With text that is not oversimplified, but well written and surprisingly complete, the book shows King as what he was: a martyr for civil rights. The book is intended as a read aloud for younger readers. However, the style and tone of the narrative is appropriate for older readers, too. The gouache folk art of Zeldis is bright and contrasts with the story—a technique sure to encourage questions. Their comparison with photographic images of the times in which Martin Luther King's story is set would provide another style and tone for readers to consider.

Arousing and holding a reader's interest may tempt a writer to use inappropriate tone.

Writers of biography may use all of the devices of style available to writers and illustrators of other genres. Jen Bryant used onomatopoeic language in her free verse describing William Carlos Williams's experiences with nature – the sounds of the river (*A River of Words*). Faith Ringgold employs dream sequences (*My Dream of Martin Luther King*) and fantasy (*If a Bus Could Talk* and *Dinner at Aunt Connie's*) to make historic contributions of African Americans accessible to younger readers.

Facing the need to arouse and hold the reader's interest in yet another collection of stories about U.S. presidents, Judith St. George (*So You Want to Be President?*) created a book discussing the attributes needed for this office amid carefully selected biographical facts about particular presidents. David Small reinforced the humorous tone with illustrations in the style of political cartoons, very much a part of our culture. This feature gives the book broader appeal. Similarly, Hanoch Piven (*What Presidents Are Made Of*) adds sophistication to biographical information about U.S. presidents. Each president is described with representative anecdotes; but the danger of sweeping generalizations confusing to readers is erased with the very humorous illustrations. Piven's three-dimensional collage-style models not only match the concepts in each narrative, but also show objects associated with important events and interests in their lives. The facts are there, but the humorous style sets them apart.

Catherine Thimmesh has twice teamed with collage artists to present collections of short biographies of women and girls who have realized dreams of discovery and invention. Boys and girls of all ages will be interested to learn of the many contributions made to everyday life—from home, to industry, to the world at large—by women and girls who have received little recognition. Here again, the collages add style and create a tone of marvel at what was previously unknown.

INQUIRY POINT

Listed are a few pairs of biographies with contrasting style and tone. Choose one or two and do a compare and contrast. What are the similarities? The differences? What is the effect for the reader? Be sure to consider illustration, if it enters into the biography. Create a pair of your own to discuss and share.

McCully, Emily Arnold. *Marvelous Mattie: How Margaret E. Knight Became an Inventor.* Farrar, Straus and Giroux, 2006.

Thimmesh, Catherine. "Margaret E. Knight: Paper Bags." *Girls Think of Everything: Stories of Ingenious Inventions by Women.* Melissa Sweet, Illus. Houghton Mifflin, 2000, pp. 35–38.

Baretta, Gene. *Now and Ben: The Modern Inventions of Benjamin Franklin.* Henry Holt, 2006.

Harness, Cheryl. *The Remarkable Benjamin Franklin.* National Geographic, 2005.

Myers, Walter Dean. *Muhammad Ali: The People's Champion.* Alix Dilinois, Illus. Collins, 2009.

Winter, Jonah. *Muhammad Ali: Champion of the World.* Francois Roca, Illus. Schwartz and Wade, 2008.

Anderson, Jameson. *Amelia Earhart: Legendary Aviator (Graphic Biographies).* Rod Whigham, Illus. Capstone, 2006.

Tanaka, Shelley. *Amelia Earhart: The Legend of the Lost Aviator.* David Craig, Illus. Abrams, 2008.

Raven, Margot Theis. *Mercedes and the Chocolate Pilot.* Sleeping Bear Press, 2002.

Tunnel, Michael O. *Candy Bomber: The Story of the Berlin Airlift's "Chocolate Pilot."* Charlesbridge, 2010.

Concepts

Concept is needed in biography as it is in other literature; a preoccupation with facts should not override the main idea implicit in a good story. Chris Raschka creates an impression of Thelonius Monk's conception of jazz as "freedom" by taking artistic liberties with biography. Raschka's exceptionally short story-biography presents the syllables of each word as musical notes, climbing up and falling down the page. Small stylized pianos and images of the hip Thelonius Monk are interspersed. This is a small book, abstract enough for young adults; it develops the concepts of freedom, jazz, and Thelonius visually and musically.

Doreen Rappaport is a master at developing a concept of her biographical subjects. In addition to the previously discussed *Eleanor, Quiet No More*, Rappaport successfully introduced her trademark style of integrating narrative text, representative quotes, and brilliant illustration in *Martin's Big Words: The Life of Martin Luther King.* Bryan Collier's watercolor and collage art made this an award winner. Readers see the importance King placed on speaking, as well as the importance of a strong vocabulary. Music lovers will appreciate Rapports treatment of Beatle, John Lennon's brief life, *John's Secret Dreams: The Life of John Lennon* also illustrated by Bryan Collier. This is an interpretive tribute to Lennon's contributions that downplays more controversial actions associated with Lennon. Kadir Nelson illustrated Rappaport's *Abe's Honest Words: The Life of Abraham Lincoln*, in his well-respected realism style. Reading these biographies all written by the same biographer creates an opportunity for young readers to understand not only how Rappaport builds a big idea, but also the power of pairing books.

Biography needs not only facts, but also a reason for the choice of subject.

A biography of a historical figure that builds an important concept can bring to life a whole historical period, as does the biography of Marian Anderson. It was Eleanor Roosevelt whose strong commitment to civil rights shamed the Daughters of the American Revolution for refusing to host Marian Anderson's concert in Constitution Hall. Russell Freedman opens *The Voice That Challenged a Nation: Marian Anderson and the Struggle for Equal Rights* with an exciting glimpse of 75,000 people waiting on the Mall in Washington, D.C., to hear "one of the great voices of the time." The president's wife had arranged for Anderson to give a free concert before the Lincoln Memorial, where the audience was much larger. Because Freedman often quotes from Anderson's autobiography, the great singer becomes a real person, revealing the regular slights and hardship associated with racial discrimination. For example, Marian was initially given one or two dollars for her singing, but she nonetheless shared it with her sisters, or with her mother who was taking in laundry and scrubbing floors. On some Sundays, the pastor took up a collection to buy Marian a dress to perform in. When she applied for admission to a music school, she was ignored until all applicants were heard, then she was asked, "What do you want?" Anderson was a striking performer in a society that did not respect or even recognize the many talents and contributions of African Americans.

The concept underlying Ruby Bridges's autobiography *Through My Eyes* might be stated in this way: "Being the first African American child to integrate New Orleans schools had its effect on me as well as on the nation." In a thoroughly illustrated book, Ruby remembers her preschool years working at home in the garden and kitchen, then

text continues on page 301

TEXTSET

Abraham Lincoln

In the flood of interest surrounding the 200th birthday of Abraham Lincoln, a significant number of biographies were published in his honor. Though there has not been a shortage of books about Lincoln for children, the increased range of formats and styles for children's biographies has expanded the possibilities for readers interested in his life, the people that surrounded him, and the context in which he lived. The textset reinforces the importance of combining books to get a better picture of a biographical subject, as well as the importance of understanding the level of fictionalizing in an account of a person's life. A well-rounded selection can avoid the tendency to either demonize or create a "halo effect" for an admired subject from history. The books in this textset include biographies with varied amounts of fictionalizing, authentic biography, poetry, and historical fiction. There is much more available on the subject of Abraham Lincoln to easily enhance and personalize this set, which ranges from preschool to young adult selections.

Adler, David. *A Picture Book of Abraham Lincoln.* John Wallner and Alexandra Wallner, Illus. Sagebrush, 1990.

The classic biographer for children, David Adler, succeeded in creating a style of authentic biography beneficial to younger readers. Chronological in style, timeline included, clear text and illustration show highlights from youth to career height. Cartoon style appeals to children but provides a tone contrast with the writing.

Borden, Louise. *A. Lincoln and Me.* Ted Lewin, Illus. Scholastic, 1999.

Borden mixes contemporary realism with nonfiction about Abraham Lincoln. Color-coding visually shows younger readers when the information is historical and when it is a part of the main storyline. Historical information is factual, well-accepted main ideas about Lincoln.

Bryant, Jen. *Abe's Fish: A Boyhood Tale of Abraham Lincoln.* Amy June Bates, Illus. Sterling, 2009.

This biography is a too-good-to-be-true version of a fictitious day in the life of young Abraham Lincoln; it is based on an actual event from Lincoln's boyhood. The book's elongated design and the cartoonish illustrations that focus on Lincoln's facial expressions (countering the serious tone of the text) is a good way to introduce students to the way biographies can create a "halo effect" for their subjects—or even cast them more as a tall tale.

Burleigh, Robert. *Abraham Lincoln Comes Home.* Wendell Minor, Illus. Henry Holt, 2008.

A historical event presented through the perspective of a young boy. This nonfiction narrative is well researched in both text and illustration—even the endpapers have significance. The gouache paintings show details from the official scale model of Lincoln's funeral train. This important episode enriches our understanding of Lincoln through the reactions of others. Includes back matter to ground the story.

D'Aulaire, Ingri. *Abraham Lincoln.* Ingri and Edgar D'Aulaire, Illus. Beautiful Feet Books, 2008.

In honor of the bicentennial of Lincoln's birth, this is the original 1940 printing. Stone lithography illustra-

tions were known for their vivid lasting color—traced drawings on Bavarian limestone. A well-researched chronology with beautiful, straightforward narrative style. Not overly sentimental, but there is a bit of a halo effect: the D'Aulaires' saw in Lincoln the archetypal American hero.

Freedman, Russell. *Lincoln: A Photobiography.* Clarion, 1987.

Chronological, authentic biography well supported with primary source materials, photographs and drawings. A useful feature is Freedman's contrasting of Lincoln as legend with Lincoln as fact at the opening of the book. Freedman's research is extensive; quotations from original sources (letters, contemporary newspaper articles, etc.) help to make this a top choice.

Geary, Rick. *The Murder of Abraham Lincoln: A Chronicle of 62 Days in the Life of the American Republic, March 4–May 4, 1865.* ComicsLit, 2005.

This graphic novel format uses meticulous research and vivid graphic art for a fascinating narrative spanning the sixty-two days between March 4 and May 4, 1865. For older readers interested in the assassination of Abraham Lincoln and the context in which it was carried out. Raises unanswered questions, leaving readers with the sense that there is more inquiry to be done. Only the image of Booth being shot is blatantly fictionalized. Style recalls Victorian-era newspapers and the illustration panels are very effective in visualizing the space in which the murder took place.

Harness, Cheryl. *Young Abe Lincoln: The Frontier Days: 1809–1837.* National Geographic, 1996.

Harness, Cheryl. *Abe Lincoln Goes to Washington: 1837–1865.* National Geographic, 1999.

This is a sequel to *Young Abe Lincoln;* the paperback version has a new cover that would be interesting for children to examine, then discuss the connotations each brings to understanding Lincoln during this segment of his life. This book features Harness's trademark illustrations, which are quite detailed; they create separate storylines. Presents multiple sides of Lincoln, preventing the story from becoming too romanticized.

Hopkinson, Deborah. *Abe Lincoln Crosses a Creek: A Tall, Thin Tale.* John Hendrix, Illus. Schwartz and Wade, 2008.

This is a participatory tale with naïve art that fits the style of this story. This historical fiction story is a great example of authorial and illustrator intervention that increases students' awareness of the decisions that go into writing and illustrating a story—even one that is supposedly true. A moral is provided at the end, setting it more as a legend than biography; it is a good example of metafiction for children and of the way subjects of biographies can become legends through repeated telling and exaggeration of their accomplishments.

Livingston, Myra Cohn. *Abraham Lincoln: A Man for All the People: A Ballad.* Samuel Byrd, Illus. Holiday House, 1993.

This folk ballad's quatrain stanzas incorporate well-known details of Lincoln's life and quotations from famous speeches. Beautifully done; the lofty tone fits this interpretation of Lincoln as a genuine hero. Livingston includes careful source notes. Difficult to find new.

Pascal, Janet, and Nancy Harrison. *Who Was Abraham Lincoln?* Grosset and Dunlap, 2008.

Part of the Who Was series; includes over 100 black and white illustrations and maps. A chronological story with expressionistic, almost cartoon art that shows exaggeration.

Percoco, James A. *Summers with Lincoln: Looking for the Man in the Monuments.* Fordham University Press, 2008.

This is a wonderful chronicle of a teacher's four summers on the road looking for Lincoln stories in some of the 200 statues erected in honor of Lincoln. Percoco chronicles the history of each monument, spotlighting its artistic, social, political, and cultural origins. A great choice for adult and young adult readers; this is an excellent model for inquiry. The approach of looking at Lincoln and how he was portrayed—and therefore how he was perceived—in different eras such as the Great Depression works well with monuments. It would work well for illustrations, too.

Pingry, Patricia A. *The Story of Abraham Lincoln.* Stephanie McFetridge Britt, Illus. Candy Cane Press, 2001.

Board book format using bright watercolors and told in 200 words for very young. Features main highlights rather than a story of an episode that might be pleasing to this younger (preschool) reader.

Polacco, Patricia. *Just in Time, Abraham Lincoln.* Putnam, 2011.

Polacco's trademark expressive paintings show a young museum visitor going back in time to meet Lincoln in 1863. An historical fiction selection with a touch of fantasy, it would be a nice companion book to Louise Borden's *Abe Lincoln and Me.* Patricia Polacco alludes to Abraham Lincoln in her historical fiction picturebooks for older readers, *Pink and Say* and *Sparrow Boy.*

Rabin, Staton. *Mr. Lincoln's Boys.* Bagram Ibatoulline, Illus. Viking, 2008.

Beautifully illustrated, this biographical story has an introduction and extensive back matter (author's note and thumbnail biographical sketches of the story characters) that provides important background of the characters and the times. The book is told through the first-person voice of Lincoln's son Tad. Fictionalized dialogue is through a limited omniscient perspective that is believable to the reader. The story creates the feeling of mischief from the boys and a caring father role for Lincoln.

Rappaport, Doreen. *Abe's Honest Words.* Kadir Nelson, Illus. Hyperion, 2008.

A chronological biography, with outstanding illustrations by Kadir Nelson. Excellent format providing an overriding theme, since Rappaport introduces the biography's concept in her titles. Illustrators for each of her biographies are chosen specifically for their ability to represent the main idea visually. Here the cover is draped in an American flag.

St. George, Judith. *Stand Tall, Abe Lincoln.* Matt Faulkner, Illus. Philomel, 2008.

In the semi-humorous, personal tone of St. George, this episodic biography focuses on the impact of Lincoln's stepmother in his early years and how it changed the way he saw himself. A picturebook, the style is somewhat expressionistic to reveal Lincoln's personality.

Steers, Edward Jr. *Lincoln Legends: Myths, Hoaxes, and Confabulations Associated with Our Greatest President.* The University Press of Kentucky, 2007.

An adult or young adult nonfiction book that clarifies common myths about Abraham Lincoln and the events of his life. The format is myth/rebuttal or confirmation/narrative. This would be a great source for analyzing picturebooks and other historical fiction and biographies for their accuracy. The text is quite detailed, but interesting and useful for adults wanting to dispel myths and avoid stereotypical treatment.

Sullivan, George. *Abraham Lincoln: In Their Own Words.* Scholastic, 2001.

Part of a series, this bio relies on speeches and letters for primary sources. This is a traditional biography, but it is well written with a fast moving storyline. Its readability and length should appeal to many students somewhere between Adler's picturebook bio and Freedman's photobiography. This book features black-and-white photos and re-productions, a useful index and short bibliography, and the primary and secondary resources (which are defined for readers).

Thomson, Sarah L. *What Lincoln Said.* James Ransome, Illus. Collins, 2008.

Ransome's book jacket previews the humorous ap-proach to this book and the illustrations throughout are purposely exaggerated to show his larger-than-life persona; Thomson builds a portrait and reveals character using Lincoln's words. Sources for the quotes are not given and might be an inquiry for the reader to pursue.

Turner, Ann. *Abe Lincoln Remembers.* Wendell Minor, Illus. HarperCollins, 2000.

Ann Turner's fictionalized memoir is told in an immediate first-person adult point of view and includes some narrative biography at the end to fill in gaps. Factual picturebooks for children are often considered too simple, but *Abe Lincoln*

Remembers (like many picturebook bios) can be both a pleasurable read and an important source for inquiry.

Van Steenwyk, Elizabeth. *Abraham Talked to the Trees.* Bill Farnsworth, Illus. Eerdmans, 2000.

This biography is an amiable story with warm pictures done in impressionistic style, with a brief focus on Lincoln as a young adult during years when he was at home with his stepmother, Sarah. Readers see his love of reading.

Wells, Rosemary. *Lincoln and His Boys.* P. J. Lynch, Illus. Candlewick, 2008.

This account was inspired by writings of one of Lincoln's sons; it introduces Lincoln from the perspectives of his sons, Will and Tad. This is accomplished through three vignettes that show the relationship between Lincoln and two of his sons. Well-researched oil paintings reflect mas-tery with light, perspective, and portraiture by the illustrator.

Winnick, Karen B. *Mr. Lincoln's Whiskers.* Boyds Mills Press, 1996.

Story of an eleven-year old girl who writes Lincoln to suggest the value of growing a beard; letters verifying this story are reproduced at the end of this interesting picturebook. Simple and authentic episode revealing Lincoln's character; he intro-duces himself to Grace Bedell on a campaign trip. Strong girl protagonist missing from many histori-cal stories; uses imagination to travel back in time; important to younger readers.

Winters, Kay. *Abe Lincoln: The Boy Who Loved Books.* Nancy Carpenter, Illus. Simon and Schuster, 2003.

This episodic biography presents Lincoln's childhood from Kentucky and Indiana and his young adulthood in New Salem, Illinois. Lincoln's love of books and reading is emphasized. Expressive oil paintings remind us of paintings of Grandma Moses's work and narrative verse. An author's note fleshes out the story.

being escorted to school by federal marshals as she walked through the crowds of racist cries and threats. Now a mature adult, she recounts the legal and judicial issues and remembers the loneliness of being the only child in her classroom. She shares her surprise that a few white children were coming to her school, but she remained the only child in the room. Her close relationship with her teacher influenced her to unwittingly adopt Boston speech. Throughout the book, running comments at the bottom of pages quote the reaction of the *New York Times*, the descriptions John Steinbeck wrote of angry taunts from racist neighbors in the school yard, as well as statements made by sympathetic people like Eleanor Roosevelt and the loving teacher Lucille Bridges. The final comment from Martin Luther King Jr. emphasizes a nation can be improved only by both "Negroes and white people of good will."

Biography may inspire positive role models, but should not be used for didactic purposes.

SUMMARY

Biography is the true account or story of the life or a segment of the life of an individual. Autobiographies and memoirs are written by or in collaboration with the subject, often from a first-person perspective. In a biography the story engages the reader through facts that are relayed with style, and the portrayal should avoid stereotyping and show the subject as unique. Readers choose biography out of curiosity about a person, curiosity aroused perhaps by having read a reference to that person, or to a discovery or a period in time. A well-written biography helps the reader toward knowledge, as contrasted to mere information or fact. Naturally, techniques of writing and illustration should be employed to this end. A good biography should also make clear the sources used to authenticate the work, especially since biographies for young children may include a certain degree of fictionalizing when complete information is unavailable. Any invention needs to be acknowledged.

Within each biography, the reader seeks facts, concepts, and the writer's attitude toward the subject. Curiosity or wonder, one motivation for children, is stimulated by the quality of what they read, tempting them to discover more about people and their relationships to far-off times, scientific concepts, or ways of solving society's problems.

Since the order in which facts and concepts are presented influences how well readers understand, a chronological narrative is often suited to younger children. Tone influences biography, just as it does imaginative literature. Style, although it must be clear and factual, need not be banal or trite; imagery, figurative language, and varied sentence structure stimulate a reader's response: I want to know more. This desire can be better met through the careful pairing of biographies, assisting readers to appreciate the genre, and to understand the subject through the many techniques writers and illustrators use.

Biographies should create a well-rounded subject, including information that is less flattering to the subject. Even with this expectation, readers still expect a biography to inspire positive role models without didacticism. The styles of biography are increasingly inviting for young readers, and illustration can show much about the personality and social context in which the biographical subject lives. Contemporary biographies provide stories of people previously left out of this genre, and many more subjects have more than one biography, improving the opportunity for readers to create a unified view.

NOTES

1. This book is recommended by and can be purchased through www.oyate.com.
2. For a comparison of Lincoln biographies for children, see Henry Mayer, "Abe, Honestly and Otherwise," *New York Times Book Review,* February 12, 1989, p. 24.
3. Herbert Kohl, *Should We Burn Babar?* (New York: The New Press, 2005).

RECOMMENDED BOOKS

BRAY, ROSEMARY L. *Martin Luther King.* Illustrated by Malcah Zeldis. Greenwillow, 1995.

BREWSTER, HUGH. *The Other Mozart: The Life of the Famous Chevalier de St. George.* Illustrated by Eric Velasquez. Abrams, 2006.

BRIDGES, RUBY. *Through My Eyes.* Scholastic, 1999.

BRYANT, JEN. *Abe's Fish: A Boyhood Tale of Abraham Lincoln.* Illustrated by Amy June Bates. Sterling, 2009.

BRYANT, JEN. *River of Words: The Story of William Carlos Williams.* Illustrated by Melissa Sweet. Eerdmans, 2008.

CUNXIN, LI. *Dancing to Freedom: The True Story of Mao's Last Dancer.* Illustrated by Anne Spudvilas. Walker Books, 2008.

DAHL, ROALD. *Boy: Tales of Childhood.* Penguin, 1988.

DEEDY, CARMEN AGRA, AND WILSON KIMELI NAIYOMAH. *14 Cows for America.* Illustrated by Thomas Gonzalez. Peachtree, 2009.

FREEDMAN, RUSSELL. *Babe Didrikson Zaharias: The Making of a Champion.* Houghton Mifflin, 1999.

FREEDMAN, RUSSELL. *Eleanor Roosevelt: A Life of Discovery.* Houghton Mifflin, 1993.

FREEDMAN, RUSSELL. *Lincoln: A Photobiography.* Tichnor and Fields, 1987.

FREEDMAN, RUSSELL. *Martha Graham: A Dancer's Life.* Houghton Mifflin, 1998.

FREEDMAN, RUSSELL. *The Voice That Challenged the Nation: Marian Anderson and the Struggle for Equal Rights.* Clarion, 2004.

GREEN, JAN, AND SANDRA JORDAN. *Ballet for Martha: Making Appalachian Spring.* Illustrated by Brian Floca. Flash Point, 2010.

GRIMES, NIKKI. *Rosa.* Illustrated by Bryan Collier. Henry Holt, 2005.

HOOSE, PHILLIP. *Claudette Colvin: Twice Toward Justice.* Farrar, Straus and Giroux, 2009.

KERLEY, BARBARA. *The Dinosaurs of Waterhouse Hawkins.* Illustrated by Brian Selznick. Scholastic, 2001.

KRULL, KATHLEEN. *Lives of the Artists: Masterpieces, Messes (and What the Neighbors Thought).* Harcourt Brace, 1995.

LESTER, JULIUS. *To Be a Slave.* Illustrated by Tom Feelings. Dial, 1968,

MARZOLLO, JEAN. *Happy Birthday, Martin Luther King.* Illustrated by Brian Pinkney. Scholastic, 1993.

MICHAEL, PAMELA, AND ROBERT HAAS. *River of Words: Young Poets and Authors on the Nature of Things.* Milkweed Editions, 2008.

PIVEN, HANOCH. *What Presidents Are Made Of.* Atheneum, 2004.

RAPPAPORT, DOREEN. *Abe's Honest Words.* Illustrated by Kadir Nelson. Hyperion, 2008.

RAPPAPORT, DOREEN. *Eleanor, Quiet No More.* Illustrated by Gary Kelley. Hyperion, 2009.

RAPPAPORT, DOREEN. *John's Secret Dreams: The Life of John Lennon.* Illustrated by Bryan Collier. Hyperion, 2004.

RAPPAPORT, DOREEN. *Martin's Big Words: The Life of Martin Luther King.* Illustrated by Bryan Collier. Hyperion, 2001.

REICH, SUSANNA. *Clara Schumann: Piano Virtuoso.* Houghton Mifflin, 1999.

RINGGOLD, FAITH. *Dinner at Aunt Connie's.* Hyperion, 1993.

RINGGOLD, FAITH. *If a Bus Could Talk.* Perfection, 2003.

RINGGOLD, FAITH. *My Dream of Martin Luther King.* Crown, 1991.

RUMFORD, JAMES. *Sequoyah: The Cherokee Man Who Gave His People Writing.* Translated by Anna Sixkiller Huckaby. Houghton Mifflin, 2004.

SIEGEL, SIENA CHERSON. *To Dance: A Ballerina's Graphic Novel.* Atheneum, 2006.

SÍS, PETER. *Play, Mozart, Play!* Greenwillow, 2006.

SÍS, PETER. *The Wall: Growing Up Behind the Iron Curtain.* Farrar, Straus and Giroux, 2007.

ST. GEORGE, JUDITH. *So You Want to Be President?* Illustrated by David Small. Philomel, 2004.

STANLEY, DIANE. *Mozart: The Wonder Child: A Puppet Play in Three Acts.* Collins, 2009.

STONE, TANYA LEE. *Almost Astronauts: 13 Women Who Dared to Dream.* Candlewick Press, 2009.

STONE, TANYA LEE. *Sandy's Circus.* Illustrated by Boris Kulikov. Viking, 2008.

THIMMESH, CATHERINE. *Girls Think of Everything: Stories of Ingenious Inventions by Women.* Illustrated by Melissa Sweet. Houghton Mifflin, 2000.

THIMMESH, CATHERINE. *The Sky's the Limit: Stories of Discovery by Women and Girls.* Illustrated by Melissa Sweet. Perfection, 2004.

WINTERS, KAY. *Abe Lincoln: The Boy Who Loved Books.* Illustrated by Nancy Carpenter. Simon and Schuster, 2003.

MyEducationKit™

Go to the topic "Nonfiction" on the MyEducationKit for this text, where you can:

- Search the Children's Literature Database, housing more than 22,000 titles searchable in every genre by authors or illustrators, by awards won, by year published, and by topic and description.
- Explore genre-related Assignments and Activities, assignable exercises showing concepts in action through database use, video, cases, and student and teacher artifacts.
- Listen to podcasts and read interviews from some of the brightest and most enduring stars of children's literature in the Conversations.
- Discover web links that will lead you to sites representing the authors you learn about in these pages, classrooms with powerful children's literature connections, and literature awards.

So You Want to Be President?

Judith St. George / Illustrated by David Small

Nonfiction must have a high standard of accuracy; photography is a preferred media for this genre. Contemporary nonfiction includes other illustrative styles and media, including cartoon art. David Small's cartoon art befits the political humor in *So You Want to Be President?*

CHAPTER THIRTEEN

Information Books

In this age of the Internet, what do informational books do for a child? Check for bias when generalizations seem unsupported by information.

Adults range widely in their reading interests, from the financial page of the daily newspaper to a favorite comic strip, and on to particular curiosities about extreme weather, political history, or the study of Malian art. In between, they experience floods of enthusiasm for "everything a particular writer ever wrote" to "anything about global warming." Yet we are continually surprised at the diversity in children's tastes or at their sudden enthusiasm for rocks, rockets, or rugby players. Often we find that the interesting adult with a multitude of curiosities is the grown child whose reading may have begun with an omnivorous—and simultaneous—devouring of Henry and Mudge stories by Cynthia Rylant and every information book available about reptiles.

Why Read Information Books?

What *does* interest a child about information books? Of course, older children may go in search of information required by their schoolwork, and some younger children find nonfiction by mistake, because they happen upon a nonfiction library shelf. But many children—perhaps most children—will need their parents, guardians, and teachers to introduce them to books that tell "true stories." These children need adults to read aloud to them some of the beautifully written and intriguingly illustrated information texts being published today, so they can see that these books have been carefully made not only to inform but also to delight them.

Teachers and parents need also to encourage children to get to know the nonfiction section of the library, and to follow up on subjects that interest them. Using sets of texts on related themes or topics in the classroom is another way to help children learn that reading one information book on a subject suggests some answers, but that reading two or three on the same subject provides a more interesting picture.

For example, if a fifth-grade teacher reads the controversial historical picture-book about zoo animals during wartime, *The Faithful Elephants,* aloud to students, he or she might also introduce them to the story of zoo animals in a more recent war: William Sumner's *Saving the Bagdad Zoo: A True Story of Hope and Heroes.* Filled with fine photographs (an enormous bear in a cage being lowered into a transport truck; a camel's mud-matted fur), this second book shows how Sumner and his team nursed thirty-two creatures left in the Baghdad Zoo after the Iraq War, providing a hopeful counterpoint to the sad story in *The Faithful Elephants.*

It's wise to have many levels of information books available to children in a classroom, too: David Macaulay's amazing *The New Way Things Work* was written for middle schoolers, but the interested second grader—the one fascinated by his flashlight and his parents' vacuum cleaner—may pore over Macaulay's intricate pictures of can openers, microscopes, scissors, binoculars, and levers in an effort to teach himself how these objects function. Whether the child understands how the book's format and design works, he may be led by his curiosity to dive into it, though he may need an adult to help him make clearer sense of it.

There are information books on so many curious topics—award-winning picturebooks about *Kakapo Rescue* and *Lizards;* books about honeybee catastrophes and bat scientists; books about *Toilets, Bathtubs, Sinks, and Sewers;* about Barbie, about dust, and about *The Kid Who Invented the Popsicle*—that there is every reason for children, with a little nudge from their teachers, to become interested in this genre.

It is true that books for very young children sometimes simplify the information they provide so much that the information can't be called completely true—the book borders on the fictional. It's also true that fiction can be read for the information it provides. After all, we learn about spinnerets and the parts of the spider's legs in *Charlotte's Web.* But when we discuss nonfiction, we want information to be explained as clearly as it can be, while keeping the complexities of real science, history, or mathematics intact. We are also less interested in character and more in discovery of the relationship and application of concepts to society or the natural world.

Often the writer uses a chronological or narrative arrangement of some kind that makes the nonfiction resemble fiction, or the writer combines an overtly fictional element with the factual information he or she wants to share. However, fiction and poetry are created to help people understand what it means to be human, while the purpose of nonfiction is to discover some part of the real world. Although we read these types of books in different ways, looking for slightly different things from each, both types should provide pleasure, surprise, and delight.

Using sets of texts on related topics helps children learn that reading two or three information books on a subject provides an interesting picture.

There are information books on many curious topics.

The pages that follow will make clear that writers and designers of information books are concerned with shaping a discussion of information in such a way that the facts presented are enlightening and encourage readers' excitement about the content. Facts must be accurate, up-to-date, and based on the most recent research, of course, but a good information book must provide something more than this information: the writer or designer of a good information book tries to show the reader that this information leads to an idea in which the reader should invest him or herself.

In addition, a good information book should introduce child readers to the community and practices of the discipline it is describing to children.[1] For example, a historical information book should present that information in a way that is true to the ways historians work, as Jim Murphy does when he writes about *The Great Fire* and *An American Plague*.[2] Older children, especially, should be able to use a good information book as an example of the kinds of research, information synthesis, and writing they might imitate. And last but certainly not least—because it affects readers' curiosity about and acceptance of facts, concepts, and disciplinary ways of thinking—is tone, the writer and photographer or illustrator's attitude toward his or her subject and readers.

What a Good Information Book Can Do

Anyone who has spent time with a child knows that children have enormous curiosity, and that they need to satisfy that curiosity. They are filled with questions that lead to more questions that, when answered, lead to still other questions. Many of these questions can be answered by the right informational book, whether it is the *Guinness Book of World Records*, which lists odd and fascinating facts; a book about the noises farm animals make, which the littlest children love to review again and again; a book telling readers how to make objects out of origami or 101 ways to draw a car; a cookbook that helps a boy make brownies with his mom; or one of the many carefully designed, researched, and written idea packages that information books are now becoming. As Margery Fisher says in *Matters of Fact*,[3] an information book evokes many responses:

> A child uses information books to assemble what he knows, what he feels, what he sees, as well as to collect new facts. His reaction to something as ordinary as a loaf [of bread] may be, at one time or another, one of wonder, excitement, interest, aesthetic pleasure, physical satisfaction, curiosity.

When adults seek answers, they may turn to the Internet. Most adults have learned how to sift out the specific items they need from the mass of constant and sometimes erroneous information that can be found there; they can extract the essential from the nonessential, the credible from the confounding, the clear from the too complex. The child, to whom the world is new and perhaps confusing, needs more context and assistance with organizing the information he or she finds in the world. If a child's parents own and allow use of a computer, he or she may be tempted to search the Internet to answer any question. What, then, can an information book provide that the Internet cannot?

A good information book can separate fact from theory (which the Internet may not do), order information and connect it to previously understood concepts (which the Internet may not do), and help the curious child move from order to comparison and on to new understanding. A good information book is carefully crafted by its author, designer, illustrator, and publisher to provide a child with a sense of the varied textures of the information in our world. Information books can promote certain values and ways of seeing the world, and provide context and elaboration in the form of carefully chosen photographs, reprints of actual documents, or smoothly textured, brightly colored paintings. The writer of a good information book lists the resources he or she used to create the book, so children get a sense of the research process; the designer or illustrator works to make the visual tone of that book pleasing, not condescending or flat. A child deserves information books that combine individuality with clarity in words and art, give significance to the subject, represent the reality of a sometimes complex topic, and show respect for the reader, whatever his or her age.

> A good information book is a beautifully designed and carefully researched package.

Three Good Information Books

Curiosity may be the force that leads a child to an information book; it is certainly the force that leads to discovery of all kinds. It leads an archeologist to look for dinosaur bones, and an artist to imagine what dinosaurs looked like when they were here, creating 3D models of the creatures (as we know from Barbara Kerley's biography, *The Dinosaurs of Waterhouse Hawkins*); it leads a sailor to travel the oceans, and a Japanese boy to board a whaling ship (as we know from Rhoda Blumberg's *Shipwrecked! The True Adventures of a Japanese Boy*). Curiosity leads an astronaut to fly into space, a historian to conduct research about a legend, a performer to attempt a death-defying stunt, and a child to learn about strange creatures in forests far away. Below we provide examples of three information books that recount information clearly and thoroughly, teach about communities, and are artistically designed and illustrated. All promote particular values as well as information. All satisfy and stimulate curiosity.

In *Quest for the Tree Kangaroo*, Sy Montgomery introduces readers to Lisa Dabek, a scientist who fell in love with animals when she was very young, even though she grew up in New York City. She became a scientist, hiking through the mountains to find animals, even though she grew up with a severe case of asthma. This beautifully photographed tale of attempts to save a dying species shows children that adult interests begin early, and that they can become anything, even if they have difficulties to overcome. It also shows what real scientists look like and how they work—in teams in villages and forests, not in isolated laboratories. When we travel with the group—which includes the author and the photographer of this book—up into the cloud forests of Papua New Guinea, we meet children who live there and learn that the people of Yawan are concerned about conservation of their forests, too. Village women look after the party of researchers as they climb into the misty mountains to observe the tree kangaroo. When the scientists catch three tree kangaroos forty feet up in a *Euodia* tree, they care for and study them, then place radio collars on them so they can track and learn more about the lives of these rare creatures. The book ends with lists of references: places to find more information about tree kangaroos; translations of Tok Pisin, the language of the people of the Huon Peninsula; information about conservation; and "Lisa's Advice for Kids," such as join an organization like Conservation International, find out what's happening in your favorite animal's home, and, most importantly, "Follow your passion!"

While Montgomery stimulates wonder, curiosity, and confidence in one way, the picturebook discussed in Chapter 7, *The Man Who Walked Between the Towers*, stimulates wonder in another way. This 2004 Caldecott Award winner is the true story of Phillipe Petit, a French street performer who, in 1974, decided to walk between the twin towers of the World Trade Center, as he had walked between the spires of the Notre Dame in Paris. The book describes the trouble Petit went to in order to perform this illegal, risky feat: he and friends posed as construction workers and took a 440-pound cable up 180 stairs to the roof of one tower and spent three hours attaching the cable from one tower to another, working across what author Mordecai Gerstein paints as a deep purple and blue sky, finishing the job just as the darkness deepens. Petit didn't just walk across the wire then, but danced, saluted, and lay down, letting the birds fly over and under him, as more and more passersby looked up to see him against the sky. Gerstein provides pictures, done in ink and oil, with heart-stopping perspectives: the sky and the buildings of Manhattan and the Statue of Liberty in the harbor as they must have looked from Petit's perspective; Petit on the wire as he looked from the persepective of the people below. The book ends with a simple reminder that the towers are no longer there. This information book combines wit, suspense, poetic words, and deep, swirling pictures together in a true story that will resonate both with the five-to-eight-year-olds it was written for and the adults who share it with them.

Ain't Nothing but a Man: My Quest to Find the Real John Henry allows us to follow a researcher's curiosity and wonder about the legend of the steel-drivin' man, John Henry. This book is indicative of a trend in information books toward genre-blending: it is partly the first-person record of a hunt through research, partly a history of the building of the railroads right after the Civil War. In it, historian Scott Reynolds Nelson tells how he became intrigued by the story of John Henry. He describes how he searched through the many folk songs about John Henry, traveled to the places the legend might have worked, looked through coal-blackened prison records, and answered many of his questions but also found some new ones. The book includes folk songs, diagrams showing how steam engines worked, illustrations of railroad workers from the 1880s, and a photograph of the man who may be the real John Henry. Best of all, this accessible, clearly written book shows older children how a historian works—using the Internet; chasing down suspicions; synthesizing information from visuals, old documents, and conversations; and looking for another way to discover the answers after hitting dead ends. Nelson demystifies the process of learning about the past, including a section called "How to Be a Historian," in which he gives readers a list of principles to follow when doing their own historical research. He instills confidence in his readers that they, too, can become historians. He also teaches them a lot about the men who worked on the railroad. Pair this book with Julius Lester and Jerry Pinckney's fine picturebook biography of the legend to encourage students to ask questions about history's relationship to story and song.

Each of these three information books shows us what such books should be at their best: intriguing, personal, exhaustively researched, and beautifully designed. Each of these books inspires the reader to reach for more; each is written with strict attention not only to factual accuracy, but also to tone and style that attract and lead to discovery.[4] These books inform readers and encourage them to learn more.

Expository Styles

Facts cannot be dumped on a reader all at one time, or we would have to make order out of masses of information—a task for an authority, not an inquirer. The writer of nonfiction must select the key ideas, put them in simple forms, relate them to facts already known or to concepts already understood, and from this point begin to clarify. Breaking down the ideas into component parts that can be easily understood by the audience, the writer arranges them in ways according to purpose.

Some writers arrange information in an expository, or non-narrative, fashion.

The writer who chooses to organize information in an **expository** or non-narrative fashion has many organizational forms to choose from. Perhaps the writer forms the information into a coherent sequence from simplest to most complex, from familiar to unfamiliar, or from early development to later development. A writer might use many other expository ways of presenting information as well. For example, a writer might use a descriptive text structure, with a main topic and subtopics described in detail (this structure is used in Karen Magnuson Bell's 2006 *Fire in Their Eyes*); a cause–effect structure (as in Jim Murphy's *An American Plague: The True and Terrifying Story of the Yellow Fever Epidemic of 1793*); or an expository text structure that conveys a problem and then describes a solution or a possible or attempted solution (as we find in the *Forbidden Schoolhouse: The True and Dramatic Story of Prudence Crandall and Her Students* by Suzanne Jurmain).

Other expository ways of organizing informational books include the question–answer structure (as we see in Seymour Simon's 1991 *Earthquakes*), the comparison/contrast structure (as we find in Elaine Scott's *Poles Apart: Why Penguins and Polar Bears Will Never Be Neighbors*), and the spatial structure (as we might call David Macaulay's 1976 *Underground*). The writer organizes the materials he or she has found, cutting out sections and revising until the book is organized in the way that best fits his or her audience and purposes. Many information books for older children include a combination of structures.[5]

Or, the writer might organize information in a web-like fashion, as is increasingly common in information books. In *What Goes on in My Head?* by Robert Winston, information is presented in small bits—not just in sidebars and bars running at the bottom of a two-page spread, but upside down in circles, too, with speech balloons coming out of cartoon character's mouths explaining that "If the brain's surface was smooth and flat, rather than folded, your head would have to be as big as a beach ball to fit the same area of the cortex inside it." This kind of structure—a web-like organization, graphically presented—allows the young reader to decide where to begin reading, what direction to read in, and which bits of information to take in first. This kind of text simulates the experience of moving from link to link on the Internet.

Chronological

We have many wonderful writers of many different kinds of nonfiction for young people these days, and many who organize their information in an expository way. One of the best for older children is Russell Freedman, whose *The War to End All Wars* is worth placing in any middle school library. In this book, the history of

World War I is organized in an obvious way: chronologically, from beginning to end. But look at the startling language Freedman uses to title some of his chapters: "Murder in Sarajevo," "The Most Terrible August in the History of the World," "The Technology of Death and Destruction," "Mutiny, Revolution, and the Collapse of Armies." Freedman begins his tale by explaining the blundering and mistaken way it began ("And so Europe was caught up in a war that few had expected and almost no one wanted"); moving on to describe trench warfare ("Officers and men alike shared their trenches with rats and frogs, with slugs and horned beetles that burrowed into the trench walls, with lice that infested every man's clothing. Rats as big as cats scampered across sleeping men's faces at night . . ."); the Battle of Verdun and the Battle of the Somme; and the sad ending of the war ("Among the combatant nations in Europe, there was scarcely a family that had not lost a son, a brother, or a father. Today, the entire length of the Western Front is marked by hundreds of graveyards and memorials to the soldiers who lost their lives fighting there"). This overview of the war contains powerful visual elements—a photograph of bearded soldiers standing around an armed snowman, a man in the trenches, shooting, while the legs of another man lie in the muck beside him—and maps that show the way the war changed countries' boundaries. Pair this book with *Truce*, Jim Murphy's Orbis Pictus Award–winning narrative of "the day the soldiers stopped fighting," to provide middle school students with a close up of one aspect of the war that Freedman describes glancingly in his overview.

Like Murphy in *Truce*, Susan Goldman Rubin chooses to focus on one part of a very long story in her picturebook *The Yellow House: Vincent Van Gogh and Paul Gauguin Side by Side*. Rather than telling the familiar stories about the time Van Gogh cut off his ear or when Gauguin lived in Tahiti, Rubin chooses to describe a short, relatively unknown period when Van Gogh and Gauguin lived and painted together. The short picturebook is organized as a narrative, but one with a comparison-and-contrast structure as well, as it shows the reader the differences and similarities of its two main characters. Rubin describes the different ways the two men painted—Van Gogh quickly, in dots and dashes, Gauguin slowly spreading the paint on the canvas. She places reproductions of the two men's paintings of the same subjects side by side—two very different paintings of women in a garden, and two very different paintings of the wife of the owner of a café. The book ends when their time together ended, and, as a good informational book should, contains a page that tells the entire life story of each man, along with notes about the book and a selected bibliography of texts from which Rubin drew her information.

Comparison/Contrast

Another book about Van Gogh is organized in a completely different way. In *What Makes a Van Gogh a Van Gogh?* written by Richard Mulberger and published by the Metropolitan Museum of Art, the text is organized around twelve different paintings by Van Gogh. For each painting, Mulberger provides a reproduction and sometimes sketches made as the artist was thinking about the painting. He also provides a short history of the circumstances surrounding the creation of each painting and the aspects of the painting that are unique to Van Gogh's style and vision. In the ending chapter Mulberger brings together all the aspects of Van Gogh's talent he has shown in the book, explaining just what makes a Van Gogh a Van Gogh. This more expository organizational framework makes it a little more difficult for even an older child to read, but it suits the writer's pedagogical aim perfectly, and serves to show children how a great artist thought about his work. Pairing this book with *The Yellow House* and any of the other fine information books about Van Gogh (*Vincent Van Gogh: Portrait of an Artist* by Jan Greenberg and *Vincent Van Gogh* from Mike Venzia's *Getting to Know the World's Greatest Artists* series, for example) will deepen students' knowledge and help them understand this organizational structure.

> Expository texts can be organized in many logical ways.

George vs. George: The American Revolution as Seen from Both Sides introduces us to an information book organized in a clear comparison/contrast fashion. By looking at the lives of King George of Great Britain and his countrymen versus George Washington and his countrymen, explaining how the two different governments worked, then showing us the two different men's perspectives on taxes, tea, and the revolutionary war itself, Rosalyn Schanzer complicates what we thought we knew about the country and the king the United States fought with so long ago. Enlivened by witty pictures, speech bubbles, and direct quotations, this comparison/contrast information book reminds children that there are usually two—and sometimes more than two—sides to a story.

Varied Styles

Organizing text from early to later developments is clearly shown in David Macaulay's *Cathedral*. Beginning with the gratitude of some thirteenth-century French villagers for peace, health, and plenty, we learn how a medieval architect is hired to design a cathedral to the glory of God. He hires the master craftsmen who own shops staffed with apprentices learning trades, as well as laborers, many just returning from the Crusades. The building of the cathedral moves from cutting the timber, quarrying the stone, clearing the site, building workshops and forges, and digging the foundation to building walls, piers, buttresses, temporary wooden frames, and then arches, beams, vaulted ceilings, and towers, and finally to placing sculpture in niches. This book is organized according to the chronology of the process of creating the cathedral, from beginning to end.

Another book about building is organized in a different way. *Built to Last: Building America's Amazing Bridges, Dams, Tunnels, and Skyscrapers* by George Sullivan is ordered both chronologically and by problem and solution. Beginning with "The Early Republic, 1790–1850," and ending with "Megaprojects 1990–Present," the book's main structure is chronological. Each time period is then separated into pages about the most important construction work that occurred during that time, usually beginning with the problem that the construction was supposed to solve. When we read about the period Sullivan calls "Invention and Discovery," we learn the amazing stories of the building of the Brooklyn Bridge and the transcontinental railroad, complete with a photograph of the pounding of the Gold Spike in Utah. We learn about the building of the Empire State Building and what difficulties the Hoover Dam solved during the "Hard Times," from 1920 through 1940. We learn about exactly what materials and feats of engineering went into the building of the St. Louis Arch, the Chesapeake Bay Bridge-Tunnel, and the Sears Tower during the 1950s and 1960s. In the section about "Megaprojects," we read about City Tunnel Number 3, which is still under construction in New York. Along the way Sullivan provides interesting short facts on the bottom of most pages. This organizational structure, along with graphic elements such as bright, big photographs and occasional small, set-off narratives, helps the reader make sense of the wealth of information provided in this lively book.

Stephen Biesty's *Castle*, from his *Cross-Sections* series, is organized in yet another way. Every right-hand page shows a full-page, incredibly detailed drawing of a castle, with the walls of the building lifted off so readers can see what people are doing inside. Each two-page spread shows one aspect of life in the castle, based on questions Biesty thought children might ask about castle life. The first section describes what it was like when the castle was under siege, the second where they put prisoners from that siege and what they were fed, the third outlines the building of the castle, another what the people who lived in the castle ate. This organizational structure might be called a form of question–answer format, as the book answers implicit questions such as, Why were castles built the way they were? Where in the castle did the people live? How did they eat? When did they play? Pair this book with David Macaulay's 1982 Caldecott Honor book of the same title for a complex understanding of life in medieval England.

Informational books that are organized in an expository fashion, as most of the books listed above are, can be difficult for children to read because so many of the organizational structures that surround children are narratives. We use narrative when we tell a friend a story, when we watch a drama or comedy on television, when we read a child a picturebook or encourage them to study a novel in school. Because children are so much more comfortable with the narrative structure, it is very important that teachers provide them with multiple and continuing experiences with texts organized in expository fashion, especially because most of the texts they read when they are out in the world at work or in college will be organized this way. Teachers can help children understand the various ways expository texts are organized by reading such texts aloud to them, by showing them how to use graphic organizers, and of course, by encouraging children to read many differently organized expository texts on the same subject, as in a textset.

INQUIRY POINT

Find three information books on a topic you are curious about or interested in working with. Notice the organization patterns of each. Is the organizational structure comparison/contrast, cause–effect, question–answer, chronological, or a combination of these? How could you best help students understand the books' organizational structures? ⚙

Narrative Styles

Because the narrative form is so familiar to us all, many writers of books for children weave information into narrative form. The nonfiction text *Christmas in the Big House, Christmas in the Quarters* deserves a mention here. In the authors' note at the beginning of the book, the writers explain that "the events and customs we describe are historically accurate. The conversations and dialogue are real; so is the setting. However, everything we use could not and would not have happened on one plantation." Bibliographical notes and lists of resources at the back of the book explain where the authors conducted their research. This kind of explanation is what we expect of good nonfiction literature for children. *Christmas in the Big House, Christmas in the Quarters* is a historical narrative, telling the story of

Christmas in 1859, but it's a narrative with a difference: the story switches back and forth from the experiences of people living in the big house to the experiences of people living in the slave quarters; it is a prime example of the comparison–contrast format for informational text.

The Magic School Bus series by Joanna Cole and Bruce Degen is an example of information text organized partly in narrative form: two stories parallel each other throughout the books, one a fantasy narrative and the other a factual expository text. The delight of these books is highly dependent on the wacky character of the teacher Ms. Frizzle: the narrative of each book in the series describes a trip she takes with her students in her magic school bus. For example, in *The Magic School Bus Inside a Hurricane*, Ms. Frizzle takes her students to a weather station where they learn—partly by flying straight into a hurricane—that nearly all hurricanes start over warm tropical oceans, that the eye is the quiet part of a hurricane, and that tornadoes often occur at the edges of hurricanes. Along the way, sometimes in small reports written on lined paper and placed on the corner of a page, readers learn small facts about weather—the definition of the word tornado, for example, or a simple explanation of the difference between tornadoes and hurricanes. Part of the fun of these books is the predictability of the characters: Ms Frizzle's clothes are wild, her school bus is wacky, and her class trips are weird, and Arnold always wants to go home. Another example of the genre blend, this informative book with its parallel narrative contains fantasy elements as well—a bus that flies and becomes a boat when it needs to. These ingenious books have made learning about weather, the human body, the solar system, the earth—and recently, the climate change challenge—vital and engaging for the youngest children.

Many writers weave information into narrative form.

Another information book organized in narrative fashion is Hudson Talbott's wonderful *Safari Journal*. This narrative of a trip to Kenya is told in an engaging, natural, and colloquial way by the fictional Casey Monroe, whose handwritten journal we read as he grumps about taking this trip with his wacky Aunt Elaine. Casey's tone is what you might imagine a sixth grader's would be as he travels around Kenya: first bored, sitting next to "Dr. Fatso" on the plane, then thrilled by the sight of an elephant lumbering along the road at sunrise. In his journal, Casey includes the photograph he took of the elephant and the mountain in the distance; we see a torn piece from Casey's spiral notebook where he has noted that Mt. Kilimanjaro is 19,340 feet high. Casey sees and writes about and takes photographs of rhinoceros, cheetahs, giraffe, and buffalo. He marks on a map all the places he's been. He visits the "mayatta" of his friends Mutongai and his son Pilot, who are both Massai, and watches the morani, young men in their late teens, celebrate with the laibon (when he hears the laibon has come Casey says, "Cool! . . . What's a laibon?"). All the way through, the book has a lighthearted tone: "Kenya isn't really like Tarzan movies. It's more like National Geographic with smells." The book is remarkable not just for its genre-blending text or the amount of information a reader would learn from it, but from its imaginative use of graphics: Casey's handwritten journal includes stunning photographs and maps to progressively show his route. In addition to adventure and information, the book contains lessons about respect for the animals of Kenya, as well as some suspenseful detective work, as Casey and his friends take off after Dr. Fatso, who is trying to poach rhinos' ivory tusks.

Writers use narratives, and organize their information in narrative ways, as they write about different topics. Below we show how a few great writers use narratives in their writing about fires, both historical and contemporary; and about natural science, both the investigators who work in the field, and the creatures they sometimes study.

Books about Fires

The Great Fire by Jim Murphy is a remarkable effort to show the devastation of the Great Fire of Chicago in 1871. The many illustrations and news stories taken from periodicals of the day, quoted personal recollections of fire survivors, and carefully researched facts about a Chicago made almost entirely of wood before the fire all add up to a complex description of this disaster's effect on real people. *The Great Fire* owes much of its success to Murphy's use of concrete and specific language to make the fire credible. What history portrays as a city's disaster becomes a personal disaster for individuals who lose lives, homes, livestock, and businesses. For example, the first call of "Fire!" is made by Daniel "Peg Leg" Sullivan, whose wooden leg gets caught in the uneven floor of the O'Leary barn; hopping on his other leg, he is hit by a calf racing for the door, hangs on to it, and is saved. Accounts of efforts to save the sick or infirm, the animals, homes, and businesses are interesting in themselves. The many individual stories Murphy provides helps readers see that, in history, there is never a single best narrative. A reader learns something else about the work historians do from this text: they see the many different and conflicting sources from which a historian must weave his or her final story. Unlike many writers of history, Murphy provides multisensory information—descriptions of sounds, smells, visions—that help the reader place the experience in context. For example, William Lee, checking on his crying seventeen-month-old child, looks out the window and sees the sky lit by flames that generated flying embers:

> Lee hesitated a moment, shouting to his wife to take care of the baby and rushed out of the house. He ran the three blocks to Bruno Goll's drugstore, determined to do what no one else in the neighborhood had thought about doing: turn in a fire alarm. At this point, the fire was barely fifteen minutes old. What followed was a series of fatal errors that set the fire free and doomed the city to a fiery death.

Murphy thus shows readers not just this complicated moment in history but also how a community of historians best conduct their work.

An interesting book to pair with Murphy's description of the devastation wrought by a long-ago fire might be the Orbis Pictus winner *Fire in Their Eyes: Wildfires and the People Who Fight Them* by Karen Magnuson Bell. Though her main structure is descriptive/expository, not narrative, Bell weaves the narratives of firefighters into her story, making it come alive. In five succinct chapters Bell presents us with the work that firefighters do for us, including their training, tools, and triumphs. She explains the science behind a burn, using comparisons that will be helpful to children, describing the temperature of an average flame front as much hotter than the temperature of a self-cleaning oven. She shows the extraordinary measures firefighters must take, using the technology developed to help them do their jobs—the foldable aluminum foil-and-glass fire shelters that they crawl into in cases of extreme danger; the Pulaski, a "combination axe and hoe," which helps firefighters mop up after a burn; and the PG bags smokejumpers sew for themselves. The heart of the book is its narratives, though, as Bell briefly and sometimes not-so-briefly recounts the stories of firefighters: a white woman who works as a fire management officer and another, Stephanie Nelson, who fights fires

Good information writers provide sensory information about their topics.

with Idaho's Sawtooth Hotshots; a Pueblo Indian man, Ken Seonia, who but for his calm and quick thinking would have died when he was fighting a fire in the Santa Fe National Forest on Earth Day 1993; and a white man who spends his winters building sets for the Metropolitan Opera. These details bring vibrancy and complexity to work that is far removed from many children's lives, and to workers who could easily be stereotyped as heroic white men. Bell's emphasis on the friendship and trust that develops between these workers provides a counterbalance to our American tendency to valorize individuals, rather than to see how often progress and safety depends on the skills and communication of a group of people.

Books about Science

Nic Bishop is highly successful at weaving the facts of nature into narrative form. In *Digging for Bird-Dinosaurs*, part of Houghton Mifflin's excellent *Scientists in the Field* series, he shows a modern-day scientist at work—not a stereotypical nerd in a lab coat, but a hard-working woman in shorts and a tank top scraping away at rocks out in the desert. In telling the story of one expedition, Bishop also tells a partial story of the scientist's life, explaining how she first became interested in bird-dinosaurs and where and what she studied in school. Within the narrative form, *Digging for Bird-Dinosaurs* is factually accurate, but it is also an accurate presentation of the way science works—with a question, a theory, and a community's gradual acceptance of that theory as fact.[6] Bishop's *Spiders,* for younger children, won an Orbis Pictus award in 2008, and with its full-page, brightly colored, detailed photographs, would be an interesting text to use alongside *Charlotte's Web*. The book includes a glossary and information about Bishop's research and photography.

 Style

How the writer uses language is style. In nonfiction, as in fiction or poetry, style is an integral part of meaning, and not merely decoration or embellishment added to explanations and descriptions. Style is part of all written matter. Some writers of nonfiction ignore artistry in language as a means of making their subjects interesting. Others are keenly aware of their responsibility to use language effectively.

Nonfiction should assist children's understanding with interesting and descriptive sentences. Brief sentences might actually take away from a reader's ability to understand a topic; informative detail is an important trait in nonfiction. For example, in Larry Dane Brimner's *Birmingham Sunday*, Brimner provides detail to explain exactly what was happening when, in 1963, Birmingham's Sixteenth Street Baptist Church was bombed:

> When Denise walked into the women's bathroom, Cynthia and Carole were fussing and primping. Sarah was washing her hands at the sink. The sash on Denise's dress had come undone, so she asked Addie Mae to retie the bow for her.
>
> Suddenly, a blast ripped through the building. Windows shattered. And thirty-inch-thick stone and brick walls thundered. Reverend John Cross, the church pastor, said, "It sounded like the whole world was shaking, and the building, I thought, was going to collapse." The clock in the main worship hall froze at 10:22.

Or, as a different example of careful writing, look at the language of *What a Great Idea!*, Stephen Tomecek's book about inventions through the ages. This book, divided into five time periods, combines history and science. Tomacek provides information about each time period and, in two-page spreads, information about inventions created during that time, from the earliest (the spear) in "The Ancient World" to the most recent (the computer and the laser) in "The Age of the Atom." In Chapter 4, "The Age of Electricity and Communication, 1799–1887," Tomecek uses an amusing internal rhyme to tell us about the battery: "Today, it's hard to imagine a world without electricity. We use it for almost everything, including lighting, writing, cleaning, preening, cooking, and looking (at movies and television)." In each section of this lively book, Tomecek tells how a particular invention works, what its impact has been, and who its "children" are—an interesting metaphor.

Look also at the detailed, clear, and contextualized description of the school Prudence Crandall ran before she decided to open her *Forbidden Schoolhouse*, a school for black girls in Connecticut in 1831. This brief passage creates a specific picture and gives us a sense of the ways in which Prudence was ahead of her times:

> If Prudence looked out at her classroom window on a sunny afternoon, she could see the girls in their long skirts and bonnets chattering as they walked in the garden or sat under the big chestnut tree doing their lessons. And they had plenty of lessons. Although many nineteenth-century people thought educating women was a waste, Prudence didn't agree. She expected her girls to learn. Reading, writing, math, geography, history, philosophy, chemistry, and astronomy were part of the school's curriculum.

Variety in sentence length and construction gives interest to this passage.

Illustration, Artwork, Photography, and Graphics

In this visual age, varied forms of visual art are becoming increasingly important in nonfiction for children. Creators of information books are using photographs, paintings, maps, pop-up art, and crayon drawings to present a sense of a book—and a sense of information itself, perhaps—as being full of different textures. Writers of nonfiction for children have begun making scrapbooks, books with flaps that lift to reveal secrets, books that glow in the dark, books full of maps that open into foldout pages, books with fur covers or envelopes stuffed with corduroy squares, as well as books illustrated by paintings worthy of being placed in an art museum.

In addition, creators of information books are using graphic elements not simply to bold important words and set off one section from another, but also to circle important words, point arrows at a person in a photograph, underline or cross out or scribble over old definitions, or annotate the text. Some brief examples of information books—not especially new ones, either—in which graphic elements are used imaginatively include a book in which a plastic overlay changes a bowl of fruit into the painter Arcimbodo's self-portrait; one that reveals the organs beneath the muscles beneath the skin through transparent pages; and Jean

Good information writers know they are responsible for using language effectively.

Fritz and Hudson Talbott's wonderful *Leonardo's Horse*, in which the cover of the book itself and all its pages are curved at the top. Children could also read a book like the wonderful *Linnea in Monet's Garden*, which includes reproductions of Monet's paintings, photographs of the artist and his garden, and the cheerfully cartoon-like little girl Linnea occasionally running across the photographs or paintings.

In Jennifer Armstrong's 1998 award winner, *Shipwreck at the Bottom of the World*, Frank Hurley's photographs from the expedition are used to great advantage: the famous photograph of the ship covered in frost, against a black sky; the ship tipped on its side; the first officer with a beard and mustache of icicles; the men waving as the rescue ship rows toward them. In Sylvia A. Johnson's *Mapping the World* the text primarily serves to explain the art—those beautiful, strange, worn representations of the world as people saw it long ago. In *The Day-Glo Brothers: The True Story of Bob and Joe Switzer's Bright Ideas and Brand-New Colors*, Chris Barton and Tony Persiani accent the book's pictures with hot pink, dazzling green, and eye-popping orange and yellow so readers can really see the fluorescent paint the brothers invented.

Steve Jenkins' 2010 Caldecott-Honor-Winning *Bones: Skeletons and How They Work* uses collage art, cut paper of different hues and textures to create the skeletons described in this beautifully made, witty book. The words are few, but illuminating; it's the pictures that matter: paper cut into differently sized and shaped skulls of parrot, butterfly fish, dog, armadillo, wild pig, and human; a human elbow joint, actual size; a skeletal rhino chasing a running skeleton man, and the 206 bones of an adult human body laid out against a black background and ready to be assembled into the grinning, waving skeleton we find, set against a jewel-red background, when we open the folded pages.

We Are the Ship: The Story of Negro League Baseball by Kadir Nelson is another book that features rich, luscious art. Nelson's paintings invite readers into a different world: in a two-page spread we see Josh Gibson watch Satchel Paige pitch: we see Gibson's arms and back ripple with muscles as he casually swings three bats in one hand; Satchel Paige is in motion, one arm slung back, about to spin a ball, the crowds in the stands a gray blur. Nelson's paintings are particularly noteworthy for the way he presents the reader with each ballplayer's direct gaze; the painted ballplayer's direct eye contact engages the reader, confronting him with the accomplishments and pride of these men who shaped the sport of baseball. In one of the book's two-page spreads, a single magnified ticket to the first Colored World Series folds out, revealing a panoramic view—four pages wide—of thirty-three white-suited ballplayers, the K.C. Monarchs and the Hilldale Club, staring solemnly out of the page in Kansas City's Muehleback Field in 1924. The effect is like stepping into a color photograph.[7]

Predictably, information books come in graphic format as well. A description of one such book will stand in for many: Mark Schultz's *The Stuff of Life: A Graphic Guide to Genetics and DNA* is wacky, visually interesting, and informative. It is ostensibly the report of an alien, Bloort 138, on the "universal regenerative and reproductive strategy of life on the planet Earth, satellite of sol." As Bloort 138 takes his Supreme Highness through this "edifying and sometimes shocking exploration of the great diversity, tenacity, and inventiveness" of life on Earth, he shows us "DNA from a human perspective," "How the System Works: Sex and the Cellular Life," "The Story of Unraveling the Chromosome," and "The Politics of Genetics." He

Varied forms of visual art are increasingly important in nonfiction for children.

INQUIRY POINT

Find three information picturebooks that have been illustrated in very different ways. Nonfiction readers may associate this genre only with photography or realistic pictures, but designers of nonfiction books use many kinds of artwork. For example, Judith St. George's, *So You Want to Be President?* uses David Small's cartoon art instead of realistic paintings.

Note the style of art or the design elements of each book. Refer to terms for types of art used in Chapter 3, "Picturebooks." If you cannot find out how the artist created his or her pictures, research your book or its illustrator and learn more about the book and how it was illustrated or designed. Share what you've learned with others.

An example:

What Presidents Are Made Of by Hanoch Piven, Atheneum, 2004.

So You Want to Be President? by Judith St. George, David Small, Illus., Penguin, 2004.

The Buck Stops Here by Alice Provenson, Viking, 2010.

introduces us to a sexy RNA nucleotide; tells us the story of Watson, Crick, and Franklin; explains prokaryote and eukaryote DNA; and introduces us to Gregor Mendel ("Hard to believe it took a humble monk to figure this out"), a group of misunderstood mutants, and the International HapMap Project. The black-and-white cartoons are lively, which makes the information interesting, and charts, checklists, models, and pictures clarify the difficult concepts. Information books are well served by graphic art. It will be interesting to see where this booming format goes next.

Other Considerations for Information Books

Tone

Tone is important to nonfiction, just as it is to fiction. Some children involve themselves more easily in nonfiction if they feel that a real person is conveying the facts to them. Writers may become persons in their own accounts by using the pronouns "we" and "you." To further satisfy this need for personal tone, the writer may adopt a particular attitude toward the facts and the readers, as we see in the examples that follow.

Information books can be written in tones that are clear, friendly, and respectful. In *We Are the Ship*, Kadir Nelson uses the word "we" and calls the members of the Negro League "our guys," which has the effect of encouraging African American readers to take particular pride in the sports history he tells. And look at Nelson's tone as he describes the players' experiences in Latin America:

But in Latin America, you had to produce. . . . And, man, they went wild if you hit a home run. In Cuba, they would give you beer or money if you hit one. They'd give you a car in Puerto Rico if you hit twenty-five of 'em. That's right, a car. A Hudson.

In the author's note at the end of the book, Nelson tells readers that his tone was a conscious choice: "I chose to present the voice of the narrator as a collective voice, the voice of every player, the voice of we." In his research, he says, he read many interviews and spoke with many players about past times, and so "it became clear that hearing the story of Negro League baseball directly from those who experienced it firsthand made it more real, more accessible." Readers of this magnificent book can attest that his decision was the right one. This book has an important visual aspect—the players make eye contact with the reader in a way that is mesmerizing and revealing, and that invites the reader to become one with the players, to become "we."

Jim Murphy's tone in *An American Plague: The True and Terrifying Story of the Yellow Fever Epidemic of 1793* is very different from Nelson's, which is as it should be, as his topic is very different. This is an attractive book about a most unpleasant subject. Illustrations are many, showing everything from the front pages of newspapers to plague victims themselves, portraits of researchers, and government proclamations. Chapters, which begin with the day's date and show how rapidly the disease traveled, have as titles quotations from observers: "This Unmerciful Enemy," "A Modern Day Time Bomb." Other chapter titles are clearly informational: "Improvements and the Public Gratitude." Murphy describes the disease: "The sickness began with chills, headache, and a painful aching in the back, arms, and legs. A high fever developed accompanied by constipation." A doctor describes his illness: "These sweats were so offensive . . . as to cause me to draw the bedclothes close to my neck, to defend myself from their smell." Origin of the plague was a mystery, so people blamed almost anything—immigrants or tobacco, bad smells or humid air—and tried almost anything to dispel it, including fires in the streets, and gunshots into the air. One newspaper contributor calling himself A.B. did suggest that a gill (about four ounces) of oil poured on rain barrels might kill mosquitoes, a possible disease origin. People scoffed. The city of Philadelphia emptied of citizens, while a few physicians struggled on.

Picturebooks express tone in artwork as well as in words. In Alice Provensen's *The Buck Stops Here: The Presidents of the United States*, we see how the tones of the paintings representing each president differ: the colors decorating the page that belongs to President Nixon, called "California's tarnished star," are dark, and the faces of the people who surround him are somber; they look down or stare into space. Another good example of tone in information picturebook art can be seen in Jan Greenberg and Sandra Jordan's wonderful *Ballet for Martha: Making Appalachian Spring*. This lovely book, which celebrates the collaboration of three artists—the choreographer and dancer Martha Graham, the composer Aaron Copeland, and the studio artist Isamu Noguchi, who designed the sets for Graham's production of the ballet Appalachian Spring—contains many bright, lively watercolors of the making of the dance. On some pages, dancers' purple dresses swirl against a blue background, or theatregoers march into the 1944 performance against a yellow-gray sky. But one painting, of one of Martha's earliest dances, Heretic, is very different in tone. In this painting, dancers in black raise their arms over their head, moving forcefully toward a woman in a white dress whose arms are thrown out in the shape of a cross. The background of this page is brown. In small script at the bottom of the page the illustrator of *Ballet for Martha*, Brian Floca, has written "Heretic,

Tone or attitude is important in informational texts.

1929." The tone of this painting is, like the dance it describes, somber, powerful, an expression of a kind of ugliness that is so strong it can be seen as beautiful.

Some Problems with Tone

Some writers of children's information books narrate in ways that confuse rather than enlighten. For example, some books about animals imbue the creatures with human qualities, suggesting that animals are uninteresting in themselves and need to be jazzed up by making them more nearly human. This is **anthropomorphism,** and it introduces an incorrect way of thinking about animals into books which are supposed to be supplying factual information. In one book about dinosaurs, a brontosaurus is called "terribly dumb"; the tylosaurus, described as clever, fierce, and cruel, seems vicious rather than, more accurately, carnivorous. In *Here Come the Wild Dogs,* about the life of a fox family, we hear the father fox's thoughts about the pleasant morning.

But children's books about animals need not be written in this way. In the photographic picturebook *Chameleon, Chameleon,* Joy Cowley does not encourage her young readers to imagine that the creature thinks as humans do. The simple words next to Nic Bishop's bright, amazingly close-up photographs describe the chameleon looking for a new tree where food might be, checking for danger—creeping carefully past the poisonous scorpion—zapping a caterpillar with his long tongue, and changing colors when he sees a female chameleon. There is no indication that the chameleon feels love, or thinks about danger in any way other than the instinctual. The book ends with an explanatory note about the lives and habits of chameleons, written, perhaps, for a parent to read aloud to a child.

INQUIRY POINT

Eric Carle's *The Very Hungry Caterpillar* is a book that is loved by many adults as well as children. It has been criticized for its anthropomorphism and for creating misconceptions about the very specific foods butterfly larvae must eat in order to complete its metamorphosis. Imagine reading this fantasy book with a younger child and then reading a nonfiction book showing the life cycle of a butterfly, such as:

Diane Hutts Aston's *A Butterfly Is Patient.* Sylvia Long, Illus. Chronicle Books, 2011.

Joan C. Calder's *Airplane in the Garden: Monarch Butterflies Take Flight,* Patio, 2011.

Bobby Kalman's *The Life Cycle of a Butterfly (with CD).* Margaret Amy Reiach, Illus., Crabtree, 2007.

1. What questions could you ask about each book to help children learn about the life cycle of the butterfly?

2. What kinds of answers would you expect them to provide?

3. What kinds of questions would you ask to help them be more aware of the art in these books?

4. What scientific concepts would you want your students to come away from this reading?

Didacticism and Propaganda

Writers are usually trying to persuade their readers to think in the same way they do: some say no piece of writing is written without the desire to persuade. Even in books that seem strictly objective, information has usually been shaped to make a point. However subtly or directly a writer is attempting to persuade, he or she has an obligation to support generalizations with facts, examples, and evidence. Experiments, statistics, descriptions of studies, and references to authorities should be the meat of the book. Carefully arranged, the evidence gathers and builds to prove the point. Preaching is unnecessary.

If, however, the book lacks sufficient evidence and relies on generalizations that the writer has not bothered to support with facts, then the critical reader should ask questions: How do we know? Who says so? When did that happen? Children should be encouraged to do this kind of questioning; they need to know that any statement printed in a book isn't necessarily true. Children need to be shown how to read critically and to ask for evidence that supports general statements.

Nonfiction writers have a responsibility to foster an attitude of inquiry. When dealing with theory not fully proven, the writer is obliged to make us aware that there are theories and countertheories on the subject. We want child readers to become intrigued by questions that have not fully been answered and problems that have not fully been solved; maybe they will grow up to find the solutions.

Writers of two award-winning nonfiction books both work hard to provide specific details that support their general statements; Kadir Nelson and Tanya Lee Stone both build their arguments about the historical periods they describe carefully. In *We Are the Ship: The Story of Negro League Baseball*, Kadir Nelson gives—and provides citations for—specific details to prove his more general statements. The easy, comfortable, colloquial tone of this book does not mean that it reflects sloppy thinking. Saying the Negro Leagues were "rough," he backs up that statement with examples:

> We didn't really know how rough it was in the Negro Leagues until some of our guys went up to the majors. Play was a lot "nicer" there. In our league, everything was legal. Spitters, shine-balls, emery balls, cut balls—you name it. They cut that ball to pieces and had curveballs breaking about six feet! Throw a new white ball to the pitcher, and it would come back brown from all the tobacco juice and what-have-you. You never knew what the ball was going to do once it left the pitcher's hand.

In endnotes at the back of the book, Nelson cites Ken Burns's PBS documentary *Baseball*, Episode 4, "A National Heirloom," as the place from which the detail about the white ball turned brown comes.

In *Almost Astronauts*, Tanya Lee Stone carefully builds her argument that the women who tried to become astronauts in the 1960s were brave women, as tough as the male astronauts, and held back simply because of societal prejudice against women. Stone describes the tests these first female astronaut hopefuls took, and how well these women did. She then tells the reader how the men did. One test Stone describes is a huge gyroscope, called the MASTIF, that an astronaut trainee stood inside and controlled while it lurched up and down, swung side to side, and spun in circles. Stone tells readers that when Mercury 7 astronaut Alan Shepard first went into this contraption he "went green and pressed the red 'chicken switch.'" She describes the experience of Jerri Cobb, the first woman to take the test—strapped into leg restraints

I N Q U I R Y   P O I N T

Find the books *From Slave Ship to Freedom Road* by Julius Lester and *Life on a Plantation* by Bobbie Kalman. Look over these books, and as you read them, answer the following questions:

1. How do the pictures and their arrangement on the page affect your sense of the non-fiction story being told?

2. How do the two books present slavery differently?

3. How is the language in each book different? Remember that language is never neutral.

4. What kinds of information does each book leave out?

5. Which book do you find the most persuasive, and why?

Finally, list the points you notice, then cite information that supports your points. ◉

---

and a chest harness. The scariest roller-coaster ride ever, the MASTIF requires trainees to touch the controls carefully, with restraint and calm, as they spin around:

> The MASTIF began to move. First one cage, then the second, then the third. Soon Cobb was "twisting like a top, and going head-over-heels at the same time." Her vision "was a dizzying blur."
>
> Cobb fought the nausea. She focused her vision.
>
> She took charge of the joystick.
>
> Move by move, she brought each rotating axis under control.
>
> Cobb mastered the MASTIF. Mercury-style.

Publishing Trends

The genre of children's information books has been growing and changing in recent years. Information books for children should be the opposite of textbooks, which can be stuffy, dry, predictable, or pedantic. Information books for children are more apt to be the most carefully created, beautifully packaged, and thoughtfully written books about ideas that we have. Nowadays, information books aim to please and delight, as well as to inform; to promote questions and laughter, as well as to tell something about a truth about the world.

Currently we are seeing more and more information books that blend genres and content areas. These genre and content area blends include some of the books we've listed above: *Ain't Nothing but a Man, What Goes on in My Head?, What a Great Idea!, Safari Journal, Why Pi?,* and *The Stuff of Life.* These books combine fiction with nonfiction, engineering with history, drawings with photographs, a witty tone with a serious subject, or comic book art with sophisticated discussions of scientific research. Each of these very different books is part of the radical change we referred to in Chapter 2, a change in the way our society experiences information—information that is constantly available from the Internet and many other sources. That change in the ways we receive and experience information has influenced the kinds of information books that are published.

Other books are more traditional, but much more visual than information books were in the past. Even the most beautifully written, word-laden books that we've described in these pages—*Almost an Astronaut, The War to End All Wars, Quest for the*

Civil Rights Movement

This textset for older children and young adult readers provides only a few of the many available books about the civil rights movement and its leaders. These non-fiction books can be used as background when teaching fiction like *The Watsons Go to Birmingham—1963* or *The Gold Cadillac* or to provide texture when viewing any of the many historical fiction books about this time period. In addition, some biographies have been included here to bring some of the people involved in the civil rights movement to life.

Comparing books to see the different ways in which the same story is told will help children think critically about ways ideas are conveyed through literature. All but a few of the books listed below have won prestigious awards.

 General Overviews of the Movement

King, Casey, and Linda Barrett Osborne. *Oh, Freedom!: Kids Talk about the Civil Rights Movement with the People Who Made It Happen.* Knopf Books for Young Readers, 1997.

Question–answer structure; fourth-grade children collect thirty-one dramatic oral histories when they talk to their parents and neighbors about the part they played in the civil rights movement.

McWhorter, Diane. *A Dream of Freedom: The Civil Rights Movement from 1954 to 1968.* Scholastic, 2004.

Chronological structure; McWhorter, who grew up in Birmingham, provides insight into the feelings of Southern whites during that era. Great photographs.

Brown Versus Board of Education, 1954

Bridges, Ruby. *Through My Eyes.* Scholastic, 2007.

Autobiographical account of the experience of integrating a school in New Orleans, looking back from adulthood.

Morrison, Toni. *Remember: The Journey to School Integration.* Houghton Mifflin, 2004.

Chronological/compare–contrast structure; includes electrifying sepia photographs.

 The Montgomery Bus Boycott, 1955

Freedman, Russell. *Freedom Walkers: The Story of the Montgomery Bus Boycott.* Holiday House, 2006.

Chronological/Problem-solution structure; an Orbus Pictus Honor winner.

Pinkney, Andrea. Brian Pinkney illus. *Boycott Blues: How Rosa Parks Inspired a Nation.* Greenwillow Books, 2008.

This picturebooks tells the story of Rosa Parks in a riveting, poetic blues style. Glowing, dramatic, two-page spreads work perfectly with the rhythmic text.

Shange, Ntozake, and Kadir Nelson. *Coretta Scott.* Amistad, 2009.

Picturebook biography in poetry with magnificent paintings.

Freedom Rides, 1961

Bausum, Ann. *Freedom Riders: John Lewis and Jim Zwerg on the Front Lines of the Civil Rights Movement.* National Geographic Children's Books, 2005.

Chronological structure comparing and contrasting the experiences of two men, one black, one white, who risked their lives on the Freedom Rides.

March on Washington, D.C., 1963

Brimner, Larry Dane. *We Are One: The Story of Bayard Rustin.* Calkins Creek, 2007.

Biography of civil rights leader Bayard Rustin, with special emphasis on his work to put together the historic March on Washington, D.C.

Birmingham Bombing and Protests, 1963

Brimner, Larry Dane. *Birmingham Sunday.* Calkins Creek, 2010.

Chronological/Problem–solution structure.

Mayer, Robert H. *When the Children Marched: The Birmingham Civil Rights Movement.* Enslow, 2008.

Children played an important role in the struggle for justice in Birmingham, and this book uses photos, newspaper accounts, and stories from all sides to show how civil rights workers decided to include young people in the movement.

Civil Rights Act and Selma, 1964

Partridge, Elizabeth. *Marching for Freedom: Keep On, Children, and Don't You Grow Weary.* Viking Juvenile, 2009.

Award-winning story of the bravery of children—beginning with ten-year-old Joann Blackmun—who participated in fighting for voting rights. Exemplary bibliography, source notes, and photographs.

Tree Kangaroo, and *Truce*—use photographs to show another aspect of the reality they describe; *We Are the Ship* and *The Magic School Bus Inside a Hurricane* are two very different kinds of picturebooks with two very different, and differently intriguing, kinds of art. It will be exciting to see what new information books are published in the years to come.[8]

SUMMARY

A good information book presents up-to-date facts and a sense of the way the community being written about does its work. It should be fashioned in a tone that both satisfies and stimulates the reader, and expresses respect for the reader's intelligence.

Information books can be organized in many ways—in expository fashion, in narrative fashion, or in the newer, more complex system that simulates the Internet, with hyperlinks sending readers in many directions. Style, which cannot be separated from meaning, is as important to nonfiction as it is to fiction, and back matter listing resources and citing sources of information are as important in children's books as they are in information books for adults. New information books are about many intriguing subjects—the courage of female astronauts, honeybee kingdoms, the creation of braces, the invention of the toilet, Barbie, day-glo paint, tattoos, bats, origami, and the building of sewers, to name a few. New information books use collage, tapestry, oil paintings, woodcuts, photographs, crayon drawings, and many, many other sophisticated kinds of art to intrigue readers. It will be exciting to see where the great writers and designers of information books take this genre next.

NOTES

1. The discussions of what makes a good science text for children in this chapter are all based on Danielle J. Ford, "More Than the Facts: Reviewing Science Books," *The Horn Book Magazine*, May/June 2002, pp. 265–271.
2. The discussions of what makes good history writing, and of Jim Murphy's work in particular, are influenced by Myra Zarnowski, "History Writing That's 'Good to Think With': The Great Fire, Blizzard! And An American Plague," *Children's Literature in Education*, 40, 2009, 40, pp. 250–262.
3. Rebecca Lukens is grateful to Margery Fisher for many of the ideas throughout this chapter. Her book *Matters of Fact* (London: Brockhampton Press, 1973/1997) is an excellent discussion of what should be expected of nonfiction books for children.
4. Margery Fisher, *Matters of Fact* (London: Brockhampton Press, 1973/1997), p. 23. Fisher contrasts two terms: A starter makes the child "want to pursue it further. A stopper can be quickly skimmed and will be as quickly forgotten because it gives the deadly impression of being self-contained and yet incomplete."
5. Much of this paragraph about text structures paraphrases and takes examples from Shirley B. Ernst and Lesley Colabucci, "Literature Apprentices: Understanding Nonfiction Text Structures with Mentor Texts," *Journal of Children's Literature*, 2(34), Fall 2008.
6. The discussions of what makes a good science text for children in this chapter are all based on Danielle J. Ford, "More Than the Facts: Reviewing Science Books,"*The Horn Book Magazine*, May/June 2002, pp. 265–271.
7. This phrase, a description of this particular painting in Kadir Nelson's book *We Are the Ship*, was taken from Phil Nel, "Kadir Nelson Is the Best; or, When the Caldecott Committee Strikes Out," *Nine Kinds of Pie* [website], retrieved from www.philnel.com.
8. We are grateful to the members of the Cooperative Children's Books Center list-serv, CCBC-Net, for their Fall conversations on children's nonfiction. Much of this chapter was informed by their knowledge and wisdom. This list-serv is still going on right now.

RECOMMENDED BOOKS

ARMSTRONG, JENNIFER. *Shipwreck at the Bottom of the World*. Scholastic, 1998.

ASTON, DIANE HUTTS. *A Butterfly Is Patient*. Illustrated by Sylvia Long. Chronicle Books, 2011.

BALL, JOHNNY. *Why Pi?* DK Children, 2009.

BARTON, CHRIS. *The Day-Glo Brothers: The True Story of Bob and Joe Switzer's Bright Ideas and Brand-New Colors*. Illustrated by Tony Persiani. Charlesbridge, 2009.

BELL, KAREN MAGNUSON. *Fire in Their Eyes: Wildfires and the People Who Fight Them*. Sandpiper, 1999.

BIESTY, STEPHEN, AND RICHARD PLATT. *Castle*. DK Publishers, 1994.

BISHOP, NIC. *Digging for Bird-Dinosaurs*. Houghton Mifflin, 2002.

BISHOP, NIC. *Lizards*. Scholastic, 2010.

BISHOP, NIC. *Spiders*. Scholastic Nonfiction, 2007.

BJORK, CHRISTINA, AND LENA ANDERSON. *Linnea in Monet's Garden*. R&S Publishers, 1987.

BLUMBERG, RHODA. *Shipwrecked! The True Adventures of a Japanese Boy*. HarperCollins, 2003.

BRIMNER, LARRY DANE. *Birmingham Sunday*. Boyds Mills Press, 2010.

CALDER, JOAN C. *Airplane in the Garden: Monarch Butterflies Take Flight*. Patio, 2011.

COLE, JOANNA, AND BRUCE DEGEN. *The Magic School Bus and the Climate Challenge*. Scholastic, 2010.

COLE, JOANNA, AND BRUCE DEGEN. *The Magic School Bus Inside a Hurricane*. Scholastic, 1996.

COLMAN, PENNY. *Toilets, Bathtubs, Sinks, and Sewers: A History of the Bathroom*. Atheneum, 1995.

COWLEY, JOY. *Chameleon, Chameleon*. Scholastic, 2005.

FREEDMAN, RUSSELL. *Freedom Walkers: The Story of the Montgomery Bus Boycott*. Scholastic, 2006.

FREEDMAN, RUSSELL. *The War to End All Wars*. Houghton Mifflin, 2010.

FRITZ, JEAN, AND HUDSON TALBOTT. *Leonardo's Horse*. Putnam Juvenile, 2001.

GERSTEIN, MORDECAI. *The Man Who Walked Between the Towers*. Square Fish, 2007.

GREENBERG, JAN. *Vincent Van Gogh: Portrait of an Artist*. Yearling, 2002.

GREENBERG, JAN, AND SANDRA JORDAN. *Ballet for Martha: Making Appalachian Spring*. Illustrated by Brian Floca. New York: Roaring Brook Press, 2010.

JENKINS, STEVE. *Bones: Skeletons and How They Work*. Scholastic, 2010.

JOHNSON, SYLVIA. *Mapping the World*. Atheneum, 1999.

JURMAIN, SUZANNE. *Forbidden Schoolhouse: The True and Dramatic Story of Prudence Crandall and Her Students*. Houghton Mifflin, 2005.

KALMAN, BOBBY. *The Life Cycle of a Butterfly (with CD)*. Illustrated by Margaret Amy Reiach, Crabtree, 2007.

KERLEY, BARBARA. *The Dinosaurs of Waterhouse Hawkins*. Scholastic Press, 2001.

LAUBER, PATRICIA. *Volcano: The Eruption and Healing of Mount St. Helens*. Bradbury, 1986.

LESTER, JULIUS. *John Henry*. Illustrated by Jerry Pinkney. Puffin, 1999.

MACAULAY, DAVID. *Castle*. Graphia, 1982.

MACAULAY, DAVID. *Cathedral*. Houghton Mifflin, 1973.

MACAULAY, DAVID. *The New Way Things Work*. Houghton Mifflin, 1998.

MACAULAY, DAVID. *Underground*. Houghton Mifflin, 1976.

McKISSACK, PATRICIA C., AND FREDRICK McKISSACK. *Christmas in the Big House, Christmas in the Quarters*. Scholastic, 2002.

MELTZER, MILTON. *All Times, All Peoples: A World History of Slavery*. Harper & Row, 1980.

MONTGOMERY, SY. *Kakapo Rescue: Saving the World's Strangest Parrot*. Illustrated by Nic Bishop. Houghton Mifflin, 2010.

MONTGOMERY, SY. *Quest for the Tree Kangaroo: An Expedition to the Cloud Forest of New Guinea*. Houghton Mifflin, 2006.

MULBERGER, RICHARD. *What Makes a Van Gogh a Van Gogh?* Viking Juvenile, 2001.

MURPHY, JIM. *An American Plague: The True and Terrifying Story of the Yellow Fever Epidemic of 1793*. Houghton Mifflin, 2003.

MURPHY, JIM. *The Great Fire*. Scholastic, 1995.

MURPHY, JIM. *Truce: The Day the Soldiers Stopped Fighting*. Houghton Mifflin, 2009.

NELSON, KADIR. *We Are the Ship: The Story of Negro League Baseball*. Hyperion, 2008.

NELSON, SCOTT REYNOLDS, AND MARC ARONSON. *Ain't Nothing but a Man: My Quest to Find the Real John Henry*. National Geographic, 2008.

PIVEN, HANOCH. *What Presidents Are Made Of*. Atheneum, 2004.

PROVENSON, ALICE. *The Buck Stops Here*. Viking, 2010.

RUBALCABA, JILL. *Every Bone Tells a Story: Hominin Discoveries, Deductions and Debates*. Illustrated by Peter Robertshaw. Charlesbridge, 2010.

RUBIN, SUSAN GOLDMAN. *The Yellow House: Vincent Van Gogh and Paul Gauguin Side by Side*. Harry N. Abrams, 2001.

SCHANZER, ROSALYN. *George vs. George: The American Revolution as Seen from Both Sides*. National Geographic Children's Books, 2007.

SCHULTZ, MARK. *The Stuff of Life: A Graphic Guide to Genetics and DNA*. Hill & Wang, 2009.

SCOTT, ELAINE. *Poles Apart: Why Penguins and Polar Bears Will Never Be Neighbors*. Viking Juvenile, 2004.

SIMON, SEYMOUR. *Earthquakes*. Perfection Learning, 2006.

SIMON, SEYMOUR. *Oceans*. Morrow, 1990.

STANLEY, JERRY. *Children of the Dust Bowl: The True Story of the School at Weedpatch Camp*. Scholastic. 2005.

STONE, TANYA LEE. *Almost Astronauts: Thirteen Women Who Dared to Dream*. Candlewick, 2009.

SULLIVAN, GEORGE. *Built to Last: Building America's Amazing Bridges, Dams, Tunnels, and Skyscrapers*. Scholastic Nonfiction, 2005.

SUMNER, WILLIAM. *Saving the Baghdad Zoo: A True Story of Hope and Heroes*. HarperCollins, 2010.

TALBOTT, HUDSON. *Safari Journal*. Harcourt Books, 2003.

TOMECEK, STEPHEN. *What a Great Idea!: Inventions That Changed the World*. Scholastic, 2003.

TSUCHIYA, YUKIO, AND TED LEWIN. *The Faithful Elephants*. Sandpiper, 1997.

VENZIA, MIKE. *Vincent Van Gogh: Getting to Know the World's Great Artists*. Children's Press, 1989.

WHITE, E. B. *Charlotte's Web*. HarperCollins, 1999.

WINSTON, ROBERT. *What Goes on in My Head?* DK Publishing, 2010.

WULFFSON, DON L. *The Kid Who Invented the Popsicle: And Other Surprising Stories about Inventions*. Puffin, 1999.

MyEducationKit™

Go to the topic "Nonfiction" on the MyEducationKit for this text, where you can:

- Search the Children's Literature Database, housing more than 22,000 titles searchable in every genre by authors or illustrators, by awards won, by year published, and by topic and description.

- Explore genre-related Assignments and Activities, assignable exercises showing concepts in action through database use, video, cases, and student and teacher artifacts.

- Listen to podcasts and read interviews from some of the brightest and most enduring stars of children's literature in the Conversations.

- Discover web links that will lead you to sites representing the authors you learn about in these pages, classrooms with powerful children's literature connections, and literature awards.

Pecan Pie Baby

Jacqueline Woodson / Illustrated by Sophie Blackall

Reading aloud is an interactive event. Realistic contemporary stories that resonate with adults and children can encourage discussion during the reading event.

CHAPTER FOURTEEN

A Lifetime of Reading

How can we help students become lifelong readers? There are at least three ways: conducting interactive read-alouds, discussing books, and encouraging independent reading.

In this final chapter we will describe some of the ways we believe that the astonishing, complex, witty, and artful children's and young adult books we have been listing in this handbook—the classics and the postmodern, the picturebooks and the informational—should be used in the classroom. We will also explain a bit about our beliefs about reading and describe ways teachers can encourage their students to become lifelong readers.

In his book *On Reading*, Ken Goodman writes, "The sense you make of a text does not depend first of all on the marks on the paper. It depends first on the sense you bring to it."[1] This is a somewhat new way of looking at reading. Rather than expecting the student to ferret out the one true meaning the writer intended when he or she put words on paper, this newer way of thinking about reading, a way influenced by Louise Rosenblatt, among others, sees reading as a meaning-making process in which the context and the reader are as important as the text.

This newer way of thinking about how reading works makes the cultural background or personal history each reader brings to the marks on the paper much more important than researchers and teachers previously thought. This newer way of thinking about how reading works also makes the context of reading more important than it was before. In part because the reader and context are considered more important, and in part because of understandings that new research has brought us, a focus on student talk has become increasingly important when teachers organize their language arts classrooms.

The connection between student talk and learning to love reading is not always easy to see. We have long thought of the reader as the loner, friendless, hidden up in his bedroom, turning the pages in silence. And yet research and new understandings of the way reading works completely blow apart this image.

First, talk is important to the growth of thought. Talking about books—and by this we mean *children's talk*—is the most important aspect of their learning. The Russian psychologist Lev Vygotsky has shown that "thought does not express itself in words, but rather *realizes* itself in them."[2] That is, until we talk, we cannot really know what we think. Because of Vygotsky's work, teachers now know that using language in a social context helps students develop their memories, their attention spans, their decision-making skills, and their overall understanding of language.[3] Or, as Lawrence Sipe puts it, "oral language in social settings is a profoundly critical component of [children's] cognitive development and one of the most important factors in their learning."[4]

Some researchers claim, in fact, that the sense of being part of a literate community is the most important thing a teacher can provide for students.[5] If, as Louise Rosenblatt put it, a text is just a "blueprint, a guide for the selecting, rejecting, and ordering of what is being called forth" in the reader's mind,[6] then providing children with a chance to talk about what is being called forth by a text is one of the best things we can do for them. Some parents provide a family community in which children have others to talk to about books. They read aloud to their children before bedtime, talk about what they've read over the supper table, or help their children find books they might like at the library. But most children will need to find this kind of literate community at school.

We also now know that children's attitudes toward language are heavily influenced by the communities in which they live. In 1983 the linguist and anthropologist Shirley Brice Heath showed teachers how children from two different rural southern, U.S. cultures learned language. In *Ways with Words: Language, Life, and Work in Communities and Classrooms*, Heath described two groups of children, both living in communities that were below the poverty line. Neither group had attitudes toward language that fit in with the middle class attitudes toward language learning these children found prevalent when they went to school. One group of children inherited a rich verbal tradition. They were constantly surrounded by their extended families' conversations from an early age. Boys in this community learned to respond to adults' verbal challenges and teasing by challenging or teasing them back. They breathed in their elders' constant telling of humorous folktales and stories that were elaborate, funny, and not necessarily true. Girls in this community learned language from talking playfully with their elders and from patty-cake games and jump-rope songs. In the second community, children spent much time alone with their mothers, and were taught to listen and behave. They learned language they heard in church, and their parents read to them from the Bible; as they grew older they learned simple Bible verses. Telling the literal truth in a story was an important value children in this community learned. Both groups of children learned to verbalize their ideas, but the communities' different conceptions of childhood, and different ideas about appropriate language use meant that the children's attitudes toward language—and

Until recently, we have thought of the reader as a loner.

Until we talk, we cannot really know what we think.

their experiences in school—were very different as they grew up.[7] It is important for teachers to understand that different communities have different attitudes toward language learning. To say this a different way, different cultures and social classes have particular rules for talk: Some children, for example, are taught that interrupting when others talk is impolite; for others, overlapping talk is just the way conversation works. Language differences must be respected; however, students may need to be taught how to conduct successful classroom conversations.[8]

Language differences must be respected.

It is in this context—the context of understanding the importance of students' talk, understanding the influence of students' varied cultural backgrounds, and understanding reading as a meaning-making process—that we discuss three ways that students can be encouraged to become lifelong readers. First, teachers can read aloud to their students every day, and make sure these read-aloud times are "interactive." Second, teachers can help students learn how to discuss texts they read with others in an exploratory, collaborative fashion. Third, teachers can help students organize their personal reading by fashioning structured independent reading programs.

The Importance of Interactive Read-Alouds

Teacher read-alouds in the classroom—that is, in the elementary and middle school classroom—can provide much to students. Teacher read-alouds can, first of all, show children that reading is something to enjoy; their teacher can be a model of enthusiasm about reading, especially when children are still struggling with the hard work of learning to read. Teacher read-alouds can help children learn new vocabulary, show them how to correct reading mistakes as they go along, provide a comforting ritual, and, perhaps most important of all, encourage children to think of themselves as part of a community of people who read and think and talk about literature.

During their read-aloud time, teachers must first "work to establish a climate of mutual respect where ideas and opinions are heard and valued."[9] Teachers must show that they value children's exploratory talk—that is, their "rough draft conversation" in which they "try out new ideas on the listener."[10] This exploratory talk, and this respect for students' responses, is an important part of an "interactive" read-aloud. Still, there are many other reasons that read-aloud time is important. One of the reasons is simple and clear: By reading aloud, a teacher provides a child, as Jim Trelease says, the best "advertisement for reading."[11] Seeing a teacher's enthusiasm for reading, learning that he or she sets aside time every day to read aloud to them, shows the value of reading to students. One teacher calls her read-aloud time "more seduction than instruction."[12] From read-aloud time children can learn the pleasure of hearing the words of a story wash over them.

Encourage children to talk in exploratory ways.

In addition, learning to read is difficult work. Children, even late-elementary and middle-school children, will be able to understand far more than they are able to read. By reading aloud to children and preteens the teacher shows them the benefits that will come from their hard work, and entices them into a world of literacy.

A second important reason to read aloud to children is to teach them new words. Regular daily or school life will not provide children the kinds of access to new vocabulary that hearing good literature will. Parents do not use as many words in everyday talk as children will hear when fine children's literature is read aloud to them. Television shows, plays, movies, computer games, even the teacher in school—none of these provide the nuanced, surprising, useful kinds of vocabulary words that good literature does.

The greater a person's vocabulary, the greater and more nuanced is his capacity to express himself. The greater a person's vocabulary, the more possible it is for that person to understand her own emotions and express them in ways other than physical action. The greater the capacity for verbal expression, the greater the possibility for growth in intelligence, as well as in understanding of new concepts and of other humans. Reading fine literature aloud to children provides all of this.

By reading aloud in the classroom at a regularly scheduled time every day, a teacher also provides students with a model of how to read and respond to a book. He or she can help students learn how to look through a book—its peritextual structures, pictures, chapters, even the headers and resource pages of an information book. In addition to modeling how to read a text, a teacher can show children how to think through reading problems by providing a weekly or monthly "think-aloud," in which the teacher verbalizes how she understands the text. The teacher might explain how she has created pictures in her mind as she reads the words, how she determines the meaning of a word from its context in the sentence, how she skims or scans, or how she decides whether to look up a new word or make meaning of the sentence without knowing that word's particular definition. This more formal teaching of reading should not be the major focus of read-aloud time, but should continue occurring occasionally through elementary school and into middle school, where children will be reading increasingly sophisticated and dense texts.

In later elementary and middle school, when children are no longer reading as many picturebooks, the ritual of read-aloud is still important. During read-aloud time with older children, the teacher can encourage students to read more closely, asking them why they think the writer chose that particular word or that exact metaphor to describe an event; she can point out the benefits or complexities of the writer's organization of time in the story's plot; she can compare the text she is reading to other texts the class is reading and encourage children to do the same; and she can perhaps ask big questions about the meaning of life or the inevitability of death with her fifth-, sixth-, or seventh-grade students. If the class is organized so that students read different novels in different small literature study groups, a text that is read aloud might be the only one all students share, and thus becomes an important touchstone for conversation.

Finally, and perhaps most importantly, reading aloud to children daily—and hearing and validating their responses to that read-aloud—provides them with the sense that, along with the teacher, they are part of a community of people who read and think and talk about literature together. Reading, even for the youngest children, is a much more social experience than has previously been thought. The closeness of reader and children as they focus together on a story has emotional benefits as well. The feeling of a communal understanding wraps children in the comfort of the story. Once children meet words, ideas, and experiences that expand their awareness of the world and what's in it, their growth can be almost infinite.

INQUIRY POINT

We're willing to bet that if you think back, you'll find that most of your reading is somehow socially motivated. You may have read the latest novel because a friend said it was great, or skimmed through an information book because a classmate talked about it, or found a book because of an article you read in the newspaper. Like the children we describe in this chapter, most of us read something because of interactions with people and places in the world around us. Younger readers can be encouraged to read when you use the kinds of book discussions and experiences we describe throughout this chapter. You can encourage interactive reading explicitly, as well. Try reading some of these books with another reader, and see if you agree.

Fleischman, Paul. *Big Talk, Poems for Four Voices.* Beppe Giacobbe, Illus. Candlewick, 2000.

Fleischman, Paul. *I Am Phoenix: Poems for Two Voices.* Ken Nutt, Illus. HarperCollins, 1989.

Fleischman, Paul. *Joyful Noise: Poems for Two Voices.* Eric Beddows, Illus. Turtleback, 1992.

Hoberman, Mary Ann. *You Read to Me, I'll Read to You: Very Short Fairy Tales to Read Together*, Michael Emberly, Illus. Little, Brown, 2004.

Hoberman, Mary Ann. *You Read to Me, I'll Read to You: Very Short Mother Goose to Read Together.* Michael Emberly, Illus. Little, Brown, 2001.

Hoberman, Mary Ann. *You Read to Me, I'll Read to You: Very Short Scary Stories to Read Together.* Michael Emberly, Illus. Little, Brown, 2007.

O'Malley, Kevin. *Once Upon a Cool Motorcycle Dude.* Carol Heyer and Scott Goto, Illus. Walker, 2010.

O'Malley, Kevin. *Once Upon a Royal Superbaby.* Carol Heyer and Scott Goto, Illus. Walker, 2005.

Pappas, Theoni. *Math Talk: Mathematical Ideas in Poems for Two Voices.* Wide World, 1993.

Schlitz, Laura Amy. *Good Masters, Sweet Ladies: Voices from a Medieval Village.* Robert Byrd, Illus. Candlewick, 2007.

Singer, Marilyn. *Mirror, Mirror: A Book of Reversible Verse.* Josee Massee, Illus. Dutton, 2010.

Stein, David Ezra. *Interrupting Chicken.* Candlewick, 2010.

Van Steenwyk, Elizabeth. *One Fine Day: A Radio Play.* Bill Farnsworth, Illus. Eerdmans, 2003. ◉

How to Conduct Read-Alouds

Read-alouds should occur every day, building from five to thirty minutes daily as children's stamina for listening develops. A read-aloud should be a special, highly valued time as well as a comfortable, community experience. Some teachers set aside a particular place in their classrooms for reading aloud and provide students with pillows to lie on; some teachers place lighted candles around their read-aloud corner.[13]

Children should be expected to be truly listening, involved, and responsive to the picturebook or story being read, and the teacher should read with expression, drama, and excitement in order to help the children listen well. A story should never be read in a monotone. Some teachers use different voices for different characters when they read aloud; some mark up the book they plan to read to help them remember which words to say loudly and which to whisper. Most teachers practice their read-alouds before entering the classroom.

But a teacher provides her own interpretation of the story simply by the way she reads aloud her chosen book. This makes it all the more important that children be made comfortable enough that they can disagree with the teacher's read-aloud interpretation of the story, showing that the teacher's sense of the story is not the only right one.[14] The teacher needs to remember to give children's responses her full attention.[15] Some teachers mark up a book to remind themselves when to pause so that children can respond; some decide on questions they will ask their students before class as well. As we have said before, and perhaps cannot say too often, the children's talk about the reading is one of the most important aspects of read-aloud time.

The importance of students' talk to their cognitive growth and to their understanding of story is one of the reasons Lawrence Sipe (among many others) places such great value on what he calls "interactive read-alouds."[16] In an interactive read-aloud the teacher does not expect children to listen quietly to her story and to save their responses until the story is finished, but rather encourages children to break into the story and respond "in the moment." Sipe and others explain that a teacher misses many valuable ideas and opportunities to help children learn through speaking if she insists that they wait until the end of the story to speak.

Read-alouds should be interactive.

And, in their talk, children may have much to teach us about the literature we read to them. Research by Morag Styles and Evelyn Arzipe has shown us that children can be more insightful readers—particularly of visual texts—than their teachers are. Perhaps because children have grown up in a digital age, they are more attuned to the visual than their teachers are. Certainly, because they have grown up in a digital age, their responses to literature will be different from their teacher's. Children's different responses should be honored. In "A Gorilla with 'Grandpa's Eyes': How Children Interpret Visual Texts," Styles and Arzipe describe children's responses to Anthony Browne's picturebook *Zoo*. They describe Browne himself saying that "children are capable of much more than people think they are . . . the creative aspect of children's minds is very exciting." Browne is also quoted as saying that in his books he tries to say things in "the gap between the pictures and the words. . . it makes them [children] concentrate on looking well . . . [they] are taught that looking isn't as important. It's the most important thing in the world."

In their research into how children read Browne's picturebook *Zoo*, Styles and Arzipe discovered that

> while some children who were fluent readers of print were also good at reading images . . . it was also noticeable that many children in their study labeled as below average readers . . . were capable of subtle and engaged analysis of visual texts within an enabling environment.

Most particularly, these researchers say, students need to be provided with visually interesting and sophisticated texts, "an interested, experienced reader who listens carefully to their responses and gives them time to think,"[17] and a classroom where open-ended (that is, *exploratory*) talk is valued.

In his research Lawrence Sipe has watched many teachers who are, in this same way, attuned to the importance of students' talk during read-aloud time. He has seen teachers who allow for exploratory talk, and who listen carefully to children's responses, play five different recognizable roles when conducting story read-aloud time. These teachers act as *readers, managers, clarifiers, fellow wonderers,* and *extenders.*[18] Whitmore says that during read-aloud time these attuned teachers move "in and out of students' talk, and make split-second decisions about how to participate." They may respond to the literature more "as a reader than as a teacher," and they may shift over time from "teacher-generated, open-ended questions to child-generated questions as initiations for discussion."[19]

Sipe suggests that one of the benefits of story read-aloud time is that it is the only time in a school day when children are allowed to interrupt their teacher with responses *during* reading. Sensitive and thoughtful teachers allow children to respond in a variety of ways during read-aloud. Sipe and others suggest that teachers need to understand that children may respond to reading in unexpected ways. In his research into read-alouds in elementary classrooms, Sipe saw children respond to read-alouds in five different ways:

- *Analytically.* Taking the book apart; that is, discussing the structure of the text and its traditional elements such as setting, plot, and theme
- *Intertextually.* Reflecting on ways in which the story being read reminded them of other stories, movies, television shows, or cultural artifacts they had experienced
- *Personally.* Connecting what they had heard in the story to experiences they had had themselves
- *Transparently.* Responding in such a way that it is clear that the story world is more real to the child than the "real" world of the classroom, as when a child shouts "Don't open the door!" to Coraline as she investigates her new house
- *Performatively.* Responding by manipulating the text, using it playfully or as a platform for humor, irony, or creativity[20]

Teachers must allow students to respond before and after read-aloud time as well, of course. Styles and Arizpe's research also shows that some children may respond more intuitively through drawing than they do through talk.[21] Patricia Enciso's strategy of providing children with markers and paper and asking them to draw themselves into one scene of the story, called symbolic story representation, also shows the value of using art to help children articulate their ideas about their experience of reading. Jeff Wilhelm has described ways in which drama—asking children to create frozen snapshots of certain scenes, enact tableaux dramas or role-play newscasts based on a plot, or write letters to or from story characters—can help older students *"be* the book."[22] Encourage children and young teens to talk as you read aloud, and provide them with many avenues for response during and after your read-aloud time, and you will be amazed at what you learn.

The Importance of Discussing Books

Literature study groups are another way to encourage students to talk about books and to encourage them to become lifelong readers. Harvey Daniels, Susan Mahon, Taffy Raphael, and others have increased teachers' awareness of the value of providing small, carefully organized groups of elementary school students with time to talk about books they choose. Again, these researchers emphasize the importance of talking about the texts being read, and the importance of helping students feel they belong to a literate community of people who talk about books. Lawrence Sipe paraphrases Patti Lather, who suggested that the way we talk and write about the social world actually creates that world.[23] If this is so, then children's sense of belonging in a world of conversation is ever more important.

Whitmore provides a helpful definition of the literature study group: "Literature study groups are small, self-selected groups of children who read various texts together, talk, and think critically about books."[24] Literature study groups, Whitmore

TEXTSET

Joyce Sidman

In this handbook we have provided examples of textsets, but once you have a classroom, you will be able to make textsets of your own. Listening to and responding to your students during read-aloud time can provide you with ideas about your students' interests, which you can use to create textsets for small-group discussions. At any rate, when you read a great book to your students, take your time, help them luxuriate in the experience, and let their interests guide you.

For example, when reading aloud Joyce Sidman's beautiful book *Dark Emperor & Other Poems of the Night*, a teacher might first ask children if they have ideas about why the first pages of the book are dark purple, and the last pages of the book pale orange. A teacher might simply hold up the first two-page spread—of an eagle swooping across a meadow as the sun goes down—and ask

children to talk about what they see. A teacher and her students could spend weeks with this book, with its fine woodcuts and its interesting mix of poetry about creatures of the night and scientific information about those same creatures. A teacher could read the book straight through, poem to poem, skipping the informative text (although that would be a great loss) if her students were more interested in the poetry than the information. She could stop after reading Sidman's lovely "Snail at Moonrise" and the corresponding information about snails, and help children find other books to teach them more about these strange woodland creatures. The teacher could, if children respond enthusiastically to Sidman's "Bat Wraps Up," read aloud and talk with children about other interesting poems about bats, like *The Bat-Poet* by Randall Jarrell.

If children became interested in Sidman's description of the predaceous diving beetle whose "food-sharing rules" Sidman describes in her book about life in a pond, *Song of the Water Boatman*, they might also be interested in hearing what she has to say about beetles in another book, her recent award-winning *Ubiquitous: Celebrating Nature's Survivors*. Reading Sidman's profound poem, "Scarab," aloud from that book will encourage many questions, and reading about how beetles' hardened forewings have helped them become survivors will promote inquiry as well. Perhaps a beetle-loving student will be able to provide more information about these creatures to her peers.

Children could compare Beckie Prange's art in *Ubiquitous* to her work in *Song of the Water Boatman*. They could discuss the different kinds of knowledge they receive from Sidman's concrete poem about a shark and the information text that goes along with that poem. How do these two perspectives on sharks make them think? Children could spend a long time just looking and talking about the peritextual pages of *Ubiquitous*, deciding how long a time is represented there—how many millions of years was it before lichens appeared on the earth?

When using rich and imaginative texts like Sidman's, a teacher does not need to read in a linear way. Her reading and discussions with children can branch out, focusing on one topic more deeply than others, and then moving in another direction (discussing ways that children could explore local pond life as they are reading *Song of the Water Boatman*, for example) based on children's interests. In this way read-aloud time can help teachers learn what their students might like to read during small-group discussions; it can also lead children into new and interesting conversations, branching off from each node of interest like a rhizoid.

Sidman, Joyce. *Butterfly Eyes and Other Secrets of the Meadow*. Beth Krommes, Illus. Houghton Mifflin, 2006.

Sidman, Joyce. *Dark Emperor & Other Poems of the Night*. Rick Allen, Illus. Houghton Mifflin, 2010.

Sidman, Joyce. *Song of the Water Boatman & Other Pond Poems*. Beckie Prange, Illus. Houghton Mifflin, 2005.

Sidman, Joyce. *Swirl by Swirl*. Beth Krommes, Illus. Houghton Mifflin, 2011.

Sidman, Joyce. *Ubiquitous: Celebrating Nature's Survivors*. Beckie Prange, Illus. Houghton Mifflin, 2010.

tells us, are organized more around students' interest in certain topics and materials than they are around students' abilities. Literature study groups meet for approximately thirty to fifty minutes, depending on the age and attention spans of the children, and the focus of the study of literature is always on the discussion among the readers.

Whitmore tells us that literature study groups are built with three key principles in mind:

- Reading is a process of constructing meaning
- Literacy is social and classroom talk is important
- Teacher and students need to negotiate power issues so that their community can be more equal and dynamic[25]

This last principle can be difficult for teachers to put into action in the classroom. In "Making the Most of Talk," Carol Gilles[26] suggests that students need to be taught how to collectively make meaning from a book. Gilles suggests that, with careful scaffolding, children in literature study groups can be provided more and more freedom to build ideas about the text together. Gilles tells about how one sixth-grade teacher, Stephanie, helped her students learn how to engage in exploratory, purposeful, supportive, idea-building conversations about books. She created a four-week unit designed purely to teach students how to talk about books; believing that what is not assessed is not valued, she and the children both assessed what the children had learned about conversation at the end of the unit.

First Stephanie provided children with short articles to mark up; they were told to write their questions and responses right on the articles. She then paired students. All students then met in a fishbowl circle—one member of the pair in the inner circle, the other member of the pair in the outer circle—in which the members of the outer circle kept track of how their partners in the inner circle contributed to a discussion about the marked-up articles.

After the fishbowl conversation was over, children answered questions about their partners' contributions to the conversation. Questions were focused at least as much about how the conversation was conducted as they were on the content of the discussion. Were all members of the group respectful of one another? What kinds of comments stopped the conversation? How did children refocus themselves on the text? Did children disagree with each other politely? Who listened well? What new ideas emerged from the conversation?

> New ideas can emerge from children's conversations about books.

After the children debriefed and assessed their own and others' roles in the conversation about books, they thought about how to ask deeper questions, keep their conversation focused on the text, build on each other's answers, and create new meanings during the conversation. The next time they formally talked, the children tried out the strategies they had decided on and were assessed on their attempts. After one four-week unit about how to conduct text-centered, purposeful, exploratory, collaborative conversations, students were ready to work in literature study groups, with only occasional debriefing sessions, for the rest of the school year.

While teaching children the rules for attentive, collaborative conversations and assessing their growth as they learn those rules is important, some teachers believe that children need more guidance as they read; the balance between leading and following students will be different for each teacher and with each group of students. In Cynthia Lewis's[27] beautiful book *Literacy Practices as Social Acts: Power, Status and Cultural Norms in the Classroom*, Lewis quotes Julia, the fifth- and sixth-grade teacher in whose classroom she spent a year. Julia uses student or teacher-led literature study groups and teacher read-alouds almost exclusively and yet, Lewis writes

> Julia felt strongly about her role as an active member of literature discussion groups and defined these groups as teacher-led despite reservations about her degree of involvement. Although she believed that children need time to construct knowledge together without the interference and control adults often impose she also felt that, as adults, teachers must offer children knowledge and guidance.

In these teacher-led discussion groups, Julia sometimes brought her students back to the text, refusing to allow them to conduct "empty chatter about books," by asking questions that required close reading, such as "What exact words did [Lindgren] use to make us all decide Hubert is a traitor?"

Other times Julia reprimanded her students for treating the characters in the books without respect. When children laughed after she read about a man's head bouncing from his body during the American Revolution, "Julia stared at them in silence . . . This was not Wiley Coyote, she told them, but a human life."

Still other times Julia asked her students critical questions, like the ones Vasquez[28] describes in her book *Getting Beyond "I Like the Book": Creating Space for Critical Literacy in K–6 Classrooms*. In the first chapter of this book Vasquez explains the idea that literacy is never neutral.[29] This simply means that one way of thinking about reading, called "critical literacy," begins with the idea that any text anyone reads has been created by someone for some reason. That is, a text is not transparent or necessarily authoritative. It has been created from a particular perspective, and is an attempt to persuade a reader to that perspective. It is easy to see this when we think about advertising—for example, how a particular deodorant commercial is trying to persuade watchers or readers to buy that particular deodorant—but this persuasive intent is a little more difficult to see in children's books. Some children's books want to persuade children to believe that they should, for example, never disagree with their elders. By teaching children to see and interrogate such ideas in books, they are taught to read the world in a critical, questioning, thoughtful fashion.

In her powerful little book *Reading Otherways*, Lissa Paul suggests a series of questions children can be taught to ask, in order to help them become more aware of what a text is trying to persuade them to believe. These questions include the following:

- Whose story is this? (For example, is *Sleeping Beauty* the Prince's story or is it Sleeping Beauty's story?)
- Who is the reader of the story? (For example, a young woman might read and interpret this story very differently from an older woman, a young man might interpret it very differently from a young woman)
- When and where was the reading produced? (For example, reading the story in 2011, when women's lives have been influenced by the feminist movement, produces a very different interpretation than reading it in 1900)
- Who acts? Who is acted upon? (What does Sleeping Beauty do, other than sleep?)
- Whose voice is heard? Whose voice is silent? (Do we ever hear Sleeping Beauty talk?)
- Who is named? Who is not?
- Whose reality is presented? Whose reality is ignored? (What might this story look like told from the evil fairy's point of view?)
- Whose voice is being ignored in this story? (Do Sleeping Beauty's parents have voices in this story?)[30]

Some of the fairy tale variants that we have described in this handbook—*The True Story of the Three Little Pigs!* by Jon Scieszka, in which the story is told from the point of view of the wolf, for example—can be seen as writers' answers to these kinds of questions.

Literature study groups may be student led all of the time, or sometimes teacher led; literature study groups may be centered around texts that encourage students to ask critical questions, or around more traditional, classic works. Students' work may be assessed every time they have conversations in a literature study group or only some of the time. The important point is that children need time to talk together about texts they have some choice over. They need time to talk in an exploratory, idea-building fashion, because it is only through such talk that they can learn what they really think, and it is only through thinking that they can invest themselves in and make meaning from texts.

INQUIRY POINT

The last time you watched a movie, whether at the theater, at home on television, or at home on a rented DVD, did you watch the movie with friends or family? If so, did you discuss the movie together afterwards? Did one person know a bit more about the director than others did? Did another person remember and describe movies the star had been in? Did another tell about a critical movie review she'd read? This kind of conversation—in which each person brings a different bit of knowledge or a slightly different perspective on the text to the discussion—is the kind of conversation we hope students become part of when they create meaning together out of the texts they read and discuss in literature study groups.[31]

TEXTSET

Critical Reading

It's important to choose carefully the texts you read aloud with students. Choose the kinds of books we've described in this handbook—texts that can be read again and again, texts that promote questions, texts that are surprising or multi-layered. Choose texts that will promote the kinds of conversations you want to have with your students. For example, a book like *Tricycle* by Elisa Amado could promote interesting conversations about socioeconomic differences—what kind of house does Margarita live in? What kind of house do Rosario and Chepe, who steal Margarita's trike, live in? This book could promote conversations about right and wrong—was it wrong for Rosario and Chepe to take Margarita's trike? Was it wrong for Margarita to protect them by lying about what happened to her trike? Which action is worse? What do students think about Senora Alejos saying that the poor people "should all be shot"? If students mention a fear of violence, or some thoughts about the causes of violence, the teacher could show them a wordless picturebook like *Why?* by Nikolai Popov. This simple book is rich with meanings on every page. Children could ask questions about the behaviors of the mouse, who wants the frog's flower, or the teacher could ask questions to prompt her students to read the visual story aloud together, deciding between them what they see hidden in the pages as they move through the story. A discussion about the causes and futility of war might ensue, possibly with references back to the book *Tricycle*. Students might decide on some sort of action they could take, such as joining with another classroom to set up a box where old winter clothes could be donated to poor children. The following are some children's books to consider.

Amado, Elisa. *Tricycle*. Alfonso Ruano, Illus. Groundwood Books, 2007.

Browne, Anthony. *Voices in the Park*. Turtleback, 2001.

Browne, Anthony. *Zoo*. Knopf, 1993.

Ewart, Marcus. *10,000 Dresses*. Rex Ray, Illus. Seven Stories Press, 2008.

Hole, Stian. *Garmann's Street*. Eerdman's, 2008.

Hole, Stian. *Garmann's Summer*. Eerdman's, 2006.

Popov, Nikolai. *Why?* NorthSouth, 1997.

Skarmeta, Antonio. *The Composition*. Alfonso Ruano, Illus. Groundwood, 2000.

Wild, Margaret. *Woolvs in the Sitee*. Anne Spudvilas, Illus. Boyds Mills, 2007.

The Importance of Independent Reading Experiences

Where does independent reading fit in with this new sense we have of reading as a process of making meaning and as a social, perhaps communal, act? Researchers have found that having students read silently and completely on their own, as schools have been doing for many years in Sustained Silent Reading (SSR) or Drop Everything and Read (DEAR) type programs, is not as successful as had been expected. Perhaps this is in part because the social aspect of reading has been neglected when teachers or administrators enact these programs. Several researchers, most particularly Barbara Moss and Terrell A. Young in their 2010 book *Creating Lifelong Readers Through Independent Reading*,[32] suggest ways of structuring independent reading experiences so that students are more excited about reading on their own.

Independent reading time should be carefully structured.

According to Moss and Young, there are a few key components of an independent reading program. One of these components is what they call "community reading time," which includes:

- Book talks
- Book sharing
- Interactive read-alouds
- Time for reading

The purpose of a teacher- or student-given book talk is to generate enthusiasm for the book, not to report in a teacher-approved way about what has been read. Book talks should include summaries of the plot that stop at an exciting point without giving away the ending, descriptions of intriguing characters, questions to the audience that help them make personal connections to the book, suggestions of questions students might be able to answer if they read the book, and perhaps a dramatic reading of a script based on a book. These book talks are intended to entice students into the classroom community of readers.

Book sharing provides students with an opportunity to share with their peers the book that they are reading silently. A student might read a short, interesting excerpt of his book to the class, use a camera to photograph and share her favorite illustrations in the book, or retell parts of the story to his peers. Small literature circles might also provide ways for students to share what they have been reading independently of each other.

Moss and Young also suggest that teachers need to educate students about how to conduct their independent reading in small "focus lessons," which should be another component of a structured independent reading program. Some topics teachers can present in these lessons include:

- How to select a book that is appropriate for them
- How to evaluate peer-recommended texts
- How to use online resources to select books

Other topics for such focus lessons might include helping students with aspects of reading itself, such as:

- How to use headings to organize the reading of informational texts
- How to think about characters as they read

Finally, Moss and Young discuss the importance of "student–teacher conferences" as a component of independent reading programs. Student–teacher conferences are useful in helping young students decide how to choose a book to read, and in providing the teacher time to listen to her students read and assess their comprehension. Student–teacher conferences are also important in helping the student feel like he or she is part of a literate community: the conference provides time for the teacher to show she is interested in what her students are reading and how they are responding to that reading.

In Donalyn Miller's[33] new book *The Book Whisperer,* she describes beginning each year with new sixth graders by allowing them to choose books from her fully stocked classroom library. She makes suggestions to them as they go through the books she has. "Has anyone read this? I loved it!" she describes herself asking the class as she waves Cornelia Funke's *The Thief Lord* over her head. She describes opening plastic tubs filled with copies of Jerry Spinelli's *Stargirl* and E. L. Konigsburg's *The View from Saturday,* and letting her students have at it, in a kind of "book frenzy." By beginning the school year with this crazy, joyous book binge, she shares her enthusiasm for reading with her students, provides them choices in their reading, makes it clear that she believes in them as readers, and starts them on their way to becoming a community of curious, thoughtful, insightful, critical, meaning-making readers. This sharing, this enthusiasm, this confidence, and this community is what we believe all teachers should give to their students.

SUMMARY

Because we cannot really know what we think until we hear what we say, and because reading is meaning making (rather than pulling from a text a meaning that the writer put there), reading is a much more social experience than researchers thought it was in the past. This is one reason that it is important to encourage students to engage in purposeful, supportive, exploratory talk about texts in the classroom. This chapter provided brief summaries of three ways in which teachers can encourage that meaning-making talk. These ways include conducting interactive read-alouds every day, helping children learn how to participate well in productive, small literature study groups, and structuring independent reading time carefully. We want to suggest you use great children's books that provide new insights to you and your students each time you reread them; books that are visually interesting and gracefully, sharply, imaginatively written, and that show respect for the intelligence of the children who will read them. We suggest you choose books like the ones we've described in this handbook, and, through talking with and listening to what your students make of those books, help them learn about new worlds and find what it means to be human.

Great children's books can help children and young teens learn what it means to be human.

NOTES

1. Ken Goodman, *On Reading* (1996) Heinemann, 1996. Quoted in Kathy Whitemore, "Literature Study Groups: Support for Community Building in Democratic Classrooms," *Talking Points,* 1(17), October 2005, p. 15. Copyright owned by National Council of Teachers of English.

2. L. S. Vygotsky, *Thought and Language* (Cambridge, MA: MIT Press, 1986). Quoted in Shelby Wolf, *Interpreting Literature with Children* (Mahwah, NJ: Routledge, 2003), p. 94.

3. A description of what talk can do for children this way can be found in Susan McMahon and Taffy

Raphael, *The Book Club Connection* (New York: Teachers College Press, 1997), p. 8.

4. Lawrence Sipe, *Storytime: Young Children's Literary Understanding in the Classroom* (New York: Teachers College Press, 2008), p. 37.

5. Ralph Peterson, *Life in a Crowded Place* (Portsmouth, NH: Heinemann, 1992). Cited in Kathy Whitmore, "Literature Study Groups: Support for Community Building in Democratic Classrooms," *Talking Points*, 1(17), October 2005, pp. 13–22. Copyright owned by National Council of Teachers of English.

6. Louise Rosenblatt, *The Reader, the Text, the Poem: The Transactional Theory of the Literary Work* (Carbondale: Southern Illinois Press, 1994). Quoted in Lawrence Sipe, *Storytime: Young Children's Literary Understanding in the Classroom* (New York: Teachers College Press, 2008), p. 57.

7. A classic text that all future educators should read is Shirley Brice Heath, *Ways with Words: Language, Life, and Work in Communities and Classrooms* (New York: Cambridge University Press, 1983). Students can learn more about Shirley Brice Heath's recent work, and her forthcoming update of the research that made up *Ways with Words,* by accessing her website, www.shirley briceheath.net.

8. This discussion of the importance of teaching children appropriate talk rules is from Carol Gilles, "Making the Most of Talk," *Voices in the Middle,* 2(18), December 2010, pp. 9–15.

9. Shelby Wolf, *Interpreting Literature with Children* (Mahwah, NJ: Routledge, 2003). Wolf quotes from Glenna Sloan, *The Child as Critic: Teaching Literature in Elementary and Middle Schools* (New York: Teachers College Press, 1991).

10. This definition of exploratory talk is from Carol Gilles, "Making the Most of Talk," *Voices in the Middle,* 2(18), December 2010, pp. 9–15.

11. Every elementary school teacher should own Jim Trelease, *Read Aloud Handbook,* 6th ed. (New York: Penguin, 2006). Explore Trelease's website, www.trealease-on-reading.com.

12. This is said by the sixth-grade teacher Julia when she is talking about the ritual of read-aloud in her classroom, in Cynthia Lewis's *Literacy Practices as Social Acts: Power, Status, and Cultural Norms in the Classroom* (Mahwah, NJ: Laurence Erlbaum, 2001), p. 78.

13. These ideas for making read-aloud time comfortable are taken from Shelby Wolf's *Interpreting Literature with Children* (Mahwah, NJ: Lawrence Erlbaum, 2004).

14. These two paragraphs contain much information take from Lawrence Sipe, *Storytime: Young Children's Literary Understanding in the Classroom* (New York: Teachers College Press, 2008).

15. Lawrence Sipe, *Storytime: Young Children's Literary Understanding in the Classroom* (New York: Teachers College Press, 2008).

16. Lawrence Sipe, *Storytime: Young Children's Literary Understanding in the Classroom* (New York: Teachers College Press, 2008).

17. Morag Styles and Evelyn Arizpe, "A Gorilla with 'Grandpa's Eyes': How Children Interpret Visual Texts—A Case Study of Anthony Browne's *Zoo,*" *Children's Literature in Education,* 4(32), December 2001, pp. 261–275.

18. Lawrence Sipe, *Storytime: Young Children's Literary Understanding in the Classroom* (New York: Teachers College, 2008).

19. Kathy Whitmore, "Literature Study Groups: Support for Community Building in Democratic Classrooms" *Talking Points,* 1(17), October 2005, pp. 13–22. Copyright owned by National Council of Teachers of English.

20. These paragraphs paraphrase and condense work from Lawrence Sipe, *Storytime: Young Children's Literary Understanding in the Classroom* (New York: Teachers College Press, 2008), pp. 181–183.

21. Morag Styles and Evelyn Arizpe, "A Gorilla with 'Grandpa's Eyes': How Children Interpret Visual Texts—A Case Study of Anthony Browne's *Zoo,*" *Children's Literature in Education,* 4(32), pp. 261–275.

22. These ideas come from Jeffrey Wilhelm, *You Gotta Be the Book: Teaching Engaged and Reflective Reading with Adolescents* (New York: Teachers College Press, 2007).

23. Lawrence Sipe, *Storytime*: Young Children's Literary Understanding in the Classroom (New York: Teachers College Press, 2008), p. 37. Quoted from Patti Lather, "Issues of Validity in Openly Ideological Research: Between a Rock and a Soft Place," *Interchange,* 17, pp. 63–84.

24. Kathy Whitmore, "Literature Study Groups: Support for Community Building in Democratic Classrooms," *Talking Points*, 17(1), October 2005, pp. 13–22. Copyright owned by National Council of Teachers of English.

25. Kathy Whitmore, "Literature Study Groups: Support for Community Building in Democratic Classrooms," *Talking Points*, 17(1), October 2005, pp. 13–22. Copyright owned by National Council of Teachers of English.

26. Carol Gilles, "Making the Most of Talk," *Voices in the Middle,* 2(18), December 2010, pp. 9–15.

27. Cynthia Lewis, *Literacy Practices as Social Acts: Power, Status, and Cultural Norms in the Classroom* (Mahwah, NJ: Laurence Erlbaum, 2001), pp. 120, 68, 63.

28. This discussion of critical literacy and critical questions is from the first chapter of Vivian Vasquez's *Getting Beyond "I Like the Book": Creating Space for Critical Literacy in K–6 Classrooms*, 2nd ed. (Newark, DE: International Reading Association, 2010).

29. Luke & Freebody, 1999

30. Lissa Paul, *Reading Otherways* (Portland, ME: Calendar Islands Publishers, 1998), pp. 15–17.

31. This inquiry point was inspired by a comparison made in Kathy Whitmore, "Literature Study Groups: Support for Community Building in Democratic Classrooms," *Talking Points*, 1(17), October 2005, pp. 13–22. Copyright owned by National Council of Teachers of English.

32. This discussion of structured independent reading is paraphrased and condensed from Barbara Moss and Terrell A. Young, *Creating Lifelong Readers Through Independent Reading* (Newark, DE: International Reading Association, 2010).

33. This story is paraphrased from Donalyn Miller, *The Book Whisperer: Awakening the Inner Reader in Every Child* (San Francisco, CA: Jossey-Bass, 2009), pp. 21–23.

MyEducationKit™

Go to the topic "Evaluating Children's Literature" on the MyEducationKit for this text, where you can:

- Search the Children's Literature Database, housing more than 22,000 titles searchable in every genre by authors or illustrators, by awards won, by year published, and by topic and description.

- Explore genre-related Assignments and Activities, assignable exercises showing concepts in action through database use, video, cases, and student and teacher artifacts.

- Listen to podcasts and read interviews from some of the brightest and most enduring stars of children's literature in the Conversations.

- Discover web links that will lead you to sites representing the authors you learn about in these pages, classrooms with powerful children's literature connections, and literature awards.

Children's Book Awards

Children's book awards are listed on the Internet. See the Children's Literature Web Guide: Internet Resources Related to Books for Children and Young Adults at http://people.ucalgary.ca/~dkbrown/index.html (Children's Book Awards page, copyright © 1994–2001 David K. Brown). Listed below in alphabetical order is a representative group.

Australian Children's Books of the Year Awards

The third week in August the Children's Book Council of Australia (CBCA) announces an award for the Best children's books in five categories: Older Readers, Younger Readers, Early Childhood, Picture Books, and Information Books. Each award category primarily considers literary merit, but the quality of illustrations is also important in the Early Childhood category. The Picture Book category is different: the text and the illustrations must achieve artistic and literary unity. For Information books, there are additional criteria relating to the accuracy and accessibility of the information.

Links to lists of past award winners and notables as well as the current short-lists for each category can be easily accessed on the CBCA website: http://cbca.org.au/awards.htm

Boston Globe–Horn Book Awards

The Boston Globe–Horn Book Awards for excellence in children's and young adult literature have been awarded annually since 1967 by the *Boston Globe* and *The Horn Book Magazine*. Through 1975, two awards were given—one for outstanding text and the other for outstanding illustration. In 1976 the award categories were changed to Outstanding Fiction or Poetry, Outstanding Nonfiction, and Outstanding Illustration. Books published in the United States but written by non-Americans are also eligible.

Awarded in June, lists of current winners and notables, as well as links to past winners can be accessed via the *Horn Book* website: www.hbook.com/bghb/current.asp

The Caldecott Medal

Since 1938, the Association of Library Service to Children of the American Library Association has annually awarded the Caldecott Medal to the illustrator of the most distinguished picture book published in the United States in the preceding year. In addition to the medalist, Caldecott Honor Books are also named during the American Library Association (ALA) Midwinter Meeting every January. The recipients must be citizens or residents of the United States. The medal is named in tribute to the well-loved English illustrator Randolph Caldecott (1846–1886).

Complete information related to this coveted children's book award is available on the Association for Library Service to Children (ALSC) website: www.ala.org/ala/mgrps/divs/alsc/awardsgrants/bookmedia/caldecottmedal/caldecottmedal.cfm

The Canadian Library Awards

This award has been given each year since 1947 by the Canadian Library Association (CLA) to a distinguished children's book authored by a citizen or permanent resident of Canada. All genres—fiction, poetry, narrative, nonfiction, retelling of traditional literature—are eligible regardless of published format. A similar medal has been given annually since 1954 to a significant children's book published in the French language.

The Book of the Year Award is described and listed on the CLA website: www.cla.ca/AM/Template.cfm?Section=Book_of_the_Year_for_Children_Award

The complete discussion of the CLA Awards can be accessed on their official website: www.cla.ca/AM/Template.cfm?Section=Awards_Scholarships_Grants&Template=/CM/HTMLDisplay.cfm&ContentID=10584

Coretta Scott King Award

Established in 1969, this award commemorates the life and work of Martin Luther King Jr. and honors Coretta Scott King "for her courage and determination to continue the work for peace and world brotherhood." It is presented annually by the American Library Association to an African American author and an African American illustrator whose works "encourage and promote" world unity and peace, and serve as an inspiration to young people in the achievement of their goals. A plaque, honorarium, and an encyclopedia are presented as gifts to the award winners and honor books.

Access information about this award at: www.ala.org/ala/mgrps/rts/emiert/cskbookawards/about.cfm

Lists of past winners can be found at: www.ala.org/ala/mgrps/rts/emiert/cskbookawards/recipients.cfm

The Geisel Award

The Geisel Award is in honor of Theodore Geisel (Dr. Seuss). It is awarded yearly to the author(s) and illustrator(s) of the most distinguished American book for beginning readers published in English in the United States during the preceding year. Information about this award and details of current winners can be accessed at: www.ala.org/ala/mgrps/divs/alsc/awardsgrants/bookmedia/geiselaward/index.cfm

A complete list of past winners and honor books can be accessed at: www.ala
.org/ala/mgrps/divs/alsc/awardsgrants/bookmedia/geiselaward/geiselaward
pastwinners/index.cfm

Hans Christian Andersen Award

Every other year IBBY (International Board on Books for Young People) presents the
Hans Christian Andersen Award to a living author and a living illustrator whose
complete works have made lasting contributions to the field of children's literature.
It is considered to be the highest international recognition given to an author (1956)
and illustrator (1966) of children's books.

The IBBY website provides complete lists of current and past winners of this
award: www.ibby.org/index.php?id=273

International Reading Association Children's Book Award

Given for the first time in 1975, this award is presented annually for a book published in the preceding year and written by a newly published author "who shows
unusual promise in the children's book field." Sponsored by the Institute for Reading
Research, the award is administered by the International Reading Association (IRA).
This award is given for fiction and nonfiction in each of three categories: primary,
intermediate, and young adult.

Current and past winners for each category can be found on the official IRA website: www.reading.org/Resources/AwardsandGrants/childrens_ira.aspx

The Kate Greenaway Medal

The Kate Greenaway Medal, given annually by the British Library Association, recognizes the outstanding illustration of a children's book first published originally for
children or young people in English or in Dual Language (in which one language is
English). Recipients are books published in the United Kingdom in the year preceding
the award. Recent winners are posted on The Kate Greenaway Medal website where
viewers can also access the link to a full list of winners: www.carnegiegreenaway.org
.uk/greenaway/recent_winners.php

The Laura Ingalls Wilder Award

This award is given to a children's author or illustrator whose work, over a period of
time, has made a substantial contribution to literature for children. The Laura Ingalls
Wilder Award is for books published in the United States. From its start in 1954 until
1960 it was presented every five years. Beginning in 1980 the award was given every

three years; it is now given every two years. This award is administered through the Association for Library Service to Children, a division of the American Library Association. Information about the award, and links to past winners can be found by visiting the ALSC website: www.ala.org/ala/mgrps/divs/alsc/awardsgrants/bookmedia/wildermedal/wilderabout/index.cfm

The Mildred L. Batchelder Award

This award is given by the Association for Library Service to Children for the best translation of a work originally published in a language other than English and subsequently translated into English and published in the United States. Discussion of the recent winner and honor books is found on the ALSC website: www.ala.org/ala/mgrps/divs/alsc/awardsgrants/bookmedia/batchelderaward/index.cfm

The National Book Award for Young People's Literature

This award, formerly a National Book Award/American Book Award from 1969 to 1983, was added to the National Book Awards (NBA) in 1996. Presented each year, the Young People's category recognizes outstanding contributions to literature for children and young adults in various genres by writers in the United States. Current and past winners can be found at the NBA website: www.nationalbook.org/nba2010.html

National Council of Teachers of English Award for Excellence in Poetry for Children

This award is presented by the National Council of Teachers of English (NCTE) to a living American poet in recognition of the poet's aggregate body of work in children's literature. It was given annually until 1982, and now is presented every three years. Information about this award and links to the biographical information for current and past winners can be found on the NCTE website: www.ncte.org/awards/poetry

The John Newbery Medal

Named in honor of John Newbery (1713–1767), the first English publisher of children's books, this medal has been given annually since 1922 by the American Library Association's Association for Library Service to Children. The recipient is recognized as the author of the most distinguished book in children's literature published in the United States in the preceding year. The award is limited to citizens or residents of the United States. In addition to the medalist, the selection committee recognizes Newbery Honor books from the finalists they review. This highest honor for children's literature is described and lists of current and past winners and honor books are available at the ALA/ALSC website: www.ala.org/ala/mgrps/divs/alsc/awardsgrants/bookmedia/newberymedal/newberymedal.cfm

The Phoenix Award

The Phoenix Award is given by the Children's Literature Association (ChLA) to a book published twenty years earlier that was originally published in English, but did not receive any major award when it was first released. The award is named after "the fabled bird that rose from its ashes with renewed life and beauty." Books selected for this award are recognized for their ability to motivate serious study of children's literature. The ChLA website provides descriptions and lists of current and former winners of this award via the Book Awards link: www.childlitassn.org/index.php?page=about&family=awards&category=06--Phoenix_Award&display=27#offset1

The Pura Belpré Award

This award is named for Pura Belpré, the first Latina librarian at the New York Public Library. The Pura Belpré Award, established in 1996, is presented annually to a Latino/Latina writer and a Latino/Latina illustrator whose work best portrays, affirms, and celebrates the Latino cultural experience in an outstanding work of literature for children and youth. It is cosponsored by the Association for Library Service to Children, a division of the American Library Association, and REFORMA, the National Association to Promote Library and Information Services to Latinos and the Spanish-Speaking, an ALA affiliate. The medalist and honor books for both author and illustrator categories are provided on the ALA/ALSC website: www.ala.org/ala/mgrps/divs/alsc/awardsgrants/bookmedia/belpremedal/index.cfm

The Scott O'Dell Award for Historical Fiction

The award was established in 1981 by Scott O'Dell and is administered by the advisory committee of the Bulletin of the Center for Children's Books. The book must be historical fiction, have unusual literary merit, be written by a citizen of the United States, and be set in the New World. It must have been published in the previous year by a U.S. publisher and must be written for children or young adults. The award has been given yearly since 1984. The winners can be found on the award's website: www.scottodell.com/pages/ScottO%27DellAwardforHistoricalFiction.aspx

The Orbis Pictus Award for Outstanding Nonfiction

This award, established in 1990 by the National Council of Teachers of English to recognize excellence in nonfiction writing, commemorates *Orbis Pictus* (1657), considered the first informational book written for children. The medalist and honor books are awarded annually in the fall. Annotated bibliographies are available on the NCTE website: www.ncte.org/awards/orbispictus

Robert F. Sibert Medal Informational Book Award

The Robert F. Sibert Informational Book Medal is presented annually to the author(s) and illustrator(s) of the most distinguished informational book published in English during the preceding year. The ALSC administers the award. The American Library Association/Association for Library Service to Children website provides information about the award and current winners as well as a link to previous winners and honor books at the award website: www.ala.org/ala/mgrps/divs/alsc/awardsgrants/bookmedia/sibertmedal/index.cfm

The Stonewall Book Awards

The Stonewall Book Award for Children's & Young Adult Literature is awarded annually to books published in English for their merit relating to the gay/lesbian/bisexual/transgendered experience. The American Library Association sponsors this Award for a medalist and honor books in January of each year. Complete descriptions and lists of winners can be found on the ALA website: www.ala.org/ala/mgrps/rts/glbtrt/stonewall/honored/index.cfm

Selected Children's Magazines

Appleseeds Magazine (award-winning social studies topics for ages 7 to 9). Carus Publishing Company 30 Grove St., Suite C, Peterborough, NH 03458
www.cobblestonepub.com/magazine/APP

Boy's Life (ages 8 to 12). Boy Scouts of America, P.O. Box 15279, Irving, TX 75015
www.boyslife.org

Calliope (explores how events from world history intertwine using themed issues for ages 9 to 14). Cobblestone Publishing Co., 30 Grove Street, Peterborough, NH 03458
www.cobblestonepub.com/magazine/CAL

Chickadee (fun, interesting facts about animals and people for ages 5 to 9). Owlkids, 10 Lower Spadina Avenue, Suite 400, Toronto, Ontario, Canada, M5V 2Z2
www.owlkids.com/chickaDEE/index.html

Cobblestone (American history for ages 8 to 14). Cobblestone Publishing Co., 30 Grove Street, Peterborough, NH 03458
www.cobblestonepub.com/magazine/COB

Cousteau Kids (nature and science around the world for ages 8 to 12). Cousteau Society, Membership Department, 710 Settlers Landing Road, Hampton, VA 23669.
www.cousteau.org/media/cousteau-kids

Cricket (children's literature, poems, stories, articles, songs, crafts and jokes for children ages 8 to 12). Cobblestone Publishing Co., 30 Grove Street, Peterborough, NH 03458
www.cobblestonepub.com/magazine/CKT

Faces: Peoples, Places and Cultures (anthropology and natural history for ages 9 to 14). Cobblestone Publishing Co., 30 Grove Street, Peterborough, NH 03458
www.cobblestonepub.com/magazine/FAC

Footsteps (African American heritage for ages 9 to 14). Cobblestone Publishing Co., 30 Grove Street, Peterborough, NH 03458
www.footstepsmagazine.com

Girls Life (ages 10 to 15). 4529 Harford Road, Baltimore, MD 21214
www.girlslife.com

Highlights for Children (activities for ages 4 to 12). P.O. Box 269, Columbus, OH 43272
www.highlights.com

Hopscotch (stories and activities for ages 6 to 12). P.O. Box 1292, Saratoga Springs, NY 12866
www.hopscotchmagazine.com

Ladybug (stories and activities for ages 2 to 7). Cobblestone Publishing Co., 30 Grove Street, Peterborough, NH 03458
www.cobblestonepub.com/magazine/LYB

National Geographic Kids (covers a wide variety of topics, but focuses on geography, nature, and science for ages of 8 to 14). P.O. Box 64066, Tampa, FL 33664
www.nationalgeographic.com/ngkids

New Moon (featuring girl editors, ages 8 to 14, and girl contributors from around the world). New Moon Publishing Company, 34 E. Superior Street, Suite 200, Duluth, MN 55802
www.newmoon.org

Odyssey (science for ages 10 to 16.). Cobblestone Publishing Co., 30 Grove Street, Peterborough, NH 03458
www.cobblestonepub.com/magazine/ODY

Owl (science and nature for children over 8). Owlkids, 10 Lower Spadina Avenue, Suite 400, Toronto, Ontario, Canada M5V 2Z2
www.owlkids.com

Ranger Rick (animals and environment for ages 7 and up). National Wildlife Federation, 11100 Wildlife Center Drive, Reston, VA 20190
www.nwf.org/gowild

Skipping Stones (an international multicultural magazine for sharing ideas and experiences among children from different lands and backgrounds). P.O. Box 3939, Eugene, OR 97403
www.skippingstones.org

Spider (literature and art for ages 6 to 9). Cobblestone Publishing Co., 30 Grove Street, Peterborough, NH 03458
www.cobblestonepub.com/magazine/SDR

Stone Soup (an international magazine illustrated and written by children, age 8 to 13). Stone Soup, P.O. Box 83, Santa Cruz, CA 95063
www.stonesoup.com

Your Big Backyard (nature for ages 3 to 7). National Wildlife Federation, 11100 Wildlife Center Drive, Reston, VA 20190
www.nwf.org/yourbigbackyard

ZooBooks (nature and animals for ages 6 to 12). Zoobooks magazine, Wildlife Education, Ltd. 4110 Progress Blvd., Suite 2A, Peru, IL 61354
www.zoobooks.com

Selected Reviewing Media
for Children's Books

The ALAN Review

American Library Association (ALA)

Appraisal (science books)

Australian Children's Book Council (ACBC)

Booklist Bulletin of the Center for Children's Books

Children's Book Council (CBC)

Children's Catalog

Children's Literature Assembly (CLA)

Children's Literature Association Quarterly

The Horn Book Magazine

Kirkus Reviews

Language Arts

Library Journal

Library Talk

The New Advocate

The New York Times Book Reviews

Oyate

Parents' Choice

Publishers Weekly

The Reading Teacher

School Library Journal

Science Books and Films

Voice of Youth Advocates (VOYA)

Wilson Library Journal

APPENDIX D

Selected Websites about Children's Literature

American Library Association
www.ala.org/ala/awardsgrants/index.cfm

Association for Library Service to Children
www.ala.org/ala/mgrps/divs/alsc/index.cfm

The Bank Street Center for Children's Literature
www.bankstreet.edu/center-childrens-literature

Canadian Library Association Book of the Year for Children Award
www.cla.ca/awards/boyc.htm

Children's Book Council
www.cbcbooks.org

The Children's Literature Association
www.childlitassn.org

The Children's Literature Web Guide
http://people.ucalgary.ca/~dkbrown

Children's Picture Book Database
www.lib.muohio.edu/pictbks

Database of Award-Winning Children's Literature
www.dawcl.com

International Board on Books for Young People
www.ibby.org

International Children's Digital Library
http://en.childrenslibrary.org

International Reading Association
www.reading.org

Kay Vandergrift's Children's Literature Page
www.scils.rutgers.edu/~kvander/ChildrenLit/index.html

Kay Vandergrift's Social History of Children's Literature
www.scils.rutgers.edu/~kvander/HistoryofChildLit/index.html

National Book Award for Young People's Literature
www.nationalbook.org/nbawinners_category.html#yp

National Book Award Winners
www.nationalbook.org

National Council for the Social Studies
www.ncss.org

National Council of Teachers of English
www.ncte.org

National Council of Teachers of Mathematics
www.nctm.org

National Science Teachers Association
www.nsta.org

Oyate
www.oyate.org

TeachingBooks.Net
www.teachingbooks.net

The Young Adult Library Services Association
www.ala.org/yalsa

Glossary of Literary Terms

Allegory a literary work in which characters and actions represent abstractions

Alliteration repetition of initial consonant sound

Allusion indirect reference to something or someone outside the literary work

Animal realism literary work in which animals and their relationships to humans are important and realistic

Antagonist force in conflict with protagonist; usually designated as self, another person, society, or nature

Anthropomorphism the giving of human qualities to animals or objects

Assonance repetition of vowel sound

Authentic biography a biography whose facts and assertions are well-documented and the research process is available to the reader

Autobiography the story of a person's life written by the subject or in conjunction with the subject, sometimes referred to as a *memoir*

Backdrop setting generalized or relatively unimportant setting

Ballad verse narrative of love, courage, the supernatural; may be of folk origin

Biographical fiction much like historical fiction; a biography where reasonably accurate information is added to fill gaps in a subject's life story

Biography the story of an individual's life, told by another person

Bleed when an illustration extends to the edge of the page with no white spaces

Cadence rhythmic flow in prose

Character human being, real or personified animal, or object taking a role in literature

Character development filling out a variety of character traits to provide the complexity of a human being

Chronological order related in the order of their happening; timeline

Classic a literary work that lives to be read and reread

Cliché overused term that has lost significance

Cliffhanger unresolved suspense that concludes a chapter

Climax action that precipitates resolution of conflict

Closed ending conclusion leaving no plot questions unanswered

Coincidence chance concurrence of events

Complication early action; part of rising plot

Concept an idea around which a work may be written

Concrete poetry poetry that is also visual art, using the shapes of words and letters to make a picture that represents the essence of the poem

Condescension an attitude or tone that underestimates the reader

Conflict struggle between protagonist and opposing force, frequently the antagonist

Connotation associative or emotional meaning of a word

Consonance repetition of consonant sound in phrase

Cumulative tale a story, often folk in origin, that continually repeats a series, then adds a new item

Denotation explicit or dictionary meaning of a word

Denouement final or closing action following the climax

Diction choice of words or wording

Didacticism in literature, an instructive or moralistic lesson often given at the expense of entertainment

Distanced tone an attitude of objectivity through which a story is told

Dramatic (objective) point of view third-person narration in which actions and speeches are recorded without interpretation; picturebook illustrations complicate this point of view

Dual point of view a story told from two perspectives

Dust jacket paper cover surrounding a hardcover book for protection and design; also referred to as book jacket or cover

Dynamic character one who changes over the course of the story

Dystopian literature dystopia literally means "bad place"; dystopian literature describes imaginary, usually future, worlds in which present tendencies are carried to an extreme to create a very unpleasant society

End papers paper glued to casing of hardbound book, in picturebooks they often contain meaningful information for the reader

End rhyme rhyming words at the ends of poetic lines

Epic long narrative poem about a heroic figure whose actions reveal the values of the culture

Episodic biography a biography based on a portion of a subject's life

Episodic plot plot with short, independent chapters linked by characters or theme more than by action

Explicit theme theme stated clearly in the story

Exposition presentation of essential information needed for understanding the action

Expository one of the four main kinds of composition, used to explain (the others are narration, argumentation, and description)

Extended metaphor a comparison developed at great length

Fable brief story, usually with animal characters, that states a didactic theme or moral

Fairy tale short stories within the folktale category of folklore; characterized by magic

Falling action final or closing action following climax; denouement

Fantasy story about the nonexistent or unreal in which action may depend on magic or the supernatural

Fictionalized biography a biography where specific information is unavailable about a subject and biographers use the best possible information to create the story; fictionalizing should be purposeful and acknowledged

Figurative language devices making comparisons, saying one thing in terms of another

First-person point of view "I" narration in which a person's experiences, thoughts, and feelings are told by him- or herself

Flashback return to event that occurred before present scene; retrospect

Flat character one that is little developed

Foil a character whose contrasting traits highlight those of a central character

Folk epic long narrative poem passed down by word of mouth, often about a hero

Folktale story passed down by word of mouth; includes fairy tales, noodlehead tales, talking beast tales, cumulative stories, and tall tales

Foreshadowing literary technique using symbols and events as hints of what is to come

Format the physical structure of a printed work (e.g., graphic novels and picturebooks are formats that span all genres)

Genre a kind or type of literature that has a common set of characteristics

Graphic novel a novel presented in the format similar to a comic book; varied styles of graphic art that has representation in all genres

Gutter the middle groove where pages are bound in a book; the white space between frames in a graphic novel

Haiku a form of Japanese poetry, usually formatted in three lines of five, seven, and five syllables

High fantasy a type of fantasy characterized by conflict between good and evil, closely patterned after folklore such as mythologies and quest tales

Hyperbole exaggeration or overstatement

Hypertext written or pictorial material interconnected in a complex way that is not easily represented on paper

Imagery verbal description or visual element appeals to the senses

Implicit theme theme implied from the story's context

Integral setting essential and specific setting that influences character, plot, and theme

Internal rhymes rhymes in a line that are after first and before last words

Interpretive biography a biography that has been tweaked, facts and events arranged in a way that creates a particular interpretation of the subject for the reader

Intertextuality Julia Kristeva's idea that every text is the absorption and transformation of another text

Irony recognition of reality different from what it truly is

Legend a traditional narrative of a people, often with some basis in historical truth

Limerick five-line humorous verse with strict traditional rhythm and rhyme pattern

Limited omniscient point of view third-person narration in which story is seen through the mind(s) of one or a few characters

Literary lore stories that are written by a known author who carefully mimics the formulas of traditional literature such as Hans Christian Andersen's popular fairy tales

Lyric poetry songlike poetry with a compact expression of feeling

Manga a Japanese style of comic; modern form is post–World War II

Memoir a subgenre of autobiography with a more narrow focus and personal tone

Mentor text a text that serves as a good teacher; a timeless text superlative in its elegance, wit, or wisdom

Metafiction a work of fiction that reveals the act of writing fiction

Metaphor an implied comparison important to the compact nature of children's literature

Meter somewhat regular rhythm pattern of stressed and unstressed syllables in a line of poetry

Mise-en-abyme a visual or verbal text placed inside another text as its smaller replica; story within a story or picture within a picture

Myth story originating in folk beliefs showing how the world works; can include supernatural forces cooperating with animals and humans

Narration one of the four main types of composition (the others are exposition, description, and argumentation); storytelling through words

Narrative order sequence in which events are commonly recounted

Narrative poetry poetry that tells a story

Noodlehead stories gently humorous folktales featuring a dim-witted person who usually wins in the end, despite being foolish

Nursery rhymes brief stories that have been passed orally from generation to generation that are told in brief rhyming verse; sometimes considered simplest introduction to poetry

Objective (or dramatic) point of view third-person narration in which actions and speeches are recorded without interpretation; picturebook illustrations complicate this point of view

Off rhymes imperfect rhymes, sometimes called "slant rhymes"; for example, ground and cloud

Omniscient point of view third-person narration in which action is told by an all-knowing writer

Onomatopoeia words that sound like their meanings, such as *meow, moo, clickety-clack*

Open ending conclusion in which the final outcome of conflict is unknown

Parody imitation of known form for comic effect or to make a subtle commentary

Peritext everything other than the printed text in a book—dust jacket, end pages, title page, covers, etc.; often referred to as paratext

Person-against-nature a main character struggles against an aspect of nature

Person-against-person a main character is in conflict with another main character

Person-against-self a main character is conflicted inside, struggling against an aspect of him- or herself

Person-against-society a main character struggles against an aspect of society, trying to change society or keep from being changed by society

Personification giving human traits to nonhumans or objects

Picture book a book that relies on pictures to enlarge, illuminate, or contrast with the text; the pictures may be in many different relationships to the text

Picturebook replaces the term *picture book* in contemporary books to emphasize that pictures carry at least half the meaning in a true picturebook; the term indicates the synergy that is created when art and text are combined

Plot sequence of events involving character in conflict

Poetry distilled and imaginative expression of feeling

Point of view the mind(s) through which the reader sees the story

Postmodernism a theory that emerged after WWII, which rejects traditions and universal truths and inserts fragmentation, change, play, and antiauthoritarianism

Pourquoi stories tales, often about natural phenomena, that answer the question "why?"

Primary theme major underlying and unifying truth of a story

Progressive plot plot with central climax

Protagonist central character in the conflict

Realism story based on the possible, though not necessarily probable; can be contemporary or historical fiction

Resolution falling action following climax

Rhyme repetition of identical or similar stressed sounds

Rhythm recurring flow of strong and weak beats

Rising action exposition and complications that lead to the climax

Round character a fully developed or three-dimensional character

Science fantasy story that combines elements of fantasy (the impossible) with elements of science (the possible)

Science fiction story about a possible future world that relies on invention or extension of nature's laws, not on the magical; includes mind-control and future-world themes

Secondary theme less important or minor theme of a story

Sensationalism focus on the thrilling or startling

Sentiment emotion or feeling

Sentimentality overuse of sentiment; false arousal of feelings

Setting the time and place in which the action occurs

Sijo Korean poetry form; the three lines each average 14–16 syllables, for a total of 44–46

Simile stated comparison, usually using *like* or as

Sound effect any sound device that affects meaning

Static character one who does not change over the course of the story

Stereotype character possessing expected traits of a group rather than being an individual

Stock character flat character with very little development; found in numerous stories, such as folktales

Style how an author says something, as opposed to what the author says

Suspense state of uncertainty that keeps the reader reading

Symbol person, object, situation, or action operating on two levels of meaning—literal and figurative or suggestive

Synesthesia simultaneous appeal to several senses

Syntax the rule-ordered arrangement of words in sentences

Talking animal stories fantasy stories that are realistic in every way except that the animals behave like humans; Charlotte's Web is a prime example

Talking beast tales traditional or folkloric tales in which animals talk

Tall tales an American form of folktale in which characters' deeds are more magnificent than they could be in reality; the truth is stretched, hence the tale is "tall"

Textset a collection of three or more texts arranged in relationship to each other for a particular purpose

Theme statement giving the underlying truth about people, society, or the human condition, either explicitly or implicitly

Time slip story in which characters find themselves in a time period different from the one in which they began, such as moving between historical periods

Tone writer's attitude toward his or her subject and readers

Trickster archetypal character in folklore who loves to break societal rules; typically a male, tricksters can also be animals

Understatement reverse of exaggeration or playing down

Verse rhyming metrical structure with less emotional intensity than poetry

Verse novel a novel told in poetry—often blank verse—rather than prose

Word/image interaction a system developed by Nikolajeva and Scott and referred to by David Lewis, Perry Nodelman, Sylvia Pantaleo, and Lawrence Sipe to describe different dynamics between words and images in picturebooks

Wordless picturebook a book that has no written narrative but tells a story with pictures alone

CREDITS

INDEX